THE WRITER IN YOU

❖

A Writing Process Reader

BARBARA LOUNSBERRY
University of Northern Iowa

📕 HarperCollins*Publishers*

Sponsoring Editor: Patricia Rossi
Project Editor: Shuli Traub
Design Supervisor: Heather A. Ziegler
Text Design: North 7 Atelier, Ltd.
Cover Design: Jaye Zimet
Cover Photo: Will Crocker
Photo Researcher: Nina Page
Director of Production: Jeanie Berke
Production Administrator: Kathleen Donnelly/Beth Maglione
Compositor: ComCom Division of Haddon Craftsmen, Inc.
Printer and Binder: R. R. Donnelley & Sons Company
Cover Printer: The Lehigh Press, Inc.

For permission to use copyrighted material, grateful acknowledgment is made to the copyright holders on pp. 610–612, which are hereby made part of this copyright page.

The Writer in You: *A Writing Process Reader*
Copyright © 1992 by HarperCollins Publishers Inc.

All rights reserved. Printed in the United States of America. No part of this book may be used or reproduced in any manner whatsoever without written permission, except in the case of brief quotations embodied in critical articles and reviews. For information address HarperCollins Publishers Inc., 10 East 53rd Street, New York, NY 10022.

Library of Congress Cataloging-in-Publication Data
Lounsberry, Barbara.
    The writer in you : a writing process reader / Barbara Lounsberry.
      p.   cm.
    ISBN 0–06–044118–6 (student ed.).—ISBN 0–06–500447–7 (instructor's ed.)
    1. College readers.   2. English language—Rhetoric.   I. Title.
PE1417.L68   1992   91–16560
808′.0427—dc20   CIP

91 92 93 94   9 8 7 6 5 4 3 2 1

For Jackson at Northwestern

Contents

Preface ix

CHAPTER 1 **Introduction: A Writer's Beginnings** 1
- Annie Dillard AN AMERICAN CHILDHOOD 4
- Philip Roth MY BASEBALL YEARS 10
- Margaret Atwood HIGH SCHOOL BEGINNINGS 14
- John Barth SOME REASONS WHY I TELL THE STORIES I TELL THE WAY I TELL THEM RATHER THAN SOME OTHER SORT OF STORIES SOME OTHER WAY 19
- STUDENT ESSAY: Warren Wortham MUSICAL BEGINNINGS 31
- Virginia Woolf PROFESSIONS FOR WOMEN 35
- SHORT STORY: Nadine Gordimer NOT FOR PUBLICATION 41

CHAPTER 2 **Finding the Subject: The Figure in the Carpet** 55
- May Sarton JOURNAL OF A SOLITUDE 60
- Joan Didion ON KEEPING A NOTEBOOK 63
- Brenda Ueland THE IMAGINATION WORKS SLOWLY AND QUIETLY 70
- Peter Elbow THE OPEN-ENDED WRITING PROCESS 75
- STUDENT ESSAY: Kelly Linnenkamp LIFEGUARDING: FUN IN THE SUN? 81
- Plato THE ALLEGORY OF THE CAVE 86
- SHORT STORY: John Updike ONE MORE INTERVIEW 94

CHAPTER 3 **Researching: The Deeper the Richer** 105
- Henry James THE ART OF FICTION 111
- John McPhee THE SEARCH FOR MARVIN GARDENS 114
- Barbara Tuchman IN SEARCH OF HISTORY 124
- Gay Talese THE TAILORS OF MAIDA 135
- Clifford Geertz BEING THERE: ANTHROPOLOGY AND THE SCENE OF WRITING 146

STUDENT ESSAY: *Jon Shepherd*   EMPLOYEE STOCK OWNERSHIP PLANS: NEW PLAYERS IN THE LEVERAGED BUYOUT GAME   158
SHORT STORY/ESSAY: *Julian Barnes*   SHIPWRECK   174

CHAPTER 4   Finding the Form   197

Longinus   ON THE SUBLIME   202
John McNulty   "COME QUICK. INDIANS!"   207
George Lakoff and Mark Johnson   CONCEPTS WE LIVE BY   213
Anne Morrow Lindbergh   DOUBLE-SUNRISE   217
Martin Luther King, Jr.   LETTER FROM BIRMINGHAM JAIL   224
STUDENT ESSAY: *Lisa Battani*   AN ANALYSIS OF "LETTER FROM BIRMINGHAM JAIL"   240
SHORT STORY: *Alice Walker*   "REALLY, DOESN'T CRIME PAY?"   250

CHAPTER 5   Finding a Voice   261

Tom Wolfe   INTRODUCTION TO THE KANDY-KOLORED TANGERINE-FLAKE STREAMLINE BABY   264
Eudora Welty   FINDING A VOICE   270
STUDENT ESSAY: *Cordell Waldron*   SEEING RED   274
Maxine Hong Kingston   AT THE WESTERN PALACE   279
Richard Rodriguez   MR. SECRETS   308
SHORT STORY: *Donna Roazen*   MILK RUN   322
Nancy Price   ONE STORY—THIRTEEN POINTS OF VIEW   325

CHAPTER 6   One True Sentence   331

Ernest Hemingway   A MOVEABLE FEAST   335
V. S. Naipaul   FINDING THE CENTER   338
Sissela Bok   LYING   343
Carol Bly   SMALL TOWNS: A CLOSE SECOND LOOK AT A VERY GOOD PLACE   357
STUDENT ESSAY: *Cori McNeilus*   LABOR UNIONS: A PART OF OUR PAST OR FUTURE?   376
SHORT STORY: *Nancy Price*   COVER GIRL   392

CHAPTER 7   Generating   399

George Orwell   WHY I WRITE   401
Stephen Jay Gould   THE PANDA'S THUMB   409

STUDENT ESSAY: Steven W. Armbrecht   THE BRADY PLAN: AN
     ATTEMPT TO SOLVE THE MEXICAN DEBT CRISIS   416
Mihaly Csikszentmihalyi   FLOW   434
Barry Lopez   LANDSCAPE AND NARRATIVE   442
Gretel Ehrlich   ABOUT MEN   449
Anne Jardim and Margaret Hennig   THE MANAGERIAL
     WOMAN   453
SHORT STORY: Gabriel García Márquez   THE SEA OF LOST
     TIME   459

CHAPTER 8   Sustaining the Call   473

William Kloefkorn   TELLING IT LIKE IT MAYBE IS: THE POET AS
     CRITIC   475
Wendell Berry   HOME OF THE FREE   486
Aleksandr Solzhenitsyn   FIRST CELL, FIRST LOVE   491
Ruth Wisse   A ROMANCE OF THE SECRET ANNEX   500
E. B. White   DEATH OF A PIG   503
STUDENT ESSAY: Brad Williams   OF COWS AND MEN   512
SHORT STORY: Leslie Marmon Silko   YELLOW WOMAN   522

CHAPTER 9   Revising and Proofreading: Backing and Filling   531

William Zinsser   WRITING—AND REWRITING—WITH A WORD
     PROCESSOR   534
Winston Churchill   THE NATIONAL COALITION   546
Mary McCarthy   LANGUAGE AND POLITICS   560
Lewis Thomas   NOTES ON PUNCTUATION   573
Carol Kammen   CONCERNING FOOTNOTES   577
STUDENT ESSAY: Jennifer C. Miller   LIPSTICK KISSES   583
SHORT STORY: Alice Munro   MATERIAL   590

CHAPTER 10   Touchstones   605

Credits   610

Preface

"Anyone who doesn't write doesn't know how wonderful it is," wrote Anne Frank in her famous diary. "I am grateful [for] . . . this possibility of developing myself and . . . of expressing all that is in me!"*

Anne Frank's words are the touchstones of *The Writer in You: A Writing Process Reader,* designed to help students discover the wonder of writing and the writer in each of them. Writing instruction in recent years has begun to focus as much on the writing *process* as on the finished product. From studying how professional writers write, we have learned that if we can help students discover the *processes* by which they write best, they will have a "method" for approaching any writing subject, audience, or purpose.

Regrettably, college readers have not kept pace with this revolution in writing instruction. Most readers offer essays, but only in final form. Students are rarely given glimpses of work-in-progress. In addition, many readers are topical or are organized by rhetorical mode. Few readers focus primarily on the creative process.

The Writer in You seeks to fill this need. Its first nine chapters—from "A Writer's Beginnings" to "Revising and Proofreading: Backing and Filling"—offer a step-by-step guide through the stages of the writing process. In addition, professional as well as student writers provide early and final drafts of their essays or short stories, so that students can study the process of revision. John Updike supplies the hastily jotted kernel of his story "One More Interview," and invites students to observe how faithful his final story remained to his initial vision. Maxine Hong Kingston makes available an early typewritten version of "At the Western Palace," a draft with many hand corrections. Sissela Bok provides the final galley proof of her essay on "Lying" to demonstrate that authors are often making revisions in their work even at the last possible moment. Playful John Barth supplies first and final drafts of the headnote to his essay "Some Reasons Why I Tell the Stories I Tell the Way I Tell Them Rather Than Some Other Sort of Stories Some Other Way."

In addition to early and final drafts of professional and student work, *The Writer in You* also includes a photograph and headnote for each writer, student and professional. The photographs help students see that writers do not inhabit some lofty plane above them but are human beings of myriad sizes and visages—just like them. More importantly, each of the nine student writers and the living professional writers are featured in headnotes to their work in which

---

*See "A Romance of the Secret Annex" on page 500. From *The Diary of Anne Frank: The Critical Edition,* eds. David Barnouw and Gerrold van Der Stroom (New York: Doubleday, 1989): 569, 587.

they describe their own writing processes. Often they give behind-the-scenes glimpses into how the piece was written, and frequently they offer helpful tips for student writers. For the 12 writers who are no longer alive—Plato, Longinus, Henry James, Virginia Woolf, George Orwell, John McNulty, Ernest Hemingway, Winston Churchill, Martin Luther King, Jr., E. B. White, Brenda Ueland, and Barbara Tuchman—I have culled autobiographies, biographies, and letters in order to write headnotes that stress their distinctive writing processes.

Indeed, *The Writer in You* is a treasury of "insider information" on writing and the creative process. Its first two chapters, "Introduction: A Writer's Beginnings" and "Finding the Subject: The Figure in the Carpet," are devoted to prewriting invention strategies. Annie Dillard illustrates ways of "paying attention" to the world, while May Sarton recommends going back to bed after breakfast to collect the thoughts and images of the awakening consciousness. John Barth confesses that his first drafts are not so much "written" as *drawn*, and describes himself scratching and scribbling and rediagraming "in kinesthetic bliss" from after breakfast until the approach of lunch. In contrast, Philip Roth finds his beginnings by typing on one page the best sentences he finds in months of freewriting. These opening chapters place special stress on finding a quiet place and sufficient time to write—two commodities so hard for most college students to come by that they must be consciously sought.

Once writers have found and warmed to their subjects, Chapter 3 focuses on "Researching: The Deeper the Richer." Here Henry James exhorts each student to try to be "one of whom nothing is lost," while Barbara Tuchman advises on-site as well as library research whenever possible. Tuchman also stresses the importance of using primary as well as secondary sources and of researchers "distilling" what they read. Julian Barnes describes the sources he tapped to write of Géricault's famous 1819 painting *The Raft of the Medusa*, and thanks a painter friend who read an early draft of his work and made a suggestion that led Barnes to even deeper research into Géricault's artistic process.

Chapters 4 through 7—"Finding the Form," "Finding a Voice," "One True Sentence," and "Generating"—may be approached in any order. Many students will not find the best form, voice, or opening of a piece of writing until they have "generated" a great deal of material. In the writers' headnotes in these chapters, Tom Wolfe urges students to start their work as letters to a specific person as one way of finding their individual voices as writers, while Maxine Hong Kingston describes the liberation of moving from first to third person and of structuring her work in the form of an "I Love Lucy" situation comedy. Eudora Welty, Mihaly Csikszentmihalyi, and Barry Lopez all seek to describe how form and voice flow from the writer's complex adjustment of outer and inner reality.

Chapters 8 and 9 of *The Writer in You*—"Sustaining the Call" and "Revising and Proofreading: Backing and Filling"—explore ways of nourishing a piece of writing for as long as may be required, as well as specific techniques for revising and proofreading one's writing. Joan Didion, for example, will place on her study wall a photo or map that conveys the atmosphere and tone she hopes to sustain throughout her work. Thus she has a visual image for constant reference. William Zinsser explains the joys of revising and proofreading on a word processor.

The final chapter provides "Touchstones," brief inspirational quotations on all stages of the writing process. Students may wish to tap these insightful nuggets for initial inspiration and return to them—as many professional writers do—in the last stages of the revising process as final spurs to their thinking.

Because students will go through all stages of the writing process with each paper they write, the text supplies sufficient essays and short stories so that teachers can use the first essay in each chapter for the first paper, and then return for second, third, fourth, and additional cycles through the reader as the course unfolds. Such circling through the reader will reinforce the students' sense of writing as a recursive *process,* no step of which can be shortchanged.

A final special feature of *The Writer in You* are Brief Warm-up Writing Exercises, which are suggested for students to complete *before* reading each of the 63 selections. These warm-up exercises provide practice in brainstorming, mapping, freewriting, and other prewriting strategies. They are also designed to help students become fluent, to encourage them to think of writing as just one of the useful tools in their intellectual repertoire. An added benefit of assigning one or more brief warm-up writing exercises before the student begins reading a selection is that students, on occasion, may actually produce something similar to what they will read. This is usually stunning for students—and reinforcing—as they see that they actually are working along the lines of a famous or admired professional writer. Students, likewise, learn a great deal about depth of research or richness of detail by comparing their brief exercises with a polished piece on a similar theme. The Questions to Ponder following each selection lead students to these considerations, and many of the Suggested Writing Possibilities call for students to return to and revise their warm-up exercises in light of what they have discovered by reading the selection.

One final word must be added about *The Writer in You:* It is designed for the novice writer who is fearful and anxious about writing, as well as for the student already beguiled by language, form, and style. The constant theme of the selections is the importance of truth as the starting point of all writing. Indeed, selections by 25 of the included writers stress, in one form or another, the importance of having some truth to communicate. In *The Writer in You* students are repeatedly urged to probe deeply into themselves, to tap the truths of their experience, and to research extensively in the outside world as well. As Orwell so memorably stated in "Why I Write" (page 407), "When I sit down to write a book, I do not say to myself, 'I am going to produce a work of art.' I write it because there is some lie that I want to expose, some fact to which I want to draw attention, and my initial concern is to get a hearing." If we can inspire our students to be seekers of truth, in themselves and in their world, then they will produce work unthought of in their early hours.

Two of the most helpful revelations to students in a writing process course are the value of collaboration and the value of hearing the responses of others to their work. *The Writer in You* is a product of such collaboration. I cannot sufficiently express my thanks to Lucy Rosendahl, who asked me to compile this reader, or to Gay Talese, who first put me in touch with Harper & Row (now HarperCollins). HarperCollins editor Patricia Rossi has guided this reader through publication with sensitivity and dispatch, aided by creative project editor Shuli Traub and by David Munger. To them I am most grateful.

Equally fervent thanks go to the many professional writers who generously combed their files for early drafts of published essays and stories, and who wrote headnotes for this volume. Notes of encouragement from these writers now fortify my study walls. Thanks, too, to the nine students at the University of Northern Iowa who were willing not only to share early and final drafts of their work, but also to submit headnotes and even to pose for a photographer.

I wish to express special thanks to Peter Elbow, whose residency at the University of Northern Iowa in 1983 awakened me to the value of writing groups and spurred me to start a journal (called *Draftings*) of student research and writing at my university. Further thanks go to my English department colleagues Nancy Price, Charlene Eblen, and Scott Cawelti; to art department colleague Frje Echeverria, who contributed ideas and support for this reader; and to graduate assistants Elizabeth Bingham and Michael Prahl as well. I also wish to thank Dr. Jon Somervill and the University of Northern Iowa Graduate College for the research fellowship and support that allowed me to complete the reader; and my mother, Jane Palen Severin, whose careful eyes backed up my own.

Finally, I wish to thank those colleagues from other colleges and universities whose reviews of the manuscript of *The Writer in You* helped shape this reader to serve the needs of instructors across the nation: Robert J. Alexander, Point Park College; Susan Aylworth, California State University at Chico; Mary Bly, University of California at Davis; Gerry Brooks, University of Nebraska; Peggy Cole, Arapahoe Community College; Mary K. Dietz, New York University; LaVerne Gonzales, San Jose State University; Ruth Greenberg, Jefferson Community College; Karen Houck, Bellevue Community College; C. Jeriel Howard, Northeastern University; Martha Kearns, University of Nevada at Reno; Bruce Leland, Western Illinois University; Ernestine W. Pickens, Clark College; Jerrie Scott, Central State University; Jack Summers, Central Piedmont Community College; Rinda West, Oakton Community College; and Thia Wolf, California State University at Chico.

Barbara Lounsberry

CHAPTER

1

Introduction:
A Writer's Beginnings

The college writer sits poised before a blank sheet of paper or computer screen. Writer A has "always liked to write." B fears writing. Anxiety grips her stomach whenever a writing assignment is made. C is simply indifferent; he has had so few writing experiences that the joys and agonies of writing have scarcely touched him. D and E, however, dream of being writers; writing fires their deepest ambitions.

No matter where you fall on the anxiety and interest axis, you can be sure there is a writer in you. Every person has ideas and feelings to share. Only the proper subject, occasion, and impetus are needed to draw them out. The readings and exercises in this reader are designed to help you find this writer-who-is-you, learn the conditions under which you write best, and explore your own writing terrain.

Why is such effort necessary? If you are sitting in a college classroom today, you can be sure that writing will be an important part of your professional and personal life. Every professional calling will call, at special times, for the writer in you. To get that first job you will need to write a résumé and (often many) job application letters. Should you become, say, a professional athlete, you will need words and sentences for the media. Athletes are also called on to deliver speeches at banquets. Some even write books. Businesspeople write letters to clients, business reports, and even create ads and brochures. Much the same can be said of any career today. Name a profession and you will find a person writing professional letters, reports, memos, and grants. By developing the writer in you, you will come to meet, even welcome, the writing challenges called for in your chosen career. You may even become the person in your office to whom others turn when it comes to the written word. You may make yourself indispensable.

Writing will play an equally vital role in your personal life. Some of the most important writing you will do in your life may be not to show others at all, but just for yourself. You may find value in keeping a diary or journal, in order to keep track of your life and of yourself as you live it. (See Joan Didion's "On Keeping a Notebook" in Chapter 2.) At moments of stress or crisis, you may find it helpful to write down your thoughts and feelings—to release your anger or sorrow or pain or perhaps simply to clarify your thoughts on the matter. In this category belong those angry letters you will write but never mail. You feel better, however, for having written them.

Some personal writing you will do simply for pleasure as an expression of your own creativity. You might write a poem or a song, a story or a meditation. Human beings from their earliest origins have decorated their surroundings; you may find yourself embellishing your world with writings that surprise you. You did not know you had it in you, but there it is.

This sense of discovery (of yourself and your world) is what makes the writing process exciting. As Peter Elbow says in the headnote to his essay on "The Open-Ended Writing Process" in Chapter 2, "I've sensed (from my own experience and from that of writers, colleagues, and students) that perhaps the experience of *being surprised* by one's writing—having it change directions or finding oneself stumbling into something unknown—is in fact the biggest reward that writing holds for us." Equally stunning is the recognition that when you've completed a piece of writing, something existed that never existed before. You have added to the world.

Between purely personal and professional writing, there fall other kinds of more-public writing. There will be the letters you want to write to your parents, to your children, and to others whom you love. There will be birthday and holiday letters to friends and letters of inquiry (or complaint) about products you buy. There will be letters to the editor in which you try to spur your fellow citizens to understand an issue the way you do. You may find yourself supporting causes you believe in, joining organizations, and writing pamphlets, letters, and publicity materials of all kinds. And there will be forms: employment forms and unemployment forms, insurance forms, health forms, credit application forms, forms seemingly without end. Simply negotiating life in the 1990s calls for the writer in you.

If I could give only one sentence of advice to each new class of college students, it would be this: read one hour a day and write one hour a day. At first this may seem an impossible suggestion, given the pressures on many college students not only to attend class and study but also to work an outside job and juggle personal relationships as well. I can only say that it will pay. Robert Waller, a gifted essayist and fiction writer who is also a professor of management, has spoken of "the value of the small increment." You read one hour every day—either your textbooks or books and magazines of your own choosing—and at the end of the week you are a measurably more knowledgeable, deeper, richer person. At the end of a month, you are deeper and wiser yet. And in a year? Five years? The increments grow, like interest in a bank account, until you are a *qualitatively* different individual. Given the fact that most people do not read extensively, you will be richer in knowledge and wisdom than your contemporaries, and that richness will be recognized by others. The rewards will be great.

The same profits come from the hour of writing. Write course assignments or a personal journal; write letters or essays or stories or poems or whatever you feel like writing. Your reading will make you a better writer—your vocabulary will grow, for example, without your even noticing it—and your writing will make you a better writer, too. You will become fluent. Writing will become just one of the things you naturally do—like breathing. Basketball player Michael Jordan possesses astonishing natural talent, but he still practices his shots every day.

We begin our study of the writing process by exploring some writers' beginnings. Beginnings themselves are interesting. Playwright Neil Simon speaks for many when he says, "I like to read about the beginnings of things. That is why I like biographies." Of the beginnings of writers there are as many tales as there are tellers. Essayist Annie Dillard, who begins this volume, started writing to aid her drawing; written phrases preserved the observations of her conscious eye. Philip Roth recalls that baseball first held the place that literature and writing would later fill. Canadian writer Margaret Atwood got "hit by writing" during her senior year in high school. In eleventh grade she did not write. In twelfth, she did. John Barth, on the other hand, did not write until college—after a detour through the world of music. Student Warren Wortham follows Barth's essay with an essay tracing his own "Musical Beginnings." English writer Virginia Woolf follows with her first struggles as a professional writer, and South African writer Nadine Gordimer closes the chapter with a short story, "Not for Publication," which reminds us that we must all follow individual paths to our callings.

The writers in this opening section share one thing in common. They all are looking back and recalling their worlds. They have searched their memories for the images and sounds and smells, the *vivid details*, that will evoke the past for them—and for their readers.

You may want to begin your writing by doing the same, by looking back at important beginnings in your life: the first television show you remember; the first record you bought or rock concert you attended; the first book you read—or loved. You may wish to write of the first person outside your family who became a friend, or of your first sense of loss. You may want to recreate the moment when you became aware that others had thoughts and feelings—just like you. Writers start by paying attention to themselves and their world. Then they begin.

AN AMERICAN CHILDHOOD

Annie Dillard

An American Childhood *was meant to describe consciousness itself. It concentrates on a child's first awareness that she, or he, is alive—is set down, vulnerable to death, in a world already underway. The child awakens repeatedly to its own consciousness; this awakening is a crucial, and a protospiritual, sensation.*

Fortunately, before adolescent self-consciousness hits, there are some magnificent years when the child is old enough to learn and too young to worry. The child delights, then, in concentrating on the world in its multiplicity and complexity. The passages below are about concentration—on drawing and identifying "criminal suspects"; they are about unself-conscious, energetic attention.

Brief Warm-up Writing Exercises

1. Look closely at, then describe a nearby object—your shoe, your backpack or purse, the desktop on which you are writing—in precise detail.
2. Drawing only on your memory, make a list of the physical characteristics of someone in your family.
3. Describe the sport, game, or activity you enjoyed most as a child and what made it special for you.

---

1   While father was motoring down the river, my reading was giving me a turn.

2   At a neighbor boy's house, I ran into Kimon Nicolaides's *The Natural Way to Draw*. This was a manual for students who couldn't get to Nicolaides's own classes at New York's Art Students League. I was amazed that there were books about things one actually did. I had been drawing in earnest, but at random, for two years. Like all children, when I drew I tried to reproduce schema. The

idea of drawing from life had astounded me two years previously, but I had gradually let it slip, and my drawing, such as it was, had sunk back into facile sloth. Now this book would ignite my fervor for conscious drawing, and bind my attention to both the vigor and the detail of the actual world.

3   For the rest of August, and all fall, this urgent, hortatory book ran my life. I tried to follow its schedules: every day, sixty-five gesture drawings, fifteen memory drawings, an hour-long contour drawing, and "The Sustained Study in Crayon, Clothed" or "The Sustained Study in Crayon, Nude."

4   While Father was gone, I outfitted an attic bedroom as a studio, and moved in. Every summer or weekend morning at eight o'clock I taped that day's drawing schedule to a wall. Since there was no model, nude or clothed, I drew my baseball mitt.

5   I drew my baseball mitt's gesture—its tense repose, its expectancy, which ran up its hollows like a hand. I drew its contours—its flat fingertips strung on square rawhide thongs. I drew its billion grades of light and dark in detail, so the glove weighed vivid and complex on the page, and the trapezoids small as dust motes in the leather fingers cast shadows, and the pale palm leather was smooth as a belly and thick. "Draw anything," said the book. "Learning to draw is really a matter of learning to see," said the book. "Imagine that your pencil point is touching the model instead of the paper." "All the student need concern himself with is reality."

6   With my pencil point I crawled over the mitt's topology. I slithered over each dip and rise; I checked my bearings, admired the enormous view, and recorded it like Meriwether Lewis mapping the Rockies.

7   One thing struck me as odd and interesting. A gesture drawing took forty-five seconds; a Sustained Study took all morning. From any stilllife arrangement or model's pose, the artist could produce either a short study or a long one. Evidently, a given object took no particular amount of time to draw; instead the artist took the time, or didn't take it, at pleasure. And, similarly, things themselves possessed no fixed and intrinsic amount of interest; instead things were interesting as long as you had attention to give them. How long does it take to draw a baseball mitt? As much time as you care to give it. Not an infinite amount of time, but more time than you first imagined. For many days, so long as you want to keep drawing that mitt, and studying that mitt, there will always be a new and finer layer of distinction to draw out and lay in. Your attention discovers—seems thereby to produce—an array of interesting features in any object, like a lamp.

8   By noon, all this drawing would have gone to my head. I slipped into the mitt, quit the attic, quit the house, and headed up the street, looking for a ball game. . . .

9   The attic bedroom where I drew my baseball mitt was a crow's nest, a treehouse, a studio, an office, a forensic laboratory, and a fort. It interested me

especially for a totemic brown water stain on a sloping plaster wall. The stain looked like a square-rigged ship heeled over in a storm. I examined this ship for many months. It was a painting, not a drawing; it had no lines, only forms awash, which rose faintly from the plaster and deepened slowly and dramatically as I watched and the seas climbed and the wind rose before anyone could furl the sails. Those distant dashes over the water—were they men sliding overboard? Were they storm petrels flying? I knew a song whose chorus asked, What did the deep sea say?

My detective work centered around the attic, and sometimes included Pin Ford. We filed information on criminal suspects in a shoe box. We got the information by hanging around the Evergreen Café on Penn Avenue and noting suspicious activity.

One dark, rainy afternoon when I was alone, I saw a case of beer inside the trunk of a man's car. If that wasn't suspicious, I didn't know what was. I was lurking just outside the drugstore, where I could see the Evergreen Café clientele without being seen. I memorized the car license number, of course, as anyone would—but my real virtue as a detective was that I could memorize the whole man, inch by inch, by means of sentences, and later reproduce the man in a drawing.

When I came home from the dark rain that afternoon I walked through floor after floor of the lighted house, wetting the golden rugs and muttering, until I got to the attic stairs and the attic itself. There I repaired to a card table under the square-rigged ship. I wrote down the suspect's car's make and license number. I wrote down my stabs at his height and age, and a description of his clothes. Then I turned on the radio, opened a cheap drawing tablet, and relaxed to the business of drawing the man who had stepped out of the Evergreen Café and revealed a case of beer in the trunk of his car.

By accident I drew a sloppy oval that looked like his head. I copied a page of these. Paying attention, I marked off some rough ratios: the crucial intervals between eye sockets, headtop, and chin. Unconsciously again, I let my hand scribble lines for features. I sat up to play back in my head certain memorized sentences: he has a wide mouth; his mouth corners fall directly beneath eyes' outer corners; forehead is round; ears are high, triangular. My dumb hand molded the recurved facial masses and shaded the eye sockets for its own pleasure with slanting parallel lines. I sat enchanted and unwitting in a trance.

What will the weather be?
Tell us, Mister Weather Man.

The radio woman enunciated her slow, terrible song. She sounded her notes delicately, as did the idiot xylophone that preceded her. A wind was rising outside. Across the attic room, the blackened windows rattled. I saw their glossed reflections on the pale walls wag. The rain battered the roof over my head, over the waterlogged ship. I heard the bare buckeye boughs hitting the house.

15   I was drawing the head. I shut my eyes. I could not see the man's face eidetically. That is, I could not reproduce it interiorly, study it, and discover new things, as some few people can look at a page, print it, as it were, in their memories, and read it off later. I could produce stable images only rarely. But like anyone, I could recall and almost see fleet torn fragments of a scene: a raincoat sleeve's wrinkling, a blond head bending, red-lighted rain falling on asphalt, a pesteringly interesting pattern in a cordovan shoe, which rises and floats across that face I want to see. I perceived these sights as scraps that floated like blowing tissue across some hollow interior space, some space at the arching roof of the rib cage, perhaps. I swerved to study them before they slid away.

16   I hoped that the sentences would nail the blowing scraps down. I hoped that the sentences would store scenes like rolls of film, rolls of film I could simply reel off and watch. But of course, the sentences did not work that way. The sentences suggested scenes to the imagination, which were no sooner repeated than envisioned, and envisioned just as poorly and just as vividly as actual memories. Here was Raggedy Ann, say, an actual memory, with her red-and-white-striped stockings and blunt black feet. And here, say, was a barefoot boy asleep in a car, his cheeks covered thinly with blood. Which was real? The barefoot boy was just as vivid. It was easier to remember a sentence than a sight, and the sentences suggested sights new or skewed. These were dim regions, these submerged caves where waters mingled. On my cheap tablet I was drawing round lips, suns, fish in schools.

17   Soon someone would call me for dinner. But I would not come, I suddenly realized, and I would not answer the call—ever—for I would have died of starvation. They would find me, having slid off my chair, half under the card table, lying dead on the floor. And so young.

18   In the blue shoe box on the card table they would find my priceless files. I had written all my data about today's suspect, drawn his face several times from several angles, and filed it all under his car's license number. When the police needed it, it was ready.

19   Privately I thought the reference librarian at the Homewood Library was soft in the head. The week before, she had handed me, in broad daylight, the book that contained the key to Morse code. Without a word, she watched me copy it, pocket the paper, and leave.

20   I knew how to keep a code secret, if she didn't. At home I memorized Morse code promptly, and burned the paper.

21   I had read the library's collection of popular forensic medicine, its many books about Scotland Yard and the FBI, a dull biography of J. Edgar Hoover, and its Sherlock Holmes. I knew I was not alone in knowing Morse code. The FBI knew it, Scotland Yard knew it, and every sparks in the navy knew it. I read everything I could get about ham radios. All I needed was a receiver. I could

listen in on troop maneuvers, intelligence reports, and disasters at sea. And I could rescue other hams from calamity, to which, as a class, they seemed remarkably prone.

22 I knew that police artists made composite drawings of criminal suspects. Witnesses to crimes selected, from a varied assortment, a stripe of crown hair, a stripe or two of forehead, a stripe of eyes, and so forth. Police artists—of whose ranks I was an oblate—made a drawing that combined these elements; newspapers published the drawings; someone recognized the suspect and called the police.

23 When Pin Ford and I were running low on suspects, and had run out of things to communicate in Morse code, I sat at my attic table beside the shoe box file and drew a variety of such stripes. I amused myself by combining them into new faces. So God must sit in heaven, at a card table, fingering a heap of stripes—hairlines, jawlines, brows—and joining them at whim to people a world. I began wondering if the stock of individual faces on earth through all of time is infinite.

24 My sweetest ambition was to see a drawing of mine on a newspaper's front page: HAS ANYBODY SEEN THIS MAN? I didn't care about reducing crime, any more than Sherlock Holmes did. I rather wished there were more crime, and closer by. What interested me was the schematic likeness, how recognizable it was, and how startlingly few things you needed to strike a resemblance. You needed only a few major proportions in the head. The soft tissues scarcely mattered; they were merely decorations that children drew. What mattered was the framing of the skull.

25 And so in that faraway attic, among the boughs of buckeye trees, year after year, I drew. I drew formal, sustained studies of my left hand still on the card table, of my baseball mitt, a saddle shoe. I drew from memory the faces of the people I knew, my own family just downstairs in the great house—oh, but I hated these clumsy drawings, these beloved faces so rigid on the page and lacking in tenderness and irony. (Who could analyze a numb skull when all you cared about was a lively caught glance, the pleased rising of Mother's cheek, the soft amused setting of Amy's lip, Father's imagining eye in its socket?) And I drew from memory the faces of people I saw in the streets. I formed sentences about them as I looked at them, and repeated the sentences to myself as I wandered on. ❖

Questions to Ponder

1. What did Annie Dillard discover about drawing as a young girl? How long did it take to do a drawing?
2. In what ways might *writing* be like drawing? How long does it take to write about something? How many different ways are there to write about something?

3. What keeps people from giving close attention to their lives as they unfold? What conditions are necessary in order for you really to concentrate on an assignment? A person? An event?
4. How is learning to *see* related to learning to write?

Writing Possibilities

1. After reading Dillard's description of the contours, texture, and shadings of her baseball mitt, repeat your "warm-up" description of a nearby object, trying to discover new and "finer layer[s] of distinction to draw out and lay in."
2. Try to recapture your first conscious memory.
   - What was it of?
   - How old were you?
   - Is your first conscious memory of an event or of a thought, a recognition?
   - Were others involved or just you?
   - What are the specific (sensory) details (sights, sounds, smells, tastes, touches) that would bring that moment back to life for you and for a reader?
   - If this memory has a meaning to you now that it did not have at the time, what is this meaning?
3. Following Annie Dillard's lead, describe a book or an activity that dominated your waking hours as a child. Try to recapture the experience and explain its significance.
4. Make a list of all the factors that keep you from focusing, concentrating, and just generally paying attention to life. Then write a letter to yourself noting some of these distractions and offering some suggestions of ways to better "attend." Address in your letter the question of whether it really matters whether we pay attention (to ourselves and the world).

My Baseball Years
Philip Roth

Beginning a book is unpleasant. . . . Worse than not knowing your subject is not knowing how to treat it, because that's finally everything. I type out beginnings and they're awful, more of an unconscious parody of my previous book than the breakaway from it that I want. I need something driving down the center of a book, a magnet to draw everything to it—that's what I look for during the first months of writing something new. I often have to write a hundred pages or more before there's a paragraph that's alive. Okay, I say to myself, that's your beginning, start there; that's the first paragraph of the book. I'll go over the first six months of work and underline in red a paragraph, a sentence, sometimes no more than a phrase, that has some life in it, and then I'll type all these out on one page. Usually it doesn't come to more than one page, but if I'm lucky, that's the start of page one. I look for the liveliness to set the tone.

Brief Warm-up Writing Exercises

1. Write why you love (or hate) physical education.
2. Describe your most exhilarating (or disappointing) moment in sports.
3. Make a list of items and expressions you would want to mention if you were going to explain the game of baseball to a visitor from another planet.
4. Describe how you usually go about beginning a piece of writing.

1 ❖ In one of his essays George Orwell writes that, though he was not very good at the game, he had a long, hopeless love affair with cricket until he was sixteen. My relations with baseball were similar. Between the ages of nine and thirteen, I must have put in a forty-hour week during the snowless months over at the neighborhood playfield—softball, hardball, and stickball pick-up games—while simultaneously holding down a full-time job as a pupil at the local grammar school. As I remember it, news of two of the most cataclysmic public events of my childhood—the death of President Roosevelt and the

bombing of Hiroshima—reached me while I was out playing ball. My performance was uniformly erratic; generally okay for those easygoing pick-up games, but invariably lacking the calm and the expertise that the naturals displayed in stiff competition. My taste, and my talent, such as it was, was for the flashy, whiz-bang catch rather than the towering fly; running and leaping I loved, all the do-or-die stuff—somehow I lost confidence waiting and waiting for the ball lofted right at me to descend. I could never make the high school team, yet I remember that, in one of the two years I vainly (in both senses of the word) tried out, I did a good enough imitation of a baseball player's *style* to be able to fool (or amuse) the coach right down to the day he cut the last of the dreamers from the squad and gave out the uniforms.

2   Though my disappointment was keen, my misfortune did not necessitate a change in plans for the future. Playing baseball was not what the Jewish boys of our lower-middle-class neighborhood were expected to do in later life for a living. Had I been cut from the high school itself, *then* there would have been hell to pay in my house, and much confusion and shame in me. As it was, my family took my chagrin in stride and lost no more faith in me than I actually did in myself. They probably would have been shocked if I had made the team.

3   Maybe I would have been too. Surely it would have put me on a somewhat different footing with this game that I loved with all my heart, not simply for the fun of playing it (fun was secondary, really), but for the mythic and aesthetic dimension that it gave to an American boy's life—particularly to one whose grandparents could hardly speak English. For someone whose roots in America were strong but only inches deep, and who had no experience, such as a Catholic child might, of an awesome hierarchy that was real and felt, baseball was a kind of secular church that reached into every class and region of the nation and bound millions upon millions of us together in common concerns, loyalties, rituals, enthusiasms, and antagonisms. Baseball made me understand what patriotism was about, at its best.

4   Not that Hitler, the Bataan Death March, the battle for the Solomons, and the Normandy invasion didn't make of me and my contemporaries what may well have been the most patriotic generation of schoolchildren in American history (and the most willingly and successfully propagandized). But the war we entered when I was eight had thrust the country into what seemed to a child—and not only to a child—a struggle to the death between Good and Evil. Fraught with perilous, unthinkable possibilities, it inevitably nourished a patriotism grounded in moral virtue and bloody-minded hate, the patriotism that fixes a bayonet to a Bible. It seems to me that through baseball I was put in touch with a more humane and tender brand of patriotism, lyrical rather than martial or righteous in spirit, and without the reek of saintly zeal, a patriotism that could not so easily be sloganized, or contained in a high-sounding formula to which you had to pledge something vague but all-encompassing called your "allegiance."

5   To sing the National Anthem in the school auditorium every week, even during the worst of the war years, generally left me cold. The enthusiastic lady teacher waved her arms in the air and we obliged with the words: "See! Light!

Proof! Night! There!" But nothing stirred within, strident as we might be—in the end, just another school exercise. It was different, however, on Sundays out at Ruppert Stadium, a green wedge of pasture miraculously walled in among the factories, warehouses, and truck depots of industrial Newark. It would, in fact, have seemed to me an emotional thrill forsaken if, before the Newark Bears took on the hated enemy from across the marshes, the Jersey City Giants, we hadn't first to rise to our feet (my father, my brother, and I—along with our inimical countrymen, the city's Germans, Italians, Irish, Poles, and, out in the Africa of the bleachers, Newark's Negroes) to celebrate the America that had given to this unharmonious mob a game so grand and beautiful.

6   Just as I first learned the names of the great institutions of higher learning by trafficking in football pools for a neighborhood bookmaker rather than from our high school's college adviser, so my feel for the American landscape came less from what I learned in the classroom about Lewis and Clark than from following the major-league clubs on their road trips and reading about the minor leagues in the back pages of *The Sporting News*. The size of the continent got through to you finally when you had to stay up to 10:30 P.M. in New Jersey to hear via radio "ticker-tape" Cardinal pitcher Mort Cooper throw the first strike of the night to Brooklyn shortstop Pee Wee Reese out in "steamy" Sportsmen's Park in St. Louis, Missouri. And however much we might be told by teacher about the stockyards and the Haymarket riot, Chicago only began to exist for me as a real place, and to matter in American history, when I became fearful (as a Dodger fan) of the bat of Phil Cavarretta, first baseman for the Chicago Cubs.

7   Not until I got to college and was introduced to literature did I find anything with a comparable emotional atmosphere and aesthetic appeal. I don't mean to suggest that it was a simple exchange, one passion for another. Between first discovering the Newark Bears and the Brooklyn Dodgers at seven or eight and first looking into Conrad's *Lord Jim* at age eighteen, I had done some growing up. I am only saying that my discovery of literature, and fiction particularly, and the "love affair"—to some degree hopeless, but still earnest—that has ensued, derives in part from this childhood infatuation with baseball. Or, more accurately perhaps, baseball—with its lore and legends, its cultural power, its seasonal associations, its native authenticity, its simple rules and transparent strategies, its longueurs and thrills, its spaciousness, its suspensefulness, its heroics, its nuances, its lingo, its "characters," its peculiarly hypnotic tedium, its mythic transformation of the immediate—was the literature of my boyhood.

8   Baseball, as played in the big leagues, was something completely outside my own life that could nonetheless move me to ecstasy and to tears; like fiction it could excite the imagination and hold the attention as much with minutiae as with high drama. Mel Ott's cocked leg striding into the ball, Jackie Robinson's pigeon-toed shuffle as he moved out to second base, each was to be as deeply affecting over the years as that night—"inconceivable," "inscrutable," as any night Conrad's Marlow might struggle to comprehend—the night that Dodger wild man, Rex Barney (who never lived up to "our" expectations, who

should have been "our" Koufax), not only went the distance without walking in half a dozen runs, but, of all things, threw a no-hitter. A thrilling mystery, marvelously enriched by the fact that a light rain had fallen during the early evening, and Barney, figuring the game was going to be postponed, had eaten a hot dog just before being told to take the mound.

9   This detail was passed on to us by Red Barber, the Dodger radio sportscaster of the forties, a respectful, mild Southerner with a subtle rural tanginess to his vocabulary and a soft country-parson tone to his voice. For the adventures of "dem bums" of Brooklyn—a region then the very symbol of urban wackiness and tumult—to be narrated from Red Barber's highly alien but loving perspective constituted a genuine triumph of what my English professors would later teach me to call "point of view." James himself might have admired the implicit cultural ironies and the splendid possibilities for oblique moral and social commentary. And as for the detail about Rex Barney eating his hot dog, it was irresistible, joining as it did the spectacular to the mundane, and furnishing an adolescent boy with a glimpse of an unexpectedly ordinary, even humdrum, side to male heroism.

10   Of course, in time, neither the flavor and suggestiveness of Red Barber's narration nor "epiphanies" as resonant with meaning as Rex Barney's pregame hot dog could continue to satisfy a developing literary appetite; nonetheless, it was just this that helped to sustain me until I was ready to begin to respond to the great inventors of narrative detail and masters of narrative voice and perspective like James, Conrad, Dostoevsky, and Bellow. ❖

Questions to Ponder

1. To Philip Roth, how is baseball like great literature—especially great fiction? What do they have in common?
2. According to Roth, what is the source of baseball's appeal to people from all classes, races, and walks of life?
3. What does Philip Roth do in "My Baseball Years" to make baseball and his childhood come alive for you the reader?
4. Could another writer (or you) make a case for the appeal of another sport? What is the appeal of basketball? Hockey? Volleyball? Swimming?
5. Why might the patriotism fostered by baseball be "a more humane and tender" brand of patriotism than that associated with war?

Writing Possibilities

1. Using Philip Roth's essay as a model, write your own essay titled "My ———— Years."
2. Take this one (long) sentence from Philip Roth's essay as your springboard for an essay of your own on baseball:

. . . baseball—with its lore and legends, its cultural power, its seasonal associations, its native authenticity, its simple rules and transparent strategies, its longueurs and thrills, its spaciousness, its suspensefulness, its heroics, its nuances, its lingo, its "characters," its peculiarly hypnotic tedium, its mythic transformation of the immediate—was the literature of my boyhood.

Devote at least one full paragraph to each of Roth's phrases and attempt to explain to someone who knows little about the game the "lore and legends" of baseball, its "cultural power," "seasonal associations," its "characters" and "lingo," and so on. What vivid current examples can you draw on to illustrate your points? Will you want to reorder Philip Roth's descriptors? Add any new ones of your own?

3. Find out who was the greatest baseball player (or writer) in your school's history and write about his or her career for your school newspaper or alumni newsletter. (*Hint:* You will want to read old newspaper stories and school histories, and you may want to track down the person and conduct a phone interview.)

HIGH SCHOOL BEGINNINGS

Margaret Atwood

When you begin to write you're in love with the language, with the act of creation, with yourself partly; but as you go on, the writing—if you follow it—will take you places you never intended to go and show you things you would never otherwise have seen. I began as a profoundly apolitical writer, but then I began to do what all novelists and some poets do: I began to describe the world around me.

. . . where I live is where everyone lives: it isn't just a place or a region, though it is also that. . . . It's a space composed of images, experiences, the weather, your own past and your ancestors', what people say and what they look like and how they react to what you're doing, important events and trivial ones, the connections among them not always obvious. The images come from outside, they are there, they are the things we live with and must deal with. But the judgments and the connections (what does it mean?) have to be made inside your head and they are made with words: good, bad, like, dislike, whether to go, whether to stay, whether to live there any more. For me that's partly what writing is: an exploration of where in reality I live. . . .

I don't think Canada is "better" than any other place, any more than I think Canadian literature is "better"; I live in one and read the other for a simple reason: they are mine, with all the sense of territory that implies. Refusing to acknowledge where you come from . . . is an act of amputation: you may become free floating, a citizen of the world . . . but only at the cost of arms, legs or heart. By discovering your place you discover yourself.

Brief Warm-up Writing Exercises

1. Make a list of all the career possibilities you have considered in your life.
2. Describe the high-school project or event that is most memorable to you.
3. Think back and describe the moment when you did your first serious piece of writing.

1   It was in high school that I, myself, became a writer. I wasn't supposed to be a writer. I wasn't intending to be a writer. In grade school, I thought I was going to be a painter. That modified to dress designer about the eighth grade. In early high school, the reality principle set in in the shape of the Guidance book. Guidance was something that was supposed to help you decide what you were going to be if and when you grew up. Our Guidance book was gray and inside it were listed the available careers, segregated according to sex. There were only five for women: schoolteacher, nurse, airline stewardess, secretary and home economist. (This was in 1953. I'm sure all of that has changed by now.) I didn't want to be any of these things, but I figured if I had to be something I didn't want to be, I might as well choose the one that would make the most money. So I chose Home Economics as my extra option, instead of typing. Typing was suspect in those days. Girls who took typing had very thin eyebrows, and smoked cigarettes in the washroom, and chewed gum, and tended to vanish from school. So I still don't know how to touch type. I write in longhand on yellow legal-size notepads with blue lines with a roll-tip ballpoint pen. That's the answer to "how do you write?"

2   Home economics and I did not really hit it off, though I learned some things in it that are still of use to me today. For instance, always file your nails from the sides toward the center. However, Home Economics purported to be a science, and demanded a certain order and rigidity. In sewing, your garments were supposed to look as good on the inside as they did on the outside. I could never see the point of this and was always having to pick out my zippers. In cooking, you were supposed to have a green thing, a white thing, a brown

thing and a yellow thing on every dinner plate. It didn't seem to matter much what these things were or how they tasted, but they had to be those colors. I did learn to make meat loaf, applesauce, and Harvard beets, and I suppose these skills would be useful should I ever wish to use them. Also, you were not supposed to stick your finger into what you were cooking in order to taste it. We in Home Economics were very germ-conscious.

3   In twelfth grade, out of the blue, I got hit by writing. (That's an off-rhyme for lightning—deliberately.) I don't know why. This was Canada in the mid-fifties in a middle-class high school, in a middle-class suburb, in the middle of the country. The terrain around was flat, both geographically and culturally. We were not taught about any writers who were still alive, let alone Canadian. So I thought that to be a writer, you had to be dead and English. You could be a girl though, like George Eliot, which was some comfort. My point is that I had no role models. But suddenly I was writing things, without any warning. I'm happy to report that my 11th grade English teacher, while being interviewed by someone or other after I had become eminent, did not lie. Instead of saying that genius poured from my every pore, and that she always knew I'd be famous some day, she quite honestly said that under her regime, I showed no special promise. Which I think was true. But there I was, a year later, writing incomprehensible but dark and brooding poems which sounded like Edgar Allen Poe and Lord Byron since I had never been exposed to any modern poetry. All my things rhymed and scanned, which was not bad training, come to think of it. I thought these poems were wonderful; in fact they were fairly awful, though tinged with a certain *je ne sais quoi,* which may have been a hint of borderline madness. My twelfth grade English teacher, however, was a certain Miss Billings. Not only was she elegant and a good dresser—important to the ex-dress designer in me—as it showed that you didn't have to be a frump if you went literary—but she encouraged me. "I can't understand this, dear, so it must be good," is what I remember her saying. Probably she said, "I can't understand this, dear, but I think it's good." Either way, I was encouraged. I decided then and there that I was going to write the great Canadian novel, which didn't seem too hard, as there was not at that time any competition.

4   One of my first acts as a writer was to subvert the home economics class. I did it in the following way. That was the year we were supposed to be doing a special project. Our home economics teacher thought that this project should be making stuffed animals. We, however, were allowed to vote on this, and I lobbied behind the scenes and got the others to vote on my project, which was a home economics opera. Since we were living under the pretense of democracy, she had to let this go through, although her stipulation was that the subject had to be home economics. The opera was about three fabrics called Orlon, Nylon, and Dacron, who lived with their

father, Old King Coal, in a castle. Along came the hero, whose name was Sir William Wooly. He had a terrible problem: he shrank from washing. Arias were sung. The resolution of the opera was that Sir William Wooly married Orlon, and they produced a new blend called Wool-Orlene, which combines the good qualities of both fabrics. This opera, which was produced, directed, and costumed by me, as well as written by me, was a smash hit. Despite this triumph, I was faced with a dilemma. I was going to be a writer, but in those days in Canada, nobody was visibly a writer. Occasionally, you would see writers in print, mentioned in newspapers, but only on the ladies' pages. This is back when there were ladies' pages, and some charitable soul had had a tea in their honor. Apart from that they were practically invisible. They weren't reviewed very much; sometimes you might find a Canadian novel or book of poetry in something called the *Canadiana* section of a book store, along with books called "Beautiful Canada" and "Favorite Canadian Recipes," but writers did not have a very high profile, and in general, people believed that a Canadian writer was an oxymoron. You had to give up one or the other. Most moved. It was evident to me that I was unable to make a living from writing, so how was I going to support my habit? I felt that I would have to do something else.

5   First I considered journalism. I thought that had something to do with writing. But I consulted my second cousin who was a journalist, and he said, "Well, dear," (remember, this was the fifties) "If you are a woman and you go into journalism, you'll end up writing the obituaries and the ladies' page." It's true that some of my critics claim that I have been doing that ever since, but at the time this did not appeal. My second choice was botany. I was, in fact, rather good at botany. I got better marks in botany than I did in English, because in those days, they used to take marks in English off for spelling mistakes, and the fact was that I could spell perfectly well words like "scrofulariasii" but I got shot down on words like "career" and "weird." My mother used to say to me, "Dear, if you're going to be a writer, don't you think you should learn to spell?" and I said, "Other people will do that for me." And they do. My third choice was running away to England, to become a waitress, live in a garret and write masterpieces. But then I actually tried being a waitress, and it was too hard. For one thing, it puts you off your food. A great way to lose weight, being a waitress. After you've cleared off all those dog dinners on other people's plates, you really don't feel like eating very much. In the end, I settled for Honors English at the University of Toronto. I could be a university professor, I thought, which would give me time off in the summers to whip off a few *Moby Dicks* or *Middlemarches,* and anyway, I could read a lot that way, which I liked to do. I would not have been able to pursue this plan without some skills in expository writing, which demonstrates once again the practical virtues of this particular craft. ❖

Questions to Ponder

1. Why does a writer suddenly start writing? List some possible reasons.
2. Does a person have to have visible role models in order to become a writer? Would visible role models help? What other kinds of role models might there be besides visible ones?
3. What might be the effects of encouragement (or lack of encouragement) on the beginning writer?
4. How does Margaret Atwood make her "High School Beginnings" come alive for you?

Writing Possibilities

1. Using Margaret Atwood's opera as a model, sketch your ideas for an opera in your major. What would an accounting opera be like? A computer science opera? An elementary education opera? A public relations opera? Now try writing this opera.
2. Describe the direct or indirect path that has brought you to your current major or career choice. Were there crucial milestones on this journey—or forks in the road?
3. Prepare a thorough report for majors in your field, describing potential jobs available, specific education or training required, hiring trends, salary ranges, job benefits, and disadvantages. (You may want to interview professionals currently working in the field as well as read brochures and articles about it.)

Some Reasons Why I Tell the Stories I Tell the Way I Tell Them Rather Than Some Other Sort of Stories Some Other Way

John Barth

To complete a novel takes me, on the average, four years: one U.S. presidential term, or the interval between undergraduate matriculation and the baccalaureate. Between novels (and sometimes on Fridays, for diversion) it is my habit to take stock, like the electorate between elections or a newly commenced Bachelor pondering graduate school; I review where and who I've been, in hopes of learning where and who I am, to the end of laying my course for the next waypoint to wherever. So that the pump won't rust while the well refills, I do this reorientation-work by writing an essay or two until the muse of storytelling reasserts her absolute priority.

"Some Reasons . . ." is the product of one such between-books inventory, eight years ago; this headnote to it is another, two novels later. Its sentences, like all my sentences, were first essayed in looseleaf longhand fountain-pen cursive; I think of them as being not so much "written" as drawn, *the letters looping and flowing and bonding into verbal units instead of sitting discretely side by side like subway passengers, each feigning engrossment in his/her double-folded newspaper. These I scratch and scribble over and rediagram as I draw in kinesthetic bliss from after breakfast until the approach of lunch, when (these days) I transfer them to the word processor for its greater power of subsequent "processing": most often the manifold rearrangement of elements within the sentences until, several much-fussed-over printouts later, my mind and ear are equally satisfied. For the record (don't ask me whose), I end each morning's drawing with a date. (11/18/89)*

DRAFT

Headnote to "Some Reasons..."

It takes me, on the average, four years to complete a novel: any U.S. presidential term, or the interval between [illegible] and the [illegible]. Between novels (and sometimes on Fridays, for diversion) it is my habit to take stock, like a new Babylonian [illegible] [illegible] or the [illegible] between elections, to review where, good or otherwise, I've been, [illegible] in hopes of knowing where (and who) I am, at the end of logging my course for the next waypoint to wherever. To keep the fingers from rusting while the well refills, I do this reconnaissance-work by writing an essay or two before the muse of storytelling reasserts her absolute priority.

"Some Reasons..." is the product of one early priority between books; the thing [illegible] it is written, two [illegible] later. [illegible] years ago [illegible], like all my stories, were first essayed in lowercase longhand cursive (I think of them as being not so much "written" as drawn), the letters looping and flowing and bonding into words instead of neatly biscuited [illegible] side by side without touching, like [illegible] passengers each with his/her own [illegible] [illegible]. Then I scratch and scribble over and rearrange [illegible] in [illegible] from after breakfast until the afterward of lunch, when ([illegible]) I

Continued

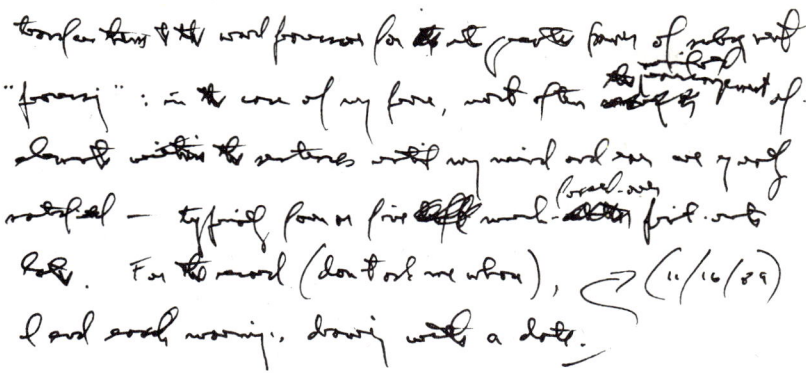

Brief Warm-up Writing Exercises

1. Write your first thoughts about your birth order. Were you the first born? An only child? A middle child? The baby of the family? Adopted? Half of a set of twins? What has your order of birth meant to you?
2. Briefly describe the landscape and climate of the place where you were born. How do you think they have affected your personality or outlook?
3. Describe your most memorable encounters with music—or musical instruments.

◆───

1   ◆ Of the making of writers there is no end till The End unmakes them. Here's how Yours Truly tells his Once upon a time:

Twins

2   It is my fate, and equally my sister's, to have been born opposite-sex twins, with an older brother and no younger siblings.
3   Much is known about "identical" (monozygotic) twins, less about fraternal (dizygotic) twins, less yet about us opposite-sexers (who, it goes without saying, are always dizygotic). But twins of any sort share the curious experiences of accommodating to a peer companion from the beginning, even in the womb; of entering the world with an established sidekick, rather than alone; of acquiring speech and the other basic skills *a deux,* in the meanwhile sharing a language before speech and beyond speech. Speech, baby twins may feel, is

for the Others. As native speakers of a dialect regard the official language, we twins may regard language itself: It is for dealing with the outsiders; between ourselves we have little need of it. One might reasonably therefore expect a twin who becomes a storyteller never to take language for granted; to be ever at it, tinkering, foregrounding it, perhaps unnaturally conscious of it. Language is for relating to the Others.

4 Now, most opposite-sex twins come soon to shrug the shoulders of their imaginations at that congenital circumstance; to regard it as a more or less amusing detail. They can do so because it was not their additional fate to have a three-year-older brother who, upon hearing the unlucky news that he had suddenly not one but a *team* of rivals for his parents' thitherto undivided attention, gamely and fatefully remarked: "Now we have a Jack and Jill."

5 Poor firstborn: Thy day in the family sun wast shadowed from that hour, but thou hadst in advance thy more than justified revenge. Jack and Jill we became, and up childhood's hill we went—in scrappy East Cambridge, a crab-and-oyster town on the Eastern Shore of Maryland—lugging between us that heavy pail. Our grade school teachers oohed and aahed (doubtless privately ughed) at the awful cuteness of our names, while alleywise classmates reddened our innocent ears with every bawdy version of the nursery rhyme. I can recite them still, those scurrilous variations; my ears still redden.

6 Language, boyoboy, c'est pour les autres: My sister and I were by it not let to forget our twinness. Until circumstance and physical maturation differentiated and tumbled us toward our separate fates—a fair benchmark is the fall of '43, when we approached both puberty and public high school in an unaffluent, semirural, semi-Southern eleven-year county system further impoverished by the war, no school band, few varsity sports, an attenuated faculty, reduced course offerings, and three curricula: the Agricultural for most of the farm boys; the Commercial for nearly all the girls and some of the boys, those who expected to go neither back to the farm nor on to college; and the Academic for the small percentage of us in that time and place whose vague ambitions did not necessarily preclude higher education (the two or three whose parents were already of the professional class were whisked out of that system and off to private preparatory schools for at least their eleventh grade and a proper twelfth)—until the Commercial course and biological womanhood befell Jill, the Academic course and biological manhood Jack, we were a Jack and Jill indeed, between whom nearly everything went without saying.

7 With those closest since, I have had sustained and intimate conversation, but seldom in words except at the beginning and end of our connection. Language is for getting to know you and getting to unknow you. We converse to convert, each the other, from an Other into an extension of ourself; and we converse conversely. Dear Reader, if I knew you better, what I'm saying would go without saying; as I do not, let me tell you a story.

8 Once upon a time, in myth, twins signified whatever dualisms a culture entertained: mortal/immortal, good/evil, creation/destruction, what had they. In western literature since the Romantic period, twins (and doubles, shadows,

mirrors) usually signify the "divided self," our secret sharer or inner adversary—even the schizophrenia some neo-Freudians maintain lies near the dark heart of writing. Aristophanes, in Plato's *Symposium,* declares we are all of us twins,* indeed a kind of Siamese twins, who have lost and who seek eternally our missing half. The loss accounts for alienation, our felt distance from man and god; the search accounts for both erotic love and the mystic's goal of divine atonement.

9   I have sometimes felt that a twin who happens to be a writer, or a writer who happens to be a twin, might take this *shtik* by the other end and use schizophrenia, say, as an image for what he knows to be his literal case: that he once was more than one person and somehow now is less. I am the least psychological of storytellers; yet even to me it is apparent that I write these words, and all the others, in part because I no longer have my twin to be wordless with, even when I'm with her. Less and less, as twins go along, goes without saying. One is in the world, talking to the Others, talking to oneself.

10 My books tend to come in parts, my sentences in twin members.

Marshes, Tides

11   Jack and Jilling was not easy in Dorchester County, Maryland, of which Cambridge is the seat. Eighty percent of that county is sub-sea level: estuarine wetlands all but uninhabited by men, but teeming like bayous and everglades with other life: the nursery of Chesapeake Bay. No hills down there to go up; and your pail of water will be salt.

12   More exactly, it will be brackish, turbid, tidal, and tepid: about the same salinity and summer temperature, I am persuaded, as the fluid we all first swam in. Unlike lake water on the one hand or ocean on the other, this will not sting your eyes. Dorchester Countians sensibly nowadays prefer swimming pools, to avoid the medusa jellyfish, or sea nettle (and the watermen, like watermen everywhere, seldom swim at all); but as summer youngsters we played in the natural element for hours and hours, eyes always open. We were often nettled but never chilled; on the other hand, we could see little farther than in the womb.

13   As a grown-up I've spent agreeable years on a mountain lake and come to enjoy the clear Caribbean, where you can see your anchor on the bottom full fathom five. Yet both seem artificial: the one a backyard pool, be it Lake Superior itself; the other a vast lighted aquarium. Only our warm green semisaline Chesapeake estuaries strike me (strike that: *caress* me) as real, for better or worse.

14   North across the Choptank from Dorchester is nearly marshless Talbot,

---

*It may be that in fact as many as 70 percent of us are. See e.g., the chapter "The Vanished Twin," in Kay Cassill's *Twins: Nature's Amazing Mystery* (New York: Atheneum, 1982).

the Gold Coast county of tidewater Maryland. Hervey Allen, author of the bestselling *Anthony Adverse,* used to live over there; James A. Michener, author of the bestselling *Chesapeake,* lives over there. A little train nicknamed The Millionaires' Special used to connect *its* county seat to New York City. Almost anyone with sense and money would prefer Talbot to Dorchester. But my father used to say that the real Eastern Shore begins on the south bank of the Choptank, and Mr. Michener himself, tisking his tongue at population pressure problems on the upper Shore, once declared to me his confidence that our lower-Shore rivers will survive "to the end of the century."

15   Eighteen more years.

16   Nearly all who took the Academic course, and many who didn't, left Dorchester County for good after graduation. Before I joined their number, I used sometimes to stand in those boundless tidal marshes, at the center of a 360-degree horizon, surrounded in the spring by maybe a quarter-million Canada geese taking off for home, and at least by age nine or ten think two clear thoughts—never clearer than upon our returning from a visit to my one connection with the larger world, a New Jersey aunt who took us marshlings to the top of the Empire State Building and *all over* the New York World's Fair of 1939/40—(1) This place speaks to me in ways that I don't even understand yet; and (2) I'm going to get out of here and become a distinguished something-or-other. My wife shakes her head at the apparent vanity of that latter. But in a landscape where nothing and almost nobody was distinguished; where for better or worse there was no pressure from nature or culture to stand out; where horizontality is so ubiquitous that anything vertical—a day beacon, a dead loblolly pine—is ipso facto interesting, the abstract wish to distinguish oneself somehow, anyhow, seems pardonable to me.

17   In Civil War times Maryland was a Border State. Mason's and Dixon's Line runs east-west across its top and then, appropriately, north-south down the Eastern Shore, which was heavily loyalist in the Revolution and Confederate in the War Between the States. Marsh country is a border state, too, between land and sea, and tide-marsh doubly so, its twin diurnal ebbs and floods continuously reorchestrating the geography. No clear demarcations here between fresh and salt, wet and dry: Many many square miles of Delaware happen to be Delaware instead of Maryland owing to a seventeenth-century surveyors' dispute about the midpoint of a line whose eastern terminus is the sharp Atlantic coast but whose western peters out in the Dorchester County marshes, where the "shoreline" at high tide may be a mile east from where it was at low, when reedy islets muddily join the main. Puberty is another border state; also twinhood, Q.E.D. Your webfoot amphibious marsh-nurtured writer will likely by mere reflex regard many conventional boundaries and distinctions as arbitrary, fluid, negotiable: form versus content, realism versus irrealism, fact versus fiction, life versus art. His favorite mark of punctuation will be the semicolon.

18   He will also carry a perpetual tide clock in his blood. My father, never a

waterman but never far from tidewater, on his one visit to the cottage I owned for years on Lake Chautauqua in west New York, could neither accept nor remember that the water level there remained the same hour after hour, day after day. Three lunchtimes into the visit he would still wonder how it could be high tide *now* when it had been at breakfast. He was polite about it, but landlocked water bored him, as it does me. How can water that doesn't chase the moon speak to the imagination? I had rather watch tides come and go from the merest muddy fingerling of a cove off a creek off a river off a bay off an ocean than own Golden Pond.

19   What mattered to me as a boy was the fact that the scruffy water in Cambridge Creek was contiguous with, say, Portugal. Years later, standing where Prince Henry the Navigator's navigators' college was, I was helped to get my bearings by the reciprocal of that fact.

20   My books and their author first located themselves in tidewater-land, then moved outside it; have lately returned; may drift off again, or not. The tide goes out, comes back, goes out, comes back. As many metaphors as boats are carried on it.

Music

21   Between Cambridge Creek and Cape St. Vincent I broke my crown in New York City at the Juilliard School of Music, into whose summer program I tumbled after high school, 17, with money I'd earned playing drums in a homegrown jazz band for the two years prior. No union rules in marshville.

22   About music my sister knew next to nothing and I less than my sister, though we'd been given piano lessons in vain right through the end of the Depression and beginning of the War; duets were thought especially apt for Jill and Jack, and we went along, she primo, I secondo. Along about V-E Day we were permitted to quit those lessons, and at once I became passionately interested in playing jazz.

23   Never a distinguished drummer (though a steady), never a soloist (a twin solo?), I was modest and middle-class enough to aspire to neither composition nor performance as a musical career, but too ambitious to consider teaching. In 1947 the big bands were still swinging; orchestration was what I went up the flyway to Juilliard to study, but we jazzfolk knew the word was *arranging*. My heroes became Pete Rugolo, Sy Oliver, Eddie Sauter, Billy Strayhorn. I would be a distinguished arranger: The term suggested something less glamorous but more dignified, daytime, and regular than *jazz drummer,* with its aura of sweat, alcohol, and "tea," as marijuana was then called. Though my father's dead brother had aspired to sculpture and my New Jersey uncle's to tournament tennis, there had never been a professional musician in the family; yet no eyebrows were raised at my ambition. There is a wonderful freedom in

having parents whose schooling ended with the eleventh grade or earlier: Merely to finish public high school is to be successful in their eyes; anything beyond it is a triumph. I could have declared that I was going to be a distinguished metaphysician, even a distinguished *poet,* and they wouldn't have minded. My New Jersey aunt spoke hopefully of, you know, studio orchestras.

24   I moved into a cockroach-and-cabbage walk-up where the subway roared out from underground near the old Juilliard on 123rd Street, took the requisite placement tests, and found myself assigned to Elementary Theory and Advanced Orchestration: rather like an apprentice writer's being assigned Bonehead English and a master class in novel-writing. I managed A's in both, learned a little about music, and for the first time confronted my limitations clearly and discovered something useful about myself.

25   My New York neighborhood, though dirty, was in 1947 wonderfully safe. I spent my best time wandering about it day and night in gritty June and grimy July, listening to black jazz blaring from the record shops on Lenox Avenue and rather enjoying my first acute loneliness. Illinois Jacquet, overblowing his tenor sax, was very big that season. Teddy Wilson was on the Juilliard summer faculty, and a number of my new classmates were young jazz players. They wore pegged pants and lapel-less jackets and saxophone straps, and they spoke hip language in New York accents, which I imitated. It impressed me that several of them were Jewish and some even black: my first real extraethnic acquaintances. They were not unfriendly.

26   Within a week I came to understand that they would be the professional musicians of their generation. I observed them; I observed me. Theirs was genuine apprentice talent, large or small; mine was makeshift amateur flair. No false modesty here: The news was nowise traumatic, but it was as unequivocal as a high-jump bar that others clear with ease or difficulty but you can't even approach. For this as well as other things, there had simply been no real standards of measurement down there in the marsh. I played with jazz groups for twenty-five years thereafter—for money in college and early teaching days, for mere pleasure later—but never after my Juilliard summer took myself seriously in that line.

27   Anyhow, I *was* lonely, even commuting in on the E L & W from my New Jersey aunt's house as I did in the latter part of my term. To have gone a whole summer without swimming in the Choptank River, to be as pale in August as I'd been in May, seemed incredible. I went home to think of some other way to be distinguished.

28   Playing jazz was agreeable for some of the same reasons being twins was: conversation in non-verbal language, the annexation of oneself to the lively organism of the group—pleasures the opposite of writing's. At heart I'm an arranger still, whose chiefest literary pleasure is to take a received melody—an old narrative poem, a classical myth, a shopworn literary convention, a shard of my experience, a *New York Times Book Review* series—and, improvising like a jazzman within its constraints, reorchestrate it to present purpose.

Learning

29 I came back crack-crowned down the flyway to find that I'd lost my tidewater girlfriend and won a scholarship I'd forgotten I had competed for, to the Johns Hopkins University. Well, now.

30 One was expected to select a major; I hadn't thought about it. Career counseling in our high school consisted of a ten-minute conversation with the phys ed teacher some time before graduation. Girls were counseled to be nurses, teachers, secretaries; boys, the farmers excepted but myself included, business administrators. As I'd been going to be a distinguished arranger, I'd dismissed that counsel. Now I shopped through the Hopkins arts and sciences catalogue, ruled out the sciences, and shrugged my shoulders at such academic majors as literature, history, philosophy, economics. A new department called Writing, Speech, and Drama listed a major in journalism; I put down Journalism and took the bus to Baltimore to become a distinguished journalist, understanding only vaguely that journalism meant newspaper work, which I had no interest in. I think I thought it meant, like, free-lancing and, uh, keeping a journal.

31 In a week I found that the Hopkins journalism major (we no longer offer it) was a hasty improvisation consisting of a guest-lecture course by a Baltimore *Sun* editor and a general curriculum in the arts and sciences, including the department's offerings in the writing of fiction and poetry. No matter: That same week I found musicians to job with for the next many seasons and settled into the task of surviving my freshman year in a serious university for which nothing since kindergarten had prepared me. (My parents had sent their children—at some sacrifice in those Depression years—to Cambridge's only kindergarten, a private, one-room affair which we loved at the time and which I see in retrospect to have been quite good. Miss Ridah Collins's Kindergarten was no playschool: we were taught reading and writing there. All my schooling between it and Johns Hopkins was a more or less benign blank of which I remember next to nothing.)

32 *What the aristocrats take for granted,* Anton Chekhov wrote to his brother, *we pay for with our youth.* What my better educated Hopkins classmates took for granted—especially the good-private-schooled ones—I paid for with my underclass years, at least. They had *heard* already about the Renaissance, the Enlightenment, and the rest; I was lost in the dark ages. They were as it were discussing the architecture while I was trying to find the men's room. Everything was news.

33 The university was small, the faculty distinguished; all of them taught us undergraduates as well as their graduate students. While looking for the men's room I found the aesthetician and historian of ideas George Boas, the philologist Leo Spitzer, the poets Pedro Salinas and Elliott Coleman, and many another inspired, inspiring teacher: never condescending, nowise palsy, utterly serious, impersonal, good humored, intellectually generous. Splendid

role models every one, who can seldom have had in their hands such unformed Silly Putty as my then mind. They were nice about it, if they noticed at all; it was their way, and I approve it, not to talk to us through Homer and Dante and Cervantes and Proust and Joyce, but to talk through us to those great ones, with whom they were at home.

34 I also found and happily lost myself in the library, a book-filer in the stacks of the Classics Department and William Foxwell Albright's Oriental Seminary, and set about the impossible task of Catching Up. No happier happenstance could have happened to me: not just the physical fact of those canyons of ancient narrative—which I managed somehow to find more inspiring than intimidating, and which it excites me still to prowl through—but the particular discoveries upon my cart of Burton's annotated *Book of the Thousand Nights and a Night,* Petronius's *Satyricon,* the *Panchatantra,* Urquhart's (misfiled) Rabelais, the eleventh-century Sanskrit *Ocean of Story.* Tales within tales within tales, told for the sake of their mere marvelousness. My literary education was, excuse me, *à la carte:* much better for a writer, maybe, than any curricular table d'hôte. I was permanently impressed with the *size* of literature and its wild variety; likewise, as I explored the larger geography of the stacks, with the variety of temperaments, histories, and circumstances from which came the literature I came to love. Book-filing made me a critical pluralist for life.

35 Finally, still looking for that men's room, I found my way into an elementary fiction-writing class presided over not by one of the gray eminences but by a gentle marine combat veteran, Poe scholar, and Faulkner fan who permitted us to call him Bob; whose Southern tongue charmed "write" into "rot," our department into Rotting Speech and Drama. Bob's course was a whole year long and repeatable; one simply turned in a story every two weeks. I wrote a story for Bob every two weeks for two years, starting from absolute scratch, trying everything and doing it all wrong over and over and over again. D's, C's, the odd B, C's, D's, through the first of those years at least. Perhaps if Bob had been a professional rotter himself, I'd have been intimidated (perhaps not; perhaps I'd have learned more, sooner, about the craft of rotting). But he was by his own confession a scholar pressed into service by a shorthanded department, and he was an excellent teacher for one who had *everything* to learn.

36 By the beginning of my junior year I was writing not much better—at best I'd climbed from absolute to relative scratch—but I had by then taken on some freight of literature both curricularly and off the cart. In particular I had discovered Faulkner, Scheherazade, Joyce, Cervantes, and Kafka, and a thing had happened curiously different from what had happened at Julliard. I was beating my head against a wall, but not breaking my crown; I was toiling uphill with much slippage and misstep, but not quite falling. Almost imperceptibly I had found my vocation, even in that term's religious sense. That I was still doing everything wrong (whereas at Juilliard I'd done some things right) scarcely mattered. As unequivocally as I'd realized I was *not* a genuine appren-

tice distinguished musician, I realized I was going to—well, not be a distinguished writer, maybe; that adjective was losing its importance; but devote my life to the practice of literature.

37   In retrospect I am impressed at the strength and depth of my then conviction, especially in the face of what I was composing. The work I did even two and three years later, in the graduate-level workshops (we were all reading *Finnegans Wake* then and had changed the department's name from Rotting Speech and Drama to Writhing, Screech, and Trauma), would not admit me today to the Hopkins seminar I preside over, some of whose members are already publishing their homework. By the time I left Baltimore in 1953 to begin a long circumstantial self-exile from home waters, I had begun to find my general subject matter, but it took me two years beyond that—of imitating Faulkner, imitating Joyce, imitating Boccaccio imitating the *Arabian Nights*—to get a bona fide handle on it: to book Ulysses and Scheherazade aboard a tidewater showboat with Yours Truly doubling at the helm and the steam calliope, arranging language no longer for the Others but for others.

Teaching

38   All of us writhers, screechers, and traumers took for granted that we'd do something else for a living while we practiced our vocation. I make that clear to my students today, at our first meeting, though it would doubtless go without saying: that even the gifted apprentice novelists among them had better plan their economic lives the way poets have had to do since the Romantic period.

39   I myself chose teaching, by a kind of passionate default or heartfelt lack of alternatives: Though demanding, it was less abusive and exhausting of my resources than the other things I'd tried—manual labor, office work—and the hours, pay, and future seemed better for a family man, which I had become, than those of a small-time pick-up musician. One last late afternoon in Baltimore, a like-minded friend and I discussed how we might honorably spend our professional academic lives while doing with our left hands the thing that mattered to us most. Ben decided he would spend his answering all rhetorical questions: If someone should ask, with a bored smile, "Who's to say, after all, what's Real and what isn't?" he'd say "Check with me" and run the questioner rigorously through the history of metaphysics. I decided I'd spend mine saying all the things that go without saying: staring first principles and basic distinctions out of countenance; facing them down, for my students' benefit and my own, until they confess new information. What is literature? What is fiction? What is a story?

40   One of those things is that some things a writer dislikes (at least wouldn't have chosen) may nevertheless be good for him, as a writer. I am an inert sort

who, left to himself, might never have exited the womb—I was as comfortable there as in turbid-tidal-tepid Langford Creek, off the Chester River, off Chesapeake Bay, where I live now, and, unlike most folks, I had company—though it is doubtless better for me, as a writer, that I was obliged to do so (a full hour and a quarter after my primo sister). I had as leave stayed on in Baltimore, but the exigencies of the academic job market took me north of Mason's and Dixon's for twenty years: first to Penn State, where I learned to love the vast multifariousness and rough democracy of big American state universities, and got so thirsty for open water that I cleared my throat and published my first three books, all set in Maryland; then to SUNY/Buffalo, where I published the next three and learned to like cities again and to savor (especially in the noisy late 1960s) another sort of border state: the visible boundary of our troubled republic and the comforting sight of great Canada across the river, where the geese come from: haven for dispossessed Americans in every upheaval since the States united. I had rather been back at Penn State (where I had rather been back at Johns Hopkins [where I had rather been back in the womb]), but as a writer I'm glad to have sniffed tear gas and to have heard—if only like Odysseus tied to the mast—the siren songs of Marshall McLuhan and my friend Leslie Fiedler.

41 It goes without saying that what the original sirens sang to that canny other sailor must have been something like "You can't go home again," and that that song ain't so very far from wrong. As with Heraclitus's man standing by the river, into the same which he cannot step twice, it isn't only the Home that changes, but the You, too, and so you can't and can.

42 I did, sort of, some years back. The tidewater I returned to was not, 30,000 tide-turns later, the tidewater I'd left, nor was the leaver the returner, though to protect the innocent no names had been changed. If between twins as they get older less and less goes without saying, in a good marriage between a man and a woman or a writer and his place so much more every season goes without saying that should I grow as old and wise as Sophocles I'll never get it all said.

43 But I intend to try. ❖

Questions to Ponder

1. In what ways do the circumstances of our birth (our birth order, for example, or the ease or difficulty of our birth) affect the kind of person we become?
2. How can a poor early education (in grade school or high school) be overcome?
3. What are some ways to tell whether you possess "genuine apprentice talent" for a field of work—or simply "makeshift amateur flair"?
4. In what ways are writers like musicians? Are writers "arrangers" of words?

Writing Possibilities

1. Project yourself into another role (or position by birth) in your family; then write a letter to your family telling them how family life will be different.
2. Choose three landmarks or physical features of the landscape in which you were raised and write how each has affected you. (Consider giving a copy of your essay to your city's historical society.)
3. Write a report for your college adviser honestly assessing the strengths and weaknesses of your precollege education. What do you most need now?
4. Write about false starts—others' and your own. Are false starts a true (and common) feature of life? Of writing? Do they need to be feared? Why or why not?

Student Essay
MUSICAL BEGINNINGS
Warren Wortham

"Musical Beginnings" was the first paper I wrote in college. It was the second week of my freshman year, and I wrote the essay to let people know how demanding and intricate writing music and being involved in the music industry can be.

In my first draft I just put my pen to the paper and tried to let my ideas flow. The reactions of my teacher and my writing group made me feel that my ideas were good. In a writing conference my teacher pushed me to say in words the central idea I wanted to communicate, and I was able to get that into my paper. In my writing group my fellow students kept pressing me for more details and explanations. In the final stages, they were a big help in helping me proofread my essay to catch mistakes in spelling, punctuation, and usage.

Here is the "Writer's Worksheet for Personal Writing" that I handed in with my first draft:

1. What is your topic? How did you decide on it?
   Writing music. I wanted to write something about my most exciting hobby.
2. The gathering strategies that I used were:
   Mapping.
   Freewriting.
3. I wrote my first draft (where and when):
   At the recording studio at 2:00 A.M.
4. After drafting, I believe that the gathering strategies that helped me the most were:
   Freewriting.
5. In this draft, I am most satisfied with:
   My decision on what to write.
6. I would like help with:
   Putting more of my ideas on paper.

Since writing the essay I have founded my own record company and have released my first group's debut album. I now play the role of record company president, producer, executive manager, promoter, and studio engineer. These new responsibilities may prompt me to use my writing process of just putting the pen to the paper and letting my thoughts flow to write another essay on my new experiences.

Brief Warm-up Writing Exercises

1. Describe the first record, tape, or album you bought—and what made you choose it.
2. Make a list of all the musical styles you can think of.
3. Describe your favorite musical artist (or group), and why you like him/her/them.

DRAFT

1   To me writing music is a way for me to turn my ideas into a type of living energy. Sometimes if you go searching for a song you won't find it. Only after relaxing and letting all thoughts flow will my ideas begin to output themselves. In writing music I simply let my thoughts control my hands and fingers.

2   Some of the material in which I write is intended for my own personal use. I use certain instrumentals of some of my work to give me ideas for other songs.

3   It is a good habit to record any idea that may surface.

1   Writing music is a way for me to turn my thoughts and ideas into a type of living energy. Writing music can sometimes be easy. Other times it is very difficult. At all times it is both a love and a business.

2   I first began writing music after the eighth grade. I had just finished my fifth year of performing in my school orchestra. Orchestra was fun, but I wanted to study the base guitar and keyboard, so over the summer and through my freshman year I taught myself to play both instruments. By my sophomore year in high school I had written twelve songs and I was putting a band together. My first songs could be categorized as pop music, but by the end of my sophomore year my band had become a Rap band. We named ourselves WORD! and performed in a talent show the last week of school. We took first place at the show, and this brought us considerable popularity. The sudden demand for our music led me to mass produce music. I suddenly became the leader, executive manager, and producer of my group, and this put a lot of pressure on my mind while I was trying to write music.

3   Sometimes when I felt under a lot of stress I would get the musician's equivalent of writer's block. However, just when it would look as if I wouldn't meet a deadline for a song, I would get a major idea and come up with a surprising new number. I learned that sometimes if you go searching for a song, you won't find it. Only after relaxing and letting all my thoughts flow will my ideas begin to find their way through my hands and fingers and control whatever instrument I hold. Some of the material I write is intended for my own listening, to give me other musical ideas. As a musician I have learned that it is a good habit to write down any idea that comes to mind.

4   Other musicians soon heard about my rap band and wanted to work with us. They doubted, however, that I could write any music besides hip-hop or rap music. I played some of my pop material and rock instrumentals and the doubters changed their views. After the word got around that I could write music in many styles, I was given the opportunity to co-write a song on an album of a band known as Kuzz.

5   Soon after this, I co-wrote a "demo," a demonstration song, with Marty Spencer, the older brother of singer Tracie Spencer. These experiences encouraged me to add rhythm and blues music to my list of styles. I also began experimenting with the blending of music styles. My first project was to put more of a rhythm and blues sound behind my rappers in the band. This took plenty of hard work and practice. In about a month we went to Grand Junction Studio and recorded a song called "Rebels in a Nightmare." This song was followed by "Main Attraction," which is about our idea of the type of girls we like, and "World Wide Enemy," which is about AIDS prevention. In writing these songs I used a method known as sampling, which is widely used to bring in people's voices and other sounds.

6   Amid all this performing I found time to produce other rap groups, along with singing groups. I also had the opportunity to do the music for radio commercials on our local black radio station, KBBG. Only near the end of my

senior year in high school did I find time to myself. During this time I continued sending demos of our songs to various record companies while brainstorming and attempting to come up with a new concept in music. My concept was to put rappers and singers together in a new way. The result was a song called "Going for Mine" and an audition for my group with Capitol Records and Suma Records.

7   The auditions were to take place in Los Angeles, and we were given the choice of transportation. We chose to go by bus. En route to Los Angeles I wrote two songs on the bus. Once we arrived we found that three more record companies wanted us to audition for them. The dates were set and we did five auditions in three days. Then we had to wait for two days for the decisions.

8   While we were waiting, however, Motown Records had us record a song which they'll release next summer called "She's Got Bass." On the last day of our stay we were told to send all of our new material to Capitol and Motown, and they would decide which songs would go onto an album to be released sometime in July.

9   Until then I will be busy writing new songs for our album, for groups that I am producing, and for other artists at different record companies. I guess the point that I really want to get across is that music is a hobby that I love and it pays off. I am not speaking from a financial point of view only. I am speaking of the fact you get the chance to let everyone hear your work. You also get the opportunity to meet and work with famous people, which can be a learning experience in itself.

10   The last time I was interviewed by our local newspaper, *The Waterloo Courier*, the reporter asked how I would respond if a record company said I needed to change my style. I simply responded: "I would say 'No Go.'" Then she asked me what I would have done if the record companies had turned us down. I told her that getting turned down would not have stopped our talents and that we would have just kept trying. Music, you see, is a love as well as a business. ❖

Questions to Ponder

1. Musicians create with notes, while writers create with words. In what ways might their composing processes be similar? Different?
2. What lessons do you think Warren Wortham has learned so far in his musical career?
3. What is the central idea (or thesis) of Warren Wortham's essay?
4. Can you imaginatively reconstruct the process Warren Wortham might have gone through to get from his first to his final draft?
5. From the evidence of "Musical Beginnings," does Warren Wortham seem to be an artist? What artistic qualities does he reveal?

Writing Possibilities

1. Using Warren Wortham's essay as a springboard, write an essay comparing and contrasting creating with music to creating with words. (Be sure to flesh out your ideas with vivid examples.)
2. Now choose another art medium (such as painting, sculpture, dance, weaving, or filmmaking) and try another comparison/contrast.
3. Choose your favorite musical artist and write an analysis of his or her work. (You may want to do research on his or her creative process and on the background of specific works you admire.)
4. From your experiences in high-school or college bands, orchestras, or choruses, write a report to your musical department presenting the history, strengths, and limitations of such programs, and any recommendations you would offer.

PROFESSIONS FOR WOMEN
Virginia Woolf

The very act of writing delighted Virginia Woolf, the great British novelist and essayist (1882–1941). She loved the feel of the pen cutting letters on the paper and invariably wrote her first drafts by hand. Then she would turn to the typewriter, typing revision after revision until the work met her exacting standards.

Woolf was a morning writer. From ten to one o'clock, her nephew said, "the great world could be ignored" (Quentin Bell, Virginia Woolf: A Biography *[New York: Harcourt Brace Jovanovich, 1972], 73). During those hours she could be found seated beside the gas fire in an old armchair, a wood board on her lap, writing and rewriting.*

At the age of nine, she began the Hyde Park Gate News, *a weekly family newspaper which she "published" for four years. She kept a journal in which she wrote scenes of rural life and descriptions of light and of mist. When she traveled she wrote descriptions of landscapes, and she composed commentaries on the books she was (always) reading.*

Woolf used a diary for a different purpose. She would open her diary after tea and write freely, for she believed this form of spontaneous composition helped to give her other works greater force and directness. Sometimes she also used her diary "to write out the pain."

In 1940, the Women's Service League invited Woolf to speak on her "professional experiences." "Professions for Women," the paper she wrote and delivered to an audience of two hundred, dealt with a subject that had concerned her since the age of fifteen, when she wrote a (now lost) History of Women. *Woolf spoke of her beginnings as a writer. She also dared to imagine women in all professions and realms of life.*

Brief Warm-up Writing Exercises

1. Describe yourself ten years from now. What would you like to be doing with your life?
2. Describe any fears you have about pursuing the career of your choice.
3. Make a list of problems people encounter in the workplace today. Choose one problem and describe it; then suggest any solutions you can imagine.

1 ❖ When your secretary invited me to come here, she told me that your Society is concerned with the employment of women and she suggested that I might tell you something about my own professional experiences. It is true I am a woman; it is true I am employed; but what professional experiences have I had? It is difficult to say. My profession is literature; and in that profession there are fewer experiences for women than in any other, with the exception of the stage—fewer, I mean, that are peculiar to women. For the road was cut many years ago—by Fanny Burney, by Aphra Behn, by Harriet Martineau, by Jane Austen, by George Eliot—many famous women, and many more unknown and forgotten, have been before me, making the path smooth, and regulating my steps. Thus, when I came to write, there were very few material obstacles in my way. Writing was a reputable and harmless occupation. The family peace was not broken by the scratching of a pen. No demand was made upon the family purse. For ten and sixpence one can buy paper enough to write all the plays of Shakespeare—if one has a mind that way. Pianos and models, Paris, Vienna and Berlin, masters and mistresses, are not needed by a writer. The cheapness of writing paper is, of course, the reason why women have succeeded as writers before they have succeeded in the other professions.

2   But to tell you my story—it is a simple one. You have only got to figure to yourselves a girl in a bedroom with a pen in her hand. She had only to move that pen from left to right—from ten o'clock to one. Then it occurred to her to do what is simple and cheap enough after all—to slip a few of those pages into an envelope, fix a penny stamp in the corner, and drop the envelope into

the red box at the corner. It was thus that I became a journalist; and my effort was rewarded on the first day of the following month—a very glorious day it was for me—by a letter from an editor containing a cheque for one pound ten shillings and sixpence. But to show you how little I deserve to be called a professional woman, how little I know of the struggles and difficulties of such lives, I have to admit that instead of spending that sum upon bread and butter, rent, shoes and stockings, or butcher's bills, I went out and bought a cat—a beautiful cat, a Persian cat, which very soon involved me in bitter disputes with my neighbors.

3   What could be easier than to write articles and to buy Persian cats with the profits? But wait a moment. Articles have to be about something. Mine, I seem to remember, was about a novel by a famous man. And while I was writing this review, I discovered that if I were going to review books I should need to do battle with a certain phantom. And the phantom was a woman, and when I came to know her better I called her after the heroine of a famous poem, The Angel in the House. It was she who used to come between me and my paper when I was writing reviews. It was she who bothered me and wasted my time and so tormented me that at last I killed her. You who come of a younger and happier generation may not have heard of her—you may not know what I mean by the Angel in the House. I will describe her as shortly as I can. She was intensely sympathetic. She was immensely charming. She was utterly unselfish. She excelled in the difficult arts of family life. She sacrificed herself daily. If there was chicken, she took the leg; if there was a draught she sat in it—in short she was so constituted that she never had a mind or a wish of her own, but preferred to sympathize always with the minds and wishes of others. Above all—I need not say it—she was pure. Her purity was supposed to be her chief beauty—her blushes, her great grace. In those days—the last of Queen Victoria—every house had its Angel. And when I came to write I encountered her with the very first words. The shadow of her wings fell on my page; I heard the rustling of her skirts in the room. Directly, that is to say, I took my pen in hand to review that novel by a famous man, she slipped behind me and whispered: "My dear, you are a young woman. You are writing about a book that has been written by a man. Be sympathetic; be tender; flatter; deceive; use all the arts and wiles of our sex. Never let anybody guess that you have a mind of your own. Above all, be pure." And she made as if to guide my pen. I now record the one act for which I take some credit to myself, though the credit rightly belongs to some excellent ancestors of mine who left me a certain sum of money—shall we say five hundred pounds a year?—so that it was not necessary for me to depend solely on charm for my living. I turned upon her and caught her by the throat. I did my best to kill her. My excuse, if I were to be had up in a court of law, would be that I acted in self-defence. Had I not killed her she would have killed me. She would have plucked the heart out of my writing. For, as I found, directly I put pen to paper, you cannot review even a novel without having a mind of your own, without expressing what you think to be the truth about human relations, morality, sex.

And all these questions, according to the Angel in the House, cannot be dealt with freely and openly by women; they must charm, they must conciliate, they must—to put it bluntly—tell lies if they are to succeed. Thus, whenever I felt the shadow of her wing or the radiance of her halo upon my page, I took up the inkpot and flung it at her. She died hard. Her fictitious nature was of great assistance to her. It is far harder to kill a phantom than a reality. She was always creeping back when I thought I had despatched her. Though I flatter myself that I killed her in the end, the struggle was severe; it took much time that had better have been spent upon learning Greek grammar; or in roaming the world in search of adventures. But it was a real experience; it was an experience that was bound to befall all women writers at that time. Killing the Angel in the House was part of the occupation of a woman writer.

4   But to continue my story. The Angel was dead; what then remained? You may say that what remained was a simple and common object—a young woman in a bedroom with an inkpot. In other words, now that she had rid herself of falsehood, that young woman had only to be herself. Ah, but what is "herself"? I mean, what is a woman? I assure you, I do not know. I do not believe that you know. I do not believe that anybody can know until she has expressed herself in all the arts and professions open to human skill. That indeed is one of the reasons why I have come here—out of respect for you, who are in process of showing us by your experiments what a woman is, who are in process of providing us, by your failures and successes, with that extremely important piece of information.

5   But to continue the story of my professional experiences. I made one pound ten and six by my first review; and I bought a Persian cat with the proceeds. Then I grew ambitious. A Persian cat is all very well, I said; but a Persian cat is not enough. I must have a motor car. And it was thus that I became a novelist—for it is a very strange thing that people will give you a motor car if you will tell them a story. It is a still stranger thing that there is nothing so delightful in the world as telling stories. It is far pleasanter than writing reviews of famous novels. And yet, if I am to obey your secretary and tell you my professional experiences as a novelist, I must tell you about a very strange experience that befell me as a novelist. And to understand it you must try first to imagine a novelist's state of mind. I hope I am not giving away professional secrets if I say that a novelist's chief desire is to be as unconscious as possible. He has to induce in himself a state of perpetual lethargy. He wants life to proceed with the utmost quiet and regularity. He wants to see the same faces, to read the same books, to do the same things day after day, month after month, while he is writing, so that nothing may break the illusion in which he is living—so that nothing may disturb or disquiet the mysterious nosings about, feelings round, darts, dashes and sudden discoveries of that very shy and illusive spirit, the imagination. I suspect that this state is the same both for men and women. Be that as it may, I want you to imagine me writing a novel in a state of trance. I want you to figure to yourselves a girl sitting with a pen in her hand, which for minutes, and indeed for hours, she never dips into the

inkpot. The image that comes to my mind when I think of this girl is the image of a fisherman lying sunk in dreams on the verge of a deep lake with a rod held out over the water. She was letting her imagination sweep unchecked round every rock and cranny of the world that lies submerged in the depths of our unconscious being. Now came the experience, the experience that I believe to be far commoner with women writers than with men. The line raced through the girl's fingers. Her imagination had rushed away. It had sought the pools, the depths, the dark places where the largest fish slumber. And then there was a smash. There was an explosion. There was foam and confusion. The imagination had dashed itself against something hard. The girl was roused from her dream. She was indeed in a state of the most acute and difficult distress. To speak without figure she had thought of something, something about the body, about the passions which it was unfitting for her as a woman to say. Men, her reason told her, would be shocked. The consciousness of what men will say of a woman who speaks the truth about her passions had roused her from her artist's state of unconsciousness. She could write no more. The trance was over. Her imagination could work no longer. This I believe to be a very common experience with women writers—they are impeded by the extreme conventionality of the other sex. For though men sensibly allow themselves great freedom in these respects, I doubt that they realize or can control the extreme severity with which they condemn such freedom in women.

6   These then were two very genuine experiences of my own. These were two of the adventures of my professional life. The first—killing the Angel in the House—I think I solved. She died. But the second, telling the truth about my own experiences as a body, I do not think I solved. I doubt that any woman has solved it yet. The obstacles against her are still immensely powerful—and yet they are very difficult to define. Outwardly, what is simpler than to write books? Outwardly, what obstacles are there for a woman rather than for a man? Inwardly, I think, the case is very different; she has still many ghosts to fight, many prejudices to overcome. Indeed it will be a long time still, I think, before a woman can sit down to write a book without finding a phantom to be slain, a rock to be dashed against. And if this is so in literature, the freest of all professions for women, how is it in the new professions which you are now for the first time entering?

7   Those are the questions that I should like, had I time, to ask you. And indeed, if I have laid stress upon these professional experiences of mine, it is because I believe that they are, though in different forms, yours also. Even when the path is nominally open—when there is nothing to prevent a woman from being a doctor, a lawyer, a civil servant—there are many phantoms and obstacles, as I believe, looming in her way. To discuss and define them is I think of great value and importance; for thus only can the labor be shared, the difficulties be solved. But besides this, it is necessary also to discuss the ends and the aims for which we are fighting, for which we are doing battle with these formidable obstacles. Those aims cannot be taken for granted; they must be perpetually questioned and examined. The whole position, as I see it—here in

this hall surrounded by women practicing for the first time in history I know not how many different professions—is one of extraordinary interest and importance. You have won rooms of your own in the house hitherto exclusively owned by men. You are able, though not without great labor and effort, to pay the rent. You are earning your five hundred pounds a year. But this freedom is only a beginning; the room is your own, but it is still bare. It has to be furnished; it has to be decorated; it has to be shared. How are you going to furnish it, how are you going to decorate it? With whom are you going to share it, and upon what terms? These, I think are questions of the utmost importance and interest. For the first time in history you are able to ask them; for the first time you are able to decide for yourselves what the answers should be. Willingly would I stay and discuss those questions and answers—but not tonight. My time is up; and I must cease. ❖

Questions to Ponder

1. What were the "phantoms" Virginia Woolf battled as a writer? When you sit down at your writing table, what "phantoms" keep *you* from having a mind of your own and expressing what you think to be the truth? Is your "phantom" some fear? Some recognizable person in your life? A representative of one or more social institutions (such as a teacher, minister, or boss)? Some part of yourself?

2. Do men have different "phantoms" to overcome than women? If so, what are they? Why might they differ?

3. Can you recall any insights you have had, or striking images or phrases that have come to you, in moments when you have let your imagination "sweep unchecked . . . in the depths of [your] unconscious"? What feelings came along with these "discoveries"?

4. Has the world changed since the 1940s, or do you think women writers are still discouraged from speaking the truth about their passions and the experiences of their bodies? Do you think men are discouraged as well? What has (or has not) changed?

5. What are the phantoms to be slain and rocks to be dashed against in other professions (besides writing)? What might they be in your major or career choice?

Writing Possibilities

1. Write a termination letter to your "phantom" or "phantoms," advising them that they are officially dismissed. (You might begin it "Dear Fear of _____," filling in the blank with your fear.)

2. Virginia Woolf likens her creative process to that of a daydreaming fisherwoman holding her rod out over the water and letting the line down deep. Describe the conditions that best allow *you* to tap your subconscious reservoirs. Discuss how you can achieve these conditions more often, or at least as often as necessary.
3. Write a speech you will deliver next week on "Professions for Men." What phantoms or obstacles do men face when embarking on careers today?
4. Write a follow-up paper on "Professions for Women" to be delivered to the Women's Service League this year. What progress (if any) would you report? (You may want to do some research on career and labor statistics, then and now.)

Short Story
NOT FOR PUBLICATION
Nadine Gordimer

"Not for Publication" was written in the 1960s and the theme came to me through my fascination with the beginnings of various African leaders. It was not a case of rags-to-riches but one of herdboy-to-president. It was also an irrefutable recognition that it doesn't take generations for people from another culture—African—to become what Europeans categorize as "civilized": which is to say competent to deal with and practice European and North American concepts of power. Many African leaders were born into humble circumstances and families in which Western education was, or seemed, an unattainable privilege. Yet in one generation the transformation was made. That it needed exceptional personal qualities in the individual concerned, since the practical obstacles were great, goes without saying. But to me it was proof that if the obstacles of poverty and poor education were removed, it would not take generations for Africans to be qualified to cope with the modern world and take their countries and their destiny in their own hands.

If herdboys could grow up to become presidents, then why should not there be a future president among the black children I saw living as vagrants in the streets of Johannesburg, my home city? That was the kernal of my story. I revise only once. Any cuts and additions are scribbled on the original, and if there are any (rare) changes in structure, they are marked. From that I type the next and final version. I worked like that in the 1960s when "Not for Publication" was written, and I still do. "Not for Publication" differs, however, from any other story I have written because my intention was to write a novel and not a story on that theme. Never before or since have I left something unfinished, or transformed it from the original medium. I gave up the idea of writing a novel about Praise because I found that I did not know enough about him—which is to say my imaginative projection could not reach deep enough—to follow him through his development.

Once this was to be a short story and not a novel, it had to concentrate on one stage in that development. Of course, a short story may make jumps and elisions to cover a lifetime, but to me this is not the true nature of the short story. An essence must be captured and distilled to strength. What would happen to a boy taken off the streets and force-fed, so to speak, with the idea of his capacities? What would the well-meaning care and even affection of white people who "rescued" him mean to him in terms of his own personality? Might it not be something quite unexpected by them? Something not taken account of?

In the answers to these questions my story took shape. The title—which I already had in mind, as usual, before I began to write—changed its meaning. If this had been a novel, the title would have referred to the fact that the President did not want his childhood as an urchin in his official biography. As the title of the story, it referred to something else: the failure of Miss Graham-Grigg and Father Audry, best forgotten.

Brief Warm-up Writing Exercises

1. Describe an experience when you were snatched from one environment and placed in another. How did you respond?
2. Make a list of the qualities of a good political leader.
3. Describe what you think would be the best education for a prime minister—or a writer.

---

1 It is not generally known—and it is never mentioned in the official biographies—that the Prime Minister spent the first eleven years of his life, as soon as he could be trusted not to get under a car, leading his uncle about the streets. His uncle was not really blind, but nearly, and he was certainly mad. He walked with his right hand on the boy's left shoulder; they kept moving part of the day, but they also had a pitch on the cold side of the street, between the legless man near the post office who sold bootlaces and copper bracelets, and the one with the doll's hand growing out of one elbow, whose pitch was

outside the YWCA. That was where Adelaide Graham-Grigg found the boy, and later he explained to her, "If you sit in the sun they don't give you anything."

2   Miss Graham-Grigg was not looking for Praise Basetse. She was in Johannesburg on one of her visits from a British Protectorate, seeing friends, pulling strings, and pursuing, on the side, her private study of following up the fate of those people of the tribe who had crossed the border and lost themselves, sometimes over several generations, in the city. As she felt down through the papers and letters in her bag to find a sixpence for the old man's hat, she heard him mumble something to the boy in the tribe's tongue—which was not in itself anything very significant in this city where many African languages could be heard. But these sounds formed in her ear as words: it was the language that she had learnt to understand a little. She asked, in English, using only the traditional form of address in the tribe's tongue, whether the old man was a tribesman. But he was mumbling the blessings that the clink of a coin started up like a kick to a worn and useless mechanism. The boy spoke to him, nudged him; he had already learnt in a rough way to be a businessman. Then the old man protested, no, no, he had come a long time from that tribe. A long, long time. He was Johannesburg. She saw that he confused the question with some routine interrogation at the pass offices, where a man from another territory was always in danger of being endorsed out to some forgotten "home." She spoke to the boy, asking him if he came from the Protectorate. He shook his head terrifiedly; once before he had been ordered off the streets by a welfare organization. "But your father? Your mother?" Miss Graham-Grigg said, smiling. She discovered that the old man had come from the Protectorate, from the very village she had made her own, and that his children had passed on to their children enough of the language for them all to continue to speak it among themselves, down to the second generation born in the alien city.

3   Now the pair were no longer beggars to be ousted from her conscience by a coin: they were members of the tribe. She found out what township they went to ground in after the day's begging, interviewed the family, established for them the old man's right to a pension in his adopted country, and, above all, did something for the boy. She never succeeded in finding out exactly who he was—she gathered he must have been the illegitimate child of one of the girls in the family, his parentage concealed so that she might go on with her schooling. Anyway, he was a descendant of the tribe, a displaced tribesman, and he could not be left to go on begging in the streets. That was as far as Miss Graham-Grigg's thoughts for him went, in the beginning. Nobody wanted him particularly, and she met with no opposition from the family when she proposed to take him back to the Protectorate and put him to school. He went with her just as he had gone through the streets of Johannesburg each day under the weight of the old man's hand.

4   The boy had never been to school before. He could not write, but Miss Graham-Grigg was astonished to discover that he could read quite fluently. Sitting beside her in her little car in the khaki shorts and shirt she had bought

him, stripped of the protection of his smelly rags and scrubbed bare to her questions, he told her that he had learnt from the newspaper vender whose pitch was on the corner: from the posters that changed several times a day, and then from the front pages of the newspapers and magazines spread there. Good God, what had he not learnt on the street! Everything from his skin out unfamiliar to him, and even that smelling strangely different—this detachment, she realized, made the child talk as he could never have done when he was himself. Without differentiation, he related the commonplaces of his life; he had also learnt from the legless copper bracelet man how to make *dagga* cigarettes and smoke them for a nice feeling. She asked him what he thought he would have done when he got older, if he had had to keep on walking with his uncle, and he said that he had wanted to belong to one of the gangs of boys, some little older than himself, who were very good at making money. They got money from white people's pockets and handbags without their even knowing it, and if the police came they began to play their penny whistles and sing. She said with a smile, "Well, you can forget all about the street, now. You don't have to think about it ever again." And he said, "Yes, med-dam," and she knew she had no idea what he was thinking—how could she? All she could offer were more unfamiliarities, the unfamiliarities of generalized encouragement, saying, "And soon you will know how to write."

5   She had noticed that he was hatefully ashamed of not being able to write. When he had had to admit it, the face that he turned open and victimized to her every time she spoke had the squinting grimace—teeth showing and a grown-up cut between the faint, child's eyebrows—of profound humiliation. Humiliation terrified Adelaide Graham-Grigg as the spectacle of savage anger terrifies others. That was one of the things she held against the missionaries: how they stressed Christ's submission to humiliation, and so had conditioned the people of Africa to humiliation by the white man.

6   Praise went to the secular school that Miss Graham-Grigg's committee of friends of the tribe in London had helped pay to set up in the village in opposition to the mission school. The sole qualified teacher was a young man who had received his training in South Africa and now had been brought back to serve his people; but it was a beginning. As Adelaide Graham-Grigg often said to the Chief, shining-eyed as any proud daughter, "By the time independence comes we'll be free not only of the British government, but of the church as well." And he always giggled a little embarrassedly, although he knew her so well and was old enough to be her father, because her own father was both a former British MP and the son of a bishop.

7   It was true that everything was a beginning; that was the beauty of it—of the smooth mud houses, red earth, flies and heat that visitors from England wondered she could bear to live with for months on end, while their palaces and cathedrals and streets choked on a thousand years of used-up endeavour were an ending. Even Praise was a beginning; one day the tribe would be economically strong enough to gather its exiles home, and it would no longer be necessary for its sons to sell their labour over that border. But it soon

became clear that Praise was also exceptional. The business of learning to read from newspaper headlines was not merely a piece of gutter wit; it proved to have been the irrepressible urge of real intelligence. In six weeks the boy could write, and from the start he could spell perfectly, while boys of sixteen and eighteen never succeeded in mastering English orthography. His arithmetic was so good that he had to be taught with the Standard Three class instead of the beginners; he grasped at once what a map was; and in his spare time showed a remarkable aptitude for understanding the workings of various mechanisms, from waterpumps to motorcycle engines. In eighteen months he had completed the Standard Five syllabus, only a year behind the average age of a city white child with all the background advantage of a literate home.

8   There was as yet no other child in the tribe's school who was ready for Standard Six. It was difficult to see what could be done now, but send Praise back over the border to school. So Miss Graham-Grigg decided it would have to be Father Audry. There was nothing else for it. The only alternative was the mission school, those damned Jesuits who'd been sitting in the Protectorate since the days when the white imperialists were on the grab, taking the tribes under their "protection"—and the children the boy would be in class with there wouldn't provide any sort of stimulation, either. So it would have to be Father Audry, and South Africa. He was a priest, too, an Anglican one, but his school was a place where at least, along with the pious pap, a black child could get an education as good as a white child's.

9   When Praise came out into the veld with the other boys his eyes screwed up against the size: the land ran away all round, and there was no other side to be seen; only the sudden appearance of the sky, that was even bigger. The wind made him snuff like a dog. He stood helpless as the country men he had seen caught by changing traffic lights in the middle of a street. The bits of space between buildings came together, ballooned uninterruptedly over him, he was lost; but there were clouds as big as the buildings had been, and even though space was vaster than any city, it was peopled by birds. If you ran for ten minutes into the veld the village was gone; but down low on the ground thousands of ants knew their way between their hard mounds that stood up endlessly as the land.

10   He went to herd cattle with the other boys early in the mornings and after school. He taught them some gambling games they had never heard of. He told them about the city they had never seen. The money in the old man's hat seemed a lot to them, who had never got more than a few pennies when the mail train stopped for water at the halt five miles away; so the sum grew in his own estimation too, and he exaggerated it a bit. In any case, he *was* forgetting about the city, in a way; not Miss Graham-Grigg's way, but in the manner of a child, who makes, like a wasp building with its own spittle, his private context within the circumstance of his surroundings, so that the space around him was reduced to the village, the pan where the cattle were taken to drink, the halt where the train went by; whatever particular patch of

sand or rough grass astir with ants the boys rolled on, heads together, among the white egrets and the cattle. He learnt from the others what roots and leaves were good to chew, and how to set wire traps for spring-hares. Though Miss Graham-Grigg had said he need not, he went to church with the children on Sundays.

11   He did not live where she did, in one of the Chief's houses, but with the family of one of the other boys; but he was at her house often. She asked him to copy letters for her. She cut things out of the newspapers she got and gave them to him to read; they were about aeroplanes, and dams being built, and the way the people lived in other countries. "Now you'll be able to tell the boys all about the Volta Dam, that is also in Africa—far from here—but still, in Africa," she said, with that sudden smile that reddened her face. She had a gramophone and she played records for him. Not only music, but people reading out poems, so that he knew that the poems in the school reader were not just short lines of words, but more like songs. She gave him tea with plenty of sugar and she asked him to help her to learn the language of the tribe, to talk to her in it. He was not allowed to call her *madam* or *missus*, as he did the white women who had put money in the hat, but had to learn to say *Miss Graham-Grigg.*

12   Although he had never known any white women before except as high-heeled shoes passing quickly in the street, he did not think that all white women must be like her; in the light of what he had seen white people, in their cars, their wealth, their distance, to be, he understood nothing that she did. She looked like them, with her blue eyes, blond hair, and skin that was not one colour but many: brown where the sun burned it, red when she blushed—but she lived here in the Chief's houses, drove him in his car, and sometimes slept out in the fields with the women when they were harvesting kaffircorn far from the village. He did not know why she had brought him there, or why she should be kind to him. But he could not ask her, any more than he would have asked her why she went out and slept in the fields when she had a gramophone and a lovely gas lamp (he had been able to repair it for her) in her room. If, when they were talking together, the talk came anywhere near the pitch outside the post office, she became slowly very red, and they went past it, either by falling silent or (on her part) talking and laughing rather fast.

13   That was why he was amazed the day she told him that he was going back to Johannesburg. As soon as she had said it she blushed darkly for it, her eyes pleading confusion: so it was really from her that the vision of the pitch outside the post office came again. But she was already speaking: ". . . to school. To a really good boarding-school, Father Audry's school, about nine miles from town. You must get your chance at a good school, Praise. We really can't teach you properly any longer. Maybe you'll be the teacher here yourself, one day. There'll be a high school, and you'll be the headmaster."

14   She succeeded in making him smile; but she looked sad, uncertain. He went on smiling because he couldn't tell her about the initiation school that he was about to begin with the other boys of his age-group. Perhaps someone

would tell her. The other women. Even the Chief. But you couldn't fool her with smiling.

15   "You'll be sorry to leave Tebedi and Joseph and the rest."

16   He stood there, smiling.

17   "Praise, I don't think you understand about yourself—about your brain." She gave a little sobbing giggle, prodded at her own head. "You've got an awfully good one. More in there than other boys—you know? It's something special—it would be such a waste. Lots of people would like to be clever like you, but it's not easy, when you are the clever one."

18   He went on smiling. He did not want her face looking into his any more and so he fixed his eyes on her feet, white feet in sandals with the veins standing out over the ankles like the feet of Christ dangling above his head in the church.

19   Adelaide Graham-Grigg had met Father Audry before, of course. All those white people who do not accept the colour bar in southern Africa seem to know each other, however different the bases of their rejection. She had sat with him on some committee or other in London a few years earlier, along with a couple of exiled white South African leftists and a black nationalist leader. Anyway, everyone knew him—from the newspapers, if nowhere else: he had been warned, in a public speech by the Prime Minister of the South African Republic, Dr. Verwocrd, that the interference of a churchman in political matters would not be tolerated. He continued to speak his mind, and (as the newspapers quoted him) "to obey the commands of God before the dictates of the State." He had close friends among African and Indian leaders, and it was said that he even got on well with certain ministers of the Dutch Reformed Church, that, in fact, *he* was behind some of the dissidents who now and then questioned Divine Sanction for the colour bar—such was the presence of his restless, black-cassocked figure, stammering eloquence, and jagged handsome face.

20   He had aged since she saw him last; he was less handsome. But he had still what he would have as long as he lived: the unconscious bearing of a natural prince among men that makes a celebrated actor, a political leader, a successful lover; an object of attraction and envy who, whatever his generosity of spirit, is careless of one cruelty for which other people will never forgive him—the distinction, the luck with which he was born.

21   He was tired and closed his eyes in a grimace straining at concentration when he talked to her, yet in spite of this, she felt the dimness of the candle of her being within his radius. Everything was right with him; nothing was quite right with her. She was only thirty-six but she had never looked any younger. Her eyes were the bright shy eyes of a young woman, but her feet and hands with their ridged nails had the look of tension and suffering of extremities that would never caress: she saw it, she saw it, she knew in his presence that they were deprived forever.

22   Her humiliation gave her force. She said, "I must tell you we want him

back in the tribe—I mean, there are terribly few with enough education even for administration. Within the next few years we'll desperately need more and more educated men. . . . We shouldn't want him to be allowed to think of becoming a priest."

23   Father Audrey smiled at what he knew he was expected to come out with: that if the boy chose the way of the Lord, etc.

24   He said, "What you want is someone who will turn out to be an able politician without challenging the tribal system."

25   They both laughed, but, again, he had unconsciously taken the advantage of admitting their deeply divergent views; he believed the chiefs must go, while she, of course, saw no reason why Africans shouldn't develop their own tribal democracy instead of taking over the Western pattern.

26   "Well, he's a little young for us to be worrying about that now, don't you think?" He smiled. There were a great many papers on his desk, and she had the sense of pressure of his preoccupation with other things. "What about the Lemeribe Mission? What's the teaching like these days—I used to know Father Chalmon when he was there—"

27   "I wouldn't send him to those people," she said spiritedly, implying that he knew her views on missionaries and their role in Africa. In this atmosphere of candour, they discussed Praise's background. Father Audry suggested that the boy should be encouraged to resume relations with his family, once he was back within reach of Johannesburg.

28   "They're pretty awful."

29   "It would be best for him to acknowledge what he was, if he is to accept what he is to become." He got up with a swish of his black skirts and strode, stooping in the opened door, to call, "Simon, bring the boy." Miss Graham-Grigg was smiling excitedly toward the doorway, all the will to love pacing behind the bars of her glance.

30   Praise entered in the navy blue shorts and white shirt of his new school uniform. The woman's kindness, the man's attention, got him in the eyes like the sun striking off the pan where the cattle had been taken to drink. Father Audry came from England, Miss Graham-Grigg had told him, like herself. That was what they were, these two white people who were not like any white people he had seen to be. What they were was being English. From far off; six thousand miles from here, as he knew from his geography book.

31   Praise did very well at the new school. He sang in the choir in the big church on Sundays; his body, that was to have been made a man's out in the bush, was hidden under the white robes. The boys smoked in the lavatories and once there was a girl who came and lay down for them in a storm-water ditch behind the workshops. He knew all about these things from before, on the streets and in the location where he had slept in one room with a whole family. But he did not tell the boys about the initiation. The women had not said anything to Miss Graham-Grigg. The Chief hadn't, either. Soon when Praise thought about it he realized that by now it must be over. Those boys

must have come back from the bush. Miss Graham-Grigg had said that after a year, when Christmas came, she would fetch him for the summer holidays. She did come and see him twice that first year, when she was down in Johannesburg, but he couldn't go back with her at Christmas because Father Audry had him in the Nativity play and was giving him personal coaching in Latin and algebra. Father Audry didn't actually teach in the school at all—it was "his" school simply because he had begun it, and it was run by the order of which he was Father Provincial—but the reports of the boy's progress were so astonishing that, as he said to Miss Graham-Grigg, one felt one must give him all the mental stimulation one could.

32 "I begin to believe we may be able to sit him for his matric when he is just sixteen." Father Audry made the pronouncement with the air of doing so at the risk of sounding ridiculous. Miss Graham-Grigg always had her hair done when she got to Johannesburg, she was looking pretty and gay. "D'you think he could do a Cambridge entrance? My committee in London would set up a scholarship, I'm sure—investment in a future prime minister for the Protectorate!"

33 When Praise was sent for, she said she hardly knew him; he hadn't grown much, but he looked so *grown-up*, with his long trousers and glasses. "You really needn't wear them when you're not working," said Father Audry. "Well, I suppose if you take 'em on and off you keep leaving them about, eh?" They both stood back, smiling, letting the phenomenon embody in the boy.

34 Praise saw that she had never been reminded by anyone about the initiation. She began to give him news of his friends, Tebedi and Joseph and the others, but when he heard their names they seemed to belong to people he couldn't see in his mind.

35 Father Audry talked to him sometimes about what Father called his "family," and when first he came to the school he had been told to write to them. It was a well-written, well-spelled letter in English, exactly the letter he presented as a school exercise when one was required in class. They didn't answer. Then Father Audry must have made private efforts to get in touch with them, because the old woman, a couple of children who had been babies when he left, and one of his grown-up "sisters" came to the school on a visiting day. They had to be pointed out to him among the other boys' visitors; he would not have known them, nor they him. He said, "Where's my uncle?"—because he would have known him at once; he had never grown out of the slight stoop of the left shoulder where the weight of the old man's hand had impressed the young bone. But the old man was dead. Father Audry came up and put a long arm round the bent shoulder and another long arm round one of the small children and said from one to the other, "Are you going to work hard and learn a lot like your brother?" And the small black child stared up into the nostrils filled with strong hair, the tufted eyebrows, the red mouth surrounded by the pale jowl dark-pored with beard beneath the skin, and then down, torn by fascination, to the string of beads that hung from the leather belt.

36 They did not come again but Praise did not much miss visitors because

he spent more and more time with Father Audry. When he was not actually being coached, he was set to work to prepare his lessons or do his reading in the Father's study, where he could concentrate as one could not hope to do up at the school. Father Audry taught him chess as a form of mental gymnastics, and was jubilant the first time Praise beat him. Praise went up to the house for a game nearly every evening after supper. He tried to teach the other boys, but after the first ten minutes of explanation of moves, someone would bring out the cards or dice and they would all play one of the old games that were played in the streets and yards and locations. Johannesburg was only nine miles away; you could see the lights.

37   Father Audry rediscovered what Miss Graham-Grigg had found—that Praise listened attentively to music, serious music. One day Father Audry handed the boy the flute that had lain for years in its velvet-lined box that bore still the little silver name-plate: Rowland Audry. He watched while Praise gave the preliminary swaying wriggle and assumed the bent-kneed stance of all the urchin performers Father Audry had seen, and then tried to blow down it in the shy, fierce attack of penny-whistle music. Father Audry took it out of his hands. "It's what you've just heard there." Bach's unaccompanied flute sonata lay on the record-player. Praise smiled and frowned, giving his glasses a lift with his nose—a habit he was developing. "But you'll soon learn to play it the right way round," said Father Audry, and with the lack of self-consciousness that comes from the habit of privilege, put the flute to his mouth and played what he remembered after ten years.

38   He taught Praise not only how to play the flute, but also the elements of musical composition, so that he should not simply play by ear, or simply listen with pleasure, but also understand what it was that he heard. The flute-playing was much more of a success with the boys than the chess had been, and on Saturday nights, when they sometimes made up concerts, he was allowed to take it to the hostel and play it for them. Once he played in a show for white people, in Johannesburg; but the boys could not come to that; he could only tell them about the big hall at the university, the jazz band, the African singers and dancers with their red lips and straightened hair, like white women.

39   The one thing that dissatisfied Father Audry was that the boy had not filled out and grown as much as one would have expected. He made it a rule that Praise must spend more time on physical exercise—the school couldn't afford a proper gymnasium, but there was some equipment outdoors. The trouble was that the boy had so little time; even with his exceptional ability, it was not going to be easy for a boy with his lack of background to matriculate at sixteen. Brother George, his form master, was certain he could be made to bring it off; there was a specially strong reason why everyone wanted him to do it since Father Audry had established that he would be eligible for an open scholarship that no black boy had ever won before—what a triumph that would be, for the boy, for the school, for all the African boys who were considered fit only for the inferior standard of "Bantu education"! Perhaps some day this beggar child from the streets of Johannesburg might even become the first black South

African to be a Rhodes Scholar. This was what Father Audry jokingly referred to as Brother George's "sin of pride." But who knew? It was not inconceivable. So far as the boy's physique was concerned—what Brother George said was probably true: "You can't feed up for those years in the streets."

40   From the beginning of the first term of the year he was fifteen Praise had to be coached, pressed on, and to work as even he had never worked before. His teachers gave him tremendous support; he seemed borne along on it by either arm so that he never looked up from his books. To encourage him, Father Audry arranged for him to compete in certain interschool scholastic contests that were really intended for the white Anglican schools—a spelling bee, a debate, a quiz contest. He sat on the platform in the polished halls of huge white schools and gave his correct answers in the African-accented English that the boys who surrounded him knew only as the accent of servants and delivery men.

41   Brother George often asked him if he were tired. But he was not tired. He only wanted to be left with his books. The boys in the hostel seemed to know this; they never asked him to play cards any more, and even when they shared smokes together in the lavatory, they passed him his drag in silence. He specially did not want Father Audry to come in with a glass of hot milk. He would rest his cheek against the pages of the books, now and then, alone in the study; that was all. The damp stone smell of the books was all he needed. Where he had once had to force himself to return again and again to the pages of things he did not grasp, gazing in blankness at the print until meaning assembled itself, he now had to force himself when it was necessary to leave the swarming facts outside which he no longer seemed to understand anything. Sometimes he could not work for minutes at a time because he was thinking that Father Audry would come in with the milk. When he did come, it was never actually so bad. But Praise couldn't look at his face. Once or twice when he had gone out again, Praise shed a few tears. He found himself praying, smiling with the tears and trembling, rubbing at the scalding water that ran down inside his nose and blotched on the books.

42   One Saturday afternoon when Father Audry had been entertaining guests at lunch he came into the study and suggested that the boy should get some fresh air—go out and join the football game for an hour or so. But Praise was struggling with geometry problems from the previous year's matriculation paper that, to Brother George's dismay, he had suddenly got all wrong, that morning.

43   Father Audry could imagine what Brother George was thinking: was this an example of the phenomenon he had met with so often with African boys of a lesser calibre—the inability, through lack of an assumed cultural background, to perform a piece of work well known to them, once it was presented in a slightly different manner outside one of their own textbooks? Nonsense, of course, in this case; everyone was overanxious about the boy. Right from the start he'd shown that there was nothing mechanistic about his thought processes; he had a brain, not just a set of conditioned reflexes.

44   "Off you go. You'll manage better when you've taken a few knocks on the field."

45   But desperation had settled on the boy's face like obstinacy. "I must, I must," he said, putting his palms down over the books.

46   "Good. Then let's see if we can tackle it together."

47   The black skirt swishing past the shiny shoes brought a smell of cigars. Praise kept his eyes on the black beads; the leather belt they hung from creaked as the big figure sat down. Father Audry took the chair on the opposite side of the table and switched the exercise book round toward himself. He scrubbed at the thick eyebrows till they stood out tangled, drew the hand down over his great nose, and then screwed his eyes closed a moment, mouth strangely open and lips drawn back in a familiar grimace. There was a jump, like a single painful hiccup, in Praise's body. The Father was explaining the problem gently, in his offhand English voice.

48   He said, "Praise? D'you follow?"—the boy seemed sluggish, almost deaf, as if the voice reached him as the light of a star reaches the earth from something already dead.

49   Father Audry put out his fine hand, in question or compassion. But the boy leapt up, dodging a blow. "Sir—no. Sir—no."

50   It was clearly hysteria; he had never addressed Father Audry as anything but "Father." It was some frightening retrogression, a reversion to the subconscious, a place of symbols and collective memory. He spoke for others, out of another time. Father Audry stood up but saw in alarm that by the boy's retreat he was made his pursuer, and he let him go blundering in clumsy panic out of the room.

51   Brother George was sent to comfort the boy. In half an hour Praise was down on the football field, running and laughing. But Father Audry took some days to get over the incident. He kept thinking how when the boy had backed away he had almost gone after him. The ugliness of the instinct repelled him; who would have thought how, at the mercy of the instinct to prey, the fox, the wild dog long for the innocence of the gentle rabbit, and the lamb. No one had shown fear of him ever before in his life. He had never given a thought to the people who were not like himself; those from whom others turn away. He felt at last a repugnant and resentful pity for them, the dripping-jawed hunters. He even thought that he would like to go into retreat for a few days, but it was inconvenient—he had so many obligations. Finally, the matter-of-factness of the boy, Praise, was the thing that restored normality. So far as the boy was concerned, one would have thought that nothing had happened. The next day he seemed to have forgotten all about it; a good thing. And so Father Audry's own inner disruption, denied by the boy's calm, sank away. He allowed the whole affair the one acknowledgement of writing to Miss Graham-Grigg—surely that was not making too much of it—to suggest that the boy was feeling the tension of his final great effort, and that a visit from her, etc.; but she was still away in England—some family troubles had kept her there for months, and in fact she had not been to see her protégé for more than a year.

52   Praise worked steadily on the last lap. Brother George and Father Audry watched him continuously. He was doing extremely well and seemed quite overcome with the weight of pride and pleasure when Father Audry presented him with a new black fountain pen: this was the pen with which he was to write the matriculation exam. On a Monday afternoon Father Audry, who had been in conference with the bishop all morning, looked in on his study, where every afternoon the boy would be seen sitting at the table that had been moved in for him. But there was no one there. The books were on the table. A chute of sunlight landed on the seat of the chair. Praise was not found again. The school was searched; and then the police were informed; the boys questioned; there were special prayers said in the mornings and evenings. He had not taken anything with him except the fountain pen.

53   When everything had been done there was nothing but silence; nobody mentioned the boy's name. But Father Audry was conducting investigations on his own. Every now and then he would get an idea that would bring a sudden hopeful relief. He wrote to Adelaide Graham-Grigg: ". . . what worries me—I believe the boy may have been on the verge of a nervous breakdown. I am hunting everywhere . . ."; was it possible that he might make his way to the Protectorate? She was acting as confidential secretary to the Chief, now, but she wrote to say that if the boy turned up she would try to make time to deal with the situation. Father Audry even sought out, at last, the "family"—the people with whom Miss Graham-Grigg had discovered Praise living as a beggar. They had been moved to a new township and it took some time to trace them. He found Number 28b, Block E, in the appropriate ethnic group. He was accustomed to going in and out of African homes and he explained his visit to the old woman in matter-of-fact terms at once, since he knew how suspicious of questioning the people would be. There were no interior doors in these houses and a woman in the inner room who was dressing moved out of the visitor's line of vision as he sat down. She heard all that passed between Father Audry and the old woman and presently she came in with mild interest. Out of a silence the old woman was saying, "My-my-my-my!"—she shook her head down into her bosom in a stylized expression of commiseration; they had not seen the boy. "And he spoke so nice, everything was so nice in the school." But they knew nothing about the boy, nothing at all. The younger woman remarked, "Maybe he's with those boys who sleep in the old empty cars there in town—you know?—there by the beer hall?" ❖

Questions to Ponder

1. What is the "initiation" Praise is about to begin when Miss Graham-Grigg takes him off to Father Audry to study? Why do you think this initiation is important to him?

2. What are the signs that Praise is not being completely transformed by Miss Graham-Grigg and Father Audry?

3. Why do you think Praise is embarrassed to have Father Audry come in with a glass of hot milk? Why does he cry, and why does he shrink in fear when Father Audry reaches out his hand?
4. What do you think happened to Praise after he left Father Audry? Where do you think he may have gone? What in the text leads you to your conclusions?
5. Why is Miss Graham-Grigg critical of the Christian missionaries who came to Africa—so critical that she has established a secular school in the tribal village in opposition to the mission school?
6. Is Father Audry right when he suggests that what Miss Graham-Grigg wants in Praise is "someone who will turn out to be an able politician without challenging the tribal system"? How does this differ from his view? What position do you take?
7. Is there just one way to make a prime minister? Or a writer? How many ways do you suppose there are?

Writing Possibilities

1. Pretend you are Prime Minister Praise Basetse and write a letter to Miss Graham-Grigg and Father Audry explaining why you did what you did.
2. Explain what "self-determination" means—for individuals and nations.
3. Write a recipe for making a political leader (Take one part———; add———; mix———, etc.)
4. Write your own recipe for becoming a writer.

CHAPTER 2

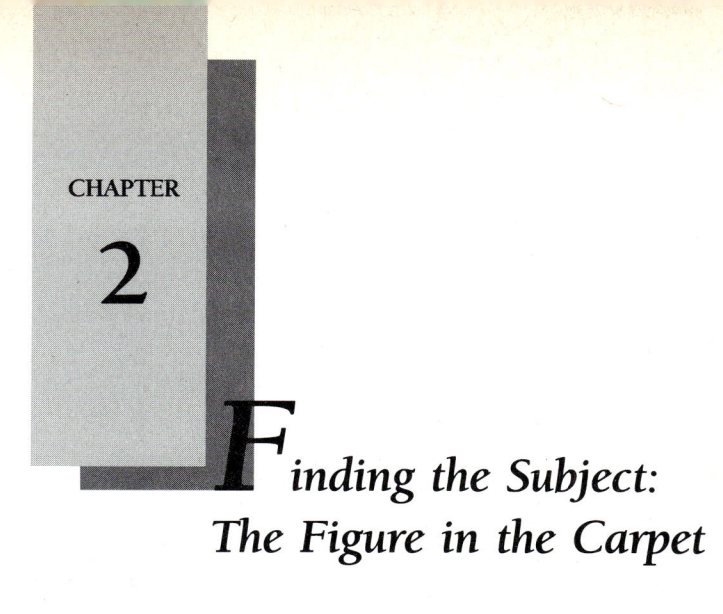

Finding the Subject: The Figure in the Carpet

Finding your subject matter as a writer is one of the most important and most enjoyable aspects of writing. When a subject suits you, it is like a new suit or pair of jeans. You are eager to put them on, show them off, even wear them out. You will spend extra hours shopping for just the right accessories, to make your suit or jeans even more attractive.

Begin, then, with this vow:

1. Never write on a subject which does not engage and excite your imagination.
2. If assigned subjects fail to excite you, modify them (with the approval of your professor or boss) until they do.

A subject which does not suit you is like your cousin's hand-me-down clothes. They may have fit your cousin, but they don't fit you. You wear them begrudgingly—if at all. If you are forced to wear them, your reluctance and discomfort show.

How do you find subjects suited to the writer in you? One way is to choose topics close to your heart. These may be events or activities you love or topics you chew over regularly with family members and friends. You can already sense the leg up you have on this material.

Your answers to the following seven questions will give you a beginning list of subjects tailored to you:

- What subjects or courses are you drawn to in school?
- What part of the newspaper do you read first?
- What topics or issues do you most often talk about with your friends?
- What do you find yourself doing in your free time?
- If money were no object, how would you spend your days?
- What do you read just for pleasure?
- What kind of videos are you most likely to rent?

Another way to begin finding what interests you as a writer is to place yourself in your student union for 20 minutes and then write about the experience. Did you write about the people in the union or the light shining through the windows? Did you write about yourself, others, the architecture of the building, or the colors and textures of the furnishings? Did you want to describe the whole building or only one small section? What you wrote reveals a great deal about what engages your attention. The next step is to pursue it.

When you are asked to select your own topics for college papers, here are six prewriting strategies you can use to help you find the ideal subject or the best approach to a subject—that figure in the carpet that you will want to follow. The advantage of all six techniques is that they can be done very quickly, most in ten minutes or less. Thus in ten minutes any fears you have had about writing the assignment will have lessened, for you see you have an abundance of material from which to write. The anxiety, in fact, may have vanished, and you will be eager to write this paper.

BRAINSTORMING

Brainstorming requires just a pencil, a piece of paper, and ten free minutes. Say you are asked to write an essay about a major turning point in your life. How do you know what to choose? In ten minutes simply jot down (as fast as you can) every turning point in your life you can remember: moving to a new town or school; meeting certain people; winning (or losing) an important game or prize; dealing with illness; choosing a college; reading a certain author or book, and so forth. The key to brainstorming is this: never reject an idea. Just get it down. You cannot know at this moment how you may use it in your creative process.

Brainstorming is the time for being bold. Write down every idea that comes to you, no matter how far afield or outrageous it may seem. Once you have your list, read it over and choose the turning point that seems to you most appealing for this assignment or the one you are most interested in exploring. If you are like most students, you will see that you have material for several papers on key turning points. This is reassuring.

MAPPING

Mapping is simply brainstorming in a slightly more organized fashion. Say you have chosen your move to a new city as the subject for your major turning point paper. Write this subject in the center of a blank sheet of paper and draw a circle around it. Then around it brainstorm all the images and feelings that you associate with this move. Often they will group together in clusters. It might look something like this schematic.

New School	New Friends	New City
Harder courses	Miss Jason	Hard to park
Volleyball team	Meet Sarah	Learning the EL
Coach Collins	Meet Jackson	The Magnificent
City leagues	Meet Steve	Mile
Scholarships	Dr. Ives	Getting lost

(MOVING TO CHICAGO)

New House	Feeling Homesick
My own room	Volleyball tryouts
Neighborhood games	Coach Collins
Big yard	His words

The advantage of mapping is that it not only helps you generate ideas but also begins to organize them as well. As you look at your clusters, you can begin to see whole sections you might write on the new school, the new house, and the new friends. You decide you might use some of the details (like getting lost and learning the El) in your introduction. However, you begin to see that the real turning point of the move to Chicago centered on Coach Collins and his words to you. You have come closer to your subject. It may be time for some freewriting.

FREEWRITING

Some people do not enjoy brainstorming and mapping. These writers can find their subjects better by simply jumping in to five or ten minutes of freewriting.

Freewriting is writing down your thoughts as they come to you without pausing and without crossing anything out. Freewriting is fun because you do not worry about spelling or perfect punctuation or form; you send your internal censors on vacation. All you are concerned about is pouring out your thoughts.

At the end of a burst of nonstop freewriting, read over what you have written. Your subject may be completely clear to you from this passage. You might circle certain sentences and phrases that you know you will want to use in your paper. Using these sentences, you may want to try another burst of freewriting to see if it will bring you even nearer to your subject and what you want to say about it. (See "The Open-ended Writing Process," page 75.)

THE REPORTER'S FORMULA

The reporter's formula is another technique for helping you quickly see your subject. Simply pretend you are a reporter and fill in the answers to the questions *who*, *what*, *where*, *when*, *why*, and *how*. As with mapping, the reporter's formula often enables you to visualize your whole paper.

>
> *Who:* Coach Collins.
> *What:* Advice on succeeding at Central High.
> *Where:* The volley ball court.
> *When:* The end of a losing match.
> *Why:* I had just lost the last point.
> *How:* Quietly, almost under his breath.

JOURNALS AND NOTEBOOKS

As May Sarton and Joan Didion explain in the essays that begin this chapter, keeping a regular diary or a writer's journal or notebook is often another helpful tool for finding your special subject matter as a writer. In diaries and journals you leave traces of who you are and what has been engaging you. In diaries and journals your material is often lying in deposit, drawing interest, ready for use whenever you are ready to use it.

However, as Brenda Ueland stresses in her essay "The Imagination Works Slowly and Quietly"—and as May Sarton implies as well—mining that subject matter takes time and patience. That is why you should make it a point of honor to start any writing assignment the day it is given you.

Never wait until the last minute! A piece of writing that begins as a map or freewrite on the first day can become a first draft after a week or ten days. Then you have the luxury of laying it aside for a day or two and of taking it out and looking at it with fresh, unhurried eyes. This opportunity for revision may cause you to add many new sentences (or sections) to your paper, move other sentences around, delete some sentences, and polish them all. A week (or a month) later, when the paper is due, you will feel good about turning it in, for it has existed for a long time in your imagination, and on paper. You will have gotten deeper into your subject (and closer to it) with every reading and revision. Actually this can be a never-ending process as student Kelly Linnenkamp reveals in the headnote to two drafts of her essay "Lifeguarding: Fun in the Sun?"

Often, however, as in Plato's famous "Allegory of the Cave," you may reach a place in your understanding of your subject when you see that what you thought was real and true was only shadow, and a new understanding will break through like the bright sun of day. For writers to achieve such breakthrough insights, sufficient quiet for writing is as important as ample time. Part of the challenge of writing will be finding a quiet place and time to work. Some writers, however, write best with music playing or even amid a hive of activity. (See May Sarton in this chapter, student Cory Waldron in Chapter 5, and E. B. White in Chapter 8.) Experiment to find times and settings that work best for you.

AUDIENCE AND PURPOSE

A final touchstone when you are searching for a subject is to consider the *audience* for your writing and your *purpose* in writing. Is your audience for this writing project your professor? Your school newspaper? Experts in your field? A potential employer? A friend? Or yourself? Do the subject and the tack you plan to take on it seem appropriate to this audience? Do they lend themselves to the purpose of the project? If you find yourself answering no to either of these questions, you may want to go back and begin brainstorming, mapping, freewriting, or mining your journal or the reporter's formula again for more fitting subjects or approaches.

Never despair, however, when hunting for a subject. Like the actor in John Updike's short story "One More Interview," which concludes this chapter, more than likely you will find yourself warming to your subject as you go along.

Journal of a Solitude

May Sarton

Generally, I get up at six—earlier in the summer—make my breakfast, go back to bed, and lie there for about an hour and think after breakfast. That's my most creative time: before I put anything down, while the subconscious is still open from the night, before anything has started to interrupt—even good things. I enjoy watching the sun rise. It's very beautiful here. Then I get up and I'm usually at my desk by half past eight. I really don't work for longer than eleven or half past eleven, but I do it every day. Then I walk Tamas [the dog] and get the mail, which is a terrible onslaught and which almost always brings something that I have to answer at once. Then I have lunch and rest. At this point, I start a whole other day, which involves household things, gardening, and similar pursuits.

I work with records playing all the time when I'm writing. Only baroque music. I love nineteenth-century music, but I can't use it when I'm working at all. I write on the typewriter directly when I'm writing a novel, but not with a poem. A poem begins with a lot of jottings, and then finally I put it on the typewriter and start revising. I try to keep the drafts of poems. I find it difficult to do because I think that everyone wants to tear up what they're casting aside. I don't always keep all the drafts, but I think that it is a good idea to do it. Sometimes it's very interesting because you go back and see how it happened.

Brief Warm-up Writing Exercises

1. Start freewriting with the words "Begin here." Then describe the weather and your immediate surroundings.
2. Describe the longest stretch of time when you have been completely alone and how you felt about this "solitude."
3. Make a list of the kinds of writing you have done in your life (keeping a diary or journal; writing letters or notes to others; writing papers or reports, newspaper articles, poems, stories, novels, plays, and so on). Beside each *form* of writing, describe the *audience* for this communication.

Now look over your list and describe the kind of writing that you enjoy most and the audience you most prefer to address.

❖ **September 15th**

1   Begin here. It is raining. I look out on the maple, where a few leaves have turned yellow, and listen to Punch, the parrot, talking to himself and to the rain ticking gently against the windows. I am here alone for the first time in weeks, to take up my "real" life again at last. That is what is strange—that friends, even passionate love, are not my real life unless there is time alone in which to explore and to discover what is happening or has happened. Without the interruptions, nourishing and maddening, this life would become arid. Yet I taste it fully only when I am alone here and "the house and I resume old conversations."

2   On my desk, small pink roses. Strange how often the autumn roses look sad, fade quickly, frost-browned at the edges! But these are lovely, bright, singing pink. On the mantel, in the Japanese jar, two sprays of white lilies, recurved, maroon pollen on the stamens, and a branch of peony leaves turned a strange pinkish-brown. It is an elegant bouquet; *shibui,* the Japanese would call it. When I am alone the flowers are really seen; I can pay attention to them. They are felt as presences. Without them I would die. Why do I say that? Partly because they change before my eyes. They live and die in a few days; they keep me closely in touch with process, with growth, and also with dying. I am floated on their moments.

3   The ambience here is order and beauty. That is what frightens me when I am first alone again. I feel inadequate. I have made an open place, a place for meditation. What if I cannot find myself inside it?

4   I think of these pages as a way of doing that. . . .

5   . . . I often feel exhausted, but it is not my work that tires (work is a rest); it is the effort of pushing away the lives and needs of others before I can come to the work with any freshness and zest.

October 11th

6   . . . I can hardly believe that relief from the anguish of these past months is here to stay, but so far it does feel like a true change of mood—or rather, a change of *being* where I can stand alone. So much of my life here is precarious. I cannot always believe even in my work. But I have come in these

last days to feel again the validity of my struggle here, that it is meaningful whether I ever "succeed" as a writer or not, and that even its failures, failures of nerve, failures due to a difficult temperament, can be meaningful. It is an age where more and more human beings are caught up in lives where fewer and fewer inward decisions can be made, where fewer and fewer real choices exist. The fact that a middle-aged, single woman, without any vestige of family left, lives in this house in a silent village and is responsible only to her own soul means something. The fact that she is a writer and can tell where she is and what it is like on the pilgrimage inward can be of comfort. It is comforting to know there are lighthouse keepers on rocky islands along the coast.

January 18th

7   . . . A strange empty day. I did not feel well, lay around, looked at daffodils against the white walls, and twice thought I must be having hallucinations because of their extraordinary scent that goes from room to room. I always forget how important the empty days are, how important it may be sometimes not to expect to produce anything, even a few lines in a journal. I am still pursued by a neurosis about work inherited from my father. A day where one has not pushed oneself to the limit seems a damaged damaging day, a sinful day. Not so! The most valuable thing we can do for the psyche, occasionally, is to let it rest, wander, live in the changing light of a room, not try to be or do anything whatever. Tonight I do feel in a state of grace, limbered up, less strained. Before supper I was able to begin to sort out poems of the last two years . . . there is quite a bunch. For my sixtieth birthday I intend to publish sixty new poems and, as I see it now, it will be a book of chiefly love poems. *Sixty at Sixty,* I call it, for fun. ❖

Questions to Ponder

1. Why is it that we often do not really "see" things until we are alone?
2. What are the benefits of making an "open place, a place for meditation" in our lives? How might writing be part of that "meditation"?
3. What aspects of your life exhaust you? What parts exhilarate you? What plan can you develop to increase the time you spend in the latter and decrease the time spent in the former?
4. Why is preparing to write—thinking, brainstorming, mapping, going over your notes, making your coffee or tea—actually an essential part of the writing process? Do you use these prewriting activities to their fullest potential?

Writing Possibilities

1. Use the "Begin here" writing you did in warm-up writing exercise 1 as the first entry in a journal that you will keep for a month. Using May Sarton's journal as a model, use your journal to describe your world and your thoughts about yourself and your work.
2. Get up a half-hour or an hour early and then follow May Sarton's example of going back to bed immediately after breakfast for a brief time of "creative revery." Afterward, jot down the ideas and images that come to you during each day's meditation.
3. Read over your journal entries, or your notes from your post-breakfast "creative reveries," and choose a recurring theme or image. Make it the subject of a reflective essay.
4. Write an essay trying to convince people of the advantages (or the disadvantages) of solitude.

ON KEEPING A NOTEBOOK

Joan Didion

I am a person whose most absorbed and passionate hours are spent arranging words on pieces of paper. I get papers of different colors: yellow paper for getting it down, for notes, for letting it run; pale blue paper when I start getting closer to it, to find the shape of the thing—the grain in the wood. And I use white paper when it seems that if, if only I could commit myself to using this expensive paper, this sixteen-weight bond with a watermark on it, maybe if I make that commitment I could get it almost right. . . .

I write entirely to find out what I'm thinking, what I'm looking at, what I see and what it means. What I want and what I fear. Why did the oil refineries around Carquinez Straits seem sinister to me in the summer of 1956? Why have the night lights in the [Berkeley] bevatron [a particle accelerator] burned in my mind for twenty years. What is going on in these pictures in my mind? . . .

Grammar is a piano I play by ear, since I seem to have been out of school the year the rules were mentioned. All I know about grammar is its infinite power. To shift the structure of a sentence alters the meaning of that sentence, as definitely and inflexibly as the position of a camera alters the meaning of the object photographed. Many people know about camera angles now, but not so many know about sentences. The arrangement of the words matters, and the arrangement you want can be found in the picture in your mind. The picture dictates the arrangement. The picture dictates whether this will be a sentence with or without clauses, a sentence that ends hard or a dying-fall sentence, long or short, active or passive. The picture tells you how to arrange the words and the arrangement of the words tells you, or tells me, what's going on in the picture.

Brief Warm-up Writing Exercises

1. If you were to keep a writer's *notebook* (instead of a daily diary or journal), brainstorm a list of the kinds of items you think you would place in it.
2. Freewrite a brief descriptive portrait of the person you were (a) at 18, (b) at 13, and (c) at a major turning point in your life.

1 " 'That woman Estelle,' " the note reads, " 'is partly the reason why George Sharp and I are separated today.' *Dirty crepe-de-Chine wrapper, hotel bar, Wilmington RR, 9:45 a.m. August Monday morning.*"

2 Since the note is in my notebook, it presumably has some meaning to me. I study it for a long while. At first I have only the most general notion of what I was doing on an August Monday morning in the bar of the hotel across from the Pennsylvania Railroad station in Wilmington, Delaware (waiting for a train? missing one? 1960? 1961? why Wilmington?), but I do remember being there. The woman in the dirty crepe-de-Chine wrapper had come down from her room for a beer, and the bartender had heard before the reason why George Sharp and she were separated today. "Sure," he said, and went on mopping the floor. "You told me." At the other end of the bar is a girl. She is talking, pointedly, not to the man beside her but to a cat lying in the triangle of sunlight cast through the open door. She is wearing a plaid silk dress from Peck & Peck, and the hem is coming down.

3 Here is what it is: the girl has been on the Eastern Shore, and now she is going back to the city, leaving the man beside her, and all she can see ahead are the viscous summer sidewalks and the 3 A.M. long-distance calls that will make her lie awake and then sleep drugged through all the steaming mornings left in August (1960? 1961?). Because she must go directly from the train to lunch in New York, she wishes that she had a safety pin for the hem of the plaid silk dress, and she also wishes that she could forget about the hem and the lunch and stay in the cool bar that smells of disinfectant and malt and make friends with the woman in the crepe-de-Chine wrapper. She is afflicted by a

little self-pity, and she wants to compare Estelles. That is what that was all about.

4   Why did I write it down? In order to remember, of course, but exactly what was it I wanted to remember? How much of it actually happened? Did any of it? Why do I keep a notebook at all? It is easy to deceive oneself on all those scores. The impulse to write things down is a peculiarly compulsive one, inexplicable to those who do not share it, useful only accidentally, only secondarily, in the way that any compulsion tries to justify itself. I suppose that it begins or does not begin in the cradle. Although I have felt compelled to write things down since I was five years old, I doubt that my daughter ever will, for she is a singularly blessed and accepting child, delighted with life exactly as life presents itself to her, unafraid to go to sleep and unafraid to wake up. Keepers of private notebooks are a different breed altogether, lonely and resistant rearrangers of things, anxious malcontents, children afflicted apparently at birth with some presentiment of loss.

5   My first notebook was a Big Five tablet, given to me by my mother with the sensible suggestion that I stop whining and learn to amuse myself by writing down my thoughts. She returned the tablet to me a few years ago; the first entry is an account of a woman who believed herself to be freezing to death in the Arctic night, only to find, when day broke, that she had stumbled onto the Sahara Desert, where she would die of the heat before lunch. I have no idea what turn of a five-year-old's mind could have prompted so insistently "ironic" and exotic a story, but it does reveal a certain predilection for the extreme which has dogged me into adult life; perhaps if I were analytically inclined I would find it a truer story than any I might have told about Donald Johnson's birthday party or the day my cousin Brenda put Kitty Litter in the aquarium.

6   So the point of my keeping a notebook has never been, nor is it now, to have an accurate factual record of what I have been doing or thinking. That would be a different impulse entirely, an instinct for reality which I sometimes envy but do not possess. At no point have I ever been able successfully to keep a diary; my approach to daily life ranges from the grossly negligent to the merely absent, and on those few occasions when I have tried dutifully to record a day's events, boredom has so overcome me that the results are mysterious at best. What is this business about "shopping, typing piece, dinner with E, depressed"? Shopping for what? Typing what piece? Who is E? Was this "E" depressed, or was I depressed? Who cares?

7   In fact I have abandoned altogether that kind of pointless entry; instead I tell what some would call lies. "That's simply not true," the members of my family frequently tell me when they come up against my memory of a shared event. "The party was *not* for you, the spider was *not* a black widow, *it wasn't that way at all.*" Very likely they are right, for not only have I always had trouble distinguishing between what happened and what merely might have happened, but I remain unconvinced that the distinction, for my purposes, mat-

ters. The cracked crab that I recall having for lunch the day my father came home from Detroit in 1945 must certainly be embroidery, worked into the day's pattern to lend verisimilitude; I was ten years old and would not now remember the cracked crab. The day's events did not turn on cracked crab. And yet it is precisely that fictitious crab that makes me see the afternoon all over again, a home movie run all too often, the father bearing gifts, the child weeping, an exercise in family love and guilt. Or that is what it was to me. Similarly, perhaps it never did snow that August in Vermont; perhaps there never were flurries in the night wind, and maybe no one else felt the ground hardening and summer already dead even as we pretended to bask in it, but that was how it felt to me, and it might as well have snowed, could have snowed, did snow.

8   *How it felt to me*: that is getting closer to the truth about a notebook. I sometimes delude myself about why I keep a notebook, imagine that some thrifty virtue derives from preserving everything observed. See enough and write it down, I tell myself, and then some morning when the world seems drained of wonder, some day when I am only going through the motions of doing what I am supposed to do, which is write—on that bankrupt morning I will simply open my notebook and there it will all be, a forgotten account with accumulated interest, paid passage back to the world out there: dialogue overheard in hotels and elevators and at the hatcheck counter in Pavillon (one middle-aged man shows his hat check to another and says, "That's my old football number"); impressions of Bettina Aptheker and Benjamin Sonnenberg and Teddy ("Mr. Acapulco") Stauffer; careful *aperçus* about tennis bums and failed fashion models and Greek shipping heiresses, one of whom taught me a significant lesson (a lesson I could have learned from F. Scott Fitzgerald, but perhaps we all must meet the very rich for ourselves) by asking, when I arrived to interview her in her orchid-filled sitting room on the second day of a paralyzing New York blizzard, whether it was snowing outside.

9   I imagine, in other words, that the notebook is about other people. But of course it is not. I have no real business with what one stranger said to another at the hat-check counter in Pavillon; in fact I suspect that the line "That's my old football number" touched not my own imagination at all, but merely some memory of something once read, probably "The Eighty-Yard Run." Nor is my concern with a woman in a dirty crepe-de-Chine wrapper in a Wilmington bar. My stake is always, of course, in the unmentioned girl in the plaid silk dress. *Remember what it was to be me*: that is always the point.

10   It is a difficult point to admit. We are brought up in the ethic that others, any others, all others, are by definition more interesting than ourselves; taught to be different, just this side of self-effacing. ("You're the least important person in the room and don't forget it," Jessica Mitford's governess would hiss in her ear on the advent of any social occasion; I copied that into my notebook because it is only recently that I have been able to enter a room without hearing some such phrase in my inner ear.) Only the very young and the very old may

recount their dreams at breakfast, dwell upon self, interrupt with memories of beach picnics and favorite Liberty lawn dresses and the rainbow trout in a creek near Colorado Springs. The rest of us are expected, rightly, to affect absorption in other people's favorite dresses, other people's trout.

11   And so we do. But our notebooks give us away, for however dutifully we record what we see around us, the common denominator of all we see is always, transparently, shamelessly, the implacable "I." We are not talking here about the kind of notebook that is patently for public consumption, a structural conceit for binding together a series of graceful *pensées;* we are talking about something private, about bits of the mind's string too short to use, an indiscriminate and erratic assemblage with meaning only for its maker.

12   And sometimes even the maker has difficulty with the meaning. There does not seem to be, for example, any point in my knowing for the rest of my life that, during 1964, 720 tons of soot fell on every square mile of New York City, yet there it is in my notebook, labeled "FACT." Nor do I really need to remember that Ambrose Bierce liked to spell Leland Stanford's name "£eland $tanford" or that "smart women almost always wear black in Cuba," a fashion hint without much potential for practical application. And does not the relevance of these notes seem marginal at best?:

> *In the basement museum of the Inyo County Courthouse in Independence, California, sign pinned to a mandarin coat:* "This MANDARIN COAT *was often worn by Mrs. Minnie S. Brooks when giving lectures on her* TEAPOT COLLECTION."
>
> *Redhead getting out of car in front of Beverly Wilshire Hotel, chinchilla stole, Vuitton bags with tags reading:*
>
> > MRS. LOU FOX
> > HOTEL SAHARA
> > VEGAS

13   Well, perhaps not entirely marginal. As a matter of fact, Mrs. Minnie S. Brooks and her MANDARIN COAT pull me back into my own childhood, for although I never knew Mrs. Brooks and did not visit Inyo County until I was thirty, I grew up in just such a world, in houses cluttered with Indian relics and bits of gold ore and ambergris and the souvenirs my Aunt Mercy Farnsworth brought back from the Orient. It is a long way from that world to Mrs. Lou Fox's world, where we all live now, and is it not just as well to remember that? Might not Mrs. Minnie S. Brooks help me to remember what I am? Might not Mrs. Lou Fox help me to remember what I am not?

14   But sometimes the point is harder to discern. What exactly did I have in mind when I noted down that it cost the father of someone I know $650 a month to light the place on the Hudson in which he lived before the Crash? What use was I planning to make of this line by Jimmy Hoffa: "I may have my

faults, but being wrong ain't one of them"? And although I think it interesting to know where the girls who travel with the Syndicate have their hair done when they find themselves on the West Coast, will I ever make suitable use of it? Might I not be better off just passing it on to John O'Hara? What is a recipe for sauerkraut doing in my notebook? What kind of magpie keeps this notebook? *"He was born the night the Titanic went down."* That seems a nice enough line, and I even recall who said it, but is it not really a better line in life than it could ever be in fiction?

15   But of course that is exactly it: not that I should ever use the line, but that I should remember the woman who said it and the afternoon I heard it. We were on her terrace by the sea, and we were finishing the wine left from lunch, trying to get what sun there was, a California winter sun. The woman whose husband was born the night the *Titanic* went down wanted to rent her house, wanted to go back to her children in Paris. I remember wishing that I could afford the house, which cost $1,000 a month. "Someday you will," she said lazily. "Someday it all comes." There in the sun on her terrace it seemed easy to believe in someday, but later I had a low-grade afternoon hangover and ran over a black snake on the way to the supermarket and was flooded with inexplicable fear when I heard the checkout clerk explaining to the man ahead of me why she was finally divorcing her husband. "He left me no choice," she said over and over as she punched the register. "He has a little seven-month-old baby by her, he left me no choice." I would like to believe that my dread then was for the human condition, but of course it was for me, because I wanted a baby and did not then have one and because I wanted to own the house that cost $1,000 a month to rent and because I had a hangover.

16   It all comes back. Perhaps it is difficult to see the value in having one's self back in that kind of mood, but I do see it; I think we are well advised to keep on nodding terms with the people we used to be, whether we find them attractive company or not. Otherwise they turn up unannounced and surprise us, come hammering on the mind's door at 4 A.M. of a bad night and demand to know who deserted them, who betrayed them, who is going to make amends. We forget all too soon the things we thought we could never forget. We forget the loves and the betrayals alike, forget what we whispered and what we screamed, forget who we were. I have already lost touch with a couple of people I used to be; one of them, a seventeen-year-old, presents little threat, although it would be of some interest to me to know again what it feels like to sit on a river levee drinking vodka-and-orange-juice and listening to Les Paul and Mary Ford and their echoes sing "How High the Moon" on the car radio. (You see I still have the scenes, but I no longer perceive myself among those present, no longer could even improvise the dialogue.) The other one, a twenty-three-year-old, bothers me more. She was always a good deal of trouble, and I suspect she will reappear when I least want to see her, skirts too long, shy to the point of aggravation, always the injured party, full of recriminations and little hurts and stories I do not want to hear again, at once

saddening me and angering me with her vulnerability and ignorance, an apparition all the more insistent for being so long banished.

17   It is a good idea, then, to keep in touch, and I suppose that keeping in touch is what notebooks are all about. And we are all on our own when it comes to keeping those lines open to ourselves: your notebook will never help me, nor mine you. *"So what's new in the whiskey business?"* What could that possibly mean to you? To me it means a blonde in a Pucci bathing suit sitting with a couple of fat men by the pool at the Beverly Hills Hotel. Another man approaches, and they all regard one another in silence for a while. "So what's new in the whiskey business?" one of the fat men finally says by way of welcome, and the blonde stands up, arches one foot and dips it in the pool, looking all the while at the cabaña where Baby Pignatari is talking on the telephone. That is all there is to that, except that several years later I saw the blonde coming out of Saks Fifth Avenue in New York with her California complexion and a voluminous mink coat. In the harsh wind that day she looked old and irrevocably tired to me, and even the skins in the mink coat were not worked the way they were doing them that year, not the way she would have wanted them done, and there is the point of the story. For a while after that I did not like to look in the mirror, and my eyes would skim the newspapers and pick out only the deaths, the cancer victims, the premature coronaries, the suicides, and I stopped riding the Lexington Avenue IRT because I noticed for the first time that all the strangers I had seen for years—the man with the seeing-eye dog, the spinster who read the classified pages every day, the fat girl who always got off with me at Grand Central—looked older than they once had.

18   It all comes back. Even that recipe for sauerkraut: even that brings it back. I was on Fire Island when I first made that sauerkraut, and it was raining, and we drank a lot of bourbon and ate the sauerkraut and went to bed at ten, and I listened to the rain and the Atlantic and felt safe. I made the sauerkraut again last night and it did not make me feel any safer, but that is, as they say, another story. ❖

Questions to Ponder

1. What can we learn about ourselves from the *facts* we jot down in our notebooks?
   - from the *scenes* and *dialogue* we record?
   - from the *sayings* we find worth noting?
2. In what ways might one writer's notebook be of value to another writer? In what respects might it be of no value at all?
3. Why is it helpful for a writer to keep in touch with his or her earlier "selves"?
4. How does Joan Didion make her notebook come alive for the reader?

Writing Possibilities

1. Using Didion's examples as models, create one *fact*, one *scene*, and one striking *saying* or line of *dialogue*. Now see if you can weave all three into one written scenario. (*Hint:* Start with either the fact or the saying and the scene may unfold naturally from them.)
2. Keep a notebook for a month, adding to it regularly anything worth noting. At the end of the month, page through your notebook as if you were a visitor from another planet doing research. Categorize the entries and analyze the person who collected them in an essay for your family titled "American [or Canadian] Magpie."
3. Take the three freewritten portraits of yourself at different ages that you wrote in warm-up writing exercise 2 and link them in one autobiographical piece. You might call it "The Three Faces of _____."

THE IMAGINATION WORKS SLOWLY AND QUIETLY

Brenda Ueland

Brenda Ueland published more than six million words before she died at the age of 93 in the 1980s. She wrote two books, many articles and short stories, and taught writing at the YWCA in Minneapolis. Along the way she was knighted by the king of Norway and set an international swimming record for persons over 80.

Ueland's inspiring book If You Want to Write: A Book about Art, Independence and Spirit *grew out of a popular lecture she gave at the University of Minnesota in the 1930s. "Be Bold, be Free, be Truthful" was Ueland's motto, and her feisty spirit leaps from her chapter titles, which encourage us to "Be careless, reckless! Be a lion, be a pirate, when you write" and to "Keep a slovenly, headlong, impulsive, honest diary."*

Ueland believed that everybody is talented, original, and has something important to say. She insisted that students can learn to work, not from "grim, dry willpower but from generosity and the fascinating search for truth."

Brief Warm-up Writing Exercises

1. Write down ideas that have been growing for a long time inside you about any of these topics: (a) college athletics, (b) college financial-aid programs, (c) student life-styles, (d) your major, (e) flag burning, (f) abortion.
2. Describe how you think a person's writing process might be affected by artificial stimulants, such as alcohol or drugs. Compare a "stimulated" writer to a writer functioning "naturally."

---

1 ❖ Now I am going to try to tell you what the creative power is, how you can detect it in yourself and separate it out from all your nervous doubts and checks. And how you can separate it from mere memory. For memory and erudition (i.e., the superimposed lumber of all the hard facts you have learned) can smother it very easily.

2 When we hear the word "inspiration" we imagine something that comes like a bolt of lightning, and at once with a rapt flashing of the eyes, tossed hair and feverish excitement, a poet or artist begins furiously to paint or write. At least I used to think sadly that that was what inspiration must be, and never experienced a thing that was one bit like it.

3 But this isn't so. Inspiration comes very slowly and quietly. Say that you want to write. Well, not much will come to you the first day. Perhaps nothing at all. You will sit before your typewriter or paper and look out of the window and begin to brush your hair absentmindedly for an hour or two. Never mind. That is all right. That is as it should be—though you must sit before your typewriter just the same and know, in this dreamy time, that you are going to write, to tell something on paper, sooner or later. And you also must know that you are going to sit here tomorrow for a while, and the next day and so on, forever and ever.

4 Our idea that we must always be energetic and active is all wrong. Bernard Shaw says that it is not true that Napoleon was always snapping out decisions to a dozen secretaries and aides-de-camp, as we are told, but that he moodled around for months. Of course he did. And that is why these smart, energetic, do-it-now, pushing people so often say: "I am not creative." They are, but they should be idle, limp and alone for much of the time, as lazy as men fishing on a levee, and quietly looking and thinking, not *willing* all the time. This quiet looking and thinking is the imagination; it is letting in ideas. Willing is doing something you know already, something you have been told by somebody else; there is no new imaginative understanding in it. And presently your soul gets frightfully sterile and dry because you are so quick, snappy and efficient about doing one thing after another that you have not time for your own ideas to come in and develop and gently shine. . . .

5   Now some people when they sit down to write and nothing special comes, no good ideas, are so frightened that they drink a lot of strong coffee to hurry them up, or smoke packages of cigarettes, or take drugs or get drunk. They do not know that good ideas come slowly, and that the more clear, tranquil and unstimulated you are, the slower the ideas come but the better they are.

6   It was Tolstoi who showed me this. I used to drink coffee all day and smoke two packages of cigarettes. I could thus pump myself up to write all day and much of the night, for a few days. But the sad part of it was, what I wrote was not very good. It came out easily, but it wasn't much good. It was interlarded with what was pretentious, commonplace and untrue.

7   This is what Tolstoi said about it:

> 'If I do not smoke I cannot write. I cannot get on. I begin and I cannot endure,' is what is usually said and what I used to say. What does it really mean?
>
> It means either that you have nothing to write, or what you wished to write has not yet matured in your consciousness, but it is only beginning dimly to present itself to you, and the appraising critic within[1] when not stupefied with tobacco, tells you so.
>
> If you did not smoke, you would either abandon what you have begun, or you would wait until your thought has cleared itself dimly in your mind; you would try to penetrate into what presents itself dimly to you—[by, as I say, idling, by a long, solitary walk, by being alone]—would consider the objects that offer themselves and would turn all your attention to the elucidation of the thought. But you smoke and the critic within you [the truth-seeking creative critic] is stupefied, and the hindrance to your work is removed. What to you, when not inebriated by tobacco, seems insignificant, again seems important; what seemed obscure, no longer seems so; the objections that present themselves vanish and you continue to write and write much and rapidly.

8   I am not urging you not to smoke. Each must find out all things for himself. But I want to show how Tolstoi knew good thoughts come slowly. And so it is nothing for you to worry about or to be afraid of, and it is even a bad plan to hurry them artificially.

9   For when you do so, there may be suddenly *many* thoughts, but that does not mean that they are specially good ones or interesting. It is just as when you give a thoughtful, slightly tired person a stiff drink. Before the drink he says

---

[1] By "critic" he means here what I call the true self, the imagination, or the Holy Ghost, or the Conscience. It is what is always searching in us and trying to free what we *really* think, from what we think we ought to think, from what is super-imposed by bossy parents, teachers or literary critics.

This critic in us all, I love. The critic I abhor is the one (inside or out) which is always measuring, comparing, cautioning and advising prudence and warning against mistakes and quoting authorities and throwing dry, anxious doubts into everyone, by showing them just the way they must go.

No, each man must go by his own Conscience, by his own creative, truth-searching critic.

nothing but what seems to him interesting and important. He mentally discards the thoughts that are not important enough to make up for the fatigue of saying them. But after the drink, all his thoughts come out head over heels, whatever crosses his mind. There are suddenly *many* thoughts; but they are just like the flutter of thoughts that come out of one of those unfortunate people who cannot keep from talking all the time. This kind of talking is not creation. It is just mental evacuation.

10   And it is Tolstoi who showed me the importance of being idle—because thoughts come so slowly. For what we write today slipped into our souls some *other* day when we were alone and doing nothing.

11   Tolstoi speaks of the hero of Dostoevsky's *Crime and Punishment.*

> *Raskolnikof lived his true life, not when he murdered the old woman or her sister. When murdering the old woman herself, and especially when murdering her sister, he did not live his true life, but acted like a machine doing what he could not help doing—discharging the cartridge with which he had long been loaded. Raskolnikof lived his true life . . . at the time when he was lying on the sofa in his room. . . . And then—in that region quite independent of animal activities—the question whether he would or would not kill the old woman was decided. That question was decided when he was doing nothing and only thinking; when only his consciousness was active and in that consciousness tiny, tiny alterations were taking place. It is at such times that one needs the greatest clearness to decide correctly the questions that have arisen, and it is just then that one glass of beer, or one cigarette, may prevent the solution of the question, may postpone the decision, stifle the voice of conscience, prompt the decision of the question in favor of one's lower animal nature, as was the case of Raskolnikof.*

12   I tell you this not to persuade you to give up drinking and smoking (though that might be a good thing too) but to show you that what you write today is the result of some span of idling yesterday, some fairly long period of protection from talking and busyness.

13   It was Raskolnikof lying on the couch, ill and miserable and in despair about his destitute mother and sister, and wondering what to do—it was then he created the murder that came many days later.

14   In the same way what you write today you thought and created in some idle time on another day. It is on another day that your ideas and visions are slowly built up, so that when you take your pencil there is something to say[2] that is not just superficial and automatic, like children yelling at a birthday party, but it is true and has been tested inwardly and is based on something.

[2]Though remember this: you may not be conscious, when you sit down, of having evolved something important to say. You will sit down as mentally blank, goodnatured and smiling as usual, and not frowning solemnly over the weight of your message. Just the same, when you begin to write, presently something will come out, something true and interesting.

15   And why it must be true I will explain later. I do not mean it must be a statement of fact such as "Columbus discovered America in 1492," but it must come from your true self and not your theoretical self, from what you really think, love and believe, not from your hope to make an impression.

16   That is why I hope you can keep up this continuity and sit for some time every day (if only for a half hour, though two hours is better and five is remarkable and eight is bliss and transfiguration!) before your typewriter—if not writing then just thoughtfully pulling your hair. If you skip for a day or two, it is hard to get started again. In a queer way you are afraid of it. It takes again an hour or two of vacant moodling, when nothing at all comes out on paper; and this is difficult always because it makes us busy, efficient Anglo-Saxons with our accomplishment-mania, feel uneasy and guilty.

17   You see, I am so afraid that you will decide that you are stupid and untalented. Or that you will put off working as so many wonderfully gifted people do, until that time when your husband can retire on full pay and all your children are out of college. ❖

Questions to Ponder

1. Why does rushing cause writers to lose ideas—or treat them superficially?
2. When a writer is given a deadline a month away for a writing assignment, when ideally should the writer begin work? Can you map out the best schedule for you for completing this project? (*Hint:* Plan time for prewriting activities, research, several drafts, revising, sharing the piece with others, revising, and proofreading.)
3. What is the best way to ensure yourself time every day to allow the imagination to work slowly and quietly?

Writing Possibilities

1. Choose one of the ideas you expressed in warm-up exercise 1 and make it the central idea (or thesis) of either (a) a letter to your campus newspaper, (b) a letter to your state senator or representative, (c) a persuasive essay, or (d) a report on the current state of affairs on your campus in respect to this issue.
2. Make a list of all the seemingly distracting or irrelevant things you do while trying to write a college paper. Then write a humorous piece titled "The Less-Than-Straight Road to Writing Success."
3. Write a dialogue between a person who thinks he or she can perform better on drugs or alcohol than "straight" and one who disputes this belief. Be sure you make each side as convincing as you can.

4. Try to recall any important ideas or insights that have come to you while you were walking or hiking alone, jogging, swimming, meditating, or just relaxing. Make a list to use in an essay stressing the value of such activities.

THE OPEN-ENDED WRITING PROCESS

Peter Elbow

"The Open-Ended Writing Process" grew out of some gradual awakenings about what actually went on in me as I went about writing. I began to accept the fact that I never seemed to have success or pleasure when I tried to write things right—that is, tried to get my meaning clear in my mind ahead of time—either by thinking hard or making a careful outline. Either I could not get my meaning clear in my mind or, if I could, I could never stick to that meaning as I proceeded to try to write it out in a draft.

This was not a merely theoretic discovery: I was having so much trouble writing that I had to drop out of graduate school, and indeed I thought perhaps I was losing my mind. But when (after five years of teaching) I returned to graduate school and began to experiment with my writing and to examine how I actually managed to get things written, I discovered that I had the best luck just plunging in and putting my initial thinking onto the paper—in the jumbled condition it was—and letting it gradually evolve on paper through messy drafts. I gave up on even trying to nail it down first.

I finally gave myself permission (and I had to finish getting my Ph.D. before I dared to think this way) to conclude that this drifting, or wandering, or mess-making technique was not just a failure on my part but could be considered a positive model: a good thing to do instead of an aberration. When I stopped being ashamed of it, I realized that it felt like an adventurous way to go about writing—and this led me, I think, to my "voyage out / voyage home" metaphor. I always enjoy my thinking most when I can ground it in some crude or physical metaphor.

Since I wrote this chapter, I've sensed (from my own experience and from that of writers, colleagues, and students) that perhaps the experience of being surprised by one's writing—having it change directions or finding oneself stumbling into something unknown—is, in fact, the biggest reward that writing holds for us. I now suspect that no one keeps up writing by choice over the years without that experience of surprise or discovery. It is this experience of meaning coming from the unknown—the experience that people over the ages have talked about with words like "inspiration" or "the muses"—that the open-ended writing process tries to promote.

Brief Warm-up Writing Exercises

1. Describe an experience (or a conversation) you have had in which you began in one mood and ended in quite another.
2. Now freewrite about an experience you have had in which you began with one idea or viewpoint and ended with a different perspective.
3. Describe your usual "mind set" at the beginning of a trip or vacation and then at the end when the car is pulling into the driveway.

1 ❖ The open-ended writing process is at the opposite extreme from the direct writing process. It is a way to bring to birth an unknown, unthought-of piece of writing a piece of writing that is not yet in you. It is a technique for thinking, seeing, and feeling new things. This process invites maximum chaos and disorientation. You have to be willing to nurse something through many stages over a long period of time and to put up with not knowing where you are going. Thus it is a process that can change you, not just your words. . . .

2 Ideally you should not choose in advance what you are going to end up with. Perhaps you start out thinking and hoping for a poem, but you may well end up with a story in prose, a letter to someone, an essay that works out one of your perplexities. The open-ended writing process goes on and on till the potential piece of writing is fully cooked and grown. Sometimes this happens quickly, sometimes you nurse it through decades (though I will suggest some ways to hasten the process a bit).

3 I think of the open-ended writing process as a voyage in two stages: a sea voyage and a coming to new land. For the sea voyage you are trying to lose sight of land—the place you began. Getting lost is the best source of new material. In coming to new land you develop a new conception of what you are writing about—a new idea or vision—and then you gradually reshape your material to fit this new vision. The sea voyage is a process of divergence, branching, proliferation, and confusion; the coming to land is a process of convergence, pruning, centralizing, and clarifying.

4 To begin the sea voyage, do a nonstop freewriting that starts from wherever you happen to be. Most often you just start with a thought or a feeling or a memory that seems for some reason important to you. But perhaps you

have something in mind for a possible piece of writing; perhaps you have some ideas for an essay; or certain images stick in mind as belonging in a poem; or certain characters or events are getting ready to make a story. You can also start by describing what you wish you could end up with. Realize of course that you probably won't just start writing.

5   The open-ended writing process is ideal for the situation where you sense you have something to write but you don't quite know what. Just start writing about anything at all. If you have special trouble with that first moment of writing—that confrontation with a blank page—ask yourself what you *don't* want to write about and start writing about it before you have a chance to resist. First thoughts. They are very likely to lead you to what you are needing to write.

6   Keep writing for at least ten or twenty or thirty minutes, depending on how much material and energy you come up with. You have to write long enough to get tired and get past what's on the top of your mind. But not so long that you start pausing in the midst of your writing.

7   Then stop, sit back, be quiet, and bring all that writing to a point. That is, by reading back or just thinking back over it, find the center or focus or point of those words and write it down in a sentence. This may mean different things: you can find the main idea that is there; or the new idea that is trying to be there; or the imaginative focus or center of gravity—an image or object or feeling, or perhaps some brand new thing occurs to you now as very important—it may even seem unrelated to what you wrote, but it comes to you now as a result of having done that burst of writing. Try to stand out of the way and let the center or focus itself decide to come forward. In any event, don't worry about it. Choose or invent something for your focus and then go on. The only requirement is that it be a single thing. Skip a few lines and write it down. Underline it or put a box around it so you can easily find it later. (Some people find it helpful to let themselves write down two or three focusing sentences.)

8   If this center of gravity is a feeling or an image, perhaps a mere phrase will do: "a feeling that something good will happen" or "mervyn the stuffed monkey slumped under the dining room table." But a complete sentence or assertion is better, especially if the focus is an idea or thought or insight. Try, that is, to get more than "economics" or "economic dimension"—since those words just vaguely point in a general direction—and try for something like "there must be an economic reason for these events."

9   You have now gone through a cycle that consists of nonstop writing and then sitting back to probe for the center. You have used two kinds of consciousness: immersion, where you have your head down and are scurrying along a trail of words in the underbrush; and perspective, where you stand back and look down on things from a height and get a sense of shape and outline.

10   Now repeat this cycle. Use the focus you just wrote down as the springboard for a new piece of nonstop writing. There are various ways in which you

can let it bounce you into new writing. Perhaps you just take it and write more about it. Or perhaps that doesn't seem right because what you already wrote has finished an idea and the focusing sentence has put the lid on it. If you wrote more about it, you would just be repeating yourself. In this case, start now with what comes next: the next step, the following thing, the reply, the answering salvo. Perhaps "what comes next" is what follows logically. Perhaps the next thing is what comes next in your mind even though it involves a jump in logic. Perhaps the next thing is a questioning or denial of what you have already written: arguments against it, writing in an opposite mood, or writing in a different mode (from prose to poetry). Stand out of the way and see what happens.

11. Whatever kind of jump it is, jump into a second burst of nonstop writing for however long you can keep it up. Long enough to get tired and lose track of where you started; not so long that you keep pausing and lose momentum. And then, again, stop and come out from the underbrush of your immersion in words, attain some calm and perspective, and find the summing up or focus or center of gravity for this second piece of writing.

12. The sea voyage consists of repeating this cycle over and over again. Keep up one session of writing long enough to get loosened up and tired—long enough in fact to make a bit of a voyage and probably to pass beyond what happened to be in mind and in mood. But usually a piece of open-ended writing takes several or even many long sittings. One of the major ingredients in the open-ended process is time and the attendant changes of mood and outlook.

13. As you change modes from writing to focusing and back to writing and back to focusing, practice letting the process itself decide what happens next—decide, for example, whether your focusing sentence springboards you into a new treatment of the same material, into a response to that material or into some other new topic or mode that "wants" to come next. If it sounds a bit mystical to say "Let it decide," I don't mean to rule out hard conscious thinking. "Letting it decide" will often mean realizing you should be rigorously logical at this point in the writing cycle. As you practice the open-ended writing process, you will get better at feeling what kind of step needs to be taken at any given point. The main thing is not to worry about doing it right. Just do it a lot.

14. As you engage in this sea voyage, invite yourself to lose sight of what you had in mind at the beginning, invite digressions, new ideas, seeds falling from unexpected sources, changes of mind. You are trying to nurse your thoughts, perceptions and feelings through a process of continual transformation—cooking and growing. . . .

15. The sea voyage is most obviously finished when you sight new land—when you get a trustworthy vision of your final piece of writing. You see that it's an argument and where it is going; or you see it is a poem and feel the general shape of it.

16. To come to land you need to get this vision clearer and more complete.

Perhaps your first glimpse showed you what is central: now you need to write out that central event or idea more fully. If what is emerging is primarily conceptual, such as an essay, you may well need to make an outline. You won't be able to see your structure clearly until you go through all you have written to find the points that feel important, write each one into a complete sentence, and then put these sentences into the most logical or easily understood order. Even for a long story or poem, you may need some kind of schematic representation of the whole so you can see it all in one glance.

17   But perhaps it is too early for any outline or overview. Perhaps you cannot really get this final vision clear and right except by plunging into a new draft in your present fame of mind—starting the first scene of the story or novel, the first line of the poem, the introductory thought for your essay—and just plowing along. Perhaps *doing it* is more helpful at this point than any method of planning or outlining.

18   What if you keep writing and writing and you sense that the sea voyage is really done, but you lack any glimpse of land. You feel you have gotten down everything you can get down, you are beginning to repeat yourself, there is no more divergence. You've succeeded in getting productively lost, but now this unknown territory starts to get depressingly familiar.

19   You can try to hasten the convergent process of coming to land. Go back over all the centers or focuses you have written down in the course of the sea voyage. Ponder them for a while. Then engage in some nonstop writing on the basis of them. Start writing "I don't yet know what all this writing is really about, but here's what the important elements seem to be: . . . ." Of course you can't put them in the right or logical order—that's just what you don't know. You are trying to bring them together into the same burst of energy and attention. You might write something like this:

> *There's writing that sounds like the writer talking, there's writing that somehow just resonates in some mysterious way, there's radio announcer speech with great energy and liveliness but sounding completely fake, there's* ———, *and there's* ———. *How can I make sense of it all?*

You are trying to get the important elements to bounce against each other in a tight place.

20   Keep up this burst of writing—this attempt to figure out what your writing is about—as long as you can. Perhaps a center will emerge. If not, go on to the step of standing back and looking for a center. If that isn't the final center, then go on to another wave of writing. Keep this up for a while. Keep up, that is, the same process you used for the sea voyage, but instead of using it for divergence and getting lost, use it for convergence and getting found. If this doesn't work, you may simply have to stop and rest. Give your writing more time in a drawer unlooked at. Anything that takes this long simply to emerge is probably important. Some complicated and important reordering of things is trying to take place inside you. ❖

Questions to Ponder

1. Why is "getting lost" one of the best ways to find new material?
2. Should writers, then, deliberately seek to lose themselves at times (so they don't know quite where they are going with a piece of writing) so that they can discover new insights or writing styles? What are some ways to do this?
3. If you always write on the surface of what you know, are you in danger of being superficial—falling into cliché (Brenda Ueland's "automatic verbiage")—instead of being profound and original?
4. How long do you find you have to work before you get past what is on top of your mind into something more unusual, unexpected, or true? What processes are involved in reaching this richer insight?
5. As you look back over the experiences you described in warm-up exercises 1 and 2, what process did your emotions or ideas go through as they passed from one state to another? What *forces* caused the changes or the deepening perspective?
6. Why is the ability to summarize and to synthesize—to find the center or point of a piece of writing—a valuable ability to have? (Note that by using the open-ended writing process, you can consciously cultivate this valuable ability.)

Writing Possibilities

1. Make a list of ideas (or feelings) that you *sense* you would like to write on or explore. Choose the one that strikes you as most appealing at this moment and try Peter Elbow's nonstop freewriting sea voyage, followed by looking back over what you have written and writing its central focus. Then springboard from this focused sentence to a new voyage of discovery.
2. Write a piece in which you deliberately turn an idea upside down. Start out by freewriting your opinion on an issue (the proper drinking age, for example), and after stopping to focus, turn in your second burst of freewriting and argue the opposite side—just as vigorously. After you pause to find the center of this second section, take the writing where it seems to want to go next.
3. Freewrite nonstop on another idea or feeling of importance to you. After the immersion in the sea voyage, step back and write down the center of gravity of what you have written. Then, for your next nonstop immersion, try to make the *same point* but *in a different form or voice*. If you wrote a short essay, now transform it into a letter or a dialogue. If your first voice was angry, now make the same point in the voice of a diplomat. Now try another burst of freewriting, exaggerating your ideas to the point of satire—or go the opposite way and explore the power of understatement.

Student Essay

LIFEGUARDING: FUN IN THE SUN?

Kelly Linnenkamp

As a first-semester sophomore, majoring in psychology and pre–physical therapy, I wrote "Lifeguarding: Fun in the Sun?" in response to the assignment of a personal experience paper. I wanted to choose a topic with which most readers are familiar, yet also be able to question a popular point of view. My first rescue as a lifeguard fit these criteria in addition to making me feel emotionally charged as I was freewriting a rough draft. Furthermore, part of my own "voice" as a writer is to use descriptions that involve the human senses, which this topic allowed me to do.

In my first draft I concentrated on vivid images and descriptions. I wasn't really sure of the overall message I wanted to convey. In revising from my first draft to my final draft, I changed my focus from how I felt about the other people involved in the rescue to how the rescue changed my own thoughts and feelings. The final draft also gave more information on lifeguard training.

If I were going to do another draft of this essay, I would use more details and figurative language to convey my own feelings of inadequacy and inferiority in relation to the other lifeguards. I think this would strengthen the overall affect of the paper. Moreover, I would tell exactly how the accident occurred rather than leave the situation as vague as in these drafts.

In my own writing I pick topics that spark interest in me. I use vivid details and descriptions, and I keep in mind that there is always room for revision.

Brief Warm-up Writing Exercises

1. Describe the most dramatic or traumatic experience you have ever had in a part-time or full-time job.
2. Describe an average day at your favorite job.
3. Freewrite on what you would consider to be the most glamorous job in the world.

DRAFT

1   Some people think that it's all glamour, glory, and good times. A "healthy" golden tan, sun-glitzed hair, and the social advantages of working at a pool make lifeguarding seem like a desirable job. While I enjoy the fringe benefits of being a lifeguard, an event that occurred during my first month in this position made me realize how much responsibility was actually upon my shoulders and that a knowledgeable team of people can act like a well-oiled machine in times of emergency.

2   "It's eleven minutes after three, ninety-eight degrees, and sunny." The D.J.'s voice faded into the familiar drone of Top 40 music that boomed out of the loudspeakers each afternoon at Byrnes Municipal Swimming Pool. Even as I sat up in the guard chair, the ever-present cocoa butter scent of tanning lotion being spread on like jelly on a slice of toast wafted up to me on the slight breeze that was blowing. Shouts and laughter of swimmers filled the air along with the constant sounds of splashing water.

3   I had to keep track of an unusually large number of swimmers, not only because of the summer heat, but also because I was used to working at a smaller, less-frequented pool. I felt nervous and inadequate among this group of well-trained swimmers. Technically, I was equally as qualified as the other guards on duty except for one crucial fact: I was inexperienced.

4   The guard that followed me in the rotation had arrived at my chair. Taking the expected precautions, we changed positions while constantly observing our area of the pool. Swiftly, I made my way through the jungle of swimmers and sunbathers to the next chair and the changing guard regiment occurred again. Pushing my sunglasses back onto my nose after they slid down on a trail of perspiration, I adjusted my towel and prepared to spend the next fifteen minutes supervising the three diving boards as well as a portion of the deep end.

5   After spending even a month as a lifeguard, the springing of a diving board after a safely exected dive or jump has a familiarity to it like that

of the voice of a parent. Several swimmers were attempting trick dives which are fun to watch, but nerve-racking because an unskilled diver is one who is likely to get hurt. While watching a group of young swimmers in the deep end, I heard the spring of the lowest, closest diving board, except with an unfamiliar thud. Instantaneously, I saw the body floundering in the water to regain buoyancy and heard a spectator saying, "She hit her head on the board." The first thought that entered my mind was that a spinal injury, since that was what I had been trained for and I had never actually seen a victim of such an accident. I gave three sharp whidtles, indicating that I had an emergency, swiftly climbed down from my chair, and slid into the water. It had occurred to me that a dive entry would have made waves that could worsen a potential spinal injury. As I approached the victim, an red-headed girl about eleven years old, she was conscious and able to swim. She was crying and holding her nose so I assisted her to the side of the pool where three other lifeguards were waiting with the spine board, although luckily it wasn't needed. With a surprising lack of bloodshed, her nose had already started to swell and turn purple, so we applied a cold pack and waited for the ambulance. Upon the arrival of the paramedics, she was diagnosed as having a broken nose.

6   Soon everything was back to normal at Byrnes Municipal Swimming Pool, but my vital signs were abnormal the rest of the day. My heart seemed to pound out of my chest and I had to grip the arms of the lifeguard chair to keep from shaking. No one ever really told me if I had done the right thing by summoning the spine board and paramedics. Still, I think I made the correct decision since the accident could have been a lot more serious, the paramedics were able to set the girl's nose before too much swelling had occurred, and the city could have had a severe lawsuit on its hands had I done nothing.

7   Several times that day and since then I have wondered how I would have reacted if the girl's injury was as serious as a severed spine. After the intense training that I've had I'm sure I would have reacted adequately. I concluded, though, that while my position is an envied one by many, there is a tremendous resposibility involved and I became

much more conscious of my actions. As I reflect back on my first rescue as a lifeguard, it took hours in my mind while in reality it took a few minutes. A team of well-trained individuals, like those I had the pleasure of working with, can make even an emergency run smoothly.

1   Some people think that it's all glamour, glory, and good times. A "healthy" golden tan, sun-glitzed hair, and the social advantages of working at a pool make lifeguarding seem like a desirable job. While I enjoy the fringe benefits of being a lifeguard, an event that occurred during my first month in this position made me realize how much responsibility was actually upon my shoulders. But it also assured me that I was capable of dealing with an emergency without panicking and making the situation even worse.

2   "It's eleven minutes after three, ninety-eight degrees, and sunny." The D.J.'s voice faded into the familiar drone of Top 40 music that boomed out of the loudspeakers each afternoon at Byrnes Municipal Swimming Pool. Even as I sat up in the guard chair, the ever-present cocoa butter scent of tanning lotion being spread on like jelly on a slice of toast wafted up to me on the slight breeze that was blowing. Shouts and laughter of swimmers filled the air along with the constant sounds of splashing water.

3   I had to keep track of an unusually large number of swimmers, not only because of the summer heat, but also because I was used to working at a smaller, less-frequented pool. I felt nervous and inadequate among this group of well-trained swimmers. Technically, I was equally as qualified as the other guards on duty except for one crucial fact: I was inexperienced. I had never really performed a rescue.

4   The guard that followed me in the rotation had arrived at my chair. Taking the expected precautions, we changed positions while constantly observing our area of the pool. Swiftly, I made my way through the jungle of swimmers and sunbathers to the next chair and the changing guard regiment occurred again. Pushing my sunglasses back onto my nose after they slid down on a trail of perspiration, I adjusted my towel and prepared to spend the next fifteen minutes supervising the three diving boards as well as a portion of the deep end.

5   After spending even a month as a lifeguard, one finds that the springing of a diving board after a safely executed dive or jump has a familiarity to it like that of the voice of a parent. Several swimmers were attempting trick dives which are fun to watch, but nerve-racking because an unskilled diver is one who is likely to get hurt. While watching a group of young swimmers in the deep end, I heard the spring of the lowest, closest diving board, except with an unfamiliar thud. Instantaneously, I saw the body floundering in the water to regain buoyancy and heard a spectator saying, "She hit her head on the board." The first thought that entered my mind was that a spinal injury had occurred. Although I had never actually seen a victim of such an accident, I

had spent several weeks learning how to deal with it. Because of the seriousness of this type of accident, especially in a pool situation, it seemed almost more emphasized in training than drowning itself. After all, if a swimmer gets water in his lungs, it can be removed, but once a person has a broken back or severed spinal cord, his life may never be the same. I gave three sharp whistles, indicating that I had an emergency, swiftly climbed down from my chair, and slid into the water. It had occurred to me that a dive entry would have made waves that could worsen a potential spinal injury. As I approached the victim, a red-headed girl about eleven years old, she was conscious and able to swim. She was crying and holding her nose so I assisted her to the side of the pool where three other lifeguards were waiting with the spine board, although luckily it wasn't needed. With a surprising lack of bloodshed, her nose had already started to swell and turn purple, so we applied a cold pack and waited for the ambulance. Upon the arrival of the paramedics, she was diagnosed as having a broken nose.

6   Soon everything was back to normal at Byrnes Municipal Swimming Pool, but my vital signs were abnormal the rest of the day. My heart seemed to pound out of my chest and I had to grip the arms of the lifeguard chair to keep from shaking. No one ever really told me if I had done the right thing by summoning the spine board and paramedics. Still, I think I made the correct decision since the accident could have been a lot more serious, perhaps even leading to a lawsuit against the city. The paramedics were able to set the girl's nose before too much swelling had occurred, but I never heard any more about her.

7   Several times that day and since then I wonder how I would have reacted if the girl's injury was as serious as a broken back or a head injury. After the intense training that I've had I'm sure I would have reacted adequately. I concluded, though, that while my position is an envied one by many, there is a tremendous responsibility involved. Even though it shook me up, I feel that my first rescue as a lifeguard made me more conscious of my actions and improved my self-confidence and performance in a job that many people feel is all fun in the sun. ❖

Questions to Ponder

1. What would you say is the "central idea," or *thesis*, of Kelly Linnenkamp's first draft? How does she refocus it by the time she's written her final draft? What is her new central idea? Why do you find the final draft stronger and more satisfying than the first draft?
2. What details in this essay reveal that Kelly was conscientious about her job?
3. Kelly says she likes to use descriptions that involve the human senses. What passages in her essay evoke the reader's sense of smell, touch, taste, sight, or hearing?

4. Is writing in any way like lifeguarding? Does our enjoyment of a good piece of writing often make us forget the considerable training and attention that goes into the attractive product?

Writing Possibilities

1. Compose a "frame" essay like Kelly Linnenkamp's in which you present in the first and final paragraphs a conclusion you've drawn about an experience you've had and in the paragraphs between these the illustrating story (narrative of the experience).
2. Brainstorm a list of jobs that look glamorous on the outside but may not be quite so attractive underneath. Classify or order your list, and then write a paper titled "All That Glitters" or, more fashionably, "All That Glitzes."
3. Now write about the hidden glamour of an ordinary job. (Choose as your audience either those currently working in this field or those who know little about this occupation.)

THE ALLEGORY OF THE CAVE
Plato

According to legend, Plato was not Plato's name at all but a nickname given to the great Greek philosopher because of his broad brow or broad shoulders. Born in 427 or 428 BCE to a distinguished Athenian family, Plato grew up listening to Socrates, who was a close friend of his uncle Charmides and his great-uncle Critias. In fact, Plato's older brothers, Glaucon and Adeimantus, were associates of Socrates, and from age 18 to 22 Plato himself was one of the group of young men who discussed with Socrates the various ethical issues that were to become the themes of Plato's more than 20 dialogues.

In disgust at the trial and execution of Socrates in 399 BCE, Plato abandoned his plans for a career in politics and decided to become a teacher of philosophy. Sick in body and spirit, he did not attend Socrates's execution but immediately left Athens for long travels in Italy, Sicily, and Egypt. When he returned in 386, he *founded the Academy, often called the first university, and taught there till his death at age 80.*

According to legend, Plato wrote poetry as a young man but destroyed his poems in his early twenties. Later he shared his insights in oral lectures, in letters, and (of course) in his famous dialogues. The dramatic dialogue, such as the famous "Allegory of the Cave" reprinted here, was particularly suited to Plato's experience and to his age. No one, ancient or modern, rivals Plato in its use. As Irwin Edman has noted, Plato lived in an age of discussion under government by discussion. What form, then, could be more suitable than the dialogue? Athenians, indeed, liked their writers to incorporate a dramatic element into their works because of the vivid impression it created. Plato's use of the dramatic dialogue also permitted him to put forth ideas tentatively, for examination, without being personally committed to them. They helped him feel his way toward the truth of his subject. Through the dialogues he could also immortalize his great teacher, Socrates.

The production of dialogues in ancient times has many parallels with the writing process today. Plato's dialogues were probably first performed or read aloud in chosen assemblies, and a few copies were made and circulated. The contents were modified in successive copyings or presentations, and only at a later stage did the dialogues become widely available as texts that one might buy or have specially copied for one's own use.

As I hope the following translation from The Republic *will reveal, along with the dialogue Plato also had the beautiful and austere Greek language to employ. We are lovers of beauty with economy, asserted the Greek leader Pericles. Words were to be used sparingly, and Greek writing was to be as simple and unadorned as Greek architecture and sculpture. Edith Hamilton has noted that the Greek writer "lifts one corner of the curtain only. A glimpse is given, no more, but by it the mind is fired to see for itself what lies behind. . . . The English method is to fill the mind with beauty; the Greek method was to set the mind to work"* (The Greek Way to Western Civilization *[New York: New American Library, 1958], 57).*

Brief Warm-up Writing Exercises

1. Describe what life might be like for a person born and raised deep inside a cave and not allowed ever to leave it.
2. Now imagine and describe what would happen if that person were suddenly freed and allowed to walk out into the sun.
3. Brainstorm a list of qualities of an ideal political leader.

1   And now, I said, let me show in a figure how far our nature is enlightened or unenlightened:—Behold! human beings living in an underground den, which has a mouth open towards the light and reaching all along the den; here they have been from their childhood, and have their legs and necks chained so that they

cannot move, and can only see before them, being prevented by the chains from turning round their heads. Above and behind them a fire is blazing at a distance, and between the fire and the prisoners there is a raised way; and you will see, if you look, a low wall built along the way, like the screen which marionette players have in front of them, over which they show the puppets.

2   I see.
3   And do you see, I said, men passing along the wall carrying all sorts of vessels, and statues and figures of animals made of wood and stone and various materials, which appear over the wall? Some of them are talking, others silent.
4   You have shown me a strange image, and they are strange prisoners.
5   Like ourselves, I replied; and they see only their own shadows, or the shadows of one another, which the fire throws on the opposite wall of the cave?
6   True, he said; how could they see anything but the shadows if they were never allowed to move their heads?
7   And of the objects which are being carried in like manner they would only see the shadows?
8   Yes, he said.
9   And if they were able to converse with one another, would they not suppose that they were naming what was actually before them?
10 Very true.
11 And suppose further that the prison had an echo which came from the other side, would they not be sure to fancy when one of the passers-by spoke that the voice which they heard came from the passing shadow?
12 No question, he replied.
13 To them, I said, the truth would be literally nothing but the shadows of the images.
14 That is certain.
15 And now look again, and see what will naturally follow if the prisoners are released and disabused of their error. At first, when any of them is liberated and compelled suddenly to stand up and turn his neck round and walk and look towards the light, he will suffer sharp pains; the glare will distress him, and he will be unable to see the realities of which in his former state he had seen the shadows; and then conceive some one saying to him, that what he saw before was an illusion, but that now, when he is approaching nearer to being and his eye is turned towards more real existence, he has a clearer vision—what will be his reply? And you may further imagine that his instructor is pointing to the objects as they pass and requiring him to name them—will he not be perplexed? Will he not fancy that the shadows which he formerly saw are truer than the objects which are now shown to him?
16 Far truer.
17 And if he is compelled to look straight at the light, will he not have a pain in his eyes which will make him turn away to take refuge in the objects of vision which he can see, and which he will conceive to be in reality clearer than the things which are now being shown to him?

18   True, he said.
19   And suppose once more, that he is reluctantly dragged up a steep and rugged ascent, and held fast until he is forced into the presence of the sun himself, is he not likely to be pained and irritated? When he approaches the light his eyes will be dazzled, and he will not be able to see anything at all of what are now called realities.
20   Not all in a moment, he said.
21   He will require to grow accustomed to the sight of the upper world. And first he will see the shadows best, next the reflections of men and other objects in the water, and then the objects themselves; then he will gaze upon the light of the moon and the stars and the spangled heaven; and he will see the sky and the stars by night better than the sun or the light of the sun by day?
22   Certainly.
23   Last of all he will be able to see the sun, and not mere reflections of him in the water, but he will see him in his own proper place, and not in another; and he will contemplate him as he is.
24   Certainly.
25   He will then proceed to argue that this is he who gives the season and the years, and is the guardian of all that is in the visible world, and in a certain way the cause of all things which he and his fellows have been accustomed to behold?
26   Clearly, he said, he would first see the sun and then reason about him.
27   And when he remembered his old habitation, and the wisdom of the den and his fellow prisoners, do you not suppose that he would felicitate himself on the change, and pity them?
28   Certainly, he would.
29   And if they were in the habit of conferring honors among themselves on those who were quickest to observe the passing shadows and to remark which of them went before, and which followed after, and which were together; and who were therefore best able to draw conclusions as to the future, do you think that he would care for such honors and glories, or envy the possessors of them? Would he not say with Homer,

Better to be the poor servant of a poor master,

and to endure anything, rather than think as they do and live after their manner?
30   Yes, he said, I think that he would rather suffer anything than entertain these false notions and live in this miserable manner.
31   Imagine once more, I said, such an one coming suddenly out of the sun to be replaced in his old situation; would he not be certain to have his eyes full of darkness?
32   To be sure, he said.
33   And if there were a contest, and he had to compete in measuring the shadows with the prisoners who had never moved out of the den, while his

sight was still weak, and before his eyes had become steady (and the time which would be needed to acquire this new habit of sight might be very considerable), would he not be ridiculous? Men would say of him that up he went and down he came without his eyes; and that it was better not even to think of ascending; and if any one tried to loose another and lead him up to the light, let them only catch the offender, and they would put him to death.

34   No question, he said.

35   This entire allegory, I said, you may now append, dear Glaucon, to the previous argument; the prison house is the world of sight, the light of the fire is the sun, and you will not misapprehend me if you interpret the journey upwards to be the ascent of the soul into the intellectual world according to my poor belief, which, at your desire, I have expressed—whether rightly or wrongly God knows. But, whether true or false, my opinion is that in the world of knowledge the idea of good appears last of all, and is seen only with an effort; and, when seen, is also inferred to be the universal author of all things beautiful and right, parent of light and of the lord of light in this visible world, and the immediate source of reason and truth in the intellectual; and that this is the power upon which he who would act rationally either in public or private life must have his eye fixed.

36   I agree, he said, as far as I am able to understand you.

37   Moreover, I said, you must not wonder that those who attain to this beatific vision are unwilling to descend to human affairs; for their souls are ever hastening into the upper world where they desire to dwell; which desire of theirs is very natural, if our allegory may be trusted.

38   Yes, very natural.

39   And is there anything surprising in one who passes from divine contemplations to the evil state of man, misbehaving himself in a ridiculous manner; if, while his eyes are blinking and before he has become accustomed to the surrounding darkness, he is compelled to fight in courts of law, or in other places, about the images or the shadows of images of justice, and is endeavoring to meet the conceptions of those who have never yet seen absolute justice?

40   Anything but surprising, he replied.

41   Anyone who has common sense will remember that the bewilderments of the eyes are of two kinds, and arise from two causes, either from coming out of the light or from going into the light, which is true of the mind's eye, quite as much as of the bodily eye; and he who remembers this when he sees anyone whose vision is perplexed and weak, will not be too ready to laugh; he will first ask whether that soul of man has come out of the brighter life, and is unable to see because unaccustomed to the dark, or having turned from darkness to the day is dazzled by excess of light. And he will count the one happy in his condition and state of being, and he will pity the other; or, if he have a mind to laugh at the soul which comes from below into the light, there will be more reason in this than in the laugh which greets him who returns from above out of the light into the den.

42   That, he said, is a very just distinction.

43   But then, if I am right, certain professors of education must be wrong when

they say that they can put a knowledge into the soul which was not there before, like sight into blind eyes.
44   They undoubtedly say this, he replied.
45   Whereas, our argument shows that the power and capacity of learning exists in the soul already; and that just as the eye was unable to turn from darkness to light without the whole body, so too the instrument of knowledge can only by the movement of the whole soul be turned from the world of becoming into that of being, and learn by degrees to endure the sight of being, and of the brightest and best of being, or in other words, of the good.
46   Very true.
47   And must there not be some art which will effect conversion in the easiest and quickest manner; not implanting the faculty of sight, for that exists already, but has been turned in the wrong direction, and is looking away from the truth?
48   Yes, he said, such an art may be presumed.
49   And whereas the other so-called virtues of the soul seem to be akin to bodily qualities, for even when they are not originally innate they can be implanted later by habit and exercise, the virtue of wisdom more than anything else contains a divine element which always remains, and by this conversion is rendered useful and profitable; or, on the other hand, hurtful and useless. Did you never observe the narrow intelligence flashing from the keen eye of a clever rogue—how eager he is, how clearly his paltry soul sees the way to his end; he is the reverse of blind, but his keen eyesight is forced into the service of evil, and he is mischievous in proportion to his cleverness?
50   Very true, he said.
51   But what if there had been a circumcision of such natures in the days of their youth; and they had been severed from those sensual pleasures, such as eating and drinking, which, like leaden weights, were attached to them at their birth, and which drag them down and turn the vision of their souls upon the things that are below—if, I say, they had been released from these impediments and turned in the opposite direction, the very same faculty in them would have seen the truth as keenly as they see what their eyes are turned to now.
52   Very likely.
53   Yes, I said; and there is another thing which is likely, or rather a necessary inference from what has preceded, that neither the uneducated and uninformed of the truth, nor yet those who never make an end of their education, will be able ministers of State, not the former, because they have no single aim of duty which is the rule of all their actions, private as well as public, nor the latter, because they will not act at all except upon compulsion, fancying that they are already dwelling apart in the islands of the blessed.
54   Very true, he replied.
55   Then, I said, the business of us who are the founders of the State will be to compel the best minds to attain that knowledge which we have already shown to be the greatest of all—they must continue to ascend until they arrive at the good; but when they have ascended and seen enough we must not allow them to do as they do now.

56 What do you mean?

57 I mean that they remain in the upper world: but this must not be allowed; they must be made to descend again among the prisoners in the den, and partake of their labors and honors, whether they are worth having or not.

58 But is not this unjust? he said; ought we to give them a worse life, when they might have a better?

59 You have again forgotten, my friend, I said, the intention of the legislator, who did not aim at making any one class in the State happy above the rest; the happiness was to be in the whole State, and he held the citizens together by persuasion and necessity, making them benefactors of the State, and therefore benefactors of one another; to this end he created them, not to please themselves, but to be his instruments in binding up the State.

60 True, he said, I had forgotten.

61 Observe, Glaucon, that there will be no injustice in compelling our philosophers to have a care and providence of others; we shall explain to them that in other States, men of their class are not obliged to share in the toils of politics: and this is reasonable, for they grow up at their own sweet will, and the government would rather not have them. Being self-taught, they cannot be expected to show any gratitude for a culture which they have never received. But we have brought you into the world to be rulers of the hive, kings of yourselves and of the other citizens, and have educated you far better and more perfectly than they have been educated, and you are better able to share in the double duty. Wherefore each of you, when his turn comes, must go down to the general underground abode, and get the habit of seeing in the dark. When you have acquired the habit, you will see ten thousand times better than the inhabitants of the den, and you will know what the several images are, and what they represent, because you have seen the beautiful and just and good in their truth. And thus our State, which is also yours, will be a reality, and not a dream only, and will be administered in a spirit unlike that of other States, in which men fight with one another about shadows only and are distracted in the struggle for power, which in their eyes is a great good. Whereas the truth is that the State in which the rulers are most reluctant to govern is always the best and most quietly governed, and the State in which they are most eager, the worst.

62 Quite true, he replied.

63 And will our pupils, when they hear this, refuse to take their turn at the toils of State, when they are allowed to spend the greater part of their time with one another in the heavenly light?

64 Impossible, he answered; for they are just men, and the commands which we impose upon them are just; there can be no doubt that every one of them will take office as a stern necessity, and not after the fashion of our present rulers of State.

65 Yes, my friend, I said; and there lies the point. You must contrive for your future rulers another and a better life than that of a ruler, and then you may have a well-ordered State; for only in the State which offers this, will they rule who are truly rich, not in silver and gold, but in virtue and wisdom, which are

the true blessings of life. Whereas if they go to the administration of public affairs, poor and hungering after their own private advantage, thinking that hence they are to snatch the chief good, order there can never be; for they will be fighting about office, and the civil and domestic broils which thus arise will be the ruin of the rulers themselves and of the whole State.

66   Most true, he replied.

67   And the only life which looks down upon the life of political ambition is that of true philosophy. Do you know of any other?

68   Indeed, I do not, he said. ❖

Questions to Ponder

1. What is an *allegory*? Why is allegory sometimes useful for a writer?
2. If people knew only a dark and chained existence, why would they want to change their condition?
3. Is it possible to be "in the dark" on some topics and "enlightened" about others? Name some topics about which you feel ignorant and others about which you feel relatively enlightened.
4. What steps are necessary for "enlightenment"?
5. What is the responsibility of those who have become enlightened?
6. Why does Plato believe political leadership should be required of enlightened ones? Do you agree with him?

Writing Possibilities

1. Write an essay in which Plato's cave would represent your knowledge and values in high school and the world outside would represent the world of college.
2. Alternatively, interpret Plato's allegory of the chained people watching shadows on the wall as a comment on the television generation. (Your audience for this essay might be the readers of *TV Guide*.)
3. Write an honest assessment of where you think you are at this moment on Plato's path from imprisonment to understanding of the "idea of the good" (the sun). Are you still chained? Unchained but still in the cave? Blinking frantically at the cave entrance? Farther along? (Give reasons and examples to support your views.)
4. Rewrite this Platonic dialogue between Socrates and Glaucon substituting your own vision of the human predicament and the educational process. (Can you devise an allegory that would illustrate your view?)

Short Story

ONE MORE INTERVIEW

John Updike

As a student might imagine, there was an actual interview, and perhaps more than one, in which I observed my own lack of interest in talking about myself grow in the course of an hour into a downright enthusiasm, so that I was actually disappointed when the interviewer expressed—politely, of course—satiation and boredom. Even a slightly famous person is invited to give a lot of interviews, and if your business is writing words, as carefully as you can, you resent the importance that is given to words you toss off under the stress of inappropriate questions and a tense social situation. Human beings want to please, even interviewees do, and one ends up being more "giving" and indiscreet than had been originally intended.

The town evoked is one of many versions, in my fiction, of Shillington, which I was to evoke under its own name a few years later, in the long essay "A Soft Spring Night in Shillington," which became the first chapter in my memoirs, Self-Consciousness. Our home towns hold the meaning of our lives, it sometimes seems, and our excitement over the mundane reminiscent facts about them continues decades after we have left them. Indeed, our leaving preserves them intact in our minds—their riddles unplumbed, their magic forever potent.

The story wrote itself fairly easily; I have preserved the piece of yellow paper upon which I, at the moment of inspiration, wrote down its first sentences, and the points I wished to cover. . . . Here it is. I have transcribed my hurried handwriting, line for line. Students can judge how closely I adhered to my original outline:

> The actor's tour took him to a city fifty miles from the small town where he had grown up, and an interviewer suggested they visit there. The interviewer was from the city's surviving morning paper, and there was a good chance of syndication, and the actor was at that awkward age almost too old for romantic leads but not old enough for character parts, so he accepted.
>
> Has to drive . . .

"Of course," he said as he approached the town, "all this was trees and fields then.

high school—learned that something takes over
terrible acne (make-up)
finds old necking spot
the girl's house
fills with a real need for the girl, a lust that is tragic, for she has long gone, vanished
interviewer gets bored as he grows excited

DRAFT

Continued

finds the nesting spot
the girl's house
fills with a real need for the
girl, a lust that is tragic, for
she was long gone, vanished
interviewer gets bored as he grows excited

Brief Warm-up Writing Exercises

1. Pretend you are a reporter driving with a famous actor through the actor's old hometown. Brainstorm a list of the questions you would want to ask during the interview.
2. Now pretend you are a celebrity returning to your hometown. Freewrite the driving tour you would make, including all the landmarks you would hope to see.
3. Recall interviews that you have read or seen on television. Describe the qualities of a good interview.

---

1 The actor's tour had taken him to a Midwestern city fifteen miles from the small town where he had grown up, and an interviewer called suggesting that they visit there together. "It would provide, you know," he said, "an angle." The newspaper the interviewer worked for was the only one left in the city, and this gave it an aura of absolute power, of final opportunity. The actor was at that awkward age almost too old for romantic leads but not old enough for character parts. Opportunity, his agent had more than once told him, doesn't knock forever. He could use the publicity.

2 "I can't stand interviews," he said.

3 The prospective interviewer said nothing, just waited.

4 "They're so intrinsically imprecise," the actor went on. "So sadly prurient." The presence on the other end of the line stuck to its silence. The female exclamations of another conversation faintly wafted into the braided wires. "O.K.," the actor said, and they set a time to meet on the hotel parking lot.

5 The interviewer stood beside a little mustard-colored car; he wore dun bell-bottoms and a denim jacket cut as short as a waiter's jacket. He was a trim, tight young man with an exceptionally small mouth and wiry black hair that had about it, without being exactly kinky, a glisten of contained energy, a kind of silent acrylic crackle that declared it would never decompose. There would be no mercy, the actor saw. He would have to watch what he said as carefully as if he were in court. Unfortunate words had a way of passing into print from a single absent-minded nod politely granted an impudent question. The actor

had a number of former wives, each equipped with vigilant lawyers, and he moved through the dark skies of private life, it sometimes seemed to him, like a comet trailing stiff white envelopes of legal stationery. So: no politeness today, no ridiculous "givingness," no charming sharing of indiscretions with this person to whom he was not a person, after all, but a name, an object to be exploited, a walking slag heap to be sifted for ore one more time.

6   "Would you like me to drive, so you can take notes?" the actor asked. He was a big-boned, coarse-skinned man offstage, and he took pleasure in menacing at the outset, with such extravagant coöperation, his wiry little persecutor.

7   "Why, yes, that might be nice, come to think of it."

8   The car was a Japanese model, as cunning and tawdry as a music-box. It had four forward gears and a reverse tucked somewhere in the lower right quadrant, where New Zealand is on a map. The dashboard hummed and spelled out monosyllables of instruction and warning. The actor felt clumsy. "I don't drive much anymore," he explained. "I'm just dragged around by these limousines."

9   "What about at your summer place in Amagansett?" the interviewer asked, having already produced a notebook.

10 "My last wife got that, as you probably know. The place, the Porsche, the works."

11 "No, I didn't know." The man wrote busily.

12 "Don't put that in—Christ," the actor begged, shifting from first gear straight into fourth, with a fearful laboring of the engine.

13 "It's on the record, isn't it, elsewhere?"

14 "Well, let's not put it on again. Makes it look as though I have nothing else to talk about."

15 "Of course," the interviewer said. He put the notebook away and gazed out the window.

16 The actor didn't like this swift, prim docility, either; it seemed stagy. From the side, the other man's mouth was a mere irritated nick in his profile; he resented having been ousted from the driver's seat.

17 "This wasn't meant to be so much a personal piece about you and your, uh, affairs," the interviewer said, "as about the place. You in regard to the place you grew up in."

18 "It's not much of a place, that was its charm," the actor said, and added, "Don't put that in, either."

19 The miles went by. Inner suburbs gave way to outer, and then there was something like countryside, behind the roadside gas stations and the old stone farmhouses with reflecting balls in their front yards. The interviewer sat silent, in what seemed to be a sulk. The strange impression grew upon the actor that this man had been a high-school athlete, a second-baseman: quick on the pivot and pesky at the plate. Determined to be entertaining, to charm away the sulk, the actor talked about the play he was in, leading actresses he had worked with, his theories of stagecraft, his philosophy of professional ups and downs. The interviewer kept his notebook tucked away. The little automobile had become

quite responsive to the actor's touch, and began to swing along curves he knew by heart, having driven them as a child, first with his father at the wheel and then with himself in control. "Of course," the actor explained, as they approached the town limits, "all this was trees and fields then. That mall didn't exist. That mess of ticky-tacky houses over there was just a dairy farm with a little creek that ran through a pasture where my mother's quainter relatives used to gather watercress. There was a dam and a pond back in there where the tough boys and the pretty girls used to go swimming. I never did. My mother thought I might drown or lose my virginity or have people think I did, which would be even worse."

20   "Uh-huh," the interviewer said, as though he had heard this before.

21   "Don't put that in about my mother and virginity," the actor asked. "She still has cousins in the area, in nursing homes mostly. There used to be a diner here," he announced abruptly, "that stayed open all night. At two in the morning you could go there, after a date, all lightheaded and your face full of lipstick, and eat a hamburger. That was my idea of the sophisticated life, eating a hamburger at two in the morning. A man called Smoky Moser ran it. He never seemed to sleep. We kids loved him. Loved him like a father, you could say. He was the father I yearned for."

22   "Is that a fact?"

23   "I exaggerate a little. Smoky was O.K., though. Died young, of some disease nobody would ever name. Better skip that: he may have a widow."

24   Grudgingly the interviewer had got out his notebook and made a few notes. The gravel lot that had surrounded the diner was occupied now by a great cube of brown-tinted glass, the branch of a statewide bank. Yellow arrows painted on the smooth asphalt told automobiles how to proceed to the drive-in windows. The actor studied the faces of the people moving in and out of the bank and recognized none of them, though there was something he did recognize—a tone, a pallor and density of flesh in their arms and faces, a way of suddenly looking behind and above them, unsmilingly, fearing the worst out of the sky, the weather of the world. "Up here, there was a feed mill, where . . ."

25   Where some of the faster girls had supposedly let it be done to them, that fabled thing, in the weedy area between two asbestos-shingled walls. The actor was surprised, after the more than a decade since he had last visited, by how sexy the town was, how saturated with love and that psychosomatic quickening which love brings. The cotton-wool sky, the heavy dusty trees, the very tone of dull red in the bricks arrived in unison at something like one's own exact body temperature. Surrounded by farm country, it was a kind of hill town, divided in the middle by an avenue that followed the curve of an abandoned railroad bed. The town's lower part, south of the avenue, had been built solid in the years just before the Depression in rows of brick semi-detached houses, houses with symmetrical big living-room windows and square-pillared front porches. There was a security here, in these ruddy rows, block after block, each with its little apron of terraced lawn, and two concrete

steps leading up to the first terrace, and little pansy beds or barberry hedges along the walk. The rectilinear, repetitive streets were high-crowned, and the actor was made to remember the rhythm imparted to a car, the soft braking and dipping, as the intersections were cautiously traversed. Many an afternoon, many a Sunday, he had cruised these streets in his parents' old tan Dodge, and then in the navy-blue Chrysler with the iridescent touched-up patch on the fender, looking for the action, for a familiar car parked outside a house he knew, which might signal an afternoon of canasta or an evening of laughing at Liberace or the roller derby on that new toy called television. Any excuse for a party, a party wherever two or three got together.

26 "This side of town hasn't changed much at all," he told the interviewer. "How could it? They didn't leave any vacant lots." Each of the thickset duplexes was like a married couple, it occurred to him now, the rumblings and spats on one side of the wall impossible not to hear on the other. "For some reason," the actor said, "the terrific-looking girls all tended to live over in this section. My family lived in a house all alone on its lot, on the older side of town. There's a distinct change once you cross the avenue. The houses, a lot of them, are wood, and look—how can I say?—gaunt. Pinched. Scary, even. Don't put that in."

27 He steered the nimble little car through a stoplight that hadn't been there thirty years ago and drove uphill, out of the cozy low-lying area of red brick rows, into the slanting neighborhood where he had been raised. "That used to be a barber shop," he said, driving up Liberty Street. "You can still see the striped pole, though Jake's been dead for years now. Apoplexy, if memory serves. Can you spell it?" Haircuts—the long wait and then the sitting so still as metal gnashed across your scalp—had filled the actor as a child with a gloom and suspense bordering on terror. There had been a big plate-glass window, and as the scissors interminably clicked, the sunshine and the traffic on the other side had seemed an unattainable paradise. Now that big window held Venetian blinds and a sign proclaiming that gold and silver could be bought and sold here. He suddenly remembered the octagonal green-and-cream pattern of the linoleum floor, dotted with hair clippings, where Jake would tap-dance. Not tap-dance, perhaps, but do a spry and comical shuffle-and-slide on that slick floor. Jake had hated Roosevelt—the thought of the man had made him apoplectic—and in the fury of his shrill tirades must have felt the danger of driving customers away, for he would suddenly relent, and change the poisoned subject, and go into his little comical steps, sometimes with the broom as partner. "And where you see that marquee with 'Bingo' on it was the old movie house, where I learned to dream," the actor said. "To dream and to pose, you could put it." Actually, the sign said INGO, and the look of disuse in its new role as a gambling hall had overtaken the theatre. The old glass cases where the movie posters—Alan Ladd, Lana Turner, Lassie—had been different every week were empty of any advertisement and had been defaced with illegible spray-painted swirls.

28 "Which was your house?" the interviewer asked.

29   "That one."
30   "Which one?"
31   "You missed it. It looks just like the ones around it."
32   "I thought you said it stood so alone on its lot."
33   "They were small lots." Why was he being perverse, the actor wondered—denying this infielder the small intrusion of gazing upon his averagely shabby and plain birthplace? Was it that the house itself, in his own quick glimpse of it, seemed to beg that he not give it away? It was wearing a new color of paint—a bright lime green—like a desperate disguise. Or was it that he himself was ashamed, of it, because it in fact had *not* been just like the ones around it? The house had been and still was slightly smaller than its flanking neighbors, those better-kept and higher-gabled houses owned in his boyhood by the Behns and the Murchisons, who looked down on them, his mother had felt, because his father worked with his hands, because his father was unemployed, because his father came home drunk and could be heard cursing out on the lawn. . . . There were many reasons why the Behns and the Murchisons might look down on them.

34   The actor's furtive glimpse had not been so quick, however, that he did not spy in the shrubbery around the front porch, with its jigsawed banister uprights, the invisible ghosts that had kept him company when he hid there, there where the earth had been too packed and sheltered to give weeds a purchase, like a hard floor. The spaces between the bushes had been like a set of little rooms only he lived in, and where he entertained voices. Who had these presences been that had spoken back to the voice inside his head? They were still there, crowded around the porch, calling out to him. There were even a few at the side of the house, where his mother had tried to grow peonies against the brick foundation, and it had proved too shady. Or had she planted the roots too deep? Mrs. Behn told her she had, and they didn't speak for a year. Imagine, his mother had said, her spying down on me from those parlor windows and not saying a word until it was too late and the peonies were dug in. The cement walk along here, in the shadows, used to accumulate anthills in the cracks, as well as neighborhood bitterness. Out back, there had been a sandbox, and its little ridges had been dunes in the Sahara, and the green lead tanks had been chasing Rommel. The voices the actor had heard while playing in the sandbox had been different; they had been news voices, broadcast from overseas.

35   "You said you learned to dream and to pose in the movie house," the interviewer prompted.

36   They were driving down another block, and his old home was sealed safe behind them. "And in the high school," the actor said. "I'll take you by it. They built it up on top of the hill; the only thing higher in town is the cemetery. Here's a confession for you. You like confessions, don't you?"

37   That silence again.

38   "I had terrible acne as a kid, from about fourteen on. Just like my father. He was all pockmarked. Well, when I put on makeup for some assembly play in about ninth grade, my own skin disappeared! For as long as I was onstage,

I was like everybody else: I was human. So I said to myself, 'Hey. The actor's life for me.'"

39 "Many adolescent boys have acne, don't they?" There seemed a reprimand in this, a call back to relativity.

40 "I don't know. Did you?"

41 "Not so bad, actually."

42 "Well, then. I bet you were quite a smooth jock in your time."

43 "Well, I was . . ."

44 "Don't be modest. You played second base, didn't you?"

45 "Center field, usually."

46 "Same idea. Anyway, I didn't care what other boys had. They were them and I was me. Leave that grammar just the way I said it."

47 "Yes. I don't know that I can use everything you say; you've already been quite generous with your time."

48 "Also, I loved having a role; it wasn't just the makeup. The whole role was like a mask, a spiritual mask I was safe behind. If people laughed, it wasn't at me, exactly. I loved to hear them laugh. Let's hear you laugh."

49 Silence.

50 "Come on. For me."

51 It was a dry, embarrassed noise.

52 "I love it," the actor complimented him. "There you see the high school. The old style, Roman pillars and all. They say when you come back to a place things look smaller, but it looks bigger than ever to me. It looks huge. I hear they don't have students to fill it now." He swung the corner, racily. "This little bug really has some zip, doesn't it? There used to be a variety store here, with the steps at an angle and the little overhang, and paper pumpkins in the window at the appropriate time of year, and then Christmas cards and Easter eggs. . . . It was a kind of 3-D calendar you could walk into and take a stool. There was a counter we could sit up at and smoke. And look at ourselves smoking in the mirror. I bet you never smoked, did you?"

53 "No. As you guessed, I was big into sports."

54 "God, I used to smoke. Anything to keep a mask in front of my face. It's gone now. The store."

55 The new owners had painted everything white, even the display windows, so no one could look in. Somebody must be living behind those blank windows. The people who had descended upon the town to live in it since the actor had left were aliens from space; he could not imagine their lives. "Now we're getting into a part of town that was new then—rich houses, we thought they were, though they don't look so rich now. The section was called Oak Slope. To live in Oak Slope was about the ritziest thing I could imagine, to live in Oak Slope and have huge closets of clothes, with a different corduroy shirt for every day of the week. Corduroy shirts—that dates me. And we used to wear reindeer sweaters; I don't suppose you know what a reindeer sweater was, do you?"

56 "I can imagine."

57 "I'm not sure you can. The sharp guys, there was a word then, 'snazzy,' s-n-a-z-z-y, the snazzy guys, whose fathers sold real estate or were foremen at the mill, owned a lot of them, beautifully knitted, with different things, it wasn't just reindeer—snowflakes, butterflies...."

58 "They're still around."

59 "It's not the same. I used to wear the one I had inside out some days, as if it was another sweater. It didn't fool anybody but made me feel slightly, you could say, snazzy. I'll be honest about it: I was pathetic. More than that, I was obnoxious. With acne yet. Just driving around Oak Slope makes me *feel* obnoxious. How am I acting?" He got no answer. "Now, down here," the actor announced, "this curving street, when I was a lad—another funny old-fashioned word, l-a-d—past the last new house built, there used to be a kind of dirt road that didn't go anywhere much and was a great place to park, if you had a girl."

60 At the age of seventeen, he had acquired a girl, Ermajean Willis. "For heaven's sake," the actor exclaimed, without acting, his exclamation honest. "It's still here. I would have thought it'd been built up ages ago."

61 The necking place. The spatial feeling of the spot—with a tall bank of earth on one side, freshly bulldozed then and still rather raw and scraggly now, and a lower rise on the other side, deep green from the time when this had been a hillside hayfield—was unaltered, uncorrupted, sexy. In his excitement the actor braked; the interviewer glanced over, worried. "Amazing," said the actor, spacing his syllables, back in performance. "I wonder if it's still used."

62 "I see a few beer bottles," said the interviewer uneasily.

63 "You don't understand what a lovely surprise this is. For a space like this to last, in modern America. The cops used to check it out once in a while and shine a flashlight in the windows." The little unpaved road that generations of furtive, love-craving cars had worn into the earth continued for a few yards between the two sheltering grassy shoulders and then dipped down to rejoin a side street called Button. Button led into Maple, Maple crossed the avenue, and two more blocks took you into Sycamore; Ermajean used to live at the corner of Sycamore and Pierce. A kind of hazy warmth, as when he would show up after midnight at Smoky's diner, had been laid across the actor's face. Without his realizing it, the little Japanese car had under his hands driven itself along the remembered route, into that inviting red realm of the two-family brick houses in rows. The car had come to the corner of Pierce and Sycamore, to the big house whose retaining walls were ornamented with mossy concrete balls and whose side entrance was a set of steps with an iron railing he had often grasped; he softly braked. She would come down those very steps for a date, all starchy and perfumed and hopeful, though what had he had to offer her but a second-run movie and an ice-cream soda afterwards? As she hurried across the street to the old Chrysler with the patched fender, her pastel dress would be flattened against her thighs by her hurrying, by the soft wind she made in her haste to be with him.

64 "My girl friend used to live here," he confessed to his interviewer.

65 "You had only one?"

66   "Well, yes. How many do you recommend? I thought I was lucky to have even one. She was a grade behind me at school, and after I graduated I lost track of her. Married, I suppose, somewhere." The actor was incredulous that the interviewer could be blind to the glory around them, the railings and retaining walls and little laplike lawns of these solid, unchanging homes, rows that at any moment might release Ermajean, racing lightly toward them with her hair in barrettes and her round young legs tipped by the kind of open-toed white heels women in Hollywood comedies wore—Jean Arthur, Rosalind Russell. The actor felt swamped by love; he was physically sickened, to think that such a scene had once been real, and that a self of his had been there to play a part.

67   His foot eased the clutch back in, and the car moved off reluctantly. "Let me show you some more of the town," he offered. "There's a quarry where we used to ice-skate. And a playground. A block from here, where they put the new annex on the town hall, there used to be the strangest little structure, like something out of Disneyland, a sort of stone tower where you paid your water bills."

68   Ermajean loved butter-pecan ice cream, he remembered, in a vanilla soda, and always debated with him whether she should have onion on her hamburger. If he would, she would. And her skin—all of his life since, he had been dealing with women who were doctoring their skins—vitamin-E cream, pancake makeup, moisturizers. Ermajean's skin had been utterly neutral in shade, neutral and natural, tinted by nothing, pure trusting female skin beneath her pastel clothes. The actor's face felt hot; he wanted to cruise forever through this half of town, the car dipping in a kind of obeisance at every intersection.

69   The interviewer cleared his throat and said, "I think maybe I've seen enough. This is only for a sidebar, you know."

70   "Wait. How about coming with me to my old luncheonette and having a bite to eat? How about some butter-pecan ice cream?"

71   The other man laughed, stiffly, as when commanded to laugh before. "And then there's a time problem," he said. "If I don't get this in tonight, your show won't still be around."

72   "That's O.K. The luncheonette is a flower shop now anyway. Please, don't put my old girl friend's name in the article."

73   "You never mentioned it."

74   "Ermajean Willis. E-r-m-a-j-e-a-n. Isn't that a wonderful funky name?"

75   "Maybe it'd be easier if I drove now."

76   "No. Keep your pencil out. You son of a bitch, I'm going to tell you the names of every family that used to live in this entire block." ❖

Questions to Ponder

1. What are the qualities of a good journalist? How does the newspaper reporter in this story measure up to these qualities?

2. In the first four paragraphs of the story what signs are there that the actor and the reporter have different language styles? Is this significant? What does the language of each reveal about him?
3. How does the actor's attitude toward his subject change as the story unfolds? What happens to him? Why do *writers* often warm to their subjects as they get into them?
4. What evidence is there in the story that the actor has kept in touch with (or lost touch with) the "selves" he was as a teen?

Writing Possibilities

1. Pretend you are the reporter in the story and write up the interview for tomorrow's paper.
2. Now pretend you are the garrulous actor's publicity agent and write the newspaper interview as he or she would. (Would your interview article get longer and more dramatic?)
3. Using John Updike's story as a model, write a reflective driving tour of your hometown, trying to recapture its special character and the important landmarks of your youth.
4. Now take the newspaper article you wrote in writing possibility 1, and transform it into a short story. Retell the story as if you were the bored newspaper reporter recounting the interview for your buddies over a beer at the end of the day.

CHAPTER 3

Researching:
The Deeper the Richer

Once you have found your subject, the next step is to have something to say on that subject. This is where many beginning writers come up dry. However, there are many ways to fill the well, so you will feel you are writing from an abundance (not a scarcity) of material. These ways all involve a new understanding of the word *re-search*.

Research provides two priceless gifts to a writer: material and options. When researching, you are like an archeologist: in general, the deeper you dig, the richer the find. You can find whole civilizations under the one you think you are inhabiting. Furthermore, deep digging will increase your freedom as a writer. If you dig a shallow trench, you will hardly be able to move. Dig deeply and you may uncover a whole underground network with many entrances and exits.

When writer Gay Talese wanted to write about a dramatic editorial conference at the climax of his history of *The New York Times* called *The Kingdom and the Power*, he interviewed individually all ten editors at the meeting. This thorough research provided him with rich material on the event and allowed him to verify his facts and impressions. Yet it did even more: it gave him the option of writing about the meeting through the eyes of any one of the ten editors. Had his research been less thorough, he would have limited his options. (See the results of Talese's most recent research, into his own family history, in "The Tailors of Maida" in this chapter.)

RESEARCHING TOPICS OF PERSONAL EXPERIENCE AND OPINION

When you are asked to write about your personal experiences or opinions, you can take confidence in knowing that mere experience in living will increase your store of material to tap—without your even noticing. College coaches often say, "The best thing about freshmen is that they become sophomores," and this is true in writing as well as in athletics. Nineteen-year-old sophomores usually have more to say than 18-year-old freshmen just by virtue of the extra year of living, thinking, and articulating ideas.* Increased material is just one of the benefits of aging!

Nevertheless, research is essential when writing of personal experiences or opinions—even when these assignments require no "outside" or library research. With these assignments *research* means "re-search"; it means searching through your memories trying to recall the precise details that will breathe life into the personal experience you are trying to evoke or the opinion you are trying to express. The hours you might spend in the library investigating a subject must be spent instead sitting and staring, combing your memory for the images, for the words, for the feelings that will make your memory (of your father, or your first dance) come alive on paper and be true, new, and important.

You may find you do this kind of memory *re-search* best by taking long walks, or when jogging, rather than by sitting and staring into space. You may wish to tap your unconscious by thinking of your past experience right before you go to sleep and immediately after you wake up—when you are in twilight consciousness.

Use the same lengthy re-search process when trying to flesh out your personal opinions on a subject. These, too, will come to life only through concrete, sensory details, as well as through thoughtful expansion of implications. However you loaf and invite your soul for these personal subjects, realize that you are doing essential re-search.

Prewriting techniques such as brainstorming, mapping, and freewriting may help you revive and flesh out your memories and opinions. Suddenly you also see your old diary in a new light: as an invaluable source of your past! Do not hesitate also to call up (literally) those involved in your past experience, to get their versions of the event. They may mention a detail that will unlock the moment for you or remind you of a facet you have overlooked. If you are re-searching a personal-opinion paper, try out your views on your roommate, your parents, on anyone, in short, who will listen. Students writing personal-experience or personal-opinion papers generally do not spend enough time deeply re-searching themselves—or interrogating others. As Henry James

---

*If they are reading an hour a day and writing an hour a day, this is doubly true.

observes in the short opening excerpt in this chapter, a writer should strive to be "one of whom nothing is lost."

RESEARCHING TOPICS OUTSIDE YOURSELF

When confronted with a topic calling for outside research, beginning writers often make another kind of error: they go to the library too soon. As a general rule, never begin your formal research until you know just what you are looking for. This means narrowing your topic and, if possible, even having a general sense of the central idea (thesis) you hope to convey in your paper. If you keep yourself from the library until this narrowing and framing are done, you will save yourself hours and hours of valuable time.

Say you have decided to write on the destruction of the rain forest. A little reflection at your desk will lead you to the conclusion that your deadline in three weeks will not give you time enough to read and write about rain forests in general. You decide you can probably make the same points by focusing on the Brazilian rain forest. Note the immediate benefits of this decision. You no longer have committed yourself to reading everything on rain forests—only on the rain forests of Brazil!

From past newspaper articles and a television documentary, you have a general notion that rain forests are not faring well in Brazil. (The documentary is what got you interested in the topic in the first place.) Thus, you take the following as your *provisional* central idea: destruction of Brazil's rain forests will damage world ecology. Suddenly you have a sharp focus and you are ready to do efficient library research.

You may decide to spend the first minutes in the library reading an encyclopedia entry on rain forests to gain a general overview of the subject. Then you will turn to the card catalog and write down (or print out, if you are fortunate enough to be using a computerized card catalog) any books on Brazil's rain forests. Bring these books to your writing desk and skim briefly through their tables of contents to gain a sense of what is in them. Then turn immediately to search for magazine, journal, and newspaper articles on Brazil's rain forests. These sources may give you more timely or late-breaking information on your subject than the books you have at hand. Many libraries now have the *Reader's Guide to Periodical Literature*, the *Business Periodicals Index*, the *Humanities Index*, the *Social Science Index*, the *General Science Index*, and the *Applied Science and Technology Index* on compact disc. Whether these indexes are in traditional volumes or on compact disc, browse through them, writing down (or printing out) all relevant articles on Brazil's rain forests. You will probably want to star and go first to articles that seem to engage your central idea head on. You will want to read authors who support your position, and you know you had better read authors who take a different view! As John McPhee explains in the headnote to "The Search for Marvin Gardens," his article on New Jersey's Atlantic City, "I knew what I was looking for: anything on the streets."

This first day at the library will give you a clear idea of the kinds of information available to you. If you find few sources on Brazil's rain forests, you may decide to broaden your topic to "Amazon Rain Forests" or "South American Rain Forests." On the other hand, you may decide to narrow the focus even more to concentrate only on one specific Brazilian forest and what has happened to it. Your central idea similarly may undergo modification in light of what you find. This only makes good sense.

After surveying the kinds of material available in your library's books, journals, magazines, and newspapers, consider whether there might be important material on your subject in government documents or in the library's archives. You may find your library does not have articles or documents you need, so you will want immediately to order them through your library's interlibrary loan system or to plan a trip to another library. This is just one reason why you should never wait to the last minute to write papers!

PRIMARY SOURCES VERSUS SECONDARY SOURCES

Barbara Tuchman, the well-known historian and writer, speaks with wisdom in "In Search of History" when she urges researchers to prefer primary sources over secondary ones. *Primary sources* are the actual documents—the Declaration of Independence, for example—while *secondary sources* are summaries and commentaries on these primary texts. Primary sources include reports, letters, diaries, and other firsthand materials on an event or subject.

Regretably, students often spend too much time reading secondary analyses of such documents rather than the documents themselves. This is like relying on your roommate's interpretation of the requirements for your major rather than reading the catalog requirements yourself. It is always risky! Anyone who has been given a wrong lead knows that secondary information varies greatly in reliability and is always only as good as its source.

Writers using only secondary sources are settling for secondhand information rather than going to the source and drawing their own conclusions. This is fatal for writers who are trying to say something true, new, and important on their subjects. Why take someone else's view of the Declaration of Independence before you read it yourself and have your own reaction to it? In point of fact, there is no way to know secondhand information is bad unless you go directly to the source.

DISTILLING: THE PROCESS OF TAKING GOOD NOTES

Along with going to the library too soon, another pitfall for beginning researchers is taking too many notes. This is an incredible waste of time, and it also can lead to plagiarism. If you are copying whole pages or paragraphs from sources onto notecards, you will too easily be tempted to recopy these passages into your paper itself. Even when you reword and properly acknowledge the source of these sentences, you are probably relying too much on others. When nearly every sentence or paragraph of an essay is credited to another source, the reader rightly wonders, What part of this work is the author's?

Protect yourself from overreliance on sources by taking spare notes. Rarely use complete sentences. This will force you to use your own words in presenting the information when you come to write your paper. Jot down on your notecards only

- statistics (including dates)
- key terms and their definitions
- pithy quotations that are so wonderful you know you will want to use them
- phrases summarizing the author's position, if you think it is one you will want to acknowledge

Once you have limited your notetaking to these four items, be sure you jot down full information on the source so you will not have to return to the book or article for a volume number or a page number once you are actually writing your paper. Here is the information to write down for books, either at the bottom or the top of the notecard.

1. Author's complete name (first and last)
2. Book title *as it appears on the title page*
3. Place the book was published (often this is on the title page or close to the publisher's name; if several places are given—like Boston and London—feel free to use just one)
4. publisher's name
5. copyright year
6. page number(s) on which the specific statistic, term, quotation, or idea you plan to use (or acknowledge) appears

Here is the information to write down for articles.

1. Author's complete name (first and last)
2. Title of the article
3. Name of the magazine, journal, or newspaper in which the article appears (checking carefully to see if a "The" is used, as in *The New York Times,* or if *magazine* is an official part of the name, as it is *not* in *Time* and *Newsweek*)
4. Volume number—if there is one
5. Issue number—if there is one
6. Date of the publication
7. *Total* page numbers of the article (55–66, for example)
8. *Specific* page number of the statistic, term, quotation, or idea you wish to cite

If you get all this information the first time, you will save yourself the annoyance of going back. If you have notes of only statistics, key terms, pithy quotes, and phrases summarizing ideas, you will sit down to write free of the worries of overdependence on your sources, free to write the truth of your subject as you have come to know it. Student Jon Shepherd speaks to this challenge in the headnote to his essay "Employee Stock Ownership Plans: A New Player in the Leveraged Buyout Game."

IN CONCLUSION

Beginning researchers often say in great anguish, "I am only 18 years old. How can I contribute anything true, new, and important to this subject?" Eighteen-year-olds too often underestimate themselves. In the first place, all writers have the advantage of their individual perspectives. (See Clifford Geertz's essay "Being There: Anthropology and the Scene of Writing".) In the second place, writers have the advantage of the latest word. Your contribution might simply be to summarize, classify, or critique what has been said before on your subject, or to suggest profitable directions for further study. You may also have new information (on AIDS or physics) unknown even six months ago.

If you are clever, you will turn your youth from a disadvantage to an advantage. Most of us have read countless pieces on teenage drug use or teen pregnancy written by adult "experts." Might a piece on teen pregnancy written by a teenager bring a new and striking perspective? The same can be said of many topics, from student financial-aid policies to the volunteer army. By researching both your mind and outside sources, you may find much that is true, new, and important to say. And there is nothing like having something to say to make you want to say it.

A good standard for adequate research might be that set by the French painter Théodore Géricault when he was preparing to paint the famous canvas that Julian Barnes describes in this chapter's concluding work, "Shipwreck."

THE ART OF FICTION
Henry James

"The great thing is to be saturated with something—that is, in one way or another, with life; and I have chosen the form of my saturation," wrote American writer Henry James (Leon Edel, Henry James: A Life [New York: Harper & Row, 1985], 115). James saturated himself with art galleries, books, and plays for the first 14 years of his life. At the age of 19, he went to Harvard Law School and found, in Winthrup Square, an old house with a large desk in an alcove. It was place, he wrote, where "even so shy a dreamer as I . . . might perhaps hope to woo the muse" (Edel 64).

And woo he did, usually writing from six to eight hours a day throughout his life. James liked to take long walks before bedtime; then, after a good night's sleep, he would rise and begin writing. He considered his writing schedule the most normal thing in the world and said he never felt better or stronger than when he had completed a morning's work.

Across his long life, James knew everyone from Emerson to Virginia Woolf, and his writing style was influenced by technological change. For the first half of his life, he dispatched directly to his publishers pages written in his rapid hand. In the 1880s, when the use of the typewriter became widespread, he began sending his manuscripts to a public stenographer.

In 1896, however, James experienced a crippling pain in his right wrist—probably the result of all those hours of writing. He hired a stenographer to take down his letters in shorthand, but by the end of a month he was dictating directly to a typist sitting at a typewriter. "I can address you only through an embroidered veil of sound," he wrote a friend (Edel 456). Eventually, James became so wedded to the sound of this typewriter that when the machine broke down and another temporarily took its place, he was unable to work.

Leon Edel, James's biographer, notes that "Henry James writing, and Henry James dictating, were different persons. Some of his friends claimed they could put their finger on the exact chapter in [What] Maisie [Knew] where manual effort ceased and dictation began. After several years of consistent dictating, the 'later manner' of Henry James emerged" (456).

The spoken voice can be heard in James's later prose, not only in his sentence *rhythms but also in his use of more colloquial words.* "And doubtless having a companion always in his work-room had its effect," stresses Edel. "The actor in him could not resist exhibitory flourishes" (456).

Primarily, however, the typewriter enabled James to revise as he never had before. He revised constantly, and while revising inserted new metaphors and long similes into his texts. "The value of that process for me is in its help to do over, for which it is extremely adapted, and which is the only way I can do at all," wrote James (Edel 554). Servants would hear James pacing constantly in rhythm with the keys of the typewriter, and they would hear his voice dictating—with long pauses.

Whether writing by hand or dictating, however, James always had a rich supply of material from which to draw. "I have too much material," he wrote to a friend. "In the way of observation I lay it in at the rate of a ton a day, and already am much embarrassed for storage room" (Edel 227).

Brief Warm-up Writing Exercises

1. Brainstorm a list of everything you would include if you were told to capture a moment in a college writing class.
2. Try to capture in words your surroundings at this very moment.

---

1 ❖ ... Experience is never limited, and it is never complete; it is an immense sensibility, a kind of huge spiderweb of the finest silken threads suspended in the chamber of consciousness, and catching every airborne particle in its tissue. It is the very atmosphere of the mind; and when the mind is imaginative—much more when it happens to be that of a man of genius—it takes to itself the faintest hints of life, it converts the very pulses of the air into revelations. The young lady living in a village has only to be a damsel upon whom nothing is lost to make it quite unfair (as it seems to me) to declare to her that she shall have nothing to say about the military. Greater miracles have been seen than that, imagination assisting, she should speak the truth about some of these gentlemen. I remember an English novelist, a woman of genius, telling me that she was much commended for the impression she had managed to give in one of her tales of the nature and way of life of the French Protestant youth. She had been asked where she learned so much about this recondite being, she had been congratulated on her peculiar opportunities. These opportunities consisted in her having once, in Paris, as she ascended a staircase, passed an open door where, in the household of a *pasteur*, some of the young Protestants were seated at table round a finished meal. The glimpse made a picture; it lasted only a moment, but that moment was experience. She had got her direct personal impression, and she turned out her type. She knew what youth was, and what Protestantism; she also had the advantage of having seen what it was to be French, so that she converted these ideas into a concrete

image and produced a reality. Above all, however, she was blessed with the faculty which when you give it an inch takes an ell, and which for the artist is a much greater source of strength than any accident of residence or of place in the social scale. The power to guess the unseen from the seen, to trace the implication of things, to judge the whole piece by the pattern, the condition of feeling life in general so completely that you are well on your way to knowing any particular corner of it—this cluster of gifts may almost be said to constitute experience, and they occur in country and in town, and in the most differing stages of education. If experience consists of impressions, it may be said that impressions *are* experience, just as (have we not seen it?) they are the very air we breathe. Therefore, if I should certainly say to a novice, "Write from experience and experience only," I should feel that this was rather a tantalizing monition if I were not careful immediately to add, "Try to be one of the people on whom nothing is lost!" ❖

Questions to Ponder

1. Why is experience never limited—or complete?
2. What are the characteristics of an imaginative person?
3. Why do you think James believes that the faculty of *boldness* ("when you give it an inch it takes an ell") is a greater source of strength in a writer than money or social postion?
4. How can we guess the unseen from the seen? When you have correctly predicted the outcome (of an athletic event, science experiment, or meeting), what factors were significant to you in making your projection?
5. What value might there be in striving to reach James's ideal of being "one on whom nothing is lost"?

Writing Possibilities

1. Write a brief description of one on whom "nothing is lost." What would such a person be like and how would he or she behave?
2. Write a dialogue between Henry James and one who would argue the dangers of being "one on whom nothing is lost." (Do you know who will win this argument until you write it?)
3. In a paragraph or brief essay, expand on James's comparison of experience to a huge spiderweb of the finest silken threads. Work out in detail what you think James might have had in mind.
4. First brainstorm a list of things people can do to improve their awareness, and then write a "how to" essay explaining how the average person can become "one on whom nothing is lost."

The Search for Marvin Gardens

John McPhee

"The Search for Marvin Gardens" was a spinoff from a long article John McPhee was writing in 1972 about the testing of new deltoid-shaped dirigibles in New Jersey. One of the testing sites for these Deltoid Pumpkin Seed[s] (as he was later to call them) was an airfield outside of Atlantic City. While McPhee was in the area, he decided to do something that had long been in his mind: walk the streets of the Monopoly game and see what would develop in his imagination. When Charles B. Darrow invented the Monopoly game in the early 1930s, he cribbed the streets from Atlantic City.

In doing research for an article, McPhee says he reads just enough to get going, and then a great deal after his on-site research. He lives in Princeton, New Jersey, and in the open stacks of the Princeton Library he "gobbled in" everything he could find on Atlantic City. "I went from book to book to book," he explains, "for I knew what I was looking for: anything that related to the streets."*

McPhee made several separate trips to Atlantic City to gather material for this article. He bought a map of the streets and walked them, but Marvin Gardens was a place he could not find. He kept asking people, "Where is Marvin Gardens?" This question aside, McPhee did very little direct interviewing for the piece. He reports that he mostly "hung around a lot" and observed. More typically he will prepare some questions in advance, but he says he does not prepare many. He prefers to be with people and see what develops.

McPhee urges students doing research never to stop at the first source but to go through as many sources as possible until they meet themselves coming out the other side. "When you keep encountering the same facts and stories again and again," he stresses, "then you know that you may be right."*

Sometimes, he notes, research will turn up information that the writer ultimately decides to exclude from the work. During his research, McPhee learned that Darrow actually spelled Marvin Gardens wrong in the Monopoly game. In reality, it is Marven Gardens, for this real estate development is located between Margate and Ventnor, thus Mar-ven rather than Marvin. At the end of his article, when he

*Telephone interview. 26 June 1990.

finally finds Marven Gardens, McPhee chose not to include this correction because it seemed too pedantic and would have upset the tone of his ending. He did, however, receive a letter from a reader accusing him, erroneously as it happened, of ignorance.

Brief Warm-up Writing Exercises

1. Describe any memories you may have of playing the game of Monopoly.
2. Describe your favorite game to play as a child or teenager and why you liked to play it.
3. Make a list of the sources you would use to learn more about your hometown.

---

1   Go. I roll the dice—a six and a two. Through the air I move my token, the flatiron, to Vermont Avenue, where dog packs range.

2   The dogs are moving (some are limping) through ruins, rubble, fire damage, open garbage. Doorways are gone. Lath is visible in the crumbling walls of the buildings. The street sparkles with shattered glass. I have never seen, anywhere, so many broken windows. A sign—"Slow, Children at Play"—has been bent backward by an automobile. At the lighthouse, the dogs turn up Pacific and disappear. George Meade, Army engineer, built the lighthouse—brick upon brick, six hundred thousand bricks, to reach up high enough to throw a beam twenty miles over the sea. Meade, seven years later, saved the Union at Gettysburg.

3   I buy Vermont Avenue for $100. My opponent is a tall, shadowy figure, across from me, but I know him well, and I know his game like a favorite tune. If he can, he will always go for the quick kill. And when it is foolish to go for the quick kill he will be foolish. On the whole, though, he is a master assessor of percentages. It is a mistake to underestimate him. His eleven carries his top hat to St. Charles Place, which he buys for $140.

4   The sidewalks of St. Charles Place have been cracked to shards by through-growing weeds. There are no buildings. Mansions, hotels once stood here. A few street lamps now drop cones of light on broken glass and vacant space behind a chain-link fence that some great machine has in places bent to the ground. Five plane trees—in full summer leaf, flecking the light—are all that live on St. Charles Place.

5   Block upon block, gradually, we are cancelling each other out—in the blues, the lavenders, the oranges, the greens. My opponent follows a plan of

his own devising. I use the Hornblower & Weeks opening and the Zuricher defense. The first game draws tight, will soon finish. In 1971, a group of people in Racine, Wisconsin, played for seven hundred and sixty-eight hours. A game begun a month later in Danville, California, lasted eight hundred and twenty hours. These are official records, and they stun us. We have been playing for eight minutes. It amazes us that Monopoly is thought of as a long game. It is possible to play to a complete, absolute, and final conclusion in less than fifteen minutes, all within the rules as written. My opponent and I have done so thousands of times. No wonder we are sitting across from each other now in this best-of-seven series for the international singles championship of the world.

•

6   On Illinois Avenue, three men lean out from second-story windows. A girl is coming down the street. She wears dungarees and a bright-red shirt, has ample breasts and a Hadendoan Afro, a black halo, two feet in diameter. Ice rattles in the glasses in the hands of the men.

7   "Hey, sister!"
8   "Come on up!"
9   She looks up, looks from one to another to the other, looks them flat in the eye.
10   "What for?" she says, and she walks on.

•

11   I buy Illinois for $240. It solidifies my chances, for I already own Kentucky and Indiana. My opponent pales. If he had landed first on Illinois, the game would have been over then and there, for he has houses built on Boardwalk and Park Place, we share the railroads equally, and we have cancelled each other everywhere else. We never trade.

•

12   In 1852, R. B. Osborne, an immigrant Englishman, civil engineer, surveyed the route of a railroad line that would run from Camden to Absecon Island, in New Jersey, traversing the state from the Delaware River to the barrier beaches of the sea. He then sketched in the plan of a "bathing village" that would surround the eastern terminus of the line. His pen flew glibly, framing and naming spacious avenues parallel to the shore—Mediterranean, Baltic, Oriental, Ventnor—and narrower transsecting avenues: North Carolina, Pennsylvania, Vermont, Connecticut, States, Virginia, Tennessee, New York, Kentucky, Indiana, Illinois. The place as a whole had no name, so when he had completed the plan Osborne wrote in large letters over the ocean, "Atlantic City." No one ever challenged the name, or the names of Osborne's streets. Monopoly was invented in the early nineteen-thirties by Charles B. Darrow, but Darrow was only transliterating what Osborne had created. The railroads, crucial to any player, were the making of Atlantic City. After the rails were down, houses and hotels burgeoned from Mediterranean and Baltic to New York and Kentucky. Properties—building lots—sold for as little as six dollars apiece and as much as a thousand dollars. The original investors in the

railroads and the real estate called themselves the Camden & Atlantic Land Company. Reverently, I repeat their names: Dwight Bell, William Coffin, John DaCosta, Daniel Deal, William Fleming, Andrew Hay, Joseph Porter, Jonathan Pitney, Samuel Richards—founders, fathers, forerunners, archetypical masters of the quick kill.

13   My opponent and I are now in a deep situation of classical Monopoly. The torsion is almost perfect—Boardwalk and Park Place versus the brilliant reds. His cash position is weak, though, and if I escape him now he may fade. I land on Luxury Tax, contiguous to but in sanctuary from his power. I have four houses on Indiana. He lands there. He concedes.

14   Indiana Avenue was the address of the Brighton Hotel, gone now. The Brighton was exclusive—a word that no longer has retail value in the city. If you arrived by automobile and tried to register at the Brighton, you were sent away. Brighton-class people came in private railroad cars. Brighton-class people had other private railroad cars for their horses—dawn rides on the firm sand at water's edge, skirts flying. Colonel Anthony J. Drexel Biddle—the sort of name that would constrict throats in Philadelphia—lived, much of the year, in the Brighton.

15   Colonel Sanders' fried chicken is on Kentucky Avenue. So is Clifton's Club Harlem, with the Sepia Revue and the Sepia Follies, featuring the Honey Bees, the Fashions, and the Lords.

16   My opponent and I, many years ago, played 2,428 games of Monopoly in a single season. He was then a recent graduate of the Harvard Law School, and he was working for a downtown firm, looking up law. Two people we knew—one from Chase Manhattan, the other from Morgan, Stanley—tried to get into the game, but after a few rounds we found that they were not in the conversation and we sent them home. Monopoly should always be *mano a mano* anyway. My opponent won 1,199 games, and so did I. Thirty were ties. He was called into the Army, and we stopped just there. Now, in Game 2 of the series, I go immediately to jail, and again to jail while my opponent seines property. He is dumbfoundingly lucky. He wins in twelve minutes.

17   Visiting hours are daily, eleven to two; Sunday, eleven to one; evenings, six to nine. "NO MINORS, NO FOOD, Immediate Family Only Allowed in Jail." All this above a blue steel door in a blue cement wall in the windowless interior of the basement of the city hall. The desk sergeant sits opposite the door to the jail. In a cigar box in front of him are pills in every color, a banquet of fruit salad an inch and a half deep—leapers, co-pilots, footballs, truck drivers, peanuts, blue angels, yellow jackets, redbirds, rainbows. Near the desk are two soldiers, waiting to go through the blue door. They are about eighteen years old. One of them is trying hard to light a cigarette. His wrists are in steel cuffs.

A military policeman waits, too. He is a year or so older than the soldiers, taller, studious in appearance, gentle, fat. On a bench against a wall sits a good-looking girl in slacks. The blue door rattles, swings heavily open. A turnkey stands in the doorway. "Don't you guys kill yourselves back there now," says the sergeant to the soldiers.

18 "One kid, he overdosed himself about ten and a half hours ago," says the M.P.

19 The M.P., the soldiers, the turnkey, and the girl on the bench are white. The sergeant is black. "If you take off the handcuffs, take off the belts," says the sergeant to the M.P. "I don't want them hanging themselves back there." The door shuts and its tumblers move. When it opens again, five minutes later, a young white man in sandals and dungarees and a blue polo shirt emerges. His hair is in a ponytail. He has no beard. He grins at the good-looking girl. She rises, joins him. The sergeant hands him a manila envelope. From it he removes his belt and a small notebook. He borrows a pencil, makes an entry in the notebook. He is out of jail, free. What did he do? He offended Atlantic City in some way. He spent a night in the jail. In the nineteen-thirties, men visiting Atlantic City went to jail, directly to jail, did not pass Go, for appearing in topless bathing suits on the beach. A city statute requiring all men to wear full-length bathing suits was not seriously challenged until 1937, and the first year in which a man could legally go bare-chested on the beach was 1940.

●

20 Game 3. After seventeen minutes, I am ready to begin construction on overpriced and sluggish Pacific, North Carolina, and Pennsylvania. Nothing else being open, opponent concedes.

●

21 The physical profile of streets perpendicular to the shore is something like a playground slide. It begins in the high skyline of Boardwalk hotels, plummets into warrens of "side-avenue" motels, crosses Pacific, slopes through church missions, convalescent homes, burlesque houses, rooming houses, and liquor stores, crosses Atlantic, and runs level through the bombed out ghetto as far—Baltic, Mediterranean—as the eye can see. North Carolina Avenue, for example, is flanked at its beach end by the Chalfonte and the Haddon Hall (908 rooms, air-conditioned), where, according to one biographer, John Philip Sousa (1854–1932) first played when he was twenty-two, insisting, even then, that everyone call him by his entire name. Behind these big hotels, motels—Barbizon, Catalina—crouch. Between Pacific and Atlantic is an occasional house from 1910—wooden porch, wooden mullions, old yellow paint—and two churches, a package store, a strip show, a dealer in fruits and vegetables. Then, beyond Atlantic Avenue, North Carolina moves on into the vast ghetto, the bulk of the city, and it looks like Metz in 1919, Cologne in 1944. Nothing has actually exploded. It is not bomb damage. It is deep and complex decay. Roofs are off. Bricks are scattered in the street. People sit on porches, six deep, at nine on a Monday morning. When they go off to wait in unemployment lines, they wait sometimes two hours. Between Mediterranean

and Baltic runs a chain-link fence, enclosing rubble. A patrol car sits idling by the curb. In the back seat is a German shepherd. A sign on the fence says, "Beware of Bad Dogs."

22 Mediterranean and Baltic are the principal avenues of the ghetto. Dogs are everywhere. A pack of seven passes me. Block after block, there are three-story brick row houses. Whole segments of them are abandoned, a thousand broken windows. Some parts are intact, occupied. A mattress lies in the street, soaking in a pool of water. Wet stuffing is coming out of the mattress. A postman is having a rye and a beer in the Plantation Bar at nine-fifteen in the morning. I ask him idly if he knows where Marvin Gardens is. He does not. "HOOKED AND NEED HELP? CONTACT N.A.R.C.O." "REVIVAL NOW GOING ON, CONDUCTED BY REVEREND H. HENDERSON OF TEXAS." These are signboards on Mediterranean and Baltic. The second one is upside down and leans against a boarded-up window of the Faith Temple Church of God in Christ. There is an old peeling poster on a warehouse wall showing a figure in an electric chair. "The Black Panther Manifesto" is the title of the poster, and its message is, or was, that "the fascists have already decided in advance to murder Chairman Bobby Seale in the electric chair." I pass an old woman who carries a bucket. She wears blue sneakers, worn through. Her feet spill out. She wears red socks, rolled at the knees. A white handkerchief, spread over her head, is knotted at the corners. Does she know where Marvin Gardens is? "I sure don't know," she says, setting down the bucket. "I sure don't know. I've heard of it somewhere, but I just can't say where." I walk on, through a block of shattered glass. The glass crunches underfoot like coarse sand. I remember when I first came here—a long train ride from Trenton, long ago, games of poker in the train—to play basketball against Atlantic City. We were half black, they were all black. We scored forty points, they scored eighty, or something like it. What I remember most is that they had glass backboards—glittering, pendent, expensive glass backboards, a rarity then in high schools, even in colleges, the only ones we played on all year.

23 I turn on Pennsylvania, and start back toward the sea. The windows of the Hotel Astoria, on Pennsylvania near Baltic, are boarded up. A sheet of unpainted plywood is the door, and in it is a triangular peephole that now frames an eye. The plywood door opens. A man answers my question. Rooms there are six, seven, and ten dollars a week. I thank him for the information and move on, emerging from the ghetto at the Catholic Daughters of America Women's Guest House, between Atlantic and Pacific. Between Pacific and the Boardwalk are the blinking vacancy signs of the Aristocrat and Colton Manor motels. Pennsylvania terminates at the Sheraton-Seaside—thirty-two dollars a day, ocean corner. I take a walk on the Boardwalk and into the Holiday Inn (twenty-three stories). A guest is registering. "You reserved for Wednesday, and this is Monday," the clerk tells him. "But that's all right. We have *plenty* of rooms." The clerk is very young, female, and has soft brown hair that hangs below her waist. Her superior kicks her.

24   He is a middle-aged man with red spiderwebs in his face. He is jacketed and tied. He takes her aside. "Don't say 'plenty,'" he says. "Say 'You are fortunate, sir. We have rooms available.'"

25   The face of the young woman turns sour. "We have all the rooms you need," she says to the customer, and, to her superior, "How's that?"

•

26   Game 4. My opponent's luck has become abrasive. He has Boardwalk and Park Place, and has sealed the board.

•

27   Darrow was a plumber. He was, specifically, a radiator repairman who lived in Germantown, Pennsylvania. His first Monopoly board was a sheet of linoleum. On it he placed houses and hotels that he had carved from blocks of wood. The game he thus invented was brilliantly conceived, for it was an uncannily exact reflection of the business milieu at large. In its depth, range, and subtlety, in its luck-skill ratio, in its sense of infrastructure and socioeconomic parameters, in its philosophical characteristics, it reached to the profundity of the financial community. It was as scientific as the stock market. It suggested the manner and means through which an underdeveloped world had been developed. It was chess at Wall Street level. "Advance token to the nearest Railroad and pay owner twice the rental to which he is otherwise entitled. If Railroad is unowned, you may buy it from the Bank. Get out of Jail, free. Advance token to nearest Utility. If unowned, you may buy it from Bank. If owned, throw dice and pay owner a total ten times the amount thrown. You are assessed for street repairs: $40 per house, $115 per hotel. Pay poor tax of $15. Go to Jail. Go directly to Jail. Do not pass Go. Do not collect $200."

•

28   The turnkey opens the blue door. The turnkey is known to the inmates as Sidney K. Above his desk are ten closed-circuit-TV screens—assorted viewpoints of the jail. There are three cellblocks—men, women, juvenile boys. Six days is the average stay. Showers twice a week. The steel doors and the equipment that operates them were made in San Antonio. The prisoners sleep on bunks of butcher block. There are no mattresses. There are three prisoners to a cell. In winter, it is cold in here. Prisoners burn newspapers to keep warm. Cell corners are black with smudge. The jail is three years old. The men's block echoes with chatter. The man in the cell nearest Sidney K. is pacing. His shirt is covered with broad stains of blood. The block for juvenile boys is, by contrast, utterly silent—empty corridor, empty cells. There is only one prisoner. He is small and black and appears to be thirteen. He says he is sixteen and that he has been alone in here for three days.

29   "Why are you here? What did you do?"

30   "I hit a jitney driver."

•

31   The series stands at three all. We have split the fifth and sixth games. We are scrambling for property. Around the board we fairly fly. We move so fast

because we do our own banking and search our own deeds. My opponent grows tense.

●

32 Ventnor Avenue, a street of delicatessens and doctors' offices, is leafy with plane trees and hydrangeas, the city flower. Water Works is on the mainland. The water comes over in submarine pipes. Electric Company gets power from across the state, on the Delaware River, in Deepwater. States Avenue, now a wasteland like St. Charles, once had gardens running down the middle of the street, a horse-drawn trolley, private homes. States Avenue was as exclusive as the Brighton. Only an apartment house, a small motel, and the All Wars Memorial Building—monadnocks spaced widely apart—stand along States Avenue now. Pawnshops, convalescent homes, and the Paradise Soul Saving Station are on Virginia Avenue. The soul-saving station is pink, orange, and yellow. In the windows flanking the door of the Virginia Money Loan Office are Nikons, Polaroids, Yashicas, Sony TVs, Underwood typewriters, Singer sewing machines, and pictures of Christ. On the far side of town, beside a single track and locked up most of the time, is the new railroad station, a small hut made of glazed firebrick, all that is left of the lines that built the city. An authentic phrenologist works on New York Avenue close to Frank's Extra Dry Bar and a church where the sermon today is "Death in the Pot." The church is of pink brick, has blue and amber windows and two red doors. St. James Place, narrow and twisting, is lined with boarding houses that have wooden porches on each of three stories, suggesting a New Orleans made of salt-bleached pine. In a vacant lot on Tennessee is a white Ford station wagon stripped to the chassis. The windows are smashed. A plastic Clorox bottle sits on the driver's seat. The wind has pressed newspaper against the chain-link fence around the lot. Atlantic Avenue, the city's principal thoroughfare, could be seventeen American Main Streets placed end to end—discount vitamins and Vienna Corset shops, movie theatres, shoe stores, and funeral homes. The Boardwalk is made of yellow pine and Douglas fir, soaked in pentachlorophenol. Downbeach, it reaches far beyond the city. Signs everywhere—on windows, lampposts, trash baskets—proclaim "Bienvenue Canadiens!" The salt air is full of Canadian French. In the Claridge Hotel, on Park Place, I ask a clerk if she knows where Marvin Gardens is. She says, "Is it a floral shop?" I ask a cabdriver, parked outside. He says, "Never heard of it." Park Place is one block long. Pacific to Boardwalk. On the roof of the Claridge is the Solarium, the highest point in town—panoramic view of the ocean, the bay, the salt-water ghetto. I look down at the rooftops of the side-avenue motels and into swimming pools. There are hundreds of people around the rooftop pools, sunbathing, reading—many more people than are on the beach. Walls, windows, and a block of sky are all that is visible from these pools—no sand, no sea. The pools are craters, and with the people around them they are countersunk into the motels.

●

33 The seventh, and final, game is ten minutes old and I have hotels on Oriental, Vermont, and Connecticut. I have Tennessee and St. James. I have

North Carolina and Pacific. I have Boardwalk, Atlantic, Ventnor, Illinois, Indiana. My fingers are forming a "V." I have mortgaged most of these properties in order to pay for others, and I have mortgaged the others to pay for the hotels. I have seven dollars. I will pay off the mortgages and build my reserves with income from the three hotels. My cash position may be low, but I feel like a rocket in an underground silo. Meanwhile, if I could just go to jail for a time I could pause there, wait there, until my opponent, in his inescapable rounds, pays the rates of my hotels. Jail, at times, is the strategic place to be. I roll boxcars from the Reading and move the flatiron to Community Chest. "Go to Jail. Go directly to Jail."

34   The prisoners, of course, have no pens and no pencils. They take paper napkins, roll them tight as crayons, char the ends with matches, and write on the walls. The things they write are not entirely idiomatic; for example, "In God We Trust." All is in carbon. Time is required in the writing. "Only humanity could know of such pain." "God So Loved the World." "There is no greater pain than life itself." In the women's block now, there are six blacks, giggling, and a white asleep in red shoes. She is drunk. The others are pushers, prostitutes, an auto thief, a burglar caught with pistol in purse. A sixteen-year-old accused of murder was in here last week. These words are written on the wall of a now empty cell: "Laying here I see two bunks about six inches thick, not counting the one I'm laying on, which is hard as brick. No cushion for my back. No pillow for my head. Just a couple scratchy blankets which is best to use it's said. I wake up in the morning so shivery and cold, waiting and waiting till I am told the food is coming. It's on its way. It's not worth waiting for, but I eat it anyway. I know one thing when they set me free I'm gonna be good if it kills me."

35   How many years must a game be played to produce an Anthony J. Drexel Biddle and chestnut geldings on the beach? About half a century was the original answer, from the first railroad to Biddle at his peak. Biddle, at his peak, hit an Atlantic City streetcar conductor with his fist, laid him out with one punch. This increased Biddle's legend. He did not go to jail. While John Philip Sousa led his band along the Boardwalk playing "The Stars and Stripes Forever" and Jack Dempsey ran up and down in training for his fight with Gene Tunney, the city crossed the high curve of its parabola. Al Capone held conventions here—upstairs with his sleeves rolled, apportioning among his lieutenant governors the states of the Eastern seaboard. The natural history of an American resort proceeds from Indians to French Canadians via Biddles and Capones. French Canadians, whatever they may be at home, are Visigoths here. Bienvenue Visigoths!

36   My opponent plods along incredibly well. He has got his fourth railroad, and patiently, unbelievably, he has picked up my potential winners until he has blocked me everywhere but Marvin Gardens. He has avoided, in the fifty-dollar zoning, my increasingly petty hotels. His cash flow swells. His railroads are

costing me two hundred dollars a minute. He is building hotels on States, Virginia, and St. Charles. He has temporarily reversed the current. With the yellow monopolies and my blue monopolies, I could probably defeat his lavenders and his railroads. I have Atlantic and Ventnor. I need Marvin Gardens. My only hope is Marvin Gardens.

37   There is a plaque at Boardwalk and Park Place, and on it in relief is the leonine profile of a man who looks like an officer in a metropolitan bank—"Charles B. Darrow, 1889–1967, inventor of the game of Monopoly." "Darrow," I address him, aloud. "Where is Marvin Gardens?" There is, of course, no answer. Bronze, impassive, Darrow looks south down the Boardwalk. "Mr. Darrow, please, where is Marvin Gardens?" Nothing. Not a sign. He just looks south down the Boardwalk.

38   My opponent accepts the trophy with his natural ease and I make, from notes, remarks that are even less graceful than his.

39   Marvin Gardens is the one color-block Monopoly property that is not in Atlantic City. It is a suburb within a suburb, secluded. It is a planned compound of seventy-two handsome houses set on curvilinear private streets under yews and cedars, poplars and willows. The compound was built around 1920, in Margate, New Jersey, and consists of solid buildings of stucco, brick, and wood, with slate roofs, tile roofs, multimullioned porches, Giraldic towers, and Spanish grilles. Marvin Gardens, the ultimate outwash of Monopoly, is a citadel and sanctuary of the middle class. "We're heavily patrolled by police here. We don't take no chances. Me? I'm living here nine years. I paid seventeen thousand dollars and I've been offered thirty. Number one, I don't want to move. Number two, I don't need the money. I have four bedrooms, two and a half baths, front den, back den. No basement. The Atlantic is down there. Six feet down and you float. A lot of people have a hard time finding this place. People that lived in Atlantic City all their life don't know how to find it. They don't know where the hell they're going. They just know it's south, down the Boardwalk."

Questions to Ponder

1. What kinds of research are showcased in this article?
2. In what ways does John McPhee seem to be one on whom nothing is lost?
3. Where would you look to find information about Charles Darrow and the invention of the Monopoly Game? About other inventors or famous people?
4. What details suggest that McPhee is fantasizing his "best-of-seven series for the international Monopoly singles championship of the world"?

Writing Possibilities

1. Using "The Search for Marvin Gardens" as a model, select a different game and weave the playing of it with a more serious story of your country—or of your family.
2. Literally walk the path of historical development of your hometown and write of your discoveries. Like McPhee, do research before and after your walks. Do you need to take several walks? Share the article you write with your city historical society and with your local newspaper. You may have to shorten and revise your piece for the latter.
3. Do research into the invention and history of a game you like to play. Then interview players of all ages. Combine the resulting information in an interesting way, perhaps for a newspaper or a magazine.

IN SEARCH OF HISTORY

Barbara Tuchman

To a historian libraries are food, shelter, and even muse. They are of two kinds: the library of published material—books, pamphlets, periodicals, etc.—and the archive of unpublished papers and documents. . . .

[Furthermore] to visit the [historical] scene before writing, even the scene of long-dead adventures, is, as it were, to start business with money in the bank. . . . On the terrain motives become clear, reasons and explanations and origins of things emerge that might otherwise have remained obscure. As a source of understanding, not to mention as a corrective for fixed ideas and mistaken notions, nothing is more valuable than knowing the scene in person, and, even more so, living the life that belongs to it. . . .

Distillation is selection, and selection, as I am hardly the first to affirm, is the essence of writing history. It is the cardinal process of composition, the most difficult, the most delicate, the most fraught with error as well as art. Ability to distinguish what is significant from what is insignificant is sine qua non. Failure to do so means that the point of the story, not to mention the reader's interest, *becomes lost in a morass of undifferentiated matter. What is required is simply the courage and self-confidence to make choices and, above all, to leave things out.*

Finally, the historian cannot do without imagination. [Francis] Parkman, intense as always in his effort to make the reader "feel the situation," chose to picture the land between the Hudson and Montreal as it would look to a wild goose flying northward in spring. . . . It would not be remarkable for one of us who has traveled in airplanes to think of the device of the bird's-eye view, but Parkman had never been off the ground. It was a pure effort of imagination to put himself behind the eye of the goose, to see the flag as a flickering white speck and the mountains, in that perfect phrase, as "a stormy sea congealed."

Brief Warm-up Writing Exercises

1. Brainstorm a list of events from history that interest you.
2. Now choose one event from your list and freewrite about it, telling why it interests you, what particularly about it arouses your imagination.
3. Freewrite a description of your research methods: how do you proceed and how do you keep track of the information you collect?

---

1   History began to exert its fascination upon me when I was about six, through the medium of the Twins series by Lucy Fitch Perkins. I became absorbed in the fortunes of the Dutch Twins; the Twins of the American Revolution, who daringly painted the name *Modeerf,* or "freedom" spelled backward, on their row boat; and especially the Belgian Twins, who suffered under the German occupation of Brussels in 1914.

2   After the Twins, I went through a G. A. Henty period and bled with Wolfe in Canada. Then came a prolonged Dumas period, during which I became so intimate with the Valois kings, queens, royal mistresses, and various Ducs de Guise that when we visited the French *châteaux* I was able to point out to my family just who had stabbed whom in which room. Conan Doyle's *The White Company* and, above all, Jane Porter's *The Scottish Chiefs* were the definitive influence. As the noble Wallace, in tartan and velvet ram, I went to my first masquerade party, stalking in silent tragedy among the twelve-year-old Florence Nightingales and Juliets. In the book the treachery of the Countess of Mar, who betrayed Wallace, carried a footnote that left its mark on me. "The crimes of this wicked woman," it said darkly, "are verified by history."

3   By the time I reached Radcliffe, I had no difficulty in choosing a field of concentration, although it turned out to be History and Lit rather than pure history. I experienced at college no moment of revelation that determined me to write historical narrative. When that precise moment occurred I cannot say; it just developed and there was a considerable time lag. What Radcliffe *did* give

me, however, was an *impetus* (not to mention an education, but I suppose that goes without saying). Part of the impetus came from great courses and great professors. Of the three to which I owe most, two, curiously enough, were in literature rather than history. They were Irving Babbitt's Comp Lit 11 and John Livingston Lowes's English 72, which included his spectacular tour de force on the origins of "The Ancient Mariner" and "Kubla Khan." He waved at Wordsworth, bowed briefly to Keats and Shelley, and really let himself go through twelve weeks of lectures, tracing the sources of Coleridge's imagery, and spending at least a week on the fatal apparition of the person from Porlock. What kept us, at least me, on the edge of my seat throughout this exploit was Lowes's enthusiasm for his subject.

4   This quality was the essence, too, of Professor C. H. McIlwain's Constitutional History of England, which came up as far as Magna Carta. It did not matter to McIlwain, a renowned scholar and historian, that only four of us were taking his course, or that he had already given it at Harvard and had to come over to repeat it to us (yes, that was the quaint custom of the time). It did not matter because McIlwain was conducting a passionate love affair with the laws of the Angles and the articles of the Charter, especially, as I remember, Article 39. Like any person in love, he wanted to let everyone know how beautiful was the object of his affections. He had white hair and pink cheeks and the brightest blue eyes I ever saw, and though I cannot remember a word of Article 39, I do remember how his blue eyes blazed as he discussed it and how I sat on the edge of my seat then too, and how, to show my appreciation, I would have given anything to write a brilliant exam paper, only to find that half the exam questions were in Anglo-Saxon, about which he had neglected to forewarn us. That did not matter either, because he gave all four of us A's anyway, perhaps out of gratitude for our affording him another opportunity to talk about his beloved Charter.

5   Professor Babbitt, on the other hand, being a classicist and antiromantic, frowned on enthusiasm. But his contempt for zeal was so zealous, so vigorous and learned, pouring out in a great organ fugue of erudition, that it amounted to enthusiasm in the end and held not only me, but all his listeners, rapt.

6   Although I did not know it or formulate it consciously at the time, it is this quality of being in love with your subject that is indispensable for writing good history—or good anything, for that matter. A few months ago when giving a talk at another college, I was invited to meet the faculty and other guests at dinner. One young member of the History Department who said he envied my subject in *The Guns of August* confessed to being bogged down and brought to a dead stop halfway through his doctoral thesis. It dealt, he told me, with an early missionary in the Congo who had never been "done" before. I asked what was the difficulty. With a dreary wave of his cocktail he said, "I just don't like him." I felt really distressed and depressed—both for him and for the conditions of scholarship. I do not know how many of you are going, or will go, to graduate school, but when you come to write that thesis on, let us say, "The Underwater Imagery Derived from the Battle of Lepanto in the Later

Poetic Dramas of Lope de Vega," I hope it will be because you care passionately about this imagery rather than because your department has suggested it as an original subject.

7   In the process of doing my own thesis—not for a Ph.D., because I never took a graduate degree, but just my undergraduate honors thesis—the single most formative experience in my career took place. It was not a tutor or a teacher or a fellow student or a great book or the shining example of some famous visiting lecturer—like Sir Charles Webster, for instance, brilliant as he was. It was the stacks at Widener. They were *my* Archimedes's bathtub, my burning bush, my dish of mold where I found my personal penicillin. I was allowed to have as my own one of those little cubicles with a table under a window, queerly called, as I have since learned, carrels, a word I never knew when I sat in one. Mine was deep in among the 942s (British History, that is) and I could roam at liberty through the rich stacks, taking whatever I wanted. The experience was marvelous, a word I use in its exact sense meaning full of marvels. The happiest days of my intellectual life, until I began writing history again some fifteen years later, were spent in the stacks at Widener. My daughter Lucy, class of '61, once said to me that she could not enter the labyrinth of Widener's stacks without feeling that she ought to carry a compass, a sandwich, and a whistle. I too was never altogether sure I could find the way out, but I was blissful as a cow put to graze in a field of fresh clover and would not have cared if I had been locked in for the night.

8   Once I stayed so late that I came out after dark, long after the dinner hour at the dorm, and found to my horror that I had only a nickel in my purse. The weather was freezing and I was very hungry. I could not decide whether to spend the nickel on a chocolate bar and walk home in the cold or take the Mass Avenue trolley and go home hungry. This story ends like "The Lady or the Tiger," because although I remember the agony of having to choose, I cannot remember how it came out.

9   My thesis, the fruit of those hours in the stacks, was my first sustained attempt at writing history. It was called "The Moral Justification for the British Empire," an unattractive title and, besides, inaccurate, because what I meant was the moral *justifying* of empire by the imperialists. It was for me a wonderful and terrible experience. Wonderful because finding the material, and following where it led, was constantly exciting and because I was fascinated by the subject, which I had thought up for myself—much to the disapproval of my tutor, who was in English Lit, not History, and interested only in Walter Pater—or was it Walter Savage Landor? Anyway, it was *not* the British Empire, and since our meetings were consequently rather painfully uncommunicative, I think he was relieved when I took to skipping them.

10   The experience was terrible because I could not make the piece sound, or rather read, the way I wanted it to. The writing fell so far short of the ideas. The characters, who were so vivid inside my head, seemed so stilted when I got them on paper. I finished it, dissatisfied. So was the department: "Style undistinguished," it noted. A few years ago, when I unearthed the thesis to look

up a reference, that impression was confirmed. It reminded me of *The Importance of Being Earnest*, when Cecily says that the letters she wrote to herself from her imaginary fiancé when she broke off their imaginary engagement were so beautiful and so badly spelled she could not reread them without crying. I felt the same way about my thesis: so beautiful—in intent—and so badly written. Enthusiasm had not been enough; one must also know how to use the language.

11   One learns to write, I have since discovered, in the practice thereof. After seven years' apprenticeship in journalism I discovered that an essential element for good writing is a good ear. One must *listen* to the sound of one's own prose. This, I think, is one of the failings of much American writing. Too many writers do not listen to the sound of their own words. For example, listen to this sentence from the organ of my own discipline, the *American Historical Review:* "His presentation is not vitiated historically by efforts at expository simplicity." In one short sentence five long Latin words of four or five syllables each. One has to read it three times over and take time out to think, before one can even make out what it means.

12   In my opinion, short words are always preferable to long ones; the fewer syllables the better, and monosyllables, beautiful and pure like "bread" and "sun" and "grass," are the best of all. Emerson, using almost entirely one-syllable words, wrote what I believe are among the finest lines in English:

> *By the rude bridge that arched the flood,*
> *Their flag to April's breeze unfurled,*
> *Here once the embattled farmers stood*
> *And fired the shot heard round the world.*

Out of twenty-eight words, twenty-four are monosyllables. It is English at its purest, though hardly characteristic of its author.

13   Or take this:

> *On desperate seas long wont to roam,*
>   *Thy hyacinth hair, thy classic face,*
> *Thy Naiad airs have brought me home*
>   *To the glory that was Greece*
>   *And the grandeur that was Rome.*

Imagine how it must feel to have composed those lines! Though coming from a writer satisfied with the easy rhythms of "The Raven" and "Annabel Lee," they represent, I fear, a fluke. To quote poetry, you will say, is not a fair comparison. True, but what a lesson those stanzas are in the sound of words! What superb use of that magnificent instrument that lies at the command of all of us—the English language. Quite by chance both practitioners in these samples happen to be Americans, and both, curiously enough, writing about history.

14   To write history so as to enthrall the reader and make the subject as captivating and exciting to him as it is to me has been my goal since that initial failure with my thesis. A prerequisite, as I have said, is to be enthralled one's self and to feel a compulsion to communicate the magic. Communicate to whom? We arrive now at the reader, a person whom I keep constantly in mind. Catherine Drinker Bowen has said that she writes her books with a sign pinned up over her desk asking, "Will the reader turn the page?"

15   The writer of history, I believe, has a number of duties vis-à-vis the reader, if he wants to keep him reading. The first is to distill. He must do the preliminary work for the reader, assemble the information, make sense of it, select the essential, discard the irrelevant—above all, discard the irrelevant—and put the rest together so that it forms a developing dramatic narrative. Narrative, it has been said, is the lifeblood of history. To offer a mass of undigested facts, of names not identified and places not located, is of no use to the reader and is simple laziness on the part of the author, or pedantry to show how much he has read. To discard the unnecessary requires courage and also extra work, as exemplified by Pascal's effort to explain an idea to a friend in a letter which rambled on for pages and ended, "I am sorry to have worried you with so long a letter but I did not have time to write you a short one." The historian is continually being beguiled down fascinating byways and sidetracks. But the art of writing—the test of the artist—is to resist the beguilement and cleave to the subject.

16   Should the historian be an artist? Certainly a conscious art should be part of his equipment. Macaulay describes him as half poet, half philosopher. I do not aspire to either of these heights. I think of myself as a storyteller, a narrator, who deals in true stories, not fiction. The distinction is not one of relative values; it is simply that history interests me more than fiction. I agree with Leopold von Ranke, the great nineteenth-century German historian, who said that when he compared the portrait of Louis XI in Scott's *Quentin Durward* with the portrait of the same king in the memoirs of Philippe de Comines, Louis's minister, he found "the truth more interesting and beautiful than the romance."

17   It was Ranke, too, who set the historian's task: to find out *wie as eigentlich gewesen ist,* what really happened, or, literally, how it really was. His goal is one that will remain forever just beyond our grasp for reasons I explained in a "Note on Sources" in *The Guns of August* (a paragraph that no one ever reads but *I* think is the best thing in the book). Summarized, the reasons are that we who write about the past were not there. We can never be certain that we have recaptured it as it really was. But the least we can do is to stay within the evidence.

18   I do not invent anything, even the weather. One of my readers told me he particularly liked a passage in *The Guns* which tells how the British Army landed in France and how on that afternoon there was a sound of summer thunder in the air and the sun went down in a blood-red glow. He thought it an artistic touch of doom, but the fact is it was true. I found it in the memoirs

of a British officer who landed on that day and heard the thunder and saw the blood-red sunset. The art, if any, consisted only in selecting it and ultimately using it in the right place.

19   Selection is what determines the ultimate product, and that is why I use material from primary sources only. My feeling about secondary sources is that they are helpful but pernicious. I use them as guides at the start of a project to find out the general scheme of what happened, but I do not take notes from them because I do not want to end up simply rewriting someone else's book. Furthermore, the facts in a secondary source have already been pre-selected, so that in using them one misses the opportunity of selecting one's own.

20   I plunge as soon as I can into the primary sources: the memoirs and the letters, the generals' own accounts of their campaigns, however tendentious, not to say mendacious, they may be. Even an untrustworthy source is valuable for what it reveals about the personality of the author, especially if he is an actor in the events, as in the case of Sir John French, for example. Bias in a primary source is to be expected. One allows for it and corrects it by reading another version. I try always to read two or more for every episode. Even if an event is not controversial, it will have been seen and remembered from different angles of view by different observers. If the event *is* in dispute, one has extra obligation to examine both sides. As the lion in Aesop said to the Man, "There are many statues of men slaying lions, but if only the lions were sculptors there might be quite a different set of statues."

21   The most primary source of all is unpublished material: private letters and diaries or the reports, orders, and messages in government archives. There is an immediacy and intimacy about them that reveals character and makes circumstances come alive. I remember Secretary of State Robert Lansing's desk diary, which I used when I was working on *The Zimmermann Telegram*. The man himself seemed to step right out from his tiny neat handwriting and his precise notations of every visitor and each subject discussed. Each day's record opened and closed with the Secretary's time of arrival and departure from the office. He even entered the time of his lunch hour, which invariably lasted sixty minutes: "Left at 1:10; returned at 2:10." Once, when he was forced to record his morning arrival at 10:15, he added, with a worried eye on posterity, "Car broke down."

22   Inside the National Archives even the memory of Widener paled. Nothing can compare with the fascination of examining material in the very paper and ink of its original issue. A report from a field agent with marginal comments by the Secretary of War, his routing directions to State and Commerce, and the scribbled initials of subsequent readers can be a little history in itself. In the Archives I found the original decode of the Zimmermann Telegram, which I was able to have declassified and photostated for the cover of my book.

23   Even more immediate is research on the spot. Before writing *The Guns* I rented a little Renault and in another August drove over the battle areas of August 1914, following the track of the German invasion through Luxembourg, Belgium, and northern France. Besides obtaining a feeling of the geog-

raphy, distances, and terrain involved in military movements, I saw the fields ripe with grain which the cavalry would have trampled, measured the great width of the Meuse at Liège, and saw how the lost territory of Alsace looked to the French soldiers who gazed down upon it from the heights of the Vosges. I learned the discomfort of the Belgian *pavé* and discovered, in the course of losing my way almost permanently in a tangle of country roads in a hunt for the house that had been British Headquarters, why a British motorcycle dispatch rider in 1914 had taken three hours to cover twenty-five miles. Clearly, owing to the British officers' preference for country houses, he had not been able to find Headquarters either. French army commanders, I noticed, located themselves in *towns,* with railroad stations and telegraph offices.

24 As to the mechanics of research, I take notes on four-by-six index cards, reminding myself about once an hour of a rule I read long ago in a research manual, "Never write on the back of anything." Since copying is a chore and a bore, use of the cards, the smaller the better, forces one to extract the strictly relevant, to distill from the very beginning, to pass the material through the grinder of one's own mind, so to speak. Eventually, as the cards fall into groups according to subject or person or chronological sequence, the pattern of my story will emerge. Besides, they are convenient, as they can be filed in a shoebox and carried around in a pocketbook. When ready to write I need only take along a packet of them, representing a chapter, and I am equipped to work anywhere; whereas if one writes surrounded by a pile of books, one is tied to a single place, and furthermore likely to be too much influenced by other authors.

25 The most important thing about research is to know when to stop. How does one recognize the moment? When I was eighteen or thereabouts, my mother told me that when out with a young man I should always leave a half-hour before I wanted to. Although I was not sure how this might be accomplished, I recognized the advice as sound, and exactly the same rule applies to research. One must stop *before* one has finished; otherwise, one will never stop and never finish. I had an object lesson in this once in Washington at the Archives. I was looking for documents in the case of Perdicaris, an American—or supposed American—who was captured by Moroccan brigands in 1904. The Archives people introduced me to a lady professor who had been doing research in United States relations with Morocco all her life. She had written her Ph.D. thesis on the subject back in, I think, 1936, and was still coming for six months each year to work in the Archives. She was in her seventies and, they told me, had recently suffered a heart attack. When I asked her what year was her cut-off point, she looked at me in surprise and said she kept a file of newspaper clippings right up to the moment. I am sure she knew more about United States–Moroccan relations than anyone alive, but would she ever leave off her research in time to write that definitive history and tell the world what she knew? I feared the answer. Yet I know how she felt. I too feel compelled to follow every lead and learn everything about a subject, but fortunately I have an even more overwhelming compulsion to see my work in print. That is the only thing that saves me.

26   Research is endlessly seductive; writing is hard work. One has to sit down on that chair and think and transform thought into readable, conservative, interesting sentences that both make sense and make the reader turn the page. It is laborious, slow, often painful, sometimes agony. It means rearrangement, revision, adding, cutting, rewriting. But it brings a sense of excitement, almost of rapture; a moment on Olympus. In short, it is an act of creation.

27   I had of course a tremendous head start in having for *The Guns of August* a spectacular subject. The first month of the First World War, as Winston Churchill said, was "a drama never surpassed." It has that heroic quality that lifts the subject above the petty and that is necessary to great tragedy. In the month of August 1914 there was something looming, inescapable, universal, that involved us all. Something in that awful gulf between perfect plans and fallible men that makes one tremble with a sense of "There but for the Grace of God go we."

28   It was not until the end, until I was actually writing the Epilogue, that I fully realized all the implications of the story I had been writing for two years. Then I began to feel I had not done it justice. But now it was too late to go back and put in the significance, like the girl in the writing course whose professor said now they would go back over her novel and put in the symbolism.

29   One of the difficulties in writing history is the problem of how to keep up suspense in a narrative whose outcome is known. I worried about this a good deal at the beginning, but after a while the actual process of writing, as so often happens, produced the solution. I found that if one writes *as of the time*, without using the benefit of hindsight, resisting always the temptation to refer to events still ahead, the suspense will build itself up naturally. Sometimes the temptation to point out to the reader the significance of an act or event in terms of what later happened is almost irresistible. But I tried to be strong. I went back and cut out all references but one of the Battle of the Marne, in the chapters leading up to the battle. Though it may seem absurd, I even cut any references to the ultimate defeat of Germany. I wrote as if I did not know who would win, and I can only tell you that the method worked. I used to become tense with anxiety myself, as the moments of crisis approached. There was Joffre, for instance, sitting under the shade tree outside Headquarters, all that hot afternoon, considering whether to continue the retreat of the French armies to the Seine or, as Gallieni is pleading, turn around now and counterattack at the Marne. The German right wing is sliding by in front of Paris, exposing its flank. The moment is escaping. Joffre still sits and ponders. Even though one knows the outcome, the suspense is almost unbearable, because one knows that if he had made the wrong decision, you and I might not be here today—or, if we were, history would have been written by others.

30   This brings me to a matter currently rather moot—the nature of history. Today the battle rages, as you know, between the big thinkers or Toynbees or systematizers on the one hand and the humanists, if I may so designate them—using the word to mean concerned with human nature, not with the humanities—on the other. The genus Toynbee is obsessed and oppressed by

the need to find an explanation for history. They arrange systems and cycles into which history must be squeezed so that it will come out evenly and have pattern and a meaning. When history, wickedly disobliging, pops up in the wrong places, the systematizers hurriedly explain any such aberrant behavior by the climate. They need not reach so far; it is a matter of people. As Sir Charles Oman, the great historian of the art of war, said some time ago, "The human record is illogical . . . and history is a series of happenings with no inevitability about it."

31   Prefabricated systems make me suspicious and science applied to history makes me wince. The nearest anyone has come to explaining history is, I think, Leon Trotsky, who both made history and wrote it. Cause in history, he said, "refracts itself through a natural selection of accidents." The more one ponders that statement the more truth one finds. More recently an anonymous reviewer in the *Times Literary Supplement* disposed of the systematizers beyond refute. "The historian," he said, "who puts his system first can hardly escape the heresy of preferring the facts which suit his system best." And he concluded, "Such explanation as there is must arise in the mind of the reader of history." That is the motto on my banner.

32   To find out what happened in history is enough at the outset without trying too soon to make sure of the "why." I believe it is safer to leave the "why" alone until after one has not only gathered the facts but arranged them in sequence; to be exact, in sentences, paragraphs, and chapters. The very process of transforming a collection of personalities, dates, gun calibers, letters, and speeches into a narrative eventually forces the "why" to the surface. It will emerge of itself one fine day from the story of what happened. It will suddenly appear and tap one on the shoulder, but not if one chases after it first, *before* one knows what happened. Then it will elude one forever.

33   If the historian will submit himself *to* his material instead of trying to impose himself *on* his material, then the material will ultimately speak to him and supply the answers. It has happened to me more than once. In somebody's memoirs I found that the Grand Duke Nicholas wept when he was named Russian Commander-in-Chief in 1914, because, said the memoirist, he felt inadequate for the job. That sounded to me like one of those bits of malice one has to watch out for in contemporary observers; it did not ring true. The Grand Duke was said to be the only "man" in the royal family; he was known for his exceedingly tough manners, was admired by the common soldier and feared at court. I did not believe he felt inadequate, but then why should he weep? I could have left out this bit of information, but I did not want to. I wanted to find the explanation that would make it fit. (Leaving things out because they do not fit is writing fiction, not history.) I carried the note about the Grand Duke around with me for days, worrying about it. Then I remembered other tears. I went through my notes and found an account of Churchill weeping and also Messimy, the French War Minister. All at once I understood that it was not the individuals but the *times* that were the stuff for tears. My next sentence almost wrote itself: "There was an aura about 1914 that caused those who

sensed it to shiver for mankind." Afterward I realized that this sentence expressed why I had wanted to write the book in the first place. The "why," you see, had emerged all by itself.

34   The same thing happened with Joffre's battle order on the eve of the Marne. I had intended to make this my climax, a final bugle call, as it were. But the order was curiously toneless and flat and refused utterly to rise to the occasion. I tried translating it a dozen different ways, but nothing helped. I grew really angry over that battle order. Then, one day, when I was rereading it for the twentieth time, it suddenly spoke. I discovered that its very flatness *was* its significance. Now I was able to quote it at the end of the last chapter and add, "It did not shout 'Forward!' or summon men to glory. After the first thirty days of war in 1914, there was a premonition that little glory lay ahead."

35   As, in this way, the explanation conveys itself to the writer, so will the implications or meaning for our time arise in the mind of the reader. But such lessons, if present and valid, must emerge from the material, not the writer. I did not write to instruct but to tell a story. The implications are what the thoughtful reader himself takes out of the book. This is as it should be, I think, because the best book is a collaboration between author and reader. ❖

Questions to Ponder

1. What are the purposes and value of the four kinds of sources Barbara Tuchman describes: (1) secondary sources; (2) primary sources; (3) unpublished material; and (4) on-the-spot research?
2. What can a researcher do to "distill" information?
3. When is research completed on a writing project?
4. What is the danger of using too many four- and five-syllable Latin words in your sentences?

Writing Possibilities

1. Choose one year in your school's history and gather all the information you can about it from books and articles (secondary sources); official documents and private diaries, letters, and autobiographies (primary sources); and onsite observations. Distill the information you gather into a short historical narrative.
2. Try to discover your college's response to the Vietnam War. Look through school newspapers and local newspapers and interview any direct participants you can identify. Write a short article for your school newspaper to be run on the anniversary of the end of the war. Write a longer essay for a historical journal and for your school's archives.

3. Try to discover your hometown's response to Prohibition. Read town histories, local newspapers, and look in church archives for sermons on the subject. Interview citizens who may have personal memories of the times. Share your findings in an essay for your historical society.

The Tailors of Maida

Gay Talese

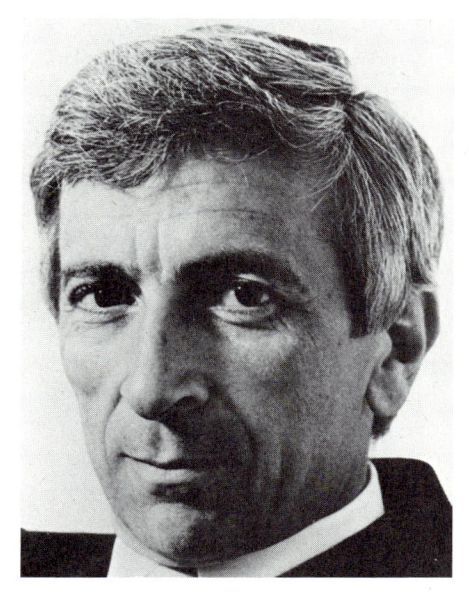

In 1982, having written about The New York Times *in* The Kingdom and the Power, *the Mafia in* Honor Thy Father, *and sex and censorship in America in* Thy Neighbor's Wife, *I decided it was time for me to turn from spectator to subject. For 37 years I had been a sympathetic observer of other people's challenges and conflicts. Now I would turn the spotlight on my family and myself in order to tell the story of Italian immigration to America.*

The intoxication of research is that you never know where it will take you. From 1982 to 1987 I made three trips to a remote mountain village in southern Italy called Maida, which lies amid eroding rock and fallen columns of antiquity. It was there my ancestors had settled centuries ago and where many of my relatives live to this day. I hired an Italian interpreter, and during the days I would interview my relatives (through the interpreter) about every facet of our family history. At night I would read histories of Italy and Europe to absorb a sense of the larger events, the historical stage on which my ancestors were merely players—minor players but worthy of notice nevertheless.

Following the trail of my father's immigration to America, I stopped in Paris and then spent eight months in Ambler, Pennsylvania, a small suburb north of Philadelphia where many southern Italian stonecutters like my namesake, my grandfather Gaetano, found work. From Ambler, I took the train my father took in 1922 to Ocean City, New Jersey, a resort island south of Atlantic City, where he would make his home, establishing a tailor shop at exactly the latitude of his home village in Italy.

It was in one of the hundreds of interviews I conducted with my father, Joseph Talese, now in his eighties, that I first heard the story of "The Tailors of Maida."

Brief Warm-up Writing Exercises

1. Describe a moment of embarrassment or the biggest scrape you got into as a child.
2. Freewrite the most dramatic family story you know.
3. Make a list of the kinds of sources you would use if you were going to trace your family's history back to its origins.

❖

1   There is a certain type of mild mental disorder that is endemic in the tailoring trade, and it began to weave its way into my father's psyche during his apprentice days in Italy, when he worked in the shop of a volatile craftsman named Francesco Cristiani, whose male forebears had been tailors for four successive generations and had, without exception, exhibited symptoms of this occupational malady.

2   Although it has never attracted scientific curiosity and therefore cannot be classified by an official name, my father once described it as a form of prolonged melancholia that occasionally erupted into cantankerous fits—the result, my father suggested, of excessive hours of slow, exacting, microscopic work that proceeds stitch by stitch, inch by inch, mesmerizing the tailor in the reflected light of a needle flickering in and out of the fabric.

3   A tailor's eye must follow a seam precisely, but his pattern of thought is free to veer off in different directions, to delve into his life, to ponder his past, to lament lost opportunities, create dramas, imagine slights, brood, exaggerate—in simple terms, the tailor when sewing has too much time in which to think.

4   My father, who served as an apprentice each day before and after school, was aware that certain tailors could sit quietly at the workbench for hours, cradling a garment between their bowed heads and crossed knees and sew without surcease, without exercise or much physical movement, without any surge of fresh oxygen to clear their brains—and *then*, with inexplicable suddenness, my father would see one of these men jump to his feet and take wild umbrage at a casual comment of a coworker, a trivial exchange that was not intended to provoke. And my father would often cower in a corner as spools and steel thimbles flew around the room—and, if goaded on by insensitive colleagues, the aroused tailor might reach for the workroom's favorite instrument of terror, the sword-length scissors.

5   There were also confrontations in the front of the store in which my father worked, disputes between the customers and the proprietor—the diminutive and vain-glorious Francesco Cristiani, who took enormous pride in his occupation and believed that he, and the tailors under his supervision, were incapable of making a serious mistake; or, if they were, he was not likely to acknowledge it.

6   Once when a customer came in to try on a new suit but was unable to slip into the jacket because the sleeves were too narrow, Francesco Cristiani not only failed to apologize to the client but he behaved as if he were insulted by the client's ignorance of the Cristiani shop's unique style in men's fashion. "You are not supposed to put your arms *through* the sleeves of this jacket!" Cristiani informed his client, in a superior tone. "This jacket is only designed to be worn *over the shoulders!*"

7   On another occasion, when Cristiani paused in the town square after lunch to listen to the Maida band during its midday concert, he noticed that the new uniform that had been delivered the day before to the third trumpeter showed a bulge behind the collar whenever the musician lifted the instrument to his lips.

8   Concerned that someone might notice it and cast aspersions on his status as a tailor, Cristiani quickly dispatched my father, then a skinny youth of eight years of age, to sneak up behind the bunting of the bandstand and, with furtive finesse, pull down on the end of the trumpeter's jacket whenever the bulge appeared. After the concert was over, Cristiani contrived a subtle means by which he was able to reacquire and repair the jacket.

9   But around this time, in the spring of 1911, there occurred a catastrophe in the shop for which there seemed to be no possible solution. The problem was so serious, in fact, that Cristiani's first reaction was to leave town for a while rather than remain in Maida to face the consequences. The incident that provoked such panic had taken place in Cristiani's workroom on the Saturday before Easter, and it centered around the damage done by an apprentice, accidentally but irreparably, to a new suit that had been made for one of Cristiani's most demanding customers—a man who was among the region's renowned *uomini rispettati,* men of respect; popularly known as the Mafia.

10   Before Cristiani became aware of the accident, he had enjoyed a prosperous morning in his shop collecting payment from several satisfied customers who had come in for the final try-on of their attire, which they would wear on the following day at the Easter *passeggiata,* the most exhibitionistic event of the year for the modish men of Southern Italy. While the modest women of the village—except for the bolder wives of American immigrants—would spend the day after Mass discreetly perched on their balconies, the men would stroll in the square, chatting with one another as they walked arm in arm, smoking and shiftily examining the fit of each other's new suits.

11   For despite the poverty in Southern Italy, or perhaps because of it, there was excessive emphasis on appearances—it was part of the region's *fare bella figura* syndrome; and most of the men who assembled in the piazza of Maida, and in dozens of similar squares throughout the south, were uncommonly knowledgeable about the art of fine tailoring.

12   They could assess in a few seconds the craft of another man's suit, could appraise each dexterous stitch, could appreciate the mastery of a tailor's most challenging task, the shoulder, from which more than twenty individualized parts of the jacket must hang in harmony and allow for fluidity in motion.

Almost every prideful male, when entering a shop to select fabric for a new suit, knew by heart the twelve principle measurements of his tailored body, starting with the distance between the neckline and the waist of the jacket, and ending with the exact width of the cuffs above the shoes. Among such men were many customers who had been dealing with the Cristiani family firm all of their lives, as had their fathers and grandfathers before them. Indeed, the Cristianis had been making men's clothes in southern Italy since 1804, when the region was controlled by Napoleon Bonaparte; and when Napoleon's brother-in-law, Joachim Murat, who had been installed on the Naples throne in 1808, was assassinated in 1815 by a Spanish Bourbon firing squad in the village of Pizzo, a few miles south of Maida, the wardrobe that Murat left behind included a suit made by Francesco Cristiani's grandfather.

13   But now on this Easter Saturday in 1911, Francesco Cristiani confronted a situation that could not benefit from his family's long tradition in the trade. In his hands he held a new pair of trousers that had an inch-long cut across the left knee, a cut that had been made by an apprentice who had been idling with a pair of scissors atop the table on which the trousers had been laid out for Cristiani's inspection. Although apprentices were repeatedly reminded that they were not to handle the heavy scissors—their main task was to sew on buttons and baste seams—some young men unwittingly violated the rule in their eagerness to gain tailoring experience. But what magnified the youth's delinquency in this situation was that the damaged trousers had been made for a *mafioso*, whose name was Vincenzo Castaglia.

14   A first-time customer from the nearby city of Cosenza, Vincenzo Castaglia was so blatant about his criminal profession that, while being measured for the suit one month before, he had asked Cristiani to allow ample room inside the jacket for the holstered pistol that he wore strapped around his chest. On that same occasion, however, Mr. Castaglia had made several other requests that elevated him in the eyes of his tailor as a man who had a sense of style and knew what might flatter his rather corpulent figure. For example, Mr. Castaglia had requested that the suit's shoulders be cut extra wide so that it would give his hips a more narrow appearance; and he sought to distract attention from his protruding belly by ordering a pleated waistcoat with wide pointed lapels, and also a hole in the center of the waistcoat through which a gold chain could be looped and linked to his diamond pocket-watch.

15   In addition, Mr. Castaglia specified that the hems of his trousers be turned up, in accord with the latest Continental fashion; and, as he peered into Cristiani's workroom in the back, he expressed satisfaction on observing that the tailors were all sewing by hand and not using the popularized sewing machine, which, despite its speedy stitching, lacked the capacity for the special molding and shaping of a fabric's seams and angles that was only possible in the hands of a talented tailor.

16   Bowing with appreciation, the tailor Cristiani had assured Mr. Castaglia that his shop would never succumb to the graceless mechanized invention, even though sewing machines were now widely used by some leading tailors

in Europe and also in America. With the mention of America, Mr. Castaglia smiled and said that he had once visited the New Land, and added that he had several relatives who had settled there. (Among them was a young cousin, Francesco Castaglia, who in future years, beginning in the era of Prohibition, would achieve great notoriety and wealth under the name "Frank Costello.")

17   In the weeks that followed, after Vincenzo Castaglia had placed a down payment on the suit that had been promised for Easter, and had left in a carriage driven by a rifle-bearing coachman, Cristiani devoted much attention to satisfying the *mafioso*'s specifications, and he was finally proud of the sartorial results—until, on Easter Saturday, he discovered under a paper pattern spread out on the table Mr. Castaglia's new pants with an inch-long slash across the left knee.

18   Screaming with anguish and fury, Cristiani soon obtained a confession from an apprentice who admitted to cutting discarded pieces of cloth on the edges of the pattern under which the trousers had been found. Cristiani stood silently, shaken for several minutes, surrounded by his equally concerned and speechless associates. Cristiani could, of course, run and hide in the hills, which had been his first inclination; or he could return the money to the *mafioso* after explaining what had happened, and then offer up the guilty apprentice as a sacrificial lamb to be appropriately dealt with. In this instance, however, there were special inhibiting circumstances. The culpable apprentice was the young nephew of Cristiani's wife, Maria. His wife had been born Maria Talese. She was the only sister of Cristiani's best friend, Gaetano Talese, then working in America. And Gaetano's eight-year-old son, the apprentice Joseph Talese—who would become my father—was now crying convulsively.

19   As Cristiani sought to comfort his remorseful nephew, his mind kept searching for some plausible solution. The trousers were obviously ruined beyond repair. There was no way, in the few hours remaining before Castaglia's visit, to make a second pair of trousers even if they had matching material in stock. Nor was there any way to perfectly obscure the cut in the fabric even with a marvelous job of mending.

20   While his fellow tailors kept insisting that the wisest move was to close the shop and leave a note for Mr. Castaglia pleading illness, or some other excuse that might delay a confrontation, Cristiani firmly reminded them that nothing could absolve him from his failure to deliver the *mafioso*'s suit in time for Easter and that it was mandatory to find a solution now, at once, or at least within the four hours that remained before Mr. Castaglia's expected arrival.

21   As the noon bell rang from the church in the main square, and as all the other stores in Maida began to close for the midday siesta, Cristiani grimly announced: "There will be no siesta for any of us today. This is not the time for food and rest—it is the time for sacrifice and meditation, and for discovering a solution. So I want everybody to stay where you are, and think of something that may save us from disaster . . ."

22   He was interrupted by some grumbling from the other tailors, who resented missing their lunch and afternoon nap; but Cristiani overruled them

with a raised hand, and immediately dispatched one of his apprenticed sons into the village to tell the tailors' wives not to expect the return of their husbands until sundown. Then he instructed the other apprentices, including my father, to pull the draperies across the windows and to lock the shop's front and back doors. And then for the next few minutes, Cristiani's entire staff of a dozen men and boys, as if participating in a wake, quietly congregated within the walls of the darkened shop.

23   My father sat in one corner, still stunned by the magnitude of his misdeed. Near him sat other apprentices, irritated at my father but nonetheless obedient to their master's order that they remain in confinement. In the center of the workroom, seated among his tailors, was Francesco Cristiani, a small wiry man with a tiny mustache, holding his head in his hands and looking up every few seconds to glance again at the trousers that lay before him, as if to remind himself that the knee slash was *real* and would not simply disappear with the next blink of an eye.

24   Several minutes later, however, with a snap of his fingers, Cristiani rose to his feet. Though barely five-feet six-inches tall, his erect carriage, fine styling, and panache lent substance to his presence. There was also a gleam in his eyes now as he looked around the room.

25   "I think I have thought of something," he announced slowly, pausing to let the suspense build until he had everyone's total attention.

26   "What is it?" asked his most senior tailor.

27   "What I can do," Cristiani continued, "is make a cut across the *right* knee that will exactly match the damaged left knee, and . . ."

28   "Are you crazy?" interrupted the older tailor.

29   "Let me finish you imbecile!" Cristiani shouted, pounding his small fist on the table; ". . . and then I can sew up both cuts of the trousers with decorative seams that will match exactly, and later I will explain to Mr. Castaglia that he is the first man in this part of Italy to be wearing trousers designed in the newest fashion, the knee-seamed fashion—the latest rage of Paris, or London, or Vienna, or . . ."

30   As his voice trailed off, the others listened with astonishment.

31   "But, maestro," one of the younger tailors said, in a cautious tone of respect, "won't Mr. Castaglia notice, after you introduce this 'new fashion,' that we tailors ourselves are not wearing trousers that follow this fashion?"

32   Cristiani raised his eyebrows slightly, then slowly began to nod his head.

33   "A good point," he conceded, after a pause, as a pessimistic mood returned to the room. And then again his eyes flashed, and he went on to say: "But we *will* follow the fashion! We will make cuts in *our* knees and then sew them up with seams similar to Mr. Castaglia's . . ." Before the men could protest, he quickly added: "But we will *not* be cutting up our own trousers. We'll use those trousers we keep in the widow's closet!"

34   Immediately everyone turned toward the locked door of a closet in the rear of the workroom, a closet within which were hung dozens of suits last worn by men now dead—suits that bereaving widows, not wishing to be reminded

of their departed spouses, had passed on to Cristiani in the hope that he would give the clothing away to passing strangers who might wear them in distant villages and towns.

35   Now Cristiani was planning to revive the trousers of the dead with his slashed-knee fashion; and while his fellow tailors were initially appalled by the idea, they were soon swayed by the exuberance with which he flung open the closet door, pulled several pairs of trousers off the suit hangers, and tossed them to his tailors, urging a quick try-on. He himself was already standing in his white cotton underwear and black garters, searching for a pair of trousers that might accommodate his slight stature; and when he succeeded, he slipped them on, climbed up on the table, and stood momentarily like a proud model in front of his men. "See," he said, pointing to the length and width, "a perfect fit."

36   As the other tailors began to pick and choose from the wide selection of clothing discarded by the widows, Cristiani was now down from the table, off with the trousers, and, holding a scissor in his hand, carefully beginning to cut across the right knee cap of the *mafioso's* trousers, duplicating the already damaged left knee. Then he applied similar incisions to the knees of the trousers he had chosen to wear himself.

37   "Now, pay close attention," he called out to his men as he sat on a stool in his underwear, with the two pairs of trousers spread before him. With a flourish of his silk-threaded needle, he applied the first stitch into the dead man's trousers, piercing the lower edge of the torn knee with an inner stitch that he adroitly looped to the upper edge—a bold, circular motion that he repeated several times until he had securely reunited the center of the knee with a small, round embroidered wreathlike design half the size of a dime.

38   Then he proceeded to sew, on the right side of the wreath, a half-inch seam that was slightly tapered and tilted upward at the end; and, after reproducing this seam on the left side of the wreath, he had created a minuscule image of a distant bird with spread wings, flying directly toward the viewer; a bird that most resembled a peregrine falcon. Cristiani thus originated a trouser style with wing-tipped knees.

39   "Well, what do you think?" he asked his men who surrounded him, indicating by his offhanded manner that he did not really care what they thought. As they shrugged their shoulders and murmured in the background, he peremptorily continued: "All right now, quickly, cut the knees of those trousers you'll be wearing, and stitch them together with the embroidered design you've just seen." Expecting no opposition, and receiving none, Cristiani then lowered his head to concentrate entirely on his own task: to finish the second knee of the trousers he would wear, and then to begin, meticulously, the job on Mr. Castaglia's trousers.

40   In the latter's case, Cristiani not only planned to embroider a winged design with silk thread that matched exactly the shade of the thread used on the button holes of the jacket of Mr. Castaglia's suit, but he also would insert a section of silk lining within the front part of the trousers, extending from the

thighs to the shins, that would protect Mr. Castaglia's knees from the scratchy feel of the embroidered inner stitching, and would also diminish the friction against the knee seams when Mr. Castaglia was out promenading at the *passeggiata*.

41   For the next two hours, everyone worked in feverish silence. As Cristiani and the other tailors affixed the winged design on the knees of all the trousers, the apprentices helped with the minor alterations, button-sewing, the ironing of cuffs, and other details that would make the dead men's trousers as presentable as possible on the bodies of the tailors. Francesco Cristiani, of course, allowed none but himself to handle the *mafioso*'s garments; and as the church bells rang, signaling the end of the siesta, Cristiani scrutinized with admiration the stitching that he had done, and he privately thanked his namesake in heaven, Saint Francesco di Paola, to whom he had been praying throughout this ordeal, for his inspired guidance with the needle.

42   Now there was the sound of activity in the square: the jingles of horse-drawn wagons, the cries of the food venders, the voices of shoppers passing back and forth along the cobblestone road in front of Cristiani's doorstep. The window draperies of the shop had just been opened, and my father and another apprentice were posted beyond the door with instructions to call in with words of warning as soon as they caught a glimpse of Mr. Castaglia's arriving carriage.

43   Inside, the tailors stood in a row behind Cristiani, famished and fatigued, and hardly comfortable in their dead men's trousers with winged-tipped knees; but their anxiety and fear concerning Mr. Castaglia's forthcoming reaction to his Easter suit dominated their emotions. Cristiani, on the other hand, seemed unusually calm and self-assured. In addition to his newly acquired brown trousers, the cuffs of which touched upon his buttoned shoes with cloth tops, he wore a lapeled gray waistcoat over a striped shirt with a rounded white collar adorned by a burgundy cravat and pearl stickpin. In his hand, on a wooden hanger, he held Mr. Castaglia's three-piece gray herringbone suit that, moments before, he had softly brushed and pressed for the final time. The suit was still warm.

44   At twenty minutes after four, my father came running through the door, and, in a voice that betrayed his panic, he announced: *"Sta arrivando!"*—he's coming. Moments later a black carriage, drawn by two horses, clangorously drew to a halt in front of the shop. After the rifle-toting coachman hopped off to open the door and extend his hand up toward his passenger, the portly dark figure of Vincenzo Castaglia heavily descended the two steps to the sidewalk, followed by a lean man in a wide-brimmed black hat, long cloak, and studded boots, who was his bodyguard.

45   Mr. Castaglia removed his gray fedora and, with a handkerchief, wiped the road dust from his brow. Then he entered the shop, where Cristiani hastened forward to greet him and, holding the new suit high on its hanger, proclaimed: "Your wonderful Easter costume awaits you!" Shaking hands, Mr. Castaglia examined the suit without comment; and then, after politely refusing Cris-

tiani's offer of a bit of whiskey or wine, he directed his bodyguard to help him remove his jacket so that he could immediately try on his Easter apparel.

46   Cristiani and the other tailors stood quietly nearby, watching as the holstered pistol strapped to Castaglia's chest swayed with his movements as he extended his arms and received over his shoulders the gray lapeled waistcoat, followed by the broad-shouldered jacket. Inhaling as he buttoned up his waistcoat and jacket, Mr. Castaglia turned toward the three-sectioned mirror next to the fitting room; and after inspecting and admiring the reflection of himself from every angle, and seeing as well the unblinking eyes of a half-dozen tailors, and then turning toward his bodyguard, who nodded approvingly Mr. Castaglia commented in a commanding voice: *"Perfetto!"*

47   *"Mille grazia,"* responded Cristiani, smiling, and bowing slightly as he carefully removed the trousers from the hanger and handed them to Mr. Castaglia. Excusing himself, Mr. Castaglia walked into the fitting room to try them on. He closed the door. A few of the tailors began to pace around the showroom, but Cristiani stood near the fitting room, whistling softly to himself. The bodyguard, still wearing his cloak and hat, sat comfortably in a chair, his legs crossed, smoking a thin cigar. The apprentices gathered in the back-room, out of sight, except for my nervous father, who remained in the showroom busily arranging and rearranging stacks of material on a counter, while keeping an eye focused on the fitting room.

48   For more than a minute not a word was spoken. The only sounds heard were made by Mr. Castaglia as he changed his trousers. First there was the thump of his shoes dropping to the floor. Then the faint whishing rustle of trouser legs being stepped into. Seconds later, a loud bump against the wooden partition as Mr. Castaglia presumably lost his balance while standing on one leg. After a sigh, a cough, and the creaking sound of shoe leather—more silence. But then, suddenly, a deep voice from behind the door bellowed: *"Maestro!"* Then louder: *"MAESTRO!"*

49   The door bolted open, revealing the glowering face and crouched figure of Mr. Castaglia, his fingers pointing down toward his bent knees and the winged design of the trousers. Waddling toward Cristiani, he yelled: *"Maestro—che aveta fatto aqui?"*—what have you done here?

50   The bodyguard jumped up, scowling at Cristiani. My father closed his eyes. The tailors stepped back. But Francesco Cristiani stood straight and still, remaining impassive even when the bodyguard's hand moved inside his cloak.

51   "What have you done?" Mr. Castaglia repeated, still squatting on bent knees, as if suffering from locked joints. Cristiani watched him for a second or two, still saying nothing; but finally, in the authoritarian tone of a teacher chiding a student, Cristiani responded: "Oh, how disappointed I am in you! How sad and insulted am I by your failure to appreciate the honor I was trying to bestow upon you, because I thought you deserved it—but, sadly, I was wrong . . ."

52   Before the confused Vincenzo Castaglia could open his mouth, and while everyone in the room remained stiffly still, Cristiani continued to talk, while

shaking his head: "You demanded to know what I had done with your trousers—not realizing that what I had done was introduce you to the modern world, which is where I thought you belonged. When you first entered this shop for a fitting last month, you seemed so different from the backward people of this region. So sophisticated. So individualistic. You had traveled to America, you said, had seen the New World, and I assumed that you were in touch with the contemporary spirit of freedom—but I greatly misjudged you . . . New clothes, alas, do not remake the man within . . ."

53   And then, carried away by his own grandiloquence, Cristiani turned toward his senior tailor, who stood closest to him, and he impulsively repeated an old Southern Italian proverb that he regretted uttering immediately after the words had slipped out of his mouth.

54   "Lavar la testa al'asino è acqua persa," Cristiani intoned: Washing a donkey's head is a waste of water.

55   Stunned silence swept through the entire shop. My father cringed behind the counter. Cristiani's tailors, horrified by his provocation, gasped and trembled as they saw Mr. Castaglia's face redden, his eyes narrow—and no one would have been surprised if the next sound were the explosion of a gun. Indeed, Cristiani himself lowered his head and seemed resigned to this fate—but strangely, having now gone too far to turn back, Cristiani wrecklessly repeated his words: "Lavar la testa . . ."—washing a donkey's head is a waste of water.

56   And Mr. Castaglia did not respond! He sputtered, he bit his lips, but he said not a word. Perhaps, having never before experienced such brazenness from anyone, and particularly not from a tiny tailor, Mr. Castaglia was too wonder-struck to act. Even his bodyguard, perplexed by his boss' inactivity, now seemed paralyzed, with his hand still inside his cloak. After a few more seconds of incredible silence, the eyes in Cristiani's lowered head moved tentatively upward, and he saw Mr. Castaglia standing with his shoulders slouched, his head hanging slightly, and a glazed and remorseful look in his eyes. He then looked at Cristiani, and winced. Finally, he spoke. "My late mother would use that expression when I made her angry," Mr. Castaglia confided softly. Then, after a pause, he added, "She died when I was very young . . ."

57   "Oh, I am so sorry," Cristiani said, as the tension subsided in the room, but everyone remained in their positions as he continued: "I do hope, however, that you will accept my word that we *did* try to make you a beautiful suit for Easter. I was just so disappointed that your trousers, which are designed in the latest fashion, did not appeal to you."

58   Looking down once again at the knees, Mr. Castaglia asked: "*This* is the latest fashion?"

59   "Yes, indeed," Cristiani reassured him.
60   "Where?"
61   "In the great capitals of the world."
62   "But not here?"

63   "Not yet," Cristiani said. "You are the first among the men of this region."
64   "But why does the latest fashion in this region have to begin with me?" Mr. Castaglia asked, in a voice that had lost its power and now seemed uncertain, defensive.
65   "Oh, no, it has not really begun with you," Cristiani quickly corrected him. "We tailors have *already* adopted this fashion." And holding up one of his trouser knees, he said: "See for yourself."
66   Mr. Castaglia looked down to examine Cristiani's knees; and then, as he turned to survey the entire room, he saw the other tailors, one after another, each lift a leg and, nodding, point to the now familiar wings of the approaching infinitesimal bird.
67   "I see," Mr. Castaglia said, his demeanor once again firm and confident. "And I see that I also owe you my apologies, maestro," he went on. "Sometimes it takes a while for a man to appreciate what is fashionable."
68   Then after shaking Cristiani's hand, and settling the financial account—but seemingly not wanting to linger a moment longer in this place where his uncertainty had been exposed—Mr. Castaglia summoned his obedient and speechless bodyguard, and handed him his old suit; and wearing his new suit, and tipping his hat, Mr. Castaglia headed toward his carriage through the door that had been pulled wide open by my father. ❖

Questions to Ponder

1. What sources do you think Gay Talese tapped to get and verify this story? (Cite specific details that suggest certain kinds of research.)
2. Why do you think Talese chooses to tell about the ill-fitting band jacket and the jacket with too-narrow sleeves before he gets to his major story involving the Italian *mafioso*? What does he gain by doing this?
3. Do the phrases and sentences in Italian strengthen or weaken this piece?
4. Was the tailor wrong to do what he did? Why do we find this story funny?

Writing Possibilities

1. Interview a family member about major crises, turning points, or adventures in his or her life. Choose one specific incident and, using Gay Talese's "Tailors of Maida" as a model, research it deeply in order to be able to narrate the moment in rich and vivid detail.
2. Read (and conduct interviews, if possible) about the founding of your college. Now try to narrate that founding, perhaps using an abstract, philosophical, or psychological generalization for the opening, as Talese does in "The Tailors of Maida." Upon completion, give your work to your library's archives.

3. Read in your town's histories and old newspapers (and conduct interviews) about the response of your town to women's suffrage (women getting the vote). How did the women and the men, and the town's political, religious, and social leaders respond? Report your findings in an article for your town newspaper or for your city's historical society.

BEING THERE: ANTHROPOLOGY AND THE SCENE OF WRITING

Clifford Geertz

First chapters are often written after the chapters to which they are introductions. Such was the case with "Being There," which was put together after the substantive essays on various anthropological writers which formed the body of my book [Works and Lives: The Anthropologist as Author] were completed. It was, therefore, a matter of saying more generally what I had already said more particularly; making explicit the animating ideas implicit in the concrete analyses. In one way, this is easy, for presumably one knows what one has said. In another, it is very difficult, for it involves articulating notions very hard to separate from their embodiment in specific texts—a bit like trying to describe how one rides a bicycle. It also can be chastening, when one discovers ambiguities and contradictions in essentially finished work. You can make a few corrections, but in general you have merely to live with the sense that there is inevitably a gap between what you wish you had written and what, in fact, you actually have. The only cure for this is never to write first chapters.

Brief Warm-up Writing Exercises

1. Choose a region of the United States or Canada and place it in a circle in the center of a piece of paper. Now brainstorm a list of descriptors of the people; the terrain; the agricultural, business, and cultural products; and any other categories you can think of relevant to the region.

2. If you have ever visited a foreign country or a different culture, freewrite what the experience was like for you.
3. Pretend you are going to write a report about the people of a different culture. Make a list on the left-hand side of a sheet of paper of the kinds of information you think would be vital to include. When you finish, on the right-hand side write *where* or *how* you would find each kind of information.

---

1 ❖ The illusion that ethnography is a matter of sorting strange and irregular facts into familiar and orderly categories—this is magic, that is technology—has long since been exploded. What it is instead, however, is less clear. That it might be a kind of writing, putting things to paper, has now and then occurred to those engaged in producing it, consuming it, or both. But the examination of it as such has been impeded by several considerations, none of them very reasonable.

2   One of these, especially weighty among the producers, has been simply that it is an unanthropological sort of thing to do. What a proper ethnographer ought properly to be doing is going out to places, coming back with information about how people live there, and making that information available to the professional community in practical form, not lounging about in libraries reflecting on literary questions. Excessive concern, which in practice usually means any concern at all, with how ethnographic texts are constructed seems like an unhealthy self-absorption—timewasting at best, hypochondriacal at worst. What we want to know about is the Tikopians and the Tallensi, not the narrative strategies of Raymond Firth or the rhetorical machinery of Meyer Fortes.

3   Another objection, here coming mostly from the consumer side, is that anthropological texts are not worth such delicate attention. It is one thing to investigate how a Conrad, a Flaubert, or even a Balzac, gets his effects; to engage in such an enterprise for a Lowie or a Radcliffe-Brown, to speak only of the dead, seems comic. A few anthropologists—Sapir, Benedict, Malinowski, and these days Lévi-Strauss—may be recognized as having a distinctive literary style, and not being above an occasional trope. But that is unusual and somewhat to their disadvantage—suggestive even of sharp practice. Good anthropological texts are plain texts, unpretending. They neither invite literary-critical close reading nor reward it.

4   But perhaps the most intense objection, coming from all quarters, and indeed rather general to intellectual life these days, is that concentrating our gaze on the ways in which knowledge claims are advanced undermines our capacity to take any of those claims seriously. Somehow, attention to such matters as imagery, metaphor, phraseology, or voice is supposed to lead to a corrosive relativism in which everything is but a more or less clever expression of opinion. Ethnography becomes, it is said, a mere game of words, as

poems and novels are supposed to be. Exposing how the thing is done is to suggest that, like the lady sawed in half, it isn't done at all.

5 These views are unreasonable, because they are not based on the experience of threats present and actual, or even looming, but on the imagining of possible ones that might occur were everything to be suddenly otherwise than it now is. If anthropologists were to stop reporting how things are done in Africa and Polynesia, if they were instead to spend their time trying to find double plots in Alfred Kroeber or unreliable narrators in Max Gluckman, and if they were seriously to argue that Edward Westermarck's stories about Morocco and those of Paul Bowles relate to their subject in the same way, with the same means and the same purposes, matters would indeed be in a parlous state.

6 But that all this would be brought on if anthropological writing were taken seriously as writing is hard to credit. The roots of fear must lie elsewhere: in the sense, perhaps, that should the literary character of anthropology be better understood, some professional myths about how it manages to persuade would be impossible to maintain. In particular, it might be difficult to defend the view that ethnographic texts convince, insofar as they do convince, through the sheer power of their factual substantiality. The marshaling of a very large number of highly specific cultural details has been the major way in which the look of truth—verisimilitude, *vraisemblance, Wahrscheinlichkeit*—has been sought in such texts. Whatever doubts the oddness of the material induces in the reader are to be overcome by its sheer abundance. Yet the fact is that the degree of credence, whether high, low, or otherwise, actually given to Malinowski's, Lévi-Strauss's, or anybody else's ethnography does not rest, at least not primarily, on such a basis. If it did, J. G. Frazer, or anyway Oscar Lewis, would indeed be king, and the suspension of disbelief many people (myself included) accord to Edmund Leach's data-poor *Political Systems of Highland Burma,* or Margaret Mead's impressionistic essay, *Balinese Character,* would be inexplicable. Ethnographers may indeed think they are believed for the extensiveness of their descriptions. (Leach attempted to answer the empiricist attacks on his Burma book by writing a fact-crammed one on Sri Lanka, but it has been far less attended to. Mead argued that Gregory Bateson's hundreds of photographs demonstrated her arguments, but hardly anyone, including Bateson, much agreed with her.) Perhaps ethnographers should be believed for the extensiveness of their descriptions, but that does not seem to be the way it works.

7 Just why the idea persists that it does so work is difficult to say. Perhaps old-fashioned notions about how "findings" are "established" in the harder sciences has something to do with it. In any case, the main alternative to this sort of factualist theory of how anthropological works convince, namely that they do so through the force of their theoretical arguments, is no more plausible. Malinowski's theoretical apparatus, once a proud tower indeed, lies largely in ruins, but he remains the ethnographer's ethnographer. The rather passé quality that Mead's psychological, culture-and-personality speculations

now seem to have (*Balinese Character* was supported by a grant for the study of dementia praecox, which the Balinese were supposed to display in a walking-around form) doesn't seem to detract very much from the cogency of her observations, unmatched by any of the rest of us, concerning what the Balinese are like. Some, at least, of Lévi-Strauss's work will survive the dissolution of structuralism into its all-too-eager successors. People will read *The Nuer* even if, as it has tended to, segmentary theory hardens into a dogma.

8   The ability of anthropologists to get us to take what they say seriously has less to do with either a factual look or an air of conceptual elegance than it has with their capacity to convince us that what they say is a result of their having actually penetrated (or, if you prefer, been penetrated by) another form of life, of having, one way or another, truly "been there." And that, persuading us that this offstage miracle has occurred, is where the writing comes in.

9   The crucial peculiarities of ethnographic writing are, like the purloined letter, so fully in view as to escape notice: the fact, for example, that so much of it consists in incorrigible assertion. The highly situated nature of ethnographic description—this ethnographer, in this time, in this place, with these informants, these commitments, and these experiences, a representative of a particular culture, a member of a certain class—gives to the bulk of what is said a rather take-it-or-leave-it quality. "Vas you dere, Sharlie?" as Jack Pearl's Baron Munchausen used to say.

10   Even if, as is now increasingly the case, others are working in the same area or on the same group, so that at least some general checking is possible, it is very difficult to disprove what someone not transparently uninformed has said. One can go look at Azande again, but if the complex theory of passion, knowledge, and causation that Evans-Pritchard said he discovered there isn't found, we are more likely to doubt our own powers than we are to doubt his—or perhaps simply to conclude that the Zande are no longer themselves. Whatever the state of thinking about the nature of *kula* exchange may or may not be at the moment, and it is rapidly changing, the picture of it given in *Argonauts of the Western Pacific* remains for all practical purposes ineffaceable. Those who would like to lessen its force must contrive somehow to shift our attention to other pictures. Even in the case of what in most other sorts of empirical study would be taken to be direct contradiction (Robert Redfield and Oscar Lewis on Tepotzlan, for example), the tendency, when both scholars are reputable, is to regard the problem as stemming from different sorts of minds taking hold of different parts of the elephant—a third opinion would but add to the embarrassment. It is not that everything ethnographers say is accepted once and for all simply because they say it. A very great deal, thank God, is not. It is that the grounds upon which it is or it isn't accepted are extremely person-specific. Unable to recover the immediacies of field work for empirical reinspection, we listen to some voices and ignore others.

11   This would be rather a scandal if we listened to some and not to others—the matter is relative, of course—out of whim, habit, or (a favored account

nowadays) prejudice or political desire. But if we do so because some ethnographers are more effective than others in conveying in their prose the impression that they have had close-in contact with far-out lives, the matter may be less desperate. In discovering how, in this monograph or that article, such an impression is created, we shall discover, at the same time, the criteria by which to judge them. As the criticism of fiction and poetry grows best out of an imaginative engagement with fiction and poetry themselves, not out of imported notions about what they should be, the criticism of anthropological writing (which is in a strict sense neither, and in a broad one both) ought to grow out of a similar engagement with *it*, not out of preconceptions of what it must look like to qualify as a science.

12   Given the person-specific (*not* "personal") nature of our judgments in these matters, the obvious place to begin such an engagement is with the question of what, in anthropology, an "author" is. It may be that in other realms of discourse the author (along with man, history, the self, God, and other middle-class appurtenances) is in the process of dying; but he . . . she . . . is still very much alive among anthropologists. In our ingenuous discipline, perhaps as usual an episteme behind, it still very much matters who speaks.

13   I make these irreverent allusions to Michel Foucault's famous article, "What Is an Author?" (which in fact I agree with, save for its premises, its conclusions, and its cast of mind), because, whatever one thinks of a world in which all forms of discourse would be reduced to "the anonymity of a murmur" in the interests of the dispersion of power, or of the notion that Mallarmé marks a decisive rupture in the history of literature, after which the notion of a literary work is steadily displaced by one of textual modes of domination, it does locate the question I am posing with some exactness. Foucault distinguishes there, perhaps a bit too sharply, between two realms of discourse: those, most especially fiction (though history, biography, philosophy, and poetry as well), in which what he calls the "author-function" remains, for the moment anyway, reasonably strong; and those, especially science (but also private letters, legal contracts, political broadsides), in which, for the most part, it does not. This is not a constant matter, even within our own tradition: in the Middle Ages, most tales—the *Chanson de Roland*—had no authors; most scientific treatises—the *Almagest*—had them. But

> a reversal occurred in the seventeenth or eighteenth century. Scientific discourses began to be received for themselves, in the anonymity of an established or always redemonstrable truth; their membership in a systematic ensemble, and not the reference to the individual who produced them, stood as their guarantee. The author-function faded away, and the inventor's name served only to christen a theorem, a proposition, particular effect, property, body, group of elements, or pathological syndrome. By the same token, literary discourses came to be accepted only when endowed with the author-function. We now ask of each poetic or fictional text: from where does it come, who wrote it, when, under what circumstances, or beginning with what design? The

> meaning ascribed to it and the status or value accorded it depend upon the manner in which we answer these questions. . . . As a result, the author-function today plays an important [though, again, in Foucault's view, decreasing] role in our view of literary works.[1]

14   It is clear that, in these terms, anthropology is pretty much entirely on the side of "literary" discourses rather than "scientific" ones. Personal names are attached to books and articles, more occasionally to systems of thought ("Radcliffe-Brownian Functionalism"; "Lévi-Straussian Structuralism"). They are not, with very few exceptions, connected to findings, properties, or propositions ("a Murdock Marriage" is a polemical joke; "the Westermarck Effect"—its reality aside—might just qualify). This does not make us into novelists any more than constructing hypotheses or writing formulas makes us, as some seem to think, into physicists. But it does suggest some family resemblances that we tend, like the North African mule who talks always of his mother's brother, the horse, but never of his father, the donkey, to suppress in favor of others, supposedly more reputable.

15   If, then, we admit that ethnographies tend to look at least as much like romances as they do like lab reports (though, as with our mule, not really like either), two questions, or perhaps the same one doubly asked, immediately pose themselves: (1) How is the "author-function" (or shall we, so long as we are going to be literary about the matter, just say "the author"?) made manifest in the text? (2) Just what is it—beyond the obvious tautology, "a work"—that the author authors? The first question, call it that of signature, is a matter of the construction of a writerly identity. The second, call it that of discourse, is a matter of developing a way of putting things—a vocabulary, a rhetoric, a pattern of argument—that is connected to that identity in such a way that it seems to come from it as a remark from a mind.

16   The question of signature, the establishment of an authorial presence within a text, has haunted ethnography from very early on, though for the most part it has done so in a disguised form. Disguised, because it has been generally cast not as a narratological issue, a matter of how best to get an honest story honestly told, but as an epistemological one, a matter of how to prevent subjective views from coloring objective facts. The clash between the expository conventions of author-saturated texts and those of author-evacuated ones that grows out of the particular nature of the ethnographic enterprise is imagined to be a clash between seeing things as one would have them and seeing them as they really are.

17   A number of unfortunate results have arisen from this burial of the question of how ethnographical texts are "author-ized" beneath anxieties (to my mind, rather exaggerated anxieties) about subjectivity. Among them is an

---

[1]M. Foucault, "What Is an Author?" in J. V. Harari, ed., *Textual Strategies* (Ithaca, N.Y., 1979), pp. 149–50.

empiricism extreme even for the social sciences; but one of the more mischievous has been that although the ambiguities implicit in that question have been deeply and continuously felt, it has been extremely difficult to address them directly. Anthropologists are possessed of the idea that the central methodological issues involved in ethnographic description have to do with the mechanics of knowledge—the legitimacy of "empathy," "insight," and the like as forms of cognition; the verifiability of internalist accounts of other peoples' thoughts and feelings; the ontological status of culture. Accordingly, they have traced their difficulties in constructing such descriptions to the problematics of field work rather than to those of discourse. If the relation between observer and observed (rapport) can be managed, the relation between author and text (signature) will follow—it is thought—of itself.

18 It is not merely that this is untrue, that no matter how delicate a matter facing the other might be it is not the same sort of thing as facing the page. The difficulty is that the oddity of constructing texts ostensibly scientific out of experiences broadly biographical, which is after all what ethnographers do, is thoroughly obscured. The signature issue, as the ethnographer confronts it, or as it confronts the ethnographer, demands both the Olympianism of the unauthorial physicist and the sovereign consciousness of the hyperauthorial novelist, while not in fact permitting either. The first brings charges of insensitivity, of treating people as objects, of hearing the words but not the music, and, of course, of ethnocentrism. The second brings charges of impressionism, of treating people as puppets, of hearing music that doesn't exist, and, of course, of ethnocentrism. Small wonder that most ethnographers tend to oscillate uncertainly between the two, sometimes in different books, more often in the same one. Finding somewhere to stand in a text that is supposed to be at one and the same time an intimate view and a cool assessment is almost as much of a challenge as gaining the view and making the assessment in the first place.

19 A sense for this challenge—how to sound like a pilgrim and a cartographer at the same time—and for the uneasiness it produces, as well as for the degree to which it is represented as arising from the complexities of self/other negotiations rather than those of self/text ones, is of course only to be gained from looking at ethnographies themselves. And, since the challenge and the uneasiness are obviously felt from the jacket flap on, a good place to look in looking at ethnographies is at beginnings—at the scene-setting, task-describing, self-presenting opening pages. So let me take, then, to indicate more clearly what I am talking about, two examples, one from a classic ethnography deservedly regarded as a model study, calm and magisterial, and one from a quite recent one, also very well done, that breathes the air of the nervous present.

20 The classic work is Raymond Firth's *We, the Tikopia*, first published in 1936. After two introductions, one by Malinowski, which says Firth's book "strengthens our conviction that cultural anthropology need not be a jumble of slogans or labels, a factory of impressionistic short-cuts, or guesswork

reconstructions [but rather] a social science—I almost feel tempted to say, the science among social studies," and one by Firth, which stresses the necessity of "lengthy personal contact with the people [one studies]" and apologizes for the fact that "this account represents not the field-work of yesterday but that of seven years ago," the book itself begins its first chapter, "In Primitive Polynesia":

> In the cool of the early morning, just before sunrise, the bow of the Southern Cross headed towards the eastern horizon, on which a tiny dark blue outline was faintly visible. Slowly it grew into a rugged mountain mass, standing up sheer from the ocean; then as we approached within a few miles it revealed around its base a narrow ring of low, flat land, thick with vegetation. The sullen grey day with its lowering clouds strengthened my grim impression of a solitary peak, wild and stormy, upthrust in a waste of waters.
>
> In an hour or so we were close inshore and could see canoes coming round from the south, outside the reef, on which the tide was low. The outrigger-fitted craft drew near, the men in them bare to the waist, girdled with bark-cloth, large fans stuck in the backs of their belts, tortoise-shell rings or rolls of leaf in the earlobes and nose, bearded, and with long hair flowing loosely over their shoulders. Some plied the rough heavy paddles, some had finely plaited pandanus-leaf mats resting on the thwarts beside them, some had large clubs or spears in their hands. The ship anchored on a short cable in the open bay off the coral reef. Almost before the chain was down the natives began to scramble aboard, coming over the side by any means that offered, shouting fiercely to each other and to us in a tongue of which not a word was understood by the Mota-speaking folk of the mission vessel. I wondered how such turbulent human material could ever be induced to submit to scientific study.
>
> Vahihaloa, my "boy," looked over the side from the upper deck, "My word, me fright too much," he said with a quavering laugh; "me tink this fella man he savvy kaikai me." Kaikai is the pidgin-English term for "eat." For the first time, perhaps, he began to doubt the wisdom of having left what was to him the civilization of Tulagi, the seat of Government four hundred miles away, in order to stay with me for a year in this far-off spot among such wild-looking savages. Feeling none too certain myself of the reception that awaited us— though I knew that it would stop short of cannibalism—I reassured him, and we began to get out the stores. Later we went ashore in one of the canoes. As we came to the edge of the reef our craft halted on account of the falling tide. We slipped overboard on to the coral rock and began to wade ashore hand in hand with our hosts, like children at a party, exchanging smiles in lieu of anything more intelligible or tangible at the moment. We were surrounded by crowds of naked chattering youngsters, with their pleasant light-brown velvet skins and straight hair, so different from the Melanesians we had left behind. They darted about splashing like a shoal of fish, some of them falling bodily into pools in their enthusiasm. At last the long wade ended, we climbed up the

> steeply shelving beach, crossed the soft, dry sand strewn with the brown needles of the Casuarina trees—a home-like touch; it was like a pine avenue—and were led to an old chief, clad with great dignity in a white coat and a loin-cloth, who awaited us on his stool under a large shady tree.[2]

21 There can be little doubt from this that Firth was, in every sense of the word, "there." All the fine detail, marshaled with Dickensian exuberance and Conradian fatality—the blue mass, lowering clouds, excited jabberings, velvet skins, shelved beach, needle carpet, enstooled chief—conduce to a conviction that what follows, five hundred pages of resolutely objectified description of social customs—the Tikopia do this, the Tikopia believe that—can be taken as fact. Firth's anxieties about inducing "such turbulent human material . . . to admit to scientific study" turned out to be as overdrawn as those of his "boy" that he would be eaten.

22 But they also never quite disappeared. The "this happened to me" accents reappear periodically; the text is nervously signed and re-signed throughout. To its last line, Firth struggles with his relation to what he has written, still seeing it in field-method terms. "The greatest need," that last line goes, "in the social sciences to-day is for a more refined methodology, as objective and dispassionate as possible, in which, while the assumptions due to the conditioning and personal interest of the investigator must influence his findings, that bias shall be consciously faced, the possibility of other initial assumptions be realized and allowance be made for the implications of each in the course of the analysis" (p. 488). At deeper levels his anxieties and those of his "boy" may not in fact have been so entirely different. "I give this somewhat egoistic recital," he writes apologetically after reviewing his field techniques, his language abilities, his mode of life on the island, and so forth, "not because I think that anthropology should be made light reading . . . but because some account of the relations of the anthropologist to his people is relevant to the nature of his results. It is an index to their social digestion—some folk cannot stomach an outsider, others absorb him easily" (p.11).

23 The recent text whose opening pages I want to instance as displaying the authorial uneasiness that arises from having to produce scientific texts from biographical experiences is *The Death Rituals of Rural Greece*, by a young ethnographer, Loring Danforth. Like many of his generation, weaned on *Positivismuskritik* and anti-colonialism, Danforth seems more concerned that he will swallow his subjects than that they will swallow him, but the problem is still seen to be essentially epistemological. I quote, with a good deal of ellipsis, from his introduction, called "Self and Other":

---

[2]R. Firth, *We, the Tikopia* (London, 1936), pp. 1–2. For a contextualization of this passage in "travel writing," see now M. L. Pratt, "Fieldwork in Common Places," in J. Clifford and G. E. Marcus, eds., *Writing Culture: The Poetics and Politics of Ethnography* (Berkeley, Calif., 1986), pp. 35–37.

Anthropology inevitably involves an encounter with the Other. All too often, however, the ethnographic distance that separates the reader of anthropological texts and the anthropologist himself from the Other is rigidly maintained and at times even artificially exaggerated. In many cases this distancing leads to an exclusive focus on the Other as primitive, bizarre, and exotic. The gap between a familiar "we" and an exotic "they" is a major obstacle to a meaningful understanding of the Other, an obstacle that can only be overcome through some form of participation in the world of the Other.

The maintenance of this ethnographic distance has resulted in . . . the parochialization or the folklorization of the anthropological inquiry into death. Rather than confronting the universal significance of death, anthropologists have often trivialized death by concerning themselves with the exotic, curious, and at times violent ritual practices that accompany death in many societies. . . . If, however, it is possible to reduce the distance between the anthropologist and the Other, to bridge the gap between "us" and "them," then the goal of a truly humanistic anthropology can be achieved. . . . [This] desire to collapse the distance between Self and Other which prompted [my] adoption of this [approach] springs from my fieldwork. Whenever I observed death rituals in rural Greece, I was acutely aware of a paradoxical sense of simultaneous distance and closeness, otherness and oneness. . . . To my eyes funeral laments, black mourning dress, and exhumation rites were exotic. Yet . . . I was conscious at all times that it is not just Others who die. I was aware that my friends and relatives will die, that I will die, that death comes to all, Self and Other alike.

Over the course of my fieldwork these "exotic" rites became meaningful, even attractive alternatives to the experience of death as I had known it. As I sat by the body of a man who had died several hours earlier and listened to his wife, his sisters, and his daughters lament his death, I imagined these rites being performed and these laments being sung at the death of my relatives, at my own death. . . . When the brother of the deceased entered the room, the women . . . began to sing a lament about two brothers who were violently separated as they sat clinging to each other in the branches of a tree that was being swept away by a raging torrent. I thought of my own brother and cried. The distance between Self and Other had grown small indeed.[3]

---

[3] L. Danforth, *The Death Rituals of Rural Greece* (Princeton, N.J., 1982), pp. 5–7. For a similar modern or post-modern complaint about "the anthropology of death," growing out of a personal experience, the accidental death of his wife, in the field, see R. Rosaldo, "Grief and a Headhunter's Rage: On the Cultural Force of Emotions," in E. Bruner, ed., *Text, Play, and Story, 1983 Proceedings of the American Ethnological Society* (Washington, D.C., 1984), pp. 178–95. "[In] most anthropological studies of death, analysts simply eliminate the emotions by assuming the position of the most detached observer. Their stance also equates the ritual with the obligatory, ignores the relation between ritual and everyday life, and conflates the ritual process with the process of mourning. The general rule . . . seems to be that one should tidy things up as much as possible by wiping away the tears and ignoring the tantrums" (p. 189).

24   There are of course great differences in these two scene-settings and self-locatings: one a realistic novel model (Trollope in the South Seas), the other a philosophical meditation model (Heidegger in Greece); one a scientistic worry about being insufficiently detached, the other a humanistic worry about being insufficiently engaged. Rhetorical expansiveness in 1936, rhetorical earnestness in 1982. But there are even greater similarities, all of them deriving from a common *topos*—the delicate but successful establishment of a familiar sensibility, much like our own, in an intriguing but unfamiliar place, not at all like our own. Firth's coming-into-the-country drama ends with his encounter, a royal audience almost, with the chief. After that, one knows they will come to understand one another, all will be well. Danforth's haunted reflections on Otherness end with his echoic mourning, more fantasy than empathy. After that, one knows the gap will be bridged, communion is at hand. Ethnographers need to convince us (as these two quite effectively do) not merely that they themselves have truly "been there," but (as they also do, if rather less obviously) that had we been there we should have seen what they saw, felt what they felt, concluded what they concluded.

25   Not all ethnographies, not most even, begin by grasping the horns of the signature dilemma in so emphatic a manner as do these. Most attempt rather to keep it at bay, either by starting off with extended and often enough (given what follows) overly detailed descriptions of the natural environment, population, and the like, or by extended theoretical discussions not again very much referred to. Explicit representations of authorial presence tend to be relegated, like other embarrassments, to prefaces, notes, or appendixes.

26   But the issue always appears, however resisted, however disguised. "The traveller in West Africa," Meyer Fortes writes on the first page of his Tallensi study (perhaps the most thoroughly objectivized of the great ethnographies—it reads like a law text written by a botanist) "who enters this region from the south is impressed by the contrast with the forest belt. According to his predilections he will view it with pleasure or dismay after the massive and gigantic gloom of the forest."[4] There is no doubt who that "traveller" is or whose ambivalences these are, or that we shall be hearing this note, just about this muffled, again. "Highway 61 stretches across two hundred miles of rich black land known as the Mississippi Delta," begins William Ferris's fine book of a few years ago on Black musicians in the rural south, *Blues from the Delta*, "where mile-long rows of cotton and soybeans spread out from its pavement and surround occasional towns such as Lula, Alligator, Panther Burn, Nitta Yuma, Anguilla, Arcola, and Onward."[5] It is quite clear (even if one does not know that Ferris was born in the Delta) who has been movin' down that highway.

27   Getting themselves into their text (that is, representationally into their text) may be as difficult for ethnographers as getting themselves into the

---

[4]M. Fortes, *The Dynamics of Clanship Among the Tallensi* (London, 1967), p.1.

[5]W. Ferris, *Blues from the Delta* (Garden City, N.Y., 1979), p. 1.

culture (that is, imaginatively into the culture). For some, it may be even more difficult (Gregory Bateson, whose eccentric classic, *Naven*, seems to consist mostly of false starts and second thoughts—preamble upon preamble, epilogue upon epilogue—comes to mind). But in one way or another, however unreflectively and with whatever misgivings about the propriety of it all, ethnographers all manage nevertheless to do it. There are some very dull books in anthropology, but few if any anonymous murmurs. . . .

28   "Being There" authorially, palpably on the page, is in any case as difficult a trick to bring off as "being there" personally, which after all demands at the minimum hardly more than a travel booking and permission to land; a willingness to endure a certain amount of loneliness, invasion of privacy, and physical discomfort; a relaxed way with odd growths and unexplained fevers; a capacity to stand still for artistic insults, and the sort of patience that can support an endless search for invisible needles in infinite haystacks. And the authorial sort of being there is getting more difficult all the time. The advantage of shifting at least part of our attention from the fascinations of field work, which have held us so long in thrall, to those of writing is not only that this difficulty will become more clearly understood, but also that we shall learn to read with a more percipient eye. A hundred and fifteen years (if we date our profession, as conventionally, from Tylor) of asseverational prose and literary innocence is long enough. ❖

Questions to Ponder

1. What are the challenges of doing on-site, "being there" research? What are the challenges of writing up research gathered in the field, that is, "being there" in the writing? Which kind of "being there" is easier for you?
2. What leads Clifford Geertz to suggest that researchers and writers in fields outside of English tend to pay little attention to the writing side of their work? How would this inattention affect the quality of their work?
3. In what way is the writer present in an essay even when it is written in third person?

Writing Possibilities

1. Compare and contrast the two excerpts Clifford Geertz presents of 1936 and 1986 anthropological writing. Describe the strengths and limitations of each. Which do you prefer? Why?
2. Take the map you created in warm-up exercise 1 (about a region of the United States or Canada) and, pretending you are an anthropologist, write

a brief study of the people and culture of your region. (You will probably want to do some library research as well as some interviewing to gather information for this piece.)

3. Select a specific "subculture" in your college or town and write an essay describing how you would go about researching and studying this subculture. After you have written this essay, follow your plan, do the research, and share your findings in a letter to your school newspaper or a report to the Dean of Students or your town's historical society.

Student Essay

EMPLOYEE STOCK OWNERSHIP PLANS: NEW PLAYERS IN THE LEVERAGED BUYOUT GAME

Jon Shepherd

This essay was originally written for an undergraduate course in labor economics. It was later selected to be printed in a student-run publication and went through a seemingly endless process of review and revision. However, this process turned a relatively weak essay into one that I believe is much stronger and more defined than the original.

I have found that the biggest problem, at least to me, is researching the topic on which I have chosen to focus. I tend to believe that a well-researched essay will basically write itself. One must be discriminating in choosing what information actually to include in the essay in order to write well. A well-written essay will include only that information which is relevant to the subject at hand. This is not to say, though, that the information dispensed in the essay does not have to be interesting to the reader, because it does. If the essay is not interesting, it does not matter whether it is well written because no one will read it.

After completing and organizing my research notes, I usually try to reserve an entire day that I can spend on writing a certain portion of the essay. By doing this, I avoid having to interrupt an idea, paragraph, or section in order to go do something else. I feel this allows for greater continuity and organization in my writing.

A writer who desires to write well should not be afraid of asking other people for their opinions on the essay. I have found that suggestions from friends are the most valuable tools I have when writing. Even though I greatly dislike having my writing criticized by others, it is still better to get input on ways to improve an essay during the drafting process than to be completely finished and realize that a major point that was made or a major issue that was discussed is unclear in the readers' minds. After all, I am writing the essay for an audience other than myself. The best way to determine if the people in that audience are able to understand and comprehend the material in the essay is to ask them. If an item is unclear, I then have the opportunity to correct the essay before it is finished.

This essay was the first in which I was involved in a group that was critiquing an essay. I found this to be even more useful than having people critique an essay one at a time. It seems that each person in the group would use another's suggestion on how to make the essay better and use that idea to make an even better suggestion. Based on my experiences, writing in groups is the best way to write a well-organized and interesting essay.

Brief Warm-up Writing Exercises

1. Pretend you are the owner of a major corporation. Brainstorm two lists: the *pros* and *cons* of allowing your employees to buy stock in your corporation.
2. Describe the kind of savings-and-investment plan you think the average college student should follow.
3. Brainstorm a list of sources you would tap to find financial information or information on economics.

DRAFT

1   Hostile takeover. Leveraged buyout. Almost every company chief executive hates to hear those two terms and tries to guard against his company becoming the object of an unwanted suitor. Lately, some major companies have been taking steps to protect themselves against a buyout offer, and one of the most popular defense maneuvers has been instituting employee stock ownership plans. But what are the advantages of an ESOP, and will one protect a company from a

leveraged buyout? And can an ESOP backfire and actually cause a company to be taken over?

2   Companies originally began using employee stock ownership plans in order to help motivate their employees. ESOPs lower costs for a company by allowing it to obtain special tax advantages, improve the employees' retirement security, and make employees more productive and efficient (Hammonds, 1989). Surveys by the U.S. General Accounting Office and the National Center for Employee Ownership have shown companies that begin ESOPs, share information with the employee-owners, and involve the employee-owners in participative decision-making are more profitable and more efficient than those ESOP companies which don't involve employees (Taplin, August, 1988). A survey of 400 companies by The ESOP Association found that 71% of the respondents believed their ESOP improved productivity. The same survey also showed that over one-half of those companies started their ESOPs since 1984 (Taplin, December, 1988). Loans to ESOPs skyrocketed from 1.2 billion dollars in 1986 to 5.5 billion dollars in 1987 (Employee Benefit Plan Reviews, July, 1988). This huge increase must be attributable to more factors than companies trying to boost productivity.

3   Employee stock ownership plans also strengthen companies against corporate raiders. This occurs because, in most tender offers, employees would vote their ESOP shares in favor of existing management, or because the simple presence of an ESOP would scare off any possible buyers. The best known example of this happening is Shamrock Holdings attempted takeover of Polaroid, which ended earlier this year. Polaroid enlarged its ESOP to cover 14% of its outstanding shares in order to fend off Shamrock's bid for the company. Shamrock, not giving up, sued Polaroid in the Delaware court system to block this action. The Delaware Chancery Court judge turned down Shamrock's challenge, ruling that Polaroid's ESOP was completely legal as it was in its place before the hostile bid and also because Polaroid's employees could vote their shares in confidence during a tender offer (Hammonds, 1989). This decision, as Malon Wilkus, president of an investment

banking firm which specializes in leveraged ESOPs, said "has gone much further then Congress ever would to solve the problem of hostile takeovers" in the U.S. (Hammonds, 1989). Polaroid's court victory has inspired many other companies to adopt ESOPs as a takeover defense. The Tribune Company and Lockheed Corporations recently instituted ESOPs to discourage potential purchasers; J.C. Penney borrowed 700 million dollars to buy stock through their ESOP as a defense against a rumored raider, and Proctor and Gamble's ESOP borrowed over one billion dollars, with the company guaranteeing the debt, to purchase enough stock to push its stock over 20% of all outstanding shares (Personnel Administrator, May, 1989). Polaroid's employees recently voted to take pay cuts to enlarge their ESOP's holding beyond 14% (Hammonds, 1989). And these are just a few of the many companies which began or enlarged their ESOPs after the Polaroid ruling was handed down. Obviously, ESOPs provide protection from hostile takeovers for those companies that form them.

4   Employee stock ownership plans, created to boost productivity and protect the company from leveraged buyouts, are themselves recently taking a more active role in acquiring companies through LBOs. One of the main reasons for this is the 1984 tax reform law, which provided tax incentives for ESOPs that take their companies private. Banks and insurance companies that lend to ESOPs get 50% of the resulting interest income excluded from their taxable income (Berss, April, 1989). This results in lower interest rates and payments for the ESOP which borrows to buy company stock. Secondly, once it purchases the company, the ESOP is allowed to pay the principle and the interest on the debt with pretax dollars. This serves to greatly reduce the company's tax bill and raises its profits *(ibid.)*.

5   In 1987 alone, there were ten LBOs worth more than 60 million dollars each in which ESOPs became the major, if not the only, owner (EBPR, July, 1988). The two largest LBOs involving ESOPs were Avis, whose ESOP decided to end Avis' revolving ownership plan, and HealthTrust, which became the largest ESOP majority owned company. HealthTrust's ESOP has provided a fine example of what can be done

with a company after an ESOP takes over. During the first year of the new ownership, over 11 million dollars was saved on supply costs and, at the end of the year, net revenues had increased 8.3% *(ibid.).*

6   Weirton Steel provides another example of what can happen when an ESOP decides to buy the company. In 1984, Weirton's parent corporation, National Steel, threatened to close the factory because of its losses. Weirton's employees opted to take pay cuts in order to buy the plant and keep it open. Since 1984 the company has been consistently profitable (Berss, 1989). But things at Weirton have not been as bright as they seem. Weirton's ESOP, like most LBO firms, hired outside managers to run the company, and there has been many conflicts between the employee-owners and their management team. The original ESOP agreement said the company must, in 1990, repurchase all the shares held by employees wishing to sell their shares. Weirton's managers, having no free cash, want to offer 20% of the shares in a public offering. This would not only create a market for the employee shares which must be repurchased, but would also give management part of the money needed for plant modernization. The other portion of the needed funds would be realized from a cut in the amount of profits paid to employees from the current level of 50% to only 33% (Schroeder, 1989). The workers, though, are fighting these moves. They feel, since they were the ones who originally saved the company, that they should now reap the benefits of the profitable company. Also, the employees are fearful of a corporate raider gaining control over a large block of stock and decreasing the degree of worker control over the company *(ibid.).* This entanglement gives credence to what many critics of ESOPs claim—mainly, that employee control, especially when a union is involved, inevitably conflicts with the need for strong management to have free reign to make decisions.

7   However, it is not just union-bashers who want to keep ESOPs out of the buyout game. Many union leaders don't want to get involved in purchasing companies with ESOPs. Even though the AFL-CIO estimates over 100,000 jobs have been lost in the past five years due to takeovers, labor unions are not willing to capitalize on the

opportunities available to them to increase job security because those opportunities mean risk (Berss, April, 1989). Over one-half of the 1.1 million members of the United Food and Commercial Workers Union have seen their employers acquired or merged out of existence, yet their leader still doesn't want to use the ESOPs to the fullest of all possibilities *(ibid.)*. Bill Olwell, though he wants job security, maintains, "I don't necessarily believe we have the capability to run a company." (Berss, 1989). Another theory is put forth by Malon Wilkus, president of American Capital Strategies. "Unions are reluctant to do buyouts because they see ESOPs as a tool for union busting" *(ibid.)*. This theory is based on the fact that unions are supposed to bargain with the owners for their members. But, if the employees are the owners, there ceases to be a need for the union and the union leaders find themselves without jobs. Another reason why unions seem to be reluctant to do LBOs is that it requires a too radical reversal in the ways that union leaders think. Unions have almost always prospered on an us-versus-them psychology, but ESOPs turn employees from "us" into "them" *(ibid.)*. Because of this new "worker capitalism," the adversarial tactics employed in the past are now becoming obsolete, but union leaders seem to be unable or are unwilling to change their ways of thinking.

8 Even when some union leaders want to use an ESOP to purchase a company, friction within the union occurs because other leaders wish to avoid participating in worker-led buyouts. In 1988 a hostile takeover of the Stop & Shop retail grocery chain was attempted by the Dart Group. The workers of Stop & Shop, represented by Food Workers Local 1351, attempted to be a white knight and tried to purchase the company. This ploy almost worked until the national union leaders decided to block the transaction. Stop & Shop was later acquired by Kohlberg, Kravis and Roberts, who then laid off approximately 2% of the work force (Berss, 1989). This is a good example of a national union being unresponsive to the needs of its members simply because they were afraid of opening the door to worker-ownership. Whether this was simply because they were afraid of losing their jobs or because they were unable to change

their obsolete ways of thinking, only they know. However, if the national leaders continue to be unresponsive to the needs of their local unions, the local unions can and will replace them with new leaders who just may wish to pursue their ESOP options.

9. One major factor that could cause unions to get more involved in the leveraged buyout game is that some major investment banking firms, including Lazard Freres and Drexel Burnham Lambert, the junk bond kings, are really pushing unions to get involved (Berss, 1989). Because of this and the fact that banks, because of the tax breaks to be gained by loaning money to ESOPs, are willing to loan to ESOPs, any ESOP which decides to undertake a LBO will have all the finances and financial advice to pull it off. The guarantee of success, taken by itself, is enough to tempt any ESOP into a takeover of its company.

10. All the previous involvements mentioned by ESOPs in LBOs occurred with the blessing of the companies' management. But the first hostile LBO by an ESOP could be on the horizon. Modine Manufacturing, a major maker of vehicular heat-transfer products, could have the distinction of being the first company taken private by a hostile ESOP-led buyout (Marcial, 1989). The company's workers are upset with the management because the management is not doing enough to raise the company's stock price. The company's ESOP, the biggest shareholder, filed a 13D in August, 1988, reporting a stake of over 17%. Most experts believe that the ESOP is likely to team up with an outside investor group to take the company private *(ibid.)*. Modine's management averted the immediate threat by meeting the worker's leaders and subsequently taking steps to raise the stock's price, but the long-term threat is still there and could be exercised by the ESOP at any time.

11. Why would Modine's ESOP consider a LBO and under what conditions might another ESOP undertake a leveraged buyout? First, a company's stock must be relatively undervalued. In Modine's case, the stock was selling at around twelve dollars, but it had a book value of 14 dollars and a breakup value of over 26 dollars (Marcial, 1989). Second, the stock should be selling at a big discount relative to its competitors'

shares. Modine's stock's price/earnings ration was only 8.3, but is competitors' P/E ratios ranged from 12 to 15 (*ibid.*). Third, like any other major investor in a company, the ESOP's members must be kept happy by the company's management. If management repeatedly ignores the desires of any major investor, including the ESOP, the company becomes a takeover candidate. And with all the tools being made available to ESOPs, an ESOP-led hostile takeover appears imminent somewhere in the United States.

Of the 311 billion dollars in merger deals last year, less than two percent involved ESOPs. However, there were 8800 ESOPs in operation, covering almost 9 million employees, by the end of the year (EBPR, July, 1988). Employee stock ownership plans have not yet reached their full potential, even one-half their potential, in the leveraged buyout field. ESOPs have evolved from being a primarily defensive mechanism to being a factor in friendly LBOs (those with the approval of company management). ESOPs can, and will, eventually be a major factor in hostile LBOs—the very thing they were designed to protect a company from in the first place.

Works Cited

Berss, Marcia R., "Buying Out the Boss," *Forbes,* Volume 143, No. 7 (April 3, 1989), pp. 41–42.

Employee Benefit Plan Review, "ESOP Loans Soar, But are Small Share of Buyouts," (July, 1988), p. 47

Employee Benefit Plan Review, "LBO's, ESOPs Transferring Ownership to Employees," (June, 1989), pp. 35-36.

Employee Benefit Plan Review, "Polaroid's ESOP Approved by Court," (June, 1989), pp. 36-37.

Hammonds, Keith, "A New Way to Keep Raiders at Bay," *Business Week,* (January 23, 1989), pp. 124–128.

Marcial, Gene, "An Employee LBO Could be a Buy," *Business Week,* (February 20, 1989), pp. 49–50.

Personnel Administrator, "More ESOPs Likely," Volume 34, No. 5, (May, 1989), pp. 32–33.

Schroeder, Michael, "Has Weirton's ESOP Worked Too Well?," *Business Week*, (January 23, 1989), pp. 174–176.

Taplin, Polly, "Sharing Information with Employee-Owners Imrpoves Firms' Productivity, Profitability," *Employee Benefit Plan Review*, (August, 1988), p. 34.

Taplin, Polly, "Most Managers Believe ESOPs Boost Productivity," *Employee Benefit Plan Review*, (December, 1988), pp. 38–39.

1 ❖ Hostile takeover. Leveraged buyout. Almost every company chief executive hates to hear those two terms and tries to guard against his or her company becoming the object of an unwanted suitor. Lately, some major companies have been taking steps to protect themselves against possible buyout offers, and one of the most popular defense maneuvers has been to institute employee stock ownership plans (ESOPs). Why did companies originally begin using ESOPs? Will employee stock ownership plans actually protect companies from hostile takeovers? Will ESOPs be used in friendly leveraged buyouts, or will ESOPS be used in hostile takeovers to gain control over the very companies they were originally designed to protect?

Advantages of Employee Stock Ownership Plans

2 American companies originally began using employee stock ownership plans in order to help motivate their employees. ESOPs improve employees' retirement security by providing stock that employees can purchase while working for the company and sell after retiring. ESOPs also usually make employees more productive and efficient (Hammonds 1989, p. 39). Workers, realizing they will now benefit from increased profits, will tend to work harder at their own jobs and make sure other workers are properly doing theirs. Surveys by the U.S. General Accounting Office and the National Center for Employee Ownership have shown that companies which use ESOPs that involve employee-owners in sharing information and participating in decision-making are more profitable and more efficient than those ESOP companies which do not (Taplin 1988, p. 46). A survey of 400 companies by the ESOP Association found that 71 percent of the respondents believed their ESOP improved productivity (Taplin 1988, p. 85).

3 The same survey also showed that over one-half of the 400 companies started their ESOPs since 1984 (Taplin 1988, p. 85). In 1989 alone, 70 publicly traded companies established employee stock ownership plans (Parham 1989, p. 10). Loans to ESOPs skyrocketed from $6.5 billion in 1988 to

$18 billion in the first half of 1989 (Parham 1989, p. 10). This huge increase in the use of ESOPs is surely attributable to more than companies merely trying to boost productivity. Employee stock ownership plans also strengthen companies against hostile takeovers. This occurs because, in most tender offers, employees vote their ESOP shares in favor of existing management in order to save their jobs. Even the simple presence of an ESOP may be enough to scare off possible buyers.

4   The best known example of an employee stock ownership plan blocking a takeover was Shamrock Holdings' attempted takeover of Polaroid, which ended early in 1989. Polaroid permitted its ESOP to enlarge its holdings to 14 percent of the company's outstanding shares in order to stave off Shamrock's bid. Not giving up, Shamrock sued Polaroid in the Delaware court system to block this action. The Delaware Chancery Court judge turned down Shamrock's challenge, ruling that Polaroid's ESOP was completely legal as it was in its planning stages or already partially in place before the hostile bid. The judge also noted that Polaroid's employees could vote their shares in confidence during a tender offer (Hammonds 1989, p. 39). As Malon Wilkus, president of an investment banking firm which specializes in leveraged ESOPs, has said, this court decision "has gone much further than Congress ever would to solve the problem of hostile takeovers" in the U.S. (Hammonds 1989, p. 39).

5   Polaroid's court victory has inspired many other companies to adopt ESOPs as a takeover defense. The Tribune Company and Lockheed Corporation recently instituted ESOPs to discourage potential purchasers; J.C. Penney borrowed $700 million to buy stock through its ESOP as a defense against a rumored raider; and Proctor and Gamble's ESOP borrowed over one billion dollars, with the company guaranteeing the debt, to purchase enough stock to push its stake to over 20 percent of all outstanding shares (Personnel Administrator 1989, p. 16). Polaroid's employees recently voted to take pay cuts to enlarge their ESOP's holding beyond 14 percent (Hammonds 1989, p. 39). These are just a few of the many companies which began or enlarged their ESOPs after the Polaroid ruling was handed down. Obviously, ESOPs provide some protection from hostile takeovers for those companies that form them.

Leveraged Versus Unleveraged ESOPs

6   When instituting an employee stock ownership plan, a company must decide what benefits it wishes to obtain from the plan. If protection from a takeover threat is desired, a leveraged ESOP is the correct choice. To create a leveraged ESOP, a company first establishes a trust through which it borrows enough money to purchase the amount of stock needed to reach the ESOP's planned size. Stock is then generally distributed to employees as the loan is paid off, with the plan's trustees usually keeping control of the stock before it is distributed (James 1989, p. 55). By assuming a large debt load, the company

insulates itself from a takeover because corporate raiders are usually unwilling to attempt to take over a company with a large debt.

7   Unleveraged ESOPs are usually established to improve the productivity of employees and/or their retirement security. Under these plans, the trustees purchase shares over time, which means the employer's contributions of funds for the purchase of stock can be very flexible (James 1989, p. 55). This allows the company to decrease its expenses and contributions in a poor fiscal year and increase them in periods of greater profitability. Because of this flexibility, unleveraged stock ownership plans are the correct choice for companies that have no reason, such as a takeover threat, to purchase a large block of stock at one time.

8   Employees almost always benefit when a leveraged ESOP is established to prevent a takeover attempt because they retain their jobs while also becoming stockholders. However, leveraged ESOPs almost always hurt existing stockholders because not only are they denied the premium which the raider offers for their shares, but downward pressure is exerted on the value of those shares as the company takes on debt to purchase existing stock or issues new stock. Unleveraged ESOPs, on the other hand, usually impose the burden of payment on the group receiving the benefits of the plan—the employees. Because a large block of stock does not have to be purchased at one time, the company can negotiate with employees to trade wage increases or other benefits for the establishment of an employee stock ownership plan and employer contributions to it.

The Friendly ESOP Buyout

9   Employee stock ownership plans, created to boost productivity and protect the company from hostile takeovers, are themselves recently being used in more active roles in acquiring companies through leveraged buyouts (LBOs). One of the main reasons for this is the 1984 tax reform law. This law provided opportunities for banks and insurance companies that lend to ESOPs to exclude 50 percent of the resulting interest income from their taxable income (Berss 1989, p. 41). As a result, they usually offer lower interest rates and payments for an ESOP which borrows to buy company stock than for other borrowers. Secondly, once it purchases the company, the ESOP is allowed to pay the principle and the interest on the debt with pretax dollars (Berss 1989, p. 41). This serves to reduce greatly the company's tax bill and raises its profits. Some congressional leaders, however, are currently trying to eliminate one of these tax breaks. In June 1989, bills were introduced in the Senate and House to eliminate the tax breaks available to banks that loan to ESOPs (James 1989, p. 55). This would decrease the amount of loanable funds available to ESOPS and would also serve to raise the real cost of loans: the interest rate. Both bills are currently awaiting committee action (Congressional Index 1989, pp. 28, 304, 51, 103).

10   There have been several recent examples of leveraged buyouts involving employee stock ownership plans. In 1987 alone, ten leveraged buyouts worth more than $60 million apiece involved ESOPs as the major, if not the only, owner (Employee Benefit Plan Review, July 1989, p. 22). The two largest LBOs involving ESOPs were Avis, whose plan was formed after the company had experienced its sixth owner in five years, and HealthTrust, which became the largest ESOP majority owned company. HealthTrust's recent history offers a vivid example of the opportunities that may be made available to a company after an ESOP-led acquisition. During the first year of the new ownership, the firm experienced savings of over $11 million on supply costs and, at the end of the year, net revenues had increased 8.3 percent (Employee Benefit Plan Review, June 1989, p. 35).

11   Weirton Steel provides a more sobering example of what can happen when an ESOP decides to buy its own company. In 1984, Weirton's parent corporation, National Steel, threatened to close the factory because of losses. Weirton's employees opted to take pay cuts in order to buy the plant and keep it open. Since 1984 the company has been consistently profitable (Berss 1989, p. 42). However, the situation at Weirton has not been as bright as it first seemed. Weirton's ESOP, like most LBO firms, hired outside managers to run the company, and there have been many conflicts between the employee-owners and their management team. The original ESOP agreement said the company must, in 1990, repurchase all shares held by employees wishing to sell (Schroeder 1989, p. 66). Weirton's managers, having a limited free cash flow, wished to sell 20 percent of the repurchased shares in a public offering. Not only would this plan save management money, but it would also give it part of the money needed for plant modernization. The other portion of the needed modernization funds would be realized from a cut in the amount of profits paid to employees from the current level of 50 percent to only 33 percent (Schroeder 1989, p. 66).

12   Weirton's workers are fighting these moves. They feel that since they were the ones who originally saved the company, they should now reap the benefits of profitability. Also, the employees are fearful of a corporate raider gaining control over a large block of stock and decreasing the degree of worker control over the company (Schroeder 1989, p. 67). This entanglement gives credence to what many critics of ESOPs claim: that employee control, especially when a union is involved, inevitably conflicts with the need for strong management to have free reign to make decisions (Schroeder 1989, p. 66).

Unions and ESOPs

13   Many union leaders do not want to see an ESOP in which their members are shareholders used to purchase a company. Even though the AFL-CIO estimates over 100,000 jobs have been lost in the past five years due to takeovers, many labor union leaders are still not willing to capitalize on the

opportunities to increase job security available to them through the encouragement of ESOP-led takeovers (Berss, April 1989, p. 41). More than one-half of the 1.1 million members of the United Food and Commercial Workers Union have seen their employers acquired or merged out of existence, yet their president, Bill Olwell, contends: "I don't necessarily believe we have the capability to run a company" (Berss 1989, p. 41). However, almost all LBO groups hire outside management to run the companies they purchase. Union leaders do not have to know how to run the company in order to participate in an employee-led buyout.

14   Another reason why unions do not want to encourage ESOPs to participate in leveraged buyouts is put forth by Malon Wilkus, a financial advisor to unions: "Unions are reluctant to do buyouts because they see ESOPs as a tool for union busting" (Berss 1989, p. 41). This is based on the belief that the main purpose of unions is to bargain with the owners for their members. If the employees are the owners, there ceases to be a need for the union, and union leaders find themselves without jobs. Another reason why unions seem to be reluctant to support ESOP-initiated leveraged buyouts is that it requires a radical reversal in the way union leaders think. Unions have almost always prospered on an us-versus-them psychology, but ESOPs turn employees from "us" into "them" (Berss 1989, p. 42). Because of this new "worker capitalism," the adversarial tactics employed by unions in the past are now becoming obsolete, but union leaders seem to be unable or unwilling to change their way of thinking.

15   Even when some local union members support an ESOP in its attempt to purchase a company, friction within the union often occurs because national union leaders may wish to avoid participating in worker-led buyouts. In 1988, a hostile takeover of the Stop & Shop retail grocery chain was attempted by the Dart Group. The workers of Stop & Shop, represented by Food Workers Local 1351, attempted to assume the role of white knight and purchase the company. This action almost worked until the national union leaders decided to block the transaction. Stop & Shop was later acquired by Kohlberg, Kravis and Roberts (Berss 1989, p. 41). This seems to be an example of national union leaders being unresponsive to the needs of their members. Whether this occurred simply because the national leaders were afraid of losing their jobs or because they were unable to change their way of thinking is impossible to tell. However, if national union leaders become unresponsive to the needs of their locals, members of the locals may replace them with leaders who might be more responsive to the ESOP options available to them.

16   According to Berss, one major factor that could cause unions to become more involved in the leveraged buyout game is that some major investment banking firms have a large incentive to get unions involved (Berss 1989, p. 41). This incentive is the huge fee the investment banking firms make from setting up the leveraged buyout plan and from securing the financing actually needed to take a company over. Because of this and the tax breaks to be gained, any ESOP which decides to undertake a leveraged buyout will probably have

ready access to the finances and financial advice needed to succeed. This, taken by itself, may be enough to tempt any ESOP into a takeover of its parent company.

Hostile ESOP Buyouts

17   The previously described involvements in leveraged buyouts by employee stock ownership plans occurred with the blessing of their companies' managements. However, the first hostile leveraged buyout by an ESOP could be on the horizon. Modine Manufacturing, a major maker of vehicular heat-transfer products, could have the distinction of being the first company taken private by a hostile ESOP-led buyout (Marcial 1989, p. 34). The company's workers are upset with management because it is not doing enough to raise the company's stock price. The company's ESOP, the biggest shareholder, filed a 13D in August 1988, reporting a stake of over 17 percent. A 13D is a document an investor is required to file with the Securities and Exchange Commission whenever a 13 percent or larger stake is acquired in a company. Some experts believe that the ESOP is likely to team up with an outside investor group to take the company private (Marcial 1989, p. 34). Although this has not yet happened, the threat still exists and could be exercised by the ESOP at any time.

18   Why would Modine's employee stock ownership plan consider an LBO? Under what conditions might another ESOP undertake a leveraged buyout? To make any leveraged buyout attractive, a company's stock must be relatively undervalued. In Modine's case, the stock was selling at around $12, but it had a book value of $14 and a breakup value of over $26 (Marcial 1989, p. 34). Secondly, the stock should be selling at a big discount relative to its competitors' shares. The price/earnings ratio of Modine's stock at that time was only 8.3, but its competitors' P/E ratios ranged from 12 to 15 (Marcial 1989, p. 34). Third, like any other major investor in a company, the ESOP's members must be kept happy by the company's management. If management repeatedly ignores the desires of any major investor, including the ESOP, the company may become a takeover candidate.

19   Another factor increases the possibility of an ESOP-led hostile takeover in the near future. The Internal Revenue Service has recently stated it will now allow investment bankers to sell bonds publicly to finance ESOP stock purchases (Parham 1989, p. 10). Prior to this, employee stock ownership plans, and companies establishing them, could only borrow from private lenders such as banks, insurance firms, and mutual funds. The recent IRS action greatly expands the amount of loanable funds available to ESOPs by allowing them to borrow from many more sources than before. With all the tools now available to employee stock ownership plans, ESOP-led hostile takeovers appear imminent.

Conclusion

By the end of 1989, there were over 10,000 employee stock ownership plans in operation, covering almost 10 million employees (James 1989, p. 53). Of the $311 billion in leveraged buyouts in 1989, however, fewer than 2 percent involved ESOPs (Berss 1989, p. 41). Employee stock ownership plans were originally established because employers believed them to increase the productivity of their workers and because they improved worker retirement security. Companies also began using employee stock ownership plans to protect themselves from corporate raiders. ESOPs then became active players in the leveraged buyout game by participating in friendly leveraged takeovers. However, employee stock ownership plans have not yet reached their full potential in the leveraged buyout arena. If the government refrains from intervening, employee stock ownership plans can, and will, eventually be a major factor in hostile leveraged buyouts—the very thing they were designed to protect a company from in the first place.

References

Berss, Marcia R. "Buying Out the Boss," *Forbes,* Apr. 3, 1989, 43(7), pp. 41–42.

"Eleven Owners Later, Avis Opts for ESOP," *Employee Benefit Plan Review,* Aug. 1988, 43(2), pp. 47–48.

"ESOP Loans Soar, but Are Small Share of Buyouts," *Employee Benefit Plan Review,* July 1988, 43(1), p. 22.

Hammonds, Keith. "A New Way to Keep Raiders at Bay," *Business Week,* Jan. 23, 1989, p. 39.

James, David L. "ESOP's White Knights," *Across the Board,* Oct. 1989, 26(10), pp. 52–56.

"LBOs, ESOPs Transferring Ownership to Employees," *Employee Benefit Plan Review,* June 1989, 43(12), pp. 35–36.

Marcial, Gene. "An Employee LBO Could Be a Buy," *Business Week,* Feb. 20, 1989, p. 134.

"More ESOPs Likely," *Personnel Administrator,* May 1989, 34(5), pp. 16–17.

Parham, Linda. "Congress Moves to Limit ESOPs," *Pension World,* Oct. 1989, 25(10), p. 10.

"Polaroid's ESOP Approved by Court," *Employee Benefit Plan Review,* June 1989, 43(12), pp. 36–38.

Schroeder, Michael. "Has Weirton's ESOP Worked Too Well," *Business Week,* Jan. 23, 1989, pp. 66–67.

Taplin, Polly. "Sharing Information with Employee-Owners Improves Firm's Productivity, Profitability," *Employee Benefit Plan Review,* Aug. 1988, 43(2), pp. 46–47.

———. "Most Managers Believe ESOPs Boost Productivity," *Employee Benefit Plan Review,* Dec. 1988, 43(6), pp. 84–85. ❖

Questions to Ponder

1. What are some of the best sources for finding *current* financial information?
2. Which form of internal (parenthetical) documentation is Jon Shepherd using? What kinds of information does he document?
3. Is Jon Shepherd for ESOPs? Against them? Neutral? How can you tell? List supporting details for each position before making your final decision.
4. What are the advantages of raising a series of questions in an introduction—as Jon Shepherd does at the end of his first paragraph? Are there any disadvantages? Does he ever answer his questions? Where?

Writing Possibilities

1. Write an essay aimed at first-year college students outlining the financial pitfalls that may await them and offering advice on how best to manage their college finances.
2. Brainstorm a list of advantages and disadvantages of college students joining together in investment clubs to purchase shares of stock. Then write a letter to your college newspaper favoring or opposing this student activity.
3. Conduct an informal survey of a group of your fellow college students, asking them specific questions regarding their incomes and their savings-and-spending habits. You may also want to interview your campus financial-aid office on the frequency of emergency student loans. Using the data you collect, draft either (a) a report on the state of student financial astuteness, to be presented to student government officers or (b) a letter to your campus newspaper briefly outlining your findings and making recommendations.

Short Story/Essay

SHIPWRECK

Julian Barnes

Whether ignorant or informed, amateur or professional, we all make overconfident assumptions about artistic intention. There is something so certain, so authoritative in a great painting (novel, piece of music . . .) that the work almost bullies us into believing that this, and only this, was what the artist initially planned. Even when advised that he or she started off in a completely opposite direction, we half do not believe the evidence: we persuade ourselves that surreptitiously, subconsciously, they always knew exactly what they were after. What I wanted to do in the chapter below was reassert the living process—one involving intention, to be sure, but also doubt, chance, underconfidence, overconfidence, false starts, false middles, and so on—which resulted in the painting which we know (though the artist himself did not) as The Raft of the Medusa.

Novelists write about what they want to write about, and (just as important) what they *can* write about. Géricault's picture imposed itself on me partly because it was a grandly turbulent image with which I'd been familiar since first seeing it in the Louvre at the age of 18, but also because the hazardous trail leading from a specific historical event off the coast of Africa to a finished canvas in a Paris studio was well documented. Two survivors of the Raft wrote their account of the ordeal (Savigny and Corréard's Narrative of a Voyage to Senegal: I found a 1985 American reprint of the 1818 London translation in Scribner's, Ann Arbor, during a trip to the States). Géricault met these two, and other survivors; he even employed the carpenter who had helped build the original raft to make him a scale model. As for the artistic process itself, a large number of his preliminary sketches and near-miss ideas have come down to us. So when I began, I had a nearly complete skeleton lying before me in the sand, waiting to be twitched back into life, to be refreshed and renewed.

But as with the painter, so with the writer. How could the finished product ever have been otherwise? Well, all too easily. At one time I had planned a whole book about the Géricault painting, about the seemingly mysterious way in which "catastrophe becomes art." This idea was then slimmed down and integrated into my novel to form a central, hinge chapter; even so, it was not originally shaped as it now stands. As I first saw it, the chapter would be in three sections: the two that survive, plus a third which brought the story up to date (and returned art to life) by describing the rediscovery of the frigate's wreckage off the Mauretanian coast in 1981. This third part never took off; instead, it atrophied into a couple of lines in a later chapter of the novel.

The first section of my chapter draws closely on Savigny and Corréard's book and uses (borrows, counterfeits) the early nineteenth-century English of that 1818 translation. The second leans on Lorenz Eitner's exemplary study Géricault; though here the language and formal techniques were naturally my own, and of my own times. "Research," I find, is a very double-edged matter: on the one hand it gives you confidence that you are getting things right; on the other, it is constricting, temporarily anesthetizing. If you remember an original text too well, your own writing cannot flow, and it becomes impossible to put a new shape on an old narrative. Research *often reminds me of building a compost heap: if you try to use what you've piled up too soon, all you get is a forkful of cabbage stumps, purulent apples, and unreconstructed teabags. You have to let it all settle and decompose in the mind first.*

Exploratory research, original writing, then subsequent verification. When working closely with fact, I need an outside opinion on the final product. So I showed the chapter below in draft form to two friends: an art historian (who passed it), and a painter who suggested, rather hesitantly, that there might be more about Géricault in the act of painting than I had put in. I knew he was right, and at this comparatively late stage added an extra page or so two-thirds of the way through— from "He was eight months in his studio . . ." to the end of the next paragraph but one (". . . open sea of contrary tides").

When the novel from which this chapter comes was published, the review which pleased me most appeared in a British rock magazine. It did not say much about the book, but it did firmly point out that Géricault's painting The Raft of the Medusa was best known as the cover for the Pogues's album Rum, Sodomy and the Lash.

DRAFT

Whether ignorant or informed, amateur or professional, we all make over-confident assumptions about artistic intention. There is something so certain, so authoritative in a great painting (novel, piece of music...) that the work almost bullies us into believing that this, and only this, was what the artist initially planned. Even ~~when~~ *advised* ~~advised~~ that he or she started off in a completely opposite direction, we half don't

Continued

believe the evidence: we persuade ourselves that surreptitiously, subconsciously, they always knew exactly what they were after. What I wanted to do in the chapter below was reassert the living process - one involving intention, to be sure, but also doubt, chance, under-confidence, over-confidence, false starts, false middles, and so on - which resulted in the painting which we know (though the artist himself did not) as The Raft of the Medusa.

Novelists write about what they want to write about, and (just as important) what they can write about. Géricault's picture imposed itself on me partly because it was a grandly turbulent image with which I'd been familiar since first seeing it in the Louvre at the age of 18, but also because the hazardous trail leading from a specific historical event off the coast of Africa to a finished canvas in a Paris studio was well-documented. Two survivors of the Raft wrote their account of the ordeal (Savigny and Corréard's Narrative of a Voyage to Senegal: I found a 1985 American reprint of the 1818 London translation in Scribner's, Ann Arbor, during a trip to the States). Géricault met these two and other survivors; he even employed the carpenter who had helped build the original raft to make him a scale model. As for the artistic process itself, a large number of his preliminary sketches and near-miss ideas have come down to us. So when I began, I had a nearly complete skeleton lying before me in the sand, waiting to be twitched back into life, to be refleshed and renerved.

But as with the painter, so with the writer. How could the finished product ever have been otherwise? Well, all too easily. At one time I had planned a whole book about the Géricault painting, about the seemingly mysterious way in which 'catastrophe becomes art'. This idea was then slimmed down and integrated into my novel to form a central, hinge chapter; even so, it wasn't originally shaped as it now stands. As I first saw it, the chapter would be in three sections: the two that survive, plus a third which brought the story up to date (and returned art to life) by describing the rediscovery of the frigate's wreckage off the Mauretanian coast in 1981. This third part never took off; instead, it atrophied into a couple of lines in a later chapter of the novel.

The first section of my chapter draws closely on Savigny and Corréard's book, and uses (borrows, counterfeits) the early 19th-century English of that 1818

Continued

translation. The second ~~chapter~~ leans on Lorenz Eitner's exemplary study Géricault; though here the language and formal techniques were naturally my own, and of my own times. 'Research', I find, is a very double-edged ~~process~~ matter: on the one hand it gives you confidence that you're getting things right; on the other, it is constricting, temporarily anaesthetising. If you remember an original text too well, your own writing can't flow, and it becomes impossible to put a new shape on an old narrative. 'Research' often reminds me of building a compost heap: if you try to use what you've piled up too soon, all you get is a forkful of cabbage stumps, purulent apples and unreconstructed teabags. You have to let it all settle and decompose in the mind first.

Exploratory research, original writing, then subsequent verification. When working closely with fact, I need ~~~~ an outside opinion on the final ~~~~ product. So I showed the chapter below in draft form to two friends: an art historian (who passed it), and a painter who suggested, rather hesitantly, that there might be more about Géricault in the act of painting than I'd ~~initially~~ put in. I knew he was right, and at this comparatively late stage added an extra page or so two-thirds of the way through - from 'He was eight months in his studio...' to the end of the next paragraph but one ('...open sea of contrary tides').

When the novel from which this chapter comes was published, the review which pleased me most appeared in a British rock magazine. It didn't say much about the book, but it did firmly pointed out that Géricault's painting The Raft of the Medusa was best known as the cover for the Pogues' album Rum, Sodomy and the Lash.

Julian Barnes
First North American ~~~~ Volume Rights, in The Writer in You, Only.

Brief Warm-up Writing Exercises

1. Freewrite a description of your favorite album cover, painting, film, or piece of music.
2. Make a list of the sources you would consult if you wanted to find out when and how your favorite painting, sculpture, film, or piece of music or literature was made.

3. Describe what you do when you look at a painting in a museum or art gallery—or what you would do.

❖ ──────────────────────────────────
　　I

1　　It began with a portent.
2　　They had doubled Cape Finisterre and were sailing south before a fresh wind when a school of porpoises surrounded the frigate. Those on board crowded the poop and the breastwork, marvelling at the animals' ability to circle a vessel already gaily proceeding at nine or ten knots. As they were admiring the sports of the porpoises, a cry was raised. A cabin boy had fallen through one of the fore portholes on the larboard side. A signal gun was fired, a life-raft thrown out, and the vessel hove to. But these manoeuvres were cumbrously done, and by the time the six-oared barge was let down, it was in vain. They could not find the raft, let alone the boy. He was only fifteen years old, and those who knew him maintained that he was a strong swimmer; they conjectured that he would most probably have reached the raft. If so, he doubtless perished upon it, after having experienced the most cruel sufferings.
3　　The expedition for Senegal consisted of four vessels: a frigate, a corvette, a flute and a brig. It had set sail from the Island of Aix on 17th June 1816 with 365 people on board. Now it continued south with its complement reduced by one. They provisioned at Tenerife, taking on precious wines, oranges, lemons, banian figs and vegetables of all kinds. Here they noted the depravity of the local inhabitants: the women of Saint Croix stood at their doors and urged the Frenchmen to enter, confident that their husbands' jealousies would be cured by the monks of the Inquisition who would speak disapprovingly of conjugal mania as the blinding gift of Satan. Reflective passengers ascribed such behaviour to the southern sun, whose power, it is known, weakens both natural and moral bonds.
4　　From Tenerife they sailed south-south-west. Fresh winds and navigational ineptitude scattered the flotilla. Alone, the frigate passed the tropic and rounded Cape Barbas. It was running close to the shore, at times no more than half a cannon shot away. The sea was strewn with rocks; brigantines could not frequent these seas at low water. They had doubled Cape Blanco, or so they believed, when they found themselves in shallows; the lead was cast every half-hour. At daybreak Mr. Maudet, ensign of the watch, made out the reckoning upon a chicken coop, and judged that they were on the edge of the Arguin reef. His advice was discounted. But even those unschooled in the sea could observe that the water had changed colour; weed was apparent at the ship's side, and a great many fish were being taken. In calm seas and clear weather, they were running aground. The lead announced eighteen fathoms, then shortly afterwards six fathoms. The frigate luffing, almost immediately gave a

heel; a second and third, then stopped. The sounding line showed a depth of five metres and sixty centimetres.

5   By misfortune, they had struck the reef at high tide; and the seas growing violent, attempts to free the ship failed. The frigate was assuredly lost. Since the boats it carried were not capacious enough to contain the whole personnel, it was decided to build a raft and embark upon it those who could not be put into the boats. The raft would then be towed to the shore and all would be saved. This plan was perfectly well-laid; but as two of the company were later to affirm, it was traced upon loose sand, which was dispersed by the breath of egotism.

6   The raft was made, and well made, places in the boats allotted, provisions made ready. At daybreak, with two metres and seventy centimetres of water in the hold and the pumps failing, the order was given to abandon ship. Yet disorder quickly embraced the well-laid plan. The allotment of places was ignored, and the provisions were carelessly handled, forgotten or lost in the waters. One hundred and fifty was to be the complement of the raft: one hundred and twenty soldiers including officers, twenty-nine men sailors and passengers, one woman. But scarcely had fifty men got on board this machine—whose extent was twenty metres in length and seven in breadth—than it sank to at least seventy centimetres under water. They cast off the barrels of flour which had been embarked, whereupon the level of the raft rose; the remaining people descended upon it, and it sank again. When the machine was fully laden, it was a metre beneath the surface, and those on board so crowded that they could not take a single step; at the back and front, they were in water up to the waist. Loose flour barrels were cast against them by the waves; a twenty-five pound bag of biscuit was thrown down to them, which the water converted at once into a paste.

7   It had been intended that one of the naval officers should take command of the raft; but this officer declined to come on board. At seven o'clock in the morning the signal for departure was given, and the little flotilla pulled away from the abandoned frigate. Seventeen persons had refused to leave the vessel, or had concealed themselves away, and thus remained on board to discover their fate.

8   The raft was towed by four boats in line astern, preceded by a pinnace, which made soundings. As the boats took up their positions, cries of *Vive le roi!* arose from the men on the raft, and a small white flag was raised upon the end of a musket. But it was at this instant of greatest hope and expectation for those upon the raft that the breath of egotism was added to the normal winds of the seas. One by one, whether for reason of self-interest, incompetence, misfortune or seeming necessity, the tow-ropes were cast aside.

9   The raft was barely two leagues from the frigate when it was abandoned. Those on board had wine, a little brandy, some water and a small portion of sodden biscuit. They had been given no compass or chart. With neither oars nor rudder, there was no means of controlling the raft, and little means either of controlling those upon it, who were constantly flung against one another as

the waters rolled over them. In the first night, a storm got up and threw the machine with great violence; the cries of those on board mingled with the roaring of the billows. Some attached ropes to the timbers of the craft, and held fast to these; all were buffeted without mercy. By daybreak the air was filled with lamentable cries, vows which could never be fulfilled were offered up to Heaven, and all prepared themselves for imminent death. It was impossible to form an idea of that first night which was not below the truth.

10   The next day the seas were calm, and for many hope was rekindled. Nevertheless, two young lads and a baker, convinced that there was no escape from death, bade farewell to their companions and willingly embraced the sea. It was during this day that those on the raft began to experience their first delusions. Some fancied that they saw land, others espied vessels come to save them, and the dashing of these deceptive hopes upon the rocks provoked greater despondency.

11   The second night was more terrible than the first. The seas were mountainous and the raft constantly near to being overthrown; the officers, clustered by the short mast, ordered the soldiery from one side of the machine to the other to counterbalance the energy of the waves. A group of men, certain that they were lost, broke open a cask of wine and resolved to soothe their last moments by abandoning the power of reason; in which they succeeded, until the sea water coming in through the hole they had made in the cask spoiled the wine. Thus doubly maddened, these disordered men determined to send all to a common destruction, and to this end attacked the ropes that bound the raft together. The mutineers being resisted, a pitched battle took place amid the waves and the darkness of the night. Order was restored, and there was an hour of tranquillity upon that fatal machine. But at midnight the soldiery rose again and attacked their superiors with knives and sabres; those without weapons were so deranged that they attempted to tear at the officers with their teeth, and many bites were endured. Men were thrown into the sea, bludgeoned, stabbed; two barrels of wine were thrown overboard and the last of the water. By the time the villains were subdued, the raft was laden with corpses.

12   During the first uprising, a workman by the name of Dominique, who had joined the mutineers, was cast into the sea. On hearing the piteous cries of this treacherous underling, the engineer in charge of the workmen threw himself into the water, and taking the villain by the hair, succeeded in dragging him back on board. Dominique's head had been split open by a sabre. In the darkness the wound was bound up and the wretch restored to life. But no sooner was he so revived than, ungrateful as he was, he rejoined the mutineers and rose with them again. This time he found less fortune and less mercy; he perished that night.

13   Delirium now menaced the unhappy survivors. Some threw themselves into the sea; some fell into torpor; some unfortunate wretches rushed at their comrades with sabres drawn demanding to be given *the wing of a chicken*. The engineer whose bravery had saved the workman Dominique pictured himself travelling the fine plains of Italy, and one of the officers saying to him, "I

remember that we have been deserted by the boats; but fear nothing; I have just written to the governor, and in a few hours we shall be saved." The engineer, calm in his delirium, responded thus: "Have you a pigeon to carry your orders with as much celerity?"

14   Only one cask of wine remained for the sixty still on board the raft. They collected tags from the soldiers and fashioned them into fish-hooks; they took a bayonet and bent it into such shape as to catch a shark. Whereupon a shark arrived, and seized the bayonet, and with a savage twist of its jaw straightened it fully out again, and swam away.

15   An extreme resource proved necessary to prolong their miserable existence. Some of those who had survived the night of the mutiny fell upon the corpses and hacked pieces from them, devouring the flesh on the instant. Most of the officers refused this meat; though one proposed that it should first be dried to make it more palatable. Some tried chewing swordbelts and cartouche boxes, and the leather trimmings to their hats, with little benefit. One sailor attempted to eat his own excrements, but he could not succeed.

16   The third day was calm and fine. They took repose, but cruel dreams added to the horrors already inflicted by hunger and thirst. The raft, which now carried less than one half its original complement, had risen up in the water, an unforeseen benefit of the night's mutinies. Yet those on board remained in water to the knees, and could only repose standing up, pressed against one another in a solid mass. On the fourth morning they perceived that a dozen of their fellows had died in the night; the bodies were given to the sea, except for one that was reserved against their hunger. At four o'clock that afternoon a shoal of flying fish passed over the raft, and many became ensnared in the extremities of the machine. That night they dressed the fish, but their hunger was so great and each portion so exiguous, that many of them added human flesh to the fish, and the flesh being dressed was found less repugnant. Even the officers began to eat it when presented in this form.

17   It was from this day onwards that all learned to consume human flesh. The next night was to bring a fresh supply. Some Spaniards, Italians and Negroes, who had remained neutral during the first mutinies, conspired together with the plan of throwing their superiors overboard and escaping to the shore, which they believed to be at hand, with those valuables and possessions which had been placed into a bag and hung upon the mast. Once more, a terrible combat ensued, and blood washed over the fatal raft. When this third mutiny was finally suppressed, there remained no more than thirty on board, and the raft had risen yet again in the water. Barely a man lay without wounds, into which salt water constantly flowed, and piercing cries were heard.

18   On the seventh day two soldiers concealed themselves behind the last barrel of wine. They struck a hole in it and began to drink the wine through a straw. On being discovered, the two trespassers were instantly cast into the water, in accordance with the necessary law that had been promulgated.

19   It was now that the most terrible decision came to be taken. On counting their numbers, it was found that they were twenty-seven. Fifteen of these were likely to live for some days; the rest, suffering from large wounds and many

of them delirious, had but the smallest chance of survival. In the time that might elapse before their deaths, however, they would surely diminish further the limited supply of provisions. It was calculated that they could well drink between them as many as thirty or forty bottles of wine. To put the sick on half allowance was but to kill them by degrees. And thus, after a debate in which the most dreadful despair presided, it was agreed among the fifteen healthy persons that their sick comrades must, for the common good of those who might yet survive, be cast into the sea. Three sailors and a soldier, their hearts now hardened by the constant sight of death, performed these repugnant but necessary executions. The healthy were separated from the unhealthy like the clean from the unclean.

20 After this cruel sacrifice, the last fifteen survivors threw all their arms into the water, reserving only a sabre lest some rope or wood might need cutting. There was sustenance left for six days while they awaited death.

21 There came a small event which each interpreted according to his nature. A white butterfly, of a species common in France, appeared over their heads fluttering, and settled upon the sail. To some, crazed with hunger, it seemed that even this could make a morsel. To others, the ease with which their visitor moved appeared a very mockery when they lay exhausted and almost motionless beneath it. To yet others, this simple butterfly was a sign, a messenger from Heaven as white as Noah's dove. Even those sceptical ones who declined to recognize a divine instrument knew with cautious hope that butterflies travel little distance from the dry land.

22 Yet no dry land appeared. Under the burning sun a raging thirst consumed them, until they began to moisten their lips with their own urine. They drank it from little tin cups which first they placed in water to cool their inner liquid the quicker. It happened that a man's cup might be stolen and restored to him later, but without the urine it had previously held. There was one who could not bring himself to swallow it, however thirsty he might be. A surgeon amongst them remarked that the urine of some men was more agreeable to swallow than that of others. He further remarked that the one immediate effect of drinking urine was an inclination to produce urine anew.

23 An officer of the army discovered a lemon, which he intended to reserve entirely for himself; violent entreaties persuaded him of the perils of selfishness. Thirty cloves of garlic were also found, from which arose further disputation; had all weapons but a sabre not been discarded, blood might have been shed once more. There were two phials filled with spirituous liquor for cleaning the teeth; one or two drops of this liquor, dispensed with reluctance by its possessor, produced on the tongue a delightful sensation which for a few seconds cast out thirst. Some pieces of pewter on being placed in the mouth effected a kind of coolness. An empty phial which had once contained essence of roses was passed among the survivors; they inhaled, and the remnants of perfume made a soothing impression.

24 On the tenth day several of the men, upon receiving their allotment of wine, conceived the plan of becoming intoxicated and then destroying them-

selves; they were with difficulty persuaded from this notion. Sharks surrounded the raft, and some soldiers, in their derangement, openly bathed within sight of the great fish. Eight of the men, reckoning that land could not be far distant, constructed a second raft upon which to escape. They built a narrow machine with a low mast and a hammock cloth for a sail; but as they made a trial of it, the frailty of the craft proved to them the temerity of their enterprise, and they abandoned it.

25   On the thirteenth day of their ordeal, the sun rose entirely free from clouds. The fifteen wretches had put up their prayers to the Almighty, and divided amongst them their portion of wine, when a captain of infantry, looking towards the horizon, descried a ship and announced it with an exclamation. All offered thanks to the Lord and gave way to transports of joy. They straightened barrel hoops and attached handkerchiefs to the end; one of their number mounted to the top of the mast and waved these little flags. All watched the vessel on the horizon and guessed at its progress. Some estimated that it was coming closer by the minute; others asserted that its course lay in a contrary direction. For half an hour they lay suspended between hope and fear. Then the ship disappeared from the sea.

26   From joy they fell into despondency and grief; they envied the fate of those who had died before them. Then, to find some consolation from their despair in sleep, they rigged a piece of cloth as shelter from the sun, and lay down beneath it. They proposed to write an account of their adventures, which they would all sign, and nail it to the top of the mast, hoping that it might by some means reach their families and the Government.

27   They had passed two hours among the most cruel reflections when the master gunner, wishing to go to the front of the raft, went out of the tent and saw the *Argus* half a league distant, carrying a full press of sail, and bearing down upon them. He could scarcely breathe. His hands stretched towards the sea. 'Saved!' he said. 'See the brig close upon us!' All rejoiced; even the wounded made to crawl towards the back part of the machine, the better to see their saviors approaching. They embraced one another, and their delight redoubled when they saw that they owed their deliverance to Frenchmen. They waved handkerchiefs and thanked Providence.

28   The *Argus* clewed up her sails and lay on to their starboard, half a pistol shot away. The fifteen survivors, the strongest of whom could not have lived beyond the next forty-eight hours, were taken up on board; the commander and officers of the brig, by their reiterated care, rekindled in the survivors the flame of life. Two who later wrote their account of the ordeal concluded that the manner in which they were saved was truly miraculous, and that the finger of Heaven was conspicuous in the event.

29   The voyage of the frigate had begun with a portent, and it ended with an echo. When the fatal raft, towed by its attendant vessels, had put to sea, there were seventeen persons left behind. Thus abandoned by their own choice, they straightaway examined the ship for everything that the departing had not taken and the sea had not penetrated. They found biscuit, wine, brandy and bacon,

enough to subsist for a while. At first tranquillity prevailed, for their comrades had promised to return to their rescue. But when forty-two days had passed without relief, twelve of the seventeen determined to reach land. To this end they constructed a second raft from some of the frigate's remaining timbers, which they bound together with strong ropes, and they embarked upon it. Like their predecessors, they lacked oars and navigational equipment, and possessed no more than a rudimentary sail. They took with them a small supply of provisions and what hope there was remaining. But many days later some Moors who live beside the Saharan coast and are subjects of King Zaide discovered the vestiges of their craft, and came to Andar with this information. It was believed that the men on this second raft were doubtless the prey of those sea-monsters which are found in great numbers off the shores of Africa.

30   And then finally, as if in mockery, there came the echo of an echo. Five men remained upon the frigate. Several days after the second raft had departed, a sailor who had refused to go upon it also attempted to reach the shore. Unable to construct a third raft for himself, he put to sea in a chicken coop. Perhaps it was the very cage upon which Mr. Maudet had verified the frigate's fatal course on that morning when they had struck the reef. But the chicken coop sank and the sailor perished when no more than half a cable's length from the *Medusa*.

Museé du Louvre.

II

31   How do you turn catastrophe into art?

32   Nowadays the process is automatic. A nuclear plant explodes? We'll have a play on the London stage within a year. A President is assassinated? You can have the book or the film or the filmed book or the booked film. War? Send in the novelists. A series of gruesome murders? Listen for the tramp of the poets. We have to understand it, of course, this catastrophe; to understand it, we have to imagine it, so we need the imaginative arts. But we also need to justify it and forgive it, this catastrophe, however minimally. Why did it happen, this mad act of Nature, this crazed human moment? Well, at least it produced art. Perhaps, in the end, that's what catastrophe is *for*.

33   He shaved his head before he started the picture, we all know that. Shaved his head so he wouldn't be able to see anyone, locked himself in his studio and came out when he'd finished his masterpiece. Is that what happened?

> The expedition set off on 17th June 1816.
>
> The *Medusa* struck the reef in the afternoon of 2nd July 1816.
>
> The survivors were rescued from the raft on 17th July 1816.
>
> Savigny and Corréard published their account of the voyage in November 1817.
>
> The canvas was bought on 24th February 1818.
>
> The canvas was transferred to a larger studio and restretched on 28th June 1818.
>
> The painting was finished in July 1819.
>
> On 28th August 1819, three days before the opening of the Salon, Louis XVIII examined the painting and addressed to the artist what the *Moniteur Universel* called "one of those felicitous remarks which at the same time judge the work and encourage the artist." The King said, "Monsieur Géricault, your shipwreck is certainly no disaster."

34   It begins with truth to life. The artist read Savigny and Corréard's account; he met them, interrogated them. He compiled a dossier of the case. He sought out the carpenter from the *Medusa*, who had survived, and got him to build a scale model of his original machine. On it he positioned wax models to represent the survivors. Around him in his studio he placed his own paintings of severed heads and dissected limbs, to infiltrate the air with mortality. Recognizable portraits of Savigny, Corréard and the carpenter are included in the final picture. (How did they feel about posing for this reprise of their sufferings?)

35   He was perfectly calm when painting, reported Antoine Alphonse Montfort, the pupil of Horace Vernet; there was little perceptible motion of the body or the arms, and only a slight flushing of the face to indicate his concentration. He worked directly on to the white canvas with only a rough outline to guide him. He painted for as long as there was light with a remorselessness which was also rooted in technical necessity: the heavy, fast-drying oils he used meant that each section, once begun, had to be completed that day. He had, as we know, had his head shaved of its reddish-blond curls, as a Do Not Disturb sign. But he was not solitary: models, pupils and friends continued coming to the house, which he shared with his young assistant Louis-Alexis Jamar. Among the models he used was the young Delacroix, who posed for the dead figure lying face down with his left arm extended.

36   Let us start with what he did not paint. He did not paint:

1. The *Medusa* striking the reef
2. The moment when the two-ropes were cast off and the raft abandoned
3. The mutinies in the night
4. The necessary cannibalism
5. The self-protective mass murder
6. The arrival of the butterfly
7. The survivors up to their waists, or calves, or ankles in water
8. The actual moment of rescue.

In other words his first concern was not to be (1) political; (2) symbolic; (3) theatrical; (4) shocking; (5) thrilling; (6) sentimental; (7) documentational; or (8) unambiguous.

Notes

37   1. The *Medusa* was a shipwreck, a news story and a painting; it was also a cause. Bonapartists attacked Monarchists. The behaviour of the frigate's captain illuminated (a) the incompetence and corruption of the Royalist Navy; (b) the general callousness of the ruling class towards those beneath them. Parallels with the ship of state running aground would have been both obvious and heavy-handed.

38   2. Savigny and Corréard, survivors and co-authors of the first account of the shipwreck, petitioned the government, seeking compensation for the victims and punishment for the guilty officers. Rebuffed by institutional justice, they applied to the wider courts of public opinion with their book. Corréard subsequently set up as a publisher and pamphleteer with a shop called At the Wreck of the Medusa; it became a meeting-place for political malcontents. We can imagine a painting of the moment when the tow-ropes are loosed: an axe, glittering in the sun, is being swung; an officer, turning his back on the

raft, is casually slipping a knot . . . It would make an excellent painted pamphlet.

3. The Mutiny was the scene that Géricault most nearly painted. Several preliminary drawings survive. Night, tempest, heavy seas, riven sail, raised sabres, drowning, hand-to-hand combat, naked bodies. What's wrong with all this? Mainly that it looks like one of those saloon-bar fights in B-Westerns where every single person is involved—throwing a punch, smashing a chair, breaking a bottle over an enemy's head, swinging heavy-booted from the chandelier. Too much is going on. You can tell more by showing less.

The sketches of the Mutiny that survive are held to resemble traditional versions of the Last Judgement, with its separation of the innocent from the guilty, and with the fall of the mutinous into damnation. Such an allusion would have been misleading. On the raft, it was not virtue that triumphed, but strength; and there was little mercy to be had. The sub-text of this version would say that God was on the side of the officer-class. Perhaps he used to be in those days. Was Noah officer-class?

4. There is very little cannibalism in Western art. Prudishness? This seems unlikely: Western art is not prudish about gouged eyes, severed heads in bags, sacrificial mastectomy, circumcision, crucifixion. What's more, cannibalism was a heathen practice which could be usefully condemned in paint while surreptitiously enflaming the spectator. But some subjects just seem to get painted more than others. Take officer-class Noah, for instance. There seem to be surprisingly few pictures of his Ark around. There is the odd jocular American primitive, and a murky Giacomo Bassano in the Prado, yet not much else springs to mind. Adam and Eve, the Expulsion, the Annunciation, the Last Judgment—you can have all these by major artists. But Noah and his Ark? A key moment in human history, a storm at sea, picturesque animals, divine intervention in human affairs: surely the necessary elements are there. What could account for this iconographical deficiency? Perhaps the lack of a single Ark painting great enough to give the subject impetus and popularity. Or is it something in the story itself: maybe artists agreed that the Flood doesn't show God in the best possible light?

Géricault made one sketch of cannibalism on the raft. The spotlit moment of anthropophagy shows a well-muscled survivor gnawing the elbow of a well-muscled cadaver. It is almost comic. Tone was always going to be the problem here.

5. A painting is a moment. What would we think was happening in a scene where three sailors and a soldier were throwing people off a raft into the sea? That the victims were already dead? Or if not, that they were being murdered for their jewelry? Cartoonists having trouble explaining the background to their jokes often give us newsvendors

standing by billboards on which some convenient headline is inscribed. With painting, the equivalent information would have to be given in the title: A GRIEVOUS SCENE ABOARD THE RAFT OF THE MEDUSA IN WHICH DESPERATE SURVIVORS, WRACKED BY CONSCIENCE, REALIZE THAT PROVISIONS ARE INSUFFICIENT AND TAKE THE TRAGIC BUT NECESSARY DECISION TO SACRIFICE THE WOUNDED IN ORDER THAT THEY THEMSELVES MIGHT HAVE A GREATER CHANCE OF SURVIVAL. That should just about do it.

44   The title of "The Raft of the Medusa," incidentally, is not "The Raft of the Medusa." The painting was listed in the Salon catalogue as *Scène de naufrage*—"Scene of Shipwreck." A cautious political move? Perhaps. But it's equally a useful instruction to the spectator: this is a painting, not an opinion.

45   6. It's not hard to imagine the arrival of the butterfly as depicted by other painters. But it sounds fairly coarse in its emotional appeal, doesn't it? And even if the question of tone could be overcome, there are two major difficulties. First, it wouldn't look like a true event, even though it was; what is true is not necessarily convincing. Second, a white butterfly six or eight centimetres across, alighting on a raft twenty metres long by seven metres broad, does give serious problems of scale.

46   7. If the raft is under water, you can't paint the raft. The figures would all be sprouting from the sea like a line-up of Venus Anadyomenes. Further, the lack of a raft presents formal problems: with everyone standing up because if they lay down they would drown, your painting is stiff with verticals; you have to be extra-ingenious. Better to wait until more on board have died, the raft has risen out of the water, and the horizontal plane becomes fully available.

47   8. The boat from the *Argus* pulling alongside, the survivors holding out their arms and clambering in, the pathetic contrast between the condition of the rescued and that of the rescuers, a scene of exhaustion and joy—all very affecting, no doubt about it. Géricault made several sketches of this moment of rescue. It could make a strong image; but it's a bit . . . straightforward.

48   That's what he didn't paint.

49 What did he paint, then? Well, what does it look as if he painted? Let us reimagine our eye into ignorance. We scrutinize "Scene of Shipwreck" with no knowledge of French naval history. We see survivors on a raft hailing a tiny ship on the horizon (the distant vessel, we can't help noticing, is no bigger than that butterfly would have been). Our initial presumption is that this is the moment of sighting which leads to a rescue. This feeling comes partly from a tireless preference for happy endings, but also from posing ourselves, at some level of consciousness, the following question: how would we know about these people on the raft if they had *not* been rescued?

50   What backs up this presumption? The ship is on the horizon; the sun is also on the horizon (though unseen), lightening it with yellow. Sunrise, we deduce, and the ship arriving with the sun, bringing a new day, hope and rescue; the black clouds overhead (very black) will soon disappear. However, what if it were sunset? Dawn and dusk are easily confused. What if it were sunset, with the ship about to vanish like the sun, and the castaways facing hopeless night as black as that cloud overhead? Puzzled, we might look at the raft's sail to see if the machine was being blown towards or away from its rescuer, and to judge if that baleful cloud is about to be dispelled; but we get little help—the wind is blowing not up and down the picture but from right to left, and the frame cuts us off from further knowledge of the weather to our right. Then, still undecided, a third possibility occurs: it could be sunrise, yet even so the rescuing vessel is not coming towards the shipwrecked. This would be the plainest rebuff of all from fate: the sun is rising, *but not for you.*

51   The ignorant eye yields, with a certain testy reluctance, to the informed eye. Let's check "Scene of Shipwreck" against Savigny and Corréard's narrative. It's clear at once that Géricault hasn't painted the hailing that led to the final rescue: that happened differently, with the brig suddenly close upon the raft and everyone rejoicing. No, this is the first sighting, when the *Argus* appeared on the horizon for a tantalizing half hour. Comparing paint with print, we notice at once that Géricault has not represented the survivor up the mast holding straightened-out barrel-hoops with handkerchiefs attached to them. He has opted instead for a man being held up on top of a barrel and waving a large cloth. We pause over this change, then acknowledge its advantage: reality offered him a monkey-up-a-stick image; art suggested a soldier focus and an extra vertical.

52   But let us not inform ourselves too quickly. Return the question to the tetchy ignorant eye. Forget the weather; what can be deduced from the personnel on the raft itself? Why not start with a head-count. There are twenty figures on board. Two are actively waving, one actively pointing, two vigorously supplicating, plus one offering muscular support to the hailing figure on the barrel: six in favour of hope and rescue. Then there are five figures (two prone, three supine) who look either dead or dying, plus an old greybeard with his back to the sighted *Argus* in a posture of mourning: six against. In between (we measure space as well as mood) there are eight more figures: one half-supplicating, half-supporting; three watching the hailer with non-committal expressions; one watching the hailer agonizingly; two in profile examining, respectively, waves past and waves to come; plus one obscure figure in the darkest, most damaged part of the canvas, with head in hands (and clawing at his scalp?). Six, six and eight: no overall majority.

53   (Twenty? queries the informed eye. But Savigny and Corréard said there were only fifteen survivors. So all those five figures who might only be unconscious are definitely dead? Yes. But then what about the culling which took place, when the last fifteen healthy survivors pitched their thirteen

wounded comrades into the sea? Géricault has dragged some of them back from the deep to help out with his composition. And should the dead lose their vote in the referendum over hope versus despair? Technically, yes; but not in assessing the mood of the picture.)

54   So the structure is balanced, six for, six against, eight don't knows. Our two eyes, ignorant and informed, squintily roam. Increasingly, they are drawn back from the obvious focus of attention, the hailer on the barrel, towards the mourning figure front left, the only person looking out at us. He is supporting on his lap a younger fellow who is—we have done our sums—certainly dead. The old man's back is turned against every living person on the raft: his pose is one of resignation, sorrow, despair; he is further marked out by his grey hair and the red cloth worn as a neck-protector. He might have strayed in from a different genre—some Poussin elder who had got lost, perhaps. (Nonsense, snaps the informed eye. Poussin? Guérin and Gros, if you must know. And the dead "Son"? A medley of Guérin, Girodet and Prud'hon.) What is this "Father" doing? (a) lamenting the dead man (his son? his chum?) on his lap; (b) realizing they will never be rescued; (c) reflecting that even if they are rescued it doesn't matter a damn because of the death he holds in his arms? (By the way, says the informed eye, there really are handicaps to being ignorant. You'd never, for instance, guess that the Father and Son are an attentuated cannibalistic motif, would you? As a group they first appear in Géricault's only surviving sketch of the Cannibalism scene; and any educated contemporary spectator would be assuredly reminded of Dante's description of Count Ugolino sorrowing in his Pisan tower among his dying children—whom he ate. Is that clear now?)

55   Whatever we decide that the old man is thinking, his presence becomes as powerful a force in the painting as that of the hailer. This counterbalance suggests the following deduction: that the picture represents the mid-point of that first sighting of the *Argus*. The vessel has been in view for a quarter of an hour and has another fifteen minutes to offer. Some believe it is still coming towards them; some are uncertain and waiting to see what happens; some—including the wisest head on board—know that it is heading away from them, and that they will not be saved. This figure incites us to read "Scene of Shipwreck" as an image of hope being mocked.

56   Those who saw Géricault's painting on the walls of the 1819 Salon knew, almost without exception, that they were looking at the survivors of the *Medusa*'s raft, knew that the ship on the horizon did pick them up (if not at the first attempt), and knew that what had happened on the expedition to Senegal was a major political scandal. But the painting which survives is the one that outlives its own story. Religion decays, the icon remains; a narrative is forgotten, yet its representation still magnetizes (the ignorant eye triumphs—how galling for the informed eye). Nowadays, as we examine "Scene of Shipwreck," it is hard to feel much indignation against Hugues Duroy de Chaumareys, captain of the expedition, or against the minister who appointed him captain, or the naval officer who refused to skipper the raft, or the sailors who loosed the tow-ropes, or the soldiery who mutinied. (Indeed, history

democratizes our sympathies. Had not the soldiers been brutalized by their wartime experiences? Was not the captain a victim of his own pampered upbringing? Would we bet on ourselves to behave heroically in similar circumstances?) Time dissolves the story into form, colour, emotion. Modern and ignorant, we reimagine the story: do we vote for the optimistic yellowing sky, or for the grieving greybeard? Or do we end up believing both versions? The eye can flick from one mood, and one interpretation, to the other: is this what was intended?

57   8a. He very nearly painted the following. Two oil studies of 1818, which in composition are closest of any preparatory sketches to the final image, show this significant difference: the vessel which is being hailed is much closer. We can see its outline, sails and masts. It is in profile, on the extreme right of the canvas, and has just begun a painful voyage across the painted horizon. It has clearly not yet seen the raft. The impact of these preliminary sketches is more active, kinetic: we feel as if the frantic waving by those on the raft might have some effect over the next few minutes, and that the picture, instead of being an instant of time, propels itself into its own future, asking the question, Will the ship sail off the edge of the canvas without seeing the raft? In contrast, the final version of "Shipwreck" is less active, offers a less articulated question. The signalling seems more futile, and the hazard on which the survivors' fate depends more terrifying. What is their chance of rescue? A drop in the ocean.

He was eight months in his studio. Around this time he drew a self-portrait, from which he stares out at us with the sullen, rather suspicious gaze that painters often assume when faced by a mirror; guiltily, we assume that the disapproval is aimed at us, whereas in fact it is mostly directed back at the sitter. His beard is short, and a tasselled Greek cap covers his shorn hair (we only hear of it being cropped when he began the picture, but hair grows a long way in eight months: how many extra trims did he need?). He strikes us as a piratical figure, determined and ferocious enough to take on, to board his enormous Shipwreck. The width of his brushes, by the way, was surprising. From the breadth of his manner, Montfort supposed that Géricault used very thick brushes; yet they were small compared to those of other artists. Small brushes, and heavy, fast-drying oils.

58   We must remember him at work. It is a normal temptation to schematize, reducing eight months to a finished picture and a series of preliminary sketches; but we must resist this. He is tallish, strong and slender, with admirable legs which were compared to those of the ephebe restraining the horse in the centre of his "Barberi Race." Standing before the Shipwreck, he works with an intensity of concentration and a need for absolute silence: the scratch of a chair was enough to break the invisible thread between eye and brush-tip. He is painting his large figures directly on to the canvas with only an outline drawing for assistance. When the work is half done it looks like a row of sculptures hanging on a white wall.

59   We must remember him in the confinement of his studio, at work, in motion, making mistakes. When we know the final result of his eight months, his progress towards it seems irresistible. We start with the masterpiece and work backwards through the discarded ideas and near-misses; but for him the discarded ideas began as excitements, and he saw only at the very end what we take for granted at the beginning. For us the conclusion was inevitable; not for him. We must try to allow for hazard, for lucky discovery, even for bluff. We can only explain it in words, yet we must also try to forget words. A painting may be represented as a series of decisions labelled 1 to 8a, but we should understand that these are just the annotations of feeling. We must remember nerves and emotions. The painter isn't carried fluently downstream towards the sunlit pool of that finished image, but is trying to hold a course in an open sea of contrary tides.

60   Truth to life, at the start, to be sure; yet once the process gets under way, truth to art is the greater allegiance. The incident never took place as depicted; the numbers are inaccurate; the cannibalism is reduced to a literary reference; the Father and Son group has the thinnest documentary justification, the barrel group none at all. The raft has been cleaned up as if for the state visit of some queasy-stomached monarch: the strips of human flesh have been housewifed away, and everyone's hair is as sleek as a painter's new-bought brush.

61   As Géricault approaches his final image, questions of form predominate. He pulls the focus, crops, adjusts. The horizon is raised and lowered (if the hailing figure is below the horizon, the whole raft is gloomily engulfed by the sea; if he breaks the horizon, it is like the raising of hope). Géricault cuts down the surrounding areas of sea and sky, hurling us on to the raft whether we like it or not. He stretches the distance from the shipwrecked to the rescuing vessel. He readjusts the positions of his figures. How often in a picture do so many of the chief participants have their backs to the spectator?

62   And what splendidly muscular backs they are. We feel embarrassed at this point, yet we shouldn't be. The naïve question often proves to be the central one. So go on, let's ask. *Why do the survivors look so healthy?* We admire the way Géricault sought out the *Medusa*'s carpenter and had him build a scale model of the raft . . . but . . . if he bothered to get the raft right, why couldn't he do the same with its inhabitants? We can understand why he fiddled the hailing figure into a separate vertical, why he added some supernumerary corpses to assist the formal structure. But why does everyone—even the corpses—look so muscled, so . . . healthy? Where are the wounds, the scars, the haggardness, the disease? These are men who have drunk their own urine, gnawed the leather from their hats, consumed their own comrades. Five of the fifteen did not survive their rescue very long. So why do they look as if they have just come from a body-building class?

63   When television companies make drama-docs about concentration camps, the eye—ignorant or informed—is always drawn to those pyjamaed extras. Their heads may be shaven, their shoulders hunched, all nail varnish removed, yet still they throb with vigour. As we watch them queue on screen for a bowl

of gruel into which the camp guard contemptuously spits, we imagine them offscreen gorging themselves at the catering van. Does "Scene of Shipwreck" prefigure this anomaly? With some painters we might pause and wonder. But not with Géricault, the portrayer of madness, corpses and severed heads. He once stopped a friend in the street who was yellow with jaundice and told him how handsome he was looking. Such an artist would hardly shrink from flesh at the limit of its endurance.

64   So let's imagine something else he didn't paint—"Scene of Shipwreck" with the casting redistributed among the emaciated. Shrivelled flesh, suppurating wounds, Belsen cheeks: such details would move us, without trouble, to pity. Salt water would gush from our eyes to match the salt water on the canvas. But this would be precipitate: the painting would be acting on us too directly. Withered castaways in tattered rags are in the same emotional register as that butterfly, the first impelling us to an easy desolation as the second impels us to an easy consolation. The trick is not hard to work.

65   Whereas the response Géricault seeks is one beyond mere pity and indignation, though these emotions might be picked up *en route* like hitchhikers. For all its subject-matter, "Scene of Shipwreck" is full of muscle and dynamism. The figures on the raft are like the waves: beneath them, yet also through them, surges the energy of the ocean. Were they painted in lifelike exhaustion they would be mere dribbles of spume rather than formal conduits. For the eye is washed—not teased, not persuaded, but tide-tugged—up to the peak of the hailing figure, down to the trough of the despairing elder, across to the recumbent corpse front right who links and leaks into the real tides. It is because the figures are sturdy enough to transmit such power that the canvas unlooses in us deeper, submarinous emotions, can shift us through currents of hope and despair, elation, panic and resignation.

66   What has happened? The painting has slipped history's anchor. This is no longer "Scene of Shipwreck," let alone "The Raft of the Medusa." We don't just imagine the ferocious miseries on that fatal machine; we don't just become the sufferers. They become us. And the picture's secret lies in the pattern of its energy. Look at it one more time: at the violent waterspout building up through those muscular backs as they reach for the speck of the rescuing vessel. All that straining—to what end? There is no formal response to the painting's main surge, just as there is no response to most human feelings. Not merely hope, but any burdensome yearning: ambition, hatred, love (especially love)—how rarely do our emotions meet the object they seem to deserve? How hopelessly we signal; how dark the sky; how big the waves. We are all lost at sea, washed between hope and despair, hailing something that may never come to rescue us. Catastrophe has become art; but this is no reducing process. It is freeing, enlarging, explaining. Catastrophe has become art: that is, after all, what it is for.

67   And what of that earlier catastrophe, the Flood? Well, the iconography of officer-class Noah begins as we might imagine. For the first dozen or more Christian centuries the Ark (usually represented as a mere box or sarcophagus

to indicate that Noah's salvation was a premonstration of Christ's escape from his sepulchre) appears widely in illuminated manuscripts, stained-glass windows, cathedral sculpture. Noah was a very popular fellow: we can find him on the bronze doors of San Zeno in Verona, on Nîmes cathedral's west façade and Lincoln's east; he sails into fresco at the Campo Santo in Pisa and Santa Maria Novella in Florence; he anchors in mosaic at Monreale, the Baptistery in Florence, St Mark's in Venice.

68 But where are the great paintings, the famous images that these are leading up to? What happens—does the Flood dry up? Not exactly; but the waters are diverted by Michelangelo. In the Sistine Chapel the Ark (now looking more like a floating bandstand than a ship) for the first time loses its compositional pre-eminence; here it is pushed right to the back of the scene. What fills the foreground are the anguished figures of those doomed antediluvians left to perish when the chosen Noah and his family were saved. The emphasis is on the lost, the abandoned, the discarded sinners, God's detritus. (Should we allow ourselves to postulate Michelangelo the rationalist, moved by pity to subtle condemnation of God's heartlessness? Or Michelangelo the pious, fulfilling his papal contract and showing us what might happen if we failed to mend our ways? Perhaps the decision was purely aesthetic—the artist preferring the contorted bodies of the damned to yet another dutiful representation of yet another wooden Ark.) Whatever the reason, Michelangelo reoriented—and revitalized—the subject. Baldassare Peruzzi followed him, Raphael followed him; painters and illustrators increasingly concentrated on the forsaken rather than the saved. And as this innovation became a tradition, the Ark itself sailed farther and farther away, retreating towards the horizon just as the *Argus* did when Géricault was approaching his final image. The wind continues to blow, and the tides to run: the Ark eventually reaches the horizon, and disappears over it. In Poussin's "The Deluge" the ship is nowhere to be seen; all we are left with is the tormented group of non-swimmers first brought to prominence by Michelangelo and Raphael. Old Noah has sailed out of art history.

69 Three reactions to "Scene of Shipwreck":

70 a. Salon critics complained that while they might be familiar with the events the painting referred to, there was no internal evidence from which to ascertain the nationality of the victims, the skies under which the tragedy was taking place, or the date at which it was all happening. This was, of course, the point.

71 b. Delacroix in 1855 recalled his reactions nearly forty years earlier to his first sight of the emerging "Medusa": "The impression it gave me was so strong that as I left the studio I broke into a run, and kept running like a madman all the way back to the rue de la Planche, where I then lived, at the far end of the faubourg Saint-Germain."

72 c. Géricault, on his death-bed, in reply to someone who mentioned the painting: "Bah, une vignette!"

73   And there we have it—the moment of supreme agony on the raft, taken up, transformed, justified by art, turned into a sprung and weighted image, then varnished, framed, glazed, hung in a famous art gallery to illuminate our human condition, fixed, final, always there. Is that what we have? Well, no. People die; rafts rot; and works of art are not exempt. The emotional structure of Géricault's work, the oscillation between hope and despair, is reinforced by the pigment: the raft contains areas of bright illumination violently contrasted with patches of the deepest darkness. To make the shadow as black as possible, Géricault used quantities of bitumen to give him the shimmeringly gloomy black he sought. Bitumen, however, is chemically unstable, and from the moment Louis XVIII examined the work a slow, irreparable decay of the paint surface was inevitable "No sooner do we come into this world," said Flaubert, "than bits of us start to fall off." The masterpiece, once completed, does not stop: it continues in motion, downhill. Our leading expert on Géricault confirms that the painting is "now in part a ruin." And no doubt if they examine the frame they will discover woodworm living there. ❖

Questions to Ponder

1. What evidence suggests that Géricault was a thorough researcher of his subject?
2. You learned from Julian Barnes's author's note that the paragraphs on Géricault's painting techniques were late additions. How do these paragraphs strengthen (or weaken) "Shipwreck"?
3. Why is it a good idea to share your drafts with others—particularly with experts on the subject—as Julian Barnes did?
4. Locate some examples of the nineteenth-century language Barnes adopts in Part I, and contrast this language with the twentieth-century language of Part II. Why is each form of diction suited to its part?
5. What are the similarities between Géricault's research-and-composition process as a painter and your research-and-composition process as a writer?

Writing Possibilities

1. Choose a painting, sculpture, film, piece of music, or work of literature, and research the history of its creation. Share your findings using Julian Barnes's Part II as a model.
2. Again choose an artwork, film, musical or literary work that you love, and analyze all its aspects, elements, and effects upon the perceiver—just as Barnes does with Géricault's painting.

3. Do research to uncover all the reviews that have been written about your favorite film, book, artwork, or piece of music. Then write an essay for an audience of fans detailing the critical reaction to the work over the years. What conclusions can you draw from this research?
4. Use Barnes's "Shipwreck" as a springboard for a paper comparing and contrasting the ignorant and the informed eye.

CHAPTER

4

Finding the Form

Finding the right form for what you have to say can make the difference between success and failure in your communication. Much of the writing you will do in college and your professional life will draw on forms commonly used in these arenas. Therefore, part of the work for the writer in you is to learn the conventions (or formats) of such widely used forms as the essay, the report, the critical review, the letter, and the résumé.

THE ESSAY

The essay is a walk, an unfolding. In the form most often used in college papers, it presents a central idea and then develops it. The charm of the essay, however, lies in its infinite variety. Essays can be serious or light, formal or highly personal. Longinus's "On the Sublime," which begins this chapter, is a serious essay on the qualities of great writing. John McNulty's " 'Come Quick. Indians!' " which follows, is both humorous and personal. An essay can seek to inform, to persuade, or to entertain; indeed it can strive for some combination of all three. "Concepts We Live By" is George Lakoff and Mark Johnson's attempt to persuade us that both our perception and thinking are shaped by the metaphors we use. Whatever the subject, tone, or purpose, however, the best essays offer new discoveries at every bend. We think the essayist has delivered the point, only to be captivated by a new sight, or insight. This is the joy of Anne Morrow Lindbergh's essay "Double-Sunrise," in which she uses the double-sunrise seashell as a metaphor for first love. An essay is more circular than many other writing forms. It goes around and around a subject, seeing it from as many angles as possible.

THE REPORT

The report is a form designed for conveying information. Reports do much of the work of this world. The conventions of a report include an objective tone; section headings; documentation of statistics, quotations, and ideas drawn from research; a bibliography of sources used; and such optional items as graphs, charts, or illustrations (included in the report itself or in Appendixes following the report). A report also often includes an abstract, a brief summary of the report's findings placed at the beginning of the work.

THE CRITICAL REVIEW

Formats for the critical review of a journal article or book, a common college writing assignment, include specially labeled sections presenting a *Summary* of the article or book; your analysis of the *Strengths* of the article or book; your evaluation of any weaknesses or *Limitations* of the work; and, finally, any *Recommendations* you might offer for strengthening the weaknesses you cited, for the use of the article by its intended audience, or for its adaptation to other audiences. (Note how this form—*Summary, Strengths, Limitations,* and *Recommendations*—can be used to analyze a business competitor's year-end report or speech, or a proposal by a fellow lawyer, doctor, politician, and so on.) In this chapter, student Lisa Battani presents two drafts of her critical review of the famous "Letter from Birmingham Jail" by Martin Luther King, Jr.

THE LETTER

The letter is a reader-oriented form. (You would never write the same thing to your roommate as to a potential employer, nor would you use the same voice and tone!) No matter who your reader is, however, you will probably make use of all or some of these common conventions of the letter: date, inside address, salutation, body, closing, signature, postscripts, enclosures. Martin Luther King, Jr., uses five of these eight conventions in his "Letter from Birmingham Jail."

THE RÉSUMÉ

All job hunters must have a résumé, sometimes called a vita or biographical sketch. A résumé is usually enclosed with your letter applying for a job. It begins with your name, home and school (or office) addresses and phone numbers, and then organizes the professional information you wish to convey under such headings as:

- Career Objective
- Employment History
- Educational Achievement
- Honors and Recognitions
- Memberships
- Publications
- Presentations
- Inventions (or other categories suited to your accomplishments)

Most résumés end with a section of Personal Data in which you can, if you choose, give your date of birth, your marital status, your health status, any languages you read or speak, and such information as whether you are "willing to travel" and "willing to relocate." When writing your résumé, you will adopt a terse, verb-oriented style as you describe what you were "responsible for" in each job you have held—including whether you *planned* or *designed* programs, *supervised* or *managed* personnel or budgets, or *met* with the public. You will keep adding to and changing your résumé throughout your professional life.

For most people, writing a résumé is an exciting, self-affirming process. You suddenly see how accomplished you are as you begin to document all the things you have been "responsible for," even in the most unglamorous part-time job. Similarly, becoming familiar with the other forms of writing required by colleges and employers will give you confidence that you can write the report and do the critical reviews that lie ahead. You probably noticed that the format of each of these forms helps organize the writer's material, both for the writer and for the reader. This is the chief merit of a format. Practicing these formats will also give you a feel for how you might modify, expand, even burst the boundaries of these conventional forms. (Might you, for example, offer more engaging section titles than *Summary, Strengths, Limitations,* and *Recommendations* for a critical review of a journal article?)

Some (perhaps much) of the writing you will be called upon to do will be in these rather carefully prescribed forms. Other writing in your life will be more open-ended. You will have something you wish to say and you will wonder, what is the best form for this content? Can I best say what I want to say through a letter, an essay (or its extended forms: the memoir, history, travelogue, biography, or autobiography), a report, a critical review, a poem, a short story or novel, a screenplay or drama, some combination of these, or a new form yet unseen?

In these cases finding the form often takes as much experimenting as finding the most effective voice and tone for the writing. You will try one form, take it as far as it will go, and then lay it aside and try another. Many people agree with Philip Larkin, who insisted that form and content are inseparable. Larkin worked slowly, for he said, "You're finding out what to say as well how to say it, and that takes time."*

One approach to form is to focus first on the *purpose* or *effect* you wish to achieve. Once you know the effect, the form for achieving that effect may naturally suggest itself. The *audience* you hope to reach should also be considered. What form would best be suited to this audience?

Still another approach is to consider the characteristics of each available form. Then choose the form best suited for what you have to say. Here are some ways to think of some of the common forms we have yet to discuss.

THE POEM

The poem is a quick insight. It is seeing something from the corner of your eye. Everyone may have seen it, but you catch it.

Safetypins

Gross-skulled, they grip their papers tightly,
coming from the factory in rows without expression.
Safety is their name, but holes are their trade, and holding:
they will hold forever, if necessary,
while tears widen around them,
until metal glints from some obscure corner
and there they lie in their rust—empty helmets
safely pinning ruin together.
NANCY PRICE

THE SHORT STORY

The short story is a crossroads. A choice is made and a change, no matter how small, follows. It, too, can deliver the quick insight. Alice Walker's short story

---

*"An Interview with *Paris Review*," *Required Writing: Miscellaneous Pieces 1955–1982* (New York: Farrar, Straus, & Giroux, 1982) 75.

" 'Really, *Doesn't* Crime Pay?' " which concludes this chapter, presents such a crossroads and is itself experimental in form.

THE NOVEL

Henry James said that a novel is "a capacious vessel. It can carry anything—with art and force in the stowage; nothing in this case will sink it. . . . The novel has nothing to fear but sailing too light. It will take aboard all we bring in good faith to the dock."

THE DRAMA

The drama devotes itself to dialogue and action. Dialogue, however, can conceal as well as reveal, and lack of action can be a powerful action.

 All writing forms are artificial. They change over time to match changes in culture. If you had been a writer living before the invention of the printing press in 1456, your form might well have been verse—verse drama or epic or romantic poetry. If you had lived in the nineteenth century, before records, radio, film, and television, you might have written long novels that could be serialized in magazines over many months and then published and savored in big volumes.
 Forms of writing are necessary. Nevertheless every original work requires a unique form. Finding that form may take hours of exploration. Like basketball player Michael Jordan, you will take the measure of each court, then push the edges, astonishing as you leap into new formations.

ON THE SUBLIME
Longinus

This note celebrates that great writer in history, Anonymous. Little is known about the author of the treatise On the Sublime. In fact, one-third of the manuscript has been lost; however, on the basis of internal evidence, scholars believe the author may have been a Greek rhetorician named Longinus (or pseudo-Longinus, as he is sometimes called), living in Rome in the first century CE. The earliest surviving copy of the treatise, which dates from the tenth century, was published in Switzerland in 1554. During the next one hundred years, it was known to scholars in Switzerland, Italy, and England, but it was not until the great French poet and critic Boileau issued his translation in 1674 that On the Sublime won its just recognition.

On the Sublime has forty-four sections; only sections 40 and 10 are reprinted here. Even to us today what is striking about the work is the range of Longinus's reading and his capacity for enthusiasm. Longinus loved great writing and sought to analyze what made it great. Throughout his treatise he employs quotations to illustrate the sublime and its opposite. His chief models are Homer, Plato, and Demosthenes. To Longinus, the sources of the sublime are greatness of thought, strong handling of the passions, skillful use of figures of thought and speech, proper choice of language, and composition (including musical or metrical effects in *prose). Greatness of thought may be inborn, Longinus asserted, but it also can be acquired by emulating great writers of the past.*

Longinus found sublimity in all forms of discourse. He found it in prose and in poetry, in the oratory of Demosthenes, the dialogues of Plato, the Greek drama, and the opening of the book of Genesis. The writing in On the Sublime *is itself sublime. As the British historian Edward Gibbon wrote of its anonymous author seventeen centuries after his death, "He tells me his own feelings about reading [beautiful passages], and tells them with such energy that he communicates them" (W. Hamilton Fyfe, introduction,* Aritistotle: The Poetics; "Longinus" on the Sublime; Demetrius on Style *[Cambridge: Harvard UP, 1953], xvii.).*

Brief Warm-up Writing Exercises

1. Rain or wind storms can be frightening. Brainstorm a list of words you would need to describe the most frightening storm (or act of nature) you have experienced. Then brainstorm a list beside it of words that capture your *feelings* or *actions* at the time. Now choose words from each list and combine them into one sentence that captures some aspect of the event.
2. Freewrite on what happens to your body and mind when you are in love. Be honest. Have you observed any bodily changes?

1   Among the factors which give most dignity to discourse is structure, which corresponds to the arrangement of the limbs of the body. One limb by itself, cut off from the others, is of no value, but all of them together complete and perfect the composition of the whole. So it is with great expressions: scattered here and there, apart from each other, they lose their own value and undo the greatness of the whole, but when they form a whole in close association, joined together by the bonds of melodious word-arrangement, then in the rounded structure of the whole they find their voice. A great work is like a feast to the courses of which many people contribute.

2   We have had sufficient proof that a good many writers of prose and poetry who have no natural genius—often, indeed, no great inborn talent—use commonplace, popular words, and, as a rule, no unusual language; yet by the mere arrangement and harmonizing of these words they endow their work with dignity, distinction, and the appearance of not being ordinary. After the murder of his children, Heracles says:

> *I have my load of ills, none can be added.*

3   The idea is thoroughly commonplace, but the line becomes great because the word-arrangement suits the image. If you arrange the words differently, you will see at once that Euripides is a poet in the arrangement of his words

rather than in the quality of his mind. He says of Dirce dragged away by the bull:

> And if he chanced
> To twist or turn, he dragged along as one
> The oak, the rock, the woman, intertwined.

Here the idea is grand, too, but it is made more forceful by the arrangement of the words which move slowly and are not, one might say, carried along on rollers; the collocation of sounds makes pauses inevitable between them. These support the long syllables with an effect of stable, wide-stepping grandeur. . . .

4   Let us consider now whether we can point to any other factor which can make writing great. There are, in every situation, a number of features which combine to make up the texture of events. To select the most vital of these and to relate them to one another to form a unified whole is an essential cause of great writing. One writer charms the reader by the selection of such details, another by the manner in which he presses them into close relationship.

5   Sappho, for example, selects on each occasion the emotions which accompany the frenzy of love. She takes these from among the constituent elements of the situation in actual life. How does she excel? In her skillful choice of the most important and intense details and in relating them to one another:

> *Peer of gods he seemeth to me, the blissful*
> *Man who sits and gazes at thee before him,*
> *Close beside thee sits, and in silence hears thee*
> *Silvery speaking.*
>
> *Laughing Love's low laughter. Oh this, this only*
> *Stirs the troubled heart in my breast to tremble,*
> *For should I but see thee a little moment,*
> *Straight is my voice hushed;*
>
> *Yea, my tongue is broken, and through and through me*
> *Neath the flesh, impalpable fire runs tingling;*
> *Nothing see mine eyes, and a noise of roaring*
> *Waves in my ears sounds;*
>
> *Sweat runs down in rivers, a tremor seizes*
> *All my limbs and paler than grass in autumn,*
> *Caught by pains of menacing death, I falter,*
> *Lost in the love trance.*

6   Do you not marvel how she seeks to make her mind, body, ears, tongue, eyes, and complexion, as if they were scattered elements strange to her, join together in the same moment of experience? In contradictory

phrases she describes herself as terrified and almost dead, in order to appear afflicted not by one passion but by a swarm of passions. Lovers do have all those feelings, but it is, as I said, her selection of the most vital details and her working them into one whole which produce the outstanding quality of the poem.

7   In the same way, as I believe, Homer picks out what is hardest to endure when describing a storm. The author of the *Arimaspeia,* on the other hand, thinks this awe-inspiring:

> It is a marvel to us, to our minds,
> That men should dwell at sea, so far from land.
> Unfortunate creatures, many ills are theirs,
> Their eyes fixed on the sky, their minds on the deep.
>
> Often to heaven they raise up their hands
> In a sad prayer from their heaving hearts.

8   Everyone can plainly see that there is here more froth than terror. How does Homer do it? Here is an example among many:

> He rushed upon them, as a wave storm-driven,
> Boistrous beneath black clouds, on a swift ship
> Will burst, and all is hidden in the foam;
> Meanwhile the wind tears thundering at the mast,
> And all hands tremble, pale and sore afraid,
> As they are carried close from under death.
>   *Iliad* 15.624–628

Aratus tried to adapt the same idea: "Thin planks keep death away." He has made his description trivial and smooth instead of terrifying. Indeed, he has circumscribed the danger in the words "planks keep death away," for in fact they do keep it away! Homer does not limit the danger to one moment; instead, he draws a picture of men avoiding destruction many times, at every wave; he forces and compels into unnatural union prepositions which are not easily joined together when he says *"from under* death." He has tortured his line into conformity with the impending disaster, and by the compactness of his language he brilliantly represents the calamity and almost stamps upon the words the very shape of the peril: "they are carried from under death." . . .

9   These writers have sifted out the most significant details on the basis of merit, so to speak, and joined them harmoniously without inserting between them anything irrelevant, frivolous, or artificial; such additions spoil the total effect just as the imperfect adjustment of massive stones that are fitted together into a wall spoils the whole structure if chinks and fissures are left between them. ❖

Questions to Ponder

1. In Sappho's ode, does her trembling, frenzied emotion gain force because it is contrasted with her lover's "blissful" calm? How does contrast help to accentuate emotions and descriptions?
2. How would Sappho's ode be different if she depicted both herself and her lover distraught by love's frenzy?
3. Can writers gain surprising and often stunning effects by joining words together that do not seem easily or naturally joined, like Homer's line about the sailors, "they are carried close from under death"? Does the fact that we pause and wonder what "from under death" means add to or detract from the power of the image? Why can writing be effective when it is a little strange?
4. What is meant by matching form to content?

Writing Possibilities

1. Reread your freewrite on how the emotion of love affects your body and mind. Underline the words, phrases, or sentences that seem best selected or combined. Copy these words, phrases, or sentences onto another sheet of paper and see if they seem to suggest to you a poem, an essay, a dialogue, or a story. Add on to these passages toward the form of your choice.
2. Rewrite the first five lines of Sappho's ode, turning her lover into a distraught (rather than a serene) figure. Now would you want to alter any of the later lines so that they better fit the new situation?
3. Return to your two lists of words describing a storm. Reread the sentence you wrote to see if you wish to make any revisions. Then select other words from each of your lists and join them in interesting or unusual combinations.
4. Think of an exciting experience you have had. Make a list of descriptive details; then try to recapture the experience though your selection and combination of these details. What form does your writing take?

"Come Quick. Indians!"
John McNulty

James Thurber wrote of his good friend John McNulty, "Nobody who knew McNulty . . . could ever have confused him for a moment with anybody else. His presence in a room . . . was as special as the way he put words down on paper" (James Thurber, introduction, The World of John McNulty [Garden City, New York: Doubleday, 1957], 10). McNulty was a newspaperman and writer of New Yorker sketches from the 1920s until his death in 1955. New York racetracks and Manhattan watering holes were the favored settings for McNulty sketches for he was the troubadour of cabbies, rummies, doormen, and the two-dollar bettor.

McNulty was born in Lawrence, Massachusetts, in 1895. He once wrote, "I attended four institutions of higher learning: Holy Cross, Colby, Columbia and Tim Costello's on Third Avenue. I've forgotten nearly everything I learned at the first three—but nothing I ever saw in the last" (Faith McNulty, personal interview, 5 June 1986). Besides the saloons, McNulty loved the streets of New York. He would rise at 5:00 A.M. and be out at 6:00, strolling the "avenyas" of his city, stopping to talk and to listen to everyone along the way.

A phrase would become the kernel of a McNulty article or sketch. He would hear something—like "She's a Bostonian. They call them" or "We get stranglers come in here at all hours"—and then build his piece around that line. His stories were essentially anecdotes, but anecdotes written with great humanity and art.

McNulty was that rare kind of writer who composes primarily in his head and then transfers the words to paper. He would hear a phrase, work it around in his mind for a day or two, and then type out his story in a rush in 15 or 20 minutes. Creative tension would be in the air before he would start thundering on the keys, but he rarely had to make more than a minor change or two when he pulled the finished sketch from his typewriter.

McNulty was a rewrite man at the time when this was one of the most highly regarded (and best paying) jobs on a newspaper. He was one of the fastest rewrite men around, and when, in 1944, Paramount Studios lured him to Hollywood to write for the movies, he wrote up his first script at city room speed, appalling his fellow writers, who threatened to lock him up if he did not slow his pace.

In his approach to writing McNulty was never intellectual. He loved ordinary *people and he loved language, and he regarded the latter with the eye of a perfectionist. He often reread H. L. Mencken's The American Language. McNulty also delighted in humor. Wit and satire simply did not interest him. He was one of the very few American writers of this century whose skill was balanced by an inexhaustible generosity of feeling.*

Brief Warm-up Writing Exercises

1. Describe a person (perhaps yourself) running a race. Try to imagine every step and feeling along the way, and capture them in words.
2. Describe an experience when time seemed to go in slow motion or stand completely still. (A class? A dental appointment? A moment of revelation?)

---

1 ❖ Once I was a movie piano player in the days when films were silent. This was in Andover, Massachusetts, seat of the famed Phillips Academy. The movie house was down Main Street from the Academy, the region known as "the foot of the hill." The theatre was owned by a man named Sam Resnik.

2 I admit at once that I was a singularly bad piano player. I still am, although I have turned to other trades in the intervening years. But I did get twenty-four dollars a week from Resnik for playing piano for only about seven or eight hours a day, six days a week, and that was not hay. It was not piano-playing either, it was specialized noise. Two of us made a team. One was Nick Baudo, who was the operator. Nowadays they call them projectionists. I was the other member of the team, the piano player.

3 Nicky and I were good friends and we liked working together. We both lived over in Lawrence, four miles from Andover; about eighteen minutes on the streetcar on account of the stops and all. We'd meet on Essex Street in Lawrence about twelve o'clock, get on the Andover trolley car and go over to work. When we got to Andover, the first thing we would do in Andover Square would be go to Lowe's drugstore and have a chocolate milk shake, each of us. Money meant nothing to us. We were, as they say now, in the chips. I'd get a pack of Sweet Caps on the way out of Lowe's and I recall now how swanky a way I behaved just buying the cigarettes, because I was not engaged in any ordinary trade. I was a piano player.

4 Then it would be time for us to go down the hill, at right angles to Main Street, to the railroad station and get the cans of film for that day. We had to do that on Monday, Wednesday, and Friday. Each show ran two days—two afternoons and nights—Monday and Tuesday, Wednesday and Thursday, and Friday and Saturday.

5 When Nick picked up the cans of films at the railroad station, I remember now, I often said to him, "What have we got today, Nick?" and sometimes he would reply, "Sunbonnets and cows." That was a kind of code expression

between us. It meant we had Mary Miles Minter. Miss Minter was one of the most popular stars in the Andover Theatre, as she was all over the country.

6   Sam Resnik would greet us as we got to the movie house. He was a little lame and he would come laboriously down the three or four steps from the theatre to the street and say: "Hello, boys, you got the stuff?"

7   "Hello, Mr. Resnik," Nicky and I would say in chorus. "We got it."

8   Of course, he knew we had the films. Nicky was obviously carrying them, the round silvery cans, but Resnik's question and our answer was just an exchange of words. Sam Resnik was not a voluble man, and it was hard for him to make conversation. He was a square shooter and Nicky and I both liked him.

9   One by one, or in the case of boys from the Academy, by fours and fives, the customers would start to go in. Nicky and I would stand in front, smoking. I remember how proud I was, loafing in front of the place and hearing, just often enough to make my spirits soar, someone say, nodding toward me, "That's the piano player." I'd look at Nicky then, and he'd look at me, good man that he was, and I fear I felt a little superior to my friend, because nobody ever said, "That's the operator."

10 It would get to be toward half past one. Nicky and I would go into the theatre and he would climb up the iron ladder to the operating room. On a good afternoon, by that time, there would be perhaps three hundred people seated. That was pretty good, when it is figured at fifteen cents for kids and twenty cents for grown-up people. Academy boys were estimated as grown-up people.

11 They had no popcorn machines or anything else, just a movie show, that's all. I'd take a last drag on the Sweet Caporal outside, the lights would be all on inside as I stepped in, and I would walk down the aisle in a kind of mild swagger. They'd clap. The applause was not for me. It was because they knew by my going to the piano the show was about to start. I took the applause as if it were for me, although in my head I knew better. It made me feel I was quite a guy. I was only nineteen or so.

12 The piano was an upright. It cost $268, and it came from Knuepfer & Dimmock, in Lawrence. I know because my mother had bought the same one, at two dollars a month, and that is where I had learned, if learning it could be called, to bang on the thing. It was down in a pit, but the pit had no depth. Mr. Resnik was not a stingy man, but he had to make all he could out of the theatre. So he squeezed in all the seats possible. The piano, in this pit, had its keyboard about a foot above the floor of the auditorium. So I sat on the floor. Mr. Resnik, long before, had had Nicky saw the legs off a kitchen chair and put it on the floor in front of the piano, and he bought a cushion for it. So, in a manner of speaking, I sat on the floor. On busy days, there was a spectator on either side of me, usually a kid, because only kids would want to sit that close to the screen and look directly up. Looking directly up is what I had to do all the time. Didn't bother me.

13 I'd adjust the cushion on the sawed-off kitchen chair and sit down. Overture.

14 That overture was a honey. Always march time. Frequently, in deference to the scholastic mob from Phillips Academy, I would give them a

college march tune which to this day I still hear once in a while on the newsreels.

15   Behind me, during the overture, I would hear the scuffling of feet getting into anticipatory position, and the additional patrons coming in. Nicky, up in the booth, had control of the light on the piano. Once in a while he would flick it on and off, prankishly, in a kind of hello, or as if to say, "Here we go again."

16   The show would open with a travelogue, about some strange land far from Andover. One reel. For that I played noncommittal music, neither a waltz nor a polka, nor anything. Favorite one was "Wedding of the Winds." Kind of cozy.

17   Now the big feature!

18   (Memory may trick me at this point, and I do not want to do any injustice to Miss Minter, who was good. Yet there were pictures like this feature. I couldn't make them up.)

19   I had practically only one lead-in to the feature. It was "Chinese Lullaby" from *East Is West*, starring Fay Bainter. That was good for the opening because it began in the middle of the piano with seven crashing chords, a pause, and then the same seven chords an octave higher. (For some reason, in silent-movie days, anything played hellangone up on the piano was Chinese.)

20   After the two sets of chords came an arpeggio, and then I would swing into the simple melody, carried with the left hand. All the while, on the screen so immediately above me, the titles were being shown. Behind me, the shuffling of feet was growing less and less audible. The people were settling down.

21   On the screen, the interior of a cabin. A trapper is saying goodbye to his wife. He has a buckskin jacket and pants, and a Daniel Boone hat, a rifle under his arm. On the floor is a child, apparently eight months old, playing and showing, in a close-up, a set of Birdseye frozen curls.

22   Nice quiet music then. Until the dog shows up. He comes gallumping in, and I have to shift to "Has Anybody Here Seen Rover?" That was a piece that had a whistle part in it. When I came to the whistle part, the Academy boys behind me would whistle. Good dog music, that "Rover" number.

23   At this juncture, the plot sets in in earnest. I sail into some more home-made waltzes. They all sound suspiciously like nothing, except that they are all in three-quarter time.

24   The trapper, rather abruptly, has left the cabin. We look back in there and see it still contains the wife, the baby, and the dog. The *heimgemacht* waltzes continue. Maybe once in a while *Tales from the Vienna Woods* sneaks in, since I see a tree.

25   QUICK! flash of skulking Indians. I shift remarkably quickly into what was known as "Hurry No. 63." I had a book of short bursts of music, for movie piano players, which contained numbered "hurries," or excitement music, as well as "lentos," or gentle stuff, and so on. My favorite hurry was No. 63. That was a thing played alternately with the left and right hand, agitato, as they'd call it at Carnegie Hall. At almost the same time I would work in some Indian music. That consisted mostly of banging a chord of A natural and E natural over and over with the left hand and playing any old thing with the right.

26   The Indians move near the cabin. I keep rolling on A flat with both hands. We're inside the cabin again. The wife is at her tasks. Waltz. Baby and dog are playing together. It is a lovely scene. Quick version of "Anybody Here Seen Rover?" mixed up with "Rock-a-bye Baby in the Treetop," both fast versions.

27   Back to the Indians. I have to shift fast here. The Indian music almost gets mixed up with the waltz, "Hurry No. 63," "Rover," and "Rock-a-bye," but somehow I manage it.

28   This is an exciting part, and to top it all, the light on the piano begins to blink. Nicky is keyed up too. I glance back over my shoulder and see, through the square hole in the operating room, the dark Italian eye of my pal. It is a laughing eye and it is a friendly eye, which spurs me on to new endeavor. I give the piano complete hell.

29   The Indians start shooting arrows. Not plain arrows. Arrows with lighted paper or something like it on them. The theory is that the cabin is so highly inflammable that the touch of one piece of lighted paper against it would turn it into a holocaust. It does, indeed, for one arrow, with lighted paper, hits the cabin in a close-up.

30   That calls for fire music. Easy. Just hit A flat high up and roll it. A flat rolled is fire music, I don't care what you say.

31   The Missus, as she might be called for handiness, glances through the window and sees the flames. Sees the Indians, too. I play tragic music. Very low. Very somber. Minor chords.

32   Quick shift again. The trapper's lady runs back to the baby, picks her up, clasps her in her arms. Seconds of soft music for close-up of mother and child.

33   To make everything clear, there is a close-up of the father, Boone-hat himself, taking an animal out of one of his traps. That proves, in case anyone has forgotten, that he isn't home.

34   The interior of the cabin again. She's decided what to do. She finds, right in front of our very eyes, paper and pencil. She scribbles a note. The note comes up big in a close-up. It says: "Come quick. INDIANS!"

35   She pins the note on the collar of the faithful dog, while I give them "Rover" fast again. She opens the door, the dog runs out, an Indian shoots at him, the blackguard, but misses. The cabin is flaming.

36   I am in an awful jam here, trying to figure out whether to play dog music, fire music, Indian music or mother music, and I wind up with a parlay of the whole outfit.

37   The dog, note on his collar, is shown running through the woods. I give him the full, twelve-dollar treatment of "Anybody Here Seen Rover?"

38   Next shot, stockade. Gate swinging wide open as dog enters. Complete pause on piano. Too dramatic for music.

39   Now I play a bugle call on the piano. That's while the commandant, who happens to be hanging around at the gate waiting for dogs to come in with notes on their collars, reads the tidy escriture.

40   Flash back to the cabin to prove the Indians haven't quit their nasty work. On the piano, "Under the Double Eagle." Horses and soldiers coming out through the stockade gate. "Loud and Fast" on the piano.

41   Indians almost upon the cabin, which is viciously aflame. I roll on A flat again, for fire. Indian stuff mixed in. Very exciting. Nicky blinks the light. I have no time to look back at him. I get louder and louder. "Under the Double Eagle" practically roars while the soldiers gallop up and the cowardly Indians, what are left of them, skulk away.

42   The trapper's wife, babe in arms with untouched curls, greets the soldiers. By chance, the trapper has come home at the same time. Big reunion all around.

43   I play "When You Come to the End of a Perfect Day" and Nicky and I go out and have a milk shake before the night show. ❖

Questions to Ponder

1. Why do you think John McNulty takes so much time and space describing the layout of the town of Andover, the Phillips Academy, his friend Nicky and his boss Sam Resnik before he begins telling what it was like to be a silent-movie piano player? What does he gain by this?

2. What sort of person does 19-year-old John McNulty seem to be? What words and phrases in this memoir create your picture of him? Do you like him?

3. Why does McNulty resort to so many short and abbreviated sentences in this piece, sentences like, "Nice quiet music then. Until the dog shows up." In what contexts might sentence fragments be effective?

4. John McNulty obviously has a wide-ranging vocabulary. He can speak of a "tidy escriture" and toss in an "agitato" and a *heimgemacht* when he wishes, but for most of this piece he chooses to be simple and informal, almost studiedly unstudied. Does the youthful, slangy style of this piece work for you? How is it suited to its subject? Why do you think McNulty occasionally drops high-falutin' words into this context?

5. McNulty wraps up this piece in one swift sentence. Does this work for you? Does it make an effective end?

Writing Possibilities

1. Try to imagine the plot of another silent movie (perhaps the villain tying the heroine to the train tracks), and write a description of the movie and the piano playing using McNulty's piece as a model.

2. Reread your description of the race from warm-up writing exercise 1. Try revising it, shortening some of the sentences and switching to fragments as the action accelerates. Try using several very short sentences in a row. See if you can make the pace of your sentences match the pace of the race.

3. Now switch to your description in warm-up writing exercise 2 of an endless moment when time dragged or stood still. See if you can capture

this endless feeling through your choice of details and the pace of your sentences.

Concepts We Live By
George Lakoff and Mark Johnson

Mark Johnson

George Lakoff

I first arrived in Berkeley on New Year's Day 1979 to begin a visiting appointment in the Philosophy Department at the University of California. The next morning I called George Lakoff to ask whether he would write an essay on metaphor for the anthology I was preparing, and, as he was about to do what he did nearly every morning—go out for a café au lait—we decided to meet at the Three C's café. It turned out that we both shared the same deep dissatisfaction with the dominant views of language, meaning, rationality, and knowledge within our respective traditions of philosophy and linguistics. We both felt that the pervasiveness and importance of metaphor in thought and experience had been seriously underestimated and that one's view of metaphor was a good way of testing where someone stood on a number of important philosophical issues.

George said he would be happy to write a piece for the anthology, but within a week he started calling me to talk over troubling issues that ranged across several disciplines but seemed to be intimately related to metaphor. When we met at the café again at the end of that first week, George said, "Let's do this thing together"—and he meant together. After we had talked and argued and made notes, he sat down at his Smith-Corona portable electric typewriter, I sat next to him, and we wrote the article sentence by sentence. One of us would start a sentence and the other would finish it. One would restate what the other had said, and then that would be reworked again. It all went pretty fast. We began to work out our view of human beings as metaphorizing animals whose conceptualization, reasoning, and expression are structured by systematic metaphorical mappings as basic cognitive processes.

The day in March when we finished the article, we agreed that we ought to work out the implications of this view in a book. So, we began immediately, working in the same way as before but with more intensity, more confusion, more obstacles, more pressure. Of course, this was to be expected, because we had done some hand waving about difficult philosophical problems in the paper that we could not avoid in the book. About issues where there was considerable disagreement, I decided early on to state my view and make my best argument, but not to insist on my view. I did exercise a modest amount of control, because early in the morning I would often edit and retype what we had done the night before, and then show it to George.

Toward the end, the work was incredibly intense, because I was leaving Berkeley July 1. After I finished teaching, for the last month or so, we worked together every day, sometimes 14 or 15 hours a day. Through all this we developed a deep friendship, finished the first draft, and had some great Chinese and Thai food.

Mark Johnson

Brief Warm-up Writing Exercises

1. Describe what people mean when they say of a person "He is a prince" or "She is a doll."
2. Choose the animal you think you are most like, and freewrite on why you are like this animal.
3. Choose from all the world and write on this topic: Life for me is most like a _____.

---

1 ❖ Metaphor is for most people a device of the poetic imagination and the rhetorical flourish—a matter of extraordinary rather than ordinary language. Moreover, metaphor is typically viewed as characteristic of language alone, a matter of words rather than thought or action. For this reason, most people think they can get along perfectly well without metaphor. We have found, on the contrary, that metaphor is pervasive in everyday life, not just in language but in thought and action. Our ordinary conceptual system, in terms of which we both think and act, is fundamentally metaphorical in nature.

2 The concepts that govern our thought are not just matters of the intellect. They also govern our everyday functioning, down to the most mundane details. Our concepts structure what we perceive, how we get around in the world, and how we relate to other people. Our conceptual system thus plays a central role in defining our everyday realities. If we are right in suggesting

that our conceptual system is largely metaphorical, then the way we think, what we experience, and what we do every day is very much a matter of metaphor.

3   But our conceptual system is not something we are normally aware of. In most of the little things we do every day, we simply think and act more or less automatically along certain lines. Just what these lines are is by no means obvious. One way to find out is by looking at language. Since communication is based on the same conceptual system that we use in thinking and acting, language is an important source of evidence for what that system is like.

4   Primarily on the basis of linguistic evidence, we have found that most of our ordinary conceptual system is metaphorical in nature. And we have found a way to begin to identify in detail just what the metaphors are that structure how we perceive, how we think, and what we do.

5   To give some idea of what it could mean for a concept to be metaphorical and for such a concept to structure an everyday activity, let us start with the concept ARGUMENT and the conceptual metaphor ARGUMENT IS WAR. This metaphor is reflected in our everyday language by a wide variety of expressions:

ARGUMENT IS WAR

Your claims are *indefensible.*
He *attacked every weak point* in my argument.
His criticisms were *right on target.*
I *demolished* his argument.
I've never *won* an argument with him.
You disagree? Okay, *shoot!*
If you use that *strategy,* he'll *wipe you out.*
He *shot down* all of my arguments.

6   It is important to see that we don't just *talk* about arguments in terms of war. We can actually win or lose arguments. We see the person we are arguing with as an opponent. We attack his positions and we defend our own. We gain and lose ground. We plan and use strategies. If we find a position indefensible, we can abandon it and take a new line of attack. Many of the things we *do* in arguing are partially structured by the concept of war. Though there is no physical battle, there is a verbal battle, and the structure of an argument—attack, defense, counterattack, etc.—reflects this. It is in this sense that the ARGUMENT IS WAR metaphor is one that we live by in this culture; it structures the actions we perform in arguing.

7   Try to imagine a culture where arguments are not viewed in terms of war, where no one wins or loses, where there is no sense of attacking or defending, gaining or losing ground. Imagine a culture where an argument is viewed as

a dance, the participants are seen as performers, and the goal is to perform in a balanced and aesthetically pleasing way. In such a culture, people would view arguments differently, experience them differently, carry them out differently, and talk about them differently. But *we* would probably not view them as arguing at all: they would simply be doing something different. It would seem strange even to call what they were doing "arguing." Perhaps the most neutral way of describing this difference between their culture and ours would be to say that we have a discourse form structured in terms of battle and they have one structured in terms of dance.

8   This is an example of what it means for a metaphorical concept, namely, ARGUMENT IS WAR, to structure (at least in part) what we do and how we understand what we are doing when we argue. *The essence of metaphor is understanding and experiencing one kind of thing in terms of another.* It is not that arguments are a subspecies of war. Arguments and wars are different kinds of things—verbal discourse and armed conflict—and the actions performed are different kinds of actions. But ARGUMENT is partially structured, understood, performed, and talked about in terms of WAR. The concept is metaphorically structured, the activity is metaphorically structured, and, consequently, the language is metaphorically structured.

9   Moreover, this is the *ordinary* way of having an argument and talking about one. The normal way for us to talk about attacking a position is to use the words "attack a position." Our conventional ways of talking about arguments presuppose a metaphor we are hardly ever conscious of. The metaphor is not merely in the words we use—it is in our very concept of an argument. The language of argument is not poetic, fanciful, or rhetorical; it is literal. We talk about arguments that way because we conceive of them that way—and we act according to the way we conceive of things. . . . ❖

Questions to Ponder

1. Do you agree with Lakoff and Johnson that arguing is like war? Where might the analogy collapse?
2. Do some people think of *love* as war? If your thinking is shaped by the metaphor "Love is war," what might some of your thoughts, actions, and statements be? How would they be different from those of one who thought of love as a "collaborative work of art"?
3. What do we mean in Western cultures when we use the metaphor "Time is money"? In what ways is time like money? What other ways are there to think of time?
4. What common metaphors shape *your* life?
5. In what ways is writing a "solo" activity? In what ways is it a "collaborative" process? How might it be limiting to think of writing as one or the other?

Writing Possibilities

1. To illustrate the importance of metaphors in shaping our thoughts, actions, and language, describe two hypothetical couples. The first (call them George and Martha) think of love as war. The second (call them Phil and Marlo) think of love as a collaborative work of art. Contrast how the two couples would think, act, and speak to each other.
2. Today we often hear of our "war on drugs." Make a list of the ways the U.S. "war on drugs" is like a real war. Make another list of ways in which the drug situation is *not* like a war. Then write a letter to President Bush (or to the current U.S. drug czar) advising him to accelerate or scrap the "drug war" metaphor. How is this metaphor helping or hindering U.S. efforts to deal with drugs?
3. Write a poem or a short essay that starts with this line: My house (dorm room, apartment) is a _____.

DOUBLE-SUNRISE

Anne Morrow Lindbergh

I began these pages for myself, in order to think out my own particular pattern of living, my own individual balance of life, work and human relationships. And since I think best with a pencil in my hand, I started naturally to write. I had the feeling, when the thoughts first clarified on paper, that my experience was very different from other people's. (Are we all under this illusion?) My situation had, in certain ways, more freedom than that of most people, and in certain other ways, much less.

Besides, I thought, not all women are searching for a new pattern of living, or want a contemplative corner of their own. Many women are content with their lives as they are. They manage amazingly well, far better than I, it seemed to me, looking at their lives from the outside. With envy and admiration, I observed the porcelain perfection of their smoothly ticking days. Perhaps they had no problems, or had found the answers long ago. No, I decided, these discussions would have value and interest only for myself.

But as I went on writing and simultaneously talking with other women, young and old, with different lives and experiences—those who supported themselves, those who wished careers, those who were hard-working housewives and mothers, and those with more ease—I found that my point of view was not unique. In varying settings and under different forms, I discovered that many women, and men, too, were grappling with essentially the same questions as I, and were hungry to discuss and argue and hammer out possible answers. Even those whose lives had appeared to be ticking imperturbably under their smiling clock-faces were often trying, like me, to evolve another rhythm with more creative pauses in it, more adjustment to their individual needs, and new and more alive relationships to themselves as well as others.

And so gradually, these chapters, fed by conversations, arguments and revelations from men and women of all groups, became more than my individual story, until I decided in the end to give them back to the people who had shared and stimulated many of these thoughts. Here, then, with my warm feelings of gratitude and companionship for those working along the same lines, I return my gift from the sea.

Brief Warm-up Exercises

1. Freewrite about any experiences you have had collecting seashells or rocks. What discoveries did you make?
2. Brainstorm a list of the most important relationships in your life up to this point. Choose one, and write a paragraph in which you try to capture the particular quality of this relationship.
3. Write your own personal definition of "ideal love."
4. Brainstorm a list of all the things that keep people from achieving the relationships they want.

---

1 ❖ This shell was a gift; I did not find it. It was handed to me by a friend. It is unusual on the island. One does not often come across such a perfect double-sunrise shell. Both halves of this delicate bivalve are exactly matched. Each side, like the wing of a butterfly, is marked with the same pattern; translucent white, except for three rosy rays that fan out from the golden hinge binding the two together. I hold two sunrises between my thumb and finger. Smooth, whole, unblemished shell, I wonder how its fragile perfection survived the breakers on the beach.

2   It is unusual; yet it was given to me freely. People are like that here. Strangers smile at you on the beach, come up and offer you a shell, for no reason, lightly, and then go by and leave you alone again. Nothing is demanded of you in payment, no social rite expected, no tie established. It was

a gift, freely offered, freely taken, in mutual trust. People smile at you here, like children, sure that you will not rebuff them, that you will smile back. And you do, because you know it will involve nothing. The smile, the act, the relationship is hung in space, in the immediacy and purity of the present; suspended on the still point of here and now; balanced there, on a shaft of air, like a seagull.

3   The pure relationship, how beautiful it is! How easily it is damaged, or weighed down with irrelevancies—not even irrelevancies, just life itself, the accumulations of life and of time. For the first part of every relationship is pure, whether it be with friend or lover, husband or child. It is pure, simple and unencumbered. It is like the artist's vision before he has to discipline it into form, or like the flower of love before it has ripened to the firm but heavy fruit of responsibility. Every relationship seems simple at its start. The simplicity of first love, or friendliness, the mutuality of first sympathy seems, at its initial appearance—even if merely in exciting conversation across a dinner table—to be a self-enclosed world. Two people listening to each other, two shells meeting each other, making one world between them. There are no others in the perfect unity of that instant, no other people or things or interests. It is free of ties or claims, unburdened by responsibilities, by worry about the future or debts to the past.

4   And then how swiftly, how inevitably the perfect unity is invaded; the relationship changes; it becomes complicated, encumbered by its contact with the world. I believe this is true in most relationships, with friends, with husband or wife, and with one's children. But it is the marriage relationship in which the changing pattern is shown up most clearly because it is the deepest one and the most arduous to maintain; and because, somehow, we mistakenly feel that failure to maintain its exact original pattern is tragedy.

5   It is true, of course, the original relationship is very beautiful. Its self-enclosed perfection wears the freshness of a spring morning. Forgetting about the summer to come, one often feels one would like to prolong the spring of early love, when two people stand as individuals, without past or future, facing each other. One resents any change, even though one knows that transformation is natural and part of the process of life and its evolution. Like its parallel in physical passion, the early ecstatic stage of a relationship cannot continue always at the same pitch of intensity. It moves to another phase of growth which one should not dread, but welcome as one welcomes summer after spring. But there is also a dead weight accumulation, a coating of false values, habits, and burdens which blights life. It is this smothering coat that needs constantly to be stripped off, in life as well as in relationships.

6   Both men and women feel the change in the early relationship and hunger nostalgically for its original pattern as life goes on and becomes more complicated. For inevitably, as the relationship grows, both men and women, at least to some degree, are drawn into their more specialized and functional roles: man, into his less personal work in the world; woman, into her traditional obligations with family and household. In both fields, functional relationships

tend to take the place of the early all-absorbing personal one. But woman refinds in a limited form with each new child, something resembling, at least in its absorption, the early pure relationship. In the sheltered simplicity of the first days after a baby is born, one sees again the magical closed circle, the miraculous sense of two people existing only for each other, the tranquil sky reflected on the face of the mother nursing her child. It is, however, only a brief interlude and not a substitute for the original more complete relationship.

7   But though both men and women are absorbed in their specialized roles and each misses something of the early relationship, there are great differences in their needs. While man, in his realm, has less chance for personal relations than woman, he may have more opportunity for giving himself creatively in work. Woman, on the other hand, has more chance for personal relations, but these do not give her a sense of her creative identity, the individual who has something of her own to say or to give. With each partner hungry for different reasons and each misunderstanding the other's needs, it is easy to fall apart or into late love affairs. The temptation is to blame the situation on the other person and to accept the easy solution that a new and more understanding partner will solve everything.

8   But neither woman nor man are likely to be fed by another relationship which seems easier because it is in an earlier stage. Such a love affair cannot really bring back a sense of identity. Certainly, one has the illusion that one will find oneself in being loved for what one really is, not for a collection of functions. But can one actually find oneself in someone else? In someone else's love? Or even in the mirror someone else holds up for one? I believe that true identity is found, as Eckhart once said, by "going into one's own ground and knowing oneself." It is found in creative activity springing from within. It is found, paradoxically, when one loses oneself. One must lose one's life to find it. Woman can best refind herself by losing herself in some kind of creative activity of her own. Here she will be able to refind her strength, the strength she needs to look and work at the second half of the problem—the neglected pure relationship. Only a refound person can refind a personal relationship.

9   But can the pure relationship of the sunrise shell be refound once it has become obscured? Obviously some relationships can never be recovered. It is not just a question of different needs to be understood and filled. In their changing roles the two partners may have grown in different directions or at different rates of speed. A brief double-sunrise episode may have been all they could achieve. It was an end in itself and not a foundation for a deeper relation. In a growing relationship, however, the original essence is not lost but merely buried under the impedimenta of life. The core of reality is still there and needs only to be uncovered and reaffirmed.

10   One way of rediscovering the double-sunrise is to duplicate some of its circumstances. Husband and wife can and should go off on vacations alone and also on vacations alone *together*. For if it is possible that woman can find herself by having a vacation alone, it is equally possible that the original relationship can sometimes be refound by having a vacation alone *together*.

Most married couples have felt the unexpected joy of one of these vacations. How wonderful it was to leave the children, the house, the job, and all the obligations of daily life; to go out together, whether for a month or a weekend or even just a night in an inn by themselves. How surprising it was to find the miracle of the sunrise repeated. There was the sudden pleasure of having breakfast alone with the man one fell in love with. Here at the small table, are only two people facing each other. How the table at home has grown! And how distracting it is, with four or five children, a telephone ringing in the hall, two or three school buses to catch, not to speak of the commuter's train. How all this separates one from one's husband and clogs up the pure relationship. But sitting at a table alone opposite each other, what is there to separate one? Nothing but a coffee pot, corn muffins and marmalade. A simple enough pleasure, surely, to have breakfast alone with one's husband, but how seldom married people in the midst of life achieve it.

11   Actually, I believe this temporary return to the pure relationship holds good for one's children, too. If only, I think, playing with my sunrise shell—if only we could have each of our children alone, not just for part of each day, but for part of each month, each year. Would they not be happier, stronger and, in the end, more independent because more secure? Does each child not secretly long for the pure relationship he once had with the mother, when he was "The Baby," when the nursery doors were shut and she was feeding him at her breast—*alone?* And if we were able to put into practice this belief and spend more time with each child alone—would he not only gain in security and strength, but also learn an important first lesson in his adult relationship?

12   We all wish to be loved alone. "Don't sit under the apple-tree with anyone else but me," runs the old popular song. Perhaps, as Auden says in his poem, this is a fundamental error in mankind.

> *For the error bred in the bone*
> *Of each woman and each man*
> *Craves what it cannot have,*
> *Not universal love*
> *But to be loved alone.*

13   Is it such a sin? In discussing this verse with an Indian philosopher, I had an illuminating answer. "It is all right to wish to be loved alone," he said, "mutuality is the essence of love. There cannot be others in mutuality. It is only in the time-sense that it is wrong. It is when we desire *continuity* of being loved alone that we go wrong." For not only do we insist on believing romantically in the "one-and-only"—the one-and-only love, the one-and-only mate, the one-and-only mother, the one-and-only security—we wish the "one-and-only" to be permanent, ever-present and continuous. The desire for continuity of being-loved-alone seems to me "the error bred in the bone" of man. For "there is no one-and-only," as a friend of mine once said in a similar discussion, "there are just one-and-only moments."

14 The one-and-only moments are justified. The return to them, even if temporarily, is valid. The moment over the marmalade and muffins is valid; the moment feeding the child at the breast is valid; the moment racing with him later on the beach is valid. Finding shells together, polishing chestnuts, sharing one's treasures:—all these moments of together-aloneness are valid, but not permanent.

15 One comes in the end to realize that there is no permanent pure-relationship and there should not be. It is not even something to be desired. The pure relationship is limited, in space and in time. In its essence it implies exclusion. It excludes the rest of life, other relationships, other sides of personality, other responsibilities, other possibilities in the future. It excludes growth. The other children are there clamoring outside the closed nursery door. One loves them, too. The telephone rings in the next room. One also wants to talk to friends. When the muffins are cleared away, one must think of the next meal or the next day. These are realities too, not to be excluded. Life must go on. That does not mean it is a waste of time to recreate for brief holiday periods together-alone experiences. On the contrary, these one-and-only moments are both refreshing and rewarding. The light shed over the small breakfast table illumines the day, many days. The race on the beach together renews one's youth like a dip in the sea. But we are no longer children; life is not a beach. There is no pattern here for permanent return, only for refreshment.

16 One learns to accept the fact that no permanent return is possible to an old form of relationship; and, more deeply still, that there is no holding of a relationship to a single form. This is not tragedy but part of the ever-recurrent miracle of life and growth. All living relationships are in process of change, of expansion, and must perpetually be building themselves new forms. But there is no single fixed form to express such a changing relationship. There are perhaps different forms for each successive stage; different shells I might put in a row on my desk to suggest the different stages of marriage—or indeed of any relationship.

17 My double-sunrise shell comes first. It is a valid image, I think, for the first stage: two flawless halves bound together with a single hinge, meeting each other at every point, the dawn of a new day spreading on each face. It is a world to itself. Is this not what the poets have always been attempting to describe?

> *And now good-morrow to our waking souls*
> *Which watch not one another out of fear;*
> *For love all love of other sights controls,*
> *And makes one little room an everywhere.*
> *Let sea-discoverers to new worlds have gone,*
> *Let maps to other, worlds on worlds have shown,*
> *Let us possess one world; each hath one, and is one.*

18 It is, however, a "little room," that Donne describes, a small world, that must be inevitably and happily outgrown. Beautiful, fragile, fleeting, the sun-

rise shell; but not, for all that, illusory. Because it is not lasting, let us not fall into the cynic's trap and call it an illusion. Duration is not a test of true or false. The day of the dragon-fly or the night of the Saturnid moth is not invalid simply because that phase in its life cycle is brief. Validity need have no relation to time, to duration, to continuity. It is on another plane, judged by other standards. It relates to the actual moment in time and place. "And what is actual is actual only for one time and only for one place." The sunrise shell has the eternal validity of all beautiful and fleeting things. ❖

Questions to Ponder

1. What stage of love does the double-sunrise seashell represent for Anne Morrow Lindbergh?
2. Why do you think it is important that such love be "freely given"?
3. Do you agree with Anne Morrow Lindbergh that most people wish to be "loved alone," that is, without any interference from the world and other people? Explain the reasons for your agreement or disagreement.
4. Why is it that such moments of pure love-alone cannot last?
5. Like Anne Morrow Lindbergh, do you think best with a pencil (or pen) in your hand or at a word processor? How does writing help us to know what we think and to clarify our thoughts?

Writing Possibilities

1. Write a journal entry just for yourself in which you test Anne Morrow Lindbergh's metaphor against important past relationships in your life—relationships with friends, lovers, spouses, or children. Did any of them have the perfect double-sunrise "love alone" quality that Lindbergh describes? What happened to these relationships? Did the perfection last?
2. Imagine and then describe a seashell that would be like the relationship you have with someone special to you. Would it be like the perfect double-sunrise seashell—or some other form entirely? Perhaps it is like a seashell no one yet has seen. Describe it.
3. Choose another metaphor (besides a seashell) for describing a relationship you have, or that many people have. In all the world, what is such a relationship most like?
4. Anne Morrow Lindbergh compares the early "simple and unencumbered" stage represented by the double-sunrise seashell to the artist's vision before the artist "has to discipline it [the vision] into form." Taking this comparison as a starting point, work out what this means in terms of writing.

Letter from Birmingham Jail
Martin Luther King, Jr.

Martin Luther King, Jr., and his sister, Christine, often studied together during their days at Booker T. Washington High School in Atlanta. He helped her with her math; she corrected his spelling. "I can't spell a lick," he later confessed, but his vocabulary dazzled the world (Stephen B. Oates, Let the Trumpet Sound: The Life of Martin Luther King, Jr. [New York: Harper & Row, 1982], 13).

King liked to read alone in his room, studying the way writers and orators joined words together. He later claimed that his "greatest talent, strongest tradition, and most constant interest was the eloquent statement of ideas" (Oates 16). According to lawyer William Kunstler, King used "the finest—and clearest—prose ever uttered." (Oates 178).

When King entered Morehouse College in the mid-1940s, he was shocked to discover that he read only at the eighth-grade level. Later he spoke with bitterness about the inferior education he had received in Atlanta's segregated schools. Through hard work King overcame that disadvantage and not only earned a bachelor's degree from Morehouse but was valedictorian of his Crozer Seminary class in 1951 and received his doctorate in theology from Boston University.

King's process for writing his doctoral thesis included writing to Paul Tillich and other theologians for information, reading hundreds of books and articles, and recording his findings on three-by-five-inch cards, which he collated on his living room floor. King would rise at 5:30 every morning and work on his thesis for three hours before leaving for work at his first church, the Dexter Avenue Baptist Church in Montgomery, Alabama. After a long day of church duties—marriages, funerals, counseling, visits—he would retreat to his study after dinner for three more hours of writing.

King adopted a different strategy for composing his Sunday sermons. During the first years of his ministry, he spent 15 hours a week on each sermon, closing his office door to devote himself to this work. On Tuesdays he would sketch an outline; on Wednesdays he would do research and decide what illustrations and life situations to use. On Fridays and Saturdays he would write the sermon on lined yellow paper, then memorize it, for on Sunday he would deliver the 35-to-40 minute speech without notes, astonishing his congregation. Later, when the pressure of events made him a national leader, King would speak extemporaneously from outlines, but he always longed for greater solitude for reflection, study, and writing.

On Good Friday 1963, King was arrested in Birmingham, Alabama, for leading a nonviolent protest march to end segregation in public accommodations. It was his thirteenth arrest. King was placed in solitary confinement in a narrow, dark cell. He was given no mattress, pillow, or blanket, and no one was allowed to see him. "Those were the longest, most frustrating hours I have lived," he later stated. "I was in a nightmare of despair" (Oates 221).

On Monday morning King's wife, Coretta, called Attorney General Robert Kennedy, who promised to find out why King was being kept in isolation. Suddenly King's jailors appeared with a pillow and mattress; suddenly, they allowed him to exercise and shower.

On Tuesday, King's lawyers brought him a four-day-old copy of the Birmingham News, which had printed a statement from eight white Alabama Christian and Jewish clergymen criticizing King's protest activities. As King read through their statement, an idea seized him. Why not compose a rebuttal to these clergymen in the form of an open letter such as the apostle Paul might have sent them?

With a pen smuggled in by his lawyers, King sat in the shadows of his cell and began writing on the margins of the newspaper. When he had filled the margins he continued on scraps of writing paper and toilet paper supplied by a friendly black trusty. He wrote the last section of the letter on a legal pad furnished by his lawyers.

The Birmingham police knew nothing of King's letter. His lawyers smuggled it out page by page, and it was typed in a frenzy of excitement. First published in pamphlet form by the American Friends Service Committee, "Letter from Birmingham Jail" also appeared in the Christian Century, Liberation, the New Leader, and many other magazines and journals. Almost a million copies circulated in the churches. King's "Letter from Birmingham Jail" has become a classic of protest literature, an eloquent summation of the philosophy and practice of nonviolent resistance. To date there has been no reply from the eight Alabama clergymen.

Brief Warm-up Writing Exercises

1. Freewrite all you know about Martin Luther King, Jr.
2. Can you imagine yourself in jail? Brainstorm a list of all the possible reasons you might find yourself in jail during your life. Circle the most likely reason and describe how this might come about.
3. Freewrite on why you think many people feel uncomfortable talking about racism and relations between races and nationalities.

April 16, 1963

My Dear Fellow Clergymen:

1   While confined here in the Birmingham city jail, I came across your recent statement calling my present activities "unwise and untimely." Seldom do I pause to answer criticism of my work and ideas. If I sought to answer all the criticisms that cross my desk, my secretaries would have little time for anything other than such correspondence in the course of the day, and I would have no time for constructive work. But since I feel that you are men of genuine good will and that your criticisms are sincerely set forth, I want to try to answer your statement in what I hope will be patient and reasonable terms.

2   I think I should indicate why I am here in Birmingham, since you have been influenced by the view which argues against "outsiders coming in." I have the honor of serving as president of the Southern Christian Leadership Conference, an organization operating in every southern state, with headquarters in Atlanta, Georgia. We have some eighty-five affiliated organizations across the South, and one of them is the Alabama Christian Movement for Human Rights. Frequently we share staff, educational, and financial resources with our affiliates. Several months ago the affiliate here in Birmingham asked us to be on call to engage in a nonviolent direct-action program if such were deemed necessary. We readily consented, and when the hour came we lived up to our promise. So I, along with several members of my staff, am here because I was invited here. I am here because I have organizational ties here.

3   But more basically, I am in Birmingham because injustice is here. Just as the prophets of the eighth century B.C. left their villages and carried their "thus saith the Lord" far beyond the boundaries of their home towns, and just as the Apostle Paul left his village of Tarsus and carried the gospel of Jesus Christ to the far corners of the Greco-Roman world, so am I compelled to carry the gospel of freedom beyond my own home town. Like Paul, I must constantly respond to the Macedonian call for aid.[1]

4   Moreover, I am cognizant of the interrelatedness of all communities and states. I cannot sit idly by in Atlanta and not be concerned about what happens in Birmingham. Injustice anywhere is a threat to justice everywhere. We are caught in an inescapable network of mutuality, tied in a single garment of destiny. Whatever affects one directly, affects all indirectly. Never again can we afford to live with the narrow, provincial, "outside agitator" idea. Anyone who lives inside the United States can never be considered an outsider anywhere within its bounds.

5   You deplore the demonstrations taking place in Birmingham. But your statement, I am sorry to say, fails to express a similar concern for the condi-

---

[1] Macedonia was in northern Greece. The citizens of Philippi in Macedonia were among the staunchest Christians, and Paul went frequently to their aid. He also helped resolve occasional bitter disputes within the Christian community there (see Philippians 2:2–14).

tions that brought about the demonstrations. I am sure that none of you would want to rest content with the superficial kind of social analysis that deals merely with effects and does not grapple with underlying causes. It is unfortunate that demonstrations are taking place in Birmingham, but it is even more unfortunate that the city's white power structure left the Negro community with no alternative.

6   In any nonviolent campaign there are four basic steps: collection of the facts to determine whether injustices exist; negotiation; self-purification; and direct action. We have gone through all these steps in Birmingham. There can be no gainsaying the fact that racial injustice engulfs this community. Birmingham is probably the most thoroughly segregated city in the United States. Its ugly record of brutality is widely known. Negroes have experienced grossly unjust treatment in the courts. There have been more unsolved bombings of Negro homes and churches in Birmingham than in any other city in the nation. These are the hard brutal facts of the case. On the basis of these conditions, Negro leaders sought to negotiate with the city fathers. But the latter consistently refused to engage in good-faith negotiation.

7   Then, last September, came the opportunity to talk with leaders of Birmingham's economic community. In the course of the negotiations, certain promises were made by the merchants—for example, to remove the stores' humiliating racial signs. On the basis of these promises, the Reverend Fred Shuttlesworth and the leaders of the Alabama Christian Movement for Human Rights agreed to a moratorium on all demonstrations. As the weeks and months went by, we realized that we were the victims of a broken promise. A few signs, briefly removed, returned; the others remained.

8   As in so many past experiences, our hopes had been blasted, and the shadow of deep disappointment settled upon us. We had no alternative except to prepare for direct action, whereby we would present our very bodies as a means of laying our case before the conscience of the local and the national community. Mindful of the difficulties involved, we decided to undertake a process of self-purification. We began a series of workshops on nonviolence, and we repeatedly asked ourselves: "Are you able to accept blows without retaliating?" "Are you able to endure the ordeal of jail?" We decided to schedule our direct-action program for the Easter season, realizing that except for Christmas, this is the main shopping period of the year. Knowing that a strong economic-withdrawal program would be the by-product of direct action, we felt that this would be the best time to bring pressure to bear on the merchants for the needed change.

9   Then it occurred to us that Birmingham's mayoral election was coming up in March, and we speedily decided to postpone action until after election day. When we discovered that the Commissioner of Public Safety, Eugene "Bull" Connor, had piled up enough votes to be in the run-off, we decided again to postpone action until the day after the run-off so that the demonstrations could not be used to cloud the issues. Like many others, we waited to see Mr. Connor defeated, and to this end we endured postponement after postponement.

Having aided in this community need, we felt that our direct-action program could be delayed no longer.

10   You may well ask, "Why direct action? Why sit-ins, marches, and so forth? Isn't negotiation a better path?" You are quite right in calling for negotiation. Indeed, this is the very purpose of direct action. Nonviolent direct action seeks to create such a crisis and foster such a tension that a community which has constantly refused to negotiate is forced to confront the issue. It seeks so to dramatize the issue that it can no longer be ignored. My citing the creation of tension as part of the work of the nonviolent resister may sound rather shocking. But I must confess that I am not afraid of the word "tension." I have earnestly opposed violent tension, but there is a type of constructive, nonviolent tension which is necessary for growth. Just as Socrates[2] felt that it was necessary to create a tension in the mind so that individuals could rise from the bondage of myths and half truths to the unfettered realm of creative analysis and objective appraisal, so must we see the need for nonviolent gadflies to create the kind of tension in society that will help men rise from the dark depths of prejudice and racism to the majestic heights of understanding and brotherhood.

11   The purpose of our direct-action program is to create a situation so crisis-packed that it will inevitably open the door to negotiation. I therefore concur with you in your call for negotiation. Too long has our beloved Southland been bogged down in a tragic effort to live in monologue rather than dialogue.

12   One of the basic points in your statement is that the action that I and my associates have taken in Birmingham is untimely. Some have asked: "Why didn't you give the new city administration time to act?" The only answer that I can give to this query is that the new Birmingham administration must be prodded about as much as the outgoing one, before it will act. We are sadly mistaken if we feel that the election of Albert Boutwell as mayor will bring the millennium[3] to Birmingham. While Mr. Boutwell is a much more gentle person than Mr. Connor, they are both segregationists, dedicated to maintenance of the status quo. I have hoped that Mr. Boutwell will be reasonable enough to see the futility of massive resistance to desegregation. But he will not see this without pressure from devotees of civil rights. My friends, I must say to you that we have not made a single gain in civil rights without determined legal and nonviolent pressure. Lamentably, it is an historical fact that privileged groups seldom give up their privileges voluntarily. Individuals may see the moral light and voluntarily give up their unjust posture; but, as

---

[2]King is referring here to the tension in the mind created by the question/answer technique known as the Socratic method. Note that King begins this paragraph with questions. Socrates was imprisoned and killed for his civil disobedience (see Plato's *Crito*).

[3]According to Revelation 20, the Second Coming of Christ will be followed by 1,000 years of peace, during which the devil will be incapacitated: This thousand-year period is called the millennium. After this, a final battle between good and evil will occur, followed by the Last Judgment.

Reinhold Niebuhr[4] has reminded us, groups tend to be more immoral than individuals.

13   We know through painful experience that freedom is never voluntarily given by the oppressor; it must be demanded by the oppressed. Frankly, I have yet to engage in a direct-action campaign that was "well timed" in the view of those who have not suffered unduly from the disease of segregation. For years now I have heard the word "Wait!" It rings in the ear of every Negro with piercing familiarity. This "Wait" has almost always meant "Never." We must come to see, with one of our distinguished jurists, that "justice too long delayed is justice denied."[5]

14   We have waited for more than 340 years for our constitutional and God-given rights. The nations of Asia and Africa are moving with jetlike speed toward gaining political independence, but we still creep at horse-and-buggy pace toward gaining a cup of coffee at a lunch counter. Perhaps it is easy for those who have never felt the stinging darts of segregation to say, "Wait." But when you have seen vicious mobs lynch your mothers and fathers at will and drown your sisters and brothers at whim; when you have seen hate-filled policemen curse, kick, and even kill your black brothers and sisters; when you see the vast majority of your twenty million Negro brothers smothering in an airtight cage of poverty in the midst of an affluent society; when you suddenly find your tongue twisted and your speech stammering as you seek to explain to your six-year-old daughter why she can't go to the public amusement park that has just been advertised on television, and see tears welling up in her eyes when she is told that Funtown is closed to colored children, and see ominous clouds of inferiority beginning to form in her little mental sky, and see her beginning to distort her personality by developing an unconscious bitterness toward white people; when you have to concoct an answer for a five-year-old son who is asking, "Daddy, why do white people treat colored people so mean?"; when you take a cross-country drive and find it necessary to sleep night after night in the uncomfortable corners of your automobile because no motel will accept you; when you are humiliated day in and day out by nagging signs reading "white" and "colored"; when your first name becomes "nigger," your middle name becomes "boy" (however old you are) and your last name becomes "John," and your wife and mother are never given the respected title "Mrs."; when you are harried by day and haunted by night by the fact that you are a Negro, living constantly at tiptoe stance, never quite knowing what to expect next, and are plagued with inner fears and outer resentments; when you are forever fighting a degenerating sense of "nobodiness"—then you will understand why we find it difficult to wait. There comes a time when the cup of endurance runs over, and men are no longer willing to be plunged into the

---

[4]A Protestant American philosopher who urged church members to put their beliefs into action against social injustice. See *Moral Man and Immoral Society* (1932).

[5]Chief Justice Earl Warren's expression in 1954 was adapted from English writer Walter Savage Landor's phrase, "Justice delayed is justice denied."

abyss of despair. I hope, sirs, you can understand our legitimate and unavoidable impatience.

You express a great deal of anxiety over our willingness to break laws. This is certainly a legitimate concern. Since we so diligently urge people to obey the Supreme Court's decision of 1954 outlawing segregation in the public schools, at first glance it may seem rather paradoxical for us consciously to break laws. One may well ask: "How can you advocate breaking some laws and obeying others?" The answer lies in the fact that there are two types of laws: just and unjust. I would be the first to advocate obeying just laws. One has not only a legal but a moral responsibility to obey just laws. Conversely, one has a moral responsibility to disobey unjust laws. I would agree with St. Augustine that "an unjust law is no law at all."[6]

Now, what is the difference between the two? How does one determine whether a law is just or unjust? A just law is a man-made code that squares with the moral law or the law of God. An unjust law is a code that is out of harmony with the moral law. To put it in the terms of St. Thomas Aquinas: An unjust law is a human law that is not rooted in eternal law and natural law. Any law that uplifts human personality is just. Any law that degrades human personality is unjust. All segregation statutes are unjust because segregation distorts the soul and damages the personality. It gives the segregator a false sense of superiority and the segregated a false sense of inferiority. Segregation, to use the terminology of the Jewish philosopher Martin Buber,[7] substitutes an "I-it" relationship for an "I-thou" relationship and ends up relegating persons to the status of things. Hence segregation is not only politically, economically, and sociologically unsound, it is morally wrong and sinful. Paul Tillich[8] has said that sin is separation. Is not segregation an existential expression of man's tragic separation, his awful estrangement, his terrible sinfulness? Thus it is that I can urge men to obey the 1954 decision of the Supreme Court, for it is morally right; and I can urge them to disobey segregation ordinances, for they are morally wrong.

Let us consider a more concrete example of just and unjust laws. An unjust law is a code that a numerical or power majority group compels a minority group to obey but does not make binding on itself. This is *difference* made legal. By the same token, a just law is a code that a majority compels a minority to follow and that it is willing to follow itself. This is *sameness* made legal.

Let me give another explanation. A law is unjust if it is inflicted on a minority that, as a result of being denied the right to vote, had no part in enacting or devising the law. Who can say that the legislature of Alabama which set up that state's segregation laws was democratically elected? Throughout Alabama all sorts of devious methods are used to prevent Negroes

[6]St. Augustine (CE 354–430) was an early and influential bishop of the Christian church.

[7]*I and Thou* (1923) is theologian Martin Buber's most famous book.

[8]A twentieth-century Protestant theologian.

from becoming registered voters, and there are some counties in which, even though Negroes constitute a majority of the population, not a single Negro is registered. Can any law enacted under such circumstances be considered democratically structured?

19   Sometimes a law is just on its face and unjust in its application. For instance, I have been arrested on a charge of parading without a permit. Now, there is nothing wrong in having an ordinance which requires a permit for a parade. But such an ordinance becomes unjust when it is used to maintain segregation and to deny citizens the First Amendment privilege of peaceful assembly and protest.

20   I hope you are able to see the distinction I am trying to point out. In no sense do I advocate evading or defying the law, as would the rabid segregationist. That would lead to anarchy. One who breaks an unjust law must do so openly, lovingly, and with a willingness to accept the penalty. I submit that an individual who breaks a law that conscience tells him is unjust, and who willingly accepts the penalty of imprisonment in order to arouse the conscience of the community over its injustice, is in reality expressing the highest respect for law.

21   Of course, there is nothing new about this kind of civil disobedience. It was evidenced sublimely in the refusal of Shadrach, Meshach, and Abednego to obey the laws of Nebuchadnezzar, on the ground that a higher moral law was at stake. It was practiced superbly by the early Christians, who were willing to face hungry lions and the excruciating pain of chopping blocks rather than submit to certain unjust laws of the Roman Empire. To a degree, academic freedom is a reality today because Socrates practiced civil disobedience. In our own nation, the Boston Tea Party represented a massive act of civil disobedience.

22   We should never forget that everything Adolf Hitler did in Germany was "legal" and everything the Hungarian freedom fighters[9] did in Hungary was "illegal." It was "illegal" to aid and comfort a Jew in Hitler's Germany. Even so, I am sure that, had I lived in Germany at the time, I would have aided and comforted my Jewish brothers. If today I lived in a Communist country where certain principles dear to the Christian faith are suppressed, I would openly advocate disobeying that country's antireligious laws.

23   I must make two honest confessions to you, my Christian and Jewish brothers. First, I must confess that over the past few years I have been gravely disappointed with the white moderate. I have almost reached the regrettable conclusion that the Negro's great stumbling block in his stride toward freedom is not the White Citizen's Counciler[10] or the Ku Klux Klanner, but the white moderate, who is more devoted to "order" than to justice; who prefers a

---

[9]The Hungarians rose in revolt against Soviet rule in 1956. Russian tanks put down the uprising with force that shocked the world.

[10]White citizens' councils were formed in the South in 1954 to fight school desegregation as ordered by the Supreme Court in May 1954.

negative peace which is the absence of tension to a positive peace which is the presence of justice; who constantly says, "I agree with you in the goal you seek, but I cannot agree with your methods of direct action"; who paternalistically believes he can set the timetable for another man's freedom; who lives by a mythical concept of time and who constantly advises the Negro to wait for a "more convenient season." Shallow understanding from people of good will is more frustrating than absolute misunderstanding from people of ill will. Lukewarm acceptance is much more bewildering than outright rejection.

24 I had hoped that the white moderate would understand that law and order exist for the purpose of establishing justice and that when they fail in this purpose they become the dangerously structured dams that block the flow of social progress. I had hoped that the white moderate would understand that the present tension in the South is a necessary phase of the transition from an obnoxious negative peace, in which the Negro passively accepted his unjust plight, to a substantive and positive peace, in which all men will respect the dignity and worth of human personality. Actually, we who engage in nonviolent direct action are not the creators of tension. We merely bring to the surface the hidden tension that is already alive. We bring it out in the open, where it can be seen and dealt with. Like a boil that can never be cured so long as it is covered up but must be opened with all its ugliness to the natural medicines of air and light, injustice must be exposed, with all the tension its exposure creates, to the light of human conscience and the air of national opinion, before it can be cured.

25 In your statement you assert that our actions, even though peaceful, must be condemned because they precipitate violence. But is this a logical assertion? Isn't this like condemning a robbed man because his possession of money precipitated the evil act of robbery? Isn't this like condemning Socrates because his unswerving commitment to truth and his philosophical inquiries precipitated the act by the misguided populace in which they made him drink hemlock? Isn't this like condemning Jesus because his unique God-consciousness and never-ceasing devotion to God's will precipitated the evil act of crucifixion? We must come to see that, as the federal courts have consistently affirmed, it is wrong to urge an individual to cease his efforts to gain his basic constitutional rights because the quest may precipitate violence. Society must protect the robbed and punish the robber.

26 I had also hoped that the white moderate would reject the myth concerning time in relation to the struggle for freedom. I have just received a letter from a white brother in Texas. He writes: "All Christians know that the colored people will receive equal rights eventually, but it is possible that you are in too great a religious hurry. It has taken Christianity almost two thousand years to accomplish what it has. The teachings of Christ take time to come to earth." Such an attitude stems from a tragic misconception of time, from the strangely irrational notion that there is something in the very flow of time that will inevitably cure all ills. Actually, time itself is neutral; it can be used either destructively or constructively. More and more I feel that the people of ill will

have used time much more effectively than have the people of good will. We will have to repent in this generation not merely for the hateful words and actions of the bad people, but for the appalling silence of the good people. Human progress never rolls in on wheels of inevitability; it comes through the tireless efforts of men willing to be co-workers with God, and without this hard work, time itself becomes an ally of the forces of social stagnation. We must use time creatively, in the knowledge that the time is always ripe to do right. Now is the time to make real the promise of democracy and transform our pending national elegy into a creative psalm of brotherhood. Now is the time to lift our national policy from the quicksand of racial injustice to the solid rock of human dignity.

27   You speak of our activity in Birmingham as extreme. At first I was rather disappointed that fellow clergymen would see my nonviolent efforts as those of an extremist. I began thinking about the fact that I stand in the middle of two opposing forces in the Negro community. One is a force of complacency, made up in part of Negroes who, as a result of long years of oppression, are so drained of self-respect and a sense of "somebodiness" that they have adjusted to segregation; and in part of a few middle-class Negroes who, because of a degree of academic and economic security and because in some ways they profit by segregation, have become insensitive to the problems of the masses. The other force is one of bitterness and hatred, and it comes perilously close to advocating violence. It is expressed in the various black nationalist groups that are springing up across the nation, the largest and best known being Elijah Muhammad's Muslim movement.[11] Nourished by the Negro's frustration over the continued existence of racial discrimination, this movement is made up of people who have lost faith in America, who have absolutely repudiated Christianity, and who have concluded that the white man is an incorrigible "devil."

28   I have tried to stand between these two forces, saying that we need emulate neither the "do-nothingism" of the complacent nor the hatred and despair of the black nationalist. For there is the more excellent way of love and nonviolent protest. I am grateful to God that, through the influence of the Negro church, the way of nonviolence became an integral part of our struggle.

29   If this philosophy had not emerged, by now many streets of the South would, I am convinced, be flowing with blood. And I am further convinced that if our white brothers dismiss as "rabble-rousers" and "outside agitators" those of us who employ nonviolent direct action, and if they refuse to support our nonviolent efforts, millions of Negroes will, out of frustration and despair, seek solace and security in black nationalist ideologies—a development that would inevitably lead to a frightening racial nightmare.

30   Oppressed people cannot remain oppressed forever. The yearning for freedom eventually manifests itself, and that is what has happened to the

---

[11] The Black Muslim movement began in the 1920s but flourished in the 1960s under its leader, Elijah Muhammad.

American Negro. Something within has reminded him of his birthright of freedom, and something without has reminded him that it can be gained. Consciously or unconsciously, he has been caught up by the *Zeitgeist*,[12] and with his black brothers of Africa and his brown and yellow brothers of Asia, South America, and the Caribbean, the United States Negro is moving with a sense of great urgency toward the promised land of racial justice. If one recognizes this vital urge that has engulfed the Negro community, one should readily understand why public demonstrations are taking place. The Negro has many pent-up resentments and latent frustrations, and he must release them. So let him march; let him make prayer pilgrimages to the city hall; let him go on freedom rides—and try to understand why he must do so. If his repressed emotions are not released in nonviolent ways, they will seek expression through violence; this is not a threat but a fact of history. So I have not said to my people, "Get rid of your discontent." Rather, I have tried to say that this normal and healthy discontent can be channeled into the creative outlet of nonviolent direct action. And now this approach is being termed extremist.

31   But though I was initially disappointed at being categorized as an extremist, as I continued to think about the matter I gradually gained a measure of satisfaction from the label. Was not Jesus an extremist for love: "Love your enemies, bless them that curse you, do good to them that hate you, and pray for them which despitefully use you, and persecute you." Was not Amos an extremist for justice: "Let justice roll down like waters and righteousness like an ever-flowing stream." Was not Paul an extremist for the Christian gospel: "I bear in my body the marks of the Lord Jesus." Was not Martin Luther an extremist: "Here I stand; I cannot do otherwise, so help me God." And John Bunyan: "I will stay in jail to the end of my days before I make a butchery of my conscience." And Abraham Lincoln: "This nation cannot survive half slave and half free." And Thomas Jefferson. "We hold these truths to be self-evident, that all men are created equal. . . ." So the question is not whether we will be extremists, but what kind of extremists we will be. Will we be extremists for hate or for love? Will we be extremists for the preservation of injustice or for the extension of justice? In that dramatic scene on Calvary's hill three men were crucified. We must never forget that all three were crucified for the same crime—the crime of extremism. Two were extremists for immorality, and thus fell below their environment. The other, Jesus Christ, was an extremist for love, truth, and goodness, and thereby rose above his environment. Perhaps the South, the nation, and the world are in dire need of creative extremists.

32   I had hoped that the white moderate would see this need. Perhaps I was too optimistic; perhaps I expected too much. I suppose I should have realized that few members of the oppressor race can understand the deep groans and passionate yearnings of the oppressed race, and still fewer have the vision to see that injustice must be rooted out by strong, persistent, and determined action. I am thankful, however, that some of our white brothers in the South

---

[12]German for the intellectual, moral, and cultural spirit of the times.

have grasped the meaning of this social revolution and committed themselves to it. They are still all too few in quantity, but they are big in quality. Some—such as Ralph McGill, Lillian Smith, Harry Golden, James McBride Dabbs, Ann Braden, and Sarah Patton Boyle—have written about our struggle[13] in eloquent and prophetic terms. Others have marched with us down nameless streets of the South. They have languished in filthy, roach-infested jails, suffering the abuse and brutality of policemen who view them as "dirty nigger-lovers." Unlike so many of their moderate brothers and sisters, they have recognized the urgency of the moment and sensed the need for powerful "action" antidotes to combat the disease of segregation.

33   Let me take note of my other major disappointment. I have been so greatly disappointed with the white church and its leadership. Of course, there are some notable exceptions. I am not unmindful of the fact that each of you has taken some significant stands on this issue. I commend you, Reverend Stallings, for your Christian stand on this past Sunday, in welcoming Negroes to your worship service on a nonsegregated basis. I commend the Catholic leaders of this state for integrating Spring Hill College several years ago.

34   But despite these notable exceptions, I must honestly reiterate that I have been disappointed with the church. I do not say this as one of those negative critics who can always find something wrong with the church. I say this as a minister of the gospel, who loves the church; who was nurtured in its bosom; who has been sustained by its spiritual blessings and who will remain true to it as long as the cord of life shall lengthen.

35   When I was suddenly catapulted into the leadership of the bus protest in Montgomery, Alabama, a few years ago, I felt we would be supported by the white church. I felt that the white ministers, priests, and rabbis of the South would be among our strongest allies. Instead, some have been outright opponents, refusing to understand the freedom movement and misrepresenting its leaders; all too many others have been more cautious than courageous and have remained silent behind the anesthetizing security of stained-glass windows.

36   In spite of my shattered dreams, I came to Birmingham with the hope that the white religious leadership of this community would see the justice of our cause and, with deep moral concern, would serve as the channel through which our just grievances could reach the power structure. I had hoped that each of you would understand. But again I have been disappointed. . . .

37   There was a time when the church was very powerful—in the time when the early Christians rejoiced at being deemed worthy to suffer for what they believed. In those days the church was not merely a thermometer that recorded the ideas and principles of popular opinion; it was a thermostat that transformed the mores of society. Whenever the early Christians entered a town, the people in power became disturbed and immediately sought to convict the Christians for being "disturbers of the peace" and "outside agita-

---

[13]These are all Southern writers who wrote against segregation.

tors." But the Christians pressed on, in the conviction that they were "a colony of heaven," called to obey God rather than man. Small in number, they were big in commitment. They were too God intoxicated to be "astronomically intimidated." By their effort and example they brought an end to such ancient evils as infanticide and gladiatorial contests.

38   Things are different now. So often the contemporary church is a weak, ineffectual voice with an uncertain sound. So often it is an archdefender of the status quo. Far from being disturbed by the presence of the church, the power structure of the average community is consoled by the church's silent—and often even vocal—sanction of things as they are.

39   But the judgment of God is upon the church as never before. If today's church does not recapture the sacrificial spirit of the early church, it will lose its authenticity, forfeit the loyalty of millions, and be dismissed as an irrelevant social club with no meaning for the twentieth century. Every day I meet young people whose disappointment with the church has turned into outright disgust.

40   Perhaps I have once again been too optimistic. Is organized religion too inextricably bound to the status quo to save our nation and the world? Perhaps I must turn my faith to the inner spiritual church, the church within the church, as the true *ekklesia*[14] and the hope of the world. But again I am thankful to God that some noble souls from the ranks of organized religion have broken loose from the paralyzing chains of conformity and joined us as active partners in the struggle for freedom. They have left their secure congregations and walked the streets of Albany, Georgia, with us. They have gone down the highways of the South on torturous rides for freedom. Yes, they have gone to jail with us. Some have been dismissed from their churches, have lost the support of their bishops and fellow ministers. But they have acted in the faith that right defeated is stronger than evil triumphant. Their witness has been the spiritual salt that has preserved the true meaning of the gospel in these troubled times. They have carved a tunnel of hope through the dark mountain of disappointment.

41   I hope the church as a whole will meet the challenge of this decisive hour. But even if the church does not come to the aid of justice, I have no despair about the future. I have no fear about the outcome of our struggle in Birmingham, even if our motives are at present misunderstood. We will reach the goal of freedom in Birmingham and all over the nation, because the goal of America is freedom. Abused and scorned though we may be, our destiny is tied up with America's destiny. Before the pilgrims landed at Plymouth, we were here. Before the pen of Jefferson etched the majestic words of the Declaration of Independence across the pages of history, we were here. For more than two centuries our forebears labored in this country without wages; they made cotton king; they built the homes of their masters while suffering gross injustice and shameful humiliation—and yet out of a bottomless vitality they

---

[14]The Greek word for church, which means not just the institution but the spirit of the church.

continued to thrive and develop. If the inexpressible cruelties of slavery could not stop us, the opposition we now face will surely fail. We will win our freedom because the sacred heritage of our nation and the eternal will of God are embodied in our echoing demands.

42   Before closing I feel impelled to mention one other point in your statement that has troubled me profoundly. You warmly commended the Birmingham police force for keeping "order" and "preventing violence." I doubt that you would have so warmly commended the police force if you had seen its dogs sinking their teeth into unarmed, nonviolent Negroes. I doubt that you would so quickly commend the policemen if you were to observe their ugly and inhumane treatment of Negroes here in the city jail; if you were to watch them push and curse old Negro women and young Negro girls; if you were to see them slap and kick old Negro men and young boys; if you were to observe them, as they did on two occasions, refuse to give us food because we wanted to sing our grace together. I cannot join you in your praise of the Birmingham police department.

43   It is true that the police have exercised a degree of discipline in handling the demonstrators. In this sense they have conducted themselves rather "nonviolently" in public. But for what purpose? To preserve the evil system of segregation. Over the past few years I have consistently preached that nonviolence demands that the means we use must be as pure as the ends we seek. I have tried to make clear that it is wrong to use immoral means to attain moral ends. But now I must affirm that it is just as wrong, or perhaps even more so, to use moral means to preserve immoral ends. Perhaps Mr. Connor and his policemen have been rather nonviolent in public, as was Chief Pritchett in Albany, Georgia, but they have used the moral means of nonviolence to maintain the immoral end of racial injustice. As T. S. Eliot[15] has said, "The last temptation is the greatest treason: To do the right deed for the wrong reason."

44   I wish you had commended the Negro sit-inners and demonstrators of Birmingham for their sublime courage, their willingness to suffer, and their amazing discipline in the midst of great provocation. One day the South will recognize its real heroes. They will be the James Merediths,[16] with the noble sense of purpose that enables them to face jeering and hostile mobs, and with the agonizing loneliness that characterizes the life of the pioneer. They will be old, oppressed, battered Negro women, symbolized in a seventy-two-year-old woman in Montgomery, Alabama, who rose up with a sense of dignity and with her people decided not to ride segregated buses, and who responded with ungrammatical profundity to one who inquired about her weariness: "My feets is tired, but my soul is at rest." They will be the young high school and college students, the young ministers of the gospel and a host of their elders, courageously and nonviolently sitting in at lunch counters and willingly going to jail

---

[15] A twentieth-century American poet, Eliot wrote these lines for his verse drama *Murder in the Cathedral*, which depicts the martyrdom of Saint Thomas à Becket.

[16] In 1961, Meredith became the first black to become a student at the University of Mississippi.

for conscience' sake. One day the South will know that when these disinherited children of God sat down at lunch counters, they were in reality standing up for what is best in the American dream and for the most sacred values in our Judaeo-Christian heritage, thereby bringing our nation back to those great wells of democracy which were dug deep by the founding fathers in their formulation of the Constitution and the Declaration of Independence.

45   Never before have I written so long a letter. I'm afraid it is much too long to take your precious time. I can assure you that it would have been much shorter if I had been writing from a comfortable desk, but what else can one do when he is alone in a narrow jail cell, other than write long letters, think long thoughts, and pray long prayers?

46   If I have said anything in this letter that overstates the truth and indicates an unreasonable impatience, I beg you to forgive me. If I have said anything that understates the truth and indicates my having a patience that allows me to settle for anything less than brotherhood, I beg God to forgive me.

47   I hope this letter finds you strong in the faith. I also hope that circumstances will soon make it possible for me to meet each of you, not as an integrationist or a civil rights leader but as a fellow clergyman and a Christian brother. Let us all hope that the dark clouds of racial prejudice will soon pass away and the deep fog of misunderstanding will be lifted from our fear-drenched communities, and in some not too distant tomorrow the radiant stars of love and brotherhood will shine over our great nation with all their scintillating beauty.

Yours in the cause of
Peace and Brotherhood,
MARTIN LUTHER KING, JR.

Questions to Ponder

1. What are the advantages of the *letter* as a form of communication? What does King gain by writing a letter, rather than an essay or magazine article or book?

2. What are King's four steps in a nonviolent campaign? Why is each step necessary? Do most protestors follow all four steps? Why or why not? Why are King's four steps a helpful guideline for evaluating admirable and less-than-admirable political protest?

3. What are the three distinctions King draws between "just" and "unjust" laws? Do you agree with him on this? Can you think of any laws today that would be "unjust" according to King's definitions?

4. King refers often to such great religious and political leaders of the past as Jesus, St. Paul, St. Augustine, Thomas Jefferson, and Abraham Lincoln. What does he gain by such references? Does he lose anything?
5. King repeatedly acknowledges the criticisms made of him and the Birmingham protest, and then rebuts them. Is this rhetorical technique—acknowledgment and rebuttal—an effective one? What would you lose if you gave your side first and *then* presented the other side?

Writing Possibilities

1. Write a "Letter to Martin" reporting on what has happened in the United States in terms of race relations since his death on April 4, 1968. (You may want to do some research, so you can offer facts, figures, and expert opinion along with your own personal views and experiences.)
2. King wrote that he was "an extremist for love." Think about yourself. What might you be called an "extremist" for? Develop an essay on the theme "I am an extremist for _____."
3. Make a list of current laws or social practices that you consider to be "unjust" or "immoral." Choose one and pretend you have been jailed for passively resisting this law or social practice. Using King's letter as a model, write your own "Letter from _____ Jail," explaining why you are in jail, why the law (or practice) is unjust, and what needs to be done.
4. Read Henry David Thoreau's essay on "Civil Disobedience." King read this essay while he was a student at Morehouse College. Write what you think King learned from Thoreau. How does King extend Thoreau's ideas?

Student Essay
AN ANALYSIS OF "LETTER FROM BIRMINGHAM JAIL"

Lisa Battani

It was my first college semester, and I found my college writing class very helpful in developing my writing skills. Among the papers that were assigned, the critical review was a new experience for me. My teacher said that a common writing assignment in many college majors is to analyze magazine or journal articles in the field.

I chose to analyze Martin Luther King's "Letter from Birmingham Jail" because I am a supporter of civil rights. I find that interest in the subject is a strong asset in my writing: interest keeps the ideas flowing.

I began by skimming the article, first only jotting down the main points and headings. Then I reread the piece carefully, taking detailed summary notes as I read. I also noted any strong points or weaknesses (in logic or writing) that I encountered. I then used this gathered material to write my first draft. Later, I read the article one final time to catch any nuances I might have missed. My last step included careful polishing of spelling, punctuation, and diction.

I found that writing a critical review was challenging. It was difficult to locate any weak points or limitations in King's letter. I admire his writing style; there is little room for improvement. On the other hand, his fantastic writing ability offered me quite a selection for my section on strong points—and inspiration as well.

Brief Warm-up Writing Exercises

1. Freewrite what you consider to be the main points Martin Luther King, Jr., made in his "Letter from Birmingham Jail."
2. Brainstorm a list of what you think are the *strengths* of King's letter. Then make another list of any *weaknesses* or *limitations* you find in it.
3. Write a first draft of a letter to your city's school board suggesting that King's letter be read and taught in the schools. Include your thoughts on the appropriate grade level.

DRAFT

Summary

1. Martin Luther King, Jr. writes his letter to his fellow clergymen from his cell in a Birmingham Jail, 1963. The clergymen, like many others, have criticized King's direct action program. King feels that it is necessary to answer their statement since they are men who could definitely have just reason. King is the president of the Southern Christian Leadership Conference; therefore, he says he has the responsibility of taking care of the unjustice in Birmingham, Alabama. He says that demonstrations are necessary to bring about justice there; he can't sit idle and watch injustice corrupt the lives of many. King feels that the clergymen have failed to see the conditions which brought about his actions. Through his letter he hopes to make them evident.

2. According to King, a nonviolent campaign follows four basic steps: a collection of facts to determine injustice, negotiation, self-purification, and finally direct action. King reveals that Birmingham is the most segregated city in the United States; injustice definitely exists. He says he has witnessed the failure of several negotiations. Promises were simply broken time after time; negotiation ended in failure. Finally self-purification processes began through workshops to prepare for direct nonviolent action.

3. The clergymen are opposed to this final step of direct action; they feel negotiation is a better solution. King agrees with them but he believes that there is a need for constructive tension, wich in turn can force the community to negotiate. Only by action can King produce this tension. The clergymen want King to give, the new mayor, Albert Boutwell time. King believes that time is no factor in curing segregation and a change in the administration will only occur if pressure is applied. King argues that blacks have waited far too long for justice. He suggests that whites don't know the consequences of being black, making it easy to say "wait."

4. Martin Luther King also responds to the clergymen's concern about

disobeying laws. He explains that there are two kinds of laws, the just and the unjust. Just laws agree with the laws of God, while the unjust do not. King strongly feels that one must have legal but also moral responsibility in following laws. This means that it is one's duty to disobey any unjust laws regardless of the consquences, Wich includes all segregation laws. King's direct action against these laws doesn't reflect anarchy; King is against it. Instead, he feels that one should break unjust laws openly, lovingly, and accept the penalty willingly. Instead of being an anarchist, King says that, this person has the highest respect for the law, in his mind.

5   King confesses that he is disappointed in white moderates. King feels that the white moderates are a block to a Negro's freedom; they are more devoted to order than peace. The whites condemn his action because they believe it will cause violence and disorder. King explains that his nonviolent action doesn't create the tension directly, rather it brings out the tension that already exists. King insists that time itself won't ease the tension; it takes the work and devotion of good people not the silence. He is disappointed in thier labeling him as an extremist. King explains that he stands in the middle of the silent and the violent blacks. King's public demonstrations help Negros release thier frustrations in a nonviolent way. If they are further oppressed, these frustrations could very well lead to violent measures.

6   King also confesses that he is very disappointed in the church leadership. He expected the support of his fellow brothers, but was deeply disappointed to find they were his opposition. In his opinion churches have changed since early Christian times; now churches follow public opinion. Consequently, he must turn his faith to the inner spiritual church for support.

7   King shows his feelings for the clergy's commending of the police. He is deeply disappointed in their praise for such immoral men. Knowing the violence and cruelty these men exercised upon blacks, King cannot agree with the clergymen. King believes that the real heroes are those

who have the courage to take part in these demonstrations, knowing the punishment they are willing to accept.

Strong Points

8   Martin Luther King's letter is well written. As a reader, I feel aware of his goals and I also understand the his reasoning behind them. He explains his feelings regarding the whites, the laws, the administration, and the need for direct action.

9   His organization is quite helpful to the reader. In his four steps to a nonviolent campaign, he shows the reader a step by step plan which describes the reasons for his nonviolent action. He also organizes laws into two groups, just and unjust laws. Through this classification he is able to reveal the reasoning behind his actions.

10 I find his reference to philosophers, like Socrates, quite succesful. He compares his motives to theirs; this enhances his credibility. He also gains credibility by referring to the Christian movement. He compares the Christian movement to his movement for racial justice. This comparison is especially successful considering he is addressing clergrymen.

11 Martin Luther King uses several appeals for sympathy to strengthen his viewpoint. He shows in detail the impatience shared by many Negros by discribing the "stinging darts of segregation." King shows the pain, "when you are harried by day and haunted by night by the fact that you are a Negro." These violent, cruel, and tragic descriptions definitely have power.

Limitations

12 I feel that Martin Luther King neglectes to mention others who suffer from segregation. He only refers to blacks as a minortiy. I think that it would by helpful to King if he included other minorities in his letter. By doing this he will gain the respect of others who also suffer a different, yet similar segregation problem. Some others he could have mentioned are forgein migrants, nonprotestants, and even women.

Recommendations

13 This letter could be very interesting to those involved in law and also those dealing with social work. It brings up many questions regarding what is morally and legally just and unjust.

14 King's letter has a message aimed toward society as a whole, yet it would take an upperlevel highschool reader to understand his historical references. It is crucial for these references to be understood; they enavle the reader to understand his viewpoint. The respected figures he refers to help persuade the reader to agree with his actions. That is definitely his goal in the letter.

15 This letter is something that all minorities, especially blacks, would want to read. Martin Luther King's direct nonviolent action is a new begining for justice. It is a step to unifying America as one. Likewise, Segregationists should also read this. This article will definitely help us all reach the goal of America—freedom.

❖ Summary

1 Martin Luther King, Jr., wrote his "Letter from Birmingham Jail" to eight fellow clergymen in Alabama in April 1963. These clergymen, like many others, had criticized Dr. King's nonviolent demonstrations against racial segregation. In his letter, Dr. King says he feels it is necessary to answer their statement because they are men of reason who could have justice on their side. He explains that his responsibility as president of the Southern Christian Leadership Conference is to deal with injustice, including injustice in Birmingham, Alabama. Dr. King asserts that nonviolent demonstrations are necessary to bring about justice in Alabama; indeed, he says he cannot sit idly by and watch injustice corrupt human lives. The clergymen, Dr. King suggests, have failed to see the conditions that brought about his action. Through his letter, he says he hopes to make these conditions evident.

2 According to Dr. King, a nonviolent campaign follows four basic steps: collection of facts to determine if injustice exists; negotiation to end the injustice; self-purification (if negotiation fails); and finally, nonviolent direct action. Dr. King asserts that Birmingham is the most segregated city in the United States; injustice, therefore, definitely exists. He says he has witnessed the failure of several negotiations to end the climate of racial violence and

discrimination in the city. Promises, he says, have been broken time after time. Because negotiations failed, self-purification processes began in workshops to prepare for nonviolent direct action.

3   The clergymen had opposed this final step; they had called negotiation a better solution. Dr. King says he agrees with them but that he believes there is also a need for constructive tension, which can force the community to negotiate. Only through nonviolent passive resistance, he says, can this tension be produced. Dr. King suggests that a change in the Birmingham city government will only occur if pressure is applied, and he insists that blacks have waited too long for justice. Indeed, he suggests that whites do not know the consequences of being black, making it easy for them to say "Wait."

4   Dr. King also responds to the clergymen's concern about disobeying laws. He explains that there are two kinds of laws: just laws and unjust laws. Just laws, he asserts, correspond with the laws of God, while unjust laws do not. Just laws, as a consequence, uplift human personality, while unjust laws "degrade" human personality (189). Another way Dr. King proposes to distinguish just from unjust laws is that unjust laws are laws that a majority compels a minority to follow but does not make binding on itself. Just laws, on the other hand, would be binding on *all,* the majority as well as the minority. Finally, Dr. King observes that just laws are laws minorities (as well as majorities) participate in creating, while unjust laws are those created without the participation of the minority (through denial of voting rights).

5   Dr. King thus insists that laws must have moral as well as legal foundations. This means that it is each person's moral duty to disobey unjust laws—including segregation laws—regardless of the consequences. Dr. King asserts that his nonviolent action against unjust laws is far from anarchic. Rather he asserts that one should break unjust laws openly and lovingly, and accept the penalty willingly.

6   It is then Dr. King's turn to express his own disappointments. He confesses he is disappointed in white moderates. Dr. King says white moderates are blocking Negro freedom, for they are devoted more to order than to justice. He is further disappointed in those who label him an "extremist," noting that, in fact, he stands between those Negroes who are silent and those Negroes who advocate violence. Indeed, he reinterprets the word "extremist," giving it a positive instead of negative connotation when he asserts proudly that he is "an extremist for love" (194).

7   Dr. King also confesses that he is greatly disappointed in the white church and its leadership. He says that he expected the support of his fellow clergymen and was deeply disappointed to find they were his opposition. He reminds his brother clergy that the early Christian church involved itself actively in matters of justice and urges them to return to the church's historical role.

8   Dr. King concludes his letter with one final expression of disappointment. He states that he is deeply disappointed by the commendation his fellow clergy had given the Birmingham police. Specifying acts of cruelty and violence committed by these police, Dr. King says he cannot agree with the clergymen's

praise. Instead, he asserts that the true heroes are those who have had the courage to take part in the demonstrations, knowing the punishment they must accept.

Strengths

9   To say that Martin Luther King, Jr.'s "Letter from Birmingham Jail" is well written is an understatement. After reading this letter, I feel aware of his goals and understand the reasoning behind them. Dr. King clearly and vividly explains his feelings regarding the clergymen, the laws, the Birmingham administration (including its police), the white "moderate," and the need for nonviolent direct action to bring about civil rights.

10   The organization of Dr. King's letter is logical and organic. He responds to the eight clergymen's criticisms point-by-point, persuasively refuting each one. In fact, this letter might be used as a model for critical thinking, for Dr. King takes each of the clergymen's reasons and shows its weaknesses and offers a better way of thinking. To the clergyman's suggestion that his actions have been "untimely," Dr. King responds first by asserting that the new Birmingham administration "must be prodded about as much as the outgoing one, before it will act," and then evokes the historical lesson that "privileged groups seldom give up their privileges voluntarily" (187). Dr. King then quotes Supreme Court Justice Earl Warren's famous declaration that "justice too long delayed is justice denied," noting that blacks have waited more than 340 years for their "constitutional and God-given rights" (187). And if such reasoning is not enough, he follows with a heartbreaking recital of barriers and indignities suffered by blacks of all ages, ending by stating, "There comes a time when the cup of endurance runs over, and men are no longer willing to be plunged into the abyss of despair. I hope, sirs, you can understand our legitimate and unavoidable impatience" (188). Dr. King takes similar care to analyze the clergymen's anxiety over his willingness to break the law. In the course of his exploration of this criticism, he insists upon the distinction between just and unjust laws and provides the clergymen (indeed, all readers) with precise ways of distinguishing between them.

11   Dr. King's references to philosophers and theologians, such as Socrates, St. Paul, and Martin Luther, are also highly effective. He compares his motives to theirs; this enhances his credibility and helps the reader perceive the historical precedents for his protest. He further builds support for his position by quoting St. Augustine and St. Thomas Aquinas (Catholic theologians), Martin Buber (a Jewish theologian) and Protestant theologians Reinhold Neibuhr and Paul Tillich. Such citations show particular awareness of his audience, which included Catholics, Protestants, and Jews.

12   Dr. King also makes brilliant use of sensory and emotional appeals in his letter—as well as appeals to reason. He helps readers *feel* the pain suffered by

many blacks by describing the "stinging darts of segregation" and the "smothering . . . airtight cage of poverty in the midst of an affluent society" (188). He makes us *see* the undeserved suffering of children when he speaks of "the ominous clouds of inferiority beginning to form in [his six-year-old daughter's] mental sky" when he must tell her she cannot go to the public amusement park she has just seen advertised on television (188). He makes us *hear* again and again the humiliating *sounds* of bigotry when he cries out, "your first name becomes 'nigger,' your middle name becomes 'boy' (however old you are) and your last name becomes 'John,' and your wife and mother are never given the respected title 'Mrs.' " (188). Indeed, he makes us feel the damage done to both blacks and whites when he speaks of seeing his young daughter begin "to distort her personality by developing an unconsciousness bitterness toward white people" (188). A reader cannot help but be moved by these vivid and tragic descriptions.

13   In fact, it is Dr. King's simple but eloquent language that makes his letter unforgettable. He uses simple metaphors, such as that depicting his young daughter's mental sky filled with clouds of inferiority (188). He describes Americans as "caught in an inescapable network of mutuality, tied in a single garment of destiny" (184). He frequently uses opposites in the same sentence to underscore the principles he values. "Injustice anywhere is a threat to justice everywhere," he declares, making us aware of both principles and places. Dr. King insists we cannot "use immoral means to attain moral ends" (198). He closes his letter with a vision of the brighter future he seeks:

> Let us all hope that the dark clouds of racial prejudice will soon pass away and the deep fog of misunderstanding will be lifted from our fear-drenched communities, and in some not too distant tomorrow the radiant stars of love and brotherhood will shine over our great nation with all their scintillating beauty. (199)

Limitations

14   It is difficult to find weaknesses in such a brilliantly reasoned and argued presentation. Nevertheless, I do think Dr. King might have enhanced his letter's persuasiveness by referring to others who suffer from discrimination besides blacks. I recognize that he was fighting at the moment for black civil rights; nonetheless, by focusing only on black civil rights, he misses the opportunity of gaining the respect and support of others who suffer different, yet similar, problems. Such groups might have included Hispanics, Asian-Americans, native Americans, and even women.

15   Some might argue that Dr. King's allusions to philosophers, theologians, and to the Negro's *zeitgeist* make his letter too difficult for the average reader today. If this is true, it is lamentable. I would note, however, that Dr. King's

specified audience was a jury of his peers, that is, fellow clergymen with philosophical and theological training. They certainly would find his references familiar, and perhaps even illuminating. Furthermore, his allusions to biblical and political revolutionaries help to remind every reader that Dr. King is merely arguing for principles put forth in texts dear to most Americans' hearts: the Bible and the Declaration of Independence and Constitution. I do not consider Dr. King's allusions and vocabulary a limitation; rather, his letter offers us all a valuable stretch.

Recommendations

16   Martin Luther King, Jr.'s "Letter from Birmingham Jail" is an important document of American history, for it presents in unforgettable language a picture of American segregation in the mid-twentieth century. Generations born after the civil rights victories of the 1960s may have little clear sense of the effects of segregation and other tolerated acts of racism on everyday American existence. Dr. King makes these damaging effects clear and his letter would help students gauge or raise questions regarding gains (or losses) in racial equality and human justice since Dr. King's time. I would thus recommend it as required reading for every American high-school student.

17   Besides its value as a document of American history, "Letter from Birmingham Jail" also represents a brilliant rhetorical model. Students of all ages should study it for its clear sense of subject, audience, and purpose; its painstaking definitions and distinctions; its citation of admirable supporting authorities; its vivid examples and metaphors; its eloquent language; and its persuasive tone of love.

18   I would also recommend "Letter from Birmingham Jail" to those studying law, philosophy, religion, and even social work. It raises many questions regarding what is morally and legally just—and unjust. Dr. King's four-step program of nonviolent direct action should be used as a primer for those considering or planning acts of nonviolent passive resistance. Specifically, individuals might ask themselves if each step is sufficiently pursued before passing on to the next. Indeed, Dr. King's four steps can offer helpful guidelines for evaluating the many acts of passive resistance—from protests at abortion clinics to those at nuclear power plants—that occur in today's media age. In evaluating the success or failure of a given protest, those having read Dr. King's letter might ask: Have the protestors sufficiently purified themselves that they can take verbal and physical abuse without returning it, indeed with a spirit of love? Are protestors willing to accept the consequences of breaking the law? Have "creative tensions" been set in motion by the nonviolent protest?

19   Finally, Dr. King's "Letter from Birmingham Jail" is a document all minorities and oppressed peoples would want to read. Dr. King's letter represents a new call for justice and equality. It represents an effort to unify a nation by calling forth many of that nation's most fundamental traditions.

Work Cited

King, Jr., Martin Luther. "Letter from Birmingham Jail." *A World of Ideas: Essential Readings for College Writers.* Ed. Lee A. Jacobus. New York: St. Martin's Press, 1983, pp. 183–199. ❖

Questions to Ponder

1. What are some ways to *pre-view* an essay, article, or book?
2. Why is it usually a good idea to read with a pencil or pen in hand—to mark key phrases or sentences, or to make notes to yourself in the margins?
3. How do you decide what to include and exclude when *summarizing* someone's work? What can be excluded? What must *not* be excluded?
4. What are the benefits of the four-part form Lisa Battani has chosen for her analysis?
5. When summarizing a work written in the past, what is the advantage of using the *historical present* (King *states,* he *expresses* disappointment, he *notes*) instead of the *past tense* (King *stated,* he *expressed* disappointment, he *noted*)? What does a writer gain by this?
6. Do you agree with Lisa Battani's opinions regarding the strengths and limitations of King's letter? What further examples could you cite to support her points? What other strengths and limitations might be added?

Writing Possibilities

1. Preview and then reread King's "Letter from Birmingham Jail" with an eye toward writing your own analysis. Make your own lists of *Strengths, Limitations,* and *Recommendations.* Order the items in each list in an effective manner; then write your own analysis of King's letter.
2. Preview and then read King's equally famous "I Have a Dream" speech (given in Washington, D.C., in August 1963). Now write an analysis of the speech using Lisa Battani's four-part form.
3. Choose an article by your favorite newspaper columnist or sports writer and write an analysis of it using Lisa Battani's four-part form. Note how

this format encourages you to make discoveries about this writer that you have not made before.
4. Revise, proofread, and mail the letter that you began in warm-up exercise 3 to your city's school board.

Short Story
"REALLY, DOESN'T CRIME PAY?"
Alice Walker

All I can remember about the writing of this story is that I was living in Mississippi at the time, in a very suburban neighborhood, and that friends of ours down the street lived in a large split-level house with a bright blue driveway.

Their house—much larger and finer than my own—symbolized for me the acceptance of the "nice home" as the temple of the emerging black middle class. All struggle seemed to lead to it; and, once inside, all protesting voices became muffled, if not silenced.

It was out of this feeling—of the "nice home" as prison and stifler of the creative voice—that this story " 'Really, Doesn't Crime Pay?' " was probably born.

Brief Warm-up Writing Exercises

1. Describe the setting in which you can be most creative. What is it (or would it be) like?
2. Brainstorm a list of the essential material possessions a "successful" person today would wish to have. Then write a description of this person's setting.
3. Choose any three days of a year and sketch a person's diary entries for those days is such a way that the three entries (taken together) would reveal a story.

September 1961

page 118

1   I sit here by the window in a house with a thirty-year mortgage, writing in this notebook, looking down at my Helena Rubenstein hands . . . and why not? Since I am not a serious writer my nails need not be bitten off, my cuticles need not have jagged edges. I can indulge myself—my hands—in Herbessence nail-soak, polish, lotions, and creams. The result is a truly beautiful pair of hands: sweet-smelling, small, and soft. . . .

2   I lift them from the page where I have written the line "Really, *Doesn't Crime Pay?*" and send them seeking up my shirt front (it is a white and frilly shirt) and smoothly up the column of my throat, where gardenia scent floats beneath my hairline. If I should spread my arms and legs or whirl, just for an instant, the sweet smell of my body would be more than I could bear. But I fit into my new surroundings perfectly; like a jar of cold cream melting on a mirrored vanity shelf.

page 119

3   "I have a surprise for you," Ruel said, the first time he brought me here. And you know how sick he makes me now when he grins.
4   "What is it?" I asked, not caring in the least.
5   And that is how we drove up to the house. Four bedrooms and two toilets and a half.
6   "Isn't it a beauty?" he said, not touching me, but urging me out of the car with the phony enthusiasm of his voice.
7   "Yes," I said. It is "a beauty." Like new Southern houses everywhere. The bricks resemble cubes of raw meat; the roof presses down, a field hat made of iron. The windows are narrow, beady eyes; the aluminum glints. The yard is a long undressed wound, the few trees as bereft of foliage as hairpins stuck in a mud cake.
8   "Yes," I say, "it sure is a beauty." He beams, in his chill and reassured way. I am startled that he doesn't still wear some kind of military uniform. But no. He came home from Korea a hero, and a glutton for sweet smells.
9   "Here we can forget the past," he says.

page 120

10   We have moved in and bought new furniture. The place reeks of newness, the green walls turn me bilious. He stands behind me, his hands touching the edges of my hair. I pick up my hairbrush and brush his hands away. I have

sweetened my body to such an extent that even he (especially he) may no longer touch it.

11   I do not want to forget the past; but I say "Yes," like a parrot. "We can forget the past here."

12   The past of course is Mordecai Rich, the man who, Ruel claims, caused my breakdown. The past is the night I tried to murder Ruel with one of his chain saws.

May 1958

page 2

13   Mordecai Rich

14   Mordecai does not believe Ruel Johnson is my husband. "*That* old man," he says, in a mocking, cruel way.

15   "Ruel is not old," I say. "Looking old is just his way." Just as, I thought, looking young is your way, although you're probably not much younger than Ruel.

16   Maybe it is just that Mordecai is a vagabond, scribbling down impressions of the South, from no solid place, going to none . . . and Ruel has never left Hancock County, except once, when he gallantly went off to war. He claims travel broadened him, especially his two months of European leave. He married me because although my skin is brown he thinks I look like a Frenchwoman. Sometimes he tells me I look Oriental: Korean or Japanese. I console myself with this thought: My family tends to darken and darken as we get older. One day he may wake up in bed with a complete stranger.

17   "He works in the store," I say. "He also raises a hundred acres of peanuts." Which is surely success.

18   "That many," muses Mordecai.

19   It is not pride that makes me tell him what my husband does, is. It is a way I can tell him about myself.

page 4

20   Today Mordecai is back. He tells a funny/sad story about a man in town who could not move his wife. "He huffed and puffed," laughed Mordecai, "to no avail." Then one night as he was sneaking up to her bedroom he heard joyous cries. Rushing in he found his wife in the arms of another woman! The wife calmly dressed and began to pack her bags. The husband begged and pleaded. "Anything you want," he promised. "What *do* you want?" he pleaded. The wife began to chuckle and, laughing, left the house with her friend.

21   Now the husband gets drunk every day and wants an ordinance passed.

He cannot say what the ordinance will be against, but that is what he buttonholes people to say: "I want a goddam ordinance passed!" People who know the story make jokes about him. They pity him and give him enough money to keep him drunk.

page 5

22   I think Mordecai Rich has about as much heart as a dirt-eating toad. Even when he makes me laugh I know that nobody ought to look on other people's confusion with that cold an eye.

23   "But that's what I am," he says, flipping through the pages of his scribble pad. "A cold eye. An eye looking for Beauty. An eye looking for Truth."

24   "Why don't you look for other things?" I want to know. "Like neither Truth nor Beauty, but places in people's lives where things have just slipped a good bit off the track."

25   "That's too vague," said Mordecai, frowning.

26   "So is Truth," I said. "Not to mention Beauty."

page 10

27   Ruel wants to know why "the skinny black tramp"—as he calls Mordecai—keeps hanging around. I made the mistake of telling him Mordecai is thinking of using our house as the setting for one of his Southern country stories.

28   "Mordecai is from the North," I said. "He never saw a wooden house with a toilet in the yard."

29   "Well maybe he better go back where he from," said Ruel, "and shit the way he's used to."

30   It's Ruel's pride that is hurt. He's ashamed of this house that seems perfectly adequate to me. One day we'll have a new house, he says, of brick, with a Japanese bath. How should I know why?

page 11

31   When I told Mordecai what Ruel said he smiled in that snake-eyed way he has and said, "Do *you* mind me hanging around?"

32   I didn't know what to say. I stammered something. Not because of his question but because he put his hand point-blank on my left nipple. He settled his other hand deep in my hair.

33   "I am married more thoroughly than a young boy like you could guess," I told him. But I don't expect that to stop him. Especially since the day he found out I wanted to be a writer myself.

34   It happened this way: I was writing in the grape arbor, on the ledge by the creek that is hidden from the house by trees. He was right in front of me before I could put my notebook away. He snatched it from me and began to read. What is worse, he read aloud. I was embarrassed to death.

35   "No wife of mine is going to embarrass me with a lot of foolish, vulgar stuff," Mordecai read. (This is Ruel's opinion of my writing.) *Every time he tells me how peculiar I am for wanting to write stories he brings up having a baby or going shopping, as if these things are the same. Just something to occupy my time.*

36   "If you have time on your hands," he said today, "why don't you go shopping in that new store in town."

37   I went. I bought six kinds of face cream, two eyebrow pencils, five nightgowns and a longhaired wig. Two contour sticks and a pot of gloss for my lips.

38   And all the while I was grieving over my last story. Outlined—which is as far as I take stories now—but dead in embryo. My hand stilled by cowardice, my heart the heart of a slave.

page 14

39   Of course Mordecai wanted to see the story. What did I have to lose?
40   "Flip over a few pages," I said. "It is the very skeleton of a story, but one that maybe someday I will write."
41   "The One-Legged Woman," Mordecai began to read aloud, then continued silently.

> The characters are poor dairy farmers. One morning the husband is too hung over to do the milking. His wife does it and when she has finished the cows are frightened by thunder and stampede, trampling her. She is also hooked severely in one leg. Her husband is asleep and does not hear her cry out. Finally she drags herself home and wakes him up. He washes her wounds and begs her to forgive him. He does not go for a doctor because he is afraid the doctor will accuse him of being lazy and a drunk, undeserving of his good wife. He wants the doctor to respect him. The wife, understanding, goes along with this.
>
> However, gangrene sets in and the doctor comes. He lectures the husband and amputates the leg of the wife. The wife lives and tries to forgive her husband for his weakness.
>
> While she is ill the husband tries to show he loves her, but cannot look at the missing leg. When she is well he finds he can no longer make love to her. The wife, sensing his revulsion, understands her sacrifice was for nothing. She drags herself to the barn and hangs herself.
>
> The husband, ashamed that anyone should know he was married to a one-legged woman, buries her himself and later tells everyone that she is visiting her mother.

42   While Mordecai was reading the story I looked out over the fields. If he says one good thing about what I've written, I promised myself, I will go to bed

with him. (How else could I repay him? All I owned in any supply were my jars of cold cream!) As if he read my mind he sank down on the seat beside me and looked at me strangely.

43   "*You* think about things like this?" he asked.

44   He took me in his arms, right there in the grape arbor. "You sure do have a lot of heavy, sexy hair," he said, placing me gently on the ground. After that, a miracle happened. Under Mordecai's fingers my body opened like a flower and carefully bloomed. And it was strange as well as wonderful. For I don't think love had anything to do with this at all.

page 17

45   After that, Mordecai praised me for my intelligence, my sensitivity, the depth of the work he had seen—and naturally I showed him everything I had: old journals from high school, notebooks I kept hidden under tarpaulin in the barn, stories written on paper bags, on table napkins, even on shelf paper from over the sink. I am amazed—even more amazed than Mordecai—by the amount of stuff I have written. It is over twenty years' worth, and would fill, easily, a small shed.

46   "You must give these to me," Mordecai said finally, holding three notebooks he selected from the rather messy pile. "I will see if something can't be done with them. You could be another Zora Hurston—" he smiled—"another Simone de Beauvoir!"

47   Of course I am flattered. "Take it! Take it!" I cry. Already I see myself as he sees me. A famous authoress, miles away from Ruel, miles away from anybody. I am dressed in dungarees, my hands are a mess. I smell of sweat. I glow with happiness.

48   "How could such pretty brown fingers write such ugly, deep stuff?" Mordecai asks, kissing them.

page 20

49   For a week we deny each other nothing. If Ruel knows (how could he not know? His sheets are never fresh), he says nothing. I realize now that he never considered Mordecai a threat. Because Mordecai seems to have nothing to offer but his skinny self and his funny talk. I gloat over this knowledge. Now Ruel will find that I am not a womb without a brain that can be bought with Japanese bathtubs and shopping sprees. The moment of my deliverance is at hand!

page 24

50   Mordecai did not come today. I sit in the arbor writing down those words and my throat begins to close up. I am nearly strangled by my fear.

page 56

51   I have not noticed anything for weeks. Not Ruel, not the house. Everything whispers to me that Mordecai has forgotten me. Yesterday Ruel told me not to go into town and I said I wouldn't, for I have been hunting Mordecai up and down the streets. People look at me strangely, their glances slide off me in a peculiar way. It is as if they see something on my face that embarrasses them. Does everyone know about Mordecai and me? Does good loving show so soon? . . . But it is not soon. He has been gone already longer than I have known him.

page 61

52   Ruel tells me I act like my mind's asleep. It is asleep, of course. Nothing will wake it but a letter from Mordecai telling me to pack my bags and fly to New York.

page 65

53   If I could have read Mordecai's scribble pad I would know exactly what he thought of me. But now I realize he never once offered to show it to me, though he had a chance to read every serious thought I ever had. I'm afraid to know what he thought. I feel crippled, deformed. But if he ever wrote it down, that would make it true.

page 66

54   Today Ruel brought me in from the grape arbor, out of the rain. I didn't know it was raining. "Old folks like us might catch rheumatism if we don't be careful," he joked. I don't know what he means. I am thirty-two. He is forty. I never felt old before this month.

page 79

55   Ruel came up to bed last night and actually cried in my arms! He would give anything for a child, he says.
56   "Do you think we could have one?" he said.
57   "Sure," I said. "Why not?"
58   He began to kiss me and carry on about my goodness. I began to laugh.

He became very angry, but finished what he started. He really does intend to have a child.

page 80

59   I must really think of something better to do than kill myself.

page 81

60   Ruel wants me to see a doctor about speeding up conception of the child.
61   "Will you go, honey?" he asks, like a beggar.
62   "Sure," I say. "Why not?"

page 82

63   Today at the doctor's office the magazine I was reading fell open at a story about a one-legged woman. They had a picture of her, drawn by someone who painted the cows orange and green, and painted the woman white, like a white cracker, with little slit-blue eyes. Not black and heavy like she was in the story I had in mind. But it is still my story, filled out and switched about as things are. The author is said to be Mordecai Rich. They show a little picture of him on a back page. He looks severe and has grown a beard. And underneath his picture there is that same statement he made to me about going around looking for Truth.
64   They say his next book will be called "The Black Woman's Resistance to Creativity in the Arts."

page 86

65   Last night while Ruel snored on his side of the bed I washed the prints of his hands off my body. Then I plugged in one of his chain saws and tried to slice off his head. This failed because of the noise. Ruel woke up right in the nick of time.

page 95

66   The days pass in a haze that is not unpleasant. The doctors and nurses do not take me seriously. They fill me full of drugs and never even bother to lock the door. When I think of Ruel I think of the song the British sing: "Ruel Britannia"! I can even whistle it, or drum it with my fingers.

Finding the Form

September 1961

page 218

67 People tell my husband all the time that I do not look crazy. I have been out for almost a year and he is beginning to believe them. Nights, he climbs on me with his slobber and his hope, cursing Mordecai Rich for messing up his life. I wonder if he feels our wills clashing in the dark. Sometimes I see the sparks fly inside my head. It is amazing how normal everything is.

page 223

68 The house still does not awaken to the pitter-patter of sweet little feet, because I religiously use the Pill. It is the only spot of humor in my entire day, when I am gulping that little yellow tablet and washing it down with soda pop or tea. Ruel spends long hours at the store and in the peanut field. He comes in sweaty, dirty, tired, and I wait for him smelling of Arpège, My Sin, Wind Song, and Jungle Gardenia. The women of the community feel sorry for him, to be married to such a fluff of nothing.

69 I wait, beautiful and perfect in every limb, cooking supper as if my life depended on it. Lying unresisting on his bed like a drowned body washed to shore. But he is not happy. For he knows now that I intend to do nothing but say yes until he is completely exhausted.

70 I go to the new shopping mall twice a day now; once in the morning and once in the afternoon, or at night. I buy hats I would not dream of wearing, or even owning. Dresses that are already on their way to Goodwill. Shoes that will go to mold and mildew in the cellar. And I keep the bottles of perfume, the skin softeners, the pots of gloss and eye shadow. I amuse myself painting my own face.

71 When he is quite, quite tired of me I will tell him how long I've relied on the security of the Pill. When I am quite, quite tired of the sweet, sweet smell of my body and the softness of these Helena Rubenstein hands I will leave him and this house. Leave them forever without once looking back. ❖

Questions to Ponder

1. What is innovative about the structure of this story? What two time periods does this story cover? How does the *form* of this story (dates plus page numbers) enable you to follow the time changes in this story?
2. What do you think Myrna (the narrator of this story) wants out of life? Which lines or details in the story lead you to your conclusion?

3. Compare and contrast the two men in Myrna's life. How are they different from each other? Do they have anything in common?
4. How does the story of the one-legged woman and her husband relate to Myrna and Ruel?
5. Alice Walker refers to smells often in this story. Why do you think Myrna keeps herself smothered in expensive fragrances and lotions? What smells does she really prefer?
6. Why do you think Myrna in 1958 was able to get only as far as outlines for her stories?
7. Do you think Myrna will ever leave Ruel? What does the fact that we are reading her book mean about her writing?
8. To what does the story's title, " 'Really, *Doesn't* Crime Pay?' " refer? How many crimes are there in this story?

Writing Possibilities

1. Using the form of Alice Walker's story as a model, plot out several scenes in a story, and then assign them page numbers as if they were pages in a novel. (Use date labels as well—if they are necessary for clarity.)
2. If you have told your story in chronological order, now take the same story and see how it changes if you start at a late point in the chronology and then flash back to an earlier time, like Walker does. Do you like the story better this way? What do you gain? What do you lose?
3. Try retelling this story from Ruel's point of view? How would he see it?
4. Mordecai Rich reportedly is planning to write an essay on "The Black Woman's Resistance to Creativity in the Arts." Using only the evidence in Walker's story, write your own essay explaining what you think is keeping Myrna from becoming the writer she wants to be.

CHAPTER 5

Finding a Voice

"In the right key one can say anything," said George Bernard Shaw. "In the wrong key, nothing."

Finding the right voice for what you have to say is as important as finding the most effective form in which to say it. The voice or tone can sink a piece of writing—or make it soar. A bland tone can kill the liveliest subject. A fresh voice can breathe new life into the oldest refrain.

Most readers agree that good writing has voice. Readers feel that a real person is speaking. Indeed, they feel that they know the person who is writing; they can almost picture the person from the voice and personality projected. Beginning writers should strive for voice in all their writing. They should cultivate their writing voices throughout their lives; with luck, they may even find a voice as distinctive as their signatures, one (like Hemingway's or Toni Morrison's) that readers will immediately associate with them.

For convenience we can separate three different types of voice: voice as tone, voice as narrator or character, and voice as the writer's original signature. In reality, however, the three are intimately related.

VOICE AS TONE

Like speech, even the shortest piece of writing has a tone. Your tone in an essay may be formal and polite, or it may be angry, sarcastic, complaining, whimsical, or melancholy. Like shades of color, tone can change across a written work. You may start a letter in an angry tone and close with an earnest plea. You might begin an essay in a light, humorous vein, which you will later turn upon and challenge.

The tone, or key, in which you choose to pitch your material should be as carefully and deliberately chosen as the format in which you present it. You should consider the tone before you place the first word on the page or screen. An easy way to determine the most effective tone for a piece of writing is to focus on these three matters:

- your audience
- the occasion (or context for your piece)
- your purpose (the effect you wish to achieve)

If you are writing to a potential employer to ask for a job, you will probably want to adopt a polite, respectful, and serious tone rather than an angry or challenging voice. Ten years later, you might assume a humorous, affectionate voice for a speech at a retirement roast for this same employer. For college papers, a polite, serious, formal-but-not-stuffy tone is usually best. Remember Bernard Shaw's words, "In the right key one can say anything," and invest some time searching for just that right key.

Just as tone should be considered before you start a piece of writing, it is well worth reexamining once your first draft is completed. Once your basic thoughts have been formulated, you can step back and trace the tone of your writing—from section to section, from paragraph to paragraph, even from sentence to sentence. Here is where you can get valuable feedback from a writing group or from even one other reader. Think of your readers as passengers aboard your ship (which is your piece of writing). Ask them if you have carried them with you throughout or if there are any points where they have abandoned ship or started paddling in the opposite direction from you. Ask them to point to specific passages that caused their unrest (or outright mutiny). It is here that you will want to listen carefully to your voice. Do you sound in these passages like a fast-talking salesperson? An angry parent reprimanding naughty children? A wise friend? A gentle coach? Is your tone helping you or hurting you at this moment? Often you can hear effective or ineffective shifts of voice and tone simply by reading your drafts aloud; however, running them by actual readers can sometimes help even more.

VOICE AS NARRATOR OR CHARACTER

Occasionally in a piece of writing you may wish to write in a voice not at all your own. You may wish to try to create narrators or characters with distinctive voices just as a technical experiment, or because it seems the only natural way to tell a story, create a play, or communicate what you want to say. It would be hard to imagine *The Adventures of Huckleberry Finn* coming from any voice other than Huck's innocent, ungrammatical one; nor can we think of *The Catcher in the Rye* without hearing Holden Caulfield's adolescent whine. Part of the joy of Alice Walker's *The Color Purple* is Celie's heartbreakingly honest voice.

Assuming a distinctive narrative voice or the voice of a character in a piece of writing is a bit like ventriloquism. You assume a character and then speak in his or her tongue. How can you learn to accomplish this ventriloquist's feat? How can you speak in other voices besides your own?

The best way to begin is to listen to the voices around you and take note of distinguishing characteristics. Is a friend's voice distinctive because of colorful expressions, habits of repetition, especially good or bad grammar, or length or pitch of speech? (Note how *Saturday Night Live* comedian Dana Carvey has built his imitation of President Bush on his recognition that the President often speaks in incomplete sentences.) It was at a party that Donna Roazen heard the "Milk Run" story included in this chapter. She liked it so much she rushed home and committed it to paper.

Jot down distinctive sentences or vocal mannerisms in your writer's notebook. This is a way consciously to cultivate your ear for individual idiom. Sometimes one line or phrase will stimulate your mind to create another. Before he began his interviews for *In Cold Blood,* Truman Capote consciously cultivated his memory and his ear for human speech by listening to records and to conversations of friends. After a few minutes he would stop them and write down everything he remembered. He practiced, he said, until he could transcribe lengthy conversations with 90 percent accuracy. Nancy Price practiced narrative voices a different way, by rewriting Donna Roazen's "Milk Run" from 13 other points of view.

If you have a satiric bent, you might also wish to hone in on group as well as individual voices with the goal of *re-presenting* them in your writing. Are there certain speech patterns common to teenage girls or guys, to disc jockeys, to fraternity or sorority members, or to college professors? Can you capture this in your writing—and for what purpose? Student Cory Waldron wants to give us a fresh take on the Little Red Riding Hood story through his "Seeing Red," a satiric retelling from the grandmother's point of view.

VOICE AS THE WRITER'S ORIGINAL SIGNATURE

Strange as it may seem at first, finding the most effective tone for a piece of writing and writing in the voices of others can be part of finding your own distinctive voice as a writer. Eudora Welty and Tom Wolfe say as much in their essays in this chapter. In fact, one way to find your original voice may be to try on as many voices and tones as possible. In "At the Western Palace," Maxine Hong Kingston adopts the voice of her Chinese-American ancestors to tell a moving story of the clash between two cultures. In "Mr. Secrets," Richard Rodriguez speaks at times in the voice of his Hispanic parents.

Finding your original voice means plunging in and trusting your instincts. You may begin with a certain voice or style in mind but quickly abandon it as you listen to the words that come from you and follow where they lead. Let the developing situation guide you. (See "Flow" in Chapter 7.)

Many writers find their way by a process of elimination, by ruling out what they don't want or what does not work. They have learned that if they have even the slightest misgivings about a passage, they should rule it out and try again. This philosophy makes sense. Somehow it is easier to know what you don't want, because what you *do* want is something as yet unknown. Only by trusting your instincts and by trial and error will you find it. When you finally hear it, you will know the voice or words are right. It may be a matter of outer meeting inner realities, as Eudora Welty suggests in this chapter in "Finding a Voice" and which Barry Lopez explores at greater length in "Landscape and Narrative" in Chapter 7.

INTRODUCTION TO *THE KANDY-KOLORED TANGERINE-FLAKE STREAMLINE BABY*

Tom Wolfe

When I was nine, I started writing a biography of Napoleon. He was small, and I was small. I was nine years old. It bothered me that the world was run by large people, and Napoleon was this little guy who, at one point, ran the world.

I also did an illustrated children's book at that time, about Mozart—a child prodigy—who gave concerts to tremendous *applause*. Then I had a long fascination with sportswriting. But I think that was bound up with my aspirations to be an athlete. That's who got applause in school! Not writers! . . .

Beginning writers tend to think genius is 95 percent something that's locked inside of your skull . . . and that the material is about 5 percent, just the clay that you're modeling. As you get further along in your career you begin to realize that's not the truth. In a work of genius, probably the proportion is more like 65 percent material and 35 percent whatever talent you have. I think you become more and more aware of the fact that the talent becomes useless without the material. . . .

When I'm writing I like to keep the room cold—I think between 62 to 65 degrees is the right temperature to write. It's another way of boxing myself in. . . . I try to set a quota of ten pages—I triple space on the typewriter. For me it's about 1,900 words. Any time I'm finished with that I can quit. . . . I'll try to do a page or two before lunch. I always get up earlier than normal, but nothing gets done until just before lunch. I do a page or two. At that point I go outside, just walk around the block. I try to get five pages done in the afternoon, so that working after dinner is not going to be too much of a struggle. But I usually end up working late anyway. This is not a very good way to do it. . . .

[When I write] what I try to do is re-create a scene from a triple point of view: the subject's point of view, my own, and that of the other people watching—often within a single paragraph. . . . I review my notes . . . close my eyes and try to imagine myself, as a Method actor would, into the scene . . . going crazy, for example . . . how it feels and what it's going to sound like if you translate it into words—which [is] real writing by radar. . . .

I wonder why students who are great letter writers and can just leave you in stitches, stiffen up and lose their style the minute they are assigned a piece of writing. . . . [Writing The Kandy-Kolored Tangerine-Flake Streamline Baby] broke me out of the restriction of newspaper style.

Brief Warm-up Writing Exercises

1. Describe the car that you love the most (or have loved in the past) and why you like it.
2. Make three lists: (1) *People* you write letters to or call by phone, (2) the *subjects* you usually talk about with each person, and (3) the *voice* or style of language you use with each (formal? slangy? serious? dutiful? joking? and so on).
3. Brainstorm a list of sports, life-styles, art forms, or other cultural styles that you think have been overlooked by the mass media.

---

1   I don't mean for this to sound like "I had a vision" or anything, but there was a specific starting point for practically all of these stories. I wrote them in a fifteen-month period, and the whole thing started with the afternoon I went to a Hot Rod & Custom Car show at the Coliseum in New York. Strange afternoon! I was sent up there to cover the Hot Rod & Custom Car show by the New York *Herald Tribune*, and I brought back exactly the kind of story any of the somnambulistic totem newspapers in America would have come up with. A totem newspaper is the kind people don't really buy to read but just

to *have,* physically, because they know it supports their own outlook on life. They're just like the buffalo tongues the Omaha Indians used to carry around or the dog ears the Mahili clan carried around in Bengal. There are two kinds of totem newspapers in the country. One is the symbol of the frightened chair-arm-doilie Vicks Vapo-Rub *Weltanschauung* that lies there in the solar plexus of all good gray burghers. All those nice stories on the first page of the second section about eighty-seven-year-old ladies on Gramercy Park who have one-hundred-and-two-year-old turtles or about the colorful street vendors of Havana. Mommy! This fellow Castro is in there, and revolutions may come and go, but the picturesque poor will endure, padding around in the streets selling their chestnuts and salt pretzels the world over, even in Havana, Cuba, assuring a paradise, after all, full of respect and obeisance, for all us Vicks Vapo-Rub chair-arm-doilie burghers. After all. Or another totem group buys the kind of paper they can put under their arms and have the totem for the tough-but-wholesome outlook, the Mom's Pie view of life. Everybody can go off to the bar and drink a few "brews" and retail some cynical remarks about Zora Folley and how the fight game is these days and round it off, though, with how George Chuvalo has "a lot of heart," which he got, one understands, by eating mom's pie. Anyway, I went to the Hot Rod & Custom Car show and wrote a story that would have suited any of the totem newspapers. All the totem newspapers would regard one of these shows as a sideshow, a panopticon, for creeps and kooks; not even wealthy, eccentric creeps and kooks, which would be all right, but lower class creeps and nutballs with dermatitic skin and ratty hair. The totem story usually makes what is known as "gentle fun" of this, which is a way of saying, don't worry, these people are nothing.

2   So I wrote a story about a kid who had built a golden motorcycle, which he called "The Golden Alligator." The seat was made of some kind of gold-painted leather that kept going back, on and on, as long as an alligator's tail, and had scales embossed on it, like an alligator's. The kid had made a whole golden suit for himself, like a space suit, that also looked as if it were covered with scales and he would lie down on his stomach on this long seat, stretched out full length, so that he appeared to be made into the motorcycle or something, and roar around Greenwich Village on Saturday nights, down Macdougal Street, down there in Nut Heaven, looking like a golden alligator on wheels. Nutty! He seemed like a Gentle Nut when I got through. It was a shame I wrote that sort of story, the usual totem story, because I was working for the *Herald Tribune,* and the *Herald Tribune* was the only experimental paper in town, breaking out of the totem formula. The thing was, I knew I had another story all the time, a bona fide story, the real story of the Hot Rod & Custom Car show, but I didn't know what to do with it. It was outside the system of ideas I was used to working with, even though I had been through the whole Ph.D. route at Yale, in American Studies and everything.

3   Here were all these ... *weird* ... nutty-looking, crazy baroque custom cars,

sitting in little nests of pink angora angel's hair for the purpose of "glamorous" display—but then I got to talking to one of the men who make them, a fellow named Dale Alexander. He was a very serious and soft-spoken man, about thirty, completely serious about the whole thing, in fact, and pretty soon it became clear, as I talked to this man for a while, that he had been living like the *complete artist* for years. He had starved, suffered—the whole thing—so he could sit inside a garage and create these cars which more than 99 percent of the American people would consider ridiculous, vulgar and lower-class-awful beyond comment almost. He had started off with a garage that fixed banged-up cars and everything, to pay the rent, but gradually he couldn't stand it anymore. Creativity—his own custom car art—became an obsession with him. So he became the complete custom car artist. And he said he wasn't the only one. All the great custom car designers had gone through it. It was the *only way*. *Holy beasts*. Starving artists! Inspiration! Only instead of garrets, they had these garages.

4   So I went over to *Esquire* magazine after a while and talked to them about this phenomenon, and they sent me out to California to take a look at the custom car world. Dale Alexander was from Detroit or some place, but the real center of the thing was in California, around Los Angeles. I started talking to a lot of these people, like George Barris and Ed Roth, and seeing what they were doing, and—well, eventually it became the story from which the title of this book was taken, "The Kandy-Kolored Tangerine-Flake Streamline Baby." But at first I couldn't even write the story. I came back to New York and just sat around worrying over the thing. I had a lot of trouble analyzing exactly what I had on my hands. By this time *Esquire* practically had a gun at my head because they had a two-page-wide color picture for the story locked into the printing presses and no story. Finally, I told Byron Dobell, the managing editor at *Esquire,* that I couldn't pull the thing together. O.K., he tells me, just type out my notes and send them over and he will get somebody else to write it. So about 8 o'clock that night I started typing the notes out in the form of a memorandum that began, "Dear Byron." I started typing away, starting right with the first time I saw any custom cars in California. I just started recording it all, and inside of a couple of hours, typing along like a madman, I could tell that something was beginning to happen. By midnight this memorandum to Byron was twenty pages long and I was still typing like a maniac. About 2 A.M. or something like that I turned on WABC, a radio station that plays rock and roll music all night long, and got a little more manic. I wrapped up the memorandum about 6:15 A.M., and by this time it was 49 pages long. I took it over to *Esquire* as soon as they opened up, about 9:30 A.M. About 4 P.M. I got a call from Byron Dobell. He told me they were striking out the "Dear Byron" at the top of the memorandum and running the rest of it in the magazine. That was the story, "The Kandy Kolored Tangerine-Flake Streamline Baby."

5   What had happened was that I started writing down everything I had seen the first place I went in California, this incredible event, a "Teen Fair." The details themselves, when I wrote them down, suddenly made me see what was happening. Here was this incredible combination of form plus money in a place nobody ever thought about finding it, namely, among teen-agers. Practically every style recorded in art history is the result of the same thing—a lot of attention to form, plus the money to make monuments to it. The "classic" English style of Inigo Jones, for example, places like the Covent Garden and the royal banquet hall at Whitehall, were the result of a worship of Italian Palladian grandeur . . . form . . . plus the money that began pouring in under James I and Charles I from colonial possessions. These were the kind of forms, styles, symbols . . . Palladian classicism . . . that influence a whole society. But throughout history, everywhere this kind of thing took place, China, Egypt, France under the Bourbons, every place, it has been something the aristocracy has been responsible for. What has happened in the United States since World War II, however, has broken that pattern. The war created money. It made massive infusions of money into every level of society. Suddenly classes of people whose styles of life had been practically invisible had the money to build monuments to their own styles. Among teen-agers, this took the form of custom cars, the twist, the jerk, the monkey, the shake, rock music generally, stretch pants, decal eyes—and all these things, these teen-age styles of life, like Inigo Jones's classicism, have started having an influence on the life of the whole country. It is not merely teen-agers. In the South, for example, all the proles, peasants, and petty burghers suddenly got enough money to start up their incredible car world. In fifteen years stock car racing has replaced baseball as the number one sport in the South. It doesn't make much difference what happens to baseball or stock car racing, actually, but this shift, from a fixed land sport, modeled on cricket, to this wild car sport, with standard, or standard-looking, cars that go 180 miles an hour or so—this symbolizes a radical change in the people as a whole. Practically nobody has bothered to see what these changes are all about. People have been looking at the new money since the war in economic terms only. Nobody will even take a look at our incredible new national pastimes, things like stock car racing, drag racing, demolition derbies, sports that attract five to ten million more spectators than football, baseball and basketball each year. Part of it is a built-in class bias. The educated classes in this country, as in every country, the people who grow up to control visual and printed communication media, are all plugged into what is, when one gets down to it, an ancient, aristocratic aesthetic. Stock car racing, custom cars—and, for that matter, the jerk, the monkey, rock music—still seem beneath serious consideration, still the preserve of ratty people with ratty hair and dermatitis and corroded thoracic boxes and so forth. Yet all these rancid people are creating new styles all the time and changing the life of the whole country in ways that nobody even seems to bother to record, much less analyze. ❖

Questions to Ponder

1. Why do you think Tom Wolfe had trouble at first trying to write his custom car story?
2. What was it about writing the "Dear Byron" memo that freed him to find his voice?
3. Why do you think it took a couple of hours of work before Tom Wolfe could tell that something "was beginning to happen"? What *was* beginning to happen?
4. What are some of the distinctive characteristics of Tom Wolfe's voice and writing style? (*Hint:* Look at his use of punctuation, and look at the kinds of words he uses.)

Writing Possibilities

1. Take a walk with a notepad through the student parking lots on your campus and see if you can discover any style trends in student transportation—or any remarkable vehicles worth writing about just in themselves. Now write these stories. (You may need to do some interviewing and library reading to add depth to your piece.)
2. Brainstorm a list of current campus styles in dress, dating or socializing, or studying. Using Tom Wolfe's piece as a model, interpret one or more of these fashions in an article for your student newspaper.
3. Now take the piece you wrote in writing possibility 2, and try writing it again imitating the language and style of those involved in the fashion. (*Hint:* It may help to follow Wolfe's technique of starting off the piece as a letter to someone from a participant or a participant/observer.)

FINDING A VOICE
Eudora Welty

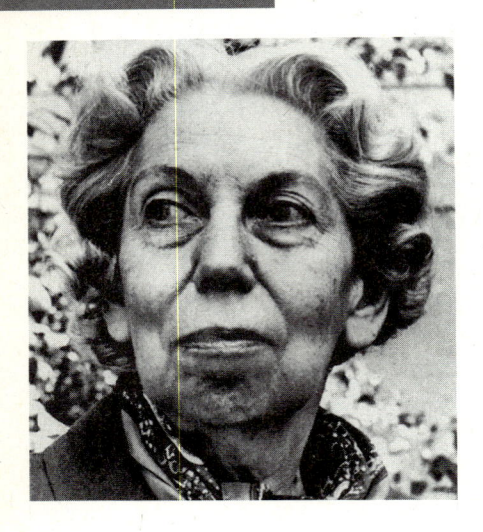

Eudora Welty considers being a Southern writer a special blessing because of the richness of Southern speech. Southerners, she has observed, delight in talking, listening, and remembering, and Southern conversation tends to take the form of stories.

> My first good story began spontaneously, in a remark repeated to me by a traveling man—our neighbor—to whom it had been spoken while he was on a trip into North Mississippi: "He's gone to borry some fire." The words, which carried such lyrical and mythological and dramatic overtones, were real and actual—their hearer repeated them to me (Eudora Welty, One Writer's Beginnings [Cambridge: Harvard UP, 1984], 87).
>
> Once you have heard certain expressions, sentences, you almost never forget them. It's like sending a bucket down the well and it always comes up full. . . . And you listen for the right word, in the present, and you hear it. . . . [W]hat you overhear on a city bus is exactly what your character would say on the page you're writing (Linda Kuehl, "The Art of Fiction XLVII: Eudora Welty." In Conversations with Eudora Welty, edited by Peggy Whitman Prenshaw [Jackson: UP of Mississippi, 1984], 77–78).

Welty finds that the stories she has written "by ear" have been the ones most easily written. In these stories, she surrenders herself to the sound of her characters' speaking voices while at the same time consciously selecting and shaping what they will say.

The rest of her stories have not been so quickly written. They "hang around" in her mind for a long time, she acknowledges, and in the writing undergo numerous revisions.

Brief Warm-up Writing Exercises

1. Make a list of the people who have been unforgettable to you because of the way they look (their facial features or expressions) or because of their

manner of speaking or moving. Then try to capture just these memorable parts (images) in vivid phrases or sentences.

2. Picture in your mind your most inward and deeply feeling self. Now freewrite the thoughts of this self.
3. Close your eyes and picture yourself walking deep into a woods. An animal appears in the path in front of you. Write what kind of animal it is and what it says to you.

❖

1   What discoveries I've made in the course of writing stories all begin with the particular, never the general. They are mostly hindsight: arrows that I now find I myself have left behind me, which have shown me some right, or wrong, way I have come. What one story may have pointed out to me is of no avail in the writing of another. But "avail" is not what I want; freedom ahead is what each story promises—beginning anew. And all the while, as further hindsight has told me, certain patterns in my work repeat themselves without my realizing. There would be no way to know this, for during the writing of any single story, there is no other existing. Each writer must find out for himself, I imagine, on what strange basis he lives with his own stories.

2   I had been writing a number of stories, more or less one after the other, before it belatedly dawned on me that some of the characters in one story were, and had been all the time, the same characters who had appeared already in another story. Only I'd written about them originally under different names, at different periods in their lives, in situations not yet interlocking but ready for it. They touched on every side. These stories were all related (and the fact was buried in their inceptions) by the strongest ties—identities, kinships, relationships, or affinities already known or remembered or foreshadowed. From story to story, connections between the characters' lives, through their motives or actions, sometimes their dreams, already existed: there to be found. Now the whole assembly—some of it still in the future—fell, by stages, into place in one location already evoked, which I saw now was a focusing point for all the stories. What had drawn the characters together there was one strong strand in them all: they lived in one way or another in a dream or in romantic aspiration, or under an illusion of what their lives were coming to, about the meaning of their (now) related lives.

3   The stories were connected most provocatively of all to me, perhaps, through the entry into my story-telling mind of another sort of tie—a shadowing of Greek mythological figures, gods and heroes that wander in various guises, at various times, in and out, emblems of the characters' heady dreams.

4   Writing these stories, which eventually appeared joined together in the book called *The Golden Apples,* was an experience in a writer's own discovery of affinities. In writing, as in life, the connections of all sorts of relationships and kinds lie in wait of discovery, and give out their signals to the Geiger counter of the charged imagination, once it is drawn into the right field.

5   The characters who go to make up my stories and novels are not portraits. Characters I invent along with the story that carries them. Attached to them are what I've borrowed, perhaps unconsciously, bit by bit, of persons I have seen or noticed or remembered in the flesh—a cast of countenance here, a manner of walking there, that jump to the visualizing mind when a story is underway. (Elizabeth Bowen said, "Physical detail cannot be invented." It can only be chosen.) I don't write by invasion into the life of a real person: my own sense of privacy is too strong for that; and I also know instinctively that living people to whom you are close—those known to you in ways too deep, too overflowing, ever to be plumbed outside love—do not yield to, could never fit into, the demands of a story. On the other hand, what I do make my stories out of is the *whole* fund of my feelings, my responses to the real experiences of my own life, to the relationships that formed and changed it, that I have given most of myself to, and so learned my way toward a dramatic counterpart. Characters take on life sometimes by luck, but I suspect it is when you can write most entirely out of yourself, inside the skin, heart, mind, and soul of a person who is not yourself, that a character becomes in his own right another human being on the page.

6   It was not my intention—it never was—to invent a character who should speak for me, the author, in person. A character is in a story to fill a role there, and the character's life along with its expression of life is defined by that surrounding—indeed is created by his own story. Yet, it seems to me now, years after I wrote *The Golden Apples,* that I did bring forth a character with whom I came to feel oddly in touch. This is Miss Eckhart, a woman who has come from away to give piano lessons to the young of Morgana. She is formidable and eccentric in the eyes of everyone, is scarcely accepted in the town. But she persisted with me, as she persisted in spite of herself with the other characters in the stories.

7   Where did the character of Miss Eckhart come from? There was my own real-life piano teacher, "eligible" to the extent that she swatted my hands at the keyboard with a fly-swatter if I made a mistake; and when she wrote "Practice" on my page of sheet music she made her "P" as Miss Eckhart did—a cat's face with a long tail. She did indeed hold a recital of her pupils every June that was a fair model for Miss Eckhart's, and of many another as well, I suppose. But the character of Miss Eckhart was miles away from that of the teacher I knew as a child, or from that of anybody I did know. Nor was she like other teacher-characters I was responsible for: my stories and novels suddenly appear to me to be full of teachers, with Miss Eckhart different from them all.

8   What the story "June Recital" most acutely shows the reader lies in her inner life. I haven't the slightest idea what my real teacher's life was like inside. But I knew what Miss Eckhart's was, for it protruded itself well enough into the story.

9   As I looked longer and longer for the origins of this passionate and strange character, at last I realized that Miss Eckhart came from me. There wasn't any resemblance in her outward identity: I am not musical, not a teacher, nor foreign

in birth; not humorless or ridiculed or missing out in love; nor have I yet let the world around me slip from my recognition. But none of that counts. What counts is only what lies at the solitary core. She derived from what I already knew for myself, even felt I had always known. What I have put into her is my passion for my own life work, my own art. Exposing yourself to risk is a truth Miss Eckhart and I had in common. What animates and possesses me is what drives Miss Eckhart, the love of her art and the love of giving it, the desire to give it until there is no more left. Even in the small and literal way, what I had done in assembling and connecting all the stories in *The Golden Apples,* and bringing them off as one, was not too unlike the June recital itself.

10   Not in Miss Eckhart as she stands solidly and almost opaquely in the surround of her story, but in the making of her character out of my most inward and most deeply feeling self, I would say I have found my voice in my fiction. ❖

Questions to Ponder

1. What words would you choose to describe the voice or tone of this memoir? Does the voice seem suitable and effective?
2. As you look back over your *own* life and work, what patterns or themes do you discover?
3. What are *your* affinities (the things you are drawn to)? Why do you think you are drawn to them?
4. In what way is the imagination like a Geiger counter?
5. Why are creators more interested in the "freedom ahead" than their work in the past? What does Eudora Welty mean when she says, "[D]uring the writing of any single story, there is no other existing"?

Writing Possibilities

1. Brainstorm a list of people you identify with in some way. They may be people you know well, such as family members, or people you have only read or heard about or seen on television or in the movies. After each, briefly write the way in which you identify with him or her.
2. Now choose one of the people on your list, and tell a story or discuss a subject as *they* would, that is, in their voice.
3. Choose a well-known fairy tale like "The Three Pigs," "Little Red Riding Hood," "Snow White and the Seven Dwarfs," or "Bambi," and choose to retell the story in the voice of one of the characters: the big, bad wolf, for example, or one of the dwarfs. How will the selection of details, focus, and voice change?

Student Essay

Seeing Red

Cordell Waldron

"Seeing Red" was originally an assigned project during an introductory college writing class. The purpose of the assignment was to develop a taste for point of view in writing. The concept is simple enough: "Little Red Riding Hood" as told by the grandmother.

The creativity lies in the characterization of the grandmother. No version of the actual story that I have heard has the grandmother cast as such an unpleasant person. With a simple change of style, the time-honored story of Little Red Riding Hood becomes something new. Point of view has this importance in literature and writing.

The original composition of the story was an in-class project and was finished in about an hour. Unfortunately this very first draft was lost. The second draft was composed about one year later at 2:00 A.M. in my dorm room. This time was ideal because I am most creative in the early hours of morning. Through talking to other writers, I have learned that this is not uncommon and that many ideas come right before the author goes to sleep. In order to get the tongue-in-cheek style that was desired, I put some light-and-lively music on (Sir Mix-a-Lot and Thomas Dolby). The point that I am trying to make is that if you have a creative time, place, and setting for writing, trust it. Do not try to write papers during what are assumed to be conventional times. The ideas just will not come; and the essay, report, or story will not be as good as it could be.

My new version of "Little Red Riding Hood" was shared with a writing group. We met every two weeks, and at each meeting I would read the story aloud and listen to the group's response. Our work was mainly that of finetuning the piece. We identified the funniest, most surprising and satisfying lines in the work, and then tried to bring all the other sentences up to that level. If a sentence was dull, we would cut it or rework it till it had more punch or patina. Through this process I found a stronger ending for "Seeing Red." The title itself was the very last addition. When I heard it, I knew it was right.

Brief Warm-up Writing Exercises

1. Freewrite the plot of your favorite television soap opera or situation comedy.
2. Freewrite your favorite fairy tale—as you remember it.
3. Brainstorm a list of details you would want to include if you were going to retell the story of Little Red Riding Hood.

DRAFT

1   Once upon a time there was a little girl walking in the forest. Her name was Little Red Riding Hood.

2   Bah. Her name was Frances Lucretia Windsworth. I should know; she was named after me and I'm her grandmother. Little Red Riding Hood my foot. What a name. Just because the little ingrate wears her expensive designer cape and not the nice blue angora that I spent two months knitting for her with my poor, decrepit fingers.

3   Anyway, she was coming to visit me with a basket of goodies. You could hardly call them goodies. Probably some instant cookies. Her mother never did listen while I tried to teach her some proper cooking. "Just pop it in the microwave," she says. She can't even cook instant cookies right. They're always burnt.

4   She was skipping along the trail, whistling merrily all the way. Probably one of those nasty new pop songs full of sex and other smutty lyrics. She always stops to dawdle along the way, picking flowers or trying to touch small animals. Mark my words one of these days she's going to git bitten. I hear there's a wolf in these parts. I told her mother to watch out and not let Frances alone in the woods. The forests around here are chock full of wolves and dragons and pigs with brick houses and Heaven knows what else. There's not always going to be a handsome prince waiting around the corner either. Just because her mother found one by kissing toads doesn't mean there's one under every rock.

5   Well, wouldn't you know it? She stops and talks to one of those

wolves. She tells it where she's going and who to see and that I live alone ever since my husband ran off with some tramp who lived with a bunch of dwarves. MALE dwarves mind you. I'm lying here in my bed and she's breaking one of the fundamental rules and talking to big ugly wolfen strangers.

6. Alas, I fretted my poor old heart away for hours waiting for Frances and then this knock comes at the door. Well, how should I know it's a wolf and not my little granddaughter? Of course I yell "Come in," expecting something other than a drooling ravenous beast. The wolf comes in and, what with me being old and not in the best of health, he eats me.

7. I guess you should expect the story to be over now, with me in the wolf's stomach and Frances Lucretia going to show up and get herself eaten, too. And rightfully so for you to think that. But noooo. I can't just die peacefully. I have to sit in the wolf's gut and hear gullible Frances Lucretia mistake a gravelly wolf's voice for mine. Obviously she got her perception from her father's side, because she can't tell that it's not me in the bed. Like I have fur and fangs and big eyes. Needless to say, the wolf eats her, too.

8. Just my lot to die in a wolf's stomach. And while I go, I've got to listen to Frances Lucretia, whining about how the big bad wolf ate her. It's her own fault, not paying attention to good advice. If she had any respect for her elders at all, she'd have come and seen me and been home hours ago. None of this would have happened.

9. Once again you'd expect me to have died away. But nooo. Along comes this hunter. Lordy knows why he was hanging around outside. He probably had his eyes on Frances Lucretia. Heaven knows she dresses to catch his eyes. Wearing those trashy red clothes. It's a wonder I'm not a great-grandmother by now. Well, he smashes through the door (Like he can't just open it.) and goes after the wolf with a knife. He makes this big bloody mess all over my poor little house and opens up the wolf from end to end. I don't think I'll ever get the floor clean. Well out I come onto the floor, with Frances Lucretia falling out on top of me. I'm lucky she didn't break my ribs.

10   Frances Lucretia ran off into the woods with that hunter. She didn't even wait around to get a stern reprimand or a spanking. A spanking would do her some good, too. She leaves me sitting here in my little old house again. And she lived happily ever after. Bah.

1   ❖ Once upon a time, there was a little girl walking in the forest. Her name was Little Red Riding Hood.
2   Bah. Her name was Frances Lucretia Windsworth. I should know; she was named after me and, after all, I am her grandmother. Little Red Riding Hood my foot. Not much of a name if you ask me. Just because the ungrateful little brat wears that expensive designer cape and not that pretty blue angora that I spent seven whole months knitting for her with my poor, arthritic fingers.
3   Anyway, she was coming to visit me with a basket of goodies. You could hardly call them goodies. Probably some of those new-fangled instant cookies. Her mother just wouldn't listen when I tried to teach her some proper cooking. "Just pop it in the microwave," she says.
4   Well, Frances Lucretia was skipping along the trail, whistling merrily all the way. Probably whistling one of those nasty new pop songs full of sex, drugs, and other smutty lyrics. She always stops to dawdle along the way, too, picking flowers or trying to touch small animals. Mark my words, one of these days she's going to get herself bitten. She'll be sorry then. Why, I even hear there's a wolf in these parts. I told her mother to watch out and not let Frances alone in the woods. But does she listen? Bah. The forests around here are chock full of wolves and dragons and pigs in brick houses and Heaven knows what else. The neighborhood just isn't what it once was—it's downright evil! There's not always going to be some handsome prince waiting around the corner to save poor Frances's skin, either. Just because her mother found one by kissing toads doesn't mean there's one under every rock.
5   Well, wouldn't you know it? She stops and talks to one of those horrible wolves. She tells him where she's going and who to see and that I live alone ever since my husband ran off with some tramp who lived with a bunch of dwarves. I'm lying here in my bed and she's breaking one of the fundamental rules and talking to big, ugly wolfen strangers.
6   Alas, I fretted my poor old heart away for hours waiting for Frances and then comes this knock on my door. Well, how should I know it's a wolf and not my little granddaughter? I just don't hear so well these days. Of course I yell "Come in," expecting something other than a ravenous drooling beast. The wolf comes in, and what with me being old and not in the best of health, he eats me. No big chase like you hear about in some stories. Just chomp chomp gulp swallow and it's all over.
7   I guess you should expect the story to be over now, what with me in the wolf's stomach and Frances Lucretia going to show up and get herself eaten,

too. And rightfully so for you think that. But noooo. I can't just die peacefully. I have to sit in the wolf's gut and hear my gullible Francis Lucretia mistake a wolf's voice for mine. Obviously she got her perception from her father's side. "What big eyes you have. What big ears you have. What big teeth you have." What a stupid little girl you are. Pay some attention. Like I have fur and fangs and big eyes. Needless to say, the wolf eats her, too.

8   Just my lot to die in a wolf's stomach. And while I go, I've got to listen to Frances Lucretia, whining about how the big bad wolf ate her. It's her own fault, not paying attention to good advice. If she had any respect for her elders at all, she'd have come and seen me and been home hours ago. None of this would have happened.

9   Once again you'd think I could just pass away. But nooo. While Frances is sitting on top of me, whining about what the wolf's stomach is doing to her Gucci cape, along comes this hunter who was hanging around outside. Heaven knows she's always dressing to catch men's eyes. Wearing those trashy red clothes. I tell you it's a wonder I'm not a great-grandmother by now. Well, he smashes through the door (like he can't just open it!) and goes after the wolf with a knife. He opens the wolf up from one end to the other and makes this big bloody mess all over my poor little house. Well, out I come onto the floor, with Frances Lucretia crashing out right on top of me. Thank my lucky stars she didn't break my ribs.

10   She makes these big eyes at the hunter and he looks back. They just stare at each other like they're in some fairy tale and haven't just about died. I try to step in and give Frances a proper lecture on minding her elders and being careful in the forest, but will she listen? Of course not. She just keeps staring at this hunter like he's going to give her a glass slipper or something. Then she starts crying about the awful shape her clothes are in and how scary it was. Heavens that girl complains a lot.

11   Well, this hunter says, "I hope everybody's okay," and heads for the door. I just about keel over dead when Frances says, "Oh, I think I need to be walked home, just in case there are any more wolves." Then the both of them go traipsing out the door without so much as a good-bye or a helping hand with the wolf. A spanking would do her some good. They leave me sitting here in my little old house, staring at the wolf guts all over my carpet. I don't think I'll ever get my floor clean again. And she lived happily ever after. But does she ever think about me? Bah. ❖

Questions to Ponder

1. How would you describe the grandmother in Cory Waldron's story? What is her personality like? How has Cory succeeded in making her voice and personality distinctive in this short piece?
2. What surprises does this story offer?

3. Do you find Cory Waldron's second closing more effective than his first? Which phrases and sentences strike you as improvements?
4. Why is humor difficult to write?

Writing Possibilities

1. Take Cory Waldron's story and tell it from Red's (Frances's) point of view—or in the wolf's voice—giving the narrator an interesting personality.
2. Take your description in warm-up writing exercise 1 of your favorite soap opera or situation comedy and revise it, writing it in the voice of one of the show's major characters.
3. Cartoon characters are often memorable to us because of their distinctive voices and mannerisms. Select several cartoon figures, and describe and analyze how their voices make them lovable—or memorable.

AT THE WESTERN PALACE
Maxine Hong Kingston

"At the Western Palace" is Chapter 4 of five chapters of The Woman Warrior—Memoirs of a Girlhood Among Ghosts. It is the most classically formed, the most excerptable piece of writing I've done. For everything else, I've had to experiment in order to create a shape that tells accurately the immensity, intricacy, and far-rangingness of lives, visions, imaginations, and cultures.

This short story is a breakthrough in my becoming a better person and a better artist. For nearly three decades—I began at age eight—I'd been writing in the first-person singular. Then four-fifths of the way through The Woman Warrior, I doubted the empathic abilities of a narrator who could not use many points of view and all the pronouns. This section is the only chapter in that book that breaks out of the first-person singular. Seeing her from the outside, the reader gets to know this girl in a social context. The insistent "I" with whom the reader identifies up to this chapter, is, after all, nobody but an ignorant girl. She has very little power in the world of adults and their transcontinental adventures, and hardly appears in this story.

Sometimes, events in real life happen to fall exactly into short-story form—or, more precisely, the sit-com form of "I Love Lucy." Keeping that half-hour in mind, I could handle four characters—Lucy and Ethel, the prototypes for Brave Orchid and Moon Orchid; and Ricky and Fred, the father and the bigamist uncle. Lucy and Ethel hatch a plot that heads for trouble, confrontation, and explosion.

The last chapter of The Woman Warrior returns to first-person narration. It opens with a paragraph that is a one-sentence rendition of "At the Western Palace": "What my brother actually said was, 'I drove Mom and Second Aunt to Los Angeles to see Aunt's husband who's got the other wife.'" I mean to show that events have many versions, that there are people who make much ado—a short story—and other people who dispense with those events as nothing much.

In my next book, China Men, I again relied on the first-person narrator to help me on the quest in the Land of Men. But in my new novel, Tripmaster Monkey—His Fake Book, at last I've been able to create a protagonist and his friends seen and told from the viewpoint of an omniscient narrator. That omniscient narrator has a personality and a memory. She knows thousands of years of Chinese history and the two hundred years of American history, and she sees a few years into the future to the end of the Vietnam War. Sometimes she controls events and characters, and sometimes she does not. She teaches, scolds, prods the characters, but mercifully, she does not let anything disastrous happen to them. As I finished the book, I thought of her as Kwan Yin, the Goddess of Mercy, and realized that "I" evolved from a self-centered child to compassionate goddess.

Brief Warm-up Writing Exercises

1. Brainstorm a list of family traditions—from ways of celebrating holidays and birthdays to favorite foods and ways of spending time.
2. Now write down as many family expressions or "sayings" as you can think of (first words mispronounced, parents' maxims, family jokes, and so on).
3. Now see if you can join any of the items in warm-up writing exercises 1 and 2 into a piece of writing.
4. Describe a happy (or disastrous) visit by a relative or neighbor.

DRAFT

Part IV

When she was about 68 years old,
Brave Orchid took a day off to wait at the San Francisco
International Airport for the plane that was bringing her sister,
Moonxxxchidx to the United States. She had not seen Moon
Orchid for thirty years. Somehowxxx If she waited for the plane,
she added her will power to keep thexplanexinxthexair it in
the air. nerhead hurt with the concentration. On the other hand,
she did notxmakexit not want to attach too much of herself on
that plane, which had to be as light as possible. At The Roar
of the other planes coming in and taking off made her dizzy, but
it was nice having the air-conditioning. These maxx airport
workers didn't have to be hotmlike field workers and laundry
workers.
 Next to Brave Orchid sat Moon Orchid's daughter only
daughter, who was helping her wait. Herxownxsonxandxdaughter Two
of her own sons and daughters ha d also come with her because
they could drive, but they had taken off to the magazine racks
and the gift shops and coffee shops. One characteristic of
her American children was that they were impatient , and could
not sit at one task for very long. She hoped they would get
back from the pay t.v.'s or the bathrooms or wherever they were, before
the plane from Hong Kong landed. If they didn't come soon, she
would go look for them. If her son thought he could hide in
the men's room, he was wrong.
 She "Are you all right, Aunt?" asked her niece.
 "No, I hurt all over sitting on these pk chairs. "Help
me pull three or four of them togethe foxxxxxxxxx so I can put
my feet up."
 She spread a blanket out ofver the chairs and made a
little bed for herself. By her side, she had two shopping bags
full of beans, rice and eggs, slivers of pork wrapped in taro
leaves. There was enough for everybody, but probably only her
niece would share them with her. Her two bad children were probably
eating hamburgers and french fries, wasting their money somehwere.
She would scold them when they came back.
 Suddenly her son and daughter came runningu "Come, Mother.
The plane's here early. I!'s landed already." They hurried
folding up the blanket, and gathering up her bags.
 She was very glad her children were good for something. They
must know what this trip was all about if they were so alert
about watching for the plane. "It's a good thing I made you
come early to wait," she s aid.
 Crowds of people gathered at the doors where the passengers would
come out. Brave Orchid pushed herxwayxtoxthexfront people out
of her way. She was going to be in front. She gave the bundles
for her children andxmakes to hold. Grabbing her neices hand,
she pushed to the front. She knew the children were too timid
to make get in front of lines and crowds.

The section where the passengers were disembarking was separated from
the people awaiting them by glass doors and walls. There were rows of people
getting their lug going though customs check. From there they had their
passports and visas checked. (Reverse). She did not see her sister anywhere
but there were still people coming in through the doors at the other end.
Here she stood at the door for four hours. Sometimes her niece
it went to ste stand by se the other two three doors for variety, but
she could watch all the doors from this one spot. She stood, her children
left and came back to check every once in a while. "Why don't you sit
down?" They asked, but "The chairs are too far away," she said.

sleep ↓

After four hours, her children gave up wandering about, gave up and drooped on the railing by the door. Who knew what they were thinking. At last her neice called out, "I see her. I see her. Mother! Mother!" She shouted whenever the doors opened, probably embarassing the American cousins, but she didn't care. Even when the doors were opened just a crack, she called out. She waited until someone came out & held the door open.

"Mama."

There are strange words in an adult voice. Many people looked to see what adult was calling like a child. Brave Orchid saw the old, old woman at a counter jerk her head up. Her little eyes glancing about in confusion. She blinked & looked all about her. She was one of those women that however old are child certain. She heard "Mama" — other neices moved, ready to jump up to take care of the child before realizing that it wasn't her. She was a tiny, tiny lady, very thin, her hair in a grey bun. She was dressed in a grey wool suit in which the top was open & there was a white silk blouse underneath. Brave Orchid saw the sister she was waiting for. The larger younger shadow she had been was like an outline around her, a dim halo. Young but so old. So old. Brave Orchid stood at the glass. That old lady? Yes, that old lady who was not looking at her or looking for whoever called "Mama" — She had learned that the children were usually calling for someone else — moved from the counter where she was having her papers stamped to the customs inspection line. She had presents in boxes, which were in foil & flower paper & the customs man was pulling out puffs of tissue. Brave Orchid could not see what was in the boxes from where she was. She wished her sister would look her way. Once or twice she seemed to look out but did not see her. Brave Orchid thought that

not very neatly wrapped perhaps because they'd already been unwrapped

Her daughter pointed towards Brave Orchid, and at last Moon
Orchid looked at her - two old women with expressions like mirrors
on their faces. One following the other, one just like the mother-
the recognition, the surprise, one was only a year or so older
than the other. The hands going out to touch the face, then to
touch one's own face, the finers along the grooves inxkxxix along
xhxxkxx the sides of their mouths. The disappointment at the
same time as the pleasure. Moon Orchid, who never understood the
gravity of things, started smiling - and laughing, pointing at
her. As if, she were laughing at a mask she had on! Yes, this
was her sister all right. She always did seem not very bright.
Sometimes Brave Orchid felt as if she went through life surrounded
by not very bright people.
    Finally Moon Orchid gathered up the rest of her stuff hodge
podge, and met her sister at the door, where they stood, blocking
the way, oblivious of other people.
    "You're an old woman," said Brave Orchid.
    "Aiaa, you're an old woman."
    "But you really are old. You can't say that about me. I'm
not old the way you're old."
    "Your hair is white and your face all wrinkled. You've gained
so much weight."
    "You're so skinny. It isn't xixhx healthy to be skinny.
Weight is beautiful."
    Her children kept pulling her out of the doorway, taking   took
packages frm and pulling at her shopping bags. One of them
had brought the car, and they xxxx put the luggage in it. They

put the two old ladies and the niece in the back seat. All
the way home, back across ~~the Sierras~~ the Bay Bridge and the Diablo
~~Mountains~~, across the San Joaquin river to the valley - all
the way home, they ~~looked at~~ exclaimed every time they turned to
look at each other about how old they had become. Brave Orchid forgot
~~they~~ she always got sick in any kind of a mechanical transportation
device. "You're so old. How did you get so old?" she'd ask
her sister. ~~She~~ Brave Orchid had tears in her eyes, but Moon
Orchid said, "You look older than me. You ~~xx~~ are older than
me," and again she'd laugh, as if it were funny, her ~~older~~ big
sister wearing a mask to tease her. Brave Orchid felt
surprised that after 30 years, ~~Kxxxxxxxxxxxxxx~~ she could get
annoyed at her sister at this odd mannerism.

Her children brought the bags into the house, which was
very crowded with things, and now very crowded with luggage for
a lifetime move all over the furniture and floor. Brave Orchid
wanted to put all the things ~~inxxxx~~ away where they belonged,
clothes into drawers, food in the kitchen, suitcases in the
basement, but Moon Orchid said, "I've got presents for everybody.
Let me get them." She started opening up boxes again, scattering
tissue paper and string everywhich way. The suitcase lids stood
open on tables and chairs. "First I've got shoes for all
of you from Lovely Orchid." She did not notice her nieces and
nephews groan.

8

Brave Orchid's husband was waiting at the gate. Moon
Orchid recognizes him from his photgraphs. He is an ~~old~~
old man, skinnier than herself, opening the gate he had built
with his own hands. Opening the gate in the twilight. "Hello.
Hello," he said ~~inxxmxiishx~~ like the English in Hong Kong.
"Hello," she said, like an English telephone operator. "Hello."
He ~~haixed~~ went to help his children ~~unxxx~~ unload the car,
~~xxxx~~ lifting great loads in ~~hixxkxx~~ with his bony fingers
~~andxbonyxxrixtx~~ the suitcases

After they ate, ~~xxxx~~ and cleaned up, Brave Orchid
said, "Now! We have to get down to suiness."
"What do you mean?" said her sister. She and and daughter
held one another's hands.
"Oh, no. I don't want to listen to this," said Brave
Orchid's husband, who left to do something else.

They sat in the kitchen with the ~~kxx~~ butcher's block and two refrigerators. There were also two stoves, one of them constantly cooking ~~khxxkinx~~ down the cannisters filled with leftovers for the chickens -cooking down leftovers into chicken food. It horrified the children when they caught your throwing chicken scraps into the chicken food.
"~~Wait until morning, Aunt,~~" ~~said Moon Orchid's~~ daughter. "Let her get some sleep."
"Yes, I do need some rest after travelling all this way," she said. "I'm here. YOu've done it and brought me here." She meant they should be satisfied with what they had already accomplished. Indeed, she ~~looked~~ stretched and appeared quite happy at sitting in this kitchen at this time. The children noticed that Brave Orchid and Moon Orchid talked very differently from one another.
"I ~~want to xxtxxd~~ go to sleep early because of jet lag," she said, but Brave Orchid, who had never been on an airplane did not let her.
"What are we going to do about your husband?" she asked quickly. That ought to wake her up.
"I don't know. Do we have to do something?"
"He does not know you're here."
Moon Orchid did not say anything. When she acknowledged receipt of the money he sent, she never mentioned that she wanted to come to the United States nor the paper machinery that Brave Orchid had set in motion to get her here. All she ever did was send him a receipt; his money had reached her.
"We have to tell him," said Brave Orchid.
Moon Orchid's eyes got big like a child's. "I shouldn't be here," she said.
"Nonsense. I want you here and your daughter wants you here."
~~IXx~~ "But that's all."
"Your husband is going to have to see you. We'll make him recognize you. Ha. Won't it be fun to see his face? You'll go to his house, and when his second wife answers the door, you say, '~~Ixdx~~ 'I want to speak to my husband,' and you give his personal name. 'Tell him I'll be sitting in the family room.' Walk past her as if she were a servant. She'll scream at him when he comes home from work, and it'll serve him right. You scream at him too."
"I'm scared. I want to go back home to Hong Kong."
"You can't. It's too late. YOu've sold your apartment. I@ve found his address. He's living in Los Angeles with his second wife, and ~~his~~ three children. Claim your rights. Those are your children. He's got two sons. you have two sons. You take them away from her. You become their mother."
"Do you really think I can be a mother of sons? Don't you think they'll be loyal to her since she gave birth to them?"

"The children will go to their true mothers ~~you~~," said Brave Orchid. "That's the way it is with mothers + children."

"Do you think he'll get angry at me that I'm here without telling him?"

"He deserves getting angry. For abandoning you, and for ~~but to think~~ abandoning your daughter."

"He didn't abandon me. He's given me so much money — I have all the food + clothing + servants ~~and~~ I've ever wanted. He and he supported our daughter too even though she's only a girl. I can't bother him. I mustn't bother him."

"How can you let him get away with this? Bother him. He deserves to be bothered. How dare he bother somebody else when he has you? How can you sit there so calmly? He wouldn't let you stay in China forever. I sent for you, and I sent for you. Urge her," she turned towards her niece. "Urge her to go look for him."

"I think you should go look for my father," she said. "I've never met him, and I'd like to see what my father looks like."

"What does it matter what he's like?" said her mother. "You're a grown woman with a husband & children of your own. You don't need a father — or a mother either. You're only being curious."

"In this country," said Brave Orchid, "Many people make their daughters their heirs. If you don't go see him, he'll give everything to the second wife's children."

"But he gives us everything anyway. What more do I have to ask for? If I saw him face to face, what is there to say?"

"I can think of hundreds of things," said Brave Orchid. "Oh, how I'd love to be in your place. What scenes I could make. I could tell him so many things. What scenes I could make. You're so wishy-washy."

"Yes, I am."

"You have to ask him why he didn't come home. Why he turned into a barbarian. Make him feel bad about leaving his mother & father. Scare him. Walk right into his house with your suitcases & boxes. Move right into the bedroom — throw her stuff out of the drawers & start putting yours in. Say, 'I am the first wife, and she is our servant.'"

"Oh, I can't do that. I can't do that at all. That's terrible."

"Of course, you can. I'll teach you. I am the first wife — and she is our servant.' And you teach the little boys to call you Mother."

"I don't think I'd be very good with little boys. Little American boys. Our bath is the only little boy I've known. Aren't they very rough and unfeeling?"

"Yes, but they're yours. Another thing I'd do if I were you, I'd get a job, and help him out. Show him I could make his life easier. How I didn't need his money."

"He has a great deal of money, doesn't he?"

"Yes, he does some job the barbarians value greatly."

"Could I find a job like that? I've never had a job."

"You could be a maid in a hotel," Brave Orchid advised. "A lot of immigrants start that way nowadays. And the maids get to bring home all the leftover soap & the clothes people leave behind."

"I would clean up after people then?"

Brave Orchid looked at this delicate sister. She was such a little old lady. She had long fingers & thin soft hands. And she had this city upper class accent from living in Hong Kong. Not a trace of the village accent remained. She had been away from the village for that long. But Brave Orchid would not relent; her dainty sister would just have to toughen up. "Immigrants also work in the campuses, where it doesn't matter if they speak Chinese. The easiest way to find a job though — and if you might want to do this — is to work in Chinatown. You get about 25¢ an hour, and usually all your meals, especially if you're working in a restaurant."

If she were in her sister's place, she would've been on the phone immediately, demanding one of these jobs. She would make the boss agree that she start in for work

[Handwritten text at top, with marginal notes:]

Marginal notes (left): "Immediate, so the key" / "got to the point" / "two" / "at the convenience who taught her"

As soon as he opened his doors in the morning, Moon Orchid's hands rubbed her forehead. She wore gold + jade rings that made her hands look very complete in the kitchen light. One of the rings was a wedding ring. Brave Orchid, who had been married for almost 50 years, did not wear any rings. They got in the way of all the work. She didn't want the gold to wear away in the dishwater + laundry water + field water. She looked at the little sister whose very wrinkles were delicate. "Forget about a job," she said, which was very ~~gosh~~ lenient of her. "You wouldn't have to work. You just go to your husband's house and demand your rights as First Wife. When you see him, you can say, 'Do you remember me?'"

"What if he doesn't?"

"Then start telling him details about your life together in China. Act like a fortune-teller. He'll be so impressed."

"Do you think he'll be glad to see me?"

"He better be glad to see you."
    So Moon Orchid began to believe that she really was going to face her husband. "He won't like me," she said.
    "Maybe you should dye your hair black so he won't think you're old. Or I have a wig you can borrow. On the other hand, he should see how you've suffered. Yes, let him see how he's made your hair turn white."
    All this time, her daughter held Moon Orchid's hand. The two of them had been separated for five years. Brave Orchid had gotten the daughter into the United States by finding her a rich and powerful ~~Chinese American husband~~ man who had gotten his citizenship papers. Her husband was a tyrant. Mother and daughter were so sorry for one another. "Let's not talk about this anymore," said Moon Orchid. "We can plan tomorrow. I want to hear about my grandchildren. Tell me about them. I have four grandchildren, don't I?" she asked her daughter.
    Brave Orchid thought that her daughter was also the small and lovely, useless type. She had spent so much time trying to toughen up these two. "They're so smart, Mother. The teachers say they are brilliant. They can speak Chinese and English. They'll be able to talk to you."
    "My children can talk to you too," said Brave Orchid. "Come. Talk to your aunt," she ordered.

1   When she was about sixty-eight years old, Brave Orchid took a day off to wait at San Francisco International Airport for the plane that was bringing her sister to the United States. She had not seen Moon Orchid for thirty years. She had begun this waiting at home, getting up a half-hour before Moon Orchid's plane took off in Hong Kong. Brave Orchid would add her will power to the forces that keep an airplane up. Her head hurt with the concentration. The plane had to be light, so no matter how tired she felt, she dared not rest her spirit on a wing but continuously and gently pushed up on the plane's belly. She had already been waiting at the airport for nine hours. She was wakeful.

2   Next to Brave Orchid sat Moon Orchid's only daughter, who was helping her aunt wait. Brave Orchid had made two of her own children come too because they could drive, but they had been lured away by the magazine racks and the gift shops and coffee shops. Her American children could not sit for very long. They did not understand sitting; they had wandering feet. She hoped they would get back from the pay TVs or the pay toilets or wherever they were spending their money before the plane arrived. If they did not come back soon, she would go look for them. If her son thought he could hide in the men's room, he was wrong. . . .

3   Suddenly her son and daughter came running. "Come, Mother. The plane's landed early. She's here already." They hurried, folding up their mother's encampment. She was glad her children were not useless. They must have known what this trip to San Francisco was about then. "It's a good thing I made you come early," she said.

4   Brave Orchid pushed to the front of the crowd. She had to be in front. The passengers were separated from the people waiting for them by glass doors and walls. Immigration Ghosts were stamping papers. The travellers crowded along some conveyor belts to have their luggage searched. Brave Orchid did not see her sister anywhere. She stood watching for four hours. Her children left and came back. "Why don't you sit down?" they asked.

5   "The chairs are too far away," she said. . . .

6   Finally Brave Orchid's children quit wandering and drooped on a railing. Who knew what they were thinking? At last the niece called out, "I see her! I see her! Mother! Mother!" Whenever the doors parted, she shouted, probably embarrassing the American cousins, but she didn't care. She called out, "Mama! Mama!" until the crack in the sliding doors became too small to let in her voice. "Mama!" What a strange word in an adult voice. Many people turned to see what adult was calling, "Mama!" like a child. Brave Orchid saw an old, old woman jerk her head up, her little eyes blinking confusedly, a woman whose nerves leapt toward the sound anytime she heard "Mama!" Then she relaxed to her own business again. She was a tiny, tiny lady, very thin, with little fluttering hands, and her hair was in a gray knot. She was dressed in a gray wool suit; she wore pearls around her neck and in her

earlobes. Moon Orchid *would* travel with her jewels showing. Brave Orchid momentarily saw, like a larger, younger outline around this old woman, the sister she had been waiting for. The familiar dim halo faded, leaving the woman so old, so gray. So old. Brave Orchid pressed against the glass. *That* old lady? Yes, that old lady facing the ghost who stamped her papers without questioning her was her sister. Then, without noticing her family, Moon Orchid walked smiling over to the Suitcase Inspector Ghost, who took her boxes apart, pulling out puffs of tissue. From where she was, Brave Orchid could not see what her sister had chosen to carry across the ocean. She wished her sister would look her way. Brave Orchid thought that if *she* were entering a new country, she would be at the windows. Instead Moon Orchid hovered over the unwrapping, surprised at each reappearance as if she were opening presents after a birthday party.

7   "Mama!" Moon Orchid's daughter kept calling. Brave Orchid said to her children, "Why don't you call your aunt too? Maybe she'll hear us if all of you call out together." But her children slunk away. Maybe that shame-face they so often wore was American politeness.

8   "Mama!" Moon Orchid's daughter called again, and this time her mother looked right at her. She left her bundles in a heap and came running. "Hey!" the Customs Ghost yelled at her. She went back to clear up her mess, talking inaudibly to her daughter all the while. Her daughter pointed toward Brave Orchid. And at last Moon Orchid looked at her—two old women with faces like mirrors.

9   Their hands reached out as if to touch the other's face, then returned to their own, the fingers checking the grooves in the forehead and along the sides of the mouth. Moon Orchid, who never understood the gravity of things, started smiling and laughing, pointing at Brave Orchid. Finally Moon Orchid gathered up her stuff, strings hanging and papers loose, and met her sister at the door, where they shook hands, oblivious to blocking the way.

10   "You're an old woman," said Brave Orchid.

11   "Aiaa. *You're* an old woman."

12   "But you are really old. Surely, you can't say that about me. I'm not old the way you're old."

13   "But *you* really are old. You're one year older than I am."

14   "Your hair is white and your face all wrinkled."

15   "You're so skinny."

16   "You're so fat."

17   "Fat women are more beautiful than skinny women."

18   The children pulled them out of the doorway. One of Brave Orchid's children brought the car from the parking lot, and the other heaved the luggage into the trunk. They put the two old ladies and the niece in the back seat. All the way home—across the Bay Bridge, over the Diablo hills, across the San Joaquin River to the valley, the valley moon so white at dusk—all the way home, the two sisters exclaimed every time they turned to look at each other, "Aiaa! How old!"

19   Brave Orchid forgot that she got sick in cars, that all vehicles but palanquins made her dizzy. "You're so old," she kept saying. "How did you get so old?"

20   Brave Orchid had tears in her eyes. But Moon Orchid said, "You look older than I. You *are* older than I," and again she'd laugh. "You're wearing an old mask to tease me." It surprised Brave Orchid that after thirty years she could still get annoyed at her sister's silliness.

21   Brave Orchid's husband was waiting under the tangerine tree. Moon Orchid recognized him as the brother-in-law in photographs, not as the young man who left on a ship. Her sister had married the ideal in masculine beauty, the thin scholar with the hollow cheeks and the long fingers. And here he was, an old man, opening the gate he had built with his own hands, his hair blowing silver in twilight. "Hello," he said like an Englishman in Hong Kong. "Hello," she said like an English telephone operator. He went to help his children unload the car, gripping the suitcase handles in his bony fingers, his bony wrists locked.

22   Brave Orchid's husband and children brought everything into the dining room, provisions for a lifetime move heaped all over the floor and furniture. Brave Orchid wanted to have a luck ceremony and then to put things away where they belonged, but Moon Orchid said, "I've got presents for everybody. Let me get them." She opened her boxes again. Her suitcase lids gaped like mouths; Brave Orchid had better hurry with the luck. . . .

23   After they ate and cleaned up, Brave Orchid said, "Now! We have to get down to business."

24   "What do you mean?" said her sister. She and her daughter held one another's hands.

25   "Oh, no. I don't want to listen to this," said Brave Orchid's husband, and left to read in bed.

26   The three women sat in the enormous kitchen with the butcher's block and two refrigerators. Brave Orchid had an inside stove in the kitchen and a stove outside on the back porch. All day long the outside stove cooked peelings and gristle into chicken feed. It horrified the children when they caught her throwing scraps of chicken into the chicken feed. Both stoves had been turned off for the night now, and the air was cooling.

27   "Wait until morning, Aunt," said Moon Orchid's daughter. "Let her get some sleep."

28   "Yes, I do need rest after travelling all the way from China," she said. "I'm here. You've done it and brought me here." Moon Orchid meant that they should be satisifed with what they had already accomplished. Indeed, she stretched happily and appeared quite satisfied to be sitting in that kitchen at that moment. "I want to go to sleep early because of jet lag," she said, but Brave Orchid, who had never been on an airplane, did not let her.

29   "What are we going to do about your husband?" Brave Orchid asked quickly. That ought to wake her up.

30   "I don't know. Do we have to do something?"
31   "He does not know you're here."
32   Moon Orchid did not say anything. For thirty years she had been receiving money from him from America. But she had never told him that she wanted to come to the United States. She waited for him to suggest it, but he never did. Nor did she tell him that her sister had been working for years to transport her here. First Brave Orchid had found a Chinese-American husband for her daughter. Then the daughter had come and had been able to sign the papers to bring Moon Orchid over.
33   "We have to tell him you've arrived," said Brave Orchid.
34   Moon Orchid's eyes got big like a child's. "I shouldn't be here," she said.
35   "Nonsense. I want you here, and your daughter wants you here."
36   "But that's all."
37   "Your husband is going to have to see you. We'll make him recognize you. Ha. Won't it be fun to see his face? You'll go to his house. And when his second wife answers the door, you say, 'I want to speak to my husband,' and you name his personal name. 'Tell him I'll be sitting in the family room.' Walk past her as if she were a servant. She'll scold him when he comes home from work, and it'll serve him right. You yell at him too."
38   "I'm scared," said Moon Orchid. "I want to go back to Hong Kong."
39   "You can't. It's too late. You've sold your apartment. See here. We know his address. He's living in Los Angeles with his second wife, and they have three children. Claim your rights. Those are *your* children. He's got two sons. *You* have two sons. You take them away from her. You become their mother."
40   "Do you really think I can be a mother of sons? Don't you think they'll be loyal to her, since she gave birth to them?"
41   "The children will go to their true mother—you," said Brave Orchid. "That's the way it is with mothers and children."
42   "Do you think he'll get angry at me because I came without telling him?"
43   "He deserves your getting angry with him. For abandoning you and for abandoning your daughter."
44   "He didn't abandon me. He's given me so much money. I've had all the food and clothes and servants I've ever wanted. And he's supported our daughter too, even though she's only a girl. He sent her to college. I can't bother him. I mustn't bother him."
45   "How can you let him get away with this? Bother him. He deserves to be bothered. How dare he marry somebody else when he has you? How can you sit there so calmly? He would've let you stay in China forever. *I* had to send for your daughter, and *I* had to send for you. Urge her," she turned to her niece. "Urge her to go look for him."
46   "I think you should go look for my father," she said. "I'd like to meet him. I'd like to see what my father looks like."
47   "What does it matter what he's like?" said her mother. "You're a grown woman with a husband and children of your own. You don't need a father—or a mother either. You're only curious."

48   "In this country," said Brave Orchid, "many people make their daughters their heirs. If you don't go see him, he'll give everything to the second wife's children."
49   "But he gives us everything anyway. What more do I have to ask for? If I see him face to face, what is there to say?"
50   "I can think of hundreds of things," said Brave Orchid. "Oh, how I'd love to be in your place. I could tell him so many things. What scenes I could make. You're so wishy-washy."
51   "Yes, I am."
52   "You have to ask him why he didn't come home. Why he turned into a barbarian. Make him feel bad about leaving his mother and father. Scare him. Walk right into his house with your suitcases and boxes. Move right into the bedroom. Throw her stuff out of the drawers and put yours in. Say, 'I am the first wife, and she is our servant.'"
53   "Oh, no, I can't do that. I can't do that at all. That's terrible."
54   "Of course you can. I'll teach you. 'I am the first wife, and she is our servant.' And you teach the little boys to call you Mother."
55   "I don't think I'd be very good with little boys. Little American boys. Our brother is the only boy I've known. Aren't they very rough and unfeeling?"
56   "Yes, but they're yours. Another thing I'd do if I were you, I'd get a job and help him out. Show him I could make his life easier; how I didn't need his money."
57   "He has a great deal of money, doesn't he?"
58   "Yes, he can do some job the barbarians value greatly."
59   "Could I find a job like that? I've never had a job."
60   "You could be a maid in a hotel," Brave Orchid advised. "A lot of immigrants start that way nowadays. And the maids get to bring home all the leftover soap and the clothes people leave behind."
61   "I would clean up after people, then?"
62   Brave Orchid looked at this delicate sister. She was such a little old lady. She had long fingers and thin, soft hands. And she had a high-class city accent from living in Hong Kong. Not a trace of village accent remained; she had been away from the village for that long. But Brave Orchid would not relent; her dainty sister would just have to toughen up. "Immigrants also work in the canneries, where it's so noisy it doesn't matter if they speak Chinese or what. The easiest way to find a job, though, is to work in Chinatown. You get twenty-five cents an hour and all your meals if you're working in a restaurant."
63   If she were in her sister's place, Brave Orchid would have been on the phone immediately, demanding one of those Chinatown jobs. She would make the boss agree that she start work as soon as he opened his doors the next morning. Immigrants nowadays were bandits, beating up store owners and stealing from them rather than working. It must've been the Communists who taught them those habits.
64   Moon Orchid rubbed her forehead. The kitchen light shined warmly on the gold and jade rings that gave her hands a completeness. One of the rings

was a wedding ring. Brave Orchid, who had been married for almost fifty years, did not wear any rings. They got in the way of all work. She did not want the gold to wash away in the dishwater and the laundry water and the field water. She looked at her younger sister whose very wrinkles were fine. "Forget about a job," she said, which was very lenient of her. "You won't have to work. You just go to your husband's house and demand your rights as First Wife. When you see him, you can say, 'Do you remember me?'"

65 "What if he doesn't?"

66 "Then start telling him details about your life together in China. Act like a fortuneteller. He'll be so impressed."

67 "Do you think he'll be glad to see me?"

68 "He better be glad to see you."

69 As midnight came, twenty-two hours after she left Hong King, Moon Orchid began to tell her sister that she really was going to face her husband. "He won't like me," she said.

70 "Maybe you should dye your hair black, so he won't think you're old. Or I have a wig you can borrow. On the other hand, he should see how you've suffered. Yes, let him see how he's made your hair turn white."

71 These many hours, her daughter held Moon Orchid's hand. The two of them had been separated for five years. Brave Orchid had mailed the daughter's young photograph to a rich and angry man with citizenship papers. He was a tyrant. Mother and daughter were sorry for one another. "Let's not talk about this anymore," said Moon Orchid. "We can plan tomorrow. I want to hear about my grandchildren. Tell me about them. I have three grandchildren, don't I?" she asked her daughter.

72 Brave Orchid thought that her niece was like her mother, the lovely, useless type. She had spent so much time trying to toughen up these two. "The children are very smart, Mother," her niece was saying. "The teachers say they are brilliant. They can speak Chinese and English. They'll be able to talk to you."

73 "My children can talk to you too," said Brave Orchid. "Come. Talk to your aunt," she ordered. . . .

74 The summer days passed while they talked about going to find Moon Orchid's husband. She felt she accomplished a great deal by folding towels. She spent the evening observing the children. She liked to figure them out. She described them aloud. "Now they're studying again. They read so much. Is it because they have enormous quantities to learn, and they're trying not to be savages? He is picking up his pencil and tapping it on the desk. Then he opens his book to page 168. His eyes begin to read. His eyes go back and forth. They go from left to right, from left to right." This makes her laugh. "How wondrous—eyes reading back and forth. Now he's writing his thoughts down. What's *that* thought?" she asked, pointing.

75 She followed her nieces and nephews about. She bent over them. "Now she is taking a machine off the shelf. She attaches two metal spiders to it. She plugs in the cord. She cracks an egg against the rim and pours the yolk and

white out of the shell into the bowl. She presses a button, and the spiders spin the eggs. What are you making?"

76 "Aunt, please take your finger out of the batter."

77 "She says, 'Aunt, please take your finger out of the batter,' " Moon Orchid repeated as she turned to follow another niece walking through the kitchen. "Now what's this one doing? Why, she's sewing a dress. She's going to try it on." Moon Orchid would walk right into the children's rooms while they were dressing. "Now she must be looking over her costumes to see which one to wear." Moon Orchid pulled out a dress. "This is nice," she suggested. "Look at all the colors."

78 "No, Aunt. That's the kind of dress for a party. I'm going to school now."

79 "Oh, she's going to school now. She's choosing a plain blue dress. She's picking up her comb and brush and shoes, and she's going to lock herself up in the bathroom. They dress in bathrooms here." She pressed her ear against the door. "She's brushing her teeth. Now she's coming out of the bathroom. She's wearing the blue dress and a white sweater. She's combed her hair and washed her face. She looks in the refrigerator and is arranging things between slices of bread. She's putting an orange and cookies in a bag. Today she's taking her green book and her blue book. And tablets and pencils. Do you take a dictionary?" Moon Orchid asked.

80 "No," said the child, rolling her eyeballs up and exhaling loudly. "We have dictionaries at school," she added before going out the door.

81 "They have dictionaries at school," said Moon Orchid, thinking this over. "She knows 'dictionary.' " Moon Orchid stood at the window peeping. "Now she's shutting the gate. She strides along like an Englishman."

82 The child married to a husband who did not speak Chinese translated for him, "Now she's saying that I'm taking a machine off the shelf and that I'm attaching two metal spiders to it. And she's saying the spiders are spinning with legs intertwined and beating the eggs electrically. Now she says I'm hunting for something in the refrigerator and—ha!—I've found it. I'm taking out butter—'cow oil.' 'They eat a lot of cow oil,' she's saying."

83 "She's driving me nuts!" the children told each other in English. . . .

84 Whenever Brave Orchid thought of it, which was everyday, she said, "Are you ready to go see your husband and claim what is yours?"

85 "Not today, but soon," Moon Orchid would reply.

86 But one day in the middle of summer, Moon Orchid's daughter said, "I have to return to my family. I promised my husband and children I'd only be gone a few weeks. I should return this week." Moon Orchid's daughter lived in Los Angeles.

87 "Good!" Brave Orchid exclaimed. "We'll all go to Los Angeles. You return to your husband, and your mother returns to hers. We only have to make one trip."

88 "You ought to leave the poor man alone," said Brave Orchid's husband. "Leave him out of women's business."

89 "When your father lived in China," Brave Orchid told the children, "he

refused to eat pastries because he didn't want to eat the dirt the women kneaded from between their fingers."

90   "But I'm happy here with you and all your children," Moon Orchid said. "I want to see how this girl's sewing turns out. I want to see your son come back from Vietnam. I want to see if this one gets good grades. There's so much to do."

91   "We're leaving on Friday," said Brave Orchid. "I'm going to escort you, and you will arrive safely."

92   On Friday Brave Orchid put on her dress-up clothes, which she wore only a few times during the year. Moon Orchid wore the same kind of clothes she wore every day and was dressed up. Brave Orchid told her oldest son he had to drive. He drove, and the two old ladies and the niece sat in the back seat.

93   They set out at gray dawn, driving between the grape trees, which hunched like dwarfs in the fields. Gnomes in serrated outfits that blew in the morning wind came out of the earth, came up in rows and columns. Everybody was only half awake. "A long time ago," began Brave Orchid, "the emperors had four wives, one at each point of the compass, and they lived in four palaces. The Empress of the West would connive for power, but the Empress of the East was good and kind and full of light. You are the Empress of the East, and the Empress of the West has imprisoned the Earth's Emperor in the Western Palace. And you, the good Empress of the East, come out of the dawn to invade her land and free the Emperor. You must break the strong spell she has cast on him that has lost him the East."

94   Brave Orchid gave her sister last-minute advice for five hundred miles. All her possessions had been packed into the trunk.

95   "Shall we go into your house together," asked Brave Orchid, "or do you want to go by yourself?"

96   "You've got to come with me. I don't know what I would say."

97   "I think it would be dramatic for you to go by yourself. He opens the door. And there you are—alive and standing on the porch with all your luggage. 'Remember me?' you say. Call him by his own name. He'll faint with shock. Maybe he'll say, 'No. Go away.' But you march right in. You push him aside and go in. Then you sit down in the most important chair, and you take off your shoes because you belong."

98   "Don't you think he'll welcome me?"

99   "She certainly wasn't very imaginative," thought Brave Orchid.

100 "It's against the law to have two wives in this country," said Moon Orchid. "I read that in the newspaper."

101 "But it's probably against the law in Singapore too. Yet our brother has two, and his sons have two each. The law doesn't matter."

102 "I'm scared. Oh, let's turn back. I don't want to see him. Suppose he throws me out? Oh, he will. He'll throw me out. And he'll have a right to throw me out, coming here, disturbing him, not waiting for him to invite me. Don't leave me by myself. You can talk louder than I can."

103 "Yes, coming with you would be exciting. I can charge through the door

and say, 'Where is your wife?' And he'll answer, 'Why, she's right here.' And I'll say, 'This isn't your wife. Where is Moon Orchid? I've come to see her. I'm her first sister, and I've come to see that she is being well taken care of.' Then I accuse him of murderous things; I'd have him arrested—and you pop up to his rescue. Or I can take a look at his wife, and I say, 'Moon Orchid, how young you've gotten.' And he'll say, 'This isn't Moon Orchid.' And you come in and say, 'No. I am.' If nobody's home, we'll climb in a window. When they get back we'll be at home; you the hostess, and I your guest. You'll be serving me cookies and coffee. And when he comes in I'll say, 'Well, I see your husband is home. Thank you so much for the visit.' And you say, 'Come again anytime.' Don't make violence. Be routine."

104   Sometimes Moon Orchid got into the mood. "Maybe I could be folding towels when he comes in. He'll think I'm so clever. I'll get to them before his wife does." But the further they came down the great central valley—green fields changing to fields of cotton on dry, brown stalks, first a stray bush here and there, then thick—the more Moon Orchid wanted to turn back. "No. I can't go through with this." She tapped her nephew on the shoulder. "Please turn back. Oh, you must turn the car around. I should be returning to China. I shouldn't be here at all. Let's go back. Do you understand me?"

105   "Don't go back," Brave Orchid ordered her son. "Keep going. She can't back out now."

106   "What do you want me to do? Make up your minds," said the son, who was getting impatient.

107   "Keep going," said Brave Orchid. "She's come this far, and we can't waste all this driving. Besides, we have to take your cousin back to her own house in Los Angeles. We have to drive to Los Angeles anyway." . . .

108   When the car stopped in front of her daughter's house, Moon Orchid asked, "May I get out to meet my grandchildren?"

109   "I told you no," said Brave Orchid. "If you do that you'll stay here, and it'll take us weeks to get up our courage again. Let's save your grandchildren as a reward. You take care of this other business, and you can play with your grandchildren without worry. Besides, you have some children to meet."

110   "Grandchildren are more wonderful than children."

111   After they left the niece's suburb, the son drove them to the address his mother had given him, which turned out to be a skyscraper in downtown Los Angeles.

112   "Don't park in front," said his mother. "Find a side street. We've got to take him by surprise. We mustn't let him spot us ahead of time. We have to catch the first look on his face."

113   "Yes, I think I would like to see the look on his face."

114   Brave Orchid's son drove up and down the side streets until he found a parking space that could not be seen from the office building.

115   "You have to compose yourself," said Brave Orchid to her sister. "You must be calm as you walk in. Oh, this is most dramatic—in broad daylight and in the middle of the city. We'll sit here for a while and look at his building."

116   "Does he own that whole building?"
117   "I don't know. Maybe so."
118   "Oh, I can't move. My knees are shaking so much I won't be able to walk. He must have servants and workers in there, and they'll stare at me. I can't bear it."
119   Brave Orchid felt a tiredness drag her down. She had to baby everyone. The traffic was rushing, Los Angeles noon-hot, and she suddenly felt carsick. No trees. No birds. Only city. "It must be the long drive," she thought. They had not eaten lunch, and the sitting had tired her out. Movement would strengthen her; she needed movement. "I want you to stay here with your aunt while I scout that building," she instructed her son. "When I come back, we'll work out a plan." She walked around the block. Indeed, she felt that her stepping on the earth, even when the earth was covered with concrete, gained strength from it. She breathed health from the air, though it was full of gasoline fumes. The bottom floor of the building housed several stores. She looked at the clothes and jewelry on display, picking out some for Moon Orchid to have when she came into her rightful place.
120   Brave Orchid rushed along beside her reflection in the glass. She used to be young and fast; she was still fast and felt young. It was mirrors, not aches and pains, that turned a person old, everywhere white hairs and wrinkles. Young people felt pain.
121   The building was a fine one; the lobby was chrome and glass; with ashtray stands and plastic couches arranged in semicircles. She waited for the elevator to fill before she got in, not wanting to operate a new machine by herself. Once on the sixth floor she searched alertly for the number in her address book.
122   How clean his building was. The rest rooms were locked, and there were square overhead lights. No windows, though. She did not like the quiet corridors with carpets but no windows. They felt like tunnels. He must be very wealthy. Good. It would serve a rich man right to be humbled. She found the door with his number on it; there was also American lettering on the glass. Apparently this was his business office. She hadn't thought of the possibility of catching him at his job. Good thing she had decided to scout. If they had arrived at his house, they would not have found him. Then they would have had to deal with *her*. And she would have phoned him, spoiled the surprise, and gotten him on her side. Brave Orchid knew how the little wives maneuvered; her father had had two little wives.
123   She entered the office, glad that it was a public place and she needn't knock. A roomful of men and women looked up from their magazines. She could tell by their eagerness for change that this was a waiting room. Behind a sliding glass partition sat a young woman in a modern nurse's uniform, not a white one, but a light blue pantsuit with white trim. She sat before an elegant telephone and an electric typewriter. The wallpaper in her cubicle was like aluminum foil, a metallic background for a tall black frame around white paint with dashes of red. The wall of the waiting room was covered with burlap, and there were plants in wooden tubs. It was an expensive waiting room. Brave Orchid approved. The patients looked well dressed, not sickly and poor.

124 "Hello. May I help you?" said the receptionist, parting the glass. Brave Orchid hesitated, and the receptionist took this to mean that she could not speak English. "Just a moment," she said, and went into an inner room. She brought back another woman, who wore a similar uniform except that it was pink trimmed in white. This woman's hair was gathered up into a bunch of curls at the back of her head; some of the curls were fake. She wore round glasses and false eyelashes, which gave her an American look. "Have you an appointment?" she asked in poor Chinese; she spoke less like a Chinese than Brave Orchid's children. "My husband, the doctor, usually does not take drop-in patients," she said. "We're booked up for about a month." Brave Orchid stared at her pink-painted fingernails, gesticulating, and thought she probably would not have given out so much information if she weren't so clumsy with language.

125 "I have the flu," Brave Orchid said.

126 "Perhaps we can give you the name of another doctor," said this woman, who was her sister-in-law. "This doctor is a brain surgeon and doesn't work with flu." Actually she said, "This doctor cuts brains," a child making up the words as she went along. She wore pink lipstick and had blue eyelids like the ghosts.

127 Brave Orchid, who had been a surgeon too, thought that her brother-in-law must be a clever man. She herself could not practice openly in the United States because the training here was so different and because she could never learn English. He was smart enough to learn ghost ways. She would have to be clever to outwit him. She needed to retreat and plan some more. "Oh, well, I'll go to another doctor, then," she said, and left.

128 She needed a new plan to get her sister and brother-in-law together. This nurse-wife was so young, and the office was so rich with wood, paintings, and fancy telephones, that Brave Orchid knew it wasn't because he couldn't get the fare together that he hadn't sent for his old wife. He had abandoned her for this modern, heartless girl. Brave Orchid wondered if the girl knew that her husband had a Chinese wife. Perhaps she should ask her.

129 But no, she mustn't spoil the surprise by giving any hints. She had to get away before he came out into the corridor, perhaps to go to one of the locked rest rooms. As she walked back to her sister, she noted corners and passageways, broom closets, other offices—ambush spots. Her sister could crouch behind a drinking fountain and wait for him to get thirsty. Waylay him.

130 "I met his second wife," she said, opening the car door.

131 "What's she like?" asked Moon Orchid. "Is she pretty?"

132 "She's very pretty and very young; just a girl. She's his nurse. He's a doctor like me. What a terrible, faithless man. You'll have to scold him for years, but first you need to sit up straight. Use my powder. Be as pretty as you can. Otherwise you won't be able to compete. You do have one advantage, however. Notice he has her be his worker. She is like a servant, so you have room to be the wife. She works at the office; you work at the house. That's almost as good as having two houses. On the other hand, a man's real partner is the

hardest worker. You couldn't learn nursing, could you? No, I guess not. It's almost as difficult as doing laundry. What a petty man he turned out to be, giving up responsibility for a pretty face." Brave Orchid reached for the door handle. "Are you ready?"

133 "For what?"

134 "To go up there, of course. We're at his office, and I think we ought to be very direct. There aren't any trees to hide you, no grass to soften your steps. So, you walk right into his office. You make an announcement to the patients and the fancy nurses. You say, 'I am the doctor's wife. I'm going to see my husband.' Then you step to the inner door and enter. Don't knock on any doors. Don't listen if the minor wife talks to you. You walk past her without changing pace. When you see him, you say, 'Surprise!' You say, 'Who is that woman out there? She claims to be your wife.' That will give him a chance to deny her on the spot."

135 "Oh, I'm so scared. I can't move. I can't do that in front of all those people—like a stage show. I won't be able to talk." And sure enough, her voice was fading into a whisper. She was shivering and small in the corner of the seat.

136 "So. A new plan, then," said Brave Orchid, looking at her son, who had his forehead on the steering wheel. "You," she said. "I want you to go up to his office and tell your uncle that there has been an accident out in the street. A woman's leg has been broken, and she's crying in pain. He'll have to come. You bring him to the car."

137 "Mother."

138 "Mm," mused Brave Orchid. "Maybe we ought to put your aunt in the middle of the street, and she can lie down with her leg bent under her." But Moon Orchid kept shaking her head in trembling no's.

139 "Why don't you push her down in the intersection and pour ketchup on her? I'll run over her a little bit," said her son.

140 "Stop being silly," she said. "You Americans don't take life seriously."

141 "Mother, this is ridiculous. This whole thing is ridiculous."

142 "Go. Do what I tell you," she said.

143 "I think your schemes will be useless, Mother."

144 "What do you know about Chinese business?" she said. "Do as I say."

145 "Don't let him bring the nurse," said Moon Orchid.

146 "Don't you want to see what she looks like?" asked Brave Orchid. "Then you'll know what he's giving up for you."

147 "No. No. She's none of my business. She's unimportant."

148 "Speak in English," Brave Orchid told her son. "Then he'll feel he has to come with you."

149 She pushed her son out of the car. "I don't want to do this," he said.

150 "You'll ruin your aunt's life if you don't. You can't understand business begun in China. Just do what I say. Go."

151 Slamming the car door behind him, he left.

152 Moon Orchid was groaning now and holding her stomach. "Straighten

up," said Brave Orchid. "He'll be here any moment." But this only made Moon Orchid groan louder, and tears seeped out between her closed eyelids.

153 "You want a husband, don't you?" said Brave Orchid. "If you don't claim him now, you'll never have a husband. Stop crying," she ordered. "Do you want him to see you with your eyes and nose swollen when that young so-called wife wears lipstick and nail polish like a movie star?"

154 Moon Orchid managed to sit upright, but she seemed stiff and frozen.

155 "You're just tired from the ride. Put some blood into your cheeks," Brave Orchid said, and pinched her sister's withered face. She held her sister's elbow and slapped the inside of her arm. If she had had time, she would have hit until the black and red dots broke out in the skin; that was the tiredness coming out. As she hit, she kept an eye on the rearview mirror. She saw her son come running, his uncle after him with a black bag in his hand. "Faster. Faster," her son was saying. He opened the car door. "Here she is," he said to his uncle. "I'll see you later." And he ran on down the street.

156 The two old ladies saw a man, authoritative in his dark western suit, start to fill the front of the car. He had black hair and no wrinkles. He looked and smelled like an American. Suddenly the two women remembered that in China families married young boys to older girls, who baby-sat their husbands their whole lives. Either that or, in this ghost country, a man could somehow keep his youth.

157 "Where's the accident?" he said in Chinese. "What is this? You don't have a broken leg."

158 Neither woman spoke. Brave Orchid held her words back. She would not let herself interfere with this meeting after long absence.

159 "What is it?" he asked. "What's wrong?" These women had such awful faces. "What is it, Grandmothers?"

160 "Grandmother?" Brave Orchid shouted. "This is your wife. I am your sister-in-law."

161 Moon Orchid started to whimper. Her husband looked at her. And recognized her. "You," he said. "What are you doing here?"

162 But all she did was open and shut her mouth without any words coming out.

163 "Why are you here?" he asked, eyes wide. Moon Orchid covered her face with one hand and motioned no with the other.

164 Brave Orchid could not keep silent. Obviously he was not glad to see his wife. "I sent for her," she burst out. "I got her name on the Red Cross list, and I sent her the plane ticket. I wrote her every day and gave her the heart to come. I told her how welcome she would be, how her family would welcome her, how her husband would welcome her. I did what you, the husband, had time to do in these last thirty years."

165 He looked directly at Moon Orchid the way the savages looked, looking for lies. "What do you want?" he asked. She shrank from his stare; it silenced her crying.

166 "You weren't supposed to come here," he said, the front seat a barrier

against the two women over whom a spell of old age had been cast. "It's a mistake for you to be here. You can't belong. You don't have the hardness for this country. I have a new life."

167 "What about me?" whispered Moon Orchid.
168 "Good," thought Brave Orchid. "Well said. Said with no guile."
169 "I have a new wife," said the man.
170 "She's only your second wife," said Brave Orchid. "This is your real wife."
171 "In this country a man may have just one wife."
172 "So you'll get rid of that creature in your office?" asked Brave Orchid.
173 He looked at Moon Orchid. Again the rude American eyes. "You go live with your daughter. I'll mail you the money I've always sent you. I could get arrested if the Americans knew about you. I'm living like an American." He talked like a child born here.
174 "How could you ruin her old age?" said Brave Orchid.
175 "She has had food. She has had servants. Her daughter went to college. There wasn't anything she thought of that she couldn't buy. I have been a good husband."
176 "You made her live like a widow."
177 "That's not true. Obviously the villagers haven't stoned her. She's not wearing mourning. The family didn't send her away to work. Look at her. She'd never fit into an American household. I have important American guests who come inside my house to eat." He turned to Moon Orchid, "You can't talk to them. You can barely talk to me."
178 Moon Orchid was so ashamed, she held her hands over her face. She wished she could also hide her dappled hands. Her husband looked like one of the ghosts passing the car windows, and she must look like a ghost from China. They had indeed entered the land of ghosts, and they had become ghosts.
179 "Do you want her to go back to China then?" Brave Orchid was asking.
180 "I wouldn't wish that on anyone. She may stay, but I do not want her in my house. She has to live with you or with her daughter, and I don't want either of you coming here anymore."
181 Suddenly his nurse was tapping on the glass. So quickly that they might have missed it, he gestured to the old women, holding a finger to his mouth for just a moment: he had never told his American wife that he had a wife in China, and they mustn't tell her either.
182 "What's happening?" she asked. "Do you need help? The appointments are piling up."
183 "No. No," he said. "This woman fainted in the street. I'll be up soon."
184 They spoke to each other in English.
185 The two old women did not call out to the young woman. Soon she left. "I'm leaving too now," said the husband.
186 "Why didn't you write to tell her once and for all you weren't coming back and you weren't sending for her?" Brave Orchid asked.

187   "I don't know," he said. "It's as if I had turned into a different person. The new life around me was so complete; it pulled me away. You became people in a book I had read a long time ago."

188   "The least you can do," said Brave Orchid, "is invite us to lunch. Aren't you inviting us to lunch? Don't you owe us a lunch? At a good restaurant?" She would not let him off easily.

189   So he bought them lunch, and when Brave Orchid's son came back to the car, he had to wait for them.

190   Moon Orchid was driven back to her daughter's house, but though she lived in Los Angeles, she never saw her husband again. "Oh, well," said Brave Orchid. "We're all under the same sky and walk the same earth; we're alive together during the same moment." Brave Orchid and her son drove back north, Brave Orchid sitting in the back seat the whole way.

191   Several months went by with no letter from Moon Orchid. When she had lived in China and in Hong Kong, she had written every other week. At last Brave Orchid telephoned long distance to find out what was happening. "I can't talk now," Moon Orchid whispered. "They're listening. Hang up quickly before they trace you." Moon Orchid hung up on Brave Orchid before the minutes she had paid for expired.

192   That week a letter came from the niece saying that Moon Orchid had become afraid. Moon Orchid said that she had overheard Mexican ghosts plotting on her life. She had been creeping along the baseboards and peeping out windows. Then she had asked her daughter to help her find an apartment at the other end of Los Angeles, where she was now hiding. Her daughter visited her every day, but Moon Orchid kept telling her, "Don't come see me because the Mexican ghosts will follow you to my new hiding place. They're watching your house."

193   Brave Orchid phoned her niece and told her to send her mother north immediately, where there were no Mexicans, she said. "This fear is an illness," she told her niece. "I will cure her." ("Long ago," she explained to her children, "when the emperors had four wives, the wife who lost in battle was sent to the Northern Palace. Her feet would sink little prints into the snow.")

194   Brave Orchid sat on a bench at the Greyhound station to wait for her sister. Her children had not come with her because the bus station was only a five-block walk from the house. Her brown paper shopping bag against her, she dozed under the fluorescent lights until her sister's bus pulled into the terminal. Moon Orchid stood blinking on the stairs, hanging tightly to the railing for old people. Brave Orchid felt the tears break inside her chest for the old feet that stepped one at a time onto the cold Greyhound cement. Her sister's skin hung loose, like a hollowed frog's, as if she had shrunken inside it. Her clothes bagged, not fitting sharply anymore. "I'm in disguise," she said. Brave Orchid put her arms around her sister to give her body warmth. She held her hand along the walk home, just as they had held hands when they were girls.

195   The house was more crowded than ever, though some of the children had

gone away to school; the jade trees were inside for the winter. Along walls and on top of tables, jade trees, whose trunks were as thick as ankles, stood stoutly, green now and without the pink skin the sun gave them in the spring.

196   "I am so afraid," said Moon Orchid.
197   "There is no one after you," said Brave Orchid. "No Mexicans."
198   "I saw some in the Greyhound station," said Moon Orchid.
199   "No. No, those were Filipinos." She held her sister's earlobes and began the healing chant for being unafraid. "There are no Mexicans after you," she said.
200   "I know. I got away from them by escaping on the bus."
201   "Yes, you escaped on the bus with the mark of the dog on it."
202   In the evening, when Moon Orchid seemed quieter, her sister probed into the cause of this trouble.
203   "What made you think anyone was after you?"
204   "I heard them talking about me. I snuck up on them and heard them."
205   "But you don't understand Mexican words."
206   "They were speaking English."
207   "You don't understand English words."
208   "This time, miraculously, I understood. I decoded their speech. I penetrated the words and understood what was happening inside."
209   Brave Orchid tweaked her sister's ears for hours, chanting her new address to her, telling her how much she loved her and how much her daughter and nephews and nieces loved her, and her brother-in-law loved her. "I won't let anything happen to you. I won't let you travel again. You're home. Stay home. Don't be afraid." Tears fell from Brave Orchid's eyes. She had whisked her sister across the ocean by jet and then made her scurry up and down the Pacific coast, back and forth across Los Angeles. Moon Orchid had misplaced herself, her spirit (her "attention," Brave Orchid called it) scattered all over the world. Brave Orchid held her sister's head as she pulled on her earlobe. She would make it up to her. For moments an attentiveness would return to Moon Orchid's face. Brave Orchid rubbed the slender hands, blew on the fingers, tried to stoke up the flickerings. She stayed home from the laundry day after day. She threw out the Thorazine and vitamin B that a doctor in Los Angeles had prescribed. She made Moon Orchid sit in the kitchen sun while she picked over the herbs in cupboards and basement and the fresh plants that grew in the winter garden. Brave Orchid chose the gentlest plants and made medicines and foods like those they had eaten in their village.
210   At night she moved from her own bedroom and slept beside Moon Orchid. "Don't be afraid to sleep," she said. "Rest. I'll be here beside you. I'll help your spirit find the place to come back to. I'll call it for you; you go to sleep." Brave Orchid stayed awake watching until dawn.
211   Moon Orchid still described aloud her nieces' and nephews' doings, but now in a monotone, and she no longer interrupted herself to ask questions. She would not go outside, even into the yard. "Why, she's mad," Brave Orchid's husband said when she was asleep.
212   Brave Orchid held her hand when she appeared vague. "Don't go away,

Little Sister. Don't go any further. Come back to us." If Moon Orchid fell asleep on the sofa, Brave Orchid sat up through the night, sometimes dozing in a chair. When Moon Orchid fell asleep in the middle of the bed, Brave Orchid made a place for herself at the foot. She would anchor her sister to this earth.

213   But each day Moon Orchid slipped further away. She said that the Mexicans had traced her to this house. That was the day she shut the drapes and blinds and locked the doors. She sidled along the walls to peep outside. Brave Orchid told her husband that he must humor his sister-in-law. It was right to shut the windows; it kept her spirit from leaking away. Then Moon Orchid went about the house turning off the lights like during air raids. The house became gloomy; no air, no light. This was very tricky, the darkness a wide way for going as well as coming back. Sometimes Brave Orchid would switch on the lights, calling her sister's name all the while. Brave Orchid's husband installed an air conditioner.

214   The children locked themselves up in their bedrooms, in the storeroom and basement, where they turned on the lights. Their aunt would come knocking on the doors and say, "Are you all right in there?"

215   "Yes, Aunt, we're all right."

216   "Beware," she'd warn. "Beware. Turn off your lights so you won't be found. Turn off the lights before they come for us."

217   The children hung blankets over the cracks in the doorjambs; they stuffed clothes along the bottoms of doors. "Chinese people are very weird," they told one another.

218   Next Moon Orchid removed all the photographs, except for those of the grandmother and grandfather, from the shelves, dressers, and walls. She gathered up the family albums. "Hide these," she whispered to Brave Orchid. "Hide these. When they find me, I don't want them to trace the rest of the family. They use photographs to trace you." Brave Orchid wrapped the pictures and the albums in flannel. "I'll carry these far away where no one will find us," she said. When Moon Orchid wasn't looking, she put them at the bottom of a storage box in the basement. She piled old clothes and old shoes on top. "If they come for me," Moon Orchid said, "everyone will be safe."

219   "We're all safe," said Brave Orchid.

220   The next odd thing Moon Orchid did was to cry whenever anyone left the house. She held on to them, pulled at their clothes, begged them not to go. The children and Brave Orchid's husband had to sneak out. "Don't let them go," pleaded Moon Orchid. "They will never come back."

221   "They will come back. Wait and see. I promise you. Watch for them. Don't watch for Mexicans. This one will be home at 3:30. This one at 5:00. Remember who left now. You'll see."

222   "We'll never see that one again," Moon Orchid wept.

223   At 3:30 Brave Orchid would remind her, "See? It's three-thirty; sure enough, here he comes." ("You children come home right after school. Don't you dare stop for a moment. No candy store. No comic book store. Do you hear?")

224   But Moon Orchid did not remember. "Who is this?" she'd ask. "Are you going to stay with us? Don't go out tonight. Don't leave in the morning."

225   She whispered to Brave Orchid that the reason the family must not go out was that "they" would take us in airplanes and fly us to Washington, D.C., where they'd turn us into ashes. Then they'd drop the ashes in the wind, leaving no evidence.

226   Brave Orchid saw that all variety had gone from her sister. She was indeed mad. "The difference between mad people and sane people," Brave Orchid explained to the children, "is that sane people have variety when they talk-story. Mad people have only one story that they talk over and over."

227   Every morning Moon Orchid stood by the front door whispering, whispering. "Don't go. The planes. Ashes. Washington, D.C. Ashes." Then, when a child managed to leave, she said, "That's the last time we'll see him again. They'll get him. They'll turn him into ashes."

228   And so Brave Orchid gave up. She was housing a mad sister who cursed the mornings for her children, the one in Vietnam too. Their aunt was saying terrible things when they needed blessing. Perhaps Moon Orchid had already left this mad old body, and it was a ghost badmouthing her children. Brave Orchid finally called her niece, who put Moon Orchid in a California state mental asylum. Then Brave Orchid opened up the windows and let the air and light come into the house again. She moved back into the bedroom with her husband. The children took the blankets and sheets down from the doorjambs and came back into the living room.

229   Brave Orchid visited her sister twice. Moon Orchid was thinner each time, shrunken to bone. But, surprisingly, she was happy and had made up a new story. She pranced like a child. "Oh, Sister, I am so happy here. No one ever leaves. Isn't that wonderful? We are all women here. Come. I want you to meet my daughters." She introduced Brave Orchid to each inmate in the ward—her daughters. She was especially proud of the pregnant ones. "My dear pregnant daughters." She touched the women on the head, straightened collars, tucked blankets. "How are you today, dear daughter?" "And, you know," she said to Brave Orchid, "we understand one another here. We speak the same language, the very same. They understand me, and I understand them." Sure enough, the women smiled back at her and reached out to touch her as she went by. She had a new story, and yet she slipped entirely away, not waking up one morning.

230   Brave Orchid told her children they must help her keep their father from marrying another woman because she didn't think she could take it any better than her sister had. If he brought another woman into the house, they were to gang up on her and play tricks on her, hit her, and trip her when she was carrying hot oil until she ran away. "I am almost seventy years old," said the father, "and haven't taken a second wife, and don't plan to now." Brave Orchid's daughters decided fiercely that they would never let men be unfaith-

ful to them. All her children made up their minds to major in science or mathematics. ❖

Questions to Ponder

1. From reading just the first paragraph of "At the Western Palace," how can the reader tell that this memoir is being told from a non-Western point of view, in a very distinctive voice? What effect does this voice have on you?
2. What is the difference between Brave Orchid and her American children? Between Brave Orchid and her sister, Moon Orchid? How does Maxine Hong Kingston convey these differences?
3. What are the small signs in Moon Orchid's first moments in the United States that her hold on reality is tenuous?
4. How might this episode be told by Moon Orchid? By Brave Orchid's daughter? By Moon Orchid's doctor-husband? In each case how would the selection of details and the voice, tone, and pace change?

Writing Possibilities

1. Tape-record your grandmother or grandfather (or some other interesting family member or neighbor) talking about the "old country," the "old ways," or their early days. Listen to this tape, jotting down unusual expressions, customs, or points of view; repeated words; and other distinctive features of their speech and story. (*Hint:* You might want to arrange these items in clusters.) Then, using Maxine Hong Kingston's memoir as a model, write about this person's experience. Use the third person, but write from their point of view, incorporating their expressions.
2. Take the piece you wrote in writing possibility 1 and treat the same material from a different point of view—perhaps that of a person who plays a major or minor role in the story. Imagine how the story might change when recounted in this voice.
3. Tape-record an interview with a student on your campus who comes from another country. Ask about the student's difficulties in learning the English language and in adjusting to American or Canadian culture. Then write an essay called "A (name of country) Student in North America" using the student's voice.
4. Describe your own experience in a different culture using a voice distinctly your own or recognizably one of your culture and background.

MR. SECRETS
Richard Rodriguez

I see myself straddling two worlds of writing: journalism and literature. There is Richard Rodriguez, the journalist—every day I spend more time reading newspapers and magazines than I do reading novels and poetry. I wander away from my desk for hours, for weeks. I want to ask questions of the stranger on the bus. I want to consider the political and social issues of the day.

Then there is Richard Rodriguez, the writer. It takes me a very long time to write. What I try to do when I write is break down the line separating the prosaic world from the poetic word. I try to write about everyday concerns—an educational issue, say, or the problems of the unemployed—but to write about them as powerfully, as richly, as well as I can.

My model in this marriage of journalism and literature is, of course, George Orwell. Orwell is the great modern example. He embarrasses other journalists by being more. He never let the urgency of the moment overwhelm his concern for literary art. But, in like measure, he embarrasses other writers because he had the courage to attend to voices outside the window; he was not afraid to look up from his papers. I hope I can be as brave in my life.

Brief Warm-up Writing Exercises

1. Freewrite about any nicknames you have had over the years and why they did or did not suit you.
2. Freewrite about a typical Christmas or other holiday celebration at your house.
3. Make a list of the different voices, expressions, and characters that might be present when a group of college "guys"—or college women—get together (*Hint:* You may want to try mapping for this.)

you have to do that? . . . Why do you need to tell the *gringos*? . . . Why do you think we're so separated as a family? Do you really think this, Richard?"

12   A new paragraph changes the tone. Soft, maternal. Worried for me she adds, "Do not punish yourself for having to give up our culture in order to 'make it' as you say. Think of all the wonderful achievements you have obtained. You should be proud. Learn Spanish better. Practice it with your dad and me. Don't worry so much. Don't get the idea that I am mad at you either.

13   "Just keep one thing in mind. Writing is one thing, the family is another. I don't want *tus hermanos* hurt by your writings. And what do you think the cousins will say when they read where you talk about how the aunts were maids? Especially I don't want the *gringos* knowing about our private affairs. Why should they? Please give this some thought. Please write about something else in the future. Do me this favor."

14   Please.

15   To the adult I am today, my mother needs to say what she would never have needed to say to her child: the boy who faithfully kept family secrets. When my fourth-grade teacher made our class write a paper about a typical evening at home, it never occurred to me actually to do so. "Describe what you do with your family," she told us. And automatically I produced a fictionalized account. I wrote that I had six brothers and sisters; I described watching my mother get dressed up in a red-sequined dress before she went with my father to a party; I even related how the imaginary baby sitter ("a high school student") taught my brother and sisters and me to make popcorn and how, later, I fell asleep before my parents returned. The nun who read what I wrote would have known that what I had written was completely imagined. But she never said anything about my contrivance. And I never expected her to either. I never thought she *really* wanted me to write about my family life. In any case, I would have been unable to do so.

16   I was very much the son of parents who regarded the most innocuous piece of information about the family to be secret. Although I had, by that time, grown easy in public, I felt that my family life was strictly private, not to be revealed to unfamiliar ears or eyes. Around the age of ten, I was held by surprise listening to my best friend tell me one day that he "hated" his father. In a furious whisper he said that when he attempted to kiss his father before going to bed, his father had laughed: "Don't you think you're getting too old for that sort of thing, son?" I was intrigued not so much by the incident as by the fact that the boy would relate it to *me*.

17   In those years I was exposed to the sliding-glass-door informality of middle-class California family life. Ringing the doorbell of a friend's house, I would hear someone inside yell out, "Come on in, Richie; door's not locked." And in I would go to discover my friend's family undisturbed by my presence. The father was in the kitchen in his underwear. The mother was in her bathrobe. Voices gathered in familiarity. A parent scolded a child in front of me; voices quarreled, then laughed; the mother told me something about her

son after he had stepped out of the room and she was sure he couldn't overhear; the father would speak to his children and to me in the same tone of voice. I was one of the family, the parents of several good friends would assure me. (Richie.)

18 My mother sometimes invited my grammar school friends to stay for dinner or even to stay overnight. But my parents never treated such visitors as part of the family, never told them they were. When a school friend ate at our table, my father spoke less than usual. (Stray, distant words.) My mother was careful to use her "visitor's voice." Sometimes, listening to her, I would feel annoyed because she wouldn't be more herself. Sometimes I'd feel embarrassed that I couldn't give to a friend at my house what I freely accepted at his.

19 I remained, nevertheless, my parents' child. At school, in sixth grade, my teacher suggested that I start keeping a diary. ("You should write down your personal experiences and reflections.") But I shied away from the idea. It was the one suggestion that the scholarship boy couldn't follow. I would not have wanted to write about the minor daily events of my life; I would never have been able to write about what most deeply, daily, concerned me during those years: I was growing away from my parents. Even if I could have been certain that no one would find my diary, even if I could have destroyed each page after I had written it, I would have felt uncomfortable writing about my home life. There seemed to me something intrinsically public about written words.

20 Writing, at any rate, was a skill I didn't regard highly. It was a grammar school skill I acquired with comparative ease. I do not remember struggling to write the way I struggled to learn how to read. The nuns would praise student papers for being neat—the handwritten letters easy for others to read; they promised that my writing style would improve as I read more and more. But that wasn't the reason I became a reader. Reading was for me the key to "knowledge"; I swallowed facts and dates and names and themes. Writing, by contrast, was an activity I thought of as a kind of report, evidence of learning. I wrote down what I heard teachers say. I wrote down things from my books. I wrote down all I knew when I was examined at the end of the school year. Writing was performed after the fact; it was not the exciting experience of learning itself. In eighth grade I read several hundred books, the titles of which I still can recall. But I cannot remember a single essay I wrote. I only remember that the most frequent kind of essay I wrote was the book report.

21 In high school there were more "creative" writing assignments. English teachers assigned the composition of short stories and poems. One sophomore story I wrote was a romance set in the Civil War South. I remember that it earned me a good enough grade, but my teacher suggested with quiet tact that next time I try writing about "something you know more about—something closer to home." Home? I wrote a short story about an old man who lived all by himself in a house down the block. That was as close as my writing ever got to my house. Still, I won prizes. When teachers suggested I contribute articles to the school literary magazine, I did so. And when I was asked to join the school newspaper, I said yes. I did not feel any great pride in my writings,

however. (My mother was the one who collected my prize-winning essays in a box she kept in her closet.) Though I remember seeing my by-line in print for the first time, and dwelling on the printing press letters with fascination: RICHARD RODRIGUEZ. The letters furnished evidence of a vast public identity writing made possible.

22   When I was a freshman in college, I began typing all my assignments. My writing speed decreased. Writing became a struggle. In high school I had been able to handwrite ten- and twenty-page papers in little more than an hour— and I never revised what I wrote. A college essay took me several nights to prepare. Suddenly everything I wrote seemed in need of revision. I became a self-conscious writer. A stylist. The change, I suspect, was the result of seeing my words ordered by the even, impersonal, anonymous typewriter print. As arranged by a machine, the words that I typed no longer seemed mine. I was able to see them with a new appreciation for how my reader would see them.

23   From grammar school to graduate school I could always name my reader. I wrote for my teacher. I could consult him or her before writing, and after. I suppose that I knew other readers could make sense of what I wrote—that, therefore, I addressed a general reader. But I didn't think very much about it. Only toward the end of my schooling and only because political issues pressed upon me did I write, and have published in magazines, essays intended for readers I never expected to meet. Now I am struck by the opportunity. I write today for a reader who exists in my mind only phantasmagorically. Someone with a face erased; someone of no particular race or sex or age or weather. A gray presence. Unknown, unfamiliar. All that I know about him is that he has had a long education and that his society, like mine, is often public (*un gringo*).

II

24   "What is psychiatry?" my mother asks. She is standing in her kitchen at the ironing board. We have been talking about nothing very important. ("Visiting.") As a result of nothing we have been saying, her question has come. But I am not surprised by it. My mother and father ask me such things. Now that they are retired they seem to think about subjects they never considered before. My father sits for hours in an armchair, wide-eyed. After my mother and I have finished discussing obligatory family news, he will approach me and wonder: When was Christianity introduced to the Asian continent? How does the brain learn things? Where is the Garden of Eden?

25   Perhaps because they consider me the family academic, my mother and father expect me to know. They do not, in any case, ask my brother and sisters the questions wild curiosity shapes. (That curiosity beats, unbeaten by age.)

26   Psychiatry? I shrug my shoulders to start with, to tell my mother that it is very hard to explain. I go on to say something about Freud. And analysis. Something about the function of a clinically trained listener. (I study my

mother's face as I speak, to see if she follows.) I compare a psychiatrist to a Catholic priest hearing Confession. But the analogy is inexact. My mother can easily speak to a priest in a darkened confessional; can easily make an act of self-revelation using the impersonal formula of ritual contrition: "Bless me, father, for I have sinned. . . ." It would be altogether different for her to address a psychiatrist in unstructured conversation, revealing those events and feelings that burn close to the heart.

27   'You mean that people tell a psychiatrist about their personal lives?'

28   Even as I begin to respond, I realize that she cannot imagine ever doing such a thing. She shakes her head sadly, bending over the ironing board to inspect a shirt with the tip of the iron she holds in her hand. Then she changes the subject. She is talking to me about one of her sisters, my aunt, who is seriously ill. Whatever it is that prompted her question about psychiatry has passed.

29   I stand there. I continue thinking about what she has asked me—and what she cannot comprehend. My parents seem to me possessed of great dignity. An aristocratic reserve. Like the very rich who live behind tall walls, my mother and father are always mindful of the line separating public from private life. Watching a celebrity talk show on television, they listen for several minutes as a movie star with bright teeth recounts details of his recent divorce. And I see my parents grow impatient. Finally, my mother gets up from her chair. Changing the channel, she says with simple disdain, "Cheap people."

30   My mother and my father are not cheap people. They never are tempted to believe that public life can also be intimate. They remain aloof from the modern temptation that captivates many in America's middle class: the temptation to relieve the anonymity of public life by trying to make it intimate. They do not understand, consequently, what so pleases the television audience listening to a movie star discuss his divorce with bogus private language. My father opens a newspaper to find an article by a politician's wife in which she reveals (actually, renders merely as gossip) intimate details of her marriage. And he looks up from the article to ask me, "Why does she do this?"

31   I find his question embarrassing. Although I know that he does not intend to embarrass me, I am forced to think about this book I have been writing. And I realize that my parents will be as puzzled by my act of self-revelation as they are by the movie star's revelations on the talk show. They never will call me cheap for publishing an autobiography. But I can well imagine their faces tightened by incomprehension as they read my words.

32   (Why does he do this?)

33   Many mornings at my desk I have been paralyzed by the thought of their faces, their eyes. I imagine their eyes moving slowly across these pages. That image has weakened my resolve. Finally, however, it has not stopped me. Despite the fact that my parents remain even now in my mind a critical, silent chorus, standing together, I continue to write. I do not make my parents' sharp distinction between public and private life. With my mother and father I scorn those who attempt to create an experience of intimacy in public. But unlike my parents, I have come to think that there is a place for the deeply personal in

public life. This is what I have learned by trying to write this book: There are things so deeply personal that they can be revealed only to strangers. I believe this. I continue to write.

34   "What is psychiatry?" my mother asks. And I wish I could tell her. (I wish she could imagine it.) "There are things that are so personal that they can only be said to someone who is not close. Someone you don't know. A person who is not an intimate friend or a relation. There are things too personal to be shared with intimates."

35   She stands at the ironing board, her tone easy because she is speaking to me. (I am her son.) For my mother that which is personal can only be said to a relative—her only intimates. She makes the single exception of confessing her sins to a Catholic priest. Otherwise, she speaks of her personal life only at home. The same is true of my father—though he is silent even with family members. Of those matters too jaggedly personal to reveal to intimates, my parents will never speak. And that seems to me an extraordinary oppression. The unspoken may well up within my mother and cause her to sigh. But beyond that sigh nothing is heard. There is no one she can address. Words never form. Silence remains to repress them. She remains quiet. My father in his chair remains quiet.

36   I wonder now what my parents' silence contains. What would be their version of the past we once shared? What memories do they carry about me? What were their feelings at many of the moments I recollect on these pages? What did my father—who had dreamed of Australia—think of his children once they forced him to change plans and remain in America? What contrary feelings did he have about our early success? How does he regard the adults his sons and daughters have become? And my mother. At what moments has she hated me? On what occasions has she been embarrassed by me? What does she recall feeling during those difficult, sullen years of my childhood? What would be her version of this book? What are my parents unable to tell me today? What things are too personal? What feelings so unruly they dare not reveal to other intimates? Or even to each other? Or to themselves?

37   Some people have told me how wonderful it is that I am the first in my family to write a book. I stand on the edge of a long silence. But I do not give voice to my parents by writing about their lives. I distinguish myself from them by writing about the life we once shared. Even when I quote them accurately, I profoundly distort my parents' words. (They were never intended to be read by the public.) So my parents do not truly speak on my pages. I may force their words to stand between quotation marks. With every word, however, I change what was said only to me.

38   "What is new with you?" My mother looks up from her ironing to ask me. (In recent years she has taken to calling me Mr. Secrets, because I tell her so little about my work in San Francisco—this book she must suspect I am writing.)

39   Nothing much, I respond.

40   I write very slowly because I write under the obligation to make myself clear to someone who knows nothing about me. It is a lonely adventure. Each

morning I make my way along a narrowing precipice of written words. I hear an echoing voice—my own resembling another's. Silent! The reader's voice silently trails every word I put down. I reread my words, and again it is the reader's voice I hear in my mind, sounding my prose.

41   When I wrote my first autobiographical essay, it was no coincidence that, from the first page, I expected to publish what I wrote. I didn't consciously determine the issue. Somehow I knew, however, that my words were meant for a public reader. Only because of that reader did the words come to the page. The reader became my excuse, my reason for writing.

42   It had taken me a long time to come to this address. There are remarkable children who very early are able to write publicly about their personal lives. Some children confide to a diary those things—like the first shuddering of sexual desire—too private to tell a parent or brother. The youthful writer addresses a stranger, the Other, with "Dear Diary" and tries to give public expression to what is intensely, privately felt. In so doing, he attempts to evade the guilt of repression. And the embarrassment of solitary feeling. For by rendering feelings in words that a stranger can understand—words that belong to the public, this Other—the young diarist no longer need feel all alone or eccentric. His feelings are capable of public intelligibility. In turn, the act of revelation helps the writer better understand his own feelings. Such is the benefit of language: By finding public words to describe one's feelings, one can describe oneself to oneself. One names what was previously only darkly felt.

43   I have come to think of myself as engaged in writing graffiti. Encouraged by physical isolation to reveal what is most personal; determined at the same time to have my words seen by strangers. I have come to understand better why works of literature—while never intimate, never individually addressed to the reader—are so often among the most personal statements we hear in our lives. Writing, I have come to value written words as never before. One can use *spoken* words to reveal one's personal self to strangers. But *written* words heighten the feeling of privacy. They permit the most thorough and careful exploration. (In the silent room, I prey upon that which is most private. Behind the closed door, I am least reticent about giving those memories expression.) The writer is freed from the obligation of finding an auditor in public. (As I use words that someone far from home can understand, I create my listener. I imagine her listening.)

44   My teachers gave me a great deal more than I knew when they taught me to write public English. I was unable then to use the skill for deeply personal purposes. I insisted upon writing impersonal essays. And I wrote always with a specific reader in mind. Nevertheless, the skill of public writing was gradually developed by the many classroom papers I had to compose. Today I *can* address an anonymous reader. And this seems to me important to say. Somehow the inclination to write about my private life in public is related to the ability to do so. It is not enough to say that my mother and father do not want to write their autobiographies. It needs also to be said that they are unable to write to a public reader. They lack the skill. Though both of them can write in

Spanish and English, they write in a hesitant manner. Their syntax is uncertain. Their vocabulary limited. They write well enough to communicate "news" to relatives in letters. And they can handle written transactions in institutional America. But the man who sits in his chair so many hours, and the woman at the ironing board—"keeping busy because I don't want to get old"—will never be able to believe that any description of their personal lives could be understood by a stranger far from home.

III

45   When my mother mentioned seeing my article seven years ago, she *wrote* to me. And I responded to her letter with one of my own. (I wrote: "I am sorry that my article bothered you . . . I had not meant to hurt . . . I think, however, that education has divided the family . . . That is something which happens in most families, though it is rarely discussed . . . I had meant to praise what I have lost . . . I continue to love you both very much.") I wrote to my mother because it would have been too difficult, too painful to hear her voice on the phone. Too unmanageable a confrontation of voices. The impersonality of the written word made it the easiest means of exchange. The remarkable thing is that nothing has been spoken about this matter by either of us in the years intervening. I know my mother suspects that I continue to write about the family. She knows that I spend months at a time "writing," but she does not press me for information. (Mr. Secrets.) She does not protest.

46   The first time I saw my mother after she had received my letter, she came with my father to lunch. I opened the door to find her smiling slightly. In an instant I tried to gather her mood. (She looked as nervous and shy as I must have seemed.) We embraced. And she said that my father was looking for a place to park the car. She came into my apartment and asked what we were having for lunch. Slowly, our voices reverted to tones we normally sound with each other. (Nothing was said of my article.) I think my mother sensed that afternoon that the person whose essay she saw in a national magazine was a person unfamiliar to her, some Other. The public person—the writer, Richard Rodriguez—would remain distant and untouchable. She never would hear his public voice across a dining room table. And that afternoon she seemed to accept the idea, granted me the right, the freedom so crucial to adulthood, to become a person very different in public from the person I am at home.

47   Intimates are not always so generous. One close friend calls to tell me she has read an essay of mine. "All that Spanish angst," she laughs. "It's not really you." Only someone very close would be tempted to say such a thing—only a person who knows who I am. From such an intimate one must sometimes escape to the company of strangers, to the liberation of the city, in order to form new versions of oneself.

48   In the company of strangers now, I do not reveal the person I am among

intimates. My brother and sisters recognize a different person, not the Richard Rodriguez in this book. I hope, when they read this, they will continue to trust the person they have known me to be. But I hope too that, like our mother, they will understand why it is that the voice I sound here I have never sounded to them. All those faraway childhood mornings in Sacramento, walking together to school, we talked but never mentioned a thing about what concerned us so much: the great event of our schooling, the change it forced on our lives. Years passed. Silence grew thicker, less penetrable. We grew older without ever speaking to each other about any of it. Intimacy grooved our voices in familiar notes; familiarity defined the limits of what could be said. Until we became adults. And now we see each other most years at noisy family gatherings where there is no place to stop the conversation, no right moment to turn the heads of listeners, no way to essay this, my voice.

49   I see them now, my brothers and sisters, two or three times every year. We do not live so very far from one another. But as an entire family, we only manage to gather for dinner on Easter. And Mother's Day. Christmas. It is usually at our parents' house that these dinners are held. Our mother invariably organizes things. Well before anyone else has the chance to make other arrangements, her voice will sound on the phone to remind us of an upcoming gathering.

50   Lately, I have begun to wonder how the family will gather even three times a year when she is not there with her phone to unite us. For the time being, however, she presides at the table. She—not my father, who sits opposite her—says the Grace before Meals. She busies herself throughout the meal. "Sit down now," somebody tells her. But she moves back and forth from the dining room table to the kitchen. Someone needs more food. (What's missing?) Something always is missing from the table. When she is seated, she listens to the conversation. But she seems lonely. (Does she think things would have been different if one of her children had brought home someone who could speak Spanish?) She does not know how or where to join in when her children are talking about Woody Allen movies or real estate tax laws or somebody's yoga class. (Does she remember how we vied with each other to sit beside her in a movie theatre?) Someone remembers at some point to include her in the conversation. Someone asks how many pounds the turkey was this year. She responds in her visitor's voice. And soon the voices ride away. She is left with the silence.

51   Sitting beside me, as usual, is my younger sister. We gossip. She tells me about her trip last week to Milan; we laugh; we talk about clothes, mutual friends in New York.

52   Other voices intrude: I hear the voices of my brother and sister and the people who have married into our family. I am the loudest talker. I am the one doing most of the talking. I talk, having learned from hundreds of cocktail parties and dinner parties how to talk with great animation about nothing

especially. I sound happy. I talk to everyone about something. And I become shy only when my older sister wonders what I am doing these days. Working in Los Angeles? Or writing again? When will she be able to see something I've published?

53   I try to change the subject.
54   "Are you writing a book?"
55   I notice, out of the corner of my eye, that my mother is nervously piling dishes and then getting up to take them out to the kitchen.
56   I say yes.
57   "Well, well, well. Let's see it. Is it going to be a love story? A romance? What's it about?"
58   She glances down at her thirteen-year-old son, her oldest. "Tommy reads and reads, just like you used to."
59   I look over at him and ask him what sort of books he likes best.
60   "Everything!" his mother answers with pride.
61   He smiles. I wonder: Am I watching myself in this boy? In this face where I can scarcely trace a family resemblance? Have I foreseen his past? He lives in a world of Little League and Pop Warner. He has spoken English all his life. His father is of German descent, a fourth-generation American. And he does not go to a Catholic school, but to a public school named after a dead politician. Still, he is someone who reads . . .
62   "He and I read all the same books," my sister informs me. And with that remark, my nephew's life slips out of my grasp to imagine.
63   Dinner progresses. There is dessert. Four cakes. Coffee. The conversation advances with remarkable ease. Talk is cheerful, the way talk is among people who rarely see one another and then are surprised that they have so much to say. Sometimes voices converge from various points around the table. Sometimes voices retreat to separate topics, two or three conversations.
64   My mother interrupts. She speaks and gets everyone's attention. Some cousin of ours is getting married next month. (Already.) And some other relative is now the mother of a nine-pound baby boy. (Already?) And some relative's son is graduating from college this year. (We haven't seen him since he was five.) And somebody else, an aunt, is retiring from her job in that candy store. And a friend of my mother's from Sacramento—Do we remember her after all these years?—died of cancer just last week. (Already!)
65   My father remains a witness to the evening. It is difficult to tell what he hears (his hearing is bad) or cannot understand (his English is bad). His face stays impassive, unless he is directly addressed. In which case he smiles and nods, too eagerly, too quickly, at what has been said. (Has he really heard?) When he has finished eating, I notice, he sits back in his chair. And his eyes move from face to face. Sometimes I feel that he is looking at me. I look over to see him, and his eyes dart away the second after I glance.
66   When Christmas dinner is finished, there are gifts to exchange in the front room. Tradition demands that my brother, the oldest, play master of ceremonies,

"Santa's helper," handing out presents with a cigar in his hand. It is the chore he has come to assume, making us laugh with his hammy asides. "This is for Richard," he says, rattling a box next to his ear, rolling his eyes. "And this one is for Mama Rodriguez." (There is the bright snap of a camera.)

67 Nowadays there is money enough for buying useless and slightly ludicrous gifts for my mother and father. (They will receive an expensive backgammon set. And airplane tickets to places they haven't the energy or the desire to visit. And they will be given a huge silver urn—"for chilling champagne.")

68 My mother is not surprised that her children are well-off. Her two daughters are business executives. Her oldest son is a lawyer. She predicted it all long ago. "Someday," she used to say when we were young, "you will all grow up and all be very rich. You'll have lots of money to buy me presents. But I'll be a little old lady. I won't have any teeth or hair. So you'll have to buy me soft food and put a blue wig on my head. And you'll buy me a big fur coat. But you'll only be able to see my eyes."

69 Every Christmas now the floor around her is carpeted with red and green wrapping paper. And her feet are wreathed with gifts.

70 By the time the last gift is unwrapped, everyone seems very tired. The room has become uncomfortably warm. The talk grows listless. ("Does anyone want coffee or more cake?" Somebody groans.) Children are falling asleep. Someone gets up to leave, prompting others to leave. ("We have to get up early tomorrow.")

71 "Another Christmas," my mother says. She says that same thing every year, so we all smile to hear it again.

72 Children are bundled up for the fast walk to the car. My mother stands by the door calling good-bye. She stands with a coat over her shoulders, looking into the dark where expensive foreign cars idle sharply. She seems, all of a sudden, very small. She looks worried.

73 "Don't come out, it's too cold," somebody shouts at her or at my father, who steps out onto the porch. I watch my younger sister in a shiny mink jacket bend slightly to kiss my mother before she rushes down the front steps. My mother stands waving toward no one in particular. She seems sad to me. How sad? Why? (Sad that we all are going home? Sad that it was not quite, can never be, the Christmas one remembers having had once?) I am tempted to ask her quietly if there is anything wrong. (But these are questions of paradise, Mama.)

74 My brother drives away.

75 "Daddy shouldn't be outside," my mother says. "Here, take this jacket out to him."

76 She steps into the warmth of the entrance hall and hands me the coat she has been wearing over her shoulders.

77 I take it to my father and place it on him. In that instant I feel the thinness

of his arms. He turns. He asks if I am going home now too. It is, I realize, the only thing he has said to me all evening. ❖

Questions to Ponder

1. Why is "Mr. Secrets" an accurate title for Richard Rodriguez's essay? Does the title have more than one meaning?
2. Why is it appropriate for someone who thinks of himself as "Mr. Secrets" to place his (often unspoken) thought in parentheses? How does *form* match *content* here? Is this often a sign of good writing?
3. Why is it that by making private feelings public through the act of writing, the young writer "no longer need feel all alone or eccentric"?
4. Why is it that the personal (the individual) can become, paradoxically, the universal? How does this happen?
5. Why is that the public voice a writer may sound in a piece of writing may not be the same voice his or her family members know and recognize? Is there something wrong or false in this?
6. How does Richard Rodriguez make the voices and personalities of himself and his family seem distinctive to us? What details and expressions help to etch them sharply in our minds?

Writing Possibilities

1. Take the description of a family holiday that you wrote for warm-up writing exercise 2 and revise it, inserting family members' voices when they would be effective.
2. Brainstorm a list of secrets that your hometown, college, or country tries to downplay or keep hidden. Choose one, and write a letter or essay to your hometown, college, or country arguing the benefits of making the truth known.
3. Make a list of the family and cultural influences that have helped shape the voices you sound in public and private encounters. In a reflective essay, analyze your own voice and describe how you wish to cultivate it in the future.
4. Using Richard Rodriguez's essay as a model, choose two different cultures, and compare and contrast their attitudes toward personal disclosure. Draw any conclusions you feel appropriate.

Short Story

MILK RUN

Donna Roazen

I am a fiction writer—short stories, novels, and novellas. While there is almost always humor in what I write, the subject matter—the human condition in the twentieth century—is a serious one. "Milk Run" is a departure from all of that and came about in what, for me, is an unusual way. One evening at a neighborhood party, I listened to a trucker from West Virginia tell a wonderful story about a hair-razing ride down the mountain with his partner. The narrator, on his third or fourth beer, felt no pain as he told his tale. I put down my own beer, listened intently, and then came home as fast as I could to write it all down as I had heard it. It was written in two drafts, with a little embellishment here and there, but what you read is essentially his speech, his vocabulary, and, I hope, his dialect and cadence.

Like most writers, I am in love with the English language, its richness and diversity. All my life I've been fascinated with dialect, both ethnic and regional. All writers are told to "Write what you know." To that I would add, if you're writing with yourself as the voice, "Write as you speak." If you're writing fiction—assuming a different persona from yourself or writing dialogue for your characters—then listen hard to the speech around you and "Write what you hear."

Brief Warm-up Writing Exercises

1. Describe your most memorable experience as either the driver or passenger in a car.
2. Think back over all the errands you've run in your life for family members or friends. Describe the most exciting experience—or the scariest, funniest, or most embarrassing *err-rand*.
3. "Chase scenes" have become almost a required part of adventure movies. Freewrite why you think the chase scene is so popular?

1 ❖ Salty Dog, he don't get too nervous about things. I mean, he has hauled everything from nitro to cut-glass and crystal and it ain't like he got his Class-One yesterday. Whatever come up, he has always took it in stride. I know of at least three jacknifes and one head-on he has walked out of with nuthin more than cuts, black eyes and a ruined disposition. So when I went with him on the milk run down Boneyard Mountain, I didn't think it was gonna be no big thing.

2   We was comin down in a non-sectioned truck full of milk cans when it seemed to me we was goin a little fast even for Salty Dog, considerin it was a narrow road with plenty of devil's hairpins and a goodly drop on my side, naturally. Salty Dog don't take to no comments on his drivin but when I noticed he was hangin on that wheel, cuttin to the right, and cuttin to the left and gettin red in the face, I says, "Salty Dog, do you have power steerin in this rig?" and he says, "Only power in this here rig is the power of Salty Dog." While that oughta been comfortin, somehow it wasn't, because we was going faster and faster and the scenery was whizzin by too fast to be admired and it did seem to me that the wheel on my side wasn't on the road too often and them run-offs looked more and more invitin only Salty Dog he never took no advantage of them and so I decided to get my mind on other things.

3   Halfway down this mountain there's this valley with meadows and farms in it and I was thinking how it might be nice to be a farmer instead of a trucker . . . just one of them crazy thoughts people get . . . and then comes this next curve and it was comin pretty fast and Salty Dog, he don't seem to take no notice of that fact and I says, "Salty Dog, there is this here curve comin up," and Salty Dog who is glassy-eyed now says, "That's too goddamned bad," and just keeps goin straight ahead which is down my side of the mountain, through a little creek, into the valley, and we're tearin across the meadow toward a pasture, through the fence, into the pasture, with the milk cans rattlin back and forth so loud you couldn't have a real conversation so I didn't ask Salty Dog why he didn't slow nor brake nor nuthin, and to tell the truth, I didn't wanna ask because I had an idea the answer would spoil my day and then we're goin for this old farmer who's just rakin away like he's got all day to get outta our way and I'm hangin out the window yellin and Salty Dog is yellin and at the very last minute, this farmer looks up and sees us. He walks . . . HE DOES NOT RUN . . . he walks slow and easy out of our way. We do not stop, we keep right on goin through his pasture, his garden, the left half of his front porch, a flock of chickens, a good part of his barn, three haystacks, and I am prayin there is a road somewhere we can get onto, and I look out of the window and it seems the farmer has now got the picture and he is not walkin no more, he is runnin shit green in circles and finally we come to a dead stop three feet from this bunch of very upset cows.

4   Well, the cows are carryin on not to mention the farmer so we roll up the

windows and lock the doors and sit there restin for a spell, Salty Dog and me, not talkin because there don't seem much to talk about except a certain embarassin puddle that each one of us is sittin in and the farmer he ain't in no mood to talk cordial, he's just screamin and jumpin up and down but we ain't listenin and finally I says, "Salty Dog, you was havin a little trouble with your brakes and your steerin, am I right?" and he just looks at me disgusted-like and don't answer and I says, "Salty Dog, what gear was you comin down in?" and he says, "13th," and I says, "Salty Dog, *why* was you comin down the side of Boneyard Mountain in 13th gear?" and he says, "Because, Willy, just before we lost the brakes and the steerin, Willy, the clutch went. Willy, so I didn't have no helluva lotta choice, now *did* I, Willy?"

5   And that seemed reasonable so I didn't say no more and we got outta the cab with our legs shakin and our stomachs upside down, past the cows and past the farmer who was still screamin and we went to check the milk, expectin it to be runnin out of all sides of the trailer but there wasn't no runnin milk, only 105 cans of Pasteurized, Homogenized, First-Class, Grade-A Cottage Cheese.

6   Which is how I come to be in the dairy business. Got this nice little store by the side of the road and I surely do enjoy watchin them trucks go by. Last time I heard of Salty Dog, he had took up with this here meditation stuff and he went and shaved his head and is on this special kinda diet . . . Fruits and nuts but no meat and no fish and especially not no milk. ❖

Questions to Ponder

1. From reading just the first paragraph, what is your impression of Salty Dog? Which specific details in the paragraph contribute to this impression?
2. What specific details in the last paragraph suggest that Salty Dog has been changed by his milk run down Boneyard Mountain?
3. How would you describe Willy, the narrator of this story? Do you think he is perceptive? Imperceptive? Naive? Ignorant? Wise? Which details in the text lead you to your conclusion?
4. What is the effect of *understatement* in this story, such as Willy's "I was thinking how it might be nice to be a farmer instead of a trucker . . ." or "I didn't want to ask because I had an idea the answer would spoil my day . . ."?
5. Do you consider the nonstandard English ("Salty Dog, he don't get too nervous . . .) and the off-color diction ("he is running shit green in

circles . . .") offensive—or necessary to this story? How would you defend your answer?

ONE STORY—THIRTEEN POINTS OF VIEW

Nancy Price

I wrote "One Story—Thirteen Points of View" as an exercise for myself as a writer, and for my writing students. The challenge was to take Donna Roazen's vivid story "Milk Run" from the claustrophobia of the interior monologue to the point at which a story almost becomes a play.

When I begin a story or novel, I let my idea for the story play in and out of every point of view I can imagine. I am looking for the distance from the action that will bring my subject into sharpest focus. Can the story be told best if readers are as close as possible to it, hearing the storyteller's stream of thought? Or will my readers feel what I have to say more strongly if they move back a bit to watch the action through one or more characters' eyes? Or shall I let the story be as unexplained as life itself, so that my readers must interpret what happens and imagine what the characters are thinking?

If your story or essay does not "work," try another vantage point, a new voice or "central consciousness." My 13 versions of "Milk Run" reveal that there are at least 13 ways to tell a story—and how different the stories are! In the first one we are right there in Willy's frantic thoughts as he whizzes with Salty Dog down Boneyard Mountain. In the last one, we are like spectators at a play or film, given nothing more than Willy and Salty Dog and Old Man Reeve in action.

We all know that writing is a richness of possibilities; perhaps it should not be call writing at all, but choosing. We arrange words as we might arrange a shop window display, selecting what will affect the viewer in exactly the way we have chosen. No other communication or art gives us such a storehouse of material: sounds, images, smells, tastes, feelings, precise thoughts, and that most elusive thing—the chooser's individual voice. When we put words together, we select each thing in our writing from every thing in the world.

1. The Storyteller Talks to Himself or Herself
   (Interior Monologue, Identified Narrator—First Person)

1   Salty Dog, he don't get too nervous about things—he has hauled everything from nitro to cut-glass and crystal and it ain't like he got his Class-One Yesterday. Whatever come up, he has always took it in stride. I know of at least three jacknifes and one head-on he has walked out of with nuthin more than cuts, black eyes, and a ruined disposition. Goin on this milk run down Boneyard Mountain, I didn't think it was gonna be no big thing. But now we're goin a little fast even for Salty Dog, considerin it's a narrow road with plenty of devil's hairpins and a goodly drop on my side, naturally, and he's not takin no comments on his drivin, but he's hanging on that wheel, cuttin to the right and cuttin to the left and gettin red in the face—Salty Dog, do you have power steerin in this rig? He says no—just the power of Salty Dog, and that ought to be comfortin, but somehow it isn't because we're going faster and faster and the scenery is whizzin by too fast to be admired and it does seem to me that the wheel on my side isn't on the road too often and them run-offs look more and more invitin only Salty Dog, he never takes any advantage of them. Maybe I can get my mind on other things. . . .

2. The Storyteller Talks to a Silent Listener
   (Dramatic Monologue, Identified Narrator—First Person)

2   Listen, Mabel, you hear that milk truck go by? Pour me another coffee, and how about a piece of that apple pie? Did I ever tell you about the time I went on the milk run with Salty Dog? You know him—he don't get too nervous about things. (Story continues.)

3. The Storyteller Writes a Letter
   (Identified Narrator—First Person)

3   Dear Joe: Remember old Salty Dog? Who'd I meet but him last Saturday, and he's shaved his head—can you believe it? Did I ever tell you about the time we took this trip down Boneyard Mountain? (Story continues.)

4. The Storyteller Keeps a Journal
   (Identified Narrator—First Person)

4   Yesterday I heard from Salty Dog. After all those years. I ought to write it all down before I forget—how we took that milk run down Boneyard Mountain. (Story continues.)

5. The Unchanged Storyteller Remembers
   (Imperceptive Nondetached Autobiography, Identified Narrator—First Person)

5   I don't know why old Salty Dog has left off running milk and shaved his head. It beats me, when he don't get too nervous about things. I mean, he has hauled everything from nitro to cut-glass and crystal and it ain't like he got his Class-One yesterday. Whatever come up, he has always took it in stride. I know of three jacknifes and one head-on he has walked out of with nuthin more than cuts, black eyes, and ruined disposition. Why, I went with him once on a milk run down Boneyard Mountain, and we came out of it all right. (Story continues.)

6. The Changed Storyteller Remembers
   (Perceptive Detached Autobiography, Identified Narrator—First Person)

6   "Milk Run" by Donna Roazen

7. A Storyteller from the Community Remembers
   (Memoir—Chorus, Identified Narrator—First Person)

7   When I was a young fellow, two characters who made milk runs down Boneyard Mountain were Salty Dog and Willy, and everybody knew what happened once when they ended up on Old Daddy Reeve's backyard. (Story continues.)

8. A Storyteller Who Saw It Happen Remembers
   (Memoir—Eyewitness, Identified Narrator—First Person)

8   About five years ago I was walking up Boneyard Mountain, and here come this truck full of milk cans burning rubber down those curves. (Story continues.)

9. A Storyteller Who Was Told About It Remembers
   (Memoir—Confidant, Identified Narrator—First Person)

9   Once when he was pretty drunk, Will told me about his milk run with Salty Dog down Boneyard Mountain. That Salty Dog, he don't get too nervous about things. (Story continues.)

10. An Invisible Storyteller: We See Through *One* Character's Eyes
   (Anonymous Narrator—Third Person)

10   When Willy went on the milk run with Salty Dog, he wasn't too nervous. Salty Dog didn't get too nervous about things. He had hauled everything from nitro to cut-glass and crystal, and it wasn't as if he'd gotten his Class-One yesterday. Willy knew that whatever came up, Salty Dog would take it in stride. There had been at least three jacknifes and one head-on that Salty Dog had walked out of with nothing more than cuts, black eyes and a ruined disposition. So when Willy went on the milk run, he didn't think it was going to be a big thing.

11   They were coming down in a nonsectioned truck full of milk cans. It seemed to Willy that they were going a little fast even for Salty Dog, considering that it was a narrow road with plenty of devil's hairpins and a goodly drop on Willy's side. Salty Dog didn't like comments on his driving, but when Willy noticed he was hanging on the wheel, cutting to the right, cutting to the left, and getting red in the face, Willy said, "Salty Dog, do you have power steerin in this rig?"

12   "Only power in this here rig is the power of Salty Dog," Salty Dog said. (Story continues.)

11. An Invisible Storyteller: We See Through *Two* Characters' Eyes
   (Anonymous Narrator—Third Person)

13   When Willy started the milk run down Boneyard Mountain with Salty Dog, he didn't think it was going to be any big thing, but Salty Dog was thinking his brakes had been acting funny. But Salty Dog didn't get too nervous about things. He'd hauled everything from nitro to cut-glass and crystal—he hadn't got his Class-One yesterday. (Story continues.)

12. An Invisible Storyteller: We See Through *More Than Two* Characters' Eyes (Anonymous Narrator—Third Person)

14   When Willy got in the milk truck with Salty Dog, he didn't think the run down Boneyard Mountain was going to be any big thing, but Salty Dog was thinking that his brakes had been acting funny. Old Man Reeve, who farmed at the bottom of Boneyard Mountain, wasn't thinking about anything in particular—he was raking his vegetable garden.

15   Willy and Salty Dog were coming down in a nonsectioned truck full of milk cans. In a while it seemed to Willy that they were going a little fast even for Salty Dog.

16   Salty Dog began to sweat. He looked ahead at all the devil's hairpins. There was a goodly drop on Willy's side.

17   Willy was getting a bit edgy, but he told himself that Salty Dog had hauled everything from nitro to cut-glass and crystal. It wasn't like Salty Dog had got his Class-One yesterday.

18   Old Man Reeve looked up at some fool of a truck driver, doing seventy-five on Boneyard Mountain. Damn fool. His back was giving him trouble again. Always fools coming down that mountain as if they thought they could fly. (Story continues.)

13. An Invisible Storyteller: We See Through *Nobody's* Eyes at All (Anonymous Narrator)

19   The truck came down Boneyard Mountain like the driver thought he had wings. The two men inside had their mouths open. Old Daddy Reeve, raking his vegetable garden in the valley below, had his mouth open too: he was singing "Abide with Me."

20   It was a narrow road, with plenty of devil's hairpins and a good drop—maybe five hundred feet in most places. The truck wheels on the drop-off side began rolling on air as much as they rolled on the road.

21   Halfway down the mountain was the valley with meadows, and Old Daddy Reeve's farm. There were plenty of run-offs down the mountain. Daddy Reeve watched. The truck didn't take any of them.

22   Salty Dog was driving, and he hung on the wheel, cutting to the right, cutting to the left, getting red in the face.

23   Salty Dog? Will said. "You have power steerin in this rig?"

24   "Only power in this rig is the power of Salty Dog." (Story continues.) ❖

Writing Possibilities

1. Choose one of Nancy Price's 13 points of view and complete her story.
2. Try making Willy the driver and Salty Dog the passenger-narrator. How would Salty Dog tell the story?
3. Tell the story of a trip you have taken—either with another person or alone—by car, truck, train, plane, motorcycle, bicycle, canoe, skateboard, red wagon, whatever. Before you start, go over Nancy Price's 13 points of view and choose to tell your story in the one you think will be most effective. (Note that as in "Milk Run," a journey does not have to be far to be filled with action and meaning.)

CHAPTER 6

One True Sentence

Having found your subject, done your research, and determined the form and voice in which you wish to speak, you come to the moment of truth, which is the first line or sentence. This chapter is devoted to the first words of a piece of writing.

TITLES AND OPENING SENTENCES

It hardly needs to be said that the title and opening sentence of a work are often the most critical words in the entire document. The fate of your communication often hangs on these words. This is because they are the first hooks for catching the reader's interest. If they are sufficiently luring, readers will not succumb to the other temptations that are constantly competing for their attention: the other articles asking to be read, the television blaring, the phone ringing, or the child pulling at the sleeve.

Writers want their titles and opening lines to be so compelling that readers will turn off the tube, unplug the phone, place the two-year-old in the playpen, and settle in for a good read. Student writers want their papers to stand out in the pile of 20 (or 200) on their professor's desk. Fortunately, recent research can help writers achieve these goals. Studies of how readers read reveal that readers' eyes tend to rest longest on the first word or two of every sentence. They rest second longest on the last word in every sentence. These pauses may be only thousandths of a second long, but they still are important. Writers should not waste these critical opening and closing sentence positions. Good writers will place strong or interesting words in these places as hooks for the reader's attention.

Which of these sentences interests you more?

> There was a fire at our library and it destroyed it.

> or

> Fire destroyed our school library.

Once again the old adage "less is more" rings true. The first sentence has not only more than twice the words of the second but also the incredibly slow opening, "There was a. . . ." Readers have to wait until the fourth word to find something worthy of their imaginations. Similarly, the important final spot is wasted on a vague, indeed ambiguous, "it." Not so the short and powerful second sentence. Didn't the opening word cause you to picture flames (and maybe even hear, smell, and feel them)? Isn't the second word ("destroyed") a more vivid verb than the weak "was" of the first sentence? Were you curious to learn what the fire destroyed—only to be handed the telegram with the sentence's final word "library"? If "Fire destroyed our school library" was the opening sentence of a work, would you want to read on to find out what was going to come next?

Good writers pay attention to the beginnings and endings of all the sentences they write. However, they give extra care to the opening words of each work because of their extra importance. Beginning writers assume that editors reading their submissions will read all the way through to the end before making a decision, but many good editors do not to do this. They say they can tell from the opening paragraph or page whether a piece is worth reading, and that will be all they will read—unless, of course, they get hooked.

Opening sentences can be short, like Melville's commanding "Call me Ishmael," and they can be intriguing, like Ralph Ellison's "I am an invisible man." Opening lines can also be long. William Kennedy has said that it was only after he wrote this opening sentence of his novel *Quinn's Book* that he knew he had a story he wanted to tell:

> I, Daniel Quinn, neither the first nor the last of a line of such Quinns, set eyes on Maud the wondrous on a late December day in 1849 on the banks of the river of aristocrats and paupers, just as the great courtesan, Magdalena Colon, also known as La Ultima, a woman whose presence turned men into spittling, masturbating pigs, boarded a skiff to carry her across the river's icy water from Albany to Greenbush, her first stop en route to the city of Troy, a community of iron, where later that evening she was scheduled to enact, yet again, her role

> as the lascivious Lais, that fabled prostitute who spurned Demosthenes' gold and yielded without fee to Diogenes, the virtuous, impecunious tubdweller.*

Readers may be breathless after reading this sentence, but most will be panting for more.

Sometimes the perfect title or opening line will come at once to a writer—like an unexpected gift. John McPhee confesses that the title for his book on tennis players Arthur Ashe and Clark Graebner was present from the beginning. "I sat down at my typewriter and typed *Levels of the Game,*" he reports. "I didn't know any of the other words in the book, but I knew the title."†

More often, however, titles and opening lines are added at the end of the writing process, when the entire piece is completed. Some writers cannot write the opening, or christen their works, till they know what they have said. There is nothing wrong with this. In fact, it is quite common. Often the title may be an important phrase or image in the work. In such cases, the work seems to name itself, but only after it is finished. Often the writer will also want to rework the opening line (or the entire introduction) to link it more firmly to what follows.

Regardless of when the opening is created, writers will devote extra time (sometimes hours, sometimes days or weeks or months) to setting the hooks. When openings or titles do not immediately come, and reading over the work produces no inspiration for titles or opening lines, writers sometimes resort to the following title types as helpful stimulants to their imaginations:

The Striking Statement

They're Freezing Tumors to Death

The Provocative or Mysterious Statement

Six Men in One Body

The Question Title

Is the Greek System Dead?

The Declarative Sentence Title

Cincinnati Cleans Its Courts

They Hunt Terrorists

Quinn's Book (New York: Penguin Books, 1988.)

†Telephone interview, 22 June 1987.

The How, Why, What Title

How to Build a Dormitory Loft
Why Jenny Can't Find a Summer Job
What the New Tax Law Will Do to Students

The Direct Address (You) Title

Your Voice Can Get You a Job
Play Winning Tennis

The Quotation Title

"They Came . . . They Saw . . . They Conquered"
"You've Come a Long Way, Baby"

The Rhyme and Alliteration Title

Boston's Billionaires
Ship for Senior Sailors
Tons of Guns

The Contrast Title

The Hard Truth about Soft Porn
Little Legends of Big Sur

The Pun, Old Song, or Maxim-with-a-Twist Title

Cut Your Hair and Have It Too
America, the Dutiful

THE TRUTH AS A GOOD BEGINNING

Whether writing the title, the opening line, or simply words to get a piece of writing going, many writers have found wisdom in Ernest Hemingway's advice in the opening selection in this chapter. Hemingway discovered that if he could only write "one true sentence," this first true sentence would lead to others. In "Finding the Center," which follows the Hemingway selection, V. S. Naipaul describes how this process worked in his own writing career.

Starting with the truth is a severe discipline. Lies, regrettably, are everywhere, as Sissela Bok observes in the selection "Lying." In her essay "Small

Towns: A Close Second Look at a Very Good Place," Carol Bly tries to look beyond the lies and easy clichés about small- and big-city living to speak the hard truth about her subject. Student Cori McNeilus does the same with the American labor movement in her essay "American Labor Unions: The Crisis and the Opportunity." In her short story, "Cover Girl," Nancy Price bares truths about America's high-fashion models.

Telling the truth should be the foremost goal of every writer. As the English novelist and essayist George Orwell put it in his essay "Why I Write" (see Chapter 7), "When I sit down to write a book, I do not say to myself, 'I am going to produce a work of art.' I write it because there is some lie that I want to expose, some fact to which I want to draw attention, and my initial concern is to get a hearing."

A Moveable Feast

Ernest Hemingway

Ernest Hemingway, who won the Nobel Prize for Literature in 1954, wrote fiction and nonfiction throughout his life. He was born in Oak Park, Illinois, and, like many writers, he learned to trim the fat from his sentences while working as a journalist. After high school, Hemingway joined the staff of the Kansas City Star. The first rule on the Star's style sheet stressed brevity, compression, and "vigorous English"—traits now considered hallmarks of Hemingway's style. "Avoid the use of adjectives," was another style sheet rule, "especially such extravagant ones as splendid, gorgeous, grand, magnificent, etc."

Hemingway liked to rise with the sun and write through the morning. Then he would savor a meal of fine foods and wine and plunge into some (usually physical) activity, such as hunting, deep-sea fishing, or swimming.

He wrote with a pencil or pen on plain newsprint or in notebooks. Occasionally he would type. He had a remarkable memory for what he had observed, and his characteristic method of writing was to add in more details as he revised, as if he were filling in the picture.

Hemingway's great concern was to record the truth as he experienced it. He was always cautioning himself to slow down, for he believed the glib and hasty line was usually a false one. Indeed, so obsessed was he to allow space in his sentences for truth to seep in that he would often leave a space before *the comma and period , as well as after , like this .*

Brief Warm-up Writing Exercises

1. Brainstorm a list of famous or striking opening or closing lines or moments—in literature, music, film, or sports.

2. Now take one of the moments or lines on your list and explain why it is so effective or memorable.

3. In five minutes make a list of all the simple true sentences you can think of. (*Hint:* Avoid clichés (overused expressions). Your sentences don't have to be grand sentences, just simple and true ones.)

---

1   ❖   When we came back to Paris it was clear and cold and lovely. The city had accommodated itself to winter, there was good wood for sale at the wood and coal place across our street, and there were braziers outside of many of the good cafés so that you could keep warm on the terraces. Our own apartment was warm and cheerful. We burned *boulets* which were molded, egg-shaped lumps of coal dust, on the wood fire, and on the streets the winter light was beautiful. Now you were accustomed to see the bare trees against the sky and you walked on the fresh-washed gravel paths through the Luxembourg gardens in the clear sharp wind. The trees were sculpture without their leaves when you were reconciled to them, and the winter winds blew across the surfaces of the ponds and the fountains blew in the bright light. All the distances were short now since we had been in the mountains.

2   Because of the change in altitude I did not notice the grade of the hills except with pleasure, and the climb up to the top floor of the hotel where I worked in a room that looked across all the roofs and the chimneys of the high hill of the quarter, was a pleasure. The fireplace drew well in the room and it was warm and pleasant to work. I brought mandarines and roasted chestnuts to the room in paper packets and peeled and ate the small tangerine-like oranges and threw their skins and spat their seeds in the fire when I ate them and roasted chestnuts when I was hungry. I was always hungry with the walking and the cold and the working. Up in the room I had a bottle of kirsch that we had brought back from the mountains and I took a drink of kirsch when I would get toward the end of a story or toward the end of the day's work. When I was through working for the day I put away the notebook, or the paper, in the drawer of the table and put any mandarines that were left in my pocket. They would freeze if they were left in the room at night.

3   It was wonderful to walk down the long flights of stairs knowing that I'd

had good luck working. I always worked until I had something done and I always stopped when I knew what was going to happen next. That way I could be sure of going on the next day. But sometimes when I was starting a new story and I could not get it going, I would sit in front of the fire and squeeze the peel of the little oranges into the edge of the flame and watch the sputter of blue that they made. I would stand and look out over the roofs of Paris and think, "Do not worry. You have always written before and you will write now. All you have to do is write one true sentence. Write the truest sentence that you know." So finally I would write one true sentence, and then go on from there. It was easy then because there was always one true sentence that I knew or had seen or had heard someone say. If I started to write elaborately, or like someone introducing or presenting something, I found that I could cut that scrollwork or ornament out and throw it away and start with the first true simple declarative sentence I had written. Up in that room I decided that I would write one story about each thing that I knew about. I was trying to do this all the time I was writing, and it was good and severe discipline.

4   It was in that room too that I learned not to think about anything that I was writing from the time I stopped writing until I started again the next day. That way my subconscious would be working on it and at the same time I would be listening to other people and noticing everything, I hoped; learning, I hoped; and I would read so that I would not think about my work and make myself impotent to do it. Going down the stairs when I had worked well, and that needed luck as well as discipline, was a wonderful feeling and I was free then to walk anywhere in Paris. ❖

Questions to Ponder

1. Why do you think Ernest Hemingway spends the first two paragraphs describing the Paris setting before he begins to talk about his writing?
2. How did Hemingway handle the moments when he had trouble getting started with a piece of writing?
3. Why might it be "good and severe discipline" to write one piece about each true thing you know?
4. Why is it often a good practice to stop work when you know what you are going to say next, or when you know where the piece of writing is going to go next?

Writing Possibilities

1. Choose the most interesting of the true sentences you wrote in warm-up writing exercise 3, and use it as the first sentence of a piece you will develop.

2. Write a "Dear Ernest" letter to Hemingway, telling him what kind of sentences would be true today—and for you.
3. Work on a story or an essay on at least four consecutive days, stopping each day when you know what is going to come next.
4. Brainstorm a list of everything you consider false. Then write an essay for your fellow students classifying the different kinds of falseness in contemporary life.

Finding the Center

V. S. Naipaul

I do not really know how I became a writer. I can give certain dates and certain facts about my career. But the process itself remains mysterious. It is mysterious, for instance, that the ambition should have come first—the wish to be a writer, to have that distinction, that fame—and that this ambition should have come long before I could think of anything to write about.

I remember, in my first term at Oxford in 1950, going for long walks—I remember the roads, the autumn leaves, the cars and trucks going by, whipping the leaves up—and wondering what I was going to write about. I had worked hard for the scholarship to go to Oxford, to be a writer. But now that I was in Oxford, I didn't know what to write about. And really, I suppose, unless I had been driven by great necessity, something even like panic, I might never have written. The idea of laying aside the ambition was very restful and tempting—the way sleep was said to be tempting to Napoleon's soldiers on the retreat from Moscow.

I felt it as artificial, that sitting down to write a book. And that is a feeling that is with me still, all these years later, at the start of a book—I am speaking of an imaginative work. There is no precise theme or story that is with me. Many things are with me: I write the artificial, self-conscious beginnings of many books; until finally some true impulse—the one I have been working toward—possesses me, and I sail away on my year's labor.

Brief Warm-up Writing Exercises

1. Freewrite a description of your neighborhood when you were a child.
2. Now write about any unusual neighbors you had.
3. Reread what you wrote for warm-up writing exercises 1 and 2, and then write one true sentence about the street or neighborhood of your youth.

---

1 ❖ It is now nearly thirty years since, in a BBC room in London, on an old BBC typewriter, and on smooth, "non-rustle" BBC script paper, I wrote the first sentence of my first publishable book. I was some three months short of my twenty-third birthday. I had left Oxford ten months before, and was living in London, trying to keep afloat and, in between, hoping to alleviate my anxiety but always only adding to it, trying to get started as a writer.

2 At Oxford I had been supported by a Trinidad government scholarship. In London I was on my own. The only money I got—eight guineas a week, less "deductions"—came from the BBC Caribbean Service. My only piece of luck in the past year, and even in the past two years, had been to get a part-time job editing and presenting a weekly literary program for the Caribbean.

3 The Caribbean Service was on the second floor of what had been the Langham Hotel, opposite Broadcasting House. On this floor the BBC had set aside a room for people like me, "freelances"—to me then not a word suggesting freedom and valor, but suggesting only people on the fringe of a mighty enterprise, a depressed and suppliant class: I would have given a lot to be "staff."

4 The freelances' room didn't encourage thoughts of radio glory; it was strictly for the production of little scripts. Something of the hotel atmosphere remained: in the great Victorian-Edwardian days of the Langham Hotel (it was mentioned in at least one Sherlock Holmes story), the freelances' room might have been a pantry. It was at the back of the heavy brick building, and gloomy when the ceiling lights were turned off. It wasn't cheerful when the lights were on: ocher walls with a pea-green dado, the gloss paint tarnished; a radiator below the window, with grit on the sill; two or three chairs, a telephone, two tables, and two old standard typewriters.

5 It was in that Victorian-Edwardian gloom, and at one of those typewriters, that late one afternoon, without having any idea where I was going, and not perhaps intending to type to the end of the page, I wrote: *Every morning when he got up Hat would sit on the banister of his back verandah and shout across, "What happening there, Bogart?"*

6 That was a Port of Spain memory. It seemed to come from far back, but it was only eleven or twelve years old. It came from the time when we—various branches of my mother's family—were living in Port of Spain, in a

house that belonged to my mother's mother. We were country people, Indians, culturally still Hindus, and this move to Port of Spain was in the nature of a migration: from the Hindu and Indian countryside to the white-negro-mulatto town. (At that time in Trinidad *black,* used by a non-black, was a word of insult; *negro* was—and remains—a polite word.)

7   Hat was our neighbor on the street. He wasn't negro or mulatto. But we thought of him as halfway there. He was a Port of Spain Indian. The Port of Spain Indians—there were pockets of them—had no country roots, were individuals, hardly a community, and were separate from us for an additional reason: many of them were Madrassis, descendants of South Indians, not Hindi-speaking, and not people of caste. We didn't see in them any of our own formalities or restrictions; and though we lived raggedly ourselves (and were far too numerous for the house), we thought of the other Indians in the street only as street people.

8   That shout of "Bogart!" was in more than one way a shout from the street. And, to add to the incongruity, it was addressed to someone in our yard: a young man, very quiet, yet another person connected in some way with my mother's family. He had come not long before from the country and was living in the separate one-room building at the back of our yard.

9   We called this room the servant room. Port of Spain houses, up to the 1930s, were built with these separate servant rooms—verandah-less little boxes, probably descended in style from the ancillary "negro houses" of slave times. I suppose that in one or two houses in our street servants of the house actually lived in the servant room. But generally it wasn't so. Servant rooms, because of the privacy they offered, were in demand, and not by servants.

10 It was wartime. The migration of my own family into the town had become part of a more general movement. People of all conditions were coming into Port of Spain to work at the two American bases. One of those bases had been built on recently reclaimed land just at the end of our street—eight houses down. Twice a day we heard the bugles; Americans, formal in their uniforms, with their khaki ties tucked into their shirts, were another part of the life of our street. The street was busy; the yards were crowded. Our yard was more crowded than most. No servant ever lodged in our servant room. Instead, the room sheltered a succession of favored transients, on their way to better things. Before the big family rush, some of these transients had been outsiders; but now they were mostly relations or people close to the family, like Bogart.

11 The connection of Bogart with my mother's family was unusual. At the turn of the century Bogart's father and my mother's father had traveled out together from India as indentured immigrants. At some time during the long and frightening journey they had sworn a bond of brotherhood; that was the bond that was being honored by their descendants.

12 Bogart's people were from the Punjab, and handsome. The two brothers we had got to know were ambitious men, rising in white-collar jobs. One was a teacher; the other (who had passed through the servant room) was a weekend sportsman who, in the cricket season, regularly got his name in the

paper. Bogart didn't have the education or the ambition of his brothers; it wasn't clear what he did for a living. He was placid, without any pronounced character, detached, and in that crowded yard oddly solitary.

13   Once he went away. When he came back, some weeks or months later, it was said that he had been "working on a ship." Port of Spain was a colonial port, and we thought of sailors as very rough, the dregs. So this business of working on a ship—though it suggested money as well as luck, for the jobs were not easy to come by—also held suggestions of danger. It was something for the reckless and the bohemian. But it must have suited Bogart, because after a time he went away—disappeared—again.

14   There was a story this time that he had gone to Venezuela. He came back; but I had no memory of his return. His adventures—if he had had any—remained unknown to me. I believe I was told that the first time he had gone away, to work on the ship, he had worked as a cook. But that might have been a story I made up myself. All that I knew of Bogart while he lived in the servant room was what, as a child, I saw from a distance. He and his comings and goings were part of the confusion and haphazardness and crowd of that time.

15   I saw a little more of him four or five years later. The war was over. The American base at the end of the street was closed. The buildings were pulled down, and the local contractor, who knew someone in our family, gave us the run of the place for a few days, to pick up what timber we wanted. My mother's extended family was breaking up into its component parts; we were all leaving my grandmother's house. My father had bought a house of his own; I used timber from the old American base to make a new front gate. Soon I had got the Trinidad government scholarship that was to take me to Oxford.

16   Bogart was still reportedly a traveler. And in Trinidad now he was able to do what perhaps he had always wanted to do: to put as much distance as possible between himself and people close to him. He was living in Carenage, a seaside village five miles or so west of Port of Spain. Carenage was a negro-mulatto place, with a Spanish flavor ('*pagnol*, in the local French patois). There were few Indians in Carenage; that would have suited Bogart.

17   With nothing to do, waiting to go away, I was restless, and I sometimes cycled out to Carenage. It was pleasant after the hot ride to splash about in the rocky sea, and pleasant after that to go and have a Coca-Cola at Bogart's. He lived in a side street, a wandering lane, with yards that were half bush, half built-up. He was a tailor now, apparently with customers; and he sat at his machine in his open shop, welcoming but undemonstrative, as placid, as without conversation, and as solitary as ever. But he was willing to play with me. He was happy to let me paint a signboard for his shop. The idea was mine, and he took it seriously. He had a carpenter build a board of new wood; and on this, over some days, after priming and painting, I did the sign. He put it up over his shop door, and I thought it looked genuine, a real sign. I was amazed; it was the first signboard I had ever done.

18   The time then came for me to go to England. I left Bogart in Carenage. And that was where he had continued to live in my memory, faintly, never a figure

in the foreground: the man who had worked on a ship, then gone to Venezuela, sitting placidly ever after at his sewing machine, below my sign, in his little concrete house-and-shop.

19 That was Bogart's story, as I knew it. And—after all our migrations within Trinidad, after my own trip to England and my time at Oxford—that was all the story I had in mind when—after two failed attempts at novels—I sat at the typewriter in the freelances' room in the Langham Hotel, to try once more to be a writer. And luck was with me that afternoon. *Every morning when he got up Hat would sit on the banister of his back verandah and shout across, "What happening there, Bogart?"* Luck was with me, because that first sentence was so direct, so uncluttered, so without complications, that it provoked the sentence that was to follow. *Bogart would turn in his bed and mumble softly, so that no one heard, "What happening there, Hat?"*

20 The first sentence was true. The second was invention. But together—to me, the writer—they had done something extraordinary. Though they had left out everything—the setting, the historical time, the racial and social complexities of the people concerned—they had suggested it all; they had created the world of the street. And together, as sentences, words, they had set up a rhythm, a speed, which dictated all that was to follow. ❖

Questions to Ponder

1. What does V. S. Naipaul's opening sentence—*"Every morning when he got up Hat would sit on the banister of his back verandah and shout across, 'What happening there, Bogart?' "*—tell us about Hat?
2. What do you think it was in Naipaul's first sentence that "provoked" his second: *"Bogart would turn in his bed and mumble softly, so that no one heard, 'What happening there, Hat?' "*
3. What does Naipaul's second sentence tell us about Bogart?
4. Does every detail of a place or subject have to be included to make a sentence true?

Writing Possibilities

1. Do some research to find out the racial and ethnic composition of your college, city, state, or region. Then write one true sentence about your findings. Does your first sentence provoke a second one—as V. S. Naipaul's did?
2. Write one true sentence that is (a) a description, (b) an astonishing or striking statement, or (c) a quiet understatement. (You might use the research you have done for writing possibility 1.)

3. Draft a letter to the president of your college. Begin it with one true sentence you would want the president to know.
4. Brainstorm a list of the qualities of a good opening sentence. Then write one true sentence about opening sentences.

LYING

Sissela Bok

The first paragraph of the Conclusion to my book Lying presented a special problem. How could I sum up what had gone before without laborious repetition? And how could I best convey the subtlety and interplay between different forms of duplicity while focusing on the role of clear-cut lying in their midst? I decided that the metaphor of a stage could serve both purposes. Yet to speak of lies, euphemisms, and other forms of deception as actors on a stage would have been farfetched and so ludicrously overspecific as to leave no room for the subtle shadings that I wanted to evoke. And so I chose to refer, instead, to the different forms of duplicity as being in the foreground or blending into the background, as clustering around and propping up lies and assuming disguises.

When I reread the manuscript in galley proofs, I felt that I needed to change the last paragraph and above all the last sentence. It spoke of a society unwilling to discuss concrete moral problems as one that "deserves the level of morality that it gets." I wanted to avoid any trace of a hortatory tone while at the same time finding a more fitting last word. In the back of my mind, I could hear my father, Gunnar Myrdal, talking about the meticulous care with which many writers he admired had chosen the last word of their texts. He would refer to the British philosopher and economist Henry Sidgwick, who had ended the first edition of his pathbreaking work, The Methods of Ethics, with the word "failure"; by the time of the seventh edition, it had changed to "scepticism." My father, not to be outdone, had concluded his book An American Dilemma with the word "Enlightenment"—one he never saw reason to change. It was in that spirit, and as a counterbalance to the title I had given to my own book, that I finally selected a last word I, too, knew was there to stay: "veracity."

Brief Warm-up Writing Exercises

1. Brainstorm a list of the different forms that lying takes in the world.
2. Freewrite about the kinds of lying and duplicity that are most common among students.
3. Describe the biggest "fib" or "lie" you have told in your life—and the consequences.

DRAFT

CONCLUSION:

> Certainly, it is heaven upon earth to have a man's mind move in charity, rest in providence, and turn upon the poles of truth.
> —Bacon, "Of Truth"

Nearly every kind of statement or action can be meant to deceive. Clearly intended lies—the most sharply etched forms of duplicity—have been in the foreground throughout this book. More marginal forms, such as evasion, euphemism, and exaggeration, have been close at hand, ready to prop up these lies or take their place. And all around have clustered the many kinds of deception intended to mislead without even marginally false statements: the changes of subject, the disguises, the gestures leading astray, all blending into the background of silence and inaction, sometimes intended only to mislead.

We lead our lives amidst all these forms of duplicity. From childhood on, we develop ways of coping with them —of believing some, seeing through others, and consciously ignoring still others. We may end by tolerating even certain practices of outright lying without knowing how to distinguish them from those that we reject out of hand/ tolerating, for instance, lies believed to serve the "best interests" of groups or individuals, those under-

[margin note: Correction of a typographical error.]

[margin note: lies]

taken for purposes of advocacy, or those construed to serve the objectives of self-defense. I have wanted to convey the *levels* of deception that we must all live with as a result and to focus on the burden they impose.

Must we take these levels of deception to be our lot? Are they somehow immutable? There is no reason to think so. They vary from one family to another, from one profession or society to the next. As a result, there is ample room for change. But how can it be brought about? What steps can individuals take by themselves, and which measures require collective action?

Individuals, without a doubt, have the power to influence the amount of duplicity in their lives and to shape their speech and action. They can decide to rule out deception wherever honest alternatives exist, and become much more adept at thinking up ~~such~~ honest ways to deal with problems. They can learn to look with much greater care at the remaining choices where deception seems the only way out. They can make use of the test of publicity to help them set standards to govern their participation in deceptive practices. Finally, they can learn to beware of efforts to dupe them, and make clear their preference for honesty even in small things.

But individuals differ greatly in their ability to carry through such changes. They differ in their knowledge of deception and its alternatives; in their desire to bring about changes; and in their understanding of what lying can do to them, either as deceiver or as deceived. Many who might be able to change the patterns of duplicity in their own lives lack any awareness of the presence of a moral problem in the first place, and thus ~~lack the ability~~ feel no need to examine their behavior and explore the alternatives carefully. Others are beyond caring.

Still another difference among individuals cuts sharply into the capacity of many to make changes: the difference in the power to carry through a change and in the freedom and security from repercussions ~~of those who~~ should they challenge deeply-rooted habits of duplicity. The lack of power and freedom to cope with the consequences of battling deceptive practices reinforces the lack of awareness or concern wherever it exists; it puts great pressure even on those least comfortable with deceit.

Thus, the ~~beginning~~ reporter who will lose his job if he is not aggressive in getting stories, or the young politician whose career depends on winning an election, may in principle be more sorely tempted to bend the truth than those whose work is secure; but this difference may be more than outweighed by the increased callousness of the latter to what they have come to regard as routine deception.

The very stress on individualism, on competition, on achieving material success which so marks our society also generates intense pressures to cut corners. To win an election, to increase one's income, to outsell competitors —such motives impel many to participate in forms of duplicity they might otherwise resist. The more widespread they judge these practices to be, the stronger will be the pressures to join, even compete, in deviousness.

The social incentives to deceit are at present very powerful; controls often weak. Many individuals feel caught up in practices they cannot change. It would be wishful thinking, therefore, to expect individuals to bring about major changes in the collective practices of deceit by themselves. Public and private institutions, with their enormous power to affect ~~individual~~ choice, must help alter the existing pressures and incentives.

What role can the government play in such efforts? First, it can look to its own practices, to the very "climate" of its dealings with the public. It will take time and great effort to try to reverse the injuries to trust and to public life of the last decades. Second, the government could move forcefully to carry out the existing laws prohibiting fraud and perjury. Here again, government members have to be the first to be held to such standards. Third, the laws and rules in our society must be examined from the point of view of whether they encourage deception needlessly. Some regulations put great pressures on individuals to deceive—in order to continue to receive welfare payments, for example, or to be allowed to have a divorce in societies with very strict rules against divorce. Some laws even *require* deception, as in those states where criminal records officials ~~in some states~~ are ~~required~~ by law to deny that certain felons have a police record when asked by prospective employers.

Private institutions can play a parallel role in reducing the incentives to cut corners. Recent studies indicate that businessmen regard unethical practices as very widespread, and pressures to conform as strong.[1] These pressures can be communicated directly from top management, with an immediate effect on lower level managers. Three quarters of those surveyed agree that, like the junior members of Nixon's reelection committee, young executives automatically go along with superiors to show loyalty. Very often, however, there is no such communication from top management; the pressures are conveyed indirectly. For example, a company may set the high goals for production or sales. When economic conditions become adverse, it may be next to impossible to meet these targets without moral compromises. If the incentives for achieving the goals—retaining one's job, most importantly, but also promotions, bonuses, or salary increases—are felt to be too compelling, the temptation to lie and to cheat can grow intolerable.

Such conditions came to light in the momentous price-fixing scandal in 1960 involving General Electric and the sale of heavy electrical machinery. For years, subordinate officials participated in illegal price-fixing activities involving sales valued at more than a billion dollars a year. By means of secret meetings, misleading code-words, falsified expense accounts, these activities were covered up, and the responsibilities passed from one manager to the next. At the very same time as top management sent around stern prohibitions of price-fixing to all subordinates, it put greater and greater pressures on each to raise the percentage of available business.²

There is ~~great~~ [strong] insistance now that business ought to have a code of ethics. But codes of ethics function all too often as shields; ~~and~~ their abstraction allows many to adhere to them while continuing their ordinary practices. In business as well as in those professions that have already developed codes, much more is needed. The codes must be but the starting point for a broad inquiry into the ethical quandaries encountered at work. Lay persons, and especially those affected by the professional practices, such as customers or patients, must be included in these efforts, and must sit on regulatory commissions. Methods of disciplining those who infringe the guidelines must be given teeth and enforced. [Insert attached page]

Educational institutions have a very large role to play as well. First of all, they, too, have to look to their own practices. How scrupulously honest are they in setting an example? How do they cope with cheating, with plagiarism, and with fraudulent research? To what extent, and in what disciplines, are deceptive techniques actually *taught* to students? [What pressures encourage such behavior?] Secondly, what can education bring to the training of students, in order that they may be more discerning, better able to cope with the various forms of duplicity that they will encounter in working life? Colleges and universities, as well as nursing schools, police academies, military academies, accounting schools, and many others need to consider how moral choice can best be studied and what standards can be expected, as well as upheld.

[What lines do law school courses, for instance, draw with respect to courtroom tactics, or business school courses with respect to bargaining and negotiation?]

Some professions such as medicine and law, have longer traditions of ethical inquiry than others; courses are springing up in these fields, and materials for teaching have been assembled. Other professions are only at the

Throughout society, then, all would benefit if the incentive structure associated with deceit were changed: if the gains from deception were lowered, and honesty made more worthwhile even in the short run. Sometimes it is easy to make such a change. Universities, for instance, have found in recent years that parents of incoming students all too often misrepresent their family income in order to gain scholarships for their children to the benefit of those in greater need of assistance. If on the other hand parents are told in advance that they may have to produce their income tax sent in or be met with misrepresentation is much less likely to take place.

Very often, however, there can be no such checks -- as where people communicate opinions or vote their preferences, or make sealed bids at auctions. In large organizations, for instance, specialists often communicate biased estimates and false probabilities in order to affect the final choices made in what they regard as the "right direction."

It might be thought to be beyond human ingenuity to devise incentives for honesty even in such circumstances. Many and Yet recent theoretical work suggests possible changes of this kind. Economists are searching for procedures that reward honesty in such activities as voting, giving expert advice, bargaining, and bidding at auctions.[3] Their efforts combine mathematical economics with policy-making in the public interest. If, as seems to be the latest changes in both social procedures so that, when people choose strategically, it is also in their best interest to be honest. In this way, social practices that have grown to bolster or alter, and that at present appear to embed deception, may be altered in such a way that all benefit thereby.

_____

3. See Jerry R. Green and Jean-Jacques Laffont, Incentives in Public Decision-Making (Amsterdam: North-Holland Publishing Company, 1979), and William Vickery, "Counterspeculation, Auctions, and Competitive Sealed Tenders," Journal of Finance, Vol. 16, no. 1, March 1961, pp. 8-37. I am indebted to David Kreps for bringing this new line of research to my attention.

beginning of such an endeavour.⁶ But in all these fields, much too little effort is being devoted to train persons who are competent to teach such courses. As a result, existing courses are often inadequate, leaving students confirmed in their suspicion that moral choice is murky and best left to intuition.

In developing courses, and in training those who will teach them, there is no need to start from scratch. We are not the first to face moral problems such as those of deception. Others have experienced them, argued about them, arrived at conclusions. The structure of lies and the possible justifications have long been studied. We need to make use of the traditional approaches. We need to consider, for example, in the context of working life, why it has been thought worse to *plan* to lie than to do so on the spur of the moment; worse to induce others to lie (and thus to *teach* deception, whether in families, work places or schools) than to do so oneself; worse to lie to those with a *right* to truthful information than to others; worse to lie to those who have entrusted you with their confidence about matters important to them than to your enemies.

We now have resources that these earlier traditions lacked. We have access to information and to methods that can sharpen and refine the very notions of what is "helpful" and what is "harmful" among the consequences of lies. There is much room for study; but we are learning, for example, what proportion of those who are very ill want to be treated truthfully; what happens to children who are deceived about the identity of their parents; how the public responds to government deceit. We are learning, also, much more about how the mechanisms of bias and rationalization work. Finally, we can go far beyond the anecdotes available to earlier thinkers in documenting the deceptive practices themselves.

These practices are not immutable. In an imperfect world, they cannot be wiped out altogether; but surely

~~moral choices be resolved with precision. But we can do much to limit the practices and to reduce the areas of difficult choice. A society that is not willing to try—that is not even willing to engage in serious discussion of concrete moral problems—deserves the level of morality that it gets.~~

they can be reduced and counteracted. I hope to have shown how often the justification they invoke is insubstantial, and how they can disguise and fuel all other wrongs. Trust and integrity are precious resources, easily squandered, hard to regain. They can thrive only on a foundation of respect for veracity.

> ❖ *Certainly, it is heaven upon earth to have a man's mind move in charity, rest in providence, and turn upon the poles of truth.*
>
> —Bacon, "Of Truth"

1   Nearly every kind of statement or action can be meant to deceive. Clearly intended lies—the most sharply etched forms of duplicity—have been in the foreground throughout this book. More marginal forms, such as evasion, euphemism, and exaggeration, have been close at hand, ready to prop up these lies or take their place. And all around have clustered the many kinds of deception intended to mislead without even marginally false statements: the changes of subject, the disguises, the gestures leading astray, all blending into the background of silence and inaction only sometimes intended to mislead.

2   We lead our lives amidst all these forms of duplicity. From childhood on, we develop ways of coping with them—of believing some, seeing through others, and consciously ignoring still others. We may end by tolerating even certain practices of outright lying without knowing how to distinguish them from those that we reject out of hand: tolerating, for instance, lies believed to serve the "best interests" of groups or individuals, those undertaken for purposes of advocacy, or those construed to serve the objectives of self-defense. I have wanted to convey the *levels* of deception that we must all live with as a result and to focus on the burden they impose.

3   Must we take these levels of deception to be our lot? Are they somehow immutable? There is no reason to think so. They vary from one family to another, from one profession or society to the next. As a result, there is ample room for change. But how can it be brought about? What steps can individuals take by themselves, and which measures require collective action?

4   Individuals, without a doubt, have the power to influence the amount of duplicity in their lives and to shape their speech and action. They can decide to rule out deception wherever honest alternatives exist, and become much more adept at thinking up honest ways to deal with problems. They can learn to look with much greater care at the remaining choices where deception seems the only way out. They can make use of the test of publicity to help them set standards to govern their participation in deceptive practices. Finally, they can learn to beware of efforts to dupe them, and make clear their preference for honesty even in small things.

5   But individuals differ greatly in their ability to carry through such changes. They differ in their knowledge of deception and its alternatives; in their desire to bring about changes; and in their understanding of what lying can do to them, either as deceiver or as deceived. Many who might be able to change the patterns of duplicity in their own lives lack any awareness of the presence of a moral problem in the first place, and thus feel no need to examine their behavior and explore the alternatives carefully. Others are beyond caring.

6   Still another difference among individuals cuts sharply into the capacity of

many to make changes: the difference in the power to carry through a change and in the freedom and security from repercussions should they challenge deeply rooted habits of duplicity. The lack of power and freedom to cope with the consequences of battling deceptive practices reinforces the lack of awareness or concern wherever it exists; it puts great pressure even on those least comfortable with deceit.

7   Thus, the cub reporter who will lose his job if he is not aggressive in getting stories, or the young politician whose career depends on winning an election, may in principle be more sorely tempted to bend the truth than those whose work is secure; but this difference may be more than outweighed by the increased callousness of the latter to what they have come to regard as routine deception.

8   The very stress on individualism, on competition, on achieving material success which so marks our society also generates intense pressures to cut corners. To win an election, to increase one's income, to outsell competitors—such motives impel many to participate in forms of duplicity they might otherwise resist. The more widespread they judge these practices to be, the stronger will be the pressures to join, even compete, in deviousness.

9   The social incentives to deceit are at present very powerful; the controls, often weak. Many individuals feel caught up in practices they cannot change. It would be wishful thinking, therefore, to expect individuals to bring about major changes in the collective practices of deceit by themselves. Public and private institutions, with their enormous power to affect personal choice, must help alter the existing pressures and incentives.

10 What role can the government play in such efforts? First, it can look to its own practices, to the very "climate" of its dealings with the public. It will take time and great effort to try to reverse the injuries to trust and to public life of the last decades. Second, the government could move forcefully to carry out the existing laws prohibiting fraud and perjury. Here again, government members have to be the first to be held to such standards. Third, the laws and rules in our society must be examined from the point of view of whether they encourage deception needlessly. Some regulations put great pressures on individuals to deceive—in order to continue to receive welfare payments, for example, or to be allowed to have a divorce in societies with very strict rules against divorce. Some laws even *require* deception, as in those states where criminal records officials are compelled by law to deny that certain felons have a police record when asked by prospective employers.

11 Private institutions can play a parallel role in reducing the incentives to cut corners. Recent studies indicate that businessmen regard unethical practices as very widespread, and pressures to conform as strong.[1] These pressures can be communicated directly from top management, with an immediate effect on

---

[1] See "The Pressure to Compromise Personal Ethics," Special Report, *Business Week,* 31 Jan. 1977:107, and Steven N. Brenner and Earl A. Molander, "Is the Ethics of Business Changing?" *Harvard Business Review* 55 (Jan.–Feb. 1977): 57–71.

lower level managers. Three quarters of those surveyed agree that, like the junior members of Nixon's reelection committee, young executives automatically go along with superiors to show loyalty. Very often, however, there is no such communication from top management; the pressures are conveyed indirectly. For example, a company may set high goals for production or sales. When economic conditions become adverse, it may be next to impossible to meet these targets without moral compromises. If the incentives for achieving the goals—retaining one's job, most importantly, but also promotions, bonuses, or salary increases—are felt to be too compelling, the temptation to lie and to cheat can grow intolerable.

12   Such conditions came to light in the momentous price-fixing scandal in 1960 involving General Electric and the sale of heavy electrical machinery. For years, subordinate officials participated in illegal price-fixing activities involving sales valued at more than a billion dollars a year. They conspired to fix prices, rig bids, split markets. By means of secret meetings, misleading codewords, falsified expense accounts, these activities were covered up, and the responsibilities passed from one manager to the next. At the very same time as top management sent around stern prohibitions of price-fixing to all subordinates, it put greater and greater pressures on each to raise the percentage of available business.[2]

13   There is strong insistence now that business ought to have a code of ethics. But codes of ethics function all too often as shields; their abstraction allows many to adhere to them while continuing their ordinary practices. In business as well as in those professions that have already developed codes, much more is needed. The codes must be but the starting point for a broad inquiry into the ethical quandaries encountered at work. Lay persons, and especially those affected by the professional practices, such as customers or patients, must be included in these efforts, and must sit on regulatory commissions. Methods of disciplining those who infringe the guidelines must be given teeth and enforced.

14   Throughout society, then, all would benefit if the incentive structure associated with deceit were changed: if the gains from deception were lowered, and honesty made more worthwhile even in the short run. Sometimes it is easy to make such a change. Universities, for instance, have found in recent years that parents of incoming students all too often misrepresent their family incomes in order to gain scholarships for their children at the expense of those in greater need of assistance. If, on the other hand, parents are told in advance that they may have to produce their income tax statements on request, such misrepresentation is much less likely to take place.

15   Very often, however, there can be no such checks—as where people communicate estimates, or vote their preference, or make sealed bids in auctions. In large organizations, for instance, specialists often communicate

---

[2] See Richard Austin Smith, "The Incredible Electrical Conspiracy," *Fortune*, April 1961: 132–37, 170–80.

skewed estimates and false prognostications in order to affect the final choices made in what they regard as the "right" direction.

16   It ought not to be beyond human ingenuity to increase the incentives for honesty even in such circumstances. Many are beginning to devote thought to possible changes of this kind. Economists, in particular, are seeking procedures that reward honesty in such activities as voting, giving expert advice, bargaining, and bidding at auctions.[3] Their efforts combine mathematical economics with policy-making in the public interest. They suggest that such changes be made in common social procedures that, when people choose strategically, it will also be in their best interest to be honest. In this way, social practices that have sprung up helter-skelter, and that at present appear to reward deception, may be altered in such a way that all benefit thereby.

17   Educational institutions have a very large role to play as well. First of all, they, too, have to look to their own practices. How scrupulously honest are they in setting an example? How do they cope with cheating, with plagiarism, and with fraudulent research? What pressures encourage such behavior? To what extent, and in what disciplines, are deceptive techniques actually *taught* to students? What lines do law school courses, for instance, draw with respect to courtroom tactics, or business school courses with respect to bargaining and negotiation? Second, what can education bring to the training of students, in order that they may be more discerning, better able to cope with the various forms of duplicity that they will encounter in working life? Colleges and universities, as well as nursing schools, police academies, military academies, accounting schools, and many others need to consider how moral choice can best be studied and what standards can be expected, as well as upheld.

18   Some professions, such as medicine and law, have longer traditions of ethical inquiry than others; courses are springing up in these fields, and materials for teaching have been assembled. Other professions are only at the beginning of such an endeavor.[4] But in all these fields, much too little effort is being devoted to train persons who are competent to teach such courses. As a result, existing courses are often inadequate, leaving students confirmed in their suspicion that moral choice is murky and best left to intuition.

19   In developing courses, and in training those who will teach them, there is no need to start from scratch. We are not the first to face moral problems such as those of deception. Others have experienced them, argued about them, arrived at conclusions. The structure of lies and the possible justifications have

---

[3] See Jerry R. Green and Jean-Jacques Laffont, *Incentives in Public Decision Making* (Amsterdam: North-Holland Publishing, 1978), and William Vickery, "Counterspeculation, Auctions, and Cooperative Sealed Tenders," *Journal of Finance* 16 (March 1961): 8–37. I am grateful to Howard Raiffa for bringing this new line of research to my attention.

[4] See Derek Bok, "Can Ethics Be Taught?" *Change* 8 (Oct. 1976): 26–30.

long been studied. We need to make use of the traditional approaches. We need to consider, for example, in the context of working life, why it has been thought worse to *plan* to lie than to do so on the spur of the moment; worse to induce others to lie (and thus to *teach* deception, whether in families, work places or schools) than to do so oneself; worse to lie to those with a *right* to truthful information than to others; worse to lie to those who have entrusted you with their confidence about matters important to them than to your enemies.

20   We now have resources that these earlier traditions lacked. We have access to information and to methods that can sharpen and refine the very notions of what is "helpful" and what is "harmful" among the consequences of lies. There is much room for study; but we are learning, for example, what proportion of those who are very ill *want* to be treated truthfully; what happens to adopted children who are deceived about the identity of their parents; how the public responds to government deceit. We are learning, also, much more about how the mechanisms of bias and rationalization work. Finally, we can go far beyond the anecdotes available to earlier thinkers in documenting the deceptive practices themselves.

21   These practices are not immutable. In an imperfect world, they cannot be wiped out altogether; but surely they can be reduced and counteracted. I hope to have shown how often the justifications they invoke are insubstantial, and how they can disguise and fuel all other wrongs. Trust and integrity are precious resources, easily squandered, hard to regain. They can thrive only on a foundation of respect for veracity. ❖

Questions to Ponder

1. Can you think of examples from your own life of each of these forms of lying?
   - Clearly intended lies
   - "White lies"
   - Exaggerations
   - Euphemisms
   - Evasions
   - Misleading gestures
   - Silence

2. Are there any kinds of "fibbing" or lying that are defensible? If you answer "yes," which kinds?
3. How can we influence the amount and kinds of duplicity in our lives?
4. What is the "test of publicity," and how can it be used to help us govern our participation in duplicity?
5. What social and institutional pressures encourage lying and duplicity?

Writing Possibilities

1. Do research and write an objective report on lying in your college or university. (You may wish to consult your student handbook for plagiarism policies, interview some faculty members and students, and even develop an informal questionnaire.) Share your report with your academic dean.
2. Now turn your report into a letter to the editor of your campus newspaper. Your letter will briefly summarize your findings and offer any recommendations you think would improve veracity on campus. Try to begin your letter with a true sentence.
3. Do research on the kinds and degrees of lying and duplicity that occur in the professional area you are preparing to enter. Develop an essay or report detailing your findings, as well as any creative solutions that occur to you.
4. Write a code of ethics (with teeth in it) for the government, a segment of the business or professional world, your college, or yourself. In what form will you present it? Will it begin with the truest sentence you know on the topic?
5. Brainstorm two lists: (1) the dangers of duplicity, and (2) the benefits of honesty in society. Then write a persuasive (or satirical) essay on the subject.

SMALL TOWNS: A CLOSE SECOND LOOK AT A VERY GOOD PLACE

Carol Bly

No one with any social or political or intellectual claims wants the social worker's car, with its license plate, parked outside the house. Certainly we aren't the kind of client who could use a social worker's applications: we know that they practice their skills with people at the bottom of the United States pile. Their guild, therefore—their profession, their trade—carries the stigma of lower class. Lower class, lower class! And so it does not easily occur to us to ask, do they by any chance teach people a very new set of skills that would help make peace? Make small towns expres-

sive? Make it easier to stay in the room and learn something, without tottering, when an enemy is holding forth? Make it easier for people to develop through the ethical stages?

It is always hard to take new wisdom from a less elegant segment of society. Northern feudal lords jeered for years at the business acumen of Florentine merchants. What the Florentines were doing, how they understood that money-makes-where-trade-breaks, worked. What the feudal lords were doing, jousting half the day, clipping the fiefs, and protecting a decorative and power-hungry religion, did not work, but it was classy.

Liberal arts people look down on social workers. That is an ugly fact. Social workers are so used to being looked down on by academics in the humanities—not to mention by government and private sector magnates—that they are surprised to hear that the "Interactional Skills" course, which they must all take in order to get a Master's Degree in Social Work, could be of use to people generally—to governments.

In the last three years of the twenty-three I spent in rural Minnesota, I began to study these Interactional Skills. I realized they would address at least three human evils of long standing: fear of making sacrifices for the community, fear of losing face if one speaks one's heart's truth, and fear of carrying on a frank conversation with a perceived enemy.

When the Iowa Humanities Board asked me to give their second annual talk, I decided to tell them about how a set of skills, which people have scarcely heard of, and which come to us from a corner we scarcely glance at, can help life in our little towns as well as in high places.

Brief Warm-up Writing Exercises

1. Write down a list of stereotypes about small towns and small-town people.
2. Now write as many *true* sentences as you can about small towns.
3. Describe an incident in which you felt put down by what someone said or did.

DRAFT

IOWA
HUM
Final ①

<u>Small towns: A Closer Look</u>

1. Let me say at the start that I <u>like</u> small-town life.

   Not everyone does. People lie about it HHH in Madison.

2. I like the lostness of midwest towns, too.
   Not the pretty, stony fields of Maine being bought up by brokers before Oct 19.

   <u>Ralph Slippy</u> — Lois's burnt arms
   Narrowed eyes
   sea of corn — our inland sea
   so hot the air constantly shook
   over the tassels
   Where are the Pilgrims? Is this what they had in mind?
   The delicate, cultural things I read about in college —
   Belgian women working lace on their aprons
   —the HUGE HISTORICAL MOMENTS...

3. Well, what's an historical moment?
   A red-faced farmer doing a speech, asking for a crop strike. Memorizing jokes...
   —John Ball in 14th c. England

IOWA HUM *Final* (1½)

4. And a second historical moment—

    Church basement. Someone's dad has died.
    Our aprons. Ground ham
    Tolling. Cars.

    The widow says, "I guess I never realized..."

5. We have heard those remarks—thousands of them
    "If I'd known then what..."
    "You don't know until you've been thr...",
    and "How would I know what goes on in her mind!"

    They say: one can't imagine...

6. Yet life is for <u>all</u> of us— life <u>imagined</u> in time so
    we live it before it's late—
SO WHAT WE GIVE TALKS ABOUT IS THE THINGS THAT NEED CHANGE

7. If that is true—not just rhetoric for a cold
    night in Greene County, what can we do to
    take hold of our lives? And make them
        — More spirited?
        — More frankly political?
            (Politics = other c̄ more than
        — More imaginative? 3)

IOWA HUM
②
Final

8. When I lived in western Minn, I was aware of our dislike of people who came from cities with a plan for us.
   We sneered.
   We said there was 0 wrong.

9. But the fact is,

   • We don't talk to one another v. happily.
     PUT DOWNS to new ideas

   • We are so afraid of disagreement, that we stick to small talk.

     Talk re delivering babies —
     "All I can say is, it looks like more snow. They can forecast what they like." instead of "God it'd be wonderful if you would shut up."

   • Or we settle for sensational distractions — ax murders — farm accidents before the cornhead had a feeder-reverser so you needn't dislodge stuck cobs with your arm.
     Or thrilling instances—true or not—of medical malpractice.

IOWA HUM.
③

5. There's not much true humanity in relating sensational info to one another.

> ● Confucius, 6th c. B.C., said the emperor Yao dressed simply and
>
> ● gave no attention to uncommon things or great happenings, nor did he value those things that were rare and peculiar."

The slight thrill of such talk is a substitute for real involvement in the conversation —

> ● and also, in those horrific events, we weren't there so the sec. after the thrill, you feel a pang of down-put — low self-image.

low self-image

6. So how shall we start to talk to each other
 ● with higher spirits?
 ● on more interesting subject? politics?
 ● on the real cares of our own lives?

↓

IOWA HUM ④

6½: <u>To stop the put-down conversations:</u>

7. We need a cure for <u>put-down</u> conversations and there is one. This is not one of those all-too-frequ griefs — which people carefully identify and then — from scratch — must forge tools for cure. The cure <u>is there</u>.

- Dial story   re courtesy + encour
- I in the end was all the <u>more</u> convinced.

8. The cure is to use 2 STEPS of current family-therapy practice — in all we do and everyone we talk to.

a) Listen for DATA
             FEELING
           + MEANING
b) Ask them a <u>FURTHER</u> ? about it.
      Always. So they can particularize.
c) Have a mental <u>picture</u> in yr head —

9. Don't be surprised if you feel a lot of resistance to this.
- I've lectured to psych + SWrs.
  Access = problem
- Who wants anything to do w SWrs?
             Not classy

IOWA
HUM
(1)

10. Tell re Hvd Med Sch's CTR FOR PSYCH. STUDIES IN A NUCLEAR AGE Dr Richard Chasin

   — 1987 Congress of Internat'l Physicians for Prevention of Nuclear War
   1493 Cambridge St
   02139

11. Let me give you an example of the NEW WAY we could talk to each other

   — remember — asking for data, feeling, meaning
   — making a mental image of it?

   Let us say we are sitting in the VFW Lounge —
     * Post commander is there
     * A failed woman who is sergeant-at-arms
     * Ralph, the careless farmhand
     * Lois, strong arms on the booth table
     * Ralph's wife, who always tells him to shut it
       Mrs Slippy

   — I know the post cdr thinks I'm a communist wtr.

   Suddenly Ralph says, "You know, them environmentalists are a bunch of communists!"

IOWA
HUM
6

Ralph's wife says, "Ralph you just shut it."

Post cdr: "I've heard there is some communism in those guys, though."

take them
thru the
conversation
{ I sue the lot — use post cdr
... Silver, his
light-colored lab...

12. How odd it sounds — to ask a thoughtful group of people to start using a family-therapy process!

→ To question people carefully when you feel like sneering — and to claim that this will help small-town life — and bring world peace!

13. In beginning I said 'The historical moment is for followers... The advice comes from the outside —

LEMMING CONDITION

1 ❖ Let me say straight off that I prefer Midwestern small towns and Midwestern countryside to cities. Human beings don't benefit from access to culture nearly so much as we pretend: children clinging high up in the bendy windbreak trees do better to imagine airships and classical storms than to be shown the Turners and Corots. And adults who never miss a serious play at the Guthrie and who have known and liked Schubert's work for decades are still perfectly capable of promoting insane public policies. Art does not keep us from running organizations which hurt the common well-being of ourselves and our planet.

2 Nor does nature, of course. People can spend all their lives among heavy woods and mist-thickened fields or on the edge of the sea and still never have a numinous idea nor any measurable urge to sacrifice self for the common good. Nature simply doesn't teach compassion. In some of the most beautiful places on our planet—the Carpathians, the steep sides of the Aegean, along the Nile—people have spent thousands of years being cruel to the pack animals who serve them.

3 If neither culture nor nature has nearly enough humane influence on us, why bother saying I prefer country to city? It is because I want to tell a truth where so many people lie. Speakers, especially, are forever "affirming the values of rural life." They assure us they will "get rid of the old stereotypes of the farmer" or the "old stereotypes of the pastoral life." Absurd: the old stereotypes have long since been got rid of by writers, artists, and sociologists. Films which claim to show the *real* country tend still to present farm people as people who feel no emotions about anything except the fate of their land. The films preserve the stereotype of farmers as people who care only for practicality.

4 There is no particular damage done by trendy attitudes towards rural life—at least not so long as these attitudes do not prevent our seeing genuine chances to make good changes. I am going to talk to you tonight about a twentieth-century psychological or socio-psychological process which I believe can make a marvelous transformation in rural life. It has to do with de-stereotyping, but on a sophisticated level. I am convinced that if we try some of the most sophisticated family-therapy processes of our time, *in our rural towns,* we can make changes which we all long for. If we love the countryside, we do long for more expressiveness and freedom.

5 Half the people who say they love the country really don't. My town, Madison, Minnesota, was charmed by a remark Hubert Humphrey made when he visited us several years ago. He started his talk by saying he did not like farming and he didn't want to live in a farmtown, and that if he did like farming and farmtowns he'd be farming and living among us. He told us he liked politics and he liked being in Washington. It was a fine breath of fresh air.

6 It also means, however, that if a speaker or writer doesn't much love the countryside, he or she won't be keen on suggesting psychological changes for us. We don't suggest psychological work except where our heart is: that's why

the best skills in interpersonal communication are practiced in group and family therapy: people's hearts are in their groups and families. In an era in which psychotherapy is leaping forward in wonderful bounds, we want to be sure to use some of it if we can. To regard country problems as merely practical (a typical city view of rural life) and not a potential user of psychological savvy is like saying—in the 1920s—that we need to rub the carriage wheels with graphite, or we need to breed faster carriage horses, instead of saying: Look, there's a new technology around here. It's called the internal combustion engine.

7   When I say I love farmtowns and the countryside I mean the towns and landscape of the Middlewest, not the picturesque ex-farms of New England, where the ancient, piled stonefence-line is kept neat by the broker or executive who owns it. I like two qualities of the Midwest which most people consider its greatest drawbacks: I like the physical lostness of the corn and soybean fields, and I like the psychological lostness of our population. We are not holding the major powerlines. We haven't much data base. Our habit is not to start changes, but to keep our chins up. We do not often look like wonderful "leadership material." If it weren't for twentieth-century process psychology, we could be written off as *followers* and clean-cut citizenry who aren't on the fast track for affecting their own ethical life, let alone national ethical life.

8   We seem simply to have to enjoy our wide sky of stars as it comes over us after the hot day's work. At night we make the best of stars: they are what we have instead of an horizonful of sea. They are our immensity. I remember finishing a day of fieldwork one hot September evening. I stood on the farm stoop with my sister-in-law. We watched a hired hand, whom I'll call Jack Slippy, bring in a disk. Jack was a man who lost more equipment in the fields than anyone else. He didn't raise the gangs on the disk, so its full width, all the wonderful sharp bottoms like cymbals, were smashing every second on the rutty road. When he got to the top of the farmyard, he made the corner around the old corncrib too tight. He let himself clip it a little, because he knew we were watching. Then he gave us, over his shoulder, the wide grin of the perfect slob.

9   My sister-in-law muttered something appropriate, and I thought, where are all the delicate cultural subjects I learned in college? Where are the Belgian women making lace on their firm aprons? Where are the huge historical moments? And what is an historical moment? Here are two. First, a farmer, a married person, is going to make his first speech asking for a crop strike. It will be either a wise or an unwise speech. He has his ironed khaki pants and an ironed, flowered sports shirt lying on the hot, double bed, in the hot, breathless, summer-oppressed little farmhouse. He is memorizing jokes which are slightly off-color, because Jack or someone who knew Jack who took a Dale Carnegie course has told him that you get the audience with you if you tell a "story." He plans to start with this remark: "I hope you won't mind if I tell you a little story." We will all be delighted: those of us who love distasteful stories know that whatever the young farmer offers will be mild stuff compared to

what we hear in the VFW Lounge. On the other hand, it is better than nothing. Those of us who don't go along with bad taste will make an exception this once: we get sick of our lives of saving our best aprons for serving at church, vacuuming out the family car after the men went and used the backseat for bringing in busted parts.

10   When he gets through with the joke, the young farmer will ask the audience to take control of their crop marketing. That is the historical moment, just as surely as the great speeches of John Ball were historical moments for fourteenth-century English farmers. We haven't got John Ball's wonderful rhetoric:

When Adam delved
And Eve span,
Who was then
The gentle-man?

But we have the same issue: making leaders out of followers.

11   There is the leader in each of us. That is the part which decides to change how human beings behave on their planet. There is also the follower in each of us: that is the part which too much respects how people have done this or that in the past. Twentieth-century learning of social and psychological skills shows us that people who once saw all change as frightening and hopeless, can be shown how to become people whose curiosity is greater than their fear of change and whose willingness to take a risk is greater than their sense of hopelessness. Twentieth-century psychological savvy says that once-diffident people can learn to see some risky project as so intriguing that they will chance a failure or two. If psychological savvy can turn a blocked person into a free person, and it sometimes can, then we need to say that we now have the savvy sometimes to turn a follower into a leader. We need, in fact, to associate the notion of *leadership* with *psychological good health*.

12   Here is a second historical moment—this time not a good one like the young farmer's girding himself to make a speech. We are in the church basement, where the doors swing between the Fellowship Hall and the kitchen. Jack Slippy's dad has died at seventy-six. In the church kitchen the long shining tables are covered with rows of round plates. The plates are piled with bun sandwiches covered with waxed paper until the very last minute. Inside each bun is a generous helping of funeral-sandwich spread. It is ground ham, ground hard-cooked egg, ground onion, some mayonnaise, and one-fourth cup of cream. Far up in the tower the bell has begun tolling. That means the funeral service for Mr. Slippy is over and the funeral director and his helpers are organizing all the cars so they will take off for the cemetery in somber, efficient order. The funeral director is putting little lavender flags on the front left fenders. The tolling tells us that it is time to change from our regular,

flower-printed work aprons into our white, lacy best serving aprons: we roll up the work aprons and jam them onto the kitchen hall shelf with our purses and jackets. People too old to get wind-chilled at the cemetery are drifting into the Fellowship Hall. Soon everyone will be back, and we will serve, making sure that everyone, especially the family's out-of-town relationship, get plenty to eat and plenty of coffee. I see Jack Slippy in a different light now: he is now two men. He is still our no-good hired hand who wrecked more machinery than anyone else, but he is also a human being who has lost his dad.

13 Eventually people begin to file past the table end where Jack's mother is sitting. If the people are uneasy in formal occasions they will give her their hand and simply say the word "Sympathy" in a very low voice. If they are comfortable in formal occasions, they will make her a little gentle speech. And then—here is the bad historical moment—Mrs. Slippy suddenly says, "I guess I never realized how much he meant to me until he was taken away."

14 It doesn't sound like much of a remark to fret over. We have heard such remarks—thousands of them. "I guess I didn't understand the value of such-and-such until it was gone." Or "You don't know what such-and-such an experience is unless you've been through it yourself." Or "If only I'd known *then* what I know now . . ." What those remarks say is, "We can't imagine life as we are living it. Imagination is nothing: only experience informs you. We waste life because we can't imagine when young what will be factual knowledge when we are old."

15 The remarks show a shocking abdication from lively mentality. Socrates wasn't mistaken in saying the unexamined life wasn't worth living. He assumed people can examine life as it goes along. He assumed one could reflect along the way. If people bother to reflect, it means they believe that imagination, as well as experience, is a teacher—a very cultivated and hope-giving and life-giving idea. If such an idea is not just rhetoric for a sharp autumn evening in Greene County, Iowa, we need to look at it seriously and consider how to put it into practice. If imagination is what is missing from rural habit, how shall we welcome it into our lives and work it up, the way a captain would want to work up a new ship someone brought into the harbor?

16 Let's ask in which ways we are not imaginative enough: we know we don't talk to one another with high enough spirits. We make hundreds and hundreds of low-spirited remarks to one another. Someone tells us a new idea: we put it down. We also *summarize* one another's conversations. Someone tells us an incident, and instead of replying in wonder: "Is that right? Is that really true? Did you really say that? Right there in front of all those people—amazing!" we start to *summarize* with "It just goes to show you." Or "That's what you can expect if you talk like that." Or we offer: "All you can do is go with the flow, I guess." Those summarizings are killers. All the joy in the room drops.

17 Likely all three of our unimaginative ways of talking to one another come of fear. We have been told that if there is open disagreement in a small town, the town will "polarize" or "the town will be blown wide open." I have never been able to picture what that would mean—having the town blown wide

open. It sounds wonderful: gentle-spoken members of the Ministerium have it out with each other openly about the women's shelter project! Heretofore stuffy business people stand in hostile groups along Main Street! Or the School Board has gone as a body to the nearest mental health outlet! It is very hard to imagine a sensible farmtown "blown wide open."

18 To prevent it, we have three kinds of conversation that are destructive of our happiness. First, we hastily summarize one another's conversations, as I have mentioned. How rude that is—without our acknowledging it! I say to you, "I saw a cat this morning, which had been struck by a car. It was trying to fling itself up off its side, on the highway. It was obviously dying, but it was trying to live." You reply: "Well, that's the sort of thing that's bound to happen when animals cross major roads." Your tone says: it is simply a practical matter. Don't waste your time with any *feeling* about the cat. Your tone says: feeling is simply useless *affect*. To see the force of this low-key summarizing and discounting, imagine children growing to the age of fourteen and fifteen and having every conversation they try on their parents and teachers be met only with wrap-up philosophies. It tells the child that wrap-up philosophies, with their flat half-interest and slight putdown, are correct—and high emotional response is not.

19 Our second bad conversational habit is that we scarcely venture out of *small talk*. It is important to realize that small talk lessens intimacy: it is not a tool of love. It is a tool of truce. When Kitty and Levin finally find each other, in *Anna Karenina,* they do not say, "You can see where someone sure didn't use enough Brass-O on the samovar!" They talk about love.

20 I have a sharp memory of small talk. I had just had a baby, safely in the small-town hospital, and now was watching a blizzard go endlessly, endlessly, solid white, past my window. All day I lay watching that snow; it looked as if it were coming unslowed all the way from Hudson's Bay. I daydreamed about it and about the baby. I was so happy that I was a little unsteady—unreliable. You wouldn't want such a person to add up columns of figures for you. Late in the afternoon a woman who had her baby two or three days before shuffled into my room. I instantly asked her to describe *her* delivery. I knew it would be unbearably self-centered if I told her about mine, straight off, but I thought I would have *earned* the right to talk about it, if I heard her out first. I wanted to hear it all—labor, delivery, stories of any other deliveries she had had. So I burst out at her from the bed, "What was your delivery like?" She gave me a look as ancient as the planet. She said, "This is another one they didn't forecast! You can say what you like about how good those forecasts are; if you ask me they don't know any better than guesswork! Look at that!" she said. We both looked out the window.

21 She hated my excitement and she certainly didn't intend to let me jubilantly pry details of her baby's birth from her. So she practiced the time-honored means of "negative reinforcement": she changed the subject from an intense, personal one, to an impersonal small-talk subject *par excellence*—the weather. If she had had one tiny lesson in interactional skills she would have

known how to handle someone like me. She would have said, in a quiet but communicative tone, "Gee, it certainly would be wonderful if you would shut up just this once."

22   Our third bad conversational habit is to settle for telling one another about *sensational events* that have nothing to do with our own lives—ax murders, farm accidents where some poor operator tried to clear out a stuck corncob, back before the picking heads had the feeder-reverser feature. Or best of all, the thrilling circumstances of medical malpractice. "They opened him up because they thought he was full of cancer but when they got in there they found a whole towel wadded up, that was marked *USS Mississippi.*"

23   There is a slight thrill to such stories. For a moment one can feel a *frisson* about the farm accident or the legendary surgical glitch, but in the end, the conversation drops our self-image lower than it was before. That is because we were not *there* in the accident or aboard ship. It is one more piece of conversation that has nothing personal to do with us. While doing a study of liberal-arts theory for Hamline University, I once added up the number of hours a college graduate has to be awake and alive, outside of work-hours or sleep-hours. If you graduate at 21 and live to be 95, work 8 hours a day between age 21 and age 65, taking regular two-week holidays throughout the working years, you have about 162,000 waking hours of life not needed for work. It sounds rather a finite number. It makes the hours sound rather precious, as if a few of them as possible should be devoted to mere pleasantries. Confucius had great respect for the ancient emperor Yao, who Confucius said "gave no attention to uncommon things or great happenings, nor did he value those things that were rare and peculiar." Confucius was saying that to a person interested in living, the things of everyday life are proper grist. One doesn't need sensation. One doesn't and shouldn't need to be thrilled at a distance. . . .

24   I have described three ways in which we damage one another's self images, day in and day out. Let me now describe two very simple, very basic social-work family-therapy processes which will be new to most Americans.

   1. When someone has just spoken, we decide to ask him or her questions, which will give us more *data* about the subject. These questions will also help that person refine or enlarge or correct the original remark. When we have found out more data, we will ask questions to find out what *feeling* the person has—and we will ask him or her if we have understood the data and the feeling correctly.
   2. All the time that anyone is speaking, we will energetically try to make a mental image of the scene being described. It means rather desperate listening, if you are not used to it.

25   The above two ideas sound like ordinary common sense and manners. In fact they are rarely practiced. Most Americans, for example, have never been asked a question about anything they have just said. They have never talked to a listener who wants them to enlarge a little on their first idea. Their

half-conscious minds have never got the message: "Oh—hear that! Someone is interested! Well!—in that case, I have stranger, more interesting less conventional things to say! I just didn't want to bring them out before, lest someone sneer or make light of them!" . . .

26   Let us say we are sitting in a classical American small-town place. It is the VFW Lounge. Here we are, with the quarter-inch woodgrain panelling, the gold-color eagle over the bar. We can have set-ups or we can have bourbon and seven, or brandy and gingerale. We are crowded warmly into a booth. The Post Commander is there. He is a grumpy fellow, I think, who is nicer to his lion-colored labrador bitch than he is to people. There is a shy woman there who is sergeant-at-arms for the VFW Auxiliary. It is curious that diffident people do that job very well: they would not be so pushy as to serve up front at the Fairstand. They don't feel comfortable with the higher-ups who dominate the church circles making Dorcas Kits. But they can take hold in a womanly way at the VFW Auxiliary meetings. I have seen them carry our gigantic fifty stars around the room, squaring the corners of their march. If they had to, they could remove the flag from a coffin, fold it into the heart-breaking triangle, and take it firmly across the undertaker's green grasscloth and present it, on behalf of the President of the United States, to someone's widow.

27   Our sergeant-at-arms is sitting here cheerfully. Jack Slippy, a man who has recently lost his aged father, is here. We know him as the dumb hand who, if you put him up on a tractor, even a comparatively simple one like a Deere 3120, can do about $500 worth of damage in an hour. But now we know him also as a person dignified by a family death. A few of you—and I—are jammed into the booth. Finally, Jack's wife, Bernice, is here. Her style with Jack is this: whenever he opens his mouth to say anything, she nudges his elbow with her elbow—an easy act since all our elbows are on the table, and Bernice says to Jack, "You just shut it, Jack."

28   Perhaps we are getting a little sauced. Even so it is an uneasy alliance, because I know the Post Commander probably thinks I am a communist. There are two levels of communist: there is an outright communist and then there is "some kind of a communist."

29   Suddenly Jack Slippy says "You know, those environmentalists are a bunch of communists!"

30   Bernice shoves her elbow into his elbow. "Jack, you just shut it," she says promptly.

31   The Post Commander says, "I've heard that some of those guys are pretty pink, though." He adds, "If you ask me."

32   This is a conversation in which none of the traditional humanities behaviors work well. If I assign to Jack the stereotype of ignorant, hostile plebe, I have dishonored him and done nothing to make any change. Worse, at the moment when I assign *him* some role like that, I am assigning *myself* the role of educated truth-knower and superior person—and that does me no good. When Bernice Slippy tells Jack to shut it, she is simply acting out of old, bad small-town values: do not talk about politics or religion. And worse, when your

husband says something with any intensity, call it off somehow. The sergeant-at-arms is enacting another small-town value: she is saying nothing because she believes that talk, whether about communists or environmentalists, isn't much.

33   I have decided to exercise my poor beginner's grasp at social-work skills.

34   "Which environmentalists did you mean, Jack?" I ask. "The ones in our county or the ones in Carver County?"

35   Jack says: "I just mean generally. Bunch of commies." Then he realizes that sounds dumb, so he gets redder in the face. "All I know," he says loudly, "is they are wrecking everything for the farmer."

36   The Post Commander says they are a bunch of city slicks who don't understand rural problems.

37   "Did you mean the environmentalists working on the slough project?" I ask. I look at Jack, since he brought it up, and he has the most noticeable feeling of anyone in the booth.

38   "All I know is," Jack shouts, "we're going to lose everything that means anything to Americans!"

39   Then he adds, "If the bank takes your relatives' farm I'm going to lose my job."

40   I recognize the first accurate thing that has been said. I also recognize genuine anger.

41   "I'd be very mad if I were going to lose my farm. Or lose my job. I'd be *very* mad," I say. "I'd also be scared, I think."

42   Jack looks at me with his jerking eyebrows. Various emotions go by like freight in his face. He looks angry still, and a little pleased, and generally pleasantly excited.

43   Now I am guessing everyone is thinking about anger and something that makes them angry. I am looking at the sergeant-at-arms, trying to guess: if she is angry about something what would that be? I pretend I am the sergeant-at-arms and I think, "So how would you like to live in this town all your life and serve in the Auxiliary and in Aid all these years and been canning for forty years if you count the summer I started helping my mother—how would you feel if some city girl, some hot-shot Home Extension agent, came to your Homemakers' Meeting and told everyone it was dangerous to do open-kettle canning? Who does she think she is with her permanent around the sides and back, and then a regular old heinie haircut in the front so she looks crazy? She is pretty, and young, and not yet tired. Anyone can do canning if they have all the fancy equipment she's got."

44   I am still day-dreaming through a possible anger for the sergeant-at-arms, when the Post Commander says, "I got to say that *everything* the environmentalists do isn't all that bad." He adds: "They are preserving the slough. I go in there a lot with Silver."

45   I swing into a question for him, for fear he will stop talking, "Is Silver your tan-colored labrador?"

46   "Silver and I," he says, "we go in there, not just to hunt, either. We go in

there pretty much all year round. She gets up birds for the fun. When it's frozen we go in on the ice."

47   The sergeant-at-arms says, "Dogs are funny on ice. They try to hang on with their toenails but they lose it anyway."

48   "We go in there," the Post Commander says, "and it is very beautiful in there."

49   What happened in this conversation, I think, is that anger which was being genuinely felt got inappropriately attached to communists and environmentalists. The anger itself, however, was genuine. It needed a little quiet questioning in order for the anger to move over to where it really belonged—about losing farm jobs. Then, when the anger was spoken about accurately, it was laid to rest: when we talk accurately about anger, much of its desperate quality disappears. It leaves space for other emotions to come take their usual, obliging places in our heads. In this conversation, the Post Commander found space to remember that he enjoys nature. Love of nature entered the booth. Amusement at dogs entered the booth. We had a mental image of the slough.

50   I have tried to move several such conversations from the original, hostile, projective remark about some supposed enemy to a particular, accurate estimate of the same subject. The invariable side effect has been gradual, affectionate recall of some more positive experience—such as prowling about a slough. The pleasant anecdote, however, never shows up until the original hostile feeling has been questioned, allowed to settle, to find its proper level. Surely—if such pathetically simple, beginners' procedures as I know of can make such change—surely it would be wise to learn all the social-work skills we can! . . .

51   We know what the blessings of country and small-town life are. They don't need reiteration. It is our griefs that want change. We are in great luck that there are ready skills developed to improve interpersonal skills. Hard-working people have these skills ready to show us. Our feelings of fear or hopelessness are not eternal truths: they are simply where we happen to be stuck for now, and we can change them.

52   I commend the wonderful know-how of social work to us all. Let's have a go at any good changes we can make, so that our lives in our countryside will be examined, reflective and passionate, and so we can take more confident action in the urgent affairs of our planet. ❖

Questions to Ponder

1. Does the first sentence of Carol Bly's essay seem to be true and strong?
2. What hard truths does Carol Bly offer in her author's note? In her essay? Do you agree with these assertions?
3. Why does Carol Bly's use of specific details of small-town life (a John Deere 3120 tractor, for example) enhance her credibility? What additional functions do such vivid specific details serve?

4. Why do you think people resort to summarizing other people's conversations, talking about sensational faraway events, or retreating into small talk rather than speaking about the truths of their hearts?
5. How does asking questions allow people to attach their feelings to their appropriate causes?
6. Does Carol Bly's blunt speaking strike you as refreshing? Is her speech an example of the practice she is advocating?

Writing Possibilities

1. Take one of the true sentences you wrote on small-town or country life in warm-up writing exercise 2 and use it as the start of an essay on the subject.
2. Take the "put down" incident you wrote about in warm-up writing exercise 3 and, using Carol Bly's essay as a model, *re-present* the incident and how it might have been salvaged or improved using Bly's questioning techniques.
3. Using Bly's essay as a model, choose another group (besides social workers and small-town residents) who are underrated by certain members of society. Defend these people in a passionate or witty essay.
4. Now turn and write blunt and vivid sentences about large cities. (*Hint:* What is rarely said about them?)

Student Essay

LABOR UNIONS: A PART OF OUR PAST OR FUTURE?

Cori McNeilus

The hardest part of writing for me is getting started. (I even fussed about what I was going to say in this headnote!) As a result, I do a lot of brainstorming and freewriting when I begin. I make lists of topics or phrases from my research, which may or may not be relevant, in order to get my thoughts moving. From these lists I make a rough outline, which provides a general order for my gathered information. Next, instead of logically trying to determine the best way to begin, I simply "go with it" and start writing. After a few pages I can relax because I am done with the difficult aspect of organization and into the fun part of writing.

Writing this essay was a challenging experience for me. I first became interested in the subject when a family member was involved with a company facing an attempted union organization. At the same time I was also taking a labor economics course, which covered labor unions. As a result, this paper gave me an opportunity to learn more about a topic that personally interested me.

Once my first draft was finished, I shared it with a writing group. I then revised and polished the essay over a period of two months, sharing each new version with the group to see if I was coming closer to meeting their needs. In response to readers' comments, I changed my opening to a blunt but true (and I hope striking) summary declaration. Indeed, I shortened my whole introduction while lengthening my essay's conclusion to acknowledge recent union successes and to try to offer more constructive suggestions for future union development. Along the way I changed the order of two of my essay's sections and broadened two section headings to make them more precise. ("Lack of Leadership" became "Unions' Failure to Adapt," and "Management Changes" became "Management and Public Policy Changes.") I also added more transitional phrases to smooth the movement of the essay from one point to the other. (See the section on "Demographic Changes" in particular). Group members also repeatedly challenged me to make my use of statistics as fair *and clear and possible, and to find other examples of union corruption besides the cases involving the Teamsters. All these changes strengthened my essay.*

For me, the most fascinating thing about my writing is that I have never considered myself a good writer! I have so many problems getting started; I pick over my wording incessantly, and I am never quite satisfied with the finished piece. Nevertheless, writing is a challenge I personally enjoy, for it is an expression of myself.

Brief Warm-up Writing Exercises

1. Freewrite your honest opinion about labor unions.
2. Brainstorm two lists: (1) the benefits of labor unions and (2) the challenges labor unions face.
3. Describe any experiences you have had with labor unions—as a member or a nonmember.

DRAFT

1. Many countries experienced a tremendous growth in technology during the industrial revolution between 1750 and 1850. As industry replaced handicrafts and factories emerged, a need arose for some form of protection for the workers who put in long hours in unsafe conditions. In the twentieth century, labor unions filled this void and strove to protect the worker. They emerged as a strong force on the side of the worker and firmly entrenched themselves as guardians of the management-employee relationship. Although the total labor force has been increasing since 1970, the number of union members in 1985 (eighteen million) is below the 1970 level of twenty-one point four million (Kovach, 1985, p. 850). The percentage of the work force in labor unions has been falling from 42 percent in 1954, 24.7 percent in 1970, 20.9 percent in 1980 (Craver, 1985, p. 210) to 16.7 percent in 1989 (Oliver, 1989).

2. Recent periods of economic decline have not helped the union situation, even though unions traditionally fare well during these periods. Therefore, union membership must increase by five hundred thousand a year in order to maintain pace with a two percent growth in the work force. However, the percentage of workers belonging to the

union is expected to decline to ten percent by 1995 (Taylor, 1989, p. 31).

What factors contributed to the decline in union membership? Several theories have been put forward to explain the decline. Those that will be discussed in this paper include: the shift from blue-collar industry dominance to white collar service dominance; increased foreign competition; increased number and percentage of women and minorities in the work force; increased government and management power over unions; and decreased leadership effectiveness. All of these factors culminated in decreased membership, decreased dues, and decreased economic power and political influence. This is witnessed by the lifting of some import quotas such as those on Japanese cars and by two more states adopting right-to-work laws since 1981 (Kovach, 1985, p. 851).

Causes

Industry Changes

In recent years, the composition of the available jobs has been changing as a shift has occurred from a predominately manufacturing society to a service-oriented society. Manufacturing jobs, the traditional stronghold of organized labor, now constitutes only 38 percent of the work force. In comparison, 42 percent of the work force is white collar and technical and 20 percent consists of craftsmen and supervisors (Carrel, 1989, p. 545). A Department of Labor Study predicts that manufacturing will generate no new jobs in the next thirteen years and as a result its contribution to GNP will be less than seventeen percent by the year 2000 (Willis, 1988, p. 14).

The increase in service jobs is problematic for organized labor since service and white collar jobs are not as receptive to unions as manufacturing once was. Of all the service workers in the work force only ten percent are unionized (Taylor, 1989, p. 31). This is a frightening figure for unions in light of the nine million new jobs in service areas such as health care, finance, real estate, and insurance (Willis, 1988, p. 14). In order to increase membership, white collar and high tech sectors must become unionized. This is especially true since most of the already organized blue collar industries have been facing a decreasing proportion of union employees. In 1961, 73 percent of blue collar industry was unionized compared to 51 percent in 1984 (Carrel, 1989, p. 521). Yet, unions are seen as too bureaucratic and seniority based for many white collar workers who have pro-management aspirations.

6   One of the causes of the decline in blue collar jobs has been increased automation. As computer-integrated robotics spreads, most manufacturing jobs will no longer be done by humans. This trend leads to a wider gap between management and the unskilled workers who lack the power to exert economic influence through strikes. As a result, industrial workers, the largest occupational group for both men and women back in 1925, have lost political power as their proportion of the total work force has declined (Drucker, 1989, p. 17).

Global Changes

7   In an increasingly global economy, U.S. industry has lost its competitive edge due to increased foreign competition. Preference for cheaper foreign goods by consumers has led industry to make several attempts to lower prices. One alternative by industry has been a large movement to the Sun Belt. In this area there is more anti-union sentiment and more right-to-work legislation. Lower labor costs in these nonunion areas allows the companies an improved chance to compete with foreign goods.

8   On an international scale, some business enterprises are becoming multinational in an effort to find lower labor costs. Also, traditional bargaining techniques fail to work against multinational corporations. If the workers strike, the company can transfer production to a division in another country, thus broadening the companies power base. It is

estimated that by 1990 most of the noncommunist world trade will be done by only three hundred companies, two-thirds of which are American (Craver, 1985, p. 213).

9   Another global change affecting unions has been the increased growth of foreign companies producing here in the U.S. For example, Japanese automakers Nissan and Toyota both have production facilities in the nonunion South. Unions failed to organize Nissan in Tennessee last July after trying for the past six years. The failure is blamed on the fact that Nissan workers earn similar wages and benefits to union workers and have not been laid off for the past ten years.

Demographic Changes

10   Changing demographics have caused higher participation in the work force from groups that are not traditionally unionized. The Hudson study predicts that between now and the year 2000 five-sixths of the new workers will be women, minority groups, and immigrants. Of those, 66 percent will be women and 29 percent will be nonwhite (Willis, 1988, p. 15). In addition, in 1950 only 24 percent of married women were in the labor force. This rose to 46 percent in 1977. Also, in 1960 30 percent of mothers worked compared to over 50 percent in 1985 (Craver, 1985, p. 211). As female participation as a percentage of the labor force increases, a problem arises for unions since only 13 to 16 percent of women workers were organized between 1878 and 1985. This is compared to 28 percent for men during this same time period (Kovach, 1985, p. 852).

11   For women, a large proportion are clumped into fields that are not highly organized such as; administrative, service, and high-tech jobs. Also, many women work part-time, temporarily, or change jobs and therefore do not view unions as helping them in the long run. Also, women may want child care and job training more than traditional union wage increases and job security. The combination of these three

factors may explain why women, an increasing percentage of the work force, are not highly organized.

12   Minorities and immigrants may resist unionization because they fear it will cost them their jobs. Faced with cultural obstacles, less education on average, and English as a second language, these people simply want to have job security. Paradoxically, this new group strongly resembles the groups which fostered the birth of unionism (Willis, 1988, p. 15). This situation provides unions with an opportunity to increase support.

Management Changes

13   Management today is more conscious of safety and health laws and is therefore more responsive to the needs of the worker than during the formative period of unions. Now, many companies have fair grievance procedures, a pleasant work environment, valid performance reviews for merit raises, and improved communication between management and workers (Carrel, 1989, p. 545). Combined with union's previous success in changing laws, almost everything that unions traditionally fought for is now law. These successes include; social security, unemployment compensation, health insurance, pension plans, child labor laws, minimum wage, occupational health and safety, and equal employment opportunities. As a consequence, government is performing the functions of protecting workers rather than the unions (Oliver, 1989). This may account for part of the decline in unionism since management and the government, rather than the unions, are now supplying the basic desires of the worker.

14   Also, modern workers want different things than their earlier counterparts. Unions must recognize this difference in order to survive. Previous union gains in wages and job security have made these demands irrelevant to today's young workers. Instead, white collar, better educated workers want better fringe benefits, personal satisfaction, and improved worker environments. Also, women,

immigrants, and uneducated minorities want child care and improved job training. Conventional union bargaining breaks down when negotiating for housing, job satisfaction, and good work environments.

Lack of Leadership Changes

15   The shift from the desires of blue collar to the desires of young "knowledge" workers has not been accompanied by a change in leadership rhetoric and idealogy which is still rooted in industrial tenets (Day, 1989, p. 19). As a result, union leaders are still using organizing techniques of the 1930-40's meant for blue collar workers. Leaders lack the exuberance and enthusiasm to get workers to participate. This may be due to leaders viewing their positions as simply jobs rather than causes to fight for (Kovach, 1985, p. 855). The result has been leaders losing contact with existing and potential members and striving for big business self-survival (Oliver, 1989). This unresponsiveness to their environment results in a lack of organization, a lack of a united front, outdated ideas, and shortsightedness.

16   Combined with the lack of motivational leadership, the public image of unions has faltered. Since 1957, the Gallup Poll's public approval rating of union labor has fallen from 76 percent to about 55 percent today (Willis, 1988, p. 14). This is partially due to young workers who view the traditional leaders as unresponsive to their needs, unorganized, and arrogant. Also, some people blame high wages, the resulting increase in prices and decrease in demand for American goods as the cause of the decline in the manufacturing industry. For example, the expensive wage contracts prior to the 1981-82 recession may have been part of the cause of the recession (Craver, 1985, p. 211).

17   Another aspect of the declining public image has been unethical leadership and numerous instances of corruption. For example, former teamster president, Jackie Presser, was indicted in 1988 for racketeering and embezzlement. In April of 1989, a former teamster

official appeared before a U.S. Senate Subcommittee concerning teamster ties to organized crime. To add insult to injury, Robert Holmes, a top Michigan Teamsters official who retired due to a racketeering lawsuit will receive an annual pension of two hundred five thousand, nine hundred sixty-four (Lippert, 1989, p. 3A).

Results

18 As a consequence of all these factors, the political power of labor unions has been drastically reduced. With employees already getting eighty percent of GNP in the form of wages in developed non-Communist countries, it is hard for them to maintain credibility and ask for more (Drucker, 1989, p. 18). The power of management combined with changes in the interpretation of labor laws are consequently aiding the union decline. For example, if a company files a bankruptcy petition, it can break the union contract and demand concessions if done in good faith. Also, a company can transfer production to a nonunion plant during the life of a contract if it is done for financial reasons and not anti-union reasons (Craver, 1985, p. 214).

19 The changes in labor law interpretations have decreased the number of enforcement personnel through decreased budgets. Also, in some instances Reagan appointees have reversed previous NLRB decisions regarding labor unions. For example, the NLRB ruled in the Milwaukee Spring Decision II, that an employer can relocate to a nonunion facility even if only to escape increased costs at a union plant, as long as this is not specifically stated in the labor agreement (Kovach, 1985, p. 853).

20 Other instances of decreased union power have occurred in the 1980's. In 1981 Reagan fired the striking members of the Professional Air Traffic Controllers Union. UAW, in 1982, agreed to three billion in wage concessions rather than losing their jobs. Eastern Airlines' 1989 strike forced the company into bankruptcy causing twenty thousand union members to lose their jobs. Amidst all of these occasions, public support was not on the side of the unions. As a result, contract wage

increases have fallen from 6.6 percent in 1982 to 2.8 percent in 1984. Far more common are wage concessions and givebacks. In the extreme cases some wage increases for nonunion members have exceeded wage increases for union members (Kovach, 1985, p. 854).

21 Due to the increasing cost of organizing workers, increasing power of employers, and the decreased cash flow for unions, there has been a wave of union mergers and acquisitions. Between 1979 and 1984 there have been thirty mergers with 35 percent of all mergers occurring since 1955 (Carrel, 1989, p. 544). Consequently, many subdivisions have closed and people have lost their jobs.

22 Another spiraling effect of decreased union power is the increased use of anti-union consultants. Hired to instruct management how to avoid unionization, consultants sometimes recommend unlawful techniques. Recently, the cost of unfair labor practice suits has been less than the cost of unionization for management. In 1970, approximately four thousand workers were unlawfully discharged. In 1980 over ten thousand workers were unlawfully discharged. Even when the companies were ordered to reinstate the workers, only 40 percent of the workers accepted and of those, 80 percent left within two years (Craver, 1985, p. 214).

Conclusion

23 As the nation prepares to enter a new decade, labor unions must look forward and adapt to changes rather than trying to fit new people, ideas, and demands into traditional molds. Unions serve a vital interest of representing workers and keeping management aware of worker's needs. They act as a buffer between the employees and management, but, they must be flexible. According to Peter F. Drucker,

> It [unions] might reinvent itself as the organ of society—and of the employing institution—concerned with building human potential and achievement, with optimizing the human resource altogether (1989, p. 22).

24   Unions must strive for a new cooperative role with management in order for the corporation to maintain a competitive edge. In this manner, the two can work together and jobs can be saved. Rather than a confrontational role unions should strive toward a participative management and employee involvement. Unions need to accept changing demographics, increased foreign competition, and the shift to service industries. They must recognize their ineffective leadership and the resulting decline in public perception and begin to work with a more responsive management.

Works Cited

Carrel, Michael K. and Kuzmits, Frank E. *Personnel Human Resource Management.* Columbus: Merrill Publishing Co., 1989, p. 514–601.

Craver, Charles B. "The Current and Future Status of Labor Organizations." *Labor Law Journal* 36 (April 1985): p. 210–225.

Day, Charles R. "We Shouldn't Let Unions Die." *Industry Week* 238 (March 20, 1989): p. 6.

Drucker, Peter F. "Will Unions Ever Again Be Useful Organs of Society?" *Industry Week* 238 (March 20, 1989): p. 17–22.

Kovach, Kenneth A. "Organized Labor's Deteriorating Condition." *Labor Law Journal* 36 (November 1985): p. 850–856.

Lippert, John. "Teamsters Official's Pension Decried." *Detroit Free Press* (February 18, 1989): p. 3A.

Nichols, Don. "Today's Unions: A Mixed Bag." *Management Review* 77 (February 1988): p. 43–44.

Nichols, Don. "Unions Play Catch-up to Today's Work Environment." *Management Review* 77 (February 1988): p. 28–29.

Personal interview with Jerry Oliver, 1 October 1989.

Taylor, Ronald A. "Why Organized Labor is Unlikely to Make a Comeback." *US News and World Report* (September 11, 1989): p. 31.

Letter to Home Shopping Network employees from Dennis Wetherell, 8 September 1989.

Willis, Rod. "Can American Unions Transform Themselves?" *Management Review* 77 (February 1988): p. 14–21.

---

1 In the past two decades unions have fallen upon hard times. Although the total labor force has been increasing since 1970, the number of union members in 1988 (17 million) (Bauman 1989, p. 4) is below the 1970 level of 21.4 million (Kovach 1985, p. 850). The percentage of the work force in labor unions has fallen from a high of 42 percent in 1954 (Carrel 1989, p. 545) to 16.8 percent in 1988 (Bauman 1989, p. 4). Furthermore, the percentage of workers belonging to unions is expected to decline to 10 percent by 1995 (Taylor 1989, p. 31).

2 Several factors have contributed to the decline of labor unions. They include the shift from blue-collar industry dominance to white-collar service industry dominance; increased foreign competition; the increased number and percentage of women and minorities in the work force; increased government and management power over unions; and the decreased effectiveness of union leadership. As a result of these factors, union membership has fallen and the economic power and political influence of organized labor has been drastically reduced.

Industry Changes

3 In recent years, the composition of available jobs in the United States has been changing as a shift has occurred from a predominately manufacturing-oriented economy to a service-oriented economy. Currently, U.S. manufacturing employs approximately 40.5 million workers as compared to approximately 69.5 million workers in wholesale, retail trade and service industries (Bauman 1989, p. 7). It is predicted that there will be no net increase in manufacturing jobs in the next ten years (Willis 1988, p. 14). As a result, manufacturing's contribution to Gross National Product will be less than 17 percent by the year 2000 (Willis 1988, p. 14) as compared to 25 percent in 1970 and 18 percent in 1987 (Economic Report of the President 1989, p. 320). The number of manufacturing employees who are unionized has been falling both proportionately and absolutely. In 1961, 73 percent of blue-collar industry was unionized compared to 51 percent in 1984 (Carrel 1989, p. 521).

4 Historically, service and white-collar workers have not been as receptive to unions as manufacturing employees. Of all the service and white-collar

workers in the work force only 10 percent are unionized (Taylor 1989, p. 31). This is a frightening figure for unions since the AFL-CIO's Committee on the Evolution of the Workforce predicted in 1985 that by 1995, 75 percent of all workers will be in the service industries (Carrel 1989, p. 545). In order to increase membership, union leaders must unionize white-collar and high-tech sectors.

Global Changes

5   In an increasingly global economy, U.S. industry is confronted with increased foreign competition. Increased consumer preference for foreign goods has led U.S. industry to make several efforts to lower costs. Some companies have moved plants to the Sun Belt states where there is more anti-union sentiment and more right-to-work legislation. Lower labor costs in these nonunion areas allow companies an improved chance to compete with foreign goods.

6   Some business enterprises are also becoming multinational in an effort to find lower labor costs. Traditional union bargaining techniques fail to work against multinational corporations. For instance, if the workers strike, the company can transfer production to a division in another country, thus broadening the company's power base.

7   Another global change affecting unions has been the increased growth of foreign companies producing in the United States. Japanese automakers Nissan and Toyota, for example, both have production facilities in the nonunion South. Unions failed to organize Nissan in Tennessee in July 1989 after trying for the previous six years. This failure was partially blamed on the fact that Nissan workers earn wages and benefits similar to union workers and have not been laid off for the past ten years (Taylor 1989, p. 31).

Demographic Changes

8   Union membership has also fallen victim to changing demographics. It is predicted that between 1990 and the year 2000, 83 percent of new workers will fall into the overlapping categories of women, minority groups, and immigrants. In 1960, 30 percent of all adult females worked compared to over 50 percent in 1985 (Craver 1985, p. 211). As female participation as a percentage of the labor force increases, the problem of organizing women arises for unions since unionized women workers were only from 13 to 16 percent of the labor force between 1978 and 1985. This is compared to 28 percent for men during this same time period (Kovach 1985, p. 852).

9   A large proportion of women workers are located in administrative, ser-

vice, and high-tech fields that have not historically been organized by unions. Many women also work part-time, temporarily, or change jobs more often than men and therefore do not view unions as helping them in the long run. In addition, many women want child care and job training rather than traditional union wage increases and job security. These factors may explain why women, an increasing percentage of the work force, are not highly unionized.

10 Minorities and immigrants, on the other hand, may resist unionization because they fear it will cost them their jobs. Faced with cultural obstacles, less education on average, and English as a second language, immigrants often simply want to have job security. Paradoxically, this group strongly resembles the groups which fostered the birth of unionism. On the positive side, minorities and immigrants desire job training to enhance their job security (Willis 1988, p. 15), a situation which provides unions with an opportunity to increase their influence.

Unions' Failure to Adapt

11 Today's workers tend to want different forms of compensation than their earlier counterparts did. Previous union gains in wages and job security enable today's young, better-educated workers to seek additional fringe benefits, personal satisfaction, and improved work environments. However, this has not been accompanied by a change in union leadership rhetoric and ideology, which is still rooted in industrial tenets (Day 1989, p. 19). Many union leaders are still using organizing techniques of the 1930s and 1940s designed for blue-collar workers. The majority of today's union leaders also seem to lack the drive and enthusiasm to get workers to participate. This may be due to leaders viewing their positions as simply jobs rather than causes for which to fight (Kovach 1985, p. 855). The result has been leaders losing contact with both existing and potential members and unions striving for survival as a business rather than as a means of protecting workers (Oliver 1989). This lack of responsiveness to a changing environment has resulted in lack of appropriate union organization, lack of a united front, outdated ideas, and shortsightedness.

12 Perhaps this less than stellar leadership has contributed to the weakened public image of unions. Since 1957, the Gallup Poll's public approval rating of labor unions has fallen from 76 percent to about 55 percent in 1988 (Willis 1988, p. 14). This is partially due to young workers who view many of the traditional leaders as unorganized, arrogant, and unresponsive to their needs. Also, some people blame union demands for the decline in the manufacturing industry. Indeed, according to Craver, the expensive wage contracts prior to the 1981–82 recession may have been part of the cause of the recession (1985, p. 211).

13 Another aspect of unions' declining public image has been evidence of

some unethical union leadership and several widely publicized instances of corruption. Former Teamster president Jackie Presser was indicted in 1988 for racketeering and embezzlement. In August 1988, fourteen New Jersey union officials were charged with labor racketeering, conspiracy, and bribery in connection with the construction industry. More than $147,000 was allegedly used for bribery purposes (ENR August 1988, p. 13). In another case, Robert Holmes, a top Michigan Teamsters official who retired due to a racketeering lawsuit, will still receive an annual pension of $205,964 (Lippert 1989, p. 3A).

Management and Public Policy Changes

14   As a general rule, management today is more conscious of safety and health issues and is therefore more responsive to the needs of the worker than during the formative period of unions. Today, many companies have fair grievance procedures, a pleasant work environment, valid performance reviews for merit raises, and improved communication between management and workers (Carrel 1989, p. 545). Combined with unions' previous successes in changing laws, many of the improvements that unions traditionally fought for are now realities. These successes include child labor laws, social security benefits, unemployment compensation, health insurance, pension plans, minimum-wage laws, occupational health and safety regulations, and equal-employment opportunities. As a consequence, it might be argued that government, rather than the unions, is performing the function of protecting workers rather than the unions (Oliver 1989).

15   Another example of decreased union power is the increased use by management of anti-union consultants. Hired to instruct management on how to avoid unionization, consultants sometimes recommend unlawful techniques. In recent years the cost for management of unfair labor practice suits has in many cases been less than the cost of unionization. In 1970, approximately 4,000 workers were unlawfully discharged. in 1980 over 10,000 workers were unlawfully fired. Even when the companies were ordered to reinstate the workers, only 40 percent of the workers accepted, and of those 80 percent left within two years (Craver 1985, p. 214).

16   Also contributing to the erosion of union power during the 1980s was the fact that many of the agencies administering the National Labor Relations Act and the Labor-Management Relations Act were faced with cuts in budgets and in the number of enforcement personnel. This decreased the number of unfair labor practice cases that were heard by these agencies. Also, several Reagan appointees to these agencies took a more pro-management stance and in some cases reversed previous long-standing decisions. According to recent rulings, if a company files a bankruptcy petition, it can break its union contract and demand concessions if done in good faith. In addition, the National Labor Relations Board reversed the 1984 Milwaukee Spring Decision II case and

stated that a company can transfer production to a nonunion plant during the life of a contract if it is done for financial reasons and not anti-union reasons (Kovach 1985, p. 853).

Conclusion

17   In 1981 Reagan fired the striking members of the Professional Air Traffic Controllers Union. In the midst of the 1982 recession, the United Auto Workers agreed to $3 billion in wage concessions rather than lose their jobs. During this same period union contract wage increases in general fell from 6.6 percent in 1982 to 2.8 percent in 1984 (Kovach 1985, p. 854). In 1989 the Eastern Airlines strike was followed by the company declaring bankruptcy. Twenty thousand union members lost their jobs. During all of these events, public support was not on the side of the unions. Altogether these events suggest the loss of union power regardless of the environment in which they happened.

18   As the nation enters a new decade, labor unions must look forward and adapt to changes rather than try to fit new people, ideas, and demands into traditional molds. Unions could serve a vital interest in representing workers and acting as a buffer between employees and management, but they must be flexible. One possibility would be for unions to strive for global unionization. Unions might try to develop ways to protect workers who are displaced due to cheaper foreign workers or focus on ways to retain those who are in a changing work climate. Also, unions might work harder to create child care facilities and flex-time benefits.

19   Rather than a confrontational role, unions should strive toward participative management and enhancing the partnership between workers and owners. This new cooperative role could assist businesses in maintaining a competitive edge and workers in maintaining job security. Union-inspired employee involvement in daily decision-making would help to increase worker self-esteem and productivity through job enrichment (Craver 1985, p. 218).

20   Although unions may seem unresponsive to a changing work environment, they are not oblivious to the challenges facing them. Changing their modes of thinking may take time, but unions are already making progress in certain segments of the workforce. For example, between 1987 and 1988, the International Union of Electronic Workers has won over 80 percent of its organizing campaigns as compared to the national average of 40 percent (Verespej 1988, p. 57). This trend could continue if unions adapt to changes in demographics, increased foreign competition, the shift to service industries, and to today's tougher legal and regulatory environment. They must change their ineffective leadership, work to improve the public perception of unions, and begin to work more effectively with a more responsive management. The 21st century could hold a promising new role for unions.

Works Cited

Bauman, Alvin. "Union Membership in 1988," *Current Wage Developments*, Feb. 1989, pp. 4–7.

Carrel, Michael K., and Kuzmits, Frank E. *Personnel Human Resource Management.* Columbus: Merrill Publishing Co., 1989.

Craver, Charles B. "The Current and Future Status of Labor Organizations," *Labor Law Journal*, Apr. 1985, 36, pp. 210–25.

Day, Charles R. "We Shouldn't Let Unions Die," *Industry Week*, Mar. 20, 1989, 238, p. 6.

Drucker, Peter F. "Will Unions Ever Again Be Useful Organs of Society?" *Industry Week*, Mar. 20, 1989, 238, pp. 17–22.

Economic Report of the President. 1989, p. 320.

"Jersey Labor Scam Charged," *ENR*, Aug. 4, 1988, pp. 13–14.

Kovach, Kenneth A. "Organized Labor's Deteriorating Condition," *Labor Law Journal*, Nov. 1985, 36, pp. 850–56.

Lippert, John. "Teamsters Official's Pension Decried," *Detroit Free Press*, Feb. 18, 1989, p. 3A.

Nichols, Don. "Today's Unions: A Mixed Bag," *Management Review*, Feb. 1988, 77, pp. 43–44.

———. "Unions Play Catch-up to Today's Work Environment," *Management Review*, Feb. 1988, 77, pp. 28–29.

Oliver, George J. Personal interview. Lawyer with Smith, Heenan, and Althen in Washington D.C., Oct. 1, 1989.

Taylor, Ronald A. "Why Organized Labor is Unlikely to Make a Comeback," *U.S. News & World Report*, Sept. 11, 1989, p. 31.

Verespej, Michael A. "Unions' Pendulum Swings," *Industry Week*, Dec. 5, 1988, pp. 57, 60–61.

Wetherll, Dennis. Letter to Home Shopping Network employees, Sept. 8, 1989.

Willis, Rod. "Can American Unions Transform Themselves?" *Management Review*, Feb. 1988, 77, pp. 14–21. ❖

Questions to Ponder

1. Compare the first draft of the opening of Cori McNeilus's essay with her final version. Which opening do you consider stronger, and why?
2. In this essay, does Cori McNeilus seem pro-union, anti-union, or neutral? On what passages do you base your opinion?
3. What techniques does Cori McNeilus use to convince us that she knows what she is talking about? Could she do anything more to enhance her credibility?

Writing Possibilities

1. Select a particular union and research its history with an eye toward how it has responded to the four challenges Cori McNeilus describes: (1) the shift from blue-collar to white-collar dominance; (2) foreign competition; (3) the increase of women, minorities, and immigrants in the workplace;

and (4) increased government and management power. Write a report presenting your findings, and share it with the union's leadership.
2. Write a utopian essay presenting your vision of the ideal union of the year 2050.
3. Consider the possibility of a labor union for college students. Do such unions exist? Brainstorm a list of the benefits and challenges of such an organization and then write an essay for your student government sharing your findings.

Short Story
COVER GIRL
Nancy Price

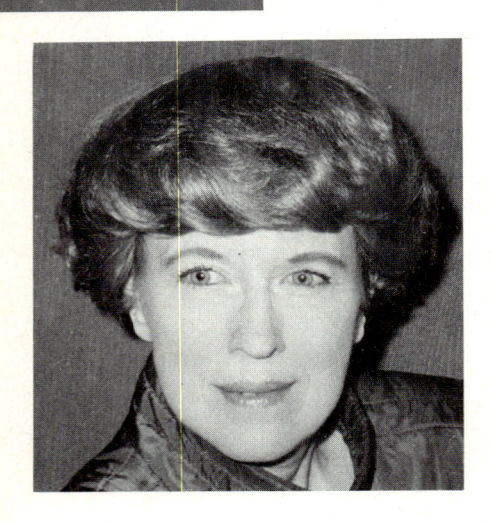

My story, "Cover Girl," was part of an assignment I gave myself: write a story about each one of the real people who describe their jobs in Studs Terkel's book Working. I wrote three, and this one is based on Terkel's "Jill Torrance," a top New York City model. It is Jill who says, "When you've worked before a camera long enough, you know what they want even though they don't . . . I think the shyest people get into show business or modeling. They were wallflowers in their classes. . . . You feel like you're someone's clothes hanger. . . . I don't like to look at my pictures. I don't like to ride by and see some advertisement and tell everyone that's me. . . . Male models. . . . You see this handsome frame and you find it empty."

I used Epcot, Walt Disney's Environmental Prototype of the Community of Tomorrow, for its immaculate facades of future and past, and added a bit of my older son's swim team and my younger son's knowledge of snapdragons. There is no substitute for the authentic fact, the one-of-a-kind real thing in poetry or fiction—perhaps that is why these stories were given prizes and appeared in newspapers coast-to-coast.

As a writer I am on the watch for such detail. I work, too, for the first sentence, the first paragraph that makes a promise the rest of the story or book will deliver.

One of my novels begins, "The two children are still alive in the oven of an August afternoon." A second book also promises violence: "The open car came over the hill too fast, fenders and running board a streak of sun. Hot summer light was brilliant on the man, woman and baby in the front seat. Halfway into the valley, sheep clogged a narrow English road—the car roared down on them, skidded to a crash on the stone bridge beyond, and burned." My novel Sleeping with the Enemy begins, "The day before Martin Burney lost his wife Sara. . . ."

Beginnings are a promise. The metallic voice of the agent doing business with beauty—and Kim's sigh—these begin "Cover Girl." I am sure I do not need to say that I did not get even one of these beginnings right, not at first. Maybe on the twentieth try . . .

Brief Warm-up Writing Exercises

1. Write as many true sentences as you can about the life of a model.
2. Brainstorm a list of qualifications for a career in modeling.
3. Describe Disneyland, Disney World, Epcot Center, or any theme park you have visited.

---

1   "Kim?" It was the metallic model agency voice on the phone; Kim gave a sigh and turned over in bed. "Be at the airport at 9:20, will you? It's Florida—Orlando. Adele Delaide's beach stuff for summer. Okay? You'll be met by Ultima Studio."

2   "Okay," Kim said. Florida. Snow flakes were melting on New York streets under her bedroom window. A cup of coffee, then she packed the makeup case and shoes, wigs, clothes. Florida.

3   She was Kim Cordelia now; she could afford a taxi, even though she had to load her cases herself, as usual. Airport magazine stands had the new *Vogue* with Kim's cruise ship series. Kim didn't buy a copy to look at her smiling face on the cover. The plane was on time; she went first class and slept.

4   "We want a 'young and carefree image,' " Adele Delaide's top man said when Kim dragged her cases upstairs to the studio. "Maybe you look too experienced."

5   The ad agency man said "young and carefree" was dated—the real seller now was "pouty and sleepy." He argued with the stylist about what was left of a bikini. The photographer said Kim looked fat.

6   Kim didn't listen much; she was running herself through a check, like a computer. They told her to stand there, sit here, look sexy, thoughtful, happy, young, carefree, pouty, sleepy . . . Kim just posed. She knew what her knees looked like from every angle, and when to tuck her toes under and how to make a pattern of herself in space.

7 The male model was bronze-brown and beautiful—he was probably local, and beach-tanned every day. If he took Kim dancing, the pair of them would look like an ad, and their conversation would sound like one, of course—an ad for him. The model put his arms around Kim and told a photographer he'd met a *marvelous* redhead hang-gliding.

8 Pairs of narrowed eyes surrounded Kim Cordelia. They looked at her as if she were the shape of a woman that would set off their arrangements of ideas, like an empty vase. When she got dressed and was ready to leave, no man at the studio asked her where she was going or if she wanted company; they were still talking about pouty and sleepy. It was always the same. When they saw the shots, they'd be satisfied, and think they'd done it all.

9 Kim went to her hotel, showered off the makeup, and ordered supper in her room. She totaled the money she'd made. She was going to sleep twelve hours, and the next day in Florida was hers. But when she crawled into bed, she dreamed all night of Kathy Knudsen of Lander, Missouri, before she was Kim Cordelia of New York. In every dream she was her old self, the Kathy who was shy and homely and hurt most of the time. There was no guy in high school who cared to get acquainted with her.

10 What a joy for her to wake late for breakfast in bed, and find Kim Cordelia's face in a mirror and Florida sunshine warming her through her silk nightgown. But her dreams had made her restless, rebellious, reckless—it was company she needed, some place with crowds where she could pick and choose. Florida was out there: toyland, girl-and-boy-land, the EPCOT Center, rubbing elbows with Disney World.

11 When Kim left her hotel in a taxi, she wasn't Kim Cordelia with her cool shine, her expensive gloss: she was just a beautiful young woman, casual enough for a college man, stylish enough for a young lawyer, smart enough to wear low-heeled shoes. Heads turned as she passed; men paused mid-word.

12 The EPCOT Center was as big as Manhattan, they said, but it was immaculate as a TV backdrop: no cigarette stubs, chipped paint, or soot—not even a dead leaf in the flower beds. Crowds poured from neatly parked cars to little trains, from trains to ticket-windows. Finally they clicked through an entrance and were in the shadow of the Spaceship Earth geosphere. Walks led to great pavilions. Kim watched crowds from the shadow of her hat, looking for the right man.

13 The first one was sitting alone in The Land pavilion. Kim watched him. He wasn't holding a table for anyone; he was busy with a platter of salad. Kim liked men who liked salads. This one had wavy, dark hair on his head, and more hair where his shirt was unbuttoned, and he had a lot of salad to eat yet.

14 Kim bought a platter of lettuce and cheese and turkey, and picked her way through a giggling, sticky grade-school class. There wasn't an empty table in sight; Kim hesitated prettily by the salad-eater's table. In only a few minutes she had her hand in his and their knees touching under their platters of fodder, and was telling her stories of his graduate student life.

15 He was very clever for somebody who only had an M.A. He could be

talking about *Antirrhinum sempervirens* or *Antirrhinum barrelieri* (he was a botanist specializing in snapdragons), but when they went on the pavilion boat tour, he was watching for dark tunnels, and could stop his Latin midword. He was a good kisser. He said she was gorgeous. He said his eyesight was extremely good, and it must have been: he managed to find deserted spots even at EPCOT, and then Kim enjoyed the kissing and quiet. But there was no point in being bored when snapdragons wilted. After an hour or two, Kim told the botanist she simply had to leave, said goodbye, and stepped into the crowd.

16   By three o'clock Kim had walked miles, and learned more than she wanted to know about insurance from a big-muscled blond. Before dinner she listened to tales of travel in Russia from a thin and wiry satyr in sandals. Both of them said at least once that she was gorgeous, and watched to see if other guys saw what they had on their arm. She ate dinner with a computer analyst who had a reservation at Les Chefs de France, but she paid her way, and heard a married tale of woe. Finally she said she really had to leave. A fife-and-drum corps conveniently marched between them at the American Experience, and when "Yankee Doodle" faded along the lagoon, the computer analyst was nowhere to be seen. Kim found a dark bench and sat down.

17   Night breezes were warm over the World Showcase lagoon. It was snowing in New York. Kim sighed and yawned. The lagoon reflected lights of a miniature Eiffel Tower, and there was a baby St. Mark's Square, and Hampton Court, and Japanese Katsura palace. Kim's feet ached: she had walked through those stage sets that were like little painted ghosts. The authentic buildings, thousands of miles away, were life-sized, stained, crumbling, real things.

18   Crowds were thinning, and most of the families with children had taken them home to bed. Kim turned her back on the baby ghosts of Europe and walked slowly through Future World, not looking at men who looked at her. Lights and colors from the Universe of Energy, the World of Motion or the Journey into Imagination spangled sidewalks and glowed in trees. Spaceship Earth shone overhead.

19   About nine-thirty Kim stopped beside a grass plot to stare at a snake of water that seemed to be alive. It jumped from one socket in grass to another: high, silvery loops that leaped overhead, fell, leaped again. Then bright arcs of water began once more a hundred feet away. How could a water jet jump like a squirrel?

20   Kim watched, fascinated. A high-school boy had timed the water's progress exactly. He leaped to meet it when it arched above him and caught the jet in one hand. Passers-by laughed and ducked. He was as expert as a baseball fielder. Kim didn't think he was good at much else. When he stood waiting for the next leaping water arc, his shoulders drooped, and so did his homely, pimpled face.

21   "You're good!" Kim said.

22   The boy turned around so quickly he almost fell. "Yeah!" he said, and ducked his head, then stared at Kim and missed the next leap of the silvery water-snake entirely.

23   "Teach me how to do it," Kim said.

24   So he taught her, and they leaped for the glittering water arcs. He finally got up nerve enough to say that he thought the water didn't travel at all: the jets jumped only once, and set off another in the line. "At least, I guess so," he said. His name was Donald Fisk, and he was getting used to looking at Kim. Would he get her a coke, she asked, sitting down to get her breath, and he came back with two cups, looking surprised that she hadn't left. She remembered how it was.

25   They sat together on a bench and drank the cokes. Don looked at her when he dared, and at his big, knobby hands when he didn't. He looked at men who passed, and they looked at her and then him. He was too dazed to even ask her name.

26   "What do you do in your spare time?" Kim said, and listened to his description of his swim team and a trophy they wanted. She wondered what would have happened if the football captain had leaned against her high-school locker one day after school while other students watched, and asked how she liked her bit part in the school play. If he'd done that once, would it have made any difference?

27   Don described how hard it was to do swimming turns; they were tricky. Kim nodded, but she was thinking about her day. She'd told every man she met that she had a "very fascinating, unique job." One man—she couldn't remember which—had said, "Oh, really?" but she'd never had to explain what her job was.

28   "My dad's going to buy me a car," Don said. "When I graduate. A new one." Kim kept a piece of ice in her mouth for a long time and thought she could have made a pretty humorous story out of Kathy Knudsen and Lander, Missouri.

29   "I've really got to go home," Kim said at last. Don's eyes were sparkling and he was pounding one big fist into the palm of the other hand, and he said please, could she stay just one minute more, because he had a favor to ask?

30   So Kim obliged. She sat on stone walls and benches. She looked up at the Geosphere and down at a bed of petunias. She knew how to do it, smiling, not looking into Don's brand new camera with flash attachment. Don asked strangers to take their picture, so Kim stood with his quivering arm around her, turning her profile to its best angle against his shirt. They traveled EPCOT walks like a firefly and his silent, smiling mate: flash, flash, flash.

31   Then Kim Cordelia kissed Don Fisk goodbye, giving him a quick lesson in the art. "I hope you'll win that swim trophy, and get your new car," she said. She smiled into his awed eyes (which she told him were handsome eyes—they were), and stroked his cheek, and ran her hands through his hair. He stood under Spaceship Earth and watched her go out in darkness toward the parking lots. He had a tremendous, triumphant smile on his face and dozens of pictures of himself and Kim Cordelia hanging around his neck.

32   Kim Cordelia turned her back on the Environmental Prototype of the Community of Tomorrow, and took a deep breath of Florida night odors: flowers

and earth and damp cement. She caught a taxi that was unloading two couples at EPCOT for late dinner. As she climbed in, the men watched. She rode back to Orlando with no expression on her photogenic face at all. ❖

Questions to Ponder

1. What details in the story reveal Kim Cordelia's attitude toward her job?
2. Which details disclose how Kim Cordelia is treated by her employers? By the men at Epcot?
3. What change takes place during this short story?
4. Do you consider Nancy Price's first sentence a true and effective opening for this story?

Writing Possibilities

1. Imitate Nancy Price's "assignment," and choose another occupation described in Studs Terkel's book *Working*. Select key details, and write a piece using these facts to add substance and authenticity to your writing.
2. Do research on the modeling schools and opportunities available in your area. (*Hint:* Look in the yellow pages of the telephone directory under "Modeling.") Interview modeling school and modeling agency heads, as well as any models you can find. Then write the truth about modeling in your area.
3. Rewrite Nancy Price's "Cover Girl" from the point of view of one (or all) of the men in the story.

CHAPTER 7

Generating

One true sentence often leads to another. Before you know it, you have composed a satisfying paragraph. Stay with it, and you have composed a work. Often, however, lines and paragraphs do not come this easily or naturally. It is reassuring to know that when inspiration wanes, there are many things you can do to get that old generator in you working.

One of the best ways is to have a regular time for writing. If you have been a dedicated jogger, you know that your body and mind become conditioned to the activity. Miss a week, and your body practically cries out to run. Those muscles long to be exercised. The same holds true for your writing muscles. Both your body and your mind will become used to writing at a given time every day, and they will come ready to work. Kurt Vonnegut says he writes every day, including Christmas. You might take holidays off, or even weekends, but a regular writing habit sets you up for regular writing.

Many people also begin their writing periods with a 15- or 20-minute stretch of reading. This warms up the language cells. You seem to ease smoothly from reading words to writing them. I like to read the prose stylists I admire most—E. B. White, Virginia Woolf, George Orwell, and Annie Dillard, to name a few. I hope that by getting their clear rhythms and polished language into my head, I can carry forward these qualities into my own work.*

---

*Sometimes, however, this can interfere with finding your own voice and style.

Another technique is to read through your notes or go over what you have previously written as a way of stoking your generator for continued output. This practice has much to recommend it. Writing often involves the unfolding of ideas. When teachers speak of admirable coherence in a paragraph, it is because the ideas seem to unfold logically (even organically) from each other. In practical terms, a writer *has* to read what comes before to find what would logically come next. The same holds true for poems or stories, which may not unfold ideas as much as project a certain mood or voice. Only by rereading can you pick up the mood, or voice, and continue it. This method of rereading and adding on, rereading and adding on, tends to bring an overall tightness and unity to the completed work, for every sentence is consciously built on what has come before.

Rereading your old material before adding to it has other benefits besides priming the engine and ensuring overall coherence. Writers often polish their past sentences as they reread them—at times in light of new visions of where the piece is going. Thus works get revised and polished as they unfold.

If you have tried a warm-up period of reading, reread your notes or work-in-progress, and are still having trouble generating what might come next, you may want to try switching technologies in hopes of surprising yourself into generation. If you write best by hand, switch to a keyboard. If you type, switch back to paper and pen. Try dictating your ideas into a tape recorder. You might be able to speak your thoughts when you were not able to write them. (Sometimes you can achieve the same effect by simply asking yourself sternly, "What are you trying to say?" You then answer, "Well, I'm trying to say that . . . ," and this answer is often exactly what you were seeking.) Do not hesitate also to return to some of your prewriting activities—like brainstorming, mapping, and freewriting—in order to generate more material for a specific section of your work.

If you have tried all these techniques and still remain blocked, decide to skip over the section that is causing so much trouble and take up another point or scene. This section may be easier to write, and in writing it, you may discover the way to approach the earlier part. If this fails, take a walk, take a shower, make yourself a cup of coffee, or water your plants, realizing that all the while your body is exerting itself, your mind is still mulling over the writing problem. In short, recognize that you are working even when you do not seem to be working!

Many writers also seek more formally to harness the creativity of the unconscious mind by thinking of their essay or story or poem just before going to sleep each night and in the twilight consciousness when they first arise. Additionally, writers should practice "imaging." In the same way as athletes project a mental image of the ball going through the hoop or out of the park just as they are stepping up to the free-throw line or the plate, writers should regularly cultivate mental images of themselves generating work. My own special image is of a typewriter spewing forth page after page of material.

George Orwell, whose essay "Why I Write" opens this chapter, found his own way of generating reviews, essays, and books. He had a strong purpose for writing, and his method was first to describe an experience and then to draw conclusions from it. This structuring device became a hallmark of his style.

Natural-history scholar Stephen Jay Gould offers an instructive case of generation in the animal kingdom: "The Panda's Thumb." The history and current difficulty of generating solutions to the debt problem in developing countries is then explored in student Steven Armbrecht's essay "The Brady Plan: An Attempt to Solve the Mexican Debt Crisis." In the excerpt from the best-selling book *Flow*, which follows, psychologist Mihaly Csikszentmihalyi explains how you can achieve creative flow by regulating the difficulty of the writing challenges you pose for yourself.

Barry Lopez describes another way of relating the outer world to the inner in "Landscape and Narrative," and Gretel Ehrlich illustrates Lopez's method in her essay "About Men." Balancing Ehrlich's essay is an excerpt from *The Managerial Woman* by Margaret Hennig and Anne Jardim. Gabriel García Márquez concludes this chapter by demonstrating in his short story "The Sea of Lost Time" that one way to generate indefinitely is to expand one's perceptions of the real.

Any writer, painter, musician, filmmaker, or inventor will tell you that you cannot wait for inspiration to practice your craft. Those who wait for inspiration never get anything done. Since there are so many ways to prime your writing generator, the best thing to do is to get yourself seated and quieted. Ultimately the best way to write is to do it.

WHY I WRITE

George Orwell

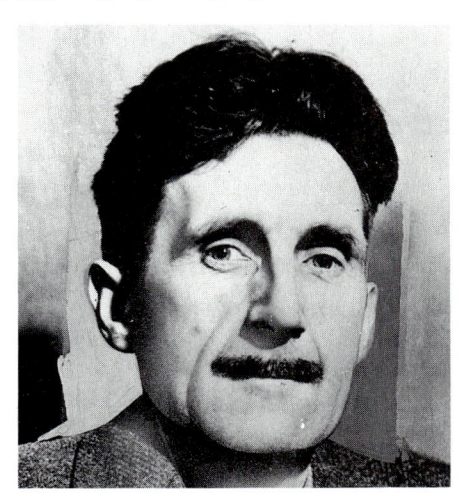

Eric Blair (who came to call himself George Orwell) first appeared in print at the age of 11 with a short patriotic poem, "Awake! Young men of England." That title would sound a life-long theme for the author of Animal Farm, an antitotalitarian fable (written in just over three months), and 1984 (drafted at least twice at the end of Orwell's all-too-brief life).

Orwell won a scholarship to Eton and while there wrote satirical verses and short stories for several college magazines. His favorite phrase was "in front of your nose," which defined both his subject matter and his method. Instead of moving on to a university following his days at Eton, at the age of 19 Orwell chose instead to join the Indian Imperial Police in Burma, plunging himself into experiences that enabled him to write two of his most famous essays, "Shooting an Elephant" and "A Hanging."

After five years in Burma, Orwell returned to England only to pursue again a subject that was in front of everyone's nose, only ignored: the life of the poor. His long autobiographical work Down and Out in Paris and London describes a period in 1929 when he lived in Paris and worked for a time as a hotel dishwasher, followed by descriptions of his travels with tramps in London and southwest England. "Poverty is what I am writing about," Orwell stated boldly (Down and Out in Paris and London [New York: Harcourt Brace Jovanovich, 1961], 9), and in 1937 he published The Road to Wagon Pier, an account of a two month sojourn in England's industrial north where he watched the unemployed picking coal at Fir Tree Siding. His next volume, Homage to Catalonia, describes his service in the Spanish Civil War.

Orwell was intensely interested in the details of daily life. He kept diaries, recording the progress of his plants and animals; indeed, it was his observation of a cart horse that gave him the idea for Animal Farm. He usually composed on a typewriter, sitting at a round table in his living room, but in the last months of his life, when he was correcting the final draft of 1984, he wrote courageously to a friend, "I don't mind being in bed as I have got used to writing there" (George Woodcock, The Crystal Spirit: A Study of George Orwell [Boston: Little, Brown, 1966], 46).

Orwell wrote, "The first thing that we ask of a writer is that he shall not tell us lies, that he shall say what he really thinks, what he really feels" (David Wykes, A Preface to Orwell [New York: Longman, 1987], 50). Orwell followed this practice throughout his life, and it is not too much to say that readers are willing to accept what he says, for he speaks out of his own hardship and suffering and as one who has faced the grimmest truths.

Orwell's friend, George Woodcock, has noted Orwell's astonishing versatility as a writer: "He rarely failed to find a subject—a popular song, an aspect of propaganda, the first toad of spring—on which there was [not] something fresh to say in a prose that, for all its ease and apparent casualness, was penetrating and direct" (Woodcock, The Crystal Spirit, 13).

Brief Warm-up Writing Exercises

1. Brainstorm a list of reasons why you write. Be honest about it.
2. Freewrite on any political or social issues that arouse your anger or support.
3. Generate as many true sentences as you can about the kinds of writing you have done up until this point in your life.

1   From a very early age, perhaps the age of five or six, I knew that when I grew up I should be a writer. Between the ages of about seventeen and twenty-four I tried to abandon this idea, but I did so with the consciousness that I was outraging my true nature and that sooner or later I should have to settle down and write books.

2   I was the middle child of three, but there was a gap of five years on either side, and I barely saw my father before I was eight. For this and other reasons I was somewhat lonely, and I soon developed disagreeable mannerisms which made me unpopular throughout my schooldays. I had the lonely child's habit of making up stories and holding conversations with imaginary persons, and I think from the very start my literary ambitions were mixed up with the feeling of being isolated and undervalued. I knew that I had a facility with words and a power of facing unpleasant facts, and I felt that this created a sort of private world in which I could get my own back for my failure in everyday life. Nevertheless the volume of serious—i.e. seriously intended—writing which I produced all through my childhood and boyhood would not amount to half a dozen pages. I wrote my first poem at the age of four or five, my mother taking it down to dictation. I cannot remember anything about it except that it was about a tiger and the tiger had "chair-like teeth"—a good enough phrase, but I fancy the poem was a plagiarism of Blake's "Tiger, Tiger." At eleven, when the war of 1914–18 broke out, I wrote a patriotic poem which was printed in the local newspaper, as was another, two years later, on the death of Kitchener. From time to time, when I was a bit older, I wrote bad and usually unfinished "nature poems" in the Georgian style. I also, about twice, attempted a short story which was a ghastly failure. That was the total of the would-be serious work that I actually set down on paper during all those years.

3   However, throughout this time I did in a sense engage in literary activities. To begin with there was the made-to-order stuff which I produced quickly, easily and without much pleasure to myself. Apart from school work, I wrote *vers d'occasion,* semi-comic poems which I could turn out at what now seems to me astonishing speed—at fourteen I wrote a whole rhyming play, in imitation of Aristophanes, in about a week—and helped to edit school magazines, both printed and in manuscript. These magazines were the most pitiful burlesque stuff that you could imagine, and I took far less trouble with them than I now would with the cheapest journalism. But side by side with all this, for fifteen years or more, I was carrying out a literary exercise of a quite different kind: this was the making up of a continuous "story" about myself, a sort of diary existing only in the mind. I believe this is a common habit of children and adolescents. As a very small child I used to imagine that I was, say, Robin Hood, and picture myself as the hero of thrilling adventures, but quite soon my "story" ceased to be narcissistic in a crude way and became more and more a mere description of what I was doing and the things I saw. For minutes at a time this kind of thing would be running through my head:

"He pushed the door open and entered the room. A yellow beam of sunlight, filtering through the muslin curtains, slanted on to the table, where a matchbox, half open, lay beside the inkpot. With his right hand in his pocket he moved across to the window. Down in the street a tortoiseshell cat was chasing a dead leaf," etc etc. This habit continued till I was about twenty-five, right through my non-literary years. Although I had to search, and did search, for the right words, I seemed to be making this descriptive effort almost against my will, under a kind of compulsion from outside. The "story" must, I suppose, have reflected the styles of the various writers I admired at different ages, but so far as I remember it always had the same meticulous descriptive quality.

4   When I was about sixteen I suddenly discovered the joy of mere words, i.e. the sounds and associations of words. The lines from *Paradise Lost,*

> *So hee with difficulty and labour hard*
> *Moved on: with difficulty and labour hee,*

which do not now seem to me so very wonderful, sent shivers down my backbone; and the spelling "hee" for "he" was an added pleasure. As for the need to describe things, I knew all about it already. So it is clear what kind of books I wanted to write, in so far as I could be said to want to write books at that time. I wanted to write enormous naturalistic novels with unhappy endings, full of detailed descriptions and arresting similes, and also full of purple passages in which words were used partly for the sake of their sound. And in fact my first completed novel, *Burmese Days,* which I wrote when I was thirty but projected much earlier, is rather that kind of book.

5   I give all this background information because I do not think one can assess a writer's motives without knowing something of his early development. His subject matter will be determined by the age he lives in—at least this is true in tumultuous, revolutionary ages like our own—but before he ever begins to write he will have acquired an emotional attitude from which he will never completely escape. It is his job, no doubt, to discipline his temperament and avoid getting stuck at some immature stage, or in some perverse mood: but if he escapes from his early influences altogether, he will have killed his impulse to write. Putting aside the need to earn a living, I think there are four great motives for writing, at any rate for writing prose. They exist in different degrees in every writer, and in any one writer the proportions will vary from time to time, according to the atmosphere in which he is living. They are:

6   1. Sheer egoism. Desire to seem clever, to be talked about, to be remembered after death, to get your own back on grown-ups who snubbed you in childhood, etc. etc. It is humbug to pretend that this is not a

motive, and a strong one. Writers share this characteristic with scientists, artists, politicians, lawyers, soldiers, successful businessmen—in short, with the whole top crust of humanity. The great mass of human beings are not acutely selfish. After the age of about thirty they abandon individual ambition—in many cases, indeed, they almost abandon the sense of being individuals at all—and live chiefly for others, or are simply smothered under drudgery. But there is also the minority of gifted, wilful people who are determined to live their own lives to the end, and writers belong in this class. Serious writers, I should say, are on the whole more vain and self-centered than journalists, though less interested in money.

7 2. Aesthetic enthusiasm. Perception of beauty in the external world, or, on the other hand, in words and their right arrangement. Pleasure in the impact of one sound on another, in the firmness of good prose or the rhythm of a good story. Desire to share an experience which one feels is valuable and ought not to be missed. The aesthetic motive is very feeble in a lot of writers, but even a pamphleteer or a writer of textbooks will have pet words and phrases which appeal to him for non-utilitarian reasons; or he may feel strongly about typography, width of margins, etc. Above the level of a railway guide, no book is quite free from aesthetic considerations.

8 3. Historical impulse. Desire to see things as they are, to find out true facts and store them up for the use of posterity.

9 4. Political purpose—using the word "political" in the widest possible sense. Desire to push the world in a certain direction, to alter other people's idea of the kind of society that they should strive after. Once again, no book is genuinely free from political bias. The opinion that art should have nothing to do with politics is itself a political attitude.

10 It can be seen how these various impulses must war against one another, and how they must fluctuate from person to person and from time to time. By nature—taking your "nature" to be the state you have attained when you are first adult—I am a person in whom the first three motives would outweigh the fourth. In a peaceful age I might have written ornate or merely descriptive books, and might have remained almost unaware of my political loyalties. As it is I have been forced into becoming a sort of pamphleteer. First I spent five years in an unsuitable profession (the Indian Imperial Police, in Burma), and then I underwent poverty and the sense of failure. This increased my natural hatred of authority and made me for the first time fully aware of the existence of the working classes, and the job in Burma had given me some understanding of the nature of imperialism: but these experiences were not enough to give me an accurate political orientation. Then came Hitler, the Spanish civil war, etc. By the end of 1935 I had still failed to reach a firm decision. I remember a little poem that I wrote at that date, expressing my dilemma:

A happy vicar I might have been
Two hundred years ago,
To preach upon eternal doom
And watch my walnuts grow;

But born, alas, in an evil time,
I missed that pleasant haven,
For the hair has grown on my upper lip
And the clergy are all clean-shaven.

And later still the times were good,
We were so easy to please,
We rocked our troubled thoughts to sleep
On the bosoms of the trees.

All ignorant we dared to own
The joys we now dissemble;
The greenfinch on the apple bough
Could make my enemies tremble.

But girls' bellies and apricots,
Roach in a shaded stream,
Horses, ducks in flight at dawn,
All these are a dream.

It is forbidden to dream again;
We maim our joys or hide them;
Horses are made of chromium steel
And little fat men shall ride them.

I am the worm who never turned,
The eunuch without a harem;
Between the priest and the commissar
I walk like Eugene Aram;

And the commissar is telling my fortune
While the radio plays,
But the priest has promised an Austin Seven,
For Duggie always pays.

I dreamed I dwelt in marble halls,
And woke to find it true;
I wasn't born for an age like this;
Was Smith? Was Jones? Were you?

The Spanish war and other events in 1936–37 turned the scale and thereafter I knew where I stood. Every line of serious work that I have written since 1936 has been written, directly or indirectly, *against* totalitarianism and *for* democratic Socialism, as I understand it. It seems to me nonsense, in a period like our own, to think that one can avoid writing of such subjects. Everyone writes of them in one guise or another. It is simply a question of which side one takes and what approach one follows. And the more one is conscious of one's political bias, the more chance one has of acting politically without sacrificing one's aesthetic and intellectual integrity.

11   What I have most wanted to do throughout the past ten years is to make political writing into an art. My starting point is always a feeling of partisanship, a sense of injustice. When I sit down to write a book, I do not say to myself, "I am going to produce a work of art." I write it because there is some lie that I want to expose, some fact to which I want to draw attention, and my initial concern is to get a hearing. But I could not do the work of writing a book, or even a long magazine article, if it were not also an aesthetic experience. Anyone who cares to examine my work will see that even when it is downright propaganda it contains much that a full-time politician would consider irrelevant. I am not able, and I do not want, completely to abandon the world-view that I acquired in childhood. So long as I remain alive and well I shall continue to feel strongly about prose style, to love the surface of the earth, and to take pleasure in solid objects and scraps of useless information. It is no use trying to suppress that side of myself. The job is to reconcile my ingrained likes and dislikes with the essentially public, non-individual activities that this age forces on all of us.

12   It is not easy. It raises problems of construction and of language, and it raises in a new way the problem of truthfulness. Let me give just one example of the cruder kind of difficulty that arises. My book about the Spanish civil war, *Homage to Catalonia,* is, of course, a frankly political book, but in the main it is written with a certain detachment and regard for form. I did try very hard in it to tell the whole truth without violating my literary instincts. But among other things it contains a long chapter, full of newspaper quotations and the like, defending the Trotskyists who were accused of plotting with Franco. Clearly such a chapter, which after a year or two would lose its interest for any ordinary reader, must ruin the book. A critic whom I respect read me a lecture about it. "Why did you put in all that stuff?" he said. "You've turned what might have been a good book into journalism." What he said was true, but I could not have done otherwise. I happened to know, what very few people in England had been allowed to know, that innocent men were being falsely accused. If I had not been angry about that I should never have written the book.

13   In one form or another this problem comes up again. The problem of language is subtler and would take too long to discuss. I will only say that of late years I have tried to write less picturesquely and more exactly. In any case I find that by the time you have perfected any style of writing, you have always

outgrown it. *Animal Farm* was the first book in which I tried, with full consciousness of what I was doing, to fuse political purpose and artistic purpose into one whole. I have not written a novel for seven years, but I hope to write another fairly soon. It is bound to be a failure, every book is a failure, but I know with some clarity what kind of book I want to write.

14   Looking back through the last page or two, I see that I have made it appear as though my motives in writing were wholly public-spirited. I don't want to leave that as the final impression. All writers are vain, selfish and lazy, and at the very bottom of their motives there lies a mystery. Writing a book is a horrible, exhausting struggle, like a long bout of some painful illness. One would never undertake such a thing if one were not driven on by some demon whom one can neither resist nor understand. For all one knows that demon is simply the same instinct that makes a baby squall for attention. And yet it is also true that one can write nothing readable unless one constantly struggles to efface one's own personality. Good prose is like a window pane. I cannot say with certainty which of my motives are the strongest, but I know which of them deserve to be followed. And looking back through my work, I see that it is invariably where I lacked a *political* purpose that I wrote lifeless books and was betrayed into purple passages, sentences without meaning, decorative adjectives and humbug generally. ❖

Questions to Ponder

1. What do you think George Orwell means when he says in paragraph 2 that he had the "power of facing unpleasant facts"? How might that be of value to a writer?
2. Do you agree with George Orwell that a writer's subject matter will be determined by the age in which he or she lives? If you agree, what are some examples of subject matter of our age?
3. Do you agree with George Orwell that writers before they even begin to write acquire an "emotional attitude" from which they will never completely escape? From this essay, what do you suspect was Orwell's emotional attitude? What is yours?
4. Do you agree with George Orwell that the majority of people abandon individual ambition by age 30 and that it is only a minority of "gifted, wilful people who are determined to live their own lives to the end . . ."? Do you consider yourself in the majority or in the minority—and why?
5. Do you endorse George Orwell's contention that the four motives for writing are (1) sheer egoism, (2) aesthetic enthusiasm, (3) historical impulse, and (4) political purpose? Can you think of any other motives for writing? Which of Orwell's four motives do you think is strongest in you?

Writing Possibilities

1. Using George Orwell's essay as a model, write your own blunt (even brutally honest) confession of why *you* write.
2. Write a "Dear George" letter telling Orwell what you value in his essay and what (if anything) you think he overlooked in his list of motives for writing.
3. Brainstorm a list of vivid examples illustrating each of Orwell's four motives for writing. They can be hypothetical or real, from your own writing or that of others. Then write an expanded essay on Orwell's four motives called, perhaps, "Orwell's Four Motives Exemplified" or "An Amplification of Orwell's Four Motives for Writing."

THE PANDA'S THUMB

Stephen Jay Gould

I was lucky to wander into evolutionary theory, one of the most exciting and important of all scientific fields. I had never heard of it when I started at a rather tender age; I was simply awed by dinosaurs. I thought paleontologists spent their lives digging up bones and putting them together, never venturing beyond the momentous issue of what connects to what. Then I discovered evolutionary theory. Ever since then, the duality of natural history—richness in particularities and potential union in underlying explanation—has propelled me. . . .

All the good natural-history writers of the past—Charles Darwin, Thomas Huxley, Charles Lyell—wrote very powerful, personal prose, and I felt I should try to do the same thing. . . . The problem is that in this country the notion of writing for the public got somehow assimilated into the notion of cheapening, simplifying, adulterating. There's no reason why it should. There's a difference between the simplification of language, which obviously you do, because people don't know the jargon, and simplification of the concepts, which you don't have to do. . . .

It's important for the lay reader [to understand how contemporary attitudes *affect scientists], because [such appreciation] debunks the notion of science as an inaccessible priesthood whose pronouncements have to be simply accepted. It may be even more important for practicing scientists, because if you want to be innovative in a science and yet think your attitude towards things is just an objective reading of nature, you're going to miss where cultural biases are affecting your work, and you may really lose opportunities for creativity.*

Brief Warm-up Writing Exercises

1. Freewrite all you know about bears in general and pandas in particular.
2. Name and describe what you consider to be the most extraordinary-looking animal, insect, or flower you have seen in books, zoos, or at large.
3. Brainstorm a list of things you have built or sewn or cooked (or otherwise concocted) in your life. Then freewrite about your favorite creation.

---

1 ❖ Few heroes lower their sights in the prime of their lives; triumph leads inexorably on, often to destruction. Alexander wept because he had no new worlds to conquer; Napoleon, overextended, sealed his doom in the depth of a Russian winter. But Charles Darwin did not follow the *Origin of Species* (1859) with a general defense of natural selection or with its evident extension to human evolution (he waited until 1871 to publish *The Descent of Man*). Instead, he wrote his most obscure work, a book entitled: *On the Various Contrivances by Which British and Foreign Orchids Are Fertilized by Insects* (1862).

2   Darwin's many excursions into the minutiae of natural history—he wrote a taxonomy of barnacles, a book on climbing plants, and a treatise on the formation of vegetable mold by earthworms—won him an undeserved reputation as an old-fashioned, somewhat doddering describer of curious plants and animals, a man who had one lucky insight at the right time. A rash of Darwinian scholarship has laid this myth firmly to rest during the past twenty years. . . . Before then, one prominent scholar spoke for many ill-informed colleagues when he judged Darwin as a "poor joiner of ideas . . . a man who does not belong with the great thinkers."

3   In fact, each of Darwin's books played its part in the grand and coherent scheme of his life's work—demonstrating the fact of evolution and defending natural selection as its primary mechanism. Darwin did not study orchids solely for their own sake. Michael Ghiselin, a California biologist who finally took the trouble to read all of Darwin's books (see his *Triumph of the Darwinian Method*), has correctly identified the treatise on orchids as an important episode in Darwin's campaign for evolution.

4   Darwin begins his orchid book with an important evolutionary premise:

continued self-fertilization is a poor strategy for long-term survival, since offspring carry only the genes of their single parent, and populations do not maintain enough variation for evolutionary flexibility in the face of environmental change. Thus, plants bearing flowers with both male and female parts usually evolve mechanisms to ensure cross-pollination. Orchids have formed an alliance with insects. They have evolved an astonishing variety of "contrivances" to attract insects, guarantee that sticky pollen adheres to their visitor, and ensure that the attached pollen comes in contact with female parts of the next orchid visited by the insect.

5   Darwin's book is a compendium of these contrivances, the botanical equivalent of a bestiary. And, like the medieval bestiaries, it is designed to instruct. The message is paradoxical but profound. Orchids manufacture their intricate devices from the common components of ordinary flowers, parts usually fitted for very different functions. If God had designed a beautiful machine to reflect his wisdom and power, surely he would not have used a collection of parts generally fashioned for other purposes. Orchids were not made by an ideal engineer; they are jury-rigged from a limited set of available components. Thus, they must have evolved from ordinary flowers.

6   Thus, the paradox, and the common theme of this trilogy of essays: Our textbooks like to illustrate evolution with examples of optimal design—nearly perfect mimicry of a dead leaf by a butterfly or of a poisonous species by a palatable relative. But ideal design is a lousy argument for evolution, for it mimics the postulated action of an omnipotent creator. Odd arrangements and funny solutions are the proof of evolution—paths that a sensible God would never tread but that a natural process, constrained by history, follows perforce. No one understood this better than Darwin. Ernst Mayr has shown how Darwin, in defending evolution, consistently turned to organic parts and geographic distributions that make the least sense. Which brings me to the giant panda and its "thumb."

7   Giant pandas are peculiar bears, members of the order Carnivora. Conventional bears are the most omnivorous representatives of their order, but pandas have restricted this catholicity of taste in the other direction—they belie the name of their order by subsisting almost entirely on bamboo. They live in dense forests of bamboo at high elevations in the mountains of western China. There they sit, largely unthreatened by predators, munching bamboo ten to twelve hours each day.

8   As a childhood fan of Andy Panda, and former owner of a stuffed toy won by some fluke when all the milk bottles actually tumbled at the county fair, I was delighted when the first fruits of our thaw with China went beyond ping pong to the shipment of two pandas to the Washington zoo. I went and watched in appropriate awe. They yawned, stretched, and ambled a bit, but they spent nearly all their time feeding on their beloved bamboo. They sat upright and manipulated the stalks with their forepaws, shedding the leaves and consuming only the shoots.

9   I was amazed by their dexterity and wondered how the scion of a stock

adapted for running could use its hands so adroitly. They held the stalks of bamboo in their paws and stripped off the leaves by passing the stalks between an apparently flexible thumb and the remaining fingers. This puzzled me. I had learned that a dexterous, opposable thumb stood among the hallmarks of human success. We had maintained, even exaggerated, this important flexibility of our primate forebears, while most mammals had sacrificed it in specializing their digits. Carnivores run, stab, and scratch. My cat may manipulate me psychologically, but he'll never type or play the piano.

10 So I counted the panda's other digits and received an even greater surprise: there were five, not four. Was the "thumb" a separately evolved sixth finger? Fortunately, the giant panda has its bible, a monograph by D. Dwight Davis, late curator of vertebrate anatomy at Chicago's Field Museum of Natural History. It is probably the greatest work of modern evolutionary comparative anatomy, and it contains more than anyone would ever want to know about pandas. Davis had the answer, of course.

11 The panda's "thumb" is not, anatomically, a finger at all. It is constructed from a bone called the radial sesamoid, normally a small component of the wrist. In pandas, the radial sesamoid is greatly enlarged and elongated until it almost equals the metapodial bones of the true digits in length. The radial sesamoid underlies a pad on the panda's forepaw; the five digits form the framework of another pad, the palmar. A shallow furrow separates the two pads and serves as a channelway for bamboo stalks.

12 The panda's thumb comes equipped not only with a bone to give it strength but also with muscles to sustain its agility. These muscles, like the radial sesamoid bone itself, did not arise *de novo*. Like the parts of Darwin's orchids, they are familiar bits of anatomy remodeled for a new function. The

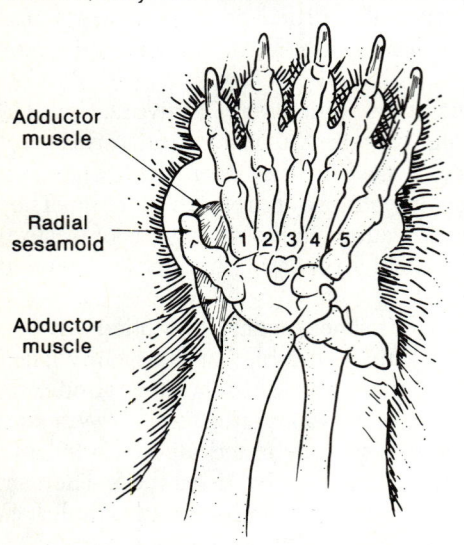

D.L. CRAMER

abductor of the radial sesamoid (the muscle that pulls it away from the true digits) bears the formidable name *abductor pollicis longus* ("the long abductor of the thumb"—*pollicis* is the genitive of *pollex,* Latin for "thumb"). Its name is a giveaway. In other carnivores, this muscle attaches to the first digit, or true thumb. Two shorter muscles run between the radial sesamoid and the pollex. They pull the sesamoid "thumb" towards the true digits.

13   Does the anatomy of other carnivores give us any clue to the origin of this odd arrangement in pandas? Davis points out that ordinary bears and raccoons, the closest relatives of giant pandas, far surpass all other carnivores in using their forelegs for manipulating objects in feeding. Pardon the backward metaphor, but pandas, thanks to their ancestry, began with a leg up for evolving greater dexterity in feeding. Moreover, ordinary bears already have a slightly enlarged radial sesamoid.

14   In most carnivores, the same muscles that move the radial sesamoid in pandas attach exclusively to the base of the pollex, or true thumb. But in ordinary bears, the long abductor muscle ends in two tendons: one inserts into the base of the thumb as in most carnivores, but the other attaches to the radial sesamoid. The two shorter muscles also attach, in part, to the radial sesamoid in bears. "Thus," Davis concludes, "the musculature for operating this remarkable new mechanism—functionally a new digit—required no intrinsic change from conditions already present in the panda's closest relatives, the bears. Furthermore, it appears that the whole sequence of events in the musculature follows automatically from simple hypertrophy of the sesamoid bone."

15   The sesamoid thumb of pandas is a complex structure formed by marked enlargement of a bone and an extensive rearrangement of musculature. Yet Davis argues that the entire apparatus arose as a mechanical response to growth of the radial sesamoid itself. Muscles shifted because the enlarged bone blocked them short of their original sites. Moreover, Davis postulates that the enlarged radial sesamoid may have been fashioned by a simple genetic change, perhaps a single mutation affecting the timing and rate of growth.

16   In a panda's foot, the counterpart of the radial sesamoid, called the tibial sesamoid, is also enlarged, although not so much as the radial sesamoid. Yet the tibial sesamoid supports no new digit, and its increased size confers no advantage, so far as we know. Davis argues that the coordinated increase of both bones, in response to natural selection upon one alone, probably reflects a simple kind of genetic change. Repeated parts of the body are not fashioned by the action of individual genes—there is no gene "for" your thumb, another for your big toe, or a third for your pinky. Repeated parts are coordinated in development; selection for a change in one element causes a corresponding modification in others. It may be genetically more complex to enlarge a thumb and *not* to modify a big toe, than to increase both together. (In the first case, a general coordination must be broken, the thumb favored separately, and correlated increase of related structures suppressed. In the second, a single gene may increase the rate of growth in a field regulating the development of corresponding digits.)

17 　　The panda's thumb provides an elegant zoological counterpart to Darwin's orchids. An engineer's best solution is debarred by history. The panda's true thumb is committed to another role, too specialized for a different function to become an opposable, manipulating digit. So the panda must use parts on hand and settle for an enlarged wrist bone and a somewhat clumsy, but quite workable, solution. The sesamoid thumb wins no prize in an engineer's derby. It is, to use Michael Ghiselin's phrase, a contraption, not a lovely contrivance. But it does its job and excites our imagination all the more because it builds on such improbable foundations.

18 　　Darwin's orchid book is filled with similar illustrations. The marsh Epipactus, for example, uses its labellum—an enlarged petal—as a trap. The labellum is divided into two parts. One, near the flower's base, forms a large cup filled with nectar—the object of an insect's visit. The other, near the flower's edge, forms a sort of landing stage. An insect alighting on this runway depresses it and thus gains entrance to the nectar cup beyond. It enters the cup, but the runway is so elastic that it instantly springs up, trapping the insect within the

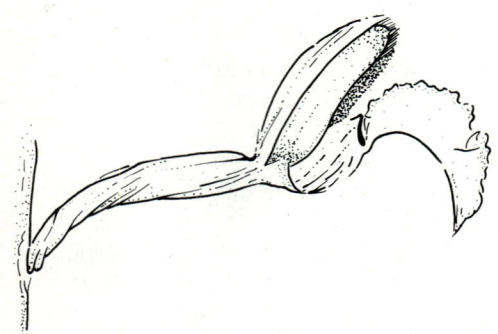

a. Runway of labellum depressed after insect lands.

D.L. CRAMER

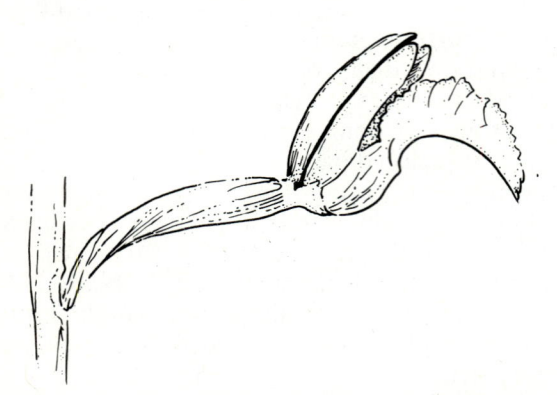

b. Runway of labellum raised after insect crawls into cup below.

D.L. CRAMER

nectar cup. The insect must then back out through the only available exit—a path that forces it to brush against the pollen masses. A remarkable machine but all developed from a conventional petal, a part readily available in an orchid's ancestor.

19   Darwin then shows how the same labellum in other orchids evolves into a series of ingenious devices to ensure cross-fertilization. It may develop a complex fold that forces an insect to detour its proboscis around and past the pollen masses in order to reach nectar. It may contain deep channels or guiding ridges that lead insects both to nectar and pollen. The channels sometimes form a tunnel, producing a tubular flower. All these adaptations have been built from a part that began as a conventional petal in some ancestral form. Yet nature can do so much with so little that it displays, in Darwin's words, "a prodigality of resources for gaining the very same end, namely, the fertilization of one flower by pollen from another plant."

20   Darwin's metaphor for organic form reflects his sense of wonder that evolution can fashion such a world of diversity and adequate design with such limited raw material:

> Although an organ may not have been originally formed for some special purpose, if it now serves for this end we are justified in saying that it is specially contrived for it. On the same principle, if a man were to make a machine for some special purpose, but were to use old wheels, springs, and pulleys, only slightly altered, the whole machine, with all its parts, might be said to be specially contrived for that purpose. Thus throughout nature almost every part of each living being has probably served, in a slightly modified condition, for diverse purposes, and has acted in the living machinery of many ancient and distinct specific forms.

21   We may not be flattered by the metaphor of refurbished wheels and pulleys, but consider how well we work. Nature is, in biologist François Jacob's words, an excellent tinkerer, not a divine artificer. And who shall sit in judgment between these exemplary skills? ❖

Questions to Ponder

1. How might writers resemble nature in being able to do amazingly much with limited raw material? How does this relate to you as a writer?
2. Should we worry about the need to "jury-rig" our writing from our (necessarily) limited set of available components? What can we do to enlarge the set of components?
3. Is "self-fertilization" as poor a strategy for long-term survival for writers as it is for orchids? How can writers achieve "cross-fertilization"?

Writing Possibilities

1. Brainstorm a list of other curious aspects of nature—such as the kangaroo's pouch and the camel's hump. Then research the topic, and using Stephen Jay Gould's essay as a model, explain to a general audience how this adaptation occurred.
2. Research the history of an intriguing invention—such as the compact disc or the permanent wave. Share your findings in an essay or report.
3. Looking over your own list of creations (which you brainstormed for warm-up writing exercise 3), analyze and describe the kind of "tinkerer" you are and the strengths and limitations of your "creations" to date.

Student Essay

THE BRADY PLAN: AN ATTEMPT TO SOLVE THE MEXICAN DEBT CRISIS

Steven W. Armbrecht

My essay on "The Brady Plan" was written as an assignment for a course in international economics. For several months before enrolling in this class, I had been reading many newspaper articles decrying the oppressive debt of developing countries. Therefore, it seemed natural to write a piece that dealt with something that was on the "front burner," so to speak, in world events. The downside of an essay like this is that politicians are constantly changing their focus. For instance, a section of this essay dealt with a plan designed 20 years ago to forgive the debt; however, it was deemed detrimental to the world economy. Now a plan is being bandied about to forgive these loans as part of the peace dividend resulting from the immense changes taking place in the world. This is what makes a current essay hard to research, write, and publish in a timely fashion.

This essay was one of the first I had written in my college career. Writing the first draft was easy. I had a master plan, similar to an outline, in my head. I just sat down one afternoon and started typing. The first two hours I typed nine pages of the first rough draft! Unfortunately, it slowed down after that as I searched for more information and polished what seemed like dozens of drafts.

Interestingly enough, I still follow this general plan of sitting down and hammering out a very rough first draft. I then can look for the pieces needed to fill out the "rough" spots. I have discovered that I would now rather research and write essays than take tests in my classes, as essay writing has become a greater challenge.

After "The Brady Plan" was shared in a writing group, it became like a child that needed constant attention. I spent many hours polishing the prose, changing words with the help of a thesaurus, and eliminating unnecessary words like *the*, *that*, *and* which. It was drawn to my attention in our group sessions that I used a lot of these words unnecessarily.

I have become very critical of my writing and read portions aloud in an attempt to discover sections that do not flow well. Beyond this, I try to have someone not very close to the subject read my work to see if it makes sense. This helps to ensure a readable product upon completion. I thank the inventor of word processors, which enable changes to be almost painless!

Brief Warm-up Writing Exercises

1. Freewrite your opinion on what role the United States (or Canada) should play in helping developing nations.
2. If you have ever had to borrow money, describe the path you followed to pay back your debt.
3. Brainstorm a list of sources you would tap in order to read about a nation's past and present economic and financial situation.

DRAFT

Introduction

1 Mexico, not entirely by its own actions, has experienced a devastating increase in foreign debt. This paper will explore the beginning, the continued expansion, and current attempts to restructure the debt. The Brady Plan, sponsored by the United States, is a big part of the restructuring process. The failure of the plan may affect the United States banking community, the International Monetary Fund, the World Bank, and the fate of Mexico as well as the less developed countries experiencing financial difficulties.

Beginning and Continued Expansion

2   The Mexican population had perceived that the rich and more industrialized nations of the world were dominaitng them, and hence the cause of their poverty. As a result President Cardenas began nationalizing the foreign owned companies during his tenure in office (1934–40) in an effort to gain support from the population. The nationalization at first helped Mexico as domestic production increased and reliance on imports fell. However, the losses incurred by the foreign investors as a result of nationalization were a source of irritation until the outbreak of WWII forced the Allies to settle their differences with Mexico. The Allies needed to utilize the Mexican oil and other productive resources against the Axis Powers. "External demand and the wartime shortage of foreign goods induced industry to operate at full capacity . . . to meet internal and external demand" (Rudolf, 167). The war years saw a tremendous inflow of capital as a result of the demand for war goods. This increased the income by the average worker increasing their demand for goods and putting an increasing strain on the productive output of the country.

3   After the war, "output was stimulated by increased domestic demand arising from the active promotion of import substitution industrialization policies" (Rudolf, 167). These policies were the direct result of the war-time cut-backs that promoted Mexican self-sufficiency. The result of this was an enlarging middle class demanding more and more goods. "The origins of Mexico's 1982 financial crisis were rooted in government policies initiated in 1978 to promote rapid economic growth and sustained following the second oil price rise in 1979–80" (Rudolf, 178). The economy had continued to expand throughout the 1970's. The government borrowed heavily to pay for expanded social programs. Financial capital was also borrowed to expand production in the newly discovered oil fields in order to capitalize on the high world oil price. "In 1981 the combination of a depressed world oil market, recession in the industiralized countries, a current account deficit that rose to US$13 billion, and higher world interest rates on the external

debt caused the public to lose confidence in the peso, and capital flight ensued" (Rudolf, 179). The lost confidence in the Mexican economy caused capital to move from Mexico to perceived safe havens like the United States or the Bahamas and forced Mexico to replace the declining revenues with borrowed funds. Mexico's debt has expanded more and more rapidly as the world oil prices have stagnated and interest rates on the borrowed money has risen.

4   The Brady Plan is an attempt to bail out the heavily debt-laden lesser developed countries like Mexico. "The heavily burdened countries of Latin America, in particular, have experienced growing social and political instability . . . as the countries have borrowed more and more, largely to keep paying off debt" (Kilborn). The plan will be put into effect first in Mexico, whose debt at the end of 1988 was approximately US$107billion.

The Brady Plan

5   The Brady Plan was announced on March 10, 1989. The plan was put forth by U.S. Treasury Secretary Nicholas Brady in an effort to avert bank failures in the United States and abroad if Mexico or any other less developed country defaults on its loans. The thrust of the plan has six main points to be addressed:

> "First, obviously, financial resources are scarce. Can they be used more effectively? Second, we must recognize that reversing capital flight offers a major opportunity, since in many cases flight capital is larger than outstanding debt. Third, there is no substitute for sound policies. Fourth, we must maintain the important role of the international financial institutions and preserve their financial integrity. Fifth, we should encourage debt and debt service reduction on a voluntary basis, while recognizing the importance of continued new lending. This should

> provide an important step back to the free
> markets, where funds abound and transactions are
> enacted in days not months. Finally, we must draw
> together these elements to provide debtor countries
> with greater hope for the future (Brady).

This speech by Mr. Brady did not promise any hard and fast monetary amounts. However, it laid the groundwork for the direction the United States was going to follow in helping alleviate the debt problems in the less developed countries.

6. A subsequent announcement by the Treasury Secretary established the rules it wished followed and gave the debt holding banks three options:

> "The accord offers bank creditors who hold
> Mexico's #54 billion of medium-term and long-term
> foreign debt three basic choices. They can either
> exchange their credits for new bonds carrying a
> fixed annual interest rate of 6.25%, compared with
> floating interest rates of more than 10%. They
> can accept a 35% reduction in the face value of
> their loans and keep floating market rates on new
> bonds issued for the remaining amount. Or, they
> can provide additional loans . . . the new bonds
> that would be used in the first two options would
> be backed by as much as $7 billion of U.S. Treasury
> Securities and escrow accounts financed by the
> International Monetary Fund, The World Bank, and
> Japan" (Truell).

The policies initiated by the plan have a sound foundation and would help Mexico and the other less developed countries if they can be implemented. "Mr. Brady said the United States and other leading democracies should emphasize helping third-world countries cut down on their debt and the interest they have to pay on it. But he said they should also keep letting them borrow to buttress their economies" (Kilborn). The options put forth in the Brady Plan are an attempt to lessen the current interest rate and the payments on these current rates. "The Mexico debt program, the first test of the so-called Brady Plan to manage Latin America's [US]$400 billion debt, has a simple premise: International backing for Mexico's market oriented economic reforms, along with a modest amount of financial aid, will trigger a surge of new investment in Mexico's prostrate economy. In particular, Mexican policy makers hope to repatriate money that their countrymen hold abroad—some $84 billion, according to a 1988 estimate by Morgan Guaranty Trust" (Moffett). As a result Mexico would have some maneuvering room in its finances. However, many problems have arisen since the plan's announcement.

Negative Results of the Brady Plan

7   The Brady Plan has asked banks to choose one of three options formed by the administration and Mexico. The hope is that the banks will follow the plan.

> "The accord, which has to be ratified by hundreds of creditor banks, should cut Mexico's interest payments to banks and provide the country with new loans. But it is unlikely to reduce Mexico's [US]$100billion foreign debt by much, bankers and official said . . . but as the Mexico accord demonstrates, the strategy now seems to be focusing mostly on cutting back interest payments on foreign bank debt and providing further loans" (Truell).

The three choices allow the banks to make a decision on how to get the largest return on their current investments. The Brady plan is attempting to reduce the interest payments but still allow Mexico to receive enough new loans to keep their economy viable.

8   In a development evidently not foreseen by the Treasury Secretary,

a fourth option was available to the banks. Chase Manhattan Corp. has begun setting up large reserves to use as a buffer to begin writing down the foreign debt as bad debt, "the move has ominous overtones for Mexico's chances of getting sufficient new bank loans to grow both economically and meet its interest payments on its debt. The move, which is likely to be copied by other banks, gives Chase the flexibility to sharply reduce new loans to developing countries" (Guenther). The bank has evidently decided to not loan any new money to Mexico. If the lead is followed by other banks Mexico will be unable to make the interest payments on its current debt. "Bankers could be under heavy pressure from shareholders not to offer new loans after taking big write downs" (Duke). If this is true, and other banks follow suit, Mexico and the other less developed countries in unstable financial positions may have to default on their loans if no financing is available to them. No matter what choice the banks make it will cause a reduction in their income from Mexico.

9   To offset this the administration offered an incentive to the banks, "The Securities and Exchange Commission accounting staff said banks won't have to automatically write down to market value debtor-country loans restructured under some of the options in Treasury Secretary Nicholas Barady's debt reduction plan. Observers said the decision could help give breathing space to banks to offer new lending to debt-laden developing countries . . . [and] the practice may let banks hide continuing loan problems" (Duke). By not having to write down the loans, the banks would be in a position to not incur as large a loss. This would have the effect of allowing the banks to keep their profits up to satisfy their stockholders. The administration is hoping that the banks will continue offering new loans with the hope that Mexico becomes economically more self-sufficient and regains the ability to rapay all the loans. If Mexico falters in its debt repayment, the source of new loans to help bail them out will be hard to find.

10   In another development the bonds that would be issued to finance the short-term debt only shift the debt from banks to the United States Treasury Bonds and the International Monetary Fund which in turn is

financed heavily by the United States. "The problem is more than academic because now that the commercial banks see their loans as a solvency problem and are reserving against them, loan portfolios of the World Bank and the International Monetary Fund are coming under pressure" (Roberts). The International Monetary Fund and the World Bank are experiencing financial difficulty, "Both institutions confront growing arrears, as their lending in recent years has increasingly been to the least creditworthy and most heavily indebted countries" (Roberts). These institutions have loaned increasing amounts to keep the debt-ridden countries from defaulting. They have had to shoulder this burden as other countries with the financial ability have shown reluctance to invest in these countries that appear to be a bad risk. It remains to be seen if the United States will continue providing financing to the World Bank and the International Monetary Fund if Mexico and other debt-ridden countries default on their loans.

11   The United States is seen by foreign investors as a safe place to invest their money. The economy is for the most part safe and the foreign investors do not need to worry about having their money taken from them. " 'The Brady Plan doesn't address the underlying structural problems that have turned the United States into one of the world's biggest tax havens,' says Mr. Henry an economist" (Moffett). By implementing the Brady Plan, Mexico hopes it will be able to show it is attempting to become a safe haven and attract some of the capital back from where it may now be sheltered.

Positive Results of the Brady Plan

12   Even though the Brady Plan does not appear to be serving the purpose intended, there is a positive indicator that Mexico's debt problem can be solved. "It triggered a surge of new optimism in the country, which helped the government reduce the high interest rates it had to pay to keep skittish investors from sending more money abroad" (Moffett). Mexico must continue on a path that will keep this optimism at an increasing level.

13   The President of Mexico has begun to implement programs designed

to influence owners of the Mexican owned capital that has been invested in the United States and other countries to reinvest in Mexico.

> "[President] Salinas has spent his first 10 months in office implementing his strategy. Despite the noisy opposition of Mexico's anachronistic left, Mexico has instituted trade liberalization, new foreign-investment regulations, the deregulation of transportation, the announced sale of state enterprises and a partial opening of Mexico's sacrosant petroleum industry to private and foreign investment. Mexico's domestic debt remains oppressive, and further privatizations in the steel, fertilizer and banking sector would enhance investor confidence" (Baer).

The opposition in Mexico is concerned that too much investment by foreigners will put Mexico back in the position it was in before the foreign owned businesses were nationalized. However, nationalized businesses have not helped solve the debt problem, in fact it may have caused the Mexican investors to invest their money out of the reach of the Mexican government. Increasing the domestic and foreign investment in the reopening industries will provide capital and create a positive environment for progress. Therefore the Brady Plan coupled with the actions taken by President Salinas should provide some respite to Mexico's debt explosion.

Conclusion

14 Even though the problem of finding financing to help Mexico is very large, it is not insurmountable. The United States, as one of the predominate world leaders, must convince the capital rich countries to invest in Mexico. If bilateral attempts do not accomplish any positive results, multilateral attempts in the United Nations must be undertaken to explain why it is in everyone's best interest to solve this growing problem. The World Bank and the International Monetary Fund must

receive increasing inflows of funds from other countries. The United States has borne a large percentage of the funds since the United Nations inception after World War II, but many nations are economically better off now than they were then and could shoulder a larger share of the burden. No country is isolated any longer in this world, in some way or another it relies on another country for something in order to survive.

15 If aid is not extended and Mexico defaults on its debt, the resulting domino effect of other less developed countries defaulting on their debt could cause a world wide depression. It is in the best interest of the United States that a solution be found as our economy may not be able to withstand the large shock that could be generated from defaults and a world wide depression.

Works Cited

Baer, M. Delal. "Mexico's Race Against the Clock". THE WALL STREET JOURNAL. 9/29/89. PA13.

Brady, Nicholas. "Excerpts from Brady Remarks on Debt." THE NEW YORK TIMES. 3/11/89. P37.

Duke, Paul Jr. "Bank Rules Are Eased On Write Downs Of Debtor-Country Loans, SEC Staff Says". THE WALL STREET JOURNAL. 9/14/89. PA11.

Guenther, Robert and Peter Truell. "Chase Manhattan Corp. Increases Loan-Loss Reserves by $1.15 Billion". THE WALL STREET JOURNAL. 9/21/89. PA3.

Kilborn, Peter, T. "Debt-Policy Shift Set on 3d World". THE NEW YORK TIMES. 3/11/89. P35.

Moffett, Matt. "Mexico's Capital Flight Still Racks Economy, Despite The Brady Plan". THE WALL STREET JOURNAL. 9/25/89. PA1.

Roberts, Paul Craig. "It's the World Bank's Turn to Adjust". THE WALL STREET JOURNAL. 10/10/89. PA14.

Rudolf, James D., Editor. MEXICO, A COUNTRY STUDY, FOREIGN AREA

STUDIES. Library of Congress Cataloging in Publication Data. Third Edition 1985.

Truell, Peter. "Mexican Pact Shows U.S. Has Refocused it Strategy Away from Debt Reduction". THE WALL STREET JOURNAL. 7/25/89. PA13

1   Mexico, not entirely by its own actions, has experienced a devastating increase in foreign debt. The country's history and policy decisions, in conjunction with actions taken by the developed world, have allowed Mexico's debt to escalate. In response, various policies and plans to restructure the debt have been essayed. The Brady Plan, introduced by the United States in 1989, was designed to be an important part of the proposed restructuring process. The failure of this plan to be implemented successfully could affect the United States' banking community, the International Monetary Fund, the World Bank, and the fate of Mexico—as well as the rest of the developing countries experiencing financial difficulties.

History of the Mexican Debt Crisis

2   In the 1930s it became evident that the rich and more industrialized nations of the world were dominating Mexico's economy. In an effort to gain public support and wrest back some control of its economy, Mexican President Lazaro Cardenas, during his tenure in office (1934–40), began nationalizing the foreign-owned companies. Nationalization, a process that put many of the private and foreign-owned businesses under direct government control, at first helped Mexico, for domestic production increased and reliance on imports fell. However, losses incurred by foreign investors as a result of nationalization were a source of irritation in international relations.

3   With the outbreak of World War II, the Allies were forced to settle their differences with Mexico in order to use its oil and productive capacity in the war effort. This induced Mexican industry to operate at full capacity to meet both external and internal demand (Rudolf 1985, p. 167). As a result of the Allied demand for war goods, there was a tremendous inflow of capital into Mexico. This increased the income of the average Mexican worker, and the resultant increase in demand for goods put an additional strain on productive capacity.

4   After the war, Mexico suddenly found that its products were no longer in great demand in the more industrialized countries. In addition, the U.S. began diverting its attention to rebuilding Japan and the war-torn nations of Europe, utilizing American rather than Mexican production facilities. As a result, Mex-

ico was left with excess productive capacity. Mexico's solution to this problem was to stimulate domestic demand by the active promotion of import substitution industrialization (ISI) policies (Rudolf 1985, p. 167). Under ISI policies, Mexico would produce domestically many of the products it had previously imported. The intention was both to become more self-sufficient and to utilize productive capacity. These ISI policies were continued from the end of the war through the early 1970s. The result was an enlarged middle class that demanded more consumer and social goods. The rising costs of social programs and falling revenues as trade declined in the middle seventies, however, caused a severe budget deficit. The Mexican government found itself in a financial predicament.

5   Mexico was forced to borrow heavily from abroad to pay for expanded social programs and to further develop its oil fields. World oil prices rose sharply in the 1970s, thus spurring Mexico to increase oil production. The rising oil price was caused by the Organization of Petroleum Exporting Countries' (OPEC) cutback in production and by the resulting increased world oil demand. Although Mexico was not a member of the OPEC cartel, it found its oil exports to the industrialized nations increasing rapidly.

6   In 1981, however, the situation drastically changed. The combination of a recession in the industrialized nations and a depressed world oil market caused Mexico's current account deficit to rise to [US] $13 billion. Also, higher world interest rates on the external debt caused the public to lose confidence in the peso, and capital flight ensued (Rudolf 1985, p. 179). Capital moved to perceived safe havens like the United States or the Bahamas and forced Mexico to replace declining revenues with borrowed funds. As the world oil price weakened in the 1980s and interest rates on borrowed money rose, Mexico's debt expanded more and more rapidly, creating concern in the lending nations.

Early Attempts to Solve the Debt Crisis

7   When the United Nations was formed after World War II, the United Nations Conference on Trade and Development (UNCTAD) was created to help the developing countries establish more favorable trade and price balances for their products in the world market. Through UNCTAD the United Nations tried to establish the New International Economic Order (NIEO) in the early 1970s. NIEO would, in essence, forgive the debts of the developing countries and create a level playing field in the world marketplace. Unfortunately, UNCTAD has not been particularly effective. Forgiving developing country debt would require huge financial losses and was no guarantee that the nations would stay out of debt because external financial resources would still be needed. Therefore this UN plan was never seriously considered by the nations holding the debt.

8   As their financial difficulties continued to mount in the 1980s, Mexico and many developing countries continued to demand financial assistance from the industrialized countries. However, these demands were not heeded. Mexico and the developing countries then turned to the International Monetary Fund for help. However, the United States and other countries providing funds to the International Monetary Fund were reluctant to increase funding to levels necessary to help all developing nations. Instead, they provided provisional loans and attempted to create an environment of free trade which they felt would help solve the debt problem by increasing the flow of external revenues to indebted nations.

9   Unfortunately, free trade cannot totally solve the debt problem. Exports from Mexico and the other developing countries are typically primary products, the prices of which are highly unstable; indeed, production increases often cause prices and revenues to fall. In effect, trade in these products does not generate cash flow fast enough or large enough to retire developing country debt.

10 The United States finally recognized the severity of Mexico's debt and, in 1982, initiated the Baker Plan, formulated by then U.S. Treasury Secretary James Baker III. The plan was based on the premise that oil prices would soon rise and generate a positive cash flow. Mexico's debt was rescheduled further into the future to allow Mexico time to reap these expected gains. However, the price of oil did not rise; in fact, it declined. The Baker Plan was a failure because the combination of further declining revenues and increased lending to repay the restructured debt forced Mexico and many other developing countries even deeper into debt.

The Brady Plan

11 As the debt in the developing countries continued to expand, U.S. Treasury Secretary Nicholas Brady presented a new plan for debt reduction on March 10, 1989. Brady's plan targeted Mexico because the Mexican debt at the end of 1988 was approximately [US] $107 billion and default on this debt could severely damage the U.S. economy.

12 The Brady Plan was devised to deter Mexico and/or any other developing country from defaulting on current external obligations. The main objectives of the plan were to:

- alleviate the scarcity of financial resources
- reverse capital flight
- maintain the important role of the international financial institutions and preserve their financial integrity
- encourage debt and debt service reduction on a voluntary basis

- recognize the importance of continued new lending
- provide free markets

If achieved in Mexico, these objectives would be implemented in the other developing countries to reduce their debts ("Excerpts From Brady Remarks on Debt" 1989, p. 37).

13   The plan recognized that financial institutions are apprehensive about lending money to the heavily indebted developing countries. It recognized as well that the International Monetary Fund and the World Bank, both created by the United Nations, face financial difficulty as more countries need money. Since these institutions are not receiving additional contributions from the member countries, financial assistance continues to be inadequate. In addition, capital flight continues to be a large problem as nationals in the financially unstable countries deposit large portions of their wealth outside the country. They have done this to keep their wealth intact and to earn higher returns than they can in the unstable domestic economy. If this capital could be reattracted to the developing countries, its investment in the domestic economy could provide a stimulant to economic growth.

14   Two solutions were put forth by Secretary Brady to solve these problems. In the long run, free markets were seen as the answer to the debt problem. Free markets with low trade barriers would increase trade between nations. By applying the theory of comparative advantage which states that a nation should export products it can produce at a relatively lower cost and import products it cannot produce as cheaply as other nations, a positive cash flow could be generated to repay the debt. This idea is not new. It has been part of many proposed solutions to Mexico's debt problem.

15   Secondly, in the short run, Treasury Secretary Brady believed debt reductions and lowered interest rates on all new loans would offer a respite until these economies could become self-sufficient and benefit from free markets. Brady recommended guidelines for U.S. banks to follow in reducing developing country debt. These guidelines consisted of three options:

1. exchange their credits for new bonds carrying a fixed annual interest rate of 6.25 percent (compared with floating interest rates of more than 10 percent)
2. accept a 35 percent reduction in the face value of their loans
3. provide additional loans. (Truell 1989, p. A13).

Under option one, the new bonds would be United States Treasury bonds. These more financially sound securities would give banks the incentive to implement the first option. Brady believed implementation of all or part of the recommended debt reduction plan (option two) would cut down the developing countries' debt and the interest paid on it, while allowing developing countries to continue borrowing to buttress their economies (option three) (Kilborn 1989, p. 35).

16   The first test of the Brady Plan to manage Latin America's $400 billion debt was to be aimed at Mexico. It was anticipated that a United States show of confidence in Mexico's ability to recover economically, along with a modest amount of financial aid, would trigger a surge of new investment. In particular, Mexico anticipated that money held by Mexicans abroad (some $84 billion, according to a 1988 estimate by Morgan Guaranty Trust) would be reinvested directly into the Mexican economy (Moffett 1989, p. A1). As a result, Mexico would have some financial maneuvering room. Once the financial sector gained some respite from the imminent short-term debt problems, new business investment would allow markets and free trade to solve a major portion of the debt crisis.

Problems with the Brady Plan

17   Unfortunately, many problems have arisen since the plan's announcement in 1989. The Bush administration and Mexico hoped that the hundreds of creditor banks would choose to follow the options proposed by the Brady Plan. This in itself was a huge supposition as banks wrestled with how to get the best return on their current investments at an acceptable risk level. Many larger banks' loan portfolios are heavily laden with loans to foreign countries. Many banks are also under heavy pressure from shareholders not to offer new loans to the developing countries (Duke 1989, p. A11). These loans were made when the rate of return was projected to be high, but now lenders are skittish because of rumors of default and interest rate restructuring, both of which will reduce banks' profits.

18   Chase Manhattan Corporation came up with its own option and began setting up large reserves to use as a buffer to write down its overseas loans. It decided not to lend any new money to Mexico or the other developing nations. If this policy persists and is followed by other banks, Mexico and the other developing countries will be unable to make interest payments on current debt and may have to default on their loans (Guenther 1989, p. A3).

19   To offset Chase Manhattan's action, the Bush administration, in September 1989, offered an incentive to the banks. The Securities and Exchange Commission (SEC) would allow banks to write down losses at a slower rate. By slowing the write down process, the banks' losses from the investments would not be as large as otherwise. By keeping their profits up, banks would appear more financially secure, satisfy their stockholders, and increase flexibility to lenders, thus allowing them to offer new loans to Mexico and other debt-laden countries as the Brady Plan intended (Duke 1989, p. A11).

20   Unfortunately, a second dilemma loomed on the horizon as it became apparent that the Brady Plan was in reality unlikely significantly to reduce

Mexico's $100 billion foreign debt. It appeared that the debt would continue to escalate even if Mexico and the other developing nations received new loans. To deal with the problem, the new focus of the Brady Plan was to cut back interest payments on foreign bank debt and provide further loans (Truell 1989, p. A13). However, these short-term fixes will do little to help Mexico provide a climate conducive to economic recovery in the markets and free trade arena. If Mexico's economy falters, new loans to help bail it out will be hard to find.

21   The United States has already issued Treasury bonds to finance some of Mexico's short-term debt. Issuing more Treasury bonds to offset the financial sectors' unwillingness to incur losses would be folly. Any additional bonds issued would only shift the debt from banks to the U.S. Treasury, or to the International Monetary Fund and World Bank, which, in turn, are heavily financed by the United States.

22   Loan portfolios of the International Monetary Fund and the World Bank are currently coming under pressure. Both institutions are faced with increased demand for loans from the developing countries as private banks have become reluctant to extend them credit. Consequently, many of the loans from these institutions have been made to the least creditworthy and most heavily indebted countries (Roberts 1989, p. A14). These loans have been made to keep debt-ridden countries from defaulting. As funds from the International Monetary Fund and the World Bank dry up, the United States may be unwilling to provide additional funds.

23   A final irony is that as economic problems have mounted in Mexico and other debt-ridden nations, the United States is seen by foreigners as a safe place to invest money. The Brady Plan does not address the underlying structural problems that have turned the United States into one of the world's biggest tax havens (Moffett 1989, p. A1). Currently, foreign investments are, for the most part, taxable only by the United States; they are protected from the tax laws of the country of origin. Mexico anticipated that the implementation of the Brady Plan would provide a positive economic climate which would attract some of the capital back from where it is sheltered.

Other Aspects of the Brady Plan

24   Even though the Brady Plan has not been implemented as planned, it has triggered a surge of economic development and new optimism in Mexico, which has deterred skittish investors from sending even more money abroad (Moffett 1989, p. A1). Mexico must continue on a path of accelerated economic development. Though reattracting the capital invested outside of the country is necessary, it is not enough. In addition, the market economy and

free trade will need to be bolstered by financial sources and/or government supported programs to help complete the recovery.

25   President Carlos Salinas de Gortari of Mexico spent his first ten months in office implementing government programs designed to influence those Mexican capitalists with wealth abroad to reinvest in Mexico. He has instituted trade liberalization and new foreign-investment regulations. He has deregulated transportation and announced the sale of some state controlled enterprises. Moreover, privatizations now under consideration in the steel, fertilizer, and banking sectors would further increase investor confidence. Even Mexico's protected petroleum industry has been partially opened to private and foreign investment (Baer 1989, p. A13). However, Mexico's domestic debt remains oppressive.

26   President Salinas and the Mexican government have not undertaken these policy changes without political and private sector opposition. The opposition is concerned that too much foreign investment will return Mexico to the position of domination by foreign-owned businesses. However, nationalized businesses have not helped solve the debt problem; in fact, they may have caused Mexican investors to invest their money out of reach of the government. Encouraging domestic and foreign investment should provide capital and create a positive environment for progress. Thus, the Brady Plan, coupled with the actions taken by President Salinas, could provide some respite from Mexico's debt crisis.

Conclusion

27   Even though the problem of finding financing to help Mexico and the other developing nations seems insurmountable, it could be alleviated by a concerted effort by all the countries of the world, not just the United States. As a major world leader, the United States must convince other capital-rich countries to invest in Mexico and other developing countries. If bilateral attempts do not achieve any positive results, multilateral attempts in the United Nations must be undertaken to demonstrate why it is in everyone's best interest to solve the developing nations' debt problems. Should sufficient financial aid not be extended and Mexico defaults on its debt, the resulting domino effect as other developing countries default could cause international monetary instability, if not world-wide depression.

28   The World Bank and the International Monetary Fund must receive increased funding from other countries. The United States has provided a large percentage of the funds to these institutions since the United Nations' inception after World War II, but many nations are economically better off now than they were then and could shoulder a larger share of the burden. Since

no country exists in isolation, all countries must cooperate in order to survive.

Works Cited

Baer, M. Delal. "Mexico's Race Against the Clock," *The Wall Street Journal,* Sept. 29, 1989, p. A13.

Duke, Paul, Jr. "Bank Rules are Eased on Write Downs of Debtor-Country Loans, SEC Staff Says," *The Wall Street Journal,* Sept. 14, 1989, p. A11.

"Excerpts from the Brady Remarks on Debt," *The New York Times,* Mar. 11, 1989, p. 37.

Guenther, Robert and Peter Truell. "Chase Manhattan Corp. Increases Loan-Loss Reserves by $1.15 Billion," *The Wall Street Journal,* Sept. 21, 1989, p. A3.

Kilborn, Peter T. "Debt-Policy Shift Set on 3rd World," *The New York Times,* Mar. 11, 1989, p. 35.

Moffett, Matt. "Mexico's Capital Flight Still Racks Economy, Despite the Brady Plan," *The Wall Street Journal,* Sept. 25, 1989, p. A14.

Roberts, Paul Craig. "It's the World Bank's Turn to Adjust," *The Wall Street Journal,* Sept. 10, 1989, p. A14.

Rudolf, James D., ed. *Mexico, A Country Study.* 3d ed. Library of Congress, 1985.

Truell, Peter. "Mexican Pact Shows U.S. Has Refocused Its Strategy Away from Debt Reduction," *The Wall Street Journal,* July 25, 1989, p. A13. ❖

Questions to Ponder

1. What function does Steven Armbrecht's early section on the "History of the Mexican Debt Crisis" serve?
2. What is the value of creating subsections with titles in an extended essay like this one?
3. What is the value of isolating and setting in specific goals and features, such as those of the Brady plan on pages 428 and 429?
4. For an audience of interested laypeople, what do you think would be the best ratio of information (facts) to analysis/interpretation? Does Steven Armbrecht generate enough of each?

Writing Possibilities

1. Using Steven Armbrecht's essay as a model, choose another developing country and research its economic history and current needs. Share your findings either in a letter or a report to your senators and representatives.

2. Explore the possibility of default of loan repayments. Will your research lead you to project a futuristic nightmare or to something else? Describe alternative scenarios in a report for the World Bank.
3. Write a satiric essay in which you would treat student loan debt as similar to developing country debt. Do the two have anything in common? Significant differences?
4. Write a letter to your parents asking for a Brady Plan for your own current debts.

FLOW
Mihaly Csikszentmihalyi

For more than two decades Professor Mihaly Csikszentmihalyi, professor and former head of the Department of Psychology at the University of Chicago, has been studying states of "optimal experience," those times when people report feelings of enjoyment, concentration, and deep involvement. During these generating experiences, which Professor Csikszentmihalyi calls "flow," people typically feel strong, alert, unself-conscious, and in effortless control. They are working at the peak of their abilities. During such moments, the sense of time seems to disappear—as do any emotional problems. Those in "flow" speak of an exhilarating feeling of transcendence, of breaking out of the boundaries of identity.

Students can learn to make these peak generating experiences a regular part of their lives, as Professor Csikszentmihalyi explains in the following essay.

Brief Warm-up Writing Exercises

1. Make a list of tasks or subjects that are so easy for you that you find them boring.
2. Now freewrite about the opposite experience of facing a task or subject that was so difficult or challenging that it created great anxiety in you.

3. Now describe any experience you have had when you were so caught up in what you were doing that you lost all track of time.

❖ ## Paths of Liberation

1   This simple truth–that the control of consciousness determines the quality of life–has been known for a long time; in fact, for as long as human records exist. The oracle's advice in ancient Delphi, "Know thyself," implied it. It was clearly recognized by Aristotle, whose notion of the "virtuous activity of the soul" in many ways prefigures the argument of this book, and it was developed by the Stoic philosophers in classical antiquity. The Christian monastic orders perfected various methods for learning how to channel thoughts and desires. Ignatius of Loyola rationalized them in his famous spiritual exercises. The last great attempt to free consciousness from the domination of impulses and social controls was psychoanalysis; as Freud pointed out, the two tyrants that fought for control over the mind were the id and the superego, the first a servant of the genes, the second a lackey of society—both representing the "Other." Opposed to them was the ego, which stood for the genuine needs of the self connected to its concrete environment.

2   In the East techniques for achieving control over consciousness proliferated and achieved levels of enormous sophistication. Although quite different from one another in many respects, the yogi disciplines in India, the Taoist approach to life developed in China, and the Zen varieties of Buddhism all seek to free consciousness from the deterministic influences of outside forces—be they biological or social in nature. Thus, for instance, a yogi disciplines his mind to ignore pain that ordinary people would have no choice but to let into their awareness; similarly he can ignore the insistent claims of hunger or sexual arousal that most people would be helpless to resist. The same effect can be achieved in different ways, either through perfecting a severe mental discipline as in Yoga or through cultivating constant spontaneity as in Zen. But the intended result is identical: to free inner life from the threat of chaos, on the one hand, and from the rigid conditioning of biological urges, on the other, and hence to become independent from the social controls that exploit both.

3   But if it is true that people have known for thousands of years what it takes to become free and in control of one's life, why haven't we made more progress in this direction? Why are we as helpless, or more so, than our ancestors were in facing the chaos that interferes with happiness? There are at least two good explanations for this failure. In the first place, the kind of knowledge—or wisdom—one needs for emancipating consciousness is not cumulative. It cannot be condensed into a formula; it cannot be memorized and then routinely applied. Like other complex forms of expertise, such as a

mature political judgment or a refined aesthetic sense, it must be earned through trial-and-error experience by each individual, generation after generation. Control over consciousness is not simply a cognitive skill. At least as much as intelligence, it requires the commitment of emotions and will. It is not enough to *know* how to do it; one must *do* it, consistently, in the same way as athletes or musicians who must keep practicing what they know in theory. And this is never easy. Progress is relatively fast in fields that apply knowledge to the material world, such as physics or genetics. But it is painfully slow when knowledge is to be applied to modify our own habits and desires.

4   Second, the knowledge of how to control consciousness must be reformulated every time the cultural context changes. The wisdom of the mystics, of the Sufi, of the great yogis, or of the Zen masters might have been excellent in their own time—and might still be the best, if we lived in those times and in those cultures. But when transplanted to contemporary California those systems lose quite a bit of their original power. They contain elements that are specific to their original contexts, and when these accidental components are not distinguished from what is essential, the path to freedom gets overgrown by brambles of meaningless mumbo jumbo. Ritual form wins over substance, and the seeker is back where he started.

5   Control over consciousness cannot be institutionalized. As soon as it becomes part of a set of social rules and norms, it ceases to be effective in the way it was originally intended to be. Routinization, unfortunately, tends to take place very rapidly. Freud was still alive when his quest for liberating the ego from its oppressors was turned into a staid ideology and a rigidly regulated profession. Marx was even less fortunate: his attempts to free consciousness from the tyranny of economic exploitation were soon turned into a system of repression that would have boggled the poor founder's mind. And as Dostoyevsky among many others observed, if Christ had returned to preach his message of liberation in the Middle Ages, he would have been crucified again and again by the leaders of that very church whose worldly power was built on his name.

6   In each new epoch—perhaps every generation, or even every few years, if the conditions in which we live change that rapidly—it becomes necessary to rethink and reformulate what it takes to establish autonomy in consciousness. Early Christianity helped the masses free themselves from the power of the ossified imperial regime and from an ideology that could give meaning only to the lives of the rich and the powerful. The Reformation liberated great numbers of people from their political and ideological exploitation by the Roman Church. The *philosophes* and later the statesmen who drafted the American Constitution resisted the controls established by kings, popes, and aristocracy. When the inhuman conditions of factory labor became the most obvious obstacles to the workers' freedom to order their own experience, as they were in nineteenth-century industrial Europe, Marx's message turned out to be especially relevant. The much more subtle but equally coercive social controls of bourgeois Vienna made Freud's road to liberation pertinent to those whose minds had been warped by such conditions. The insights of the

Gospels, of Martin Luther, of the framers of the Constitution, of Marx and Freud—just to mention a very few of those attempts that have been made in the West to increase happiness by enhancing freedom—will always be valid and useful, even though some of them have been perverted in their application. But they certainly do not exhaust either the problems or the solutions.

7   Given the recurring need to return to this central question of how to achieve mastery over one's life, what does the present state of knowledge say about it? How can it help a person learn to rid himself of anxieties and fears and thus become free of the controls of society, whose rewards he can now take or leave? As suggested before, the way is through control over consciousness, which in turn leads to control over the quality of experience. Any small gain in that direction will make life more rich, more enjoyable, more meaningful. . . .

8   We have seen how people describe the common characteristics of optimal experience: a sense that one's skills are adequate to cope with the challenges at hand, in a goal-directed, rule-bound action system that provides clear clues as to how well one is performing. Concentration is so intense that there is no attention left over to think about anything irrelevant, or to worry about problems. Self-consciousness disappears, and the sense of time becomes distorted. An activity that produces such experiences is so gratifying that people are willing to do it for its own sake, with little concern for what they will get out of it, even when it is difficult, or dangerous.

9   But how do such experiences happen? Occasionally flow may occur by chance, because of a fortunate coincidence of external and internal conditions. For instance, friends may be having dinner together, and someone brings up a topic that involves everyone in the conversation. One by one they begin to make jokes and tell stories, and pretty soon all are having fun and feeling good about one another. While such events may happen spontaneously, it is much more likely that flow will result either from a structured activity, or from an individual's ability to make flow occur, or both.

10 Why is playing a game enjoyable, while the things we have to do every day—like working or sitting at home—are often so boring? And why is it that one person will experience joy even in a concentration camp, while another gets the blahs while vacationing at a fancy resort? Answering these questions will make it easier to understand how experience can be shaped to improve the quality of life. This [section] will explore those particular activities that are likely to produce optimal experiences, and the personal traits that help people achieve flow easily.

Flow Activities

11 When describing optimal experience in this work, we have given as examples such activities as making music, rock climbing, dancing, sailing, chess, and so

forth. What makes these activities conducive to flow is that they were *designed* to make optimal experience easier to achieve. They have rules that require the learning of skills, they set up goals, they provide feedback, they make control possible. They facilitate concentration and involvement by making the activity as distinct as possible from the so-called "paramount reality" of everyday existence. For example, in each sport participants dress up in eye-catching uniforms and enter special enclaves that set them apart temporarily from ordinary mortals. For the duration of the event, players and spectators cease to act in terms of common sense, and concentrate instead on the peculiar reality of the game.

12   Such *flow activities* have as their primary function the provision of enjoyable experiences. Play, art, pageantry, ritual, and sports are some examples. Because of the way they are constructed, they help participants and spectators achieve an ordered state of mind that is highly enjoyable.

13   Roger Caillois, the French psychological anthropologist, has divided the world's games (using that word in its broadest sense to include every form of pleasurable activity) into four broad classes, depending on the kind of experiences they provide. *Agon* includes games that have competition as their main feature, such as most sports and athletic events; *alea* is the class that includes all games of chance, from dice to bingo; *ilinx*, or vertigo, is the name he gives to activities that alter consciousness by scrambling ordinary perception, such as riding a merry-go-round or skydiving; and *mimicry* is the group of activities in which alternative realities are created, such as dance, theater, and the arts in general.

14   Using this scheme, it can be said that games offer opportunities to go beyond the boundaries of ordinary experience in four different ways. In agonistic games, the participant must stretch her skills to meet the challenge provided by the skills of the opponents. The roots of the word "compete" are the Latin *con petire,* which meant "to seek together." What each person seeks is to actualize her potential, and this task is made easier when others force us to do our best. Of course, competition improves experience only as long as attention is focused primarily on the activity itself. If extrinsic goals—such as beating the opponent, wanting to impress an audience, or obtaining a big professional contract—are what one is concerned about, then competition is likely to become a distraction, rather than an incentive to focus consciousness on what is happening.

15   Aleatory games are enjoyable because they give the illusion of controlling the inscrutable future. The Plains Indians shuffled the marked rib bones of buffaloes to predict the outcome of the next hunt, the Chinese interpreted the pattern in which sticks fell, and the Ashanti of East Africa read the future in the way their sacrificed chickens died. Divination is a universal feature of culture, an attempt to break out of the constraints of the present and get a glimpse of what is going to happen. Games of chance draw on the same need. The buffalo ribs become dice, the sticks of the I Ching become playing cards,

and the ritual of divination becomes gambling—a secular activity in which people try to outsmart each other or try to outguess fate.

16   Vertigo is the most direct way to alter consciousness. Small children love to turn around in circles until they are dizzy; the whirling dervishes in the Middle East go into states of ecstasy through the same means. Any activity that transforms the way we perceive reality is enjoyable, a fact that accounts for the attraction of "consciousness-expanding" drugs of all sorts, from magic mushrooms to alcohol to the current Pandora's box of hallucinogenic chemicals. But consciousness cannot be expanded; all we can do is shuffle its content, which gives us the impression of having broadened it somehow. The price of most artificially induced alterations, however, is that we lose control over that very consciousness we were supposed to expand.

17   Mimicry makes us feel as though we are more than what we actually are through fantasy, pretense, and disguise. Our ancestors, as they danced wearing the masks of their gods, felt a sense of powerful identification with the forces that ruled the universe. By dressing like a deer, the Yaqui Indian dancer felt at one with the spirit of the animal he impersonated. The singer who blends her voice in the harmony of a choir finds chills running down her spine as she feels at one with the beautiful sound she helps create. The little girl playing with her doll and her brother pretending to be a cowboy also stretch the limits of their ordinary experience, so that they become, temporarily, someone different and more powerful—as well as learn the gender-typed adult roles of their society.

18   In our studies, we found that every flow activity, whether it involved competition, chance, or any other dimension of experience, had this in common: It provided a sense of discovery, a creative feeling of transporting the person into a new reality. It pushed the person to higher levels of performance, and led to previously undreamed-of states of consciousness. In short, it transformed the self by making it more complex. In this growth of the self lies the key to flow activities.

19   A simple diagram might help explain why this should be the case. Let us assume that the figure (p. 440) represents a specific activity—for example, the game of tennis. The two theoretically most important dimensions of the experience, challenges and skills, are represented on the two axes of the diagram. The letter A represents Alex, a boy who is learning to play tennis. The diagram shows Alex at four different points in time. When he first starts playing (A_1), Alex has practically no skills, and the only challenge he faces is hitting the ball over the net. This is not a very difficult feat, but Alex is likely to enjoy it because the difficulty is just right for his rudimentary skills. So at this point he will probably be in flow. But he cannot stay there long. After a while, if he keeps practicing, his skills are bound to improve, and then he will grow bored just batting the ball over the net (A_2). Or it might happen that he meets a more practiced opponent, in which case he will realize that there are much harder challenges for him

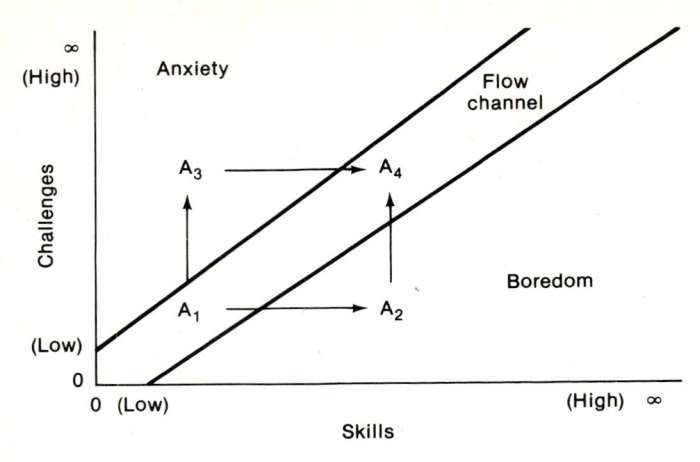

Why the complexity of consciousness increases as a result of flow experiences.

than just lobbing the ball—at that point, he will feel some anxiety (A_3) concerning his poor performance.

20   Neither boredom nor anxiety are positive experiences, so Alex will be motivated to return to the flow state. How is he to do it? Glancing again at the diagram, we see that if he is bored (A_2) and wishes to be in flow again, Alex has essentially only one choice: to increase the challenges he is facing. (He also has a second choice, which is to give up tennis altogether—in which case A would simply disappear from the diagram.) By setting himself a new and more difficult goal that matches his skills—for instance, to beat an opponent just a little more advanced than he is—Alex would be back in flow (A_4).

21   If Alex is anxious (A_3), the way back to flow requires that he increase his skills. Theoretically he could also reduce the challenges he is facing, and thus return to flow where he started (in A_1), but in practice it is difficult to ignore challenges once one is aware that they exist.

22   The diagram shows that both A_1 and A_4 represent situations in which Alex is in flow. Although both are equally enjoyable, the two states are quite different in that A_4 is a more *complex* experience than A_1. It is more complex because it involves greater challenges, and demands greater skills from the player.

23   But A_4, although complex and enjoyable, does not represent a stable situation, either. As Alex keeps playing, either he will become bored by the stale opportunities he finds at that level, or he will become anxious and frustrated by his relatively low ability. So the motivation to enjoy himself again will push him to get back into the flow channel, but now at a level of complexity even *higher* than A_4.

24   It is this dynamic feature that explains why flow activities lead to growth and discovery. One cannot enjoy doing the same thing at the same level for long. We grow either bored or frustrated; and then the desire to enjoy ourselves again pushes us to stretch our skills, or to discover new opportunities for using them. ❖

Questions to Ponder

1. Why does focusing (or concentrating) require imposing mental limits or rules?
2. What goal might you set for yourself that would be challenging—but not too challenging?
3. What kinds of feedback are there? What sorts of feedback would help you know if you are meeting your goal?
4. What might you do to increase the challenge for yourself in a certain area of your life?
5. Why do you think the experience of setting and achieving goals makes people deeper, richer, and happier human beings?

Writing Possibilities

1. Interview ten people (including yourself), asking them (a) if they have ever experienced that sense of absorbing, timeless flow; (b) to describe the experience; and (c) to explain what they think brought about the flow. Analyze and classify (if possible) the different responses. Then write a report of what you learned from your research on flow.
2. Look at the personal flow experience you described in warm-up writing exercise 3. Now try to recapture this experience using a form and language designed to simulate the experience. Be creative.
3. Select the aspect of writing that causes you most anxiety, and develop a conscious program of steps, rules, and goals to help you decrease your anxiety level, increase your skill level, and perhaps turn even writing into a "flow" experience.
4. Do research about flow as experienced by athletes or artists. Write a report sharing your findings, including a section on how nonathletes or nonartists can tap into such "highs."

Landscape and Narrative
Barry Lopez

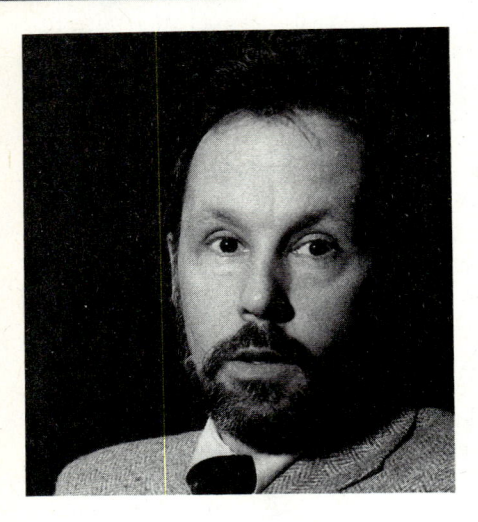

When the reader comes to a writer's work, he or she should sense, very quickly I think, the presence of a distinct personality, someone with a certain ethical, moral, and artistic dimension. And insofar as that writer is a worthy illuminator of the world for the reader, he or she continues to read the writer's work. Writing is really an extraordinary act of self-assertion. You put down on paper the way you understand the world. But, for me, there must be a point where the reader loses sight of the writer, where he gains another understanding, a vision of what lies before the writer; so that by the time the reader finishes a book or an essay, he's really thinking about his own thoughts with regard to that subject, or that place, or that set of events, and not so much about the writer's. The initial step is an act of ego, the next step a loss of ego, a sort of disappearance.

I think this is an old ideal among writers; writers pretty consistently agree among themselves, in my experience, that they are conduits, some sort of lightning rod, an instrument through which something else is passed. That doesn't mean that you're completely passive as a writer. What it means, to me, is that you bring the skills you have to bear—your insight and command of language, your ability to research, whatever your talents might be—to shape something that is moving through you.

Brief Warm-up Writing Exercises

1. Freewrite about any encounters you have had with wild animals.
2. Try to capture in words the relationship of one object in your present classroom to another: the ticking of the clock and the students' attention; the light playing on a wall poster; your teacher's clothing as it affects his or her behavior. Choose some relationship and write about it.
3. Freewrite your feelings after you've heard or read a good story. What effect does that story have on you?

1. ❖ One summer evening in a remote village in the Brooks Range of Alaska, I sat among a group of men listening to hunting stories about the trapping and pursuit of animals. I was particularly interested in several incidents involving wolverine, in part because a friend of mine was studying wolverine in Canada, among the Cree, but, too, because I find this animal such an intense creature. To hear about its life is to learn more about fierceness.

2. Wolverines are not intentionally secretive, hiding their lives from view, but they are seldom observed. The range of their known behavior is less than that of, say, bears or wolves. Still, that evening no gratuitous details were set out. This was somewhat odd, for wolverine easily excite the imagination; they can loom suddenly in the landscape with authority, with an aura larger than their compact physical dimensions, drawing one's immediate and complete attention. Wolverine also have a deserved reputation for resoluteness in the worst winters, for ferocious strength. But neither did these attributes induce the men to embellish.

3. I listened carefully to these stories, taking pleasure in the sharply observed detail surrounding the dramatic thread of events. The story I remember most vividly was about a man hunting a wolverine from a snow machine in the spring. He followed the animal's tracks for several miles over rolling tundra in a certain valley. Soon he caught sight ahead of a dark spot on the crest of a hill—the wolverine pausing to look back. The hunter was catching up, but each time he came over a rise the wolverine was looking back from the next rise, just out of range. The hunter topped one more rise and met the wolverine bounding toward him. Before he could pull his rifle from its scabbard the wolverine flew across the engine cowl and the windshield, hitting him square in the chest. The hunter scrambled his arms wildly, trying to get the wolverine out of his lap, and fell over as he did so. The wolverine jumped clear as the snow machine rolled over, and fixed the man with a stare. He had not bitten, not even scratched the man. Then the wolverine walked away. The man thought of reaching for the gun, but no, he did not.

4. The other stories were like this, not so much making a point as evoking something about contact with wild animals that would never be completely understood.

5. When the stories were over, four or five of us walked out of the home of our host. The surrounding land, in the persistent light of a far northern summer, was still visible for miles—the striated, pitched massifs of the Brooks Range; the shy, willow-lined banks of the John River flowing south from Anaktuvuk Pass; and the flat tundra plain, opening with great affirmation to the north. The landscape seemed alive because of the stories. It was precisely these ocherous tones, this kind of willow, exactly this austerity that had informed the wolverine narratives. I felt exhilaration, and a deeper confirmation of the stories. The mundane tasks which awaited me I anticipated now with pleasure. The stories had renewed in me a sense of the purpose of my life.

6   This feeling, an inexplicable renewal of enthusiasm after storytelling, is familiar to many people. It does not seem to matter greatly what the subject is, as long as the context is intimate and the story is told for its own sake, not forced to serve merely as the vehicle for an idea. The tone of the story need not be solemn. The darker aspects of life need not be ignored. But I think intimacy is indispensable—a feeling that derives from the listener's trust and a storyteller's certain knowledge of his subject and regard for his audience. This intimacy deepens if the storyteller tempers his authority with humility, or when terms of idiomatic expression, or at least the physical setting for the story, are shared.

7   I think of two landscapes—one outside the self, the other within. The external landscape is the one we see—not only the line and color of the land and its shading at different times of the day, but also its plants and animals in season, its weather, its geology, the record of its climate and evolution. If you walk up, say, a dry arroyo in the Sonoran Desert you will feel a mounding and rolling of sand and silt beneath your foot that is distinctive. You will anticipate the crumbling of the sedimentary earth in the arroyo bank as your hand reaches out, and in that tangible evidence you will sense a history of water in the region. Perhaps a black-throated sparrow lands in a paloverde bush—the resiliency of the twig under the bird, that precise shade of yellowish-green against the milk-blue sky, the fluttering whir of the arriving sparrow, are what I mean by "the landscape." Draw on the smell of creosote bush, or clack stones together in the dry air. Feel how light is the desiccated dropping of the kangaroo rat. Study an animal track obscured by the wind. These are all elements of the land, and what makes the landscape comprehensible are the relationships between them. One learns a landscape finally not by knowing the name or identity of everything in it, but by perceiving the relationships in it—like that between the sparrow and the twig. The difference between the relationships and the elements is the same as that between written history and a catalog of events.

8   The second landscape I think of is an interior one, a kind of projection within a person of a part of the exterior landscape. Relationships in the exterior landscape include those that are named and discernible, such as the nitrogen cycle, or a vertical sequence of Ordovician limestone, and others that are uncodified or ineffable, such as winter light falling on a particular kind of granite, or the effect of humidity on the frequency of a blackpoll warbler's burst of song. That these relationships have purpose and order, however inscrutable they may seem to us, is a tenet of evolution. Similarly, the speculations, intuitions, and formal ideas we refer to as "mind" are a set of relationships in the interior landscape with purpose and order; some of these are obvious, many impenetrably subtle. The shape and character of these relationships in a person's thinking, I believe, are deeply influenced by where on this earth one goes, what one touches, the patterns one observes in nature—the intricate history of one's life in the land, even a life in the city, where wind, the chirp of birds, the line of a falling leaf, are known. These thoughts are arranged,

further, according to the thread of one's moral, intellectual, and spiritual development. The interior landscape responds to the character and subtlety of an exterior landscape; the shape of the individual mind is affected by land as it is by genes.

9   In stories like those I heard at Anaktuvuk Pass about wolverine, the relationship between separate elements in the land is set forth clearly. It is put in a simple framework of sequential incidents and apposite detail. If the exterior landscape is limned well, the listener often feels that he has heard something pleasing and authentic—trustworthy. We derive this sense of confidence I think not so much from verifiable truth as from an understanding that lying has played no role in the narrative. The storyteller is obligated to engage the reader with a precise vocabulary, to set forth a coherent and dramatic rendering of incidents—and to be ingenuous.

10 When one hears a story one takes pleasure in it for different reasons—for the euphony of its phrases, an aspect of the plot, or because one identifies with one of the characters. With certain stories certain individuals may experience a deeper, more profound sense of well-being. This latter phenomenon, in my understanding, rests at the heart of storytelling as an elevated experience among aboriginal peoples. It results from bringing two landscapes together. The exterior landscape is organized according to principles or laws or tendencies beyond human control. It is understood to contain an integrity that is beyond human analysis and unimpeachable. Insofar as the storyteller depicts various subtle and obvious relationships in the exterior landscape accurately in his story, and insofar as he orders them along traditional lines of meaning to create the narrative, the narrative will "ring true." The listener who "takes the story to heart" will feel a pervasive sense of congruence within himself and also with the world.

11 Among the Navajo and, as far as I know, many other native peoples, the land is thought to exhibit a sacred order. That order is the basis of ritual. The rituals themselves reveal the power in that order. Art, architecture, vocabulary, and costume, as well as ritual, are derived from the perceived natural order of the universe—from observations and meditations on the exterior landscape. An indigenous philosophy—metaphysics, ethics, epistemology, aesthetics, and logic—may also be derived from a people's continuous attentiveness to both the obvious (scientific) and ineffable (artistic) orders of the local landscape. Each individual, further, undertakes to order his interior landscape according to the exterior landscape. To succeed in this means to achieve a balanced state of mental health.

12 I think of the Navajo for a specific reason. Among the various sung ceremonies of this people—Enemyway, Coyoteway, Red Antway, Uglyway—is one called Beautyway. In the Navajo view, the elements of one's interior life—one's psychological makeup and moral bearing—are subject to a persistent principle of disarray. Beautyway is, in part, a spiritual invocation of the order of the exterior universe, that irreducible, holy complexity that manifests itself as all things changing through time (a Navajo definition of beauty,

hózhǫ́ǫ́). The purpose of this invocation is to recreate in the individual who is the subject of the Beautyway ceremony that same order, to make the individual again a reflection of the myriad enduring relationships of the landscape.

13 I believe story functions in a similar way. A story draws on relationships in the exterior landscape and projects them onto the interior landscape. The purpose of storytelling is to achieve harmony between the two landscapes, to use all the elements of story—syntax, mood, figures of speech—in a harmonious way to reproduce the harmony of the land in the individual's interior. Inherent in story is the power to reorder a state of psychological confusion through contact with the pervasive truth of those relationships we call "the land."

14 These thoughts, of course, are susceptible to interpretation. I am convinced, however, that these observations can be applied to the kind of prose we call nonfiction as well as to traditional narrative forms such as the novel and the short story, and to some poems. Distinctions between fiction and nonfiction are sometimes obscured by arguments over what constitutes "the truth." In the aboriginal literature I am familiar with, the first distinction made among narratives is to separate the authentic from the inauthentic. Myth, which we tend to regard as fictitious or "merely metaphorical," is as authentic, as real, as the story of a wolverine in a man's lap. (A distinction is made, of course, about the elevated nature of myth—and frequently the circumstances of myth-telling are more rigorously prescribed than those for the telling of legends or vernacular stories—but all of these narratives are rooted in the local landscape. To violate *that* connection is to call the narrative itself into question.)

15 The power of narrative to nurture and heal, to repair a spirit in disarray, rests on two things: the skillful invocation of unimpeachable sources and a listener's knowledge that no hypocrisy or subterfuge is involved. This last simple fact is to me one of the most imposing aspects of the Holocene history of man.

16 We are more accustomed now to thinking of "the truth" as something that can be explicitly stated, rather than as something that can be evoked in a metaphorical way outside science and Occidental culture. Neither can truth be reduced to aphorism or formulas. It is something alive and unpronounceable. Story creates an atmosphere in which it becomes discernible as a pattern. For a storyteller to insist on relationships that do not exist is to lie. Lying is the opposite of story. (I do not mean to confuse ignorance with deception, or to imply that a storyteller can perceive all that is inherent in the land. Every storyteller falls short of a perfect limning of the landscape—perception and language both fail. But to make up something that is not there, something which can never be corroborated in the land,

to knowingly set forth a false relationship, is to be lying, no longer telling a story.)

17   Because of the intricate, complex nature of the land, it is not always possible for a storyteller to grasp what is contained in a story. The intent of the storyteller, then, must be to evoke, honestly, some single aspect of all that the land contains. The storyteller knows that because different individuals grasp the story at different levels, the focus of his regard for truth must be at the primary one—with who was there, what happened, when, where, and why things occurred. The story will then possess similar truth at other levels—the integrity inherent at the primary level of meaning will be conveyed everywhere else. As long as the storyteller carefully describes the order before him, and uses his storytelling skill to heighten and emphasize certain relationships, it is even possible for the story to be more successful than the storyteller himself is able to imagine.

18   I would like to make a final point about the wolverine stories I heard at Anaktuvuk Pass. I wrote down the details afterward, concentrating especially on aspects of the biology and ecology of the animals. I sent the information on to my friend living with the Cree. When, many months later, I saw him, I asked whether the Cree had enjoyed these insights of the Nunamiut into the nature of the wolverine. What had they said?

19   "You know," he told me, "how they are. They said, 'That could happen.' "

20   In these uncomplicated words the Cree declared their own knowledge of the wolverine. They acknowledged that although they themselves had never seen the things the Nunamiut spoke of, they accepted them as accurate observations, because they did not consider story a context for misrepresentation. They also preserved their own dignity by not overstating their confidence in the Nunamiut, a distant and unknown people.

21   Whenever I think of this courtesy on the part of the Cree I think of the dignity that is ours when we cease to demand the truth and realize that the best we can have of those substantial truths that guide our lives is metaphorical—a story. And the most of it we are likely to discern comes only when we accord one another the respect the Cree showed the Nunamiut. Beyond this—that the interior landscape is a metaphorical representation of the exterior landscape, that the truth reveals itself most fully not in dogma but in the paradox, irony, and contradictions that distinguish compelling narratives—beyond this there are only failures of imagination: reductionism in science; fundamentalism in religion; fascism in politics.

22   Our national literatures should be important to us insofar as they sustain us with illumination and heal us. They can always do that so long as they are written with respect for both the source and the reader, and with an understanding of why the human heart and the land have been brought together so regularly in human history. ❖

Questions to Ponder

1. Why do you think Barry Lopez chose to begin and end his essay with stories about the wolverine?
2. Why do beginning writers often focus too generally rather than on the specific relationship of one element to another? Why is focusing on relationships (both exterior and interior) one way to generate material?
3. In Barry Lopez's view, what are the qualities of the best storytellers?
4. Do you agree with Barry Lopez that a person's interior landscape (one's ideas, intuitions, and speculations) responds to the character of the exterior landscape? If you agree, why might this be so? If you disagree, why do you believe this interior response may not occur?
5. Do you agree with Barry Lopez that stories have the power to "nurture and heal, to repair a spirit in disarray"? How do they do this? What stories (from books, films, or life) have healed you?

Writing Possibilities

1. Write a series of paragraphs in which you try to tell the simple truths about an animal (or animals) you have seen or known—in the manner of the Nunamuit. When you finish, look back to see if you have included any unnecessary details or false relationships.
2. Write a short essay on some landscape you know, paying attention to both the obvious (scientific) order and the ineffable.
3. Attempt a piece of writing that would project the relationships of an exterior landscape into the interior landscape: the harmony of the land to a harmonious inner state, for example, or a disharmonious landscape and its effect on the inner being.

ABOUT MEN
Gretel Ehrlich

Beginning in 1976, when I went to Wyoming to make a film, I had the experience of waking up not knowing where I was, whether I was a man or a woman, or which toothbrush was mine. I had suffered a tragedy and made a drastic geographical and cultural move fairly baggageless, but I wasn't losing my grip. As Jim Bridges is reported to have said, "I wasn't lost, I just didn't know where I was for a few weeks." What I had lost (at least for a while) was my appetite for the life I had left: city surroundings, old friends, familiar comforts. It had occurred to me that comfort was only a disguise for discomfort; reference points, a disguise for what will always change.

Friends asked when I was going to stop "hiding out" in Wyoming. What appeared to them as a landscape of lunar desolation and intellectual backwardness was luxurious to me. For the first time I was able to take up residence on earth with no alibis, no self-promoting schemes.

The beginnings of this book took the form of raw journal entries sent to a friend in Hawaii. I chose her because she had been raised in a trailerhouse behind a bar in Wyoming; she then made the outlandish leap to a tropical climate and a life in academia. I was jumping in the opposite direction and suspected we might have crossed paths midair somewhere.

The sudden changes in my life brought on the usual zany dreams: road blocks were set up where I walked barefoot with a big suitcase; national boundaries changed overnight and I was forced to take a long, arbitrary detour. The detour, of course, became the actual path; the digressions in my writing, the narrative.

The truest art I would strive for in any work would be to give the page the same qualities as earth: weather would land on it harshly; light would elucidate the most difficult truths; wind would sweep away obtuse padding. Finally, the lessons of impermanence taught me this: loss constitutes an odd kind of fullness; despair empties out into an unquenchable appetite for life.

Brief Warm-up Writing Exercises

1. Brainstorm a list of the characteristics of the American or Canadian cowboy.

2. Freewrite about any experiences you have had in the American or Canadian West—or describe the Western scene of a film you remember.
3. Write about a person you know who is *not* like he or she appears to be on the surface.

1 ❖ When I'm in New York but feeling lonely for Wyoming I look for the Marlboro ads in the subway. What I'm aching to see is horseflesh, the glint of a spur, a line of distant mountains, brimming creeks, and a reminder of the ranchers and cowboys I've ridden with for the last eight years. But the men I see in those posters with their stern, humorless looks remind me of no one I know here. In our hellbent earnestness to romanticize the cowboy we've ironically disesteemed his true character. If he's "strong and silent" it's because there's probably no one to talk to. If he "rides away into the sunset" it's because he's been on horseback since four in the morning moving cattle and he's trying, fifteen hours later, to get home to his family. If he's "a rugged individualist" he's also part of a team: ranch work is teamwork and even the glorified open-range cowboys of the 1880s rode up and down the Chisholm Trail in the company of twenty or thirty other riders. Instead of the macho, trigger-happy man our culture has perversely wanted him to be, the cowboy is more apt to be convivial, quirky, and softhearted. To be "tough" on a ranch has nothing to do with conquests and displays of power. More often than not, circumstances—like the colt he's riding or an unexpected blizzard—are overpowering him. It's not toughness but "toughing it out" that counts. In other words, this macho, cultural artifact the cowboy has become is simply a man who possesses resilience, patience, and an instinct for survival. "Cowboys are just like a pile of rocks—everything happens to them. They get climbed on, kicked, rained and snowed on, scuffed up by wind. Their job is 'just to take it,' " one old-timer told me.

2 A cowboy is someone who loves his work. Since the hours are long—ten to fifteen hours a day—and the pay is $30 he has to. What's required of him is an odd mixture of physical vigor and maternalism. His part of the beef-raising industry is to birth and nurture calves and take care of their mothers. For the most part his work is done on horseback and in a lifetime he sees and comes to know more animals than people. The iconic myth surrounding him is built on American notions of heroism: the index of a man's value as measured in physical courage. Such ideas have perverted manliness into a self-absorbed race for cheap thrills. In a rancher's world, courage has less to do with facing danger than with acting spontaneously—usually on behalf of an animal or another rider. If a cow is stuck in a boghole he throws a loop around her neck, takes his dally (a half hitch around the saddle horn), and pulls her out with horsepower. If a calf is born sick, he may take her home, warm her in front of the kitchen fire, and massage her legs until dawn. One friend, whose favorite horse was trying to swim a lake with hobbles on, dove

under water and cut her legs loose with a knife, then swam her to shore, his arm around her neck lifeguard-style, and saved her from drowning. Because these incidents are usually linked to someone or something outside himself, the westerner's courage is selfless, a form of compassion.

3   The physical punishment that goes with cowboying is greatly underplayed. Once fear is dispensed with, the threshold of pain rises to meet the demands of the job. When Jane Fonda asked Robert Redford (in the film *Electric Horseman*) if he was sick as he struggled to his feet one morning, he replied, "No, just bent." For once the movies had it right. The cowboys I was sitting with laughed in agreement. Cowboys are rarely complainers; they show their stoicism by laughing at themselves.

4   If a rancher or cowboy has been thought of as a "man's man"—laconic, hard-drinking, inscrutable—there's almost no place in which the balancing act between male and female, manliness and feminity, can be more natural. If he's gruff, handsome, and physically fit on the outside, he's androgynous at the core. Ranchers are midwives, hunters, nurturers, providers, and conservationists all at once. What we've interpreted as toughness—weathered skin, calloused hands, a squint in the eye and a growl in the voice—only masks the tenderness inside. "Now don't go telling me these lambs are cute," one rancher warned me the first day I walked into the football-field-sized lambing sheds. The next thing I knew he was holding a black lamb. "Ain't this little rat good-lookin'?"

5   So many of the men who came to the West were southerners—men looking for work and a new life after the Civil War—that chivalrousness and strict codes of honor were soon thought of as western traits. There were very few women in Wyoming during territorial days, so when they did arrive (some as mail-order brides from places like Philadelphia) there was a stand-offishness between the sexes and a formality that persists now. Ranchers still tip their hats and say, "Howdy, ma'am" instead of shaking hands with me.

6   Even young cowboys are often evasive with women. It's not that they're Jekyll and Hyde creatures—gentle with animals and rough on women—but rather, that they don't know how to bring their tenderness into the house and lack the vocabulary to express the complexity of what they feel. Dancing wildly all night becomes a metaphor for the explosive emotions pent up inside, and when these are, on occasion, released, they're so battery-charged and potent that one caress of the face or one "I love you" will peal for a long while.

7   The geographical vastness and the social isolation here make emotional evolution seem impossible. Those contradictions of the heart between respectability, logic, and convention on the one hand, and impulse, passion, and intuition on the other, played out wordlessly against the paradisical beauty of the West, give cowboys a wide-eyed but drawn look. Their lips pucker up, not with kisses but with immutability. They may want to break out, staying up all night with a lover just to talk, but they don't know how and can't imagine what the consequences will be. Those rare occasions when they do bare themselves

result in confusion. "I feel as if I'd sprained my heart," one friend told me a month after such a meeting.

8   My friend Ted Hoagland wrote, "No one is as fragile as a woman but no one is as fragile as a man." For all the women here who use "fragileness" to avoid work or as a sexual ploy, there are men who try to hide theirs, all the while clinging to an adolescent dependency on women to cook their meals, wash their clothes, and keep the ranch house warm in winter. But there is true vulnerability in evidence here. Because these men work with animals, not machines or numbers, because they live outside in landscapes of torrential beauty, because they are confined to a place and a routine embellished with awesome variables, because calves die in the arms that pulled others into life, because they go to the mountains as if on a pilgrimage to find out what makes a herd of elk tick, their strength is also a softness, their toughness, a rare delicacy. ❖

Questions to Ponder

1. What traditional views of the cowboy does Gretel Ehrlich call into question in this essay?
2. By debunking the romantic myth of the cowboy does Gretel Ehrlich make the real cowboy more or less attractive to you? Why?
3. Why does being a cowboy involve generation and nurturing even more than killing and violence?
4. How can writers be nurturers of their own gifts and still be masculine—even "tough"?

Writing Possibilities

1. Read about the pioneer women of the West, and using Gretel Ehrlich's essay as a model, write about the myth of the frontier woman versus the reality as you have found it.
2. Choose another popular myth, such as that of the "dizzy blonde" or the "dumb jock." Analyze the myth, and suggest reality's greater complexity.
3. Write about the college Greek or the college independent: the myths and the complex realities. Consider writing a brief letter to the editor of your campus newspaper summarizing your view.

THE MANAGERIAL WOMAN
Anne Jardim and Margaret Hennig

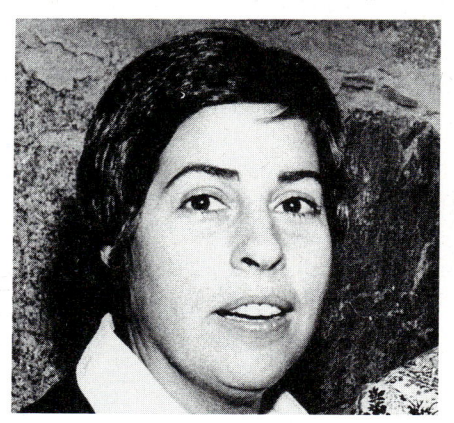

Anne Jardim

Margaret Hennig

Anne Jardim, of British Guiana, and Margaret Hennig, of New Jersey, met as doctoral students at Harvard Business School in 1964. In 1974, they founded the Simmons College Graduate School of Management in Boston.

The Managerial Woman was the outcome of research jointly begun by the two in 1973. Moving from Margaret Hennig's 1970 doctoral dissertation, which traced the careers of 25 women who became corporate senior managers before 1965, the two began traveling more than one hundred thousand miles across the United States. They conducted in-depth interviews with more than one hundred women managers in the utilities, banking, and communications industries. They led career-planning seminars with groups of women managers and seminars for more than one thousand male managers who are responsible for the identification and promotion of women in their companies. They also taught undergraduate and graduate women.

"The primary aim of [our work] is to help men and women understand the critically different beliefs and assumptions which they hold about themselves and each other, about organizations and a management career," Hennig and Jardim insist:

> These differences result in different styles, different emphases and very different ways of responding to typical management situations on a day-to-day basis. Men understand their own mind-sets but not those of women. The reverse is equally real and the outcome only too often is confusion, misunderstanding and misinterpretation. . . .
>
> The insights we have often painfully won are presented in this [work]. . . . laws legislate for equal opportunity. They do not and cannot

legislate truly equal access to that opportunity, and most important, they cannot ensure that people who have traditionally been discriminated against will immediately and automatically demonstrate the ability to take advantage of whatever access to opportunity may exist. . . . Real integration will take place when the outsider group feels strong enough and competent enough to choose to integrate—and when the system which receives them is as aware of this as they (Margaret Hennig and Anne Jardim, The Managerial Woman [New York: Pocket Books, 1978], 12–17).

Brief Warm-up Writing Exercises

1. Make a list of all the sports you have played in your life.
2. Now make two lists: (a) the *benefits* of playing football and (b) the *liabilities* of playing football.
3. Describe the qualities of a good manager.

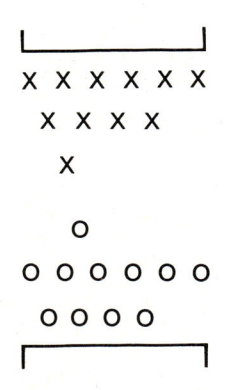

```
            |_____|
             x x x x x x
              x x x x
               x

               o
             o o o o o o
              o o o o
            |_____|
```

1. ❖ Women . . . attempt to identify what this diagram represents. Is it a game? If so, is it field hockey, football or could it be baseball? How many games need teams of eleven? Are those goal posts?
2. Men's comments are immediately evaluative: "It's football and it's a lousy play. Change the coach. Switch to another channel."
3. What lies behind this difference in response begins with small boys learning about teams, about being members of teams, about winning and losing. Their concept of strategy may at first be a very simple one: how you win may mean no more than getting the fat boys on your team so you can trample the skinny boys on the other.
4. But then it becomes more sophisticated and task specialization sets in. Runners *and* blockers are seen to be needed. The guys with the imagination

to plan and anticipate possible outcomes achieve a value of their own. A team makes it possible to become a star and one has to learn how to manage this. A team makes it possible to share a star's luster by active association, and again one can learn how to manage this. A team can even be a place to hide, a place to learn about survival—how to stay on, how to be given another chance; "After all he's too nice a guy to drop!", or "He's not really producing yet but he's learning fast, and he's a real straight player." Over and above this, there is the drive to win and of necessity win as a team, not as a lone individual independent of everyone else.

5   What do men experience, learn and then internalize as working assumptions from a game like football? And does it matter that the great majority of women share neither their experience nor their assumptions?

6   Simply as an experience, ask a man you know to try to think back to the time when he played a team game like football. What was it like? What did he begin to learn? What did he *have* to learn if he wanted to stay on the team?

7   Varying only as to form, the answers we have been given—time and time again—are:

What was it like? *What did you begin to learn?*	*What did you have to learn if you wanted to stay on the team?*
It was boys only	Competition, you had to win
Team work	Cooperation to get a job done— you had to work with guys you wouldn't choose as friends outside the team
Hard work	
Preparation and practice, practice, practice	
If you were knocked down you had to get up again	If you got swell-headed about how fast you could run then the other guys didn't block for you any more
It gave you a sense of belonging, of being part of something bigger than yourself	
	Losing, what it felt like to lose
You learned that a team needs a leader because motivation or lack of it depends on the coach	That you win some, you lose some
	How to take criticism—from the coach, your peers, the crowd
You learned fast that some people were better than others—but you had to have eleven	That you didn't get anywhere without planning and you had to have alternative plans
	Once you knew the rules you could bend them—and you could influence the referee

8   Consider these answers from two points of view: the way they define an environment and the personal skills they identify as needed to survive in it. Do they describe fairly closely a management environment in a corporate setting? Do they reflect skills an effective manager must be able to rely on?

9   Beyond individual hard work, persistence and the ability to deal with

criticism by seeing it as directed much less to the person and much more to task achievement, these answers have to do with goals and objectives; with winning and attempting to deal with loss by distancing it—you win some, you lose some; with group relationships—how to maintain and work with them; and with relationships to authority—whether it be rules or people.

10   These are personal skills. Boys begin to develop them in an outdoor classroom to which girls traditionally have had no access. After five to fifteen years of practice, men bring these skills with them to management jobs and they are skills critical to job performance once the dividing line between supervision and management is crossed.

11   Supervision typically involves responsibility for routine, predictable and specific job performance by subordinates in an area of skills with which the supervisor is extremely familiar. He or she usually "grew up" in that skill: learned it when he or she first went to work, performed it well, was promoted to supervise others to do what he or she once did.

12   Goals and plans to achieve them are usually set for the supervisor to follow. Problems are routine, predictable and can be solved as they arise.

13   Learning the more technical aspects of the job can be achieved on one's own—seminars, courses, textbooks.

14   The formal system of relationships required to do the job is typically vertical—up the line to one's boss, down the line to subordinates.

15   Crossing the line between supervision and management demands that an individual be prepared for a series of fundamental changes in the skills required to do the job, changes for which no formal training is typically available.

16   In management jobs, goals and plans to meet them are no longer as clearly set as they were for the supervisor. They are increasingly part of a manager's responsibility. Success at planning demands an awareness of group weakness and strengths and ability to balance the one against the other without destructive conflict. "Some people are better than others but you have to have eleven."

17   Goal-setting. Planning. But how do you get the plan implemented?

18   "The team needs a leader because motivation or lack of it depends on the coach." "Knowing the rules and bending them." "Influencing the referee." "Taking criticism from (your own) coach, your peers, the crowd." "Winning *and* losing." "Winning some, losing some."

19   Another required shift in skills has to do with problem-solving. The supervisor deals with more or less routine day-to-day problems susceptible to more or less tried and true solutions. The manager has to *anticipate* problems and if possible be ready with alternatives. "You don't get anywhere without planning and (when problems arise) you have to have alternative plans."

20   Yet another shift centers on the learning system. Formal learning can teach you technical skills. Dealing with people in a task setting inevitably has to be learned informally and men have already learned the ground rules on intra-group relationships among men. "Cooperation to get a job done—if you get swellheaded about how fast you can run then the other guys don't block for

you any more." "Some people are better than others but you have to have eleven."

21   Still another shift in skills has to do with the formal system of relationships. The simple vertical line typical of supervision—upward to a boss, downward to subordinates—becomes complicated by a network of lateral relationships with counterparts in other areas whose input or lack of it makes an impact in terms of both budget and productivity on what your own department or group can deliver. With *no* formal authority to force a desired result, one must fall back on influence—an outcome of friendship, persuasion, favors granted and owed, promises that must be kept if you want to be operative in the future, connections with people who already *have* influence, the way you yourself are seen—are you a winner, a member of "the club," or are you a potential loser?

22   The experience of most little girls has no parallel. The prestigious sports for girls tend to be one on one: tennis, swimming, golf, gymnastics, skating. And in the one-on-one sports, the old adage that "it's not whether you won or lost but *how* you played the game" has been so stressed that many women tennis players now in their twenties still play for "exercise"—they don't play to win. While this is changing, it is changing slowly. There cannot be many fathers with the courage to face the ridicule that must have attached to the brave man who fought the sneering insistence of the Little League coach that his daughter wear a protective cup in order to qualify for the baseball team.

23   Team sports. One team against another. Aiming to win, to reach an objective. It means one must develop a strategy that takes the environment into account. Who and what can help? Who and what can hinder? When? How much? How do I make use of this or counter that in order to get where I want to go? And if the objective is career advancement through the management ranks of today's corporation, who is most likely to win—the man who sees that world as it is, a world of winning and losing, of teams, of stars, of average and mediocre players, in essence *his* world, or the woman struggling to find a world as it should be, as it ought to be, in search of the best possible method?

24   Before we are misunderstood we want to make very clear that we are placing no value judgment whatsoever on the aim to win. We are not saying it is either good or bad. What we are saying is that it is real, very real, and that far more men feel, see and act on that reality than do women. Strategy now has a bad sound, a legacy of politicians who lost sight of moral objectives and adopted without question both the tenuous ethics of the game plan and a language drawn intact from the football field; men who took the concept of winning and made it an end in itself, never questioning the meaning of what they won since winning was enough in itself. We would guess, and it is a guess, that very few women indeed could develop a mind-set of this kind because so few women think of winning in personal terms. If anything, women tend to exemplify the other extreme—"Do the best you can and hope someone will notice you." For both men and women the answer to this dilemma of extremes probably lies somewhere in the middle ground—and if men need to lessen the drive to win, women as certainly need to develop it. ❖

Questions to Ponder

1. According to Margaret Hennig and Anne Jardim, how do early experiences with team sports contribute to the success of a manager?
2. Do you find any weaknesses in Margaret Hennig's and Anne Jardim's argument? If so, what might these be?
3. In what ways is business management *not* like team sports?
4. What are the parallels between generating in the business world and generating in writing?

Writing Possibilities

1. Conduct an informal survey like Margaret Hennig and Anne Jardim's asking men and women about their experiences with another sport (besides football). Analyze the responses, and present your findings in the form of a report to your physical education department, business department, or women's and men's studies programs.
2. Write your own recipe for producing good managers.
3. Write a critical analysis of this excerpt from *The Managerial Woman*. Include a brief *summary*, sections on the *strengths* and *limitations* of the excerpt, and a final section presenting your *conclusions* and *recommendations* to the writers for future editions or further applications.

Short Story

THE SEA OF LOST TIME

Gabriel García Márquez

Antonio Pigafetta, a Florentine navigator who went with Magellan on the first voyage around the world, wrote, upon his passage through our southern lands of America, a strictly accurate account that nonetheless resembles a venture into fantasy. In it he recorded that he had seen hogs with navels on their haunches, clawless birds whose hens laid eggs on the backs of their mates, and others still, resembling tongueless pelicans, with beaks like spoons. He wrote of having seen a misbegotten creature with the head and ears of a mule, a camel's body, the legs of a deer and the whinny of a horse. He described how the first native encountered in Patagonia was confronted with a mirror, whereupon that impassioned giant lost his senses to the terror of his own image.

This short and fascinating book, which even then contained the seeds of our present-day novels, is by no means the most staggering account of our reality in that age. The Chroniclers of the Indies left us countless others. . . .

Europeans of good will—and sometimes those of bad, as well—have been struck, with ever greater force, by the unearthly tidings of Latin America, that boundless realm of haunted men and historic women, whose unending obstinacy blurs into legend. . . .

I dare to think that it is this outsized reality, and not just its literary expression, that has deserved the attention of the Swedish Academy of Letters. A reality not of paper, but one that lives within us and determines each instant of our countless daily deaths, and that nourishes a source of insatiable creativity, full of sorrow and beauty . . . (from his lecture on receiving the Nobel Prize for Literature in 1982).

Brief Warm-up Writing Exercises

1. Freewrite about an evening when something strange comes out of the sea.
2. Now try to imagine a world under the sea. Brainstorm a list of the things that would be in this world.

3. Freewrite your understanding of the word *allegory,* along with any examples of allegory in literature or film that you know.

❖ Toward the end of January the sea was growing harsh, it was beginning to dump its heavy garbage on the town, and a few weeks later everything was contaminated with its unbearable mood. From that time on the world wasn't worth living in, at least until the following December, so no one stayed awake after eight o'clock. But the year Mr. Herbert came the sea didn't change, not even in February. On the contrary, it became smoother and more phosphorescent and during the first nights of March it gave off a fragrance of roses.

Tobías smelled it. His blood attracted crabs and he spent half the night chasing them off his bed until the breeze rose up again and he was able to sleep. During his long moments of lying awake he learned how to distinguish all the changes in the air. So that when he got a smell of roses he didn't have to open up the door to know that it was a smell from the sea.

He got up late. Clotilde was starting a fire in the courtyard. The breeze was cool and all the stars were in place, but it was hard to count them down to the horizon because of the lights from the sea. After having his coffee, Tobías could still taste a trace of night on his palate.

"Something very strange happened last night," he remembered.

Clotilde, of course, had not smelled it. She slept so heavily that she didn't even remember her dreams.

"It was a smell of roses," Tobías said, "and I'm sure it came from the sea."

"I don't know what roses smell like," said Clotilde.

She could have been right. The town was arid, with a hard soil furrowed by saltpeter, and only occasionally did someone bring a bouquet of flowers from outside to cast into the sea where they threw their dead.

"It's the smell that drowned man from Guacamayal had," Tobías said.

"Well," Clotilde said, smiling "if it was a good smell, then you can be sure it didn't come from this sea."

It really was a cruel sea. At certain times, when the nets brought in nothing but floating garbage, the streets of the town were still full of dead fish when the tide went out. Dynamite only brought the remains of old shipwrecks to the surface.

The few women left in town, like Clotilde, were boiling up with bitterness. And like her, there was old Jacob's wife, who got up earlier than usual that morning, put the house in order, and sat down to breakfast with a look of adversity.

"My last wish," she said to her husband, "is to be buried alive."

She said it as if she were on her deathbed, but she was sitting across the table in a dining room with windows through which the bright March light came pouring in and spread throughout the house. Opposite her, calming his peaceful hunger, was old Jacob, a man who had loved her so much and for so

long that he could no longer conceive of any suffering that didn't start with his wife.
15 "I want to die with the assurance that I'll be laid beneath the ground like proper people," she went on. "And the only way to be sure of it is to go around asking people to do me the blessed charity of burying me alive."
16 "You don't have to ask anybody," old Jacob said with the greatest of calm. "I'll put you there myself."
17 "Let's go, then," she said, "because I'm going to die before very long."
18 Old Jacob looked her over carefully. Her eyes were the only thing still young. Her bones had become knotted up at the joints and she had the same look of a plowed field which, when it came right down to it, she had always had.
19 "You're in better shape than ever," he told her.
20 "Last night I caught a smell of roses," she sighed.
21 "Don't pay it any mind," old Jacob said to assure her. "Things like that are always happening to poor people like us."
22 "Nothing of the sort," she said. "I've always prayed that I'd know enough ahead of time when death would come so I could die far away from this sea. A smell of roses in this town can only be a message from God."
23 All that old Jacob could think of was to ask for a little time to put things in order. He'd heard tell that people don't die when they ought to but when they want to, and he was seriously worried by his wife's premonition. He even wondered whether, when the moment came, he'd be up to burying her alive.
24 At nine o'clock he opened the place where he used to have a store. He put two chairs and a small table with the checkerboard on it by the door and he spent all morning playing opponents who happened by. From his house he looked at the ruined town, the shambles of a town with the traces of former colors that had been nibbled away by the sun and a chunk of sea at the end of the street.
25 Before lunch, as always, he played with Don Máximo Gómez. Old Jacob couldn't imagine a more humane opponent than a man who had survived two civil wars intact and had only sacrificed an eye in the third. After losing one game on purpose, he held him back for another.
26 "Tell me one thing, Don Máximo," he asked him then. "Would you be capable of burying your wife alive?"
27 "Certainly," Don Máximo Gómez answered. "You can believe me when I say that my hand wouldn't even tremble."
28 Old Jacob fell into a surprised silence. Then, after letting himself be despoiled of his best pieces, he sighed:
29 "Well, the way it looks, Petra is going to die."
30 Don Máximo Gómez didn't change his expression. "In that case," he said, "there's no reason to bury her alive." He gobbled up two pieces and crowned a king. Then he fastened an eye wet with sad waters on his opponent.
31 "What's she got?"
32 "Last night," old Jacob explained, "she caught a smell of roses."

33 "Then half the town is going to die," Don Máximo Gómez said. "That's all they've been talking about this morning."

34 It was hard for old Jacob to lose again without offending him. He brought in the table and the chairs, closed up the shop, and went about everywhere looking for someone who had caught the smell. In the end only Tobías was sure. So he asked him please to stop by his place, as if by chance, and tell his wife all about it.

35 Tobías did as he was told. At four o'clock, all dressed up in his Sunday best, he appeared on the porch where the wife had spent all afternoon getting old Jacob's widower's outfit together.

36 He had come up so quietly that the woman was startled.

37 "Mercy," she exclaimed. "I thought it was the archangel Gabriel."

38 "Well, you can see it's not," Tobías said. "It's only me and I've come to tell you something."

39 She adjusted her glasses and went back to work.

40 "I know what it's all about," she said.

41 "I bet you don't," Tobías said.

42 "You caught the smell of roses last night."

43 "How did you know?" Tobías asked in desolation.

44 "At my age," the woman said, "there's so much time left over for thinking that a person can become a regular prophet."

45 Old Jacob, who had his ear pressed against the partition wall in the back of the store, stood up in shame.

46 "You see, woman," he shouted through the wall. He made a turn and appeared on the porch. "It wasn't what you thought it was after all."

47 "This boy has been lying," she said without raising her head. "He didn't smell anything."

48 "It was around eleven o'clock," Tobías said. "I was chasing crabs away."

49 The woman finished mending a collar.

50 "Lies," she insisted. "Everybody knows you're a tricker." She bit the thread with her teeth and looked at Tobías over her glasses.

51 "What I can't understand is why you went to the trouble to put Vaseline on your hair and shine your shoes just to come and be so disrespectful to me."

52 From then on Tobías began to keep watch on the sea. He hung his hammock up on the porch by the yard and spent the night waiting, surprised by the things that go on in the world while people are asleep. For many nights he could hear the desperate scrawling of the crabs as they tried to claw-climb up the supports of the house, until so many nights went by that they got tired of trying. He came to know Clotilde's way of sleeping. He discovered how her fluty snores became more high-pitched as the heat grew more intense until they became one single languid note in the torpor of July.

53 At first Tobías kept watch on the sea the way people who know it well do, his gaze fixed on a single point of the horizon. He watched it change color. He watched it turn out its lights and become frothy and dirty and toss up its refuse-laden belches when great rainstorms agitated its digestion. Little by little

he learned to keep watch the way people who know it better do, not even looking at it but unable to forget about it even in his sleep.

54   Old Jacob's wife died in August. She died in her sleep and they had to cast her, like everyone else, into a flowerless sea. Tobías kept on waiting. He had waited so long that it was becoming his way of being. One night, while he was dozing in his hammock, he realized that something in the air had changed. It was an intermittent wave, like the time a Japanese ship had jettisoned a cargo of rotten onions at the harbor mouth. Then the smell thickened and was motionless until dawn. Only when he had the feeling that he could pick it up in his hands and exhibit it did Tobías leap out of his hammock and go into Clotilde's room. He shook her several times.

55   "Here it is," he told her.

56   Clotilde had to brush the smell away like a cobweb in order to get up. Then she fell back down on her tepid sheets.

57   "God curse it," she said.

58   Tobías leaped toward the door, ran into the middle of the street, and began to shout. He shouted with all his might, took a deep breath and shouted again, and then there was a silence and he took a deeper breath, and the smell was still on the sea. But nobody answered. Then he went about knocking on doors from house to house, even on houses that had no owners, until his uproar got entwined with that of the dogs and he woke everybody up.

59   Many of them couldn't smell it. But others, especially the old ones, went down to enjoy it on the beach. It was a compact fragrance that left no chink for any odor of the past. Some, worn out from so much smelling, went back to their houses. Most of the people stayed to finish their night's sleep on the beach. By dawn the smell was so pure that it was a pity even to breathe it.

60   Tobías slept most of the day. Clotilde caught up with him at siesta time and they spent the afternoon frolicking in bed without even closing the door to the yard. First they did it like earthworms, then like rabbits, and finally like turtles, until the world grew sad and it was dark again. There was still a trace of roses in the air. Sometimes a wave of music reached the bedroom.

61   "It's coming from Catarino's," Clotilde said. "Someone must have come to town."

62   Three men and a woman had come. Catarino thought that others might come later and he tried to fix his gramophone. Since he couldn't do it, he asked Pancho Aparecido, who did all kinds of things because he'd never owned anything, and besides, he had a box of tools and a pair of intelligent hands.

63   Catarino's place was a wooden building set apart and facing the sea. It had one large room with benches and small tables, and several bedrooms in the rear. While they watched Pancho Aparecido working, the three men and the woman drank in silence, sitting at the bar and yawning in turn.

64   The gramophone worked well after several tries. When they heard the music, distant but distinct, the people stopped chatting. They looked at one another and for a moment had nothing to say, for only then did they realize how old they had become since the last time they'd heard music.

65   Tobías found everybody still awake after nine o'clock. They were sitting in their doorways listening to Catarino's old records, with the same look of childish fatalism of people watching an eclipse. Every record reminded them of someone who had died, the taste of food after a long illness, or something they'd had to do the next day many years ago which never got done because they'd forgotten.

66   The music stopped around eleven o'clock. Many people went to bed, thinking it was going to rain because a dark cloud hung over the sea. But the cloud descended, floated for a while on the surface, and then sank into the water. Only the stars remained above. A short while later, the breeze went out from the town and came back with a smell of roses.

67   "Just what I told you, Jacob," Don Máximo Gómez exclaimed. "Here it is back with us again. I'm sure now that we're going to smell it every night."

68   "God forbid," old Jacob said. "That smell is the only thing in life that's come too late for me."

69   They'd been playing checkers in the empty store without paying any attention to the records. Their memories were so ancient that there weren't records old enough to stir them up.

70   "For my part, I don't believe much of anything about this," Don Máximo Gómez said. "After so many years of eating dust, with so many women wanting a little yard to plant flowers in, it's not strange that a person should end up smelling things like this and even thinking it's all true."

71   "But we can smell it with our own noses," old Jacob said.

72   "No matter," said Don Máximo Gómez. "During the war, when the revolution was already lost, we'd wanted a general so bad that we saw the Duke of Marlborough appear in flesh and blood. I saw him with my own eyes, Jacob."

73   It was after midnight. When he was alone, old Jacob closed his store and took his lamp to the bedroom. Through the window, outlined against the glow of the sea, he saw the crag from which they threw their dead.

74   "Petra," he called in a soft voice.

75   She couldn't hear him. At that moment she was floating along almost on the surface of the water beneath a radiant noonday sun on the Bay of Bengal. She'd lifted her head to look through the water, as through an illuminated showcase, at a huge ocean liner. But she couldn't see her husband, who at that moment on the other side of the world was starting to hear Catarino's gramophone again.

76   "Just think," old Jacob said. "Barely six months ago they thought you were crazy and now they're the ones making a festival out of the smell that brought on your death."

77   He put out the light and got into bed. He wept slowly with that graceless little whimper old people have, but soon he fell asleep.

78   "I'd get away from this town if I could," he sobbed as he tossed. "I'd go straight to hell or anywhere else if I could only get twenty pesos together."

79   From that night on and for several weeks, the smell remained on the sea. It impregnated the wood of the houses, the food, and the drinking water, and

there was nowhere to escape the odor. A lot of people were startled to find it in the vapors of their own shit. The men and the women who had come to Catarino's place left one Friday, but they were back on Saturday with a whole mob. More people arrived on Sunday. They were in and out of everywhere like ants, looking for something to eat and a place to sleep, until it got to be impossible to walk the streets.

80   More people came. The women who had left when the town died came back to Catarino's. They were fatter and wore heavier make-up, and they brought the latest records, which didn't remind anyone of anything. Some of the former inhabitants of the town returned. They'd gone off to get filthy rich somewhere else and they came back talking about their fortunes but wearing the same clothes they'd left with. Music and side shows arrived, wheels of chance, fortunetellers and gunmen and men with snakes coiled about their necks who were selling the elixir of eternal life. They kept on coming for many weeks, even after the first rains had come and the sea became rough and the smell disappeared.

81   A priest arrived among the last. He walked all over, eating bread dipped in light coffee, and little by little, he banned everything that had come before him: games of chance, the new music and the way it was danced, and even the recent custom of sleeping on the beach. One evening, at Melchor's house, he preached a sermon about the smell of the sea.

82   "Give thanks to heaven, my children," he said, "for this is the smell of God."

83   Someone interrupted him.

84   "How can you tell, Father? You haven't smelled it yet."

85   "The Holy Scriptures," he said, "are quite explicit in regard to this smell. We are living in a chosen village."

86   Tobías went about back and forth in the festival like a sleepwalker. He took Clotilde to see what money was. They made believe they were betting enormous sums at roulette, and then they figured things up and felt extremely rich with all the money they could have won. But one night not just they, the whole multitude occupying the town, saw more money in one place than they could possibly have imagined.

87   That was the night Mr. Herbert arrived. He appeared suddenly, set up a table in the middle of the street, and on top of the table placed two large trunks brimful with bank notes. There was so much money that no one noticed it at first, because they couldn't believe it was true. But when Mr. Herbert started ringing a little bell, the people had to believe him, and they went over to listen.

88   "I'm the richest man in the world," he said. "I've got so much money I haven't got room to keep it any more. And besides, since my heart's so big that there's no room for it in my chest, I have decided to travel the world over solving the problems of mankind."

89   He was tall and ruddy. He spoke in a loud voice and without any pauses, and simultaneously he waved about a pair of lukewarm, languid hands that always looked as if they'd just been shaved. He spoke for fifteen minutes and

rested. Then he rang the little bell and began to speak again. Halfway through his speech, someone in the crowd waved a hat and interrupted him.

90 "Come on, mister, don't talk so much and start handing out the money."

91 "Not so fast," Mr. Herbert replied. "Handing out money with no rhyme or reason, in addition to being an unfair way of doing things, doesn't make any sense at all."

92 With his eyes he located the man who had interrupted him, and motioned him to come forward. The crowd let him through.

93 "On the other hand," Mr. Herbert went on, "this impatient friend of ours is going to give us a chance to explain the most equitable system of the distribution of wealth." He reached out a hand and helped him up.

94 "What's your name?"

95 "Patricio."

96 "All right, Patricio," Mr. Herbert said. "Just like everybody else, you've got some problem you haven't been able to solve for some time."

97 Patricio took off his hat and confirmed it with a nod.

98 "What is it?"

99 "Well, my problem is this," Patricio said. "I haven't got any money."

100 "How much do you need?"

101 "Forty-eight pesos."

102 Mr. Herbert gave an exclamation of triumph. "Forty-eight pesos," he repeated. The crowd accompanied him in clapping.

103 "Very well, Patricio," Mr. Herbert went on. "Now, tell us one thing: what can you do?"

104 "Lots of things."

105 "Decide on one," Mr. Herbert said. "The thing you do best."

106 "Well," Patricio said, "I can do birds."

107 Applauding a second time, Mr. Herbert turned to the crowd.

108 "So, then, ladies and gentlemen, our friend Patricio, who does an extraordinary job at imitating birds, is going to imitate forty-eight different birds and in that way he will solve the great problem of his life."

109 To the startled silence of the crowd, Patricio then did his birds. Sometimes whistling, sometimes with his throat, he did all known birds and finished off the figure with others that no one was able to identify. When he was through, Mr. Herbert called for a round of applause and gave him forty-eight pesos.

110 "And now," he said, "come up one by one. I'm going to be here until tomorrow at this time solving problems."

111 Old Jacob learned about the commotion from the comments of people walking past his house. With each bit of news his heart grew bigger and bigger until he felt it burst.

112 "What do you think about this gringo?" he asked.

113 Don Máximo Gómez shrugged his shoulders. "He must be a philanthropist."

114 "If I could only do something," old Jacob said, "I could solve my little problem right now. It's nothing much: twenty pesos."

115   "You play a good game of checkers," Don Máximo Gómez said.
116   Old Jacob appeared not to have paid any attention to him, but when he was alone, he wrapped up the board and the box of checkers in a newspaper and went off to challenge Mr. Herbert. He waited until midnight for his turn. Finally Mr. Herbert had them pack up his trunks and said good-bye until the next morning.
117   He didn't go off to bed. He showed up at Catarino's place with the men who were carrying his trunks and the crowd followed him all the way there with their problems. Little by little, he went on solving them, and he solved so many that finally, in the store, the only ones left were the women and some men with their problems already solved. And in the back of the room there was a solitary woman fanning herself slowly with a cardboard advertisement.
118   "What about you?" Mr. Herbert shouted at her. "What's your problem?"
119   The woman stopped fanning herself.
120   "Don't try to get me mixed up in your fun, mister gringo," she shouted across the room. "I haven't got any kind of problem and I'm a whore because it comes out of my balls."
121   Mr. Herbert shrugged his shoulders. He went on drinking his cold beer beside the open trunks, waiting for other problems. He was sweating. A while later, a woman broke away from the group that was with her at the table and spoke to him in a low voice. She had a five-hundred-peso problem.
122   "How would you split that up?" Mr. Herbert asked her.
123   "By five."
124   "Just imagine," Mr. Herbert said. "That's a hundred men."
125   "It doesn't matter," she said. "If I can get all that money together they'll be the last hundred men of my life."
126   He looked her over. She was quite young, fragile-boned, but her eyes showed a simple decision.
127   "All right," Mr. Herbert said. "Go into your room and I'll start sending each one with his five pesos to you."
128   He went to the street door and rang his little bell.
129   At seven o'clock in the morning Tobías found Catarino's place open. All the lights were out. Half asleep and puffed up with beer, Mr. Herbert was controlling the entry of men into the girl's room.
130   Tobías went in too. The girl recognized him and was surprised to see him in her room.
131   "You too?"
132   "They told me to come in," Tobías said. "They gave me five pesos and told me not to take too long."
133   She took the soaked sheet off the bed and asked Tobías to hold the other end. It was as heavy as canvas. They squeezed it, twisting it by the ends, until it got its natural weight back. They turned the mattress over and the sweat came out the other side. Tobías did things as best he could. Before leaving he put the five pesos on the pile of bills that was growing high beside the bed.

134 "Send everybody you can," Mr. Herbert suggested to him. "Let's see if we can get this over with before noon."
135 The girl opened the door a crack and asked for a cold beer. There were still several men waiting.
136 "How many left?" she asked.
137 "Sixty-three," Mr. Herbert answered.
138 Old Jacob followed him about all day with his checkerboard. His turn came at nightfall and he laid out his problem and Mr. Herbert accepted. They put two chairs and a small table on top of the big table in the middle of the street, and old Jacob made the first move. It was the last play he was able to premeditate. He lost.
139 "Forty pesos," Mr. Herbert said, "and I'll give you a handicap of two moves."
140 He won again. His hands barely touched the checkers. He played blindfolded, guessing his opponent's moves, and still won. The crowd grew tired of watching. When old Jacob decided to give up, he was in debt to the tune of five thousand seven hundred forty-two pesos and twenty-three cents.
141 He didn't change his expression. He jotted down the figure on a piece of paper he had in his pocket. Then he folded up the board, put the checkers in their box, and wrapped everything in the newspaper.
142 "Do with me what you will," he said, "but let me have these things. I promise you that I will spend the rest of my life getting all that money together."
143 Mr. Herbert looked at his watch.
144 "I'm terribly sorry," he said. "Your time will be up in twenty minutes." He waited until he was sure that his opponent hadn't found the solution. "Don't you have anything else to offer?"
145 "My honor."
146 "I mean," Mr. Herbert explained, "something that changes color when a brush daubed with paint is passed over it."
147 "My house," old Jacob said as if he were solving a riddle. "It's not worth much, but it is a house."
148 That was how Mr. Herbert took possession of old Jacob's house. He also took possession of the houses and property of others who couldn't pay their debts, but he called for a week of music, fireworks, and acrobats and he took charge of the festivities himself.
149 It was a memorable week. Mr. Herbert spoke of the miraculous destiny of the town and he even sketched out the city of the future, great glass buildings with dance floors on top. He showed it to the crowd. They looked in astonishment, trying to find themselves among the pedestrians painted in Mr. Herbert's colors, but they were so well dressed that they couldn't recognize themselves. It pained them to be using him so much. They laughed at the urge they'd had to cry back in October and they kept on living in the mist of hope until Mr. Herbert rang his little bell and said the party was over. Only then did he get some rest.

150   "You're going to die from that life you lead," old Jacob said.
151   "I've got so much money that there's no reason for me to die," Mr. Herbert said.
152   He flopped onto his bed. He slept for days on end, snoring like a lion, and so many days went by that people grew tired of waiting on him. They had to dig crabs to eat. Catarino's new records got so old that no one could listen to them any more without tears, and he had to close his place up.
153   A long time after Mr. Herbert had fallen asleep, the priest knocked on old Jacob's door. The house was locked from the inside. As the breathing of the man asleep had been using up the air, things had lost their weight and were beginning to float about.
154   "I want to have a word with him," the priest said.
155   "You'll have to wait," said old Jacob.
156   "I haven't got much time."
157   "Have a seat, Father, and wait," old Jacob repeated. "And please talk to me in the meantime. It's been a long time since I've known what's been going on in the world."
158   "People have all scattered," the priest said. "It won't be long before the town will be the same as it was before. That's the only thing that's new."
159   "They'll come back when the sea smells of roses again," old Jacob said.
160   "But meanwhile, we've got to sustain the illusions of those who stay with something," the priest said. "It's urgent that we start building the church."
161   "That's why you've come to see Mr. Herbert," old Jacob said.
162   "That's right," said the priest. "Gringos are very charitable."
163   "Wait a bit, then, Father," old Jacob said. "He might just wake up."
164   They played checkers. It was a long and difficult game which lasted several days, but Mr. Herbert didn't wake up.
165   The priest let himself be confused by desperation. He went all over with a copper plate asking for donations to build the church, but he didn't get very much. He was getting more and more diaphanous from so much begging, his bones were starting to fill with sounds, and one Sunday he rose two hands above the ground, but nobody noticed it. Then he packed his clothes in one suitcase and the money he had collected in another and said good-bye forever.
166   "The smell won't come back," he said to those who tried to dissuade him. "You've got to face up to the fact that the town has fallen into mortal sin."
167   When Mr. Herbert woke up the town was the same as it had been before. The rain had fermented the garbage the crowds had left in the streets and the soil was as arid and hard as a brick once more.
168   "I've been asleep a long time," Mr. Herbert said, yawning.
169   "Centuries," said old Jacob.
170   "I'm starving to death."
171   "So is everybody else," old Jacob said. "There's nothing to do but go to the beach and dig for crabs."
172   Tobías found him scratching in the sand, foaming at the mouth, and he

was surprised to discover that when rich people were starving they looked so much like the poor. Mr. Herbert didn't find enough crabs. At nightfall he invited Tobías to come look for something to eat in the depths of the sea.

173 "Listen," Tobías warned him, "only the dead know what's down inside there."

174 "Scientists know too," Mr. Herbert said. "Beneath the sea of the drowned there are turtles with exquisite meat on them. Get your clothes off and let's go."

175 They went. At first they swam straight along and then down very deep to where the light of the sun stopped and then the light of the sea, and things were visible only in their own light. They passed by a submerged village with men and women on horseback turning about a musical kiosk. It was a splendid day and there were brightly colored flowers on the terraces.

176 "A Sunday sank at about eleven o'clock in the morning," Mr. Herbert said. "It must have been some cataclysm."

177 Tobías turned off toward the village, but Mr. Herbert signaled him to keep going down.

178 "There are roses there," Tobías said. "I want Clotilde to know what they are."

179 "You can come back another time at your leisure," Mr. Herbert said. "Right now I'm dying of hunger."

180 He went down like an octopus, with slow, slinky strokes of his arms. Tobías, who was trying hard not to lose sight of him, thought that it must be the way rich people swam. Little by little, they were leaving the sea of common catastrophes and entering the sea of the dead.

181 There were so many of them that Tobías thought that he'd never seen as many people on earth. They were floating motionless, face up, on different levels, and they all had the look of forgotten souls.

182 "They're very old dead," Mr. Herbert said. "It's taken them centuries to reach this state of repose."

183 Farther down, in the waters of the more recent dead, Mr. Herbert stopped. Tobías caught up with him at the instant that a very young woman passed in front of them. She was floating on her side, her eyes open, followed by a current of flowers.

184 Mr. Herbert put his finger to his lip and held it there until the last of the flowers went by.

185 "She's the most beautiful woman I've ever seen in all my life," he said.

186 "She's old Jacob's wife," Tobías said. "She must be fifty years younger, but that's her. I'm sure of it."

187 "She's done a lot of traveling," Mr. Herbert said. "She's carrying behind her flowers from all the seas of the world."

188 They reached bottom. Mr. Herbert took a few turns over earth that looked like polished slate. Tobías followed him. Only when he became accustomed to the half light of the depths did he discover that the turtles were there. There were thousands of them, flattened out on the bottom, so motionless they looked petrified.

189   "They're alive," Mr. Herbert said, "but they've been asleep for millions of years."
190   He turned one over. With a soft touch he pushed it upward and the sleeping animal left his hands and continued drifting up. Tobías let it pass by. Then he looked toward the surface and saw the whole sea upside down.
191   "It's like a dream," he said.
192   "For your own good," Mr. Herbert said, "don't tell anyone about it. Just imagine the disorder there'd be in the world if people found out about these things."
193   It was almost midnight when they got back to the village. They woke up Clotilde to boil some water. Mr. Herbert butchered the turtle, but it took all three of them to chase and kill the heart a second time as it bounced out into the courtyard while they were cutting the creature up. They ate until they couldn't breathe any more.
194   "Well, Tobías," Mr. Herbert then said, "we've got to face reality."
195   "Of course."
196   "And reality says," Mr. Herbert went on, "that the smell will never come back."
197   "It will come back."
198   "It won't come back," Clotilde put in, "among other reasons because it never really came. It was you who got everybody all worked up."
199   "You smelled it yourself," Tobías said.
200   "I was half dazed that night," Clotilde said. "But right now I'm not sure about anything that has to do with this sea."
201   "So I'll be on my way," Mr. Herbert said. "And," he added, speaking to both of them, "you should leave too. There are too many things to do in the world for you to be starving in this town."
202   He left. Tobías stayed in the yard counting the stars down to the horizon and he discovered that there were three more since last December. Clotilde called him from the bedroom, but he didn't pay any attention.
203   "Come here, you dummy," Clotilde insisted. "It's been years since we did it like rabbits."
204   Tobías waited a long time. When he finally went in, she had fallen asleep. He half woke her, but she was so tired that they both got things mixed up and they were only able to do it like earthworms.
205   "You're acting like a boob," Clotilde said grouchily. "Try to think about something else."
206   "I am thinking about something else."
207   She wanted to know what it was and he decided to tell her on the condition that she wouldn't repeat it. Clotilde promised.
208   "There's a village at the bottom of the sea," Tobías said, "with little white houses with millions of flowers on the terraces."
209   Clotilde raised her hands to her head.
210   "Oh, Tobías," she exclaimed. "Oh, Tobías, for the love of God, don't start up with those things again."

211   Tobías didn't say anything else. He rolled over to the edge of the bed and tried to go to sleep. He couldn't until dawn, when the wind changed and the crabs left him in peace. ❖

Questions to Ponder

1. Why does it seem as if Gabriel García Márquez's story could go and on and on?
2. How does Marquez seem to generate this story?
3. If an allegory is a form in which persons, objects, and actions in a story are equated with ideas outside the story itself, of what historical or political situation might "The Sea of Lost Time" be an allegory?
4. If you think of "The Sea of Lost Time" as a story of South America's (or Colombia's) plight, what might Mr. Herbert represent? His money? His sleep? The smell of roses? The sea of lost time itself? What details in the story lead you to your conclusions?
5. How does Gabriel García Márquez make his fantastical world seem real?

Writing Possibilities

1. Start a story about a town, and then keep adding episode after episode to it.
2. Now try writing a story that also is an allegory about your state's or country's role in the world. How will you represent your state or country? How will others appear in your story?
3. Write a story in which you try to make surprising and fantastical happenings seem like ordinary reality.

CHAPTER

8

Sustaining the Call

This chapter explores two different types of writing stamina: sustaining a specific piece of writing, and sustaining your calling as a writer during times of adversity.

SUSTAINING THE VAST CONTINUOUS DREAM

In the opening essay in this section, Nebraska's state poet, William Kloefkorn, suggests that a work should have magnitude; it "must be long enough to make a distinct aural impression, but short enough to be taken in by the memory." How do you keep the tone or the vision or the rhythm of a work going? In Henry James's words, how do you sustain the "vast continuous dream" from working day to working day, over the weeks, or months, or years necessary to complete a finished work?

Some writers sustain the dream by living a deliberately sedentary life. While they are finishing a piece, they do not want to go anywhere or do anything that will interfere with the creative life going on inside them. Writers at these times may seem remote or out of touch. "If you do become engaged in what is going on with other people, then you have lost the thread," explains Joan Didion. "You've turned off the computer, and it is not for that period of time making the connections it ought to be making."* While writing her novel *A Book of Common Prayer,* Didion says she almost heard a steady humming in her head when things were going well.

Another technique Didion has found to help her sustain a piece of writing is to find a picture or a phrase that captures the quality she hopes to convey. She then keeps that picture or phrase before her in her writing room, for constant reference. For *A Book of Common Prayer* she wrote this phrase on a map of Central America: "Surface like rainbow slick, shifting, fall, thrown away, irridescent." These were the qualities she was trying to capture in her writing.

Another method of sustaining a work's quality comes into play during revision. Here writers identify the parts of the work they consider the very best, then concentrate on bringing everything else up to that level. John Irving spoke to this point when asked if he felt he had to top *The World According to Garp* after it became a best-seller. Writers are always trying to top their best *sentences,* he retorted.†

SUSTAINING THE CALL IN ADVERSITY

Several essays in this chapter concern sustaining the call of writing in adversity. Aleksandr Solzhenitsyn faced this challenge when imprisoned and exiled in what he later immortalized as *The Gulag Archipelago.* His "First Cell, First Love" from that work is included here. During World War II, young Anne Frank managed to sustain the call of writing through two years of secret hiding which ended with her capture and death in the German extermination camps. These writers offer us three tips for sustaining ourselves and the call of writing in times of political repression, or simply in times of illness or distress.

Writers can sustain the call by retaining their curiosity. By maintaining a lively interest in every cell and all his fellow prisoners, Solzhenitsyn was able to keep his mind free while his body was in prison. Anne Frank did the same, daring to turn her gaze upon herself and her own developing body and mind. Student Brad Williams displays this kind of curiosity in his essay "Of Cows and Men."

Writers can also take periods when they cannot write as times to explore themselves for vital changes that will affect their work. "Your writing is yourself," insists Nancy Price, "so when you can not write, look at your life philosophy. It may be undergoing change."‡ Change for a writer is the progressive facing of truth. Writers who wish to become better writers must be ready and willing to change—and to pay attention to change. Perhaps change will be the topic of your work.

Finally, writers can sustain the call by recalling their tradition. Whether

---

*Sara Davidson, "A Visit with Joan Didion," *Joan Didion: Essays and Conversations,* ed. Ellen G. Friedman (Princeton, N.J.: Ontario Review Press, 1984), 15.

†Interview. *The Writer's Workshop.* University of South Carolina.

‡Personal Interview, 2 Oct. 1989.

your tradition, like Leslie Marmon Silko's, includes the legend of "Yellow Woman" or, like Wendell Berry's, the writings of John Milton, the tradition is there and will provide inspiration and sustenance. As Wendell Berry implies in his essay "Home of the Free," the tradition will often supply standards for judging your age and its ideas. In "Death of a Pig," E. B. White finds in the tradition of Greek tragedy a context for understanding personal grief.

In moments of oppression, writers can comfort themselves with the knowledge that the tradition will continue, regardless of temporary setbacks. As the British writer Jean Rhys has written:

> *All of writing is a huge lake. There are great rivers that feed the lake, like Tolstoy and Dostoevsky. And there are trickles, like Jean Rhys. All that matters is feeding the lake. I don't matter. The lake matters. You must keep feeding the lake. It is very important. Nothing else is important.*

TELLING IT LIKE IT MAYBE IS: THE POET AS CRITIC

William Kloefkorn

A poem is an attitude looking for something solid to sit on.

By writing the rough draft the poet makes a guess at what his attitude is; by revising he tries to move guess beyond reckon *all the way to* Yeah, that's it. *To do this he makes use of whatever literary touchstones have come his way—anything from descriptions of foundation garments in the Sears catalog to lines from Chaucer and Salinger. Add to these that multitude of other touchstones derived from the verbal experience. In my first collection,* Alvin Turner as Farmer, *I have the speaker, the farmer, conclude one of the poems by saying*

> Feed me,
> Woman,
> Then kindly step back!
> I intend to do some pretty damn fancy whistling
> While I slop the hogs.

Not "pretty fancy" or "damn fancy," because at the back of my brain I yet hear the boys in the pool hall saying "pretty damn fancy," "pretty" and "damn" therefore being a marriage made in small-town eight-ball heaven. The phrase reflects the attitude, or a part of it, I was looking for as I wrote the poem.

All writers are critics, if only of their own stuff. Especially of their own stuff. And all writers have critical yardsticks, though most of them probably do not formalize them with lists; most writers, in fact, probably use them in much the same way that they use their legs for walking or their lungs for breathing. In a moment of sophomoric affirmation I ended a poem like this:

> And O how fresh, how sweet the world is!
> It is a house of milk and tongue
> and eye and skin
> and breath and breast and quilt
> and fingertips and dung,
> and that is all it is.
>
> And that is everything!

Looking at those lines I realize that my criteria for selecting the nouns had nothing to do with either the written or the spoken touchstone—no catalog, no Chaucer, no small talk over a pool or snooker table; my touchstones were experiences to which the nouns are immeasurably attached, and to talk about these episodes would surely try the patience of Griselda.

In any case, I won the goddam hog-calling contest (see below), and later I wrote a poem about it—my attitude toward the victory having found something solid (would you believe a 900-pound Chester White?) to sit on.

Brief Warm-up Writing Exercises

1. Describe any experience you have had entering a contest or competition.
2. Freewrite on how writing might possibly be like hog calling.
3. Brainstorm a list of books or single lines (quotations) that have been important to you as "touchstones" of good writing.

1   ❖ I'm a poet, and therefore a critic, and because many of you are poets and critics, too, I'd like to tell it like it maybe really is, or was, or both.

2   To begin with, I had not intended to enter the hog-calling competition in North Platte.

3   North Platte, Nebraska, population 24,509, lies snugly and picturesquely in the western third of the state, 225 miles due west of Lincoln, near the confluence of the north and the south branches of the Platte River, a braided

stream that according to those who have never tried to navigate her at flood stage is an inch deep and a mile wide. I was in North Platte with a colleague, Charles Stubblefield, Stub for short, to present belt buckles to the poets and the storytellers whom we judged to be the winners of an annual writing contest that was part of a week-long June celebration called Buffalo Bill Days. Buffalo Bill had some roots in North Platte, and North Platte had a Buffalo Bill museum to prove it, not to mention the week-long celebration, which Stub and I that year (it was 1978) were a part of. Did I mention that the belt buckles were very large and very gaudy, gold-and-silver gaudy, spit-shine gaudy, gaudiness on a par with, say, Circus-Circus in Las Vegas, or Pat Robertson's grin? They were.

4   So we spent most of a Monday evening presenting the buckles and listening to the winning poems and stories, and before we went to bed the friends on whom we were imposing ourselves convinced us that we should stay an extra day or two and take in some of the hoopla.

5   We stayed. The first hoopla occurred early the following morning—a pork-chop breakfast on the town's most spacious mall. The event began unethically early, six A.M., but the good news was that the chops were three inches thick and lean as a rakehandle. Stub, a transplanted Texan who writes good stories and tells even better ones, allowed that he had never eaten better chops, not even in the Texas panhandle, and I agreed, though I have never eaten pork chops in the Texas panhandle.

6   After breakfast we noticed that the hooplas were rapidly proliferating. For example, a number of young women, scantily attired, were attaching large buttons to the lapels of whomever, buttons declaring that PORK IS BEAUTIFUL. These young women were Pork Queens, each identified by a purple banner that rather evenly divided the upper body diagonally into two parts; the identification specified not the name of the woman, but the area she represented: Polk County Pork Queen, Garden County, Frontier, Cherry, Holt, Boyd, Sheridan, Hooker—and towns, too, Thedford and Chadron and Hyannis and Weeping Water and Ogallala and Broken Bow. The Nebraska Pork Queen was there, and so too the National Pork Queen. As these women attached buttons to the lapels of whomever, which eventually included me and Stub, other folks brought in a covey of shoats and set up a fence around them; the Queens were later to dress these little porkers, and the most colorfully dressed would win a prize, though not a belt buckle.

7   Then as if from nowhere a flat-bed truck materialized at the center of the parking lot, a truck roughly the size of Rhode Island. Soon a wooden ladder appeared, enabling a young cowboy to climb to the bed, where he put together a microphone complete with speakers, after which he placed three metal chairs at the front of the bed, near the cab. Then—now listen to this part, because it's important—then he hauled out three gorgeous trophies, each with a golden hog adorning the top, and placed them in front of the chairs. Having tested the mike, he announced that the hog-calling competition would begin in precisely thirty minutes, and three categories were open—the Pork Queens first, the other women next, and the menfolk bringing up the rear.

8   I looked at those trophies and my desire to possess one of them amounted to lust.
9   I poked Stub in one of his Texas ribs. "If it isn't too late," I said, "let's enter and go for that trophy."
10 To my great surprise Stub declined. He said that he had never called hogs. I said that I had never called hogs, either. But just look at that trophy, buckeroo, I told him. Think how lovely it would look sitting on a shelf between *A Farewell to Arms* and the *Catcher in the Rye*. Stub admitted that, yes, such a trophy most certainly would hike the valuation of his office, but nonetheless he did not want to enter the competition.
11 I was surprised all the way into silence. Stub is a native Texan, for chrissake, and therefore an extrovert, a gambler, a man on whom very little ever is lost. But for some reason that to this day remains a mystery, he refused to enter the contest.
12 But at last he compromised. He said that if I wanted to go for the trophy (and O God I did, though as I noted earlier I had not gone to North Platte with anything of the sort in mind), he would enter my name and would coach me.
13 I agreed, and Stub disappeared into the gathering mob.
14 He returned shortly before the Pork Queens, all of them now assembled on the bed of the truck, were to begin their calling, and his grin looked like one of those belt buckles we had awarded the night before.
15 "It's all set," he said. "You're number seventeen."
16 We watched and listened closely to each Pork Queen as she advanced to the mike, identified herself by name, and did her call. Stub became the consummate critic. Did I mention that before he took to literature and to storytelling he coached defensive football at East Texas State? He did. That he was a pilot in World War Two? He was.
17 When the Pork Queen category had spent itself, Stub and I huddled. It would be about fifteen minutes, the young cowboy had said, before the women-other-than-the-Pork-Queens competition got underway, so Stub wanted to use that time to do some coaching.
18 "You notice any weakness in particular?" asked Stub.
19 "Well," I said, "one of the contestants, Miss Sheridan County, I think it was, stood too far away from the mike. I think that most of her call was wasted on those beyond the first few rows."
20 "Good," Stub said. During the contest he had been scribbling into a small notebook; now he made a check beside one of the scribbles. "Suggestion number one," he said, *"swallow the microphone."* He paused. He looked squarely at me. "You notice anything else?"
21 I tried to remember. Yes, one of the Queens had walked up to the mike, then only miniseconds later she walked away. I mentioned this to Stub.
22 "Good," he said. He made another check beside one of the scribbles. "Lesson number two," he said, *"sustain the call,* though it might seem to you that eons are passing. The call," he added, "must have magnitude; it must be

long enough to make a distinct aural impression, but short enough to be taken in by the memory."

23   I looked at my coach, who has a round friendly face, like soft leather, and blue sharp eyes that twinkle with something akin to mischief if not misdemeanor. Like me, he was wearing jeans and a cotton shirt, his yellow, mine blue. For judging the poetry and the stories we had been given belt buckles very similar to the ones we had presented to the winners, and of course we were wearing them with maybe undue pride. In any case, we fit tolerably well, I think, into the down-home congregation that was large and growing larger.

24   We studied each caller in the next category, too, women old and young and in-between, Stub scribbling like an insane critic into his little notebook. When the competition ended we huddled again.

25   "Well?" he said.

26   I tried to remember. But the looks and the calls of all those women, and there were many, began running together.

27   "Look," I said finally, "you're the goddam coach. Aren't you supposed to tell *me*?"

28   Stub smiled, I think, condescendingly. "It's the Socratic method, dummy," he said. "Now think hard. Remember the caller who stood behind the mike stiff as a two-by-six?"

29   "Yes," I said, "in fact I do. Now that you mention it."

30   "Did her stiffness strengthen her call or weaken it?"

31   "Weakened it," I said.

32   "And why do you suppose it weakened it?"

33   "Because it didn't seem natural."

34   "And what," said the master, "might she have done to appear more natural?"

35   "Relax," I said.

36   "Relax," said Stub.

37   "Yes," I said, "and maybe bend her knees a little."

38   "Bend her knees," said Socrates.

39   "Yes," I said, "and maybe do something with her hands; they hung too stiffly at her sides."

40   "Hung too stiffly," Stub said. I was impressed with his uncanny talent for repetition. Chewing his tongue now, he made a third check beside one of the hentracks. "Observation number three," he said, "*assume a pose*, somewhat bending the knees and cupping the hands to form a megaphone." He paused. He looked squarely at me. "Anything else?"

41   "Well, there was this very small girl whose call was pretty much a monotone."

42   This time Stub made the check beside the scribble before he announced the inference. Then: "Lesson number four," he said, *vary the pitch*. Vary it suddenly and drastically, providing a surprise not unlike discovery."

43 "Now see here, coach," I said, "Socrates is one thing, but Aristotle's another."

44 "Okay," said Stub, "then listen. It's about time for the male competition to begin. But before it does, I have two more pieces of advice."

45 He explained them, and I had them freshly in mind as I climbed the ladder and approached the mike. Number five: *be anecdotal;* give the three judges time to arrange their papers by telling a very brief anecdote. Also, this will make you appear more down to earth, more grassroots, more human. And number six: *be political;* identify yourself with a pork producer association.

46 I did both. I told the judges that my paternal grandfather, who farmed a quarter-section of dry land in southeastern Kansas near a small town named Cedar Vale, taught me how to call hogs, which was partly true, because I used to go with my grandfather once in a while to slop the hogs, and he would slap the slopbucket with his free hand and sort of sing out Sooooooo-eeeeee in a falsetto that always surprised me, because he had such a low voice, but he never did anything fancy—he didn't have to, because he only had half a dozen hogs, which he kept in a pen not much bigger than a bathroom, and they weren't provided with a rich Frenchman's bill of fare, so they were always hungry, meaning that even before my grandfather could slap the slop-bucket more than once, or utter more than half a syllable of Sooooooo-eeeeee, they were already on their way to the trough—and he never gave me any of what you might honestly call formal instruction. So my little anecdote was mostly untrue, but it had enough truth in it I believe to earn it a consideration in Purgatory, though I wouldn't bet the farm on it.

47 But when I moved into number six I outright lied. I said that I was a member of the Salt Valley Pork Producers Association (SVPPA), and when I said this I looked at the judges, and they seemed impressed.

48 So I turned my head and swallowed the mike and assumed a pose and let it rip—and rip and rip and rip. I went from low notes to high notes to middle C, sending out a hog call that I am firmly convinced my grandfather, dead now these twenty years, must have heard all the way to the Cedar Vale, Kansas, cemetery, a call that I hope to heaven he is proud of. What I didn't know was that CBS was taping this event, and that both my brother and my mother would see and hear it on the evening news and would call me to ask if sure enough it had happened at last: have I gone all the way crazy?

49 Coach was pleased with the performance. He had that belt-buckle grin on his round soft-leather face, and he shook my hand.

50 "If that dude from Broken Bow doesn't take us out," he said, "I think we're in."

51 The dude from Broken Bow had done what he called an Arkansas razorback call, and he had swallowed the mike and assumed a pose and had varied the pitch and had held the call long enough for it to make a distinct aural impression but not so long that it couldn't be taken in by the memory, and he had ended his call with a series of cluckcluckclucks that tapered off into silence; I personally thought that the ending of his effort would be more

effective and more appropriate for the calling of leghorn chickens, but I had to admit that it was impressive—even to the extent that it had both me and Socrates worried.

52   But when the remaining contestants had finished their calls, and the judges had done their tallying, my name was announced as the winner. The dude from Broken Bow would have to settle for second place, for which there was no trophy whatsoever.

53   The immediate consequence of my victory was that I had a tough time during the rest of the week buying myself a drink. North Platte loves a hog-caller, especially one that walks away with the gilded hog, which means that for me the remainder of Buffalo Bill Days is somewhat a blur. A lovely, slow-motion, laughter-soaked, sour-mash blur, but most definitely a blur.

54   The long-range consequence of the victory is that I now more fully realize the extent to which inference is crucial to both the poet and the critic. One learns the art of hog-calling by studying the callers and listening to the calls, not by prescribing rules that complement one's own biases. The poet reads other writers, taking from them a portion of whatever it is that causes the heart to quicken, the mind to reach, the scalp to detach itself most pleasurably and most painfully from the bone.

55   Both poet and critic have what Matthew Arnold in his essay "The Study of Poetry" called "touchstones," those lines of poetry that are in the tradition of what he labeled "poetry of the highest order," lines with the punch that gives them staying power from one age into another. He writes, "Indeed there can be no more useful help for discovering what poetry belongs to the class of the truly excellent, and can therefore do us most good, than to have always in one's mind lines and expressions of the great masters, and to apply them as a touchstone to other poetry. Of course we are not to require this other poetry to resemble them; it may be very dissimilar. But if we have any tact we shall find them, when we have lodged them well in our minds, an infallible touchstone for detecting the presence of high poetic quality, and also the degree of this quality, in all other poetry we may place beside them."

56   Arnold cites lines from Homer, Dante, Shakespeare, and Milton; he never says precisely why the lines reflect "poetry of the highest order," though he does affirm that the lines can be "recognized by being felt in the verse of the master," a recognition that perhaps owes more to osmosis than to rationality, and the matter isn't much clarified when soon thereafter he adds, "the substance and matter on the one hand, the style and manner on the other, have a mark, an accent of high beauty, worth, and power."

57   We might quarrel with some of Arnold's finer points, and we might not choose the same lines that he chose to illustrate "poetry of the highest order," but it seems to me that inevitably our touchstones do exist, not necessarily memorized, but in existence nonetheless, haunting the neocortex level of the brain, and when we are serving as poet or critic we test our writing against them, sometimes even to the extent that we slip into an unwitting imitation.

58   I have some of my own touchstones from the classics, lines that even in

translation cause the heart to quicken, the mind to reach, the scalp to detach itself most pleasurably and most painfully from the bone. When Medea, in awful conflict with herself—shall she murder her own children to spite her unfaithful husband?—says,

> "Do not, O my heart, you must not do these things!
> Poor heart, let them go, have pity upon the children,"

doesn't the reader's own heart quicken? When Orestes, in the *Libation Bearers*, having avenged his father's death by murdering his mother, says,

> "Now I can praise him, now I can stand by to mourn
> and speak before this web that killed my father; yet
> I grieve for the thing done, the death, and all our race,"

doesn't the mind reach out—especially when Orestes says, "all our race"?

59   And when Dido, feeling betrayed, says to the god-directed Aeneas,

> "Oh, I will follow
> In blackest fire, and when cold death has taken
> Spirit from body, I will be there to haunt you,
> A shade, all over the world. I will have vengeance,"

doesn't the reader's scalp detach itself most pleasurably and most painfully from the bone—pleasure because Dido has indeed been betrayed, and thus perhaps deserves to be applauded as she imagines revenge, pain because no amount of revenge can set things right between her and Virgil's protagonist?

60   My own touchstones include the moderns as well as the ancients. I read the final four lines of James Hearst's poem "Veterans' Day," for example, and I am considerably impressed with the way in which he brings Donne into the poem to reflect both anger and concern:

> *They died, goddam it, they died,*
> *the young men for whom the bells toll,*
> *never to have homes, or wives or children,*
> *or the comfort of a warm bed.*

61   I admire too the opening lines of Hearst's poem "Truth":

> *How the devil do I know*
> *if there are rocks in your field,*
> *plow it and find out.*

62   Eliot and Frost and Robinson and Gwendolyn Brooks and Marge Piercy and others, including of course such prose-poets as Twain and Faulkner and

Steinbeck and Hemingway and Salinger, have their places in my repertoire of touchstones. Hear this couplet from an Elburn, Illinois, poet, a man named Dave Etter:

> Hands that have burst their purple veins
> float on the river where I was baptized.

Or these from his "Green-Eyed Boy after Reading Whitman and Sandburg":

> Clean smell of hay. This joyful flesh.
> The sweet sound of the hermit thrush.
> A virgin river sings in my free-verse head.

63 At the outset I said, "I'm a poet, and therefore a critic," and I mean by this that I am first of all a critic of my own work. My own best judgment, however fallible, will finally either make the poem or break it. And that is true, I believe, of most poets and critics. We can help each other, certainly, but when push comes to shove we must rely upon our own sense of what constitutes excellence.

64 Frequently we arrive at that sense of excellence by way of the back door, by acknowledging and standing guard against those personal biases that flesh seems heir to. I'll discuss several of them here, and you can revise the list, taking away from or adding to it, however the shoe seems best to fit. I'll focus here upon the critic, though the poet, who is therefore a critic, should pay some attention.

65 First is the affinity that some of us have for the personal and often confessional approach. If I am the poet, then everything that happens to me should be written about, and the world should stop its humdrum spinning and read me. If I am the critic, then whatever I read matters only if it can be viewed in the light of my most immediate interest. Here is what this particular bias can lead to:

> I like Hemingway very much. I especially like his
> short story, "A Clean, Well-Lighted Place." I mean,
> the story is so real. So true. I mean, I once knew
> a waiter who had more patience than you could shake
> a stick at. To tell you the truth, I still know him,
> if you know what I mean. Anyway, he's really patient.
> He isn't as old as the waiter in Hemingway's story,
> but I say age isn't everything. Anyway, he's patient,
> and he also has insomnia. According to Webster,
> insomnia is "a chronic inability to sleep." I
> remember that once this waiter (he works at Dale's
> Drive-In) stayed up all night with me, and he didn't
> show any signs at all of being sleepy. Boy, was

he patient. I must admit, though, that he doesn't much care for "clean, well-lighted places." Wow!

66   This writer's sense of reality doesn't extend beyond the tip of her nose, which means that the personal and the confessional can overlap one's sense of reality—which means further that neither poet nor critic should be bound by the limits of his own literal experience. One critic of John Steinbeck's *Grapes of Wrath*, for example, came down hard on the book because he had spent some time in Oklahoma and had not met anyone like the Joadses. Well, I have lived twenty-six years in Nebraska, and only recently did I spend some time with a sandhills rancher. Does this mean that only now can I believe in Mari Sandoz's *Old Jules*? Of course not. Years ago she took me into the book and made me a believer, and my later experience in the sandhills only confirmed what she had shown me.

67   Next, some of us have a tendency to see things chiefly, if not only, in political and sociological terms. Such a critic might handle that Hemingway story like this:

Ernest Hemingway's "A Clean, Well-Lighted Place" is a perfect example of what is wrong with our involvement in (fill in the blank—Korea, Vietnam, Panama, Nicaragua, the Persian Gulf), and it indicates, too, the extent to which ghetto children should avoid political conventions and marijuana. The old waiter in Hemingway's story has difficulty sleeping, and one is left to ponder the question, why are so many people today so very restless? The answer, of course, lies in man's inhumanity to man, an example of which is (fill in the blank—Korea, Vietnam, Panama, Nicaragua, the Persian Gulf). I was talking to a veteran of the Korean Conflict just the other day, and he said. . . .

68   Or we might be inclined to read most things ontologically, as if we are counting a double major in theology and philosophy, with perhaps a smattering of educationese tossed in:

Beneath the surface of Ernest Hemingway's "A Clean, Well-Lighted Place" being and non-being lie like the greater part of an iceberg. The essence of the personhood of the old waiter is his primordial relationship to "nada," or "nothingness," and his quarrel with the younger waiter is suggestive of the reality of experiential monism. Metaphysically speaking. . . .

69   Not far removed from this pitfall is the predisposition of some to write and to read most things from what I call the "Jesus-Wants-Me-for-a-Sunbeam" slant. If you have not read such a work, you are either very isolated or very young—or very dead. Here is Hemingway in the clutches of such an attitude:

In the beginning God created everything: the birds, the flowers, the trees, and even man. Later, men created such things as cars and pencils, railroads and cafes. Ernest Hemingway knew all of this perhaps better than most of us, for *in his short story, "A Clean, Well-Lighted Place," he says that only through the divine light of Christ can man keep his senses and go to sleep. We all know, as Luther and others have told us, that "the light of the world is Jesus," and Hemingway's story re-affirms this age-old truth. The old waiter, for example, prays. . . .*

70   Probably the dominant urge is that of making the poem or the story fit into an aphoristic straight-jacket, an urge that both poet and critic should strain mightily to resist. So forgive me, Papa, for this one last abuse of your work:

Ernest Hemingway's "A Clean, Well-Lighted Place" dramatizes the fact that "Early to bed, early to rise, makes a man healthy, wealthy, and wise." Unfortunately, the old waiter in the story has not learned this lesson, and the upshot is that he is neither healthy nor wealthy, and his insomnia—which is the result of his guilt feeling about staying up too late—can hardly be called wise. If he is ever to achieve success, he must learn the lesson that such men as Benjamin Franklin and Horatio Alger both learned and taught: the early bird gets the worm.

71   You can take the list from here. In doing so, level with yourself; poet or critic, or both, tell it like it maybe is, acknowledging your biases and guarding against them. Then, when your own list is more or less finished, look at each point and determine its flip-side; each determination should serve then as a reasonable positive criterion for your own creating and critiquing.

72   No, I have not returned to North Platte in quest of another trophy. Yes, I do still have the trophy that I won in 1978. It is a thing of rare porcine beauty and a joy most of the time. It is in storage now and has been since last December 18 and will be until the building in which I hang out, Old Main, is properly renovated, probably next January—in time, I hope, for the start of the spring semester, though I wouldn't bet the farm on it. At that time, should that time occur, I'll return the trophy to its place on a shelf between *A Farewell to Arms* and the *Catcher in the Rye*.

73   Oh, yes. The National Pork Queen won the Pork Queen division of the hog-calling competition, and the Queen from Cherry County dressed her shoat to a fair-you-well and walked off with the first-place prize; I don't remember what the prize was, but I do know that it wasn't a belt buckle.

74   The name of her little hog was Hamlet. ❖

Questions to Ponder

1. How do William Kloefkorn's six lessons for hog calling apply to writing?
2. What is the advantage of embedding instruction in a story?
3. According to William Kloefkorn, what do writers and critics have in common?

4. This essay is the published version of a keynote speech William Kloefkorn gave at a conference of high school and college writers. What form and voice does Kloefkorn adopt for this occasion? Do you find them effective for his audience?

Writing Possibilities

1. Put on your "teacher" hat, and write an essay in which you explain how each of William Kloefkorn's lessons for successful hog calling might apply to successful writing.
2. Look back at warm-up writing exercise 1, about your experience with a contest or competition. Using Bill Kloefkorn's essay as a model, assume the voice or style of the competition you entered, and write of the experience in a way that will offer a lesson.
3. Write a serious "how to" essay for freshmen taking their first literature course. Tell them how you attack a poem, short story, novel, play, piece of nonfiction—or all of the above.
4. Using William Kloefkorn's essay as a model, write of a serious matter through deceptively folksy, down-home narration.

HOME OF THE FREE

Wendell Berry

Ignorance of books and the lack of critical consciousness of language were safe enough in primitive societies with coherent oral traditions. In our society, which exists in an atmosphere of prepared, public language—language that is either written or being read—illiteracy is both a personal and a public danger. Think how constantly "the average American" is surrounded by premeditated language, in newspapers and magazines, on signs and billboards, on TV and radio. He is forever being asked to buy or believe somebody else's line of goods. The line of goods is being sold, moreover, by men who are trained to make him buy it or believe it, whether or not he needs it or understands it or knows its value or wants it. This sort of selling is an honored profession among us. Parents who grow hysterical at the thought that their son might not cut his hair are glad to have him taught, and later employed, to lie about the quality of an automobile or the ability of a candidate.

What is our defense against this sort of language—this language-as-weapon? There is only one. We must know a better language. We must speak, and teach our children to speak, a language precise and articulate and lively enough to tell the truth about the world as we know it. And to do this we must know something of the roots and resources of our language; we must know its literature. The only defense against the worst is a knowledge of the best. By their ignorance people enfranchise their exploiters. . . .

I am saying, then, that literacy—the mastery of language and the knowledge of books—is not an ornament, but a necessity. It is impractical only by the standards of quick profit and easy power. Longer perspective will show that it alone can preserve in us the possibility of an accurate judgment of ourselves, and the possibilities of correction and renewal. Without it, we are adrift in the present, in the wreckage of yesterday, in the nighmare of tomorrow.

Brief Warm-up Writing Exercises

1. Brainstorm a list of the advertisements or commercials that you hate.
2. Freewrite about the household chore you like best to do.
3. Brainstorm two lists: the *advantages* and the *disadvantages* of "laborsaving" devices.

1   I was writing not long ago about a team of Purdue engineers who foresaw that by 2001 practically everything would be done by remote control. The question I asked—because such a "projection" *forces* one to ask it—was, Where does satisfaction come from? I concluded that there probably wouldn't be much satisfaction in such a world. There would be a lot of what passes for "efficiency," a lot of "production" and "consumption," but little satisfaction.

2   What I failed to acknowledge was that this "world of the future" is already established among us, and is growing. Two advertisements that I have lately received from correspondents make this clear, and raise the question about the sources of satisfaction more immediately and urgently than any abstract "projection" can do.

3   The first is the legend from a John Deere [tractor] display at Waterloo Municipal Airport:

    INTRODUCING SOUND-GARD BODY . . .
    A DOWN TO EARTH SPACE CAPSULE.

New Sound-Gard body from John Deere, an "earth space capsule" to protect and encourage the American farmer at his job of being "Breadwinner to a world of families."

Outside: dust, noise, heat, storm, fumes.

Inside: all's quiet, comfortable, safe.

Features include a 4 post Roll Gard, space-age metals, plastics, and fibers to isolate driver from noise, vibration, and jolts. He dials "inside weather," to his liking . . . he push buttons radio or stereo tape entertainment. He breathes filtered, conditioned air in his pressurized compartment. He has remote control over multi-ton and multi-hookups, with control tower visibility . . . from his scientifically padded seat.

4   The second is an ad for a condominium housing development:

HOME OF THE FREE.

We do the things you hate. You do the things you like. We mow the lawn, shovel the walks, paint and repair and do all exterior maintenance.

You cross-country ski, play tennis, hike, swim, work out, read or nap. Or advise our permanent maintenance staff as they do the things you hate.

5   Different as they may seem at first, these two ads make the same appeal, and they represent two aspects of the same problem: the widespread, and still spreading, assumption that we somehow have the right to be set free from anything whatsoever that we "hate" or don't want to do. According to this view, what we want to be set free from are the natural conditions of the world and the necessary work of human life; we do not want to experience temperatures that are the least bit too hot or too cold, or to work in the sun, or be exposed to wind or rain, or come in personal contact with anything describable as dirt, or provide for any of our own needs, or clean up after ourselves. Implicit in all this is the desire to be free of the "hassles" of mortality, to be "safe" from the life cycle. Such freedom and safety are always for sale. It is proposed that if we put all earthly obligations and the rites of passage into the charge of experts and machines, then life will become a permanent holiday.

6   What these people are really selling is insulation—cushions of technology, "space age" materials, and the menial work of other people—to keep fantasy in and reality out. The condominium ad says flat out that it is addressed to people who "hate" the handwork of household maintenance, and who will enjoy "advising" the people who do it for them; it is addressed, in other words, to those who think themselves too good to do work that other people are not too good to do. But it is a little surprising to realize that the John Deere ad is addressed to farmers who not only hate farming (that is, any physical contact with the ground or the weather or the crops), but also hate tractors, from the "dust," "fumes," "noise, vibration, and jolts" of which

they wish to be protected by an "earth space capsule" and a "scientifically padded seat."

7 Of course, the only real way to get this sort of freedom and safety—to escape the hassles of earthly life—is to die. And what I think we see in these advertisements is an appeal to a desire to be dead that is evidently felt by many people. These ads are addressed to the perfect consumers—the self-consumers, who have found nothing of interest here on earth, nothing to do, and are impatient to be shed of earthly concerns. And so I am at a loss to explain the delay. Why hasn't some super salesman sold every one of these people a coffin—an "earth space capsule" in which they would experience no discomfort or inconvenience whatsoever, would have to do no work that they hate, would be spared all extremes of weather and all noises, fumes, vibrations, and jolts?

8 I wish it were possible for us to let these living dead bury themselves in the earth space capsules of their choice and think no more about them. The problem is that with their insatiable desire for comfort, convenience, remote control, and the rest of it, they cause an unconscionable amount of trouble for the rest of us, who would like a fair crack at living the rest of our lives within the terms and conditions of the real world. Speaking for myself, I acknowledge that the world, the weather, and the life cycle have caused me no end of trouble, and yet I look forward to putting in another forty or so years with them because they have also given me no end of pleasure and instruction. They interest me. I want to see them thrive on their own terms. I hate to see them abused and interfered with for the comfort and convenience of a lot of spoiled people who presume to "hate" the more necessary kinds of work and all the natural consequences of working outdoors.

9 When people begin to "hate" the life cycle and to try to live outside it and to escape its responsibilities, then the corpses begin to pile up and to get into the wrong places. One of the laws that the world imposes on us is that everything must be returned to its source to be used again. But one of the first principles of the haters is to violate this law in the name of convenience or efficiency. Because it is "inconvenient" to return bottles to the beverage manufacturers, "dead soldiers" pile up in the road ditches and in the waterways. Because it is "inconvenient" to be responsible for wastes, the rivers are polluted with everything from human excrement to various carcinogens and poisons. Because it is "efficient" (by what standard?) to mass-produce meat and milk in food "factories," the animal manures that once would have fertilized the fields have instead become wastes and pollutants. And so to be "free" of "inconvenience" and "inefficiency" we are paying a high price—which the haters among us are happy to charge to posterity.

10 And what a putrid (and profitable) use they have made of the idea of freedom! What a tragic evolution has taken place when the inheritors of the Bill of Rights are told, and when some of them believe, that "the home of the free" is where somebody else will do your work!

11 Let me set beside those advertisements a sentence that I consider a responsible statement about freedom: "To be free is precisely the same thing as to be

pious, wise, just and temperate, careful of one's own, abstinent from what is another's, and thence, in fine, magnanimous and brave." That is John Milton. He is speaking out of the mainstream of our culture. Reading his sentence after those advertisements is coming home. His words have an atmosphere around them that a living human can breathe in.

12   How do you get free in Milton's sense of the word? I don't think you can do it in an earth space capsule or a space space capsule or a capsule of any kind. What Milton is saying is that you can do it only by living in this world as you find it, and by taking responsibility for the consequences of your life in it. And that means doing some chores that, highly objectionable in anybody's capsule, may not be at all unpleasant in the world.

13   Just a few days ago I finished up one of the heaviest of my spring jobs: hauling manure. On a feed lot I think this must be real drudgery even with modern labor-saving equipment—all that "waste" and no fields to put it on! But instead of a feed lot I have a small farm—what would probably be called a subsistence farm. My labor-saving equipment consists of a team of horses and a forty-year-old manure spreader. We forked the manure on by hand—forty-five loads. I made my back tired and my hands sore, but I got a considerable amount of pleasure out of it. Everywhere I spread that manure I knew it was needed. What would have been a nuisance in a feed lot was an opportunity and a benefit here. I enjoyed seeing it go out onto the ground. I was working some two-year-olds in the spreader for the first time, and I enjoyed that—mostly. And, since there were no noises, fumes, or vibrations the loading times were socially pleasant. I had some help from neighbors, from my son, and, toward the end, from my daughter who arrived home well rested from college. She helped me load, and then read *The Portrait of a Lady* while I drove up the hill to empty the spreader. I don't think many young women have read Henry James while forking manure. I enjoyed working with my daughter, and I enjoyed wondering what Henry James would have thought of her. ❖

Questions to Ponder

1. What spurred Wendell Berry to write this essay? Can advertisements and newspaper articles, television shows and films sometimes inspire fine commentary?
2. Does "free" for Wendell Berry mean free from responsibility?
3. What (and whose) definition of "freedom" does Wendell Berry contrast with the advertisements for space capsule tractors and condominiums? What are the differences between these definitions?
4. What does Wendell Berry consider necessary behavior (and thinking) for "sustaining the call."
5. Do you agree with Wendell Berry, or do you think he is too harsh with those who are seeking comfort and ease?

Writing Possibilities

1. Look at the list of advertisements you hate from warm-up writing exercise 1, and using Wendell Berry's essay as a model, write your own essay analyzing and criticizing the ads—and the assumptions behind them.
2. Write a letter to Wendell Berry defending "laborsaving" devices and the people who use them.
3. Choose a laborsaving device, and research its development, its costs to operate, and the implications of its continued use for the survival of human freedom in Wendell Berry's sense of the word. You might want to present your findings in the form of an article for *Consumer Reports*.

FIRST CELL, FIRST LOVE

Aleksandr Solzhenitsyn

From the time I was very young I had had, on my own, a longing to become a writer and had written much of the usual youthful nonsense and, in the [1930s], had made attempts to get published, but my manuscripts were not accepted anywhere. I had in mind getting a literary education, but Rostov did not offer what I wanted; to go to Moscow was impossible because of my mother's being single and ill and our very modest means . . . I enrolled in the mathematics department at Rostov University; I had considerable aptitude for mathematics, I could do it easily, but it never appealed to me as a life's work. However, it served as a benefactor in my destiny. At least twice it saved my life: probably I would not have survived eight years of the [prison] camps if, as a mathematician, I had not been assigned for four years to a so-called sharashka; and in exile I was allowed to teach mathematics and physics, which made life easier and gave me a chance to get down to the job of writing. If I had had a literary education, I doubt I would have come through my ordeals intact; I would have been under a great handicap. . . .

I was arrested on the basis of censored extracts from my correspondence with a school friend in 1944–5, basically for disrespectful remarks about Stalin, al-

though we referred to him by a pseudonym. Material complementing the "accusation" was rough drafts of stories and reflections found in my map case. Nevertheless, this was not sufficient for a "trial," and in June 1945 I was "convicted" by a procedure that was then widespread—in my absence, by a decision of OSO (an NKVD Special Tribunal). . . . [O]n March 5 [1953], the day Stalin's death was announced, I was for the first time let out on the street without guards. . . . During all the [subsequent] years in exile I taught mathematics and physics in a rural school and, given my austere and solitary way of life, secretly wrote prose (in camp, I could only compose verse by heart). I manage to preserve it and to bring it with me from exile into the European part of the country, where I continued to be outwardly busy teaching, secretly busy writing. . . .

A work of art contains its verification in itself: artificial, strained concepts do not withstand the test of being turned into images; they fall to pieces, turn out to be sickly and pale, convince no one. Works which draw on truth and present it to us in live and concentrated form grip us, compellingly involve us, and no one ever, not even ages hence, will come forth to refute them.

Brief Warm-up Writing Exercises

1. Freewrite about any experience you have had when you were confined—because of illness, weather, or punishment.
2. Brainstorm a list of things you would do to survive if you were to become a prisoner of war.
3. Freewrite all you know about the Soviet prison camps from 1917 to the 1970s.

1 ❖ How is one to take the title of this chapter? A cell and love in the same breath? Ah, well, probably it has to do with Leningrad during the blockade—and you were imprisoned in the Big House. In that case it would be very understandable. That's why you are still alive—because they shoved you in there. It was the best place in Leningrad—not only for the interrogators, who even lived there and had offices in the cellars in case of shelling. Joking aside, in Leningrad in those days no one washed and everyone's face was covered with a black crust, but in the Big House prisoners were given a hot shower every tenth day. Well, it's true that only the corridors were heated—for the jailers. The cells were left unheated, but after all, there were water pipes in the cells that worked and a toilet, and where else in Leningrad could you find that? And the bread ration was just like the ration outside—barely four and a half ounces. In addition, there was broth made from slaughtered horses once a day! And thin gruel once a day as well!

2   It was a case of the cat's being envious of the dog's life! But what about punishment cells? And what about the *"supreme measure"*—execution? No, that isn't what the chapter title is about.

3   Not at all.

4   You sit down and half-close your eyes and try to remember them all. How many different cells you were imprisoned in during your term! It is difficult even to count them. And in each one there were people, people. There might be two people in one, 150 in another. You were imprisoned for five minutes in one and all summer long in another.

5   But in every case, out of all the cells you've been in, your first cell is a very special one, the place where you first encountered others like yourself, doomed to the same fate. All your life you will remember it with an emotion that you otherwise experience only in remembering your first love. And those people, who shared with you the floor and air of that stone cubicle during those days when you rethought your entire life, will from time to time be recollected by you as members of your own family.

6   Yes, in those days they were your only family.

7   What you experience in your first interrogation cell parallels nothing in your entire *previous* life or your whole *subsequent* life. No doubt prisons have stood for thousands of years before you came along, and may continue to stand after you too—longer than one would like to think—but that first interrogation cell is unique and inimitable.

8   Maybe it was a terrible place for a human being. A lice-laden, bedbug-infested lock-up, without windows, without ventilation, without bunks, and with a dirty floor, a box called a KPZ[1] in the village soviet, at the police station, in the railroad station, or in some port. (The KPZ's and the DPZ's are scattered across the face of our land in the greatest abundance. There are masses of prisoners in them.) Or maybe it was "solitary" in the Archangel prison, where the glass had been smeared over with red lead so that the only rays of God's maimed light which crept in to you were crimson, and where a 15-watt bulb burned constantly in the ceiling, day and night. Or "solitary" in the city of Choibalsan, where, for six months at a time, fourteen of you were crowded onto seven square yards of floor space in such a way that you could only shift your bent legs in unison. Or it was one of the Lefortovo "psychological" cells, like No. 111, which was painted black and also had a day-and-night 25-watt bulb, but was in all other respects like every other Lefortovo cell: asphalt floor; the heating valve out in the corridor where only the guards had access to it; and, above all, that interminable irritating roar from the wind tunnel of the neighboring Central Aero- and Hydrodynamics Institute—a roar one could not believe was unintentional, a roar which would make a bowl or cup vibrate so violently that it would slip off the edge of the table, a roar which made it

---

[1] KPZ = Cell for Preliminary Detention. DPZ = House of Preliminary Detention. In other words, where interrogations are conducted, and where sentences are served.

useless to converse and during which one could sing at the top of one's lungs and the jailer wouldn't even hear. And then when the roar stopped, there would ensue a sense of relief and felicity superior to freedom itself.

9   But it was not the dirty floor, not the murky walls, nor the odor of the latrine bucket that you loved—but those fellow prisoners with whom you about-faced at command, and that something which beat between your heart and theirs, and their sometimes astonishing words, and then, too, the birth within you, on that very spot, of free-floating thoughts you had so recently been unable to leap up or rise to.

10 And how much it had cost you to last out until that first cell! You had been kept in a pit, or in a box, or in a cellar. No one had addressed a human word to you. No one had looked at you with a human gaze. All they did was to peck at your brain and heart with iron beaks, and when you cried out or groaned, they laughed.

11 For a week or a month you had been an abandoned waif, alone among enemies, and you had already said good-bye to reason and to life; and you had already tried to kill yourself by "falling" from the radiator in such a way as to smash your brains against the iron cone of the valve.[2] Then all of a sudden you were alive again, and were brought in to your friends. And reason returned to you.

12 That's what your first cell is!

13 You waited for that cell. You dreamed of it almost as eagerly as of freedom. Meanwhile, they kept shoving you around between cracks in the wall and holes in the ground, from Lefortovo into some legendary, diabolical Sukhanovka.

14 Sukhanovka was the most terrible prison the MGB had. Its very name was used to intimidate prisoners; interrogators would hiss it threateningly. And you'd not be able to question those who had been there: either they were insane and talking only disconnected nonsense, or they were dead.

15 Sukhanovka was a former monastery, dating back to Catherine the Great. It consisted of two buildings—one in which prisoners served out their terms, and the other a structure that contained sixty-eight monks' cells and was used for interrogations. The journey there in a Black Maria took two hours, and only a handful of people knew that the prison was really just a few miles from Lenin's Gorki estate and near the former estate of Zinaida Volkonskaya. The countryside surrounding it was beautiful.

16 There they stunned the newly arrived prisoner with a stand-up punishment cell again so narrow that when he was no longer able to stand he had to sag, supported by his bent knees propped against the wall. There was no alternative. They kept prisoners thus for more than a day to break their resistance. But they ate tender, tasty food at Sukhanovka, which was like nothing else in the MGB—because it was brought in from the Architects' Rest Home. They didn't maintain a separate kitchen to prepare hogwash. However, the amount one architect would eat—including fried potatoes and meatballs—

[2]Alexander D.

was divided among twelve prisoners. As a result the prisoners were not only always hungry but also exceedingly irritable.

17 The cells were all built for two, but prisoners under interrogation were usually kept in them singly. The dimensions were five by six and a half feet.[3] Two little round stools were welded to the stone floor, like stumps, and at night, if the guard unlocked a cylinder lock, a shelf dropped from the wall onto each stump and remained there for seven hours (in other words, during the hours of interrogation, since there was no daytime interrogation at Sukhanovka at all), and a little straw mattress large enough for a child also dropped down. During the day, the stool was exposed and free, but one was forbidden to sit on it. In addition, a table lay, like an ironing board, on four upright pipes. The "fortochka" in the window—the small hinged pane for ventilation—was always closed except for ten minutes in the morning when the guard cranked it open. The glass in the little window was reinforced. There were never any exercise periods out of doors. Prisoners were taken to the toilet at 6 A.M. only—i.e., when no one's stomach needed it. There was no toilet period in the evening. There were two guards for each block of seven cells, so that was why the prisoners could be under almost constant inspection through the peephole, the only interruption being the time it took the guard to step past two doors to a third. And that was the purpose of silent Sukhanovka: to leave the prisoner not a single moment for sleep, not a single stolen moment for privacy. You were always being watched and always in their power.

18 But if you endured the whole duel with insanity and all the trials of loneliness, and had stood firm, you deserved your first cell! And now when you got into it, your soul would heal.

19 If you had surrendered, if you had given in and betrayed everyone, you were also ready for your first cell. But it would have been better for you not to have lived until that happy moment and to have died a victor in the cellar, without having signed a single sheet of paper.

20 Now for the first time you were about to see people who were not your

---

[3]To be absolutely precise, they were 156 centimeters by 209 centimeters. How do we know? Through a triumph of engineering calculation and a strong heart that even Sukhanovka could not break. The measurements were the work of Alexander D., who would not allow them to drive him to madness or despair. He resisted by striving to use his mind to calculate distances. In Lefortovo he counted steps, converted them into kilometers, remembered from a map how many kilometers it was from Moscow to the border, and then how many across all Europe, and how many across the Atlantic Ocean. He was sustained in this by the hope of returning to America. And in one year in Lefortovo solitary he got, so to speak, halfway across the Atlantic. Thereupon they took him to Sukhanovka. Here, realizing how few would survive to tell of it—and all our information about it comes from him—he invented a method of measuring the cell. The numbers 10/22 were stamped on the bottom of his prison bowl, and he guessed that "10" was the diameter of the bottom and "22" the diameter of the outside edge. Then he pulled a thread from a towel, made himself a tape measure, and measured everything with it. Then he began to invent a way of sleeping *standing up*, propping his knees against the small chair, and of deceiving the guard into thinking his eyes were open. He succeeded in this deception, and that was how he managed not to go insane when Ryumin kept him sleepless for a month.

enemies. Now for the first time you were about to see others who were alive,[4] who were traveling your road, and whom you could join to yourself with the joyous word "we."

21   Yes, that word which you may have despised out in freedom, when they used it as a substitute for your own individuality ("All of us, like one man!" Or: "We are deeply angered!" Or: "We demand!" Or: "We swear!"), is now revealed to you as something sweet: you are not alone in the world! Wise, spiritual beings—*human beings*—still exist.

22   I had been dueling for four days with the interrogator, when the jailer, having waited until I lay down to sleep in my blindingly lit box, began to unlock my door. I heard him all right, but before he could say: "Get up! Interrogation!" I wanted to lie for another three-hundredths of a second with my head on the pillow and pretend I was sleeping. But, instead of the familiar command, the guard ordered: "Get up! Pick up your bedding!"

23   Uncomprehending, and unhappy because this was my most precious time, I wound on my footcloths, put on my boots, my overcoat, my winter cap, and clasped the government-issue mattress in my arms. The guard was walking on tiptoe and kept signaling me not to make any noise as he led me down a corridor silent as the grave, through the fourth floor of the Lubyanka, past the desk of the section supervisor, past the shiny numbers on the cells and the olive-colored covers of the peepholes, and unlocked Cell 67. I entered and he locked it behind me immediately.

24   Even though only a quarter of an hour or so had passed since the signal to go to sleep had been given, the period allotted the prisoners for sleeping was so fragile, and undependable, and brief that, by the time I arrived, the inhabitants of Cell 67 were already asleep on their metal cots with their hands on top of the blankets.[5]

25   At the sound of the door opening, all three started and raised their heads for an instant. They, too, were waiting to learn which of them might be taken to interrogation.

26   And those three lifted heads, those three unshaven, crumpled pale faces, seemed to me so human, so dear, that I stood there, hugging my mattress, and

---

[4]And if this was in the Big House in Leningrad during the siege, you may also have seen cannibals. Those who had eaten human flesh, those who had traded in human livers from dissecting rooms, were for some reason kept by the MGB with the political prisoners.

[5]New measures of oppression, additions to the traditional prison regulations, were invented only gradually in the internal prisons of the GPU-NKVID-MGB. At the beginning of the twenties, prisoners were not subjected to this particular measure, and lights were turned off at night as in the ordinary world. But they began to keep the lights on, on the logical grounds that they needed to keep the prisoners in view at all times. (When they used to turn the lights on for inspection, it had been even worse.) Arms had to be kept outside the blanket, allegedly to prevent the prisoner from strangling himself beneath the blanket and thus escaping his just interrogation. It was demonstrated experimentally that in the winter a human being always wants to keep his arms under the bedclothes for warmth; consequently the measure was made permanent.

smiled with happiness. And they smiled. And what a forgotten look that was—after only one week!

27   "Are you from freedom?" they asked me. (That was the question customarily put to a newcomer.)

28   "Nooo," I replied. And that was a newcomer's usual first reply.

29   They had in mind that I had probably been arrested recently, which meant that I came *from freedom*. And I, after ninety-six hours of interrogation, hardly considered that I was from "freedom." Was I not already a veteran prisoner? Nonetheless I was *from freedom*. The beardless old man with the black and very lively eyebrows was already asking me for military and political news. Astonishing! Even though it was late February, they knew nothing about the Yalta Conference, nor the encirclement of East Prussia, nor anything at all about our own attack below Warsaw in mid-January, nor even about the woeful December retreat of the Allies. According to regulations, those under interrogation were not supposed to know anything about the outside world. And here indeed they didn't!

30   I was prepared to spend half the night telling them all about it—with pride, as though all the victories and advances were the work of my own hands. But at this point the duty jailer brought in my cot, and I had to set it up without making any noise. I was helped by a young fellow my own age, also a military man. His tunic and aviator's cap hung on his cot. He had asked me, even before the old man spoke, not for news of the war but for tobacco. But although I felt openhearted toward my new friends, and although not many words had been exchanged in the few minutes since I joined them, I sensed something alien in this front-line soldier who was my contemporary, and, as far as he was concerned, I clammed up immediately and forever.

31   (I had not yet even heard the word "nasedka"—"stool pigeon"—nor learned that there had to be one such "stool pigeon" in each cell. And I had not yet had time to think things over and conclude that I did not like this fellow, Georgi Kramarenko. But a spiritual relay, a sensor relay, had clicked inside me, and it had closed him off from me for good and all. I would not bother to recall this event if it had been the only one of its kind. But soon, with astonishment, and alarm, I became aware of the work of this internal sensor relay as a constant, inborn trait. The years passed and I lay on the same bunks, marched in the same formations, and worked in the same work brigades with hundreds of others. And always that secret sensor relay, for whose creation I deserved not the least bit of credit, worked even before I remembered it was there, worked at the first sight of a human face and eyes, at the first sound of a voice—so that I opened my heart to that person either fully or just the width of a crack, or else shut myself off from him completely. This was so consistently unfailing that all the efforts of the State Security officers to employ stool pigeons began to seem to me as insignificant as being pestered by gnats: after all, a person who has undertaken to be a traitor always betrays the fact in his face and in his voice, and even though some were more skilled in pretense, there was always something fishy about them. On the other hand, the sensor relay helped me distinguish those to whom I could from the very

beginning of our acquaintance completely disclose my most precious depths and secrets—secrets for which heads roll. Thus it was that I got through eight years of imprisonment, three years of exile, and another six years of underground authorship, which were in no wise less dangerous. During all those seventeen years I recklessly revealed myself to dozens of people—and didn't make a misstep even once. (I have never read about this trait anywhere, and I mention it here for those interested in psychology. It seems to me that such spiritual sensors exist in many of us, but because we live in too technological and rational an age, we neglect this miracle and don't allow it to develop.)

32   We set up the cot, and I was then ready to talk—in a whisper, of course, and lying down, so as not to be sent from this cozy nest into a punishment cell. But our third cellmate, a middle-aged man whose cropped head already showed the white bristles of imminent grayness, peered at me discontentedly and said with characteristic northern severity: "Tomorrow! Night is for sleeping."

33   That was the most intelligent thing to do. At any minute, one of us could have been pulled out for interrogation and held until 6 A.M., when the interrogator would go home to sleep but we were forbidden to.

34   One night of undisturbed sleep was more important than all the fates on earth!

35   One more thing held me back, which I didn't quite catch right away but had felt nonetheless from the first words of my story, although I could not at this early date find a name for it: As each of us had been arrested, everything in our world had switched places, a 180-degree shift in all our concepts had occurred, and the good news I had begun to recount with such enthusiasm might not be good news for *us* at all.

36   My cellmates turned on their sides, covered their eyes with their handkerchiefs to keep out the light from the 200-watt bulb, wound towels around their upper arms, which were chilled from lying on top of the blankets, hid their lower arms furtively beneath them, and went to sleep.

37   And I lay there, filled to the brim with the joy of being among them. One hour ago I could not have counted on being with anyone. I could have come to my end with a bullet in the back of my head—which was what the interrogator kept promising me—without having seen anyone at all. Interrogation still hung over me, but how far it had retreated! Tomorrow I would be telling them my story (though not talking about my *case*, of course) and they would be telling me their stories too. How interesting tomorrow would be, one of the best days of my life! (Thus, very early and very clearly, I had this consciousness that prison was not an abyss for me, but the most important turning point in my life.)

38   Every detail of the cell interested me. Sleep fled, and when the peephole was not in use I studied it all furtively. Up there at the top of one wall was a small indentation the length of three bricks, covered by a dark-blue paper blind. They had already told me it was a window. Yes, there was a window in the cell. And the blind served as an air-raid blackout. Tomorrow there would

be weak daylight, and in the middle of the day they would turn off the glaring light bulb. How much that meant—to have daylight in daytime! ❖

Questions to Ponder

1. Why is Aleksandr Solzhenitsyn's double-question opening effective? How does it draw you into his essay?
2. What does Aleksandr Solzhenitsyn achieve by repeatedly addressing the reader as "you" and assuming that the reader was imprisoned too?
3. How did Aleksandr Solzhenitsyn sustain himself in prison?
4. How does Solzhenitsyn create a vivid picture of Soviet prison cells?

Writing Possibilities

1. Take your warm-up writing exercise 1 on an experience of confinement, and do a new draft, trying out Solzhenitsyn's second person ("you") address. Does this more direct and personal address make the writing flow more easily for you?
2. Choose another country and time period, and research this country's treatment of political prisoners. Share your findings in either a comparison-contrast essay (comparing your country's "cells" with Aleksandr Solzhenitsyn's), or in a separate report and analysis.
3. Write an essay or report detailing your own experiences (and perhaps that of others) with "spiritual sensors"—instinctive sensing of friends and foes. Has there been any research to document this phenomenon?
4. Using the list you generated in warm-up writing exercise 2, write an open letter to those in jail, advising them of how best to sustain themselves in adversity.

A Romance of the Secret Annex

Ruth Wisse

Ruth Wisse was born in Cernovtsy, Romania and is now a Canadian citizen. She is currently professor of Yiddish and Jewish Literature at McGill University. She has also been a senior lecturer on Yiddish literature at Tel-Aviv University and Hebrew University in Israel.

Professor Wisse's first book was her doctoral dissertation, which was published by the University of Chicago Press under the title The Schlemiel as Modern Hero. She has edited The Shtetl and Other Modern Yiddish Novellas, and her anthology of The Best of Sholom Aleichem, coedited with Irving Howe, begins with a series of letters between Howe and herself. In her second letter, her words regarding Sholom Aleichem's Tevye might apply to Anne Frank as well: "He gives proof of his creative survival even as he describes the destruction of its source" (Washington, D.C.: New Republic Books, 1979, xv).

Brief Warm-up Writing Exercises

1. Freewrite all the facts you know or have heard about Anne Frank and her diary.
2. If you have actually read *The Diary of Anne Frank* or seen the play made of her life, freewrite your initial and final impressions. What impact did the diary or the play have on you?
3. Brainstorm a list of the challenges that would confront a person in hiding with others, unable to leave for an unknown period of time.

1 ❖ In my local bookstore, *Anne Frank: The Diary of a Young Girl* is a staple of the children's section. Anne, who recorded her coming of age from shortly before she and her parents went into hiding in Amsterdam until their arrest two years later on Aug. 4, 1944, has given millions of readers their first, and

probably sharpest images of Jewish experience under Nazi occupation. Schoolchildren in all parts of the world have come to know the Holocaust as the story of that vivid girl and the events that led to her reduction to ashes in Bergen-Belsen within seven months.

2   Now there is a critical edition of the diary, with an apparatus that might put Shakespearean scholarship to shame. Published to coincide with the 60th anniversary of Anne Frank's birth, it is less a tribute to her than a response to the horror that still pursues her memory. Because the murdered Jewish girl has become a Dutch national heroine, attacks on the authenticity of the diary, part of the revisionist anti-Semitic attempt to deny the slaughter of the Jews of Europe, are also attacks on the Dutch Government. The Netherlands State Institute for War Documentation has gone to great lengths to establish the history of the Frank family and the validity of the text; the report on handwriting identification alone, a 70-page summary of which is included here, fills 270 pages. Fortunately, the bitter ironies that inspired this book have also produced a document of interest and worth.

3   To allay doubts about the diary's authorship, the editors reproduce three texts: all that was found of the original diary, of Anne's revisions, and the diary as it was edited by her father, Otto Frank, on which the standard English translation is based. The differences we discover among the versions leave the familiar author substantially unchanged, except for deepening our appreciation of her craft. When, in hiding, she heard the Dutch Minister of Education, Science and Art say in a London broadcast that the history of the war would be based not on official documents alone but on ordinary records of private individuals, Anne wrote: "Of course, they all made a rush at my diary immediately. Just imagine how interesting it would be if I were to publish a romance of the 'Secret Annexe.' The title alone would be enough to make people think it was a detective story."

4   Despite her self-mockery, she was embarked on just such a project, rewriting her diary on loose pages with an eye to its eventual publication. Writing was her vocation: "I know myself what is and what is not well written," she said. "Anyone who doesn't write doesn't know how wonderful it is. . . . I am grateful to God for giving me this gift, this possibility of developing myself and of writing, of expressing all that is in me."

5   Those who lived with her in hiding in a secret annex behind an Amsterdam warehouse, its entrance concealed by a bookcase, respected her pen sufficiently to worry about how it was presenting them.

6   In revising her diary, Anne tempered some of her outbursts. She deleted details that no longer seemed relevant, and introduced stylistic refinements. Particularly in its early parts, the original diary contained much more fancy—a daydream about figure skating, replete with a sketch of the costume she would wear; unsent letters to real and imaginary friends; an abundance of jokes. The

slightly more mature teen-ager imposed herself on this child. She pared down many paragraphs of enraged complaints about her mother the "old nanny goat" and her sister Margot whom "I'll soon tell . . . where she gets off" to a few sober sentences describing the tension between them. Anne never once reversed or significantly revised her earlier observations, but rewrote her diary with greater self-control.

7   On the whole, Otto Frank was also remarkably respectful of his daughter's artistry and truthfulness. It could not have been easy for him to expose to the world Anne's critical views of her family, including her growing impatience even with him, whom she adored. If he excised some of the harshest things Anne had to say about her mother and the others in hiding, or if he omitted the adverbial phrase from the sentence, "Daddy . . . pushed me aside very roughly," he is also to be credited with having pieced together what remained of Anne's manuscripts, and with sensitive judgment.

8   He may not be to blame, either, for the omission of Anne's most explicit passages about sex, including a wonderful discussion with her friend Peter about his cat, and a clinical analysis of her various apertures. The editors tell us that when the diary was first submitted to Dutch publishers, it was turned down because a few sexual details offended Christian sensibilities. Otto Frank knew that he would have to withhold some of Anne's observations if he wanted the manuscript to enter the public domain. The unexpurgated version included here shows just how fresh was her curiosity, and how very keen her descriptive powers.

9   The researchers tried to fill in what the diary could not tell us about the betrayal and arrest of the eight people in hiding, and of what became of them. Their reports destroy any notion of posthumous "justice." Since the newest investigation called into doubt the guilt of the warehouseman once thought to have alerted the Nazis to the hiding place, the true betrayer's identity is left murkier than before. ❖

Questions to Ponder

1. This review of *The Diary of Anne Frank: The Critical Edition* appeared in *The New York Times Book Review*. How does Ruth Wisse introduce her readers to her subject in her first two paragraphs? Do you find the introduction adequate?

2. What role do you think writing played in Anne Frank's life during her years in hiding?

3. How does Ruth Wisse structure this review? Do you find this structure effective?

4. Do you agree that history will (and should) be based on "ordinary records of private individuals"? Explain the reasons for your answer.

Writing Possibilities

1. Read *The Diary of Anne Frank: The Critical Edition,* and write your own review of the volume. (In all likelihood your opinions and emphases will differ from Ruth Wisse's.)
2. Choose a recent new edition of one of your favorite books (perhaps an old "classic"), and write a review of the new edition using Ruth Wisse's essay as a model. Are reviews one way to sustain the call of good books, films, concerts, and art exhibitions?
3. Take several diary or journal entries you have written, and revise them to make them more lasting records of your life for future readers.

DEATH OF A PIG
E. B. White

"If an unhappy childhood is indispensable for a writer, I am ill-equipped: I missed out on all that and was neither deprived nor unloved," wrote E[lwyn] B[rooks] White, the superb essayist and author of children's classics:

> It would be inaccurate, however, to say that my childhood was untroubled. The normal fears and worries of every child were in me developed to a high degree; every day was an awesome prospect. I was uneasy about practically everything: the uncertainty of the future, the dark of the attic, the panoply and discipline of school, the transitoriness of life, the mystery of the church and of God, the fraility of the body, the sadness of afternoon, the shadow of sex, the distant challenge of love and marriage, the far-off problem of a livelihood. I brooded about them all, lived with them day by day. Being the youngest in a large family, I was usually in a crowd but often felt lonely and removed. I took to writing early, to assuage my uneasiness and collect my thoughts, and I was a busy writer long before I went into long pants (Dorothy Lobrano Guth, ed., Letters of E. B. White [New York: Harper & Row, 1976], 1).

White won two scholarships to Cornell University and, once on campus, quickly began writing for the college newspaper, the Cornell Daily Sun. He contributed items to The Berry Patch, a "chatty, pseudo-literary column," which was patterned after the famous newspaper columns in New York: Franklin P. Adam's Conning Tower, Christopher Morley's Bowling Green, and Don Marquis's Sun Dial. After college, he toured America in a Model-T roadster, sending back travel sketches from stops along the way.

Back in New York, White found that the appearance of Harold Ross's New Yorker magazine in 1925 was to prove a turning point in his life. "I bought a copy of the first issue at a newsstand in Grand Central, examined Eustace Tilley and his butterfly on the cover, and was attracted to the newborn magazine not because it had any great merit but because the items were short, relaxed, and sometimes funny. I was a 'short' writer, and I lost no time in submitting squibs and poems," he recalled (Guth 72).

White soon was on the New Yorker staff, writing taglines for newsbreaks and the captions for pictures. He wrote both commentary and original pieces for the Talk of the Town; he substituted for the drama and movie critics, and did a great deal of writing to fill gaps in each issue. "The way to approach a manuscript is on all fours, in utter amazement," White wrote to Harold Ross (Guth 242).

"I discovered a long time ago that writing of the small things of the day, the trivial matters of the heart, the inconsequential but near things of this living, was the only kind of creative work which I could accomplish with any sincerity or grace," White wrote his brother (Guth 184). White had a barn for writing on his Maine farm, but he said he often preferred to write in the middle of the living room instead, "where the household tides run strongest" (Guth 388).

The character Stuart Little appeared to him in a dream, "all complete, with his hat, his cane, and his brisk manner" (Guth 193). Charlotte's Web took longer. In 1951 White wrote a friend, "I've recently finished another children's book, but have put it away for a while to ripen (let the body heat go out of it). It doesn't satisfy me the way it is and I think eventually I shall rewrite it pretty much, in order to shift the emphasis and make other reforms" (Guth 331). He came back to the story in about a year and rewrote it extensively, introducing Fern, who was not in the early drafts.

White's essay "Death of a Pig" was published in 1948. He wrote to the veterinarian in the story, "I was merely attempting to describe as accurately and factually as possible, a curious interlude in my life when comedy and tragedy seemed to cohere" (Guth 289).

Brief Warm-up Writing Exercises

1. Describe the death of a favorite pet or animal.
2. Freewrite about the behavior of another person or animal at the time of a loved one's death.
3. Make a list of all the "ingredients" you would want to go into your funeral.

1   I spent several days and nights in mid-September with an ailing pig and I feel driven to account for this stretch of time, more particularly since the pig died at last, and I lived, and things might easily have gone the other way round and none left to do the accounting. Even now, so close to the event, I cannot recall the hours sharply and am not ready to say whether death came on the third night or the fourth night. This uncertainty afflicts me with a sense of personal deterioration; if I were in decent health I would know how many nights I had sat up with a pig.

2   The scheme of buying a spring pig in blossomtime, feeding it through summer and fall, and butchering it when the solid cold weather arrives, is a familiar scheme to me and follows an antique pattern. It is a tragedy enacted on most farms with perfect fidelity to the original script. The murder, being premeditated, is in the first degree but is quick and skillful, and the smoked bacon and ham provide a ceremonial ending whose fitness is seldom questioned.

3   Once in a while something slips—one of the actors goes up in his lines and the whole performance stumbles and halts. My pig simply failed to show up for a meal. The alarm spread rapidly. The classic outline of the tragedy was lost. I found myself cast suddenly in the role of pig's friend and physician—a farcical character with an enema bag for a prop. I had a presentiment, the very first afternoon, that the play would never regain its balance and that my sympathies were now wholly with the pig. This was slapstick—the sort of dramatic treatment that instantly appealed to my old dachshund, Fred, who joined the vigil, held the bag, and, when all was over, presided at the interment. When we slid the body into the grave, we both were shaken to the core. The loss we felt was not the loss of ham but the loss of pig. He had evidently become precious to me, not that he represented a distant nourishment in a hungry time, but that he had suffered in a suffering world. But I'm running ahead of my story and shall have to go back.

4   My pigpen is at the bottom of an old orchard below the house. The pigs I have raised have lived in a faded building that once was an icehouse. There is a pleasant yard to move about in, shaded by an apple tree that overhangs the low rail fence. A pig couldn't ask for anything better—or none has, at any rate. The sawdust in the icehouse makes a comfortable bottom in which to root, and a warm bed. This sawdust, however, came under suspicion when the pig took sick. One of my neighbors said he thought the pig would have done better on new ground—the same principle that applies in planting potatoes. He said there might be something unhealthy about that sawdust, that he never thought well of sawdust.

5   It was about four o'clock in the afternoon when I first noticed that there was something wrong with the pig. He failed to appear at the trough for his supper, and when a pig (or a child) refuses supper a chill wave of fear runs through any household, or ice-household. After examining my pig, who was stretched out in the sawdust inside the building, I went to the phone and cranked it four times. Mr. Dameron answered. "What's good for a sick pig?"

I asked. (There is never any identification needed on a country phone; the person on the other end knows who is talking by the sound of the voice and by the character of the question.)

6   "I don't know, I never had a sick pig," said Mr. Dameron, "but I can find out quick enough. You hang up and I'll call Henry."

7   Mr. Dameron was back on the line again in five minutes. "Henry says roll him over on his back and give him two ounces of castor oil or sweet oil, and if that doesn't do the trick give him an injection of soapy water. He says he's almost sure the pig's plugged up, and even if he's wrong, it can't do any harm."

8   I thanked Mr. Dameron. I didn't go right down to the pig, though. I sank into a chair and sat still for a few minutes to think about my troubles, and then I got up and went to the barn, catching up on some odds and ends that needed tending to. Unconsciously I held off, for an hour, the deed by which I would officially recognize the collapse of the performance of raising a pig; I wanted no interruption in the regularity of feeding, the steadiness of growth, the even succession of days. I wanted no interruption, wanted no oil, no deviation. I just wanted to keep on raising a pig, full meal after full meal, spring into summer into fall. I didn't even know whether there were two ounces of castor oil on the place.

9   Shortly after five o'clock I remembered that we had been invited out to dinner that night and realized that if I were to dose a pig there was no time to lose. The dinner date seemed a familiar conflict: I move in a desultory society and often a week or two will roll by without my going to anybody's house to dinner or anyone's coming to mine, but when an occasion does arise, and I am summoned, something usually turns up (an hour or two in advance) to make all human intercourse seem vastly inappropriate. I have come to believe that there is in hostesses a special power of divination, and that they deliberately arrange dinners to coincide with pig failure or some other sort of failure. At any rate, it was after five o'clock and I knew I could put off no longer the evil hour.

10   When my son and I arrived at the pigyard, armed with a small bottle of castor oil and a length of clothesline, the pig had emerged from his house and was standing in the middle of his yard, listlessly. He gave us a slim greeting. I could see that he felt uncomfortable and uncertain. I had brought the clothesline thinking I'd have to tie him (the pig weighed more than a hundred pounds) but we never used it. My son reached down, grabbed both front legs, upset him quickly, and when he opened his mouth to scream I turned the oil into his throat—a pink, corrugated area I had never seen before. I had just time to read the label while the neck of the bottle was in his mouth. It said Puretest. The screams, slightly muffled by oil, were pitched in the hysterically high range of pig-sound, as though torture were being carried out, but they didn't last long: it was all over rather suddenly, and, his legs released, the pig righted himself.

11   In the upset position the corners of his mouth had been turned down, giving him a frowning expression. Back on his feet again, he regained the set

smile that a pig wears even in sickness. He stood his ground, sucking slightly at the residue of oil; a few drops leaked out of his lips while his wicked eyes, shaded by their coy little lashes, turned on me in disgust and hatred. I scratched him gently with oily fingers and he remained quiet, as though trying to recall the satisfaction of being scratched when in health, and seeming to rehearse in his mind the indignity to which he had just been subjected. I noticed, as I stood there, four or five small dark spots on his back near the tail end, reddish brown in color, each about the size of a housefly. I could not make out what they were. They did not look troublesome but at the same time they did not look like mere surface bruises or chafe marks. Rather they seemed blemishes of internal origin. His stiff white bristles almost completely hid them and I had to part the bristles with my fingers to get a good look.

12   Several hours later, a few minutes before midnight, having dined well and at someone else's expense, I returned to the pighouse with a flashlight. The patient was asleep. Kneeling, I felt his ears (as you might put your hand on the forehead of a child) and they seemed cool, and then with the light made a careful examination of the yard and the house for sign that the oil had worked. I found none and went to bed.

13   We had been having an unseasonable spell of weather—hot, close days, with the fog shutting in every night, scaling for a few hours in midday, then creeping back again at dark, drifting in first over the trees on the point, then suddenly blowing across the fields, blotting out the world and taking possession of houses, men, and animals. Everyone kept hoping for a break, but the break failed to come. Next day was another hot one. I visited the pig before breakfast and tried to tempt him with a little milk in his trough. He just stared at it, while I made a sucking sound through my teeth to remind him of past pleasures of the feast. With very small, timid pigs, weanlings, this ruse is often quite successful and will encourage them to eat; but with a large, sick pig the ruse is senseless and the sound I made must have made him feel, if anything, more miserable. He not only did not crave food, he felt a positive revulsion to it. I found a place under the apple tree where he had vomited in the night.

14   At this point, although a depression had settled over me, I didn't suppose that I was going to lose my pig. From the lustiness of a healthy pig a man derives a feeling of personal lustiness; the stuff that goes into the trough and is received with such enthusiasm is an earnest of some later feast of his own, and when this suddenly comes to an end and the food lies stale and untouched, souring in the sun, the pig's imbalance becomes the man's, vicariously, and life seems insecure, displaced, transitory.

15   As my own spirits declined, along with the pig's, the spirits of my vile old dachshund rose. The frequency of our trips down the footpath through the orchard to the pigyard delighted him, although he suffers greatly from arthritis, moves with difficulty, and would be bedridden if he could find anyone willing to serve him meals on a tray.

16   He never missed a chance to visit the pig with me, and he made many

professional calls on his own. You could see him down there at all hours, his white face parting the grass along the fence as he wobbled and stumbled about, his stethoscope dangling—a happy quack, writing his villainous prescriptions and grinning his corrosive grin. When the enema bag appeared, and the bucket of warm suds, his happiness was complete, and he managed to squeeze his enormous body between the two lowest rails of the yard and then assumed full charge of the irrigation. Once, when I lowered the bag to check the flow, he reached in and hurriedly drank a few mouthfuls of the suds to test their potency. I have noticed that Fred will feverishly consume any substance that is associated with trouble—the bitter flavor is to his liking. When the bag was above reach, he concentrated on the pig and was everywhere at once, a tower of strength and inconvenience. The pig, curiously enough, stood rather quietly through this colonic carnival, and the enema, though ineffective, was not as difficult as I had anticipated.

17   I discovered, though, that once having given a pig an enema there is no turning back, no chance of resuming one of life's more stereotyped roles. The pig's lot and mine were inextricably bound now, as though the rubber tube were the silver cord. From then until the time of his death I held the pig steadily in the bowl of my mind; the task of trying to deliver him from his misery became a strong obsession. His suffering soon became the embodiment of all earthly wretchedness. Along toward the end of the afternoon, defeated in physicking, I phoned the veterinary twenty miles away and placed the case formally in his hands. He was full of questions, and when I casually mentioned the dark spots on the pig's back, his voice changed its tone.

18   "I don't want to scare you," he said, "but when there are spots, erysipelas has to be considered."

19   Together we considered erysipelas, with frequent interruptions from the telephone operator, who wasn't sure the connection had been established.

20   "If a pig has erysipelas can he give it to a person?" I asked.

21   "Yes, he can," replied the vet.

22   "Have they answered?" asked the operator.

23   "Yes, they have," I said. Then I addressed the vet again. "You better come over here and examine this pig right away."

24   "I can't come myself," said the vet, "but McFarland can come this evening if that's all right. Mac knows more about pigs than I do anyway. You needn't worry too much about the spots. To indicate erysipelas they would have to be deep hemorrhagic infarcts."

25   "Deep hemorrhagic what?" I asked.

26   "Infarcts," said the vet.

27   "Have they answered?" asked the operator.

28   "Well," I said, "I don't know what you'd call these spots, except they're about the size of a housefly. If the pig has erysipelas I guess I have it, too, by this time, because we've been very close lately."

29   "McFarland will be over," said the vet.

30   I hung up. My throat felt dry and I went to the cupboard and got a bottle

of whiskey. Deep hemorrhagic infarcts—the phrase began fastening its hooks in my head. I had assumed that there could be nothing much wrong with a pig during the months it was being groomed for murder; my confidence in the essential health and endurance of pigs had been strong and deep, particularly in the health of pigs that belonged to me and that were part of my proud scheme. The awakening had been violent and I minded it all the more because I knew that what could be true of my pig could be true also of the rest of my tidy world. I tried to put this distasteful idea from me, but it kept recurring. I took a short drink of the whiskey and then, although I wanted to go down to the yard and look for fresh signs, I was scared to. I was certain I had erysipelas.

31   It was long after dark and the supper dishes had been put away when a car drove in and McFarland got out. He had a girl with him. I could just make her out in the darkness—she seemed young and pretty. "This is Miss Owen," he said. "We've been having a picnic supper on the shore, that's why I'm late."

32   McFarland stood in the driveway and stripped off his jacket, then his shirt. His stocky arms and capable hands showed up in my flashlight's gleam as I helped him find his coverall and get zipped up. The rear seat of his car contained an astonishing amount of paraphernalia, which he soon overhauled, selecting a chain, a syringe, a bottle of oil, a rubber tube, and some other things I couldn't identify. Miss Owen said she's go along with us and see the pig. I led the way down the warm slope of the orchard, my light picking out the path for them, and we all three climbed the fence, entered the pighouse, and squatted by the pig while McFarland took a rectal reading. My flashlight picked up the glitter of an engagement ring on the girl's hand.

33   "No elevation," said McFarland, twisting the thermometer in the light. "You needn't worry about erysipelas." He ran his hand slowly over the pig's stomach and at one point the pig cried out in pain.

34   "Poor piggledy-wiggledy!" said Miss Owne.

35   The treatment I had been giving the pig for two days was then repeated, somewhat more expertly, by the doctor, Miss Owen and I handing him things as he needed them—holding the chain that he had looped around the pig's upper jaw, holding the syringe, holding the bottle stopper, the end of the tube, all of us working in darkness and in comfort, working with the instinctive teamwork induced by emergency conditions, the pig unprotesting, the house shadowy, protecting, intimate. I went to bed tired but with a feeling of relief that I had turned over part of the responsibility of the case to a licensed doctor. I was beginning to think, though, that the pig was not going to live.

36   He died twenty-four hours later, or it might have been forty-eight—there is a blur in time here, and I may have lost or picked up a day in the telling and the pig one in the dying. At intervals during the last day I took cool fresh water down to him and at such times as he found the strength to get to his feet he would stand with head in the pail and snuffle his snout around. He drank a few sips but no more; yet it seemed to comfort him to dip his nose in water and bobble it about, sucking in and blowing out through his teeth. Much of

the time, now, he lay indoors half buried in sawdust. Once, near the last, while I was attending him I saw him try to make a bed for himself but he lacked the strength, and when he set his snout into the dust he was unable to plow even the little furrow he needed to lie down in.

37   He came out of the house to die. When I went down, before going to bed, he lay stretched in the yard a few feet from the door. I knelt, saw that he was dead, and left him there: his face had a mild look, expressive neither of deep peace nor of deep suffering, although I think he had suffered a good deal. I went back up to the house and to bed, and cried internally—deep hemorrhagic intears. I didn't wake till nearly eight the next morning, and when I looked out the open window the grave was already being dug, down beyond the dump under a wild apple. I could hear the spade strike against the small rocks that blocked the way. Never send to know for whom the grave is dug, I said to myself, it's dug for thee. Fred, I well knew, was supervising the work of digging, so I ate breakfast slowly.

38   It was a Saturday morning. The thicket in which I found the gravediggers at work was dark and warm, the sky overcast. Here, among alders and young hackmatacks, at the foot of the apple tree, Lennie had dug a beautiful hole, five feet long, three feet wide, three feet deep. He was standing in it, removing the last spadefuls of earth while Fred patrolled the brink in simple but impressive circles, disturbing the loose earth of the mound so that it trickled back in. There had been no rain in weeks and the soil, even three feet down, was dry and powdery. As I stood and stared, an enormous earthworm which had been partially exposed by the spade at the bottom dug itself deeper and made a slow withdrawal, seeking even remoter moistures at even lonelier depths. And just as Lennie stepped out and rested his spade against the tree and lit a cigarette, a small green apple separated itself from a branch overhead and fell into the hole. Everything about this last scene seemed overwritten—the dismal sky, the shabby woods, the imminence of rain, the worm (legendary bedfellow of the dead), the apple (conventional garnish of a pig).

39   But even so, there was a directness and dispatch about animal burial, I thought, that made it a more decent affair than human burial: there was no stopover in the undertaker's foul parlor, no wreath nor spray; and when we hitched a line to the pig's hind legs and dragged him swiftly from his yard, throwing our weight into the harness and leaving a wake of crushed grass and smoothed rubble over the dump, ours was a businesslike procession, with Fred, the dishonorable pallbearer, staggering along in the rear, his perverse bereavement showing in every seam in his face; and the post mortem performed handily and swiftly right at the edge of the grave, so that the inwards that had caused the pig's death preceded him into the ground and he lay at last resting squarely on the cause of his own undoing.

40   I threw in the first shovelful, and then we worked rapidly and without talk, until the job was complete. I picked up the rope, made it fast to Fred's collar (he is a notorious ghoul), and we all three filed back up the path to the house, Fred bringing up the rear and holding back every inch of the way, feigning

unusual stiffness. I noticed that although he weighed far less than the pig, he was harder to drag, being possessed of the vital spark.

41   The news of the death of my pig travelled fast and far, and I received many expressions of sympathy from friends and neighbors, for no one took the event lightly and the premature expiration of a pig is, I soon discovered, a departure which the community marks solemnly on its calendar, a sorrow in which it feels fully involved. I have written this account in penitence and in grief, as a man who failed to raise his pig, and to explain my deviation from the classic course of so many raised pigs. The grave in the woods is unmarked, but Fred can direct the mourner to it unerringly and with immense good will, and I know he and I shall often revisit it, singly and together, in seasons of reflection and despair, on flagless memorial days of our own choosing. ❖

Questions to Ponder

1. What does E. B. White gain by speaking of his own "sense of personal deterioration" as well as that of the pig?
2. Why do you think E. B. White compares his pig's death to ancient tragedy in paragraph 2 and throughout the essay? What does he gain by doing this?
3. Is Fred, the dog, a necessary character in this essay? What function does he serve?
4. Does this essay seem to have "voice"? Do you feel you know the person who wrote it? How would you describe this person and "voice"? How does White's voice suit his subject?
5. How can one sustain a call by speaking of the *failure* to do so?

Writing Possibilities

1. Take the freewrite you composed about the death of a favorite pet or animal, and revise it to include your own evolving state through the event. Do you like it better in this version?
2. Choose an animal, bird, insect, or fish, and research and write about its natural death—and any unnatural accidents that can hasten it. You may wish to share your findings in a personal essay like E. B. White's or in a more formal report for a science class.
3. Find out and write about one or more of the unnoticed people at funerals—grave diggers or florists or cemetery keepers. How might you best write about these people and their work?
4. Write a detailed analysis of E. B. White's essay. Paragraph by paragraph, what makes this simple tale so moving?

Student Essay

OF COWS AND MEN

Brad Williams

Since high school, most of my writing experience has been of the "formal" nature, so "Of Cows and Men" was a welcome change from the usual research papers. I'm generally more informal with pieces such as the "Cows," because creative writing lets me experiment with different styles. I especially like being able to enlighten readers with just enough aspects and different glimpses of my subjects that they can complete the entire picture or draw their own conclusions. My favorite method for providing glimpses is through dialogue. It is much more fun to form a mental picture of someone from hearing what they say than by having the author describe what the person is like. In fact, I always try to look at my writing through the reader's eyes to make sure that I'm providing plenty of images and suggestive insights, but not so many that they feel the story is being forced upon them. Fully achieving this effect takes many drafts as well as the continual input of anyone who is willing to read the piece; in the case of the "Cows," it took seven drafts, the second of which is reproduced below along with the final version.

Deciding on the right approach to writing about the cows was particularly challenging. My first thought was to explore and describe the different things I observed about the cows during my visits throughout the summer. I quickly decided, however, that the reader needed more than simply cows. Eventually, the story evolved as a piece about my family and our interactions with the cows, and with each other. Finding an ending was also challenging. I can remember that it just kind of came to me as I was composing at the keyboard very late one night. It was strange, I could hear the ending in my head as I was trying to type it. It was a great feeling, because I knew the ending was right. I felt like I was the guy at the keyboard in the ending of the movie *Stand by Me*. I just hope that I don't have to stay up that late every time I need an ending. That experience reinforced my belief that you shouldn't worry about the ending, or a title for that matter, until the time comes. It will usually take care of itself.

Now that I think about it, the idea for the "Cows" actually came from my mom.

Near the end of summer vacation (1989), when I was getting ready to go back to school, mom said that she thought I would be able to use the cows in a paper at college. Yeah, right, Mom. Well, I have her to thank for the wonderful idea. As it turned out, I enjoyed writing about the cows just about as much as I enjoy visiting the cows (it will be great to see them again this summer)!

Brief Warm-up Writing Exercises

1. Freewrite all you know about cows.
2. Describe one activity that you enjoy with your family.
3. Freewrite a dialogue between you and some member of your family. What would you say, and what would that person typically say?

DRAFT

1   "Would you like to go visit the cows?" Hmmm . . . did she say cows, as in C-O-W-S? Naah, must be a friend of the family that I haven't met yet, the Chows or something like that. "Uhhhhm—I don't think so, mom." After a day of 90° heat and mowing what seemed like 5,000 lawns, I was tired, hungry, and in severe need of a shower. In other words, I had no desire to go visit the Chows or anyone else for that matter.

2   In my short time home from college, I had gradually been getting back into the groove of working. My dad's lawn service had kept me busy mowing yards for the last seven summers—I truly was a seasoned mower. Even so, I still needed a little time to build up my endurance and regain my top mowing form; without this conditioning period, I would be in a perpetual state of physical exhaustion and in constant need of a shower.

3   In light of these circumstances, I didn't give a second thought to the idea of visiting *anyone*— until later the next day. After all the mowing was finished, my mom once again asked me the same puzzling question.

4   "Would you like to go visit the cows?" This time I knew that I had heard my mother correctly, but I wanted to make sure. "Mom, are you talking about *real* cows, as in the kind that go mooo?" Mom looked at me and smiled, "Yeah, moo-moo cows, what did you think I meant?" It was one of those questions that you hear, and then pretend like you

didn't. I paused, and thought for a moment . . . you "visit" people, you don't visit cows. Oh well, I was in the mood for a good joke, "Why mom, are they lonely?" Her response left me even more confused: "Well, they might be, I'm not sure—but they're probably hungry."

5   So much for the dumb-question approach. I had now established that the cows were for real, and that my mother thought that they might have feelings. I had witnessed a similar phenomenon before with my younger brother. Mom thought that he had feelings too, but I knew better—he was either 1) just hungry or 2) trying to get me into trouble. But this was different, my mother had posed a fascinating thought—cows with feelings.

6   After deciding to forego further dead-end questions, I got into the pickup truck with my mom and dad, and off we went on our trip to visit the cows. I still thought that the idea of visiting cows sounded corny, but I went along with it anyway.

7   The pickup was loaded with about a dozen tubs of grass clippings from the day's mowing. My parents explained that the cows eat the grass clippings that we bring them. In fact, they said that the cows *love* the grass clippings since it is easier for them to eat a pile of pre-cut food without having to spend the entire day grazing. I nodded, and then digested this latest bit of information. It seemed to me that mowed grass was probably like fast food for cows. I wondered if the cows watched for our pickup in the same way we watch for the Domino's delivery person. Enough speculation, I'd leave that to my mom.

8   In a few minutes, we were driving on a gravel road for about a mile and then we turned and drove up a long, curving, gravel driveway. My dad stopped and got out of the truck to unlatch a wire that was strung across our path and completed the circuit for the electric fence. He then directed me to drive the truck into the open, mostly barren area that was in front of us. I recognized the landscape as being the kind in which I could picture cows standing around and mooing at each other. But there were no cows to be seen, and thus I assumed none that we could visit. Maybe I would have to wait for another day.

9   Even though the cows were not around, my dad still wanted me to

start unloading the tubs of grass and dump them on the ground. After a few minutes, I stopped what I was doing and listened. My ears pricked up as I heard what sounded like—cows that were possessed! Not that I had heard possessed cows before, but I could tell that something wasn't quite right. What I heard was not the typical happy-cow "mooo," it was more like a screaming noise: "MOOOEEHOO!" And to top it all off, there was also a stereophonic background rumble, probably similar to what a nuclear explosion would sound like. If you hadn't guessed, this is the sound that stampeding hooves make. Terror. Horror. These were the few coherent thoughts I could manage in the span of a few seconds.

10   Panic set in instantly. I dropped my tub and turned around just in time to see a blur of brown, black, and white cows. They came charging down a small hill less than a hundred feet from our truck—(gulp)—and me. My survival reflexes took over as I jumped into the bed of the pickup. Then, at the very last second, the cows stopped on a dime, bent down, and started eating. They did not slow down and they did not skid. I would have sworn that they had anti-locking brakes or something. Much to my amazement, dad was still standing down on the ground, casually dumping grass.

11   Like I said, I was horrified. But please remember that up close and personal, these animals were *huge*. They were not the nice little cows that come to mind that you see grazing on a farm along the highway. I could feel how heavy they were just by looking at them, seeing how they pushed into each other with such tremendous force—all for the sake of getting the best pile of grass. I now knew what mom meant when she told my brother and I not to fight over food.

12   With some coaxing from my parents, I got up enough courage to get down out of the truck and finish dumping the grass. I was still scared, especially when one of the cows started to eat out of a tub that was still up in the truck. Stay calm. Don't let them know you're scared.

13   Compared to minutes earlier, everything was now silent. The loud approach of hungry cows had been replaced by the sounds of a few grunts and exhalations, the soft rustle of tongues licking up mouthfuls

of grass, and the incessant thud of cows banging their heads into each other. They were to busy eating to even give a partial mooo.

14. At first I thought that these cows might kill each other with all their heavy body slamming; and then I realized that I was standing right next to them and that I didn't care if they killed each other just as long as they didn't kill me! I stepped a safe distance back and made a few observations as I intently watched the cows. The pushing and shoving must be partly in fun, and partly a way of establishing the pecking-order. Right about now, I could imagine my mom saying "Sure, it's all in fun until some cow pokes an eye out!"

15. With all the pushing that was going on, I felt sorry for the baby calves. They didn't seem to know what all the excitement was about; plus, anytime that they tried to nibble or even sniff at the grass, some big bully cow would send them flying out of the way. Survival of the fittest I guess, but it was still a little sad to see them getting bounced around for just being curious. One of the older cows was off to the side, away from the rest of the cows that were chowing down, and she was kind of like the mom for all the baby calves. It must have been her turn to watch them and make sure they didn't get into trouble or in the way while the others ate.

16. One of the calves looked like it was only a few days old and it seemed to need a bit more supervision than the others. I don't think it knew what the fence was for yet. Every once in awhile I would see the calf squeeze under the electric wire and wander out onto the gravel driveway, but not for too long; the mom cow would mooo and it would run back in under the fence.

17. The cows had been eating for a good fifteen minutes now, and so I emptied a few more tubs of grass for them. As I did this, I noticed that they would back away from me quickly if I got near them. Amazing—the one-ton cows that had me scared out of my mind turn out to be scared of *me*, the 175-pound human. Despite the implications of this revelation, I was still more scared of the cows than they were of me. Simple logic: there were more of them, they were over ten-times my weight, and they did not speak English.

18   Given the situation of the cows possibly being scared of me, I decided that the best thing to do would be to try to make friends with them. I had a good start, they liked the food we'd brought them. But I needed something more, communication of some sort, so I tried the universal sign of friendship—petting behind the ears. Unfortunately, whenever I would reach out to touch a cow, it would run away, especially the calves. The general consensus was "no petting allowed," with the exception of one big, coal-black cow that had white patches on its lower jaw and forehead.

19   I found out from the owner that this cow was named "Pet." Not a very original name. Apparently one of his younger daughter's had raised the cow from birth and she couldn't think of a name for it, but she did know that it was like other "pets." As it turned out, the name was quite appropriate since Pet was used to being touched by humans. So I ended up petting Pet for awhile, watching its big, brown eyes blink and its massive tongue lick up grass clippings. I eventually worked up to feeding Pet grass out of my hand (very carefully) and was thus able to befriend one of the cows.

20   The tubs had been emptied and the cows were contently chomping away on what remained of the piles of grass. It was time for my parents and I to go back home for dinner; I was in severe need a shower. My first visit to the cows had been very enjoyable. A little scary, but enjoyable. Somehow I knew, and I thought that the cows knew, that we'd be seeing each other again really soon. I could visit them again tomorrow after the mowing was finished. You don't visit cows—unless they're friends that just happen to be cows.

21   After arriving back home, I asked my brother if he knew anything about the cows. He gave me his typical response to one of my questions, "Whhat?!" I didn't bother to explain any further, I just asked the magic question: "Would you like to go visit the cows? They eat the grass we mow." I got the number two answer on Brent's Top Ten Responses to Any Question: "So." That's okay, I'd ask him again tomorrow.

1 "Would you like to go visit the cows?" Hmmm . . . did she say cows, as in C-O-W-S? Naaah . . . must be a friend of the family that I haven't met yet, the Chows or something like that. "Uhhhhm—I don't think so, Mom." After a day of 90° heat and mowing what seemed like 5,000 lawns, I was tired, hungry, and in dire need of a shower. In other words, I had no desire to go visit the Chows or anyone else for that matter.

2 In my short time home from college, I had gradually been getting back into the groove of working. My dad's lawn service had kept me busy mowing yards for the last seven summers. I truly was a seasoned mower. Even so, I still needed a little time to build up my endurance and regain my top mowing form; without this conditioning period, I would be in a perpetual state of physical exhaustion.

3 In light of these circumstances, I didn't give a second thought to the idea of visiting *anyone*—until later the next day. After all the mowing was finished, my mom once again asked me the same puzzling question.

4 "Would you like to go visit the cows?" This time I knew that I had heard my mother correctly, but I wanted to make sure. "Mom, are you talking about *real* cows, as in the kind that mooo?" Mom looked at me and smiled, "Yeah, moo-moo cows, what did you think I meant?" It was one of those questions that you hear, and then pretend like you didn't. I paused, and thought for a moment. You *visit* people; you don't visit cows. Oh well, I was in the mood for a good joke. "Why Mom, are they lonely?" Her response left me even more confused: "Well, they might be, I'm not sure—but they're probably hungry."

5 So much for the dumb-question approach. I had now established that the cows were for real and that my mother thought that they might have feelings. I had witnessed a similar phenomenon before with my younger brother. Mom thought that he had feelings too, but I knew better—he was either (1) just hungry or (2) trying to get me into trouble.

6 I then went outside to help my dad load the truck. "Load the truck" was one of the three basic lawn service tasks in which dad had made certain I was expert, the other two being the easier jobs of "unload the truck" and "mow." We proceeded to lift about a dozen jam-packed tubs of grass clippings, each weighing about 75 pounds, into the bed of the pickup. Dad had made the tubs by sawing large plastic drums in half. Of course, he got me to help him.

7 The speed and eagerness that my dad showed while we loaded the truck seemed to indicate that he wasn't very reluctant about going to visit the cows. On the other hand, maybe he just wanted to get it over with as quickly as possible. I thought that I'd better find out for sure *before* I was actually committed to going, so I asked him a simple question: "Do you *like* to visit the cows?" My dad stopped what he was doing, looked at me for a few seconds and then said, "Well, yeah, I suppose you could say that." This did not sound all that convincing, so I countered with another blunt question, "Why?" I expected some sort of practical, dadlike response about it being more efficient or cost-effective. Instead, what my dad said sounded more like something my

mom would say: "The cows are fun to watch." Maybe I was better off *not* knowing what to expect.

8   Then my dad asked a familiar question that told me that I was forgetting something: "Do I have to retrain you every time?" This was his way of kidding me, and reminding me to get up in the truck and make sure that all the tubs were stacked properly. As he laughed, I smiled and said, "Why not, I get paid by the hour!" He was still laughing to himself as Mom and I got into the pickup, and then off we went on our trip to visit the cows.

9   As we were riding along, my parents explained that the cows eat the grass clippings that we bring them. In fact, they said that the cows *love* the grass clippings since it is quicker and easier for them to eat a pile of precut food without having to spend the entire day grazing. I nodded and then gave some thought to this latest bit of information. It seemed to me that mowed grass was probably like fast food for cows. I wondered if the cows watched for our pickup in the same way we watch for the Domino's delivery person.

10   Enough speculation. I'd leave that to Mom.

11   In a few minutes, we were driving on a gravel road for about a mile, and then we turned and drove up a long, curving, gravel driveway. My dad stopped and got out of the truck to unlatch a wire that was strung across our path and completed the circuit for the electric fence. I drove the truck into the open, mostly barren area that was in front of us while he latched the fence back into place. I recognized the landscape as being the kind in which I could picture cows mooing and standing around in a small circle with their backs to each other. But there were no cows to be seen and thus, I assumed, none that we could visit. Maybe I would just have to wait for another day.

12   Even though the cows were not around, my dad still wanted me to start unloading the tubs of grass and dump them on the ground. After a few minutes, I stopped what I was doing and listened. My ears pricked up as I heard what sounded like . . . cows that were possessed! What I heard was not the typical happy-cow "mooo," it was more like a screaming noise: "MOOO-EEHOO!" And to top it all off, there was also a cataclysmic background rumble, probably similar to what a nuclear explosion would sound like. This is the sound that stampeding hooves make.

13   Terror. Horror. These were the few coherent thoughts I could manage in the span of a few seconds.

14   Panic set in instantly.

15   I dropped my tub and turned around just in time to see a moving wall of brown, black, and white. About fifteen cows came charging down a small hill less than a hundred feet from our truck—(gulp)—and me. My survival reflexes took over as I jumped into the bed of the pickup. Then, at the very last second, the cows stopped, bent down, and started eating. They did not slow down. They did not skid. They just stopped.

16   Much to my amazement, Dad was still standing down on the ground diligently working on the task of dumping grass. His manner was somewhat casual. He even had a slight smile on his face.

17   Please keep in mind that up close and personal, these animals were *huge*. They were not the nice little cows that you see from a distance grazing on a farm along the highway. In reality, cows are massive. I could feel how heavy they were just by looking at them, seeing how they pushed into each other with such tremendous force—all for the sake of getting the best pile of grass. Now I knew what it must look like when Mom tells my brother and me not to fight over food.

18   "You wanna *walk* home?"

19   My dad could still kid me, even when I was obviously not in the mood, for this was my signal to get busy and help him finish dumping the grass. With a little more coaxing from my parents, I finally got up enough courage to get down out of the truck. I was still scared, especially when one of the cows started to eat out of a tub that was still up in the truck. Stay calm. Don't let them know you're scared.

20   Compared to their noisy arrival, the cows were now silent. The loud approach of hungry cows had been replaced by the sounds of a few grunts and exhalations, the soft rustle of tongues licking up mouthfuls of grass, and the incessant thud of cows banging their heads into one another.

21   At first I thought that these cows might kill one another with all their heavy body slamming. Then I realized that I was standing right next to them and all I cared about was that they didn't kill me! I stepped a safe distance back and intently watched the cows. The pushing and shoving must be partly in fun, and partly a way of establishing the pecking-order. Right about now, I could imagine my mom saying "Sure, it's all in fun until some cow pokes an eye out!"

22   With all this pushing, I felt sorry for the baby calves. They didn't seem to know what all the excitement was about, and anytime that they tried to nibble or even sniff at the grass, some big bully cow would send them flying out of the way. Survival of the fittest I guess, but it was still a little sad to see them getting bounced around for just being curious. My mom must have felt sorry for the baby calves too, because she scolded several of the "pushy" cows with a disciplinary "You quit that!" Eventually she had me help her make "baby" piles of grass for the calves to eat, away from the pushing and shoving.

23   One cow was off to the side, away from the rest of the cows that were chowing down; she was kind of like a mom for all the baby calves. It must have been her turn to calf-sit and make sure that they didn't get into trouble or in the way while the others ate. One of the calves looked like it was only a few days old, and I could tell that it had no clue what purpose the electric fence served. Every once in a while the calf would squeeze under the wire and wander out onto the gravel driveway. The calf seemed oblivious to the electric shock it received when it brushed against the wire. The calf's adventure in the outside world, however, never lasted very long. Either the mom cow would give an authoritative mooo, or more frightening yet, *my* mom would try to chase it down, and the calf would immediately scurry back in under the fence.

24   The cows had been eating for a good fifteen minutes now, and so I emptied a few more tubs of grass for them. As I did this, I noticed that they would back away from me quickly if I got near them. Amazing—the one-ton cows that had

me scared out of my mind turn out to be scared of *me*, the 175-pound human. Nevertheless, I was still scared. Simple logic: there were more of them, they were over ten times my weight, and they were hungry.

25   I decided that the best thing to do would be to try to make friends with them. I had a good start; they liked the food we'd brought them. But I needed something more, communication of some sort, so I tried the universal sign of friendship—petting behind the ears. Unfortunately, whenever I would reach out to touch a cow, it would run away, especially the calves. The general consensus was "no petting allowed," with the exception of one big, coal black cow that had snow white patches on its lower jaw and forehead.

26   I found out from the owner that this cow was named "Pet." That's right, Pet. Apparently one of his younger daughters had raised the cow from birth and she couldn't think of a name for it, but she did know that it was like other "pets." So I ended up petting Pet for awhile, watching its big, brown eyes blink and its massive tongue lick up grass clippings. Eventually, I even worked up to feeding Pet grass out of my hand—very carefully—and was thus able to befriend one of the cows.

27   The cows were contentedly chomping away on what remained of the piles of grass; my dad was just finishing loading the empty tubs, and I was hungry. It was time for my parents and me to go back home for dinner, so we got in the truck and headed home.

28   My first visit to the cows had been enjoyable, a little scary, but enjoyable. Somehow I knew, and I thought the cows knew, that we'd be seeing each other again really soon. I could visit them again tomorrow after the mowing was finished. You don't visit cows—unless they're friends that just happen to be cows.

29   After arriving back home, I asked my brother if he knew anything about the cows. He gave me his typical response to one of my questions, "Whhat?" I didn't bother to explain; I just asked the magic question: "Would you like to go visit the cows?" He gave me a blank stare, so I gave him more information. "They eat the grass we mow." Then I got the number two response on Brent's Top Ten Responses to Anything: "So." That's okay. I'd ask him again tomorrow. ❖

Questions to Ponder

1. Does Brad Williams's opening paragraph draw you into his essay? What makes it effective?
2. Why do you think Brad Williams spends so many paragraphs setting up his visit to the cows before actually getting there? Does this strengthen or weaken his essay?
3. Does this essay have "voice"? Do you feel like you know the person who wrote it? How does Brad Williams's voice differ from E. B. White's voice in "Death of a Pig"? How does Brad Williams's voice suit his subject?

4. What makes the title of this essay appropriate? Is this essay as much about men (and women) as about cows?
5. What does Brad Williams do to sustain this simple story?

Writing Possibilities

1. Brainstorm a list of unusual visits you have made. Choose one, and try to recapture the visit—and its significance—in a writing voice suited to the occasion.
2. Do some serious reading and interviewing about the social habits of a specific animal. Then share your findings in a light essay or a serious report. (*Hint:* You might want to choose a creature that has an undeserved reputation—like a wolf or spider.)
3. Spend an evening or two in your college library or union observing the study or social habits of your fellow students. Share your findings in (a) a letter to the campus newspaper, (b) a mock–anthropologist's report on the "natives" of your campus, or (c) a light or serious essay.

Short Story
YELLOW WOMAN

Leslie Marmon Silko

I am of mixed-breed ancestry, but what I know is Laguna [Pueblo]. This place I am from is everything I am as a writer and human being. I suppose at the core of my writing is the attempt to identify what it is to be a half-breed or mixed blooded person; what it is to grow up neither white nor fully traditional Indian. . . .

I attempt to say with my stories that Indian life today is full of terror and death and great suffering, but despite these tremendous odds against us for two hundred of years—the racism, the poverty, the alcoholism—we go on living. We live to celebrate the beauty of the Earth and Sky because the beauty and vitality of life, like the rainbow colored horses leaping, has never been lost. The world remains for us as it has always been. . . .

[When I was a teenager, I used to wander around down by the river] and try to imagine walking around the bend and just happening to stumble upon some beautiful man. Later on I realized that these kinds of things that I was doing when I was fifteen are exactly the kinds of things out of which stories like the Yellow Woman story [came]. I finally put the two together: the adolescent longings and the old stories, that plus the stories around Laguna at the time about people who did, in fact, just in recent times, use the river as a meeting place.

Brief Warm-up Writing Exercises

1. Freewrite any traditional stories or legends you know concerning your ancestors.
2. Describe the most unusual encounter you have ever had with a stranger.
3. Describe any experience you know of when myth became reality.

1   My thigh clung to his with dampness, and I watched the sun rising up through the tamaracks and willows. The small brown water birds came to the river and hopped across the mud, leaving brown scratches in the alkali-white crust. They bathed in the river silently. I could hear the water, almost at our feet where the narrow fast channel bubbled and washed green ragged moss and fern leaves. I looked at him beside me, rolled in the red blanket on the white river sand. I cleaned the sand out of the cracks between my toes, squinting because the sun was above the willow trees. I looked at him for the last time, sleeping on the white river sand.

2   I felt hungry and followed the river south the way we had come the afternoon before, following our footprints that were already blurred by lizard tracks and bug trails. The horses were still lying down, and the black one whinnied when he saw me but he did not get up—maybe it was because the corral was made out of thick cedar branches and the horses had not yet felt the sun like I had. I tried to look beyond the pale red mesas to the pueblo. I knew it was there, even if I could not see it, on the sandrock hill above the river, the same river that moved past me now and had reflected the moon last night.

3   The horse felt warm underneath me. He shook his head and pawed the sand. The bay whinnied and leaned against the gate trying to follow, and I remembered him asleep in the red blanket beside the river. I slid off the horse and tied him close to the other horse, I walked north with the river again, and the white sand broke loose in footprints over footprints.

4   "Wake up."

5   He moved in the blanket and turned his face to me with his eyes still closed. I knelt down to touch him.

6   "I'm leaving."

7   He smiled now, eyes still closed. "You are coming with me, remember?" He sat up now with his bare dark chest and belly in the sun.

8   "Where?"

9   "To my place."

10   "And will I come back?"

11   He pulled his pants on. I walked away from him, feeling him behind me and smelling the willows.

12   "Yellow Woman," he said.

13   I turned to face him. "Who are you?" I asked.

14   He laughed and knelt on the low, sandy bank, washing his face in the river. "Last night you guessed my name, and you knew why I had come."

15   I stared past him at the shallow moving water and tried to remember the night, but I could only see the moon in the water and remember his warmth around me.

16   "But I only said that you were him and that I was Yellow Woman—I'm not really her—I have my own name and I come from the pueblo on the other side of the mesa. Your name is Silva and you are a stranger I met by the river yesterday afternoon."

17   He laughed softly. "What happened yesterday has nothing to do with what you will do today, Yellow Woman."

18   "I know—that's what I'm saying—the old stories about the ka'tsina spirit and Yellow Woman can't mean us."

19   My old grandpa liked to tell those stories best. There is one about Badger and Coyote who went hunting and were gone all day, and when the sun was going down they found a house. There was a girl living there alone, and she had light hair and eyes and she told them that they could sleep with her. Coyote wanted to be with her all night so he sent Badger into a prairie-dog hole, telling him he thought he saw something in it. As soon as Badger crawled in, Coyote blocked up the entrance with rocks and hurried back to Yellow Woman.

20   "Come here," he said gently.

21   He touched my neck and I moved closer to him to feel his breathing and to hear his heart. I was wondering if Yellow Woman had known who she was—if she knew that she would become part of the stories. Maybe she'd had another name that her husband and relatives called her so that only the ka'tsina from the north and the storytellers would know her as Yellow Woman. But I didn't go on; I felt him all around me, pushing me down into the white river sand.

22   Yellow Woman went away with the spirit from the north and lived with him and his relatives. She was gone for a long time, but then one day she came back and she brought twin boys.

23   "Do you know the story?"

24   "What story?" He smiled and pulled me close to him as he said this. I was afraid lying there on the red blanket. All I could know was the way he felt, warm, damp, his body beside me. This is the way it happens in the stories, I

was thinking, with no thought beyond the moment she meets the ka'tsina spirit and they go.

25 "I don't have to go. What they tell in stories was real only then, back in time immemorial, like they say."

26 He stood up and pointed at my clothes tangled in the blanket. "Let's go," he said.

27 I walked beside him, breathing hard because he walked fast, his hand around my wrist. I had stopped trying to pull away from him, because his hand felt cool and the sun was high, drying the river bed into alkali. I will see someone, eventually I will see someone, and then I will be certain that he is only a man—some man from nearby—and I will be sure that I am not Yellow Woman. Because she is from out of time past and I live now and I've been to school and there are highways and pickup trucks that Yellow Woman never saw.

28 It was an easy ride north on horseback. I watched the change from the cottonwood trees along the river to the junipers that brushed past us in the foothills, and finally there were only piñons, and when I looked up at the rim of the mountain plateau I could see pine trees growing on the edge. Once I stopped to look down, but the pale sandstone had disappeared and the river was gone and the dark lava hills were all around. He touched my hand, not speaking, but always singing softly a mountain song and looking into my eyes.

29 I felt hungry and wondered what they were doing at home now—my mother, my grandmother, my husband, and the baby. Cooking breakfast, saying, "Where did she go?—maybe kidnapped." And Al going to the tribal police with the details: "She went walking along the river."

30 The house was made with black lava rock and red mud. It was high above the spreading miles of arroyos and long mesas. I smelled a mountain smell of pitch and buck brush. I stood there beside the black horse, looking down on the small, dim country we had passed, and I shivered.

31 "Yellow Woman, come inside where it's warm."

32 He lit a fire in the stove. It was an old stove with a round belly and an enamel coffeepot on top. There was only the stove, some faded Navajo blankets, and a bedroll and cardboard box. The floor was made of smooth adobe plaster, and there was one small window facing east. He pointed at the box.

33 "There's some potatoes and the frying pan." He sat on the floor with his arms around his knees pulling them close to his chest and he watched me fry the potatoes. I didn't mind him watching me because he was always watching me—he had been watching me since I came upon him sitting on the river bank trimming leaves from a willow twig with his knife. We ate from the pan and he wiped the grease from his fingers on his Levi's.

34 "Have you brought women here before?" He smiled and kept chewing, so I said, "Do you always use the same tricks?"

35 "What tricks?" He looked at me like he didn't understand.

36 "The story about being a ka'tsina from the mountains. The story about Yellow Woman."

37   Silva was silent; his face was calm.
38   "I don't believe it. Those stories couldn't happen now," I said.
39   He shook his head and said softly, "But some day they will talk about us, and they will say 'Those two lived long ago when things like that happened.'"
40   He stood up and went out. I ate the rest of the potatoes and thought about things—about the noise the stove was making and the sound of the mountain wind outside. I remembered yesterday and the day before, and then I went outside.
41   I walked past the corral to the edge where the narrow trail cut through the black rim rock. I was standing in the sky with nothing around me but the wind that came down from the blue mountain peak behind me. I could see faint mountain images in the distance miles across the vast spread of mesas and valleys and plains. I wondered who was over there to feel the mountain wind on those sheer blue edges—who walked on the pine needles in those blue mountains.
42   "Can you see the pueblo?" Silva was standing behind me.
43   I shook my head. "We're too far away."
44   "From here I can see the world." He stepped out on the edge. "The Navajo reservation begins over there." He pointed to the east. "The Pueblo boundaries are over here." He looked below us to the south, where the narrow trail seemed to come from. "The Texans have their ranches over there, starting with that valley, the Concho Valley. The Mexicans run some cattle over there too."
45   "Do you ever work for them?"
46   "I steal from them," Silva answered. The sun was dropping behind us and the shadows were filling the land below. I turned away from the edge that dropped forever into the valleys below.
47   "I'm cold," I said, "I'm going inside." I started wondering about this man who could speak the Pueblo language so well but who lived on a mountain and rustled cattle. I decided that this man Silva must be Navajo, because Pueblo men didn't do things like that.
48   "You must be a Navajo."
49   Silva shook his head gently. "Little Yellow Woman," he said, "you never give up, do you? I have told you who I am. The Navajo people know me, too." He knelt down and unrolled the bedroll and spread the extra blankets out on a piece of canvas. The sun was down, and the only light in the house came from outside—the dim orange light from sundown.
50   I stood there and waited for him to crawl under the blankets.
51   "What are you waiting for?" he said, and I lay down beside him. He undressed me slowly like the night before beside the river—kissing my face gently and running his hands up and down my belly and legs. He took off my pants and then he laughed.
52   "Why are you laughing?"
53   "You are breathing so hard."
54   I pulled away from him and turned my back to him.
55   He pulled me around and pinned me down with his arms and chest. "You don't understand, do you, little Yellow Woman? You will do what I want."

56   And again he was all around me with his skin slippery against mine, and I was afraid because I understood that his strength could hurt me. I lay underneath him and I knew that he could destroy me. But later, while he slept beside me, I touched his face and I had a feeling—the kind of feeling for him that overcame me that morning along the river. I kissed him on the forehead and he reached out for me.

57   When I woke up in the morning he was gone. It gave me a strange feeling because for a long time I sat there on the blankets and looked around the little house for some object of his—some proof that he had been there or maybe that he was coming back. Only the blankets and the cardboard box remained. The .30-30 that had been leaning in the corner was gone, and so was the knife I had used the night before. He was gone, and I had my chance to go now. But first I had to eat, because I knew it would be a long walk home.

58   I found some dried apricots in the cardboard box, and I sat down on a rock at the edge of the plateau rim. There was no wind and the sun warmed me. I was surrounded by silence. I drowsed with apricots in my mouth, and I didn't believe that there were highways or railroads or cattle to steal.

59   When I woke up, I stared down at my feet in the black mountain dirt. Little black ants were swarming over the pine needles around my foot. They must have smelled the apricots. I thought about my family far below me. They would be wondering about me, because this had never happened to me before. The tribal police would file a report. But if old Grandpa weren't dead he would tell them what happened—he would laugh and say, "Stolen by a ka'tsina, a mountain spirit. She'll come home—they usually do." There are enough of them to handle things. My mother and grandmother will raise the baby like they raised me. Al will find someone else, and they will go on like before, except that there will be a story about the day I disappeared while I was walking along the river. Silva had come for me; he said he had. I did not decide to go. I just went. Moonflowers blossom in the sand hills before dawn, just as I followed him. That's what I was thinking as I wandered along the trail through the pine trees.

60   It was noon when I got back. When I saw the stone house I remembered that I had meant to go home. But that didn't seem important any more, maybe because there were little blue flowers growing in the meadow behind the stone house and the gray squirrels were playing in the pines next to the house. The horses were standing in the corral, and there was a beef carcass hanging on the shady side of a big pine in front of the house. Flies buzzed around the clotted blood that hung from the carcass. Silva was washing his hands in a bucket full of water. He must have heard me coming because he spoke to me without turning to face me.

61   "I've been waiting for you."

62   "I went walking in the big pine trees."

63   I looked into the bucket full of bloody water with brown-and-white animal hairs floating in it. Silva stood there letting his hand drip, examining me intently.

64   "Are you coming with me?"

65 "Where?" I asked him.
66 "To sell the meat in Marquez."
67 "If you're sure it's O.K."
68 "I wouldn't ask you if it wasn't," he answered.
69 He sloshed the water around in the bucket before he dumped it out and set the bucket upside down near the door. I followed him to the corral and watched him saddle the horses. Even beside the horses he looked tall, and I asked him again if he wasn't Navajo. He didn't say anything; he just shook his head and kept cinching up the saddle.
70 "But Navajos are tall."
71 "Get on the horse," he said, "and let's go."
72 The last thing he did before we started down the steep trail was to grab the .30-30 from the corner. He slid the rifle into the scabbard that hung from his saddle.
73 "Do they ever try to catch you?" I asked.
74 "They don't know who I am."
75 "Then why did you bring the rifle?"
76 "Because we are going to Marquez where the Mexicans live."
77 The trail leveled out on a narrow ridge that was steep on both sides like an animal spine. On one side I could see where the trail went around the rocky gray hills and disappeared into the southeast where the pale sandrock mesas stood in the distance near my home. On the other side was a trail that went west, and as I looked far into the distance I thought I saw the little town. But Silva said no, that I was looking in the wrong place, that I just thought I saw houses. After that I quit looking off into the distance; it was hot and the wildflowers were closing up their deep-yellow petals. Only the waxy cactus flowers bloomed in the bright sun, and I saw every color that a cactus blossom can be; the white ones and the red ones were still buds, but the purple and the yellow were blossoms, open full and the most beautiful of all.
78 Silva saw him before I did. The white man was riding a big gray horse, coming up the trail towards us. He was traveling fast and the gray horse's feet sent rocks rolling off the trail into the dry tumbleweeds. Silva motioned for me to stop and we watched the white man. He didn't see us right away, but finally his horse whinnied at our horses and he stopped. He looked at us briefly before he lapped the gray horse across the three hundred yards that separated us. He stopped his horse in front of Silva, and his young fat face was shadowed by the brim of his hat. He didn't look mad, but his small, pale eyes moved from the blood-soaked gunny sacks hanging from my saddle to Silva's face and then back to my face.
79 "Where did you get the fresh meat?" the white man asked.
80 "I've been hunting," Silva said, and when he shifted his weight in the saddle the leather creaked.
81 "The hell you have, Indian. You've been rustling cattle. We've been looking for the thief for a long time."

82   The rancher was fat, and sweat began to soak through his white cowboy shirt and the wet cloth stuck to the thick rolls of belly fat. He almost seemed to be panting from the exertion of talking, and he smelled rancid, maybe because Silva scared him.

83   Silva turned to me and smiled. "Go back up the mountain, Yellow Woman."

84   The white man got angry when he heard Silva speak in a language he couldn't understand. "Don't try anything, Indian. Just keep riding to Marquez. We'll call the state police from there."

85   The rancher must have been unarmed because he was very frightened and if he had a gun he would have pulled it out then. I turned my horse around and the rancher yelled, "Stop!" I looked at Silva for an instant and there was something ancient and dark—something I could feel in my stomach—in his eyes, and when I glanced at his hand I saw his finger on the trigger of the .30-30 that was still in the saddle scabbard. I slapped my horse across the flank and the sacks of raw meat swung against my knees as the horse leaped up the trail. It was hard to keep my balance, and once I thought I felt the saddle slipping backward; it was because of this that I could not look back.

86   I didn't stop until I reached the ridge where the trail forked. The horse was breathing deep gasps and there was a dark film of sweat on its neck. I looked down in the direction I had come from, but I couldn't see the place. I waited. The wind came up and pushed warm air past me. I looked up at the sky, pale blue and full of thin clouds and fading vapor trails left by jets.

87   I think four shots were fired—I remember hearing four hollow explosions that reminded me of deer hunting. There could have been more shots after that, but I couldn't have heard them because my horse was running again and the loose rocks were making too much noise as they scattered around his feet.

88   Horses have a hard time running downhill, but I went that way instead of up hill to the mountain because I thought it was safer. I felt better with the horse running southeast past the round gray hills that were covered with cedar trees and black lava rock. When I got to the plain in the distance I could see the dark green patches of tamaracks that grew along the river; and beyond the river I could see the beginning of the pale sandrock mesas. I stopped the horse and looked back to see if anyone was coming; then I got off the horse and turned the horse around, wondering if it would go back to its corral under the pines on the mountain. It looked back at me for a moment and then plucked a mouthful of green tumbleweeds before it trotted back up the trail with its ears pointed forward, carrying its head daintily to one side to avoid stepping on the dragging reins. When the horse disappeared over the last hill, the gunny sacks full of meat were still swinging and bouncing.

89   I walked toward the river on a wood-hauler's road that I knew would eventually lead to the paved road. I was thinking about waiting beside the road for someone to drive by, but by the time I got to the pavement I had decided

it wasn't very far to walk if I followed the river back the way Silva and I had come.

90   The river water tasted good, and I sat in the shade under a cluster of silvery willows. I thought about Silva, and I felt sad at leaving him; still, there was something strange about him, and I tried to figure it out all the way back home.

91   I came back to the place on the river bank where he had been sitting the first time I saw him. The green willow leaves that he had trimmed from the branch were still lying there, wilted in the sand. I saw the leaves and I wanted to go back to him—to kiss him and to touch him—but the mountains were too far away now. And I told myself, because I believe it, he will come back sometime and be waiting again by the river.

92   I followed the path up from the river into the village. The sun was getting low, and I could smell supper cooking when I got to the screen door of my house. I could hear their voices inside—my mother was telling my grandmother how to fix the Jell-O and my husband, Al, was playing with the baby. I decided to tell them that some Navajo had kidnapped me, but I was sorry that old Grandpa wasn't alive to hear my story because it was the Yellow Woman stories he liked to tell best. ❖

Questions to Ponder

1. What makes Leslie Marmon Silko's opening sentence effective? Does it make you want to read on?
2. What is truth and what is legend, and where do the two intersect in this story?
3. Why do the young woman and man do what they do? Can you explain what might motivate each?
4. What feelings does Leslie Marmon Silko evoke in you through this story?

Writing Possibilities

1. Take a myth or legend (perhaps one you described in warm-up writing exercise 1), and write of a person's encounter with this legend and what happened.
2. Do research into folk stories and legends of your nationality. Choose one, and write an essay for your historical society explaining the origin of the story and its meaning to your people.
3. Write another version of "Yellow Woman" that would have a different ending.

CHAPTER

9

Revising and Proofreading: Backing and Filling

Many writers find it helpful to distinguish between *revising* and *proofreading*. *Revision* means truly trying to re-see your piece of writing with an eye toward making additions, deletions, substitutions, rearrangements, changes in voice, even changes in form: in short, substantial modifications to the draft. Julian Barnes spoke, in Chapter 3, of revising "Shipwreck" to include a new section on Géricault's painting methods after receiving a helpful suggestion to this effect from a painter. He agreed with the painter that such a section would improve his piece, so he revised accordingly. In this chapter, student Jennifer Miller decided to switch to italics to underscore *visually* the change of voices in her essay "Lipstick Kisses."

For most writers, revising begins in a serious way after the first draft of the work is finished; however, it can occur at any stage of the writing process. Some writers like to revise as they go along. Many like to get feedback from others on possibilities for revision at regular stages in a work's composition. The process of improving our work can become so satisfying, in fact, that often we would just as soon keep tinkering with a piece indefinitely. William Zinsser describes the fun of revision on the word processor in his essay "Writing—and Rewriting—with a Word Processor," which opens this chapter. Fortunately, deadlines force us finally to pull our babies from our chests and release them (often reluctantly) into the world.

Proofreading is revising on a smaller scale. It is the final process every piece of writing undergoes, during which spelling is checked and judgments are made about matters of punctuation, grammar, agreement, and other facets of standard edited English. Two decades of teaching has convinced me of two truths of college writing: (1) most students do not spend enough time on revision, and (2) most students have not been taught to be good proofreaders.

The biggest reason college students do not spend enough time on revision is that they do not start writing until the last minute. When this happens, the first draft is usually the last draft—and it shows. The student is not happy with the paper. The professor is not happy with the paper. Everybody is pretty miserable about the whole experience. What a difference it would make if students could convince themselves of the sense of well-being they would gain by writing that first draft early instead of late. With weeks to spare before the final version is due, they can put the work away to grow and settle in their imaginations, then take it out and read it with fresh eyes and make large or small revisions. Students can show their drafts to others to give them a test run, just as they would a new car. Then they can get the bugs out.

Revision is an attitude, a willingness to reevaluate; proofreading is a skill anyone can learn. The basic premise is simple: you cannot proofread a paper once and catch all the errors. You must proofread your work many times, one for each facet of writing of concern. Multiple proofreading only makes sense. Writing consists of large matters and small matters: the presentation and development of ideas or images or moods, and small matters of execution, like spelling and punctuation. In describing "The National Coalition" he put together at the beginning of World War II, Winston Churchill makes it clear that he insisted on signing off on every war directive, and each one had to be in writing. The buck started (and stopped) with Winston Churchill, and it was with Winston Churchill the writer.

Good proofreaders will follow these tips for successful proofreading:

1. *Read your work aloud.* This slows you down and enables you to hear how words and sentences sound. It also allows you better to *see* each word in order to catch spelling, typographical, or punctuation errors.
2. *Try reading your sentences from right to left (Chinese style), instead of from left to right.* When you do this, the "sense" of your writing won't distract you. It won't encourage you to see what is not there. With nothing making sense, you can concentrate on looking at the words alone. You will be surprised at the spelling, typographical, and even punctuation errors you may uncover in this fashion.
3. *Read through your work for clarity of each line or sentence*—and make changes accordingly.
4. *Read through just focusing on word choice.* Have you chosen the strongest, most precise verbs possible in every sentence? Had you better look up a word to see if you are using it correctly? Here is the time for pulling out your thesaurus and looking for another word that will better capture what you have in mind. (See Mary McCarthy's essay "Language and Politics" in this chapter.)
5. *If you are writing on a word processor, put your draft through the computer spell check, or read your work just looking at spelling.* Look up any words that you even suspect may be misspelled. When in doubt, check. Write

down your personal "problem words" in the front of your dictionary for easy reference, so you won't have to waste minutes paging through the dictionary each time.

6. *Reread your work focusing only on the punctuation.* Have you used just enough commas, but not too many? Have you remembered to place a question mark if you have asked a (nonrhetorical) question? Have you used the semicolon, the colon, ellipses, and square brackets correctly? If you have started a quotation or parenthesis, have you remembered to close it? (See Lewis Thomas's "Notes on Punctuation" in this chapter.)
7. *Reread your essay paying attention to agreement of subjects, pronouns, verbs, and nouns.* Agreement can be tricky, and the farther away your subject is from your verb, the easier it is for agreement to be lost.
8. *Go through your work just to check that any footnotes, parenthetical documentation, and bibliographical entries are handled in correct style.* You may want to doublecheck the MLA Handbook, The Publication Manual of the American Psychological Association, The Chicago Manual of Style, or another stylebook used in your discipline. (See Carol Kammen's essay "Concerning Footnotes" in this chapter.)
9. *Do one last reading, concentrating on any special writing problems you are trying to conquer.* If you are working on your sentence sense, check each sentence to make sure it is a complete sentence rather than a fragment or run-together sentence. If you are working on your grammar or wordiness or overusing *really* or *very*, concentrate only on this.

If you get into the habit of this kind of selective but multiple proofreading, you will train your eye to such a degree that a career may open up to you in copyediting.

The soundest proofreading advice I can offer, however, is this: the more important the piece of writing, the more important it is to have an outside proofreader as well as your own vigilant eyes. Ironically, writers are the worst proofreaders of their own work. That is because they are too close to the text. They have worked over the piece so much that, when proofreading, they can easily supply words that are not on the page or overlook errors clearly there. Before taking your résumé to the printer, ask a trusted friend or relative to read it over. Nobody wants one hundred beautiful and expensive copies of a flawed résumé. The same holds true for any letter of job application. Your letter will be taken by employers and search committees for what it is: a reflection of you. If your letter seems hurried, sloppy, and careless, can you expect to be hired? Even one spelling or typographical error can rule you out of a highly competitive field.

Revising and proofreading means backing and filling, but it pays. Brendan Gill described the secret of writers for *The New Yorker* as this: "One must be harder on oneself than one knows how to be."*

---

*Here at The New Yorker (New York: Berkley, 1976), 310.

Writing—and Rewriting—with a Word Processor

William Zinsser

The two paragraphs below, from the first edition of On Writing Well, *look like a first draft, but actually they have already been rewritten and retyped four or five times. With each rewrite I try to make what I have written tighter, stronger and more precise, eliminating every element that is not doing useful work. Then I go over it once more, reading it aloud, and am always amazed at how much clutter can still be cut. Today, on a word processor, no such record of my changes would exist. But the principles of editing are exactly the same.*

Writing is hard work. A clear sentence is no accident. Very few sentences come out right the first time, or even the third time. Remember this is a consolation in moments of despair. If you find that writing is hard, it's because it is hard. It's one of the hardest things that people do.

DRAFT

1 The man snoozing in his chair with an unfinished magazine open on his lap is a man who was being given too much unnecessary trouble by the writer. It won't do to say that the snoozing reader

is too dumb or too lazy to keep pace with the ~~writer's~~ train of thought. My sympathies are ~~entirely~~ with him. ~~He's not so dumb.~~ (If the reader is lost, it is generally because the writer ~~of the article~~ has not been careful enough to keep him on the ~~proper~~ path.

This carelessness can take any number of ~~different~~ forms. Perhaps a sentence is so excessively ~~long and~~ cluttered that the reader, hacking his way through ~~all~~ the verbiage, simply doesn't know what it means. Perhaps a sentence has been so shoddily constructed that the reader could read it in any of several ways. Perhaps the writer has switched pronouns in mid-sentence, or has switched tenses, so the reader loses track of who is talking, or when the action took place. Perhaps Sentence B is not a logical sequel to Sentence A -- the writer, in whose head the connection is clear, has not bothered to provide the missing link. Perhaps the writer has used an important word incorrectly by not taking the trouble to look it up. He may think that "sanguine" and "sanguinary" mean the same thing, but (the difference is a bloody big one). The reader can only infer (speaking of big differences) what the writer is trying to imply.

Brief Warm-up Writing Exercises

1. Freewrite about your first experience using a computer.
2. Brainstorm a list of writing projects for which you might use a word processor.
3. Describe your first experience trying to ride a bike, drive a car, or operate any other kind of "technology."

1   There's nobody more filled with anxiety than a writer who has been told that he should start writing with a word processor. He keeps putting it off, and when he finally runs out of excuses he goes to his fate lugging more of the classic phobias than even Freud would want to see in one patient: fear of machines, fear of failure, fear of looking stupid, fear of writing, fear of separation from all that's familiar and comfortable.

2   And there's nobody more evangelistic than a writer who has made the leap. Like all evangelists, he has been given the good news, which is that a word processor not only frees writers from the drudgery of writing and rewriting and retyping; it also makes them better writers. Not since the typewriter replaced the pen has a more exciting tool come along. I don't know a

single writer with a word processor who would dream of going back to the way he wrote before.

3   So the problem, obviously, is how to make the leap. How does the neurotic get turned into the believer? As a former neurotic I can testify that the first step is the hardest.

4   Like many writers, I'm a mechanical boob. I can't figure out how the simplest mechanism works. The stapler on my desk has been empty for a year. It's not that I haven't bought the staples; I just can't face the trauma of trying to put them in. One of the sights I most dread on the American landscape is a self-service gas station. I will drive back and forth through an entire town to find a station that has a human operator, one where I won't have to get out and stare at the pump handle, realizing—once again—that I have no idea how to release the gas. When I'm confronted by any strange contraption my hands shake and my heart begins to pound. Fear of flying, for instance, is not one of my phobias; what reduces me to panic in an airplane is trying to open those little plastic packets of food.

5   I mention this to explain that I'm a liberal arts type, with all the hang-ups that come out of that tradition—and also many of the snobberies. I'm as guilty as the next humanist of thinking that science and technology are what have made the world more cold and impersonal. I also come out of a tradition of dependence on paper. To me, paper and pencil were always holy objects. So were scissors and paste, and so were the floor and the wastebasket and all the other objects for arranging writing when it was going well and for throwing it away when it wasn't.

6   All my life I wrote by putting a piece of paper in an old Underwood standard typewriter. I would write one or two paragraphs, and then I would take the paper out and edit what I had written, and then I would put a new piece of paper in the typewriter and type what I had edited, and then I'd take *that* piece of paper out and edit it, and then I'd type it again. And again.

7   Nevertheless I began to see that a major revolution was under way in writing, editing, composition, layout, printing and publishing. Paper was out; type was out; Gutenberg was out. Electronic writing was in. Still, I tried to ignore it. Then, one day, my wife said, "You ought to write a book about how to write with a word processor." And she knows what a mechanical boob I am. But I thought: Why not? Instead of being dragged kicking and screaming into the future, I would drag everybody else kicking and screaming into the future.

8   So I went around to IBM. I'd like to say that I went the next day, but somehow I didn't. I chose IBM solely because it was one of the oldest and most respected companies in the field. I didn't want to waste time comparing brands. I also knew that if I didn't just go out and do it I would never do it at all.

9   At the showroom I was met by a young man and a young woman who showed me the IBM Displaywriter. They were impeccable in business suits. They sat me down among their gleaming terminals and I thought, "I'm not well enough dressed for the new technology. I'm a writer. God help me if I spill

some Danish pastry on this stuff." The IBM woman, whose name was Donna, started to demonstrate the equipment. As she typed and pressed other mysterious keys, her words kept popping onto the screen and off again. Meanwhile she explained what she was doing in language that wasn't comforting: words like textpack and module and diskette. (A diskette is a disk; that's part of the problem.)

10   Then she said, "Now you try it." I said "I have to go." But Donna eased me over to the keyboard and told me to write something. "You're very tense," she said. I *was* tense. My hands were clammy; any minute I'd start hyperventilating all over their shiny equipment. I took off my coat and loosened my tie, and they were shocked by that, but at least I felt more like a writer. Still, I didn't think *my* words would appear on the screen; only IBM's words would appear on the screen.

11   But I started to type, and my words *did* appear on the screen. They even looked like my words. I had thought that writing at a terminal would involve whole new mental processes—that the machine would make my writing mechanical. But it seemed quite natural. I began to play with the keys that make it possible to insert new words and sentences, or to delete them or move them around, and I got the point, and I told Donna and Robert to sign me up. (The IBM man's name was Robert; somehow I knew it wasn't going to be Skip or Bud.) We signed the contract, incidentally, with a ballpoint pen on an old-fashioned form with carbon paper. When it's legal time at IBM they want you on paper and not on a disk.

12   I arranged to have the word processor delivered to my office at the Book-of-the-Month Club and I walked out into the familiar streets of Manhattan and took a deep breath. I had faced the unknown and come out alive. But I still had to face the machine. As I waited for it to be delivered, I half hoped it would never come. When it did, I managed for a week to find reasons not to open the cartons, and when I finally had assembled the five units—the keyboard, the terminal screen, the electronic module that the screen sits on, the toaster-like unit that holds the disks, and the printer—I waited another two days before I turned the power switch to ON. That was the biggest step of all.

13   I taught myself to use the machine in about two weeks. Today I realize that it's possible to teach a writer in one hour almost everything he would need to know. But I was up against three obstacles. One was that I was an early user of a word processor; nobody else in our office had one, and there was no friend to answer my questions. Another block was that I was trying to learn from the instruction manual—one of the most forbidding swamps in the English language.

14   But the biggest block was my basic fear of machines. Every time my machine emitted a beep I jumped; every time the screen wrote me one of its punitive messages, like INVALID KEY or WRONG DISKETTE, I took it as a rebuke—I was too dumb for the new technology. In fact, I kept feeling guilty for making my word processor work so hard. I would inadvertently make some sentences disappear, and then I would have to ask the machine to get them back, and the

machine would retrieve them with a great deal of self-important clunking and I would feel terrible about putting it to so much trouble. Several weeks went by before I thought, "It's just a bunch of wires." This brilliant insight led to the first breakthrough: "I'm as smart as the machine."

15   The second breakthrough came when I realized that I didn't have to learn to do all the things the machine can do. The screen and the manuals constantly describe elaborate tasks that the word processor can perform: horrible tasks for secretaries who need to compile tables or indexes, for instance, or make blind copies of business correspondence. The breakthrough came when I thought: "I don't want to do all those tasks. I only want to write and rewrite and edit and paginate and print." At that moment the machine lost its power over me and I realized—the biggest breakthrough of all—that it's just a fancy typewriter.

16   What does a word processor do that's so helpful? It puts your words right in front of your eyes for your instant consideration—and reconsideration. Most writers don't initially say what they want to say, or say it as well as they could. The typical sentence as it first emerges almost always has something wrong with it: it's not clear; it's not logical; it's too long; it's full of clutter; it's awkward; it's pretentious; it's boring; it lacks rhythm; it could be read in several different ways; it doesn't lead the reader out of the previous sentence. As a writer you're well aware of this blunt truth and you know how to go back and make repairs. But you also know how tiring it is just to *think* about going back and making repairs. All of us have an emotional equity in our first draft—we can hardly believe that it wasn't born perfect. Beyond that, there's the fatigue of retyping the manuscript over and over. The tendency is to say, "It's good enough." Or you just run out of time.

17   But with a word processor you can play with your writing on the screen until you get it right, and the paragraphs will keep rearranging themselves, no matter how many words you change or add or cut, and you don't have to print it until it's just the way you want it. The printer will print exactly what's on the screen—word for word, line for line. It's an electronic typewriter that takes its instructions from the mother unit.

18   Imagine, for example, that you've written a paragraph. When you read it over you realize that there's something you'd like to add after the second sentence that hadn't occurred to you before. You just type it in. The existing sentences will move to the right to make room for it, and the paragraph will regroup itself with the new material added. Then let's say you read the new paragraph and find that you don't need the new sentence after all. Press the DELETE key. The sentence will vanish and the gaps will close up again. You can add or delete or move anything at all—words, phrases, sentences, paragraphs, whole pages. There's no kind of tinkering that you can't do—and undo—instantly.

19   To me this is God's gift, or technology's gift, to good writing. Because the essence of writing is rewriting. I've never thought of rewriting as an unfair burden—extra homework that I don't deserve. On the contrary, I think it's a

privilege to be able to shape my writing until it's as clean and strong as I can make it. Like a good watch, it should run smoothly and have no extra parts. Nevertheless all this rewriting is a chore. I happen to be a slow writer, and I can't write the second paragraph until I've got the first one right, or the third one until I've got the second one right. The floor around my typewriter used to be littered with crumpled earlier drafts. I consoled myself with the truism that in the act of retyping, a writer is also rewriting. But now I see that the truism is only about 10 percent true: I've spent much of my life retyping, just as I spent a lot of time washing dishes by hand before someone invented the dishwasher: it liberates you from a chore that's not creative and that saps your energy and enthusiasm.

20   Of course all writers write differently. My method of writing and rewriting one paragraph at a time is totally unlike that of the person who writes his whole first draft in one burst. Still, however you write, there's no escape from rewriting.

21   What do I mean by "rewriting"? I don't mean writing one version and then writing a whole new version from scratch, and then a third. Most rewriting consists of reshaping and polishing the raw material you wrote on your first try. This means that a certain amount of your typing has already been done. Let's look at a typical paragraph and imagine that it's the writer's first draft. There's nothing really wrong with it—it's clear and it's grammatical. But it's full of ragged edges: failures of the writer to keep the reader notified of changes in time, place and mood, or to animate his style. What I've done is to add, in brackets after each sentence, some of the thoughts that might occur to a careful writer taking a first look at this draft. After that the revised paragraph appears.

> *There used to be a time when neighbors took care of one another, he remembered.* [Put "he remembered" first to establish reflective tone.] *It no longer seemed to happen that way, however.* [The contrast supplied by "however" must start the sentence. Also establish place.] *He wondered if it was because everyone in the modern world was so busy.* [All these opening sentences are the same length and have the same dreary rhythm; turn this one around.] *It occurred to him that people today had so many things to do that they didn't have time any more for old-fashioned friendship.* [Sentence essentially repeats previous sentence; give it specific detail or kill it.] *Things didn't work that way in America in previous eras.* [Reader is still in the present tense; reverse the sentence to tell him he's now in the past. America no longer needed here if inserted earlier.] *And he knew that the situation was very different in other countries of the world, as he recalled from the years when he lived in villages in such places as Spain and Italy.* [Reader is still in America; start with a negative transition word. Sentence also too flabby. "Countries of the world" redundant.] *It almost seemed to him that as people got richer and built their houses farther apart they isolated themselves form the essentials of life.* [Plant irony early? Sharpen the paradox about richness.] *And there was another thought that troubled him.* [This is the real

point of the paragraph; signal the reader that it's important. Avoid weak "there was" construction.] *His friends had deserted him when he needed them most during his recent illness.* [Reshape the sentence so the last word is "most"; the last word is the one that lingers in the reader's ear. Hold sickness for next sentence.] *It was almost as if they found him guilty of doing something shameful.* [Introduce sickness here as the reason. Is "guilty" necessary? Implicit?] *He recalled reading somewhere about societies in primitive parts of the world in which sick people were shunned, though he had never heard of any such ritual in America.* [Sentence starts slowly and stays very windy. Break it into shorter units. Snap off the point.]

He remembered that neighbors used to take care of one another. But that no longer seemed to happen in America. Was it because everyone was so busy? Were people really so preoccupied with their TV sets and their cars and their fitness programs that they had no time for friendship? In previous eras that was never true. Nor was it how families lived in other parts of the world. Even in the poorest villages of Spain and Italy he recalled how people would drop in with a loaf of bread. An ironic idea struck him: as people got richer they cut themselves off from the richness of life. But what really troubled him was an even more shocking fact. The time when his friends deserted him was the time when he needed them most. By getting sick he almost seemed to have done something shameful. He knew that other societies had a custom of "shunning" people who were very ill. But that ritual only existed in primitive cultures. Or did it?

22   My revisions aren't necessarily the best ones that could be made—or the only ones. They're mainly matters of carpentry: fixing the structure and the flow. Much could still be done in such areas as cadence, detail and freshness of language. But my point is that most rewriting is a process of juggling elements that already exist. And I'm not just talking about polishing individual sentences. The total construction is equally important. Read your article aloud from beginning to end and put yourself in the reader's mind. You might find, for instance, that you had written two sentences like this:

The tragic hero of the play is Othello. Small and malevolent, Iago feeds his jealous suspicions.

In itself there's nothing wrong with the Iago sentence. But as a sequel to the previous sentence it's very wrong. The name lingering in the reader's ear is Othello; as the reader proceeds into the next sentence he naturally assumes that Othello is small and malevolent.

23   When you read your writing aloud with these connecting links in mind you'll find a dismaying number of places where you have lost or confused the reader, or failed to tell him the one fact he needs to know, or told him too much. With a word processor you can move through your piece easily,

patching all these trouble spots. After every patch, look at what you've done and decide whether you like it. If you don't like it, try something else. When you finish your repairs the machine will paginate your entire article, putting the same number of lines on each page, and the printer will type it while you go and have a beer. Sweeter music could hardly be sung to a writer than the sound of his article being typed exactly the way he wants it—but not by him.

24   Later you may decide that you want to add a few paragraphs of new information on, say, page 8. Just call page 8 back to the screen, add the new material, and tell the machine to repaginate the article from that point forward. If you've forgotten a footnote—and what dissertation writer hasn't?—just type it in its proper place and let the machine do the dirty work of redistributing the lines, renumbering the pages and making a clean copy. Why should a Ph.D. candidate waste his intellect on such drudgery? His thesis is two years late anyway.

25   In short, the word processor can concentrate your mind on the craft of writing, revising and editing—much more powerfully than this has ever been possible, because your words are right in front of you in all their infinite possibility, waiting to be infinitely reshaped. Technology, the great villain, turns out to be your friend. I have no patience with people who say that writing at a terminal will make our writing mechanical, or turn our children into robots. What we write still has to come out of our heads; no machine is going to do that for us.

26   For children, in fact, the word processor strikes me as an ideal tool for learning how to write. Children are natural writers—their heads are full of images and wonder and wordplay. Their hands, however, are too slow to get all the wonderful words on paper. Grimly gripping the pencil, they try to keep pace with their galloping thoughts. But it's a losing battle—the joy of writing turns to frustration and is often lost forever. This wouldn't happen if they could tap out their writing easily and see it on a screen and move their words around and substitute one for another. *That's* the joy of writing, as every poet knows: to make words dance for us in all their possible patterns. The word processor could also be a classroom tool for teaching students how to revise and rewrite. Imagine that instead of a blackboard they would see a projection of a paragraph that's been written on a terminal screen, with the teacher editing the sentences and explaining his or her reasons. It would be a dramatic exposure to the writing process.

27   In my first few weeks at a word processor I was comforted by the thought that I could always make a printout of what I had written. Then I would be able to edit it with my sacred pencil. But very soon I realized that I was editing my writing on the screen more quickly and competently, and with far less fatigue, than I ever had on paper. Visually, the words seemed clearer when they were right in front of my eyes than when they were on a piece of paper viewed from a 45-degree angle. If even one letter was wrong it jumped out at me from the screen. And to be able to change those words instantly was a miracle. Every day I would just call up what I had written the day before, read over the last

few pages and keep going. I only made a printout when somebody else needed a copy. I weaned myself from paper almost immediately.

28   But (I hear you saying) what if you decide after revising a paragraph that you liked the first version better? Especially that long opening sentence that caught the energy you were feeling at the time. And what was that elegant phrase—something about the gulls at dusk—that now seems so absolutely right, if not downright luminous? All those gems have vanished into the electricity. This question about the loss of material is the biggest factor—after the primordial fear of the machine itself—that keeps writers from even trying a word processor.

29   The question has various answers, depending on how you work. In my case, editing and revising as I go along, I almost always prefer my improvements to what they replaced. I love to see an unnecessary word or phrase evaporate at the flick of a key; I love to replace a humdrum word with one that has more precision or color. With every change I feel that I'm getting nearer to where I would finally like to arrive, and as I see the piece growing in strength, literally before my eyes, I feel a purer pleasure than I've ever had in rewriting.

30   But most writers work in a more spacious manner, freely pouring out ideas and sentences with the knowledge that they can come back later and clean up the mess. If you are this kind of writer you don't want to keep erasing what you've written; you want to save all your drafts. You can do this on paper and you can also do it on the screen. The machine requires you to give a different name to every item you create at a terminal. This is the storage system that enables you to file your work on a disk and to summon it back as often as you need it.

31   Assume that you're writing an article about automobiles. You might name your first draft CAR. It will exist for you on a disk in that form, with all its raw virtues and flaws. You can also make a printout of it so that you have it on paper. Then you might write a second draft and name it CAR2 and make a printout of that. Then you might write a third draft, CAR3, by working from the printout of CAR and CAR2, combining the best features of both. Or you might decide that your well-meant revisions have lost the freshness of the original and that CAR is the version that's truest to your intentions. Just call CAR back to the screen and make it your working version, perhaps borrowing some refinements from CAR2 and CAR3. But whatever you do, the work will be much easier and faster because the words are only images of light.

32   In certain kinds of writing you'll save incredible amounts of time and energy. I'm thinking especially of interviews and other articles that make extensive use of "quotes." The people you interview may be highly articulate; nevertheless they will digress and repeat themselves. Even if they give you all the material you need, they will never give it to you in the form in which you'll finally need it. You're stuck with the hard job of imposing a shape on the material, distilling the quotes that will tell the story best, and creating a narrative flow.

33   This can involve hours of fiddling with the quotes: putting them in and taking them back out and trying them somewhere else and substituting different ones. Often, for instance, you'll write an entire page incorporating a set of quotes that you thought was perfect for a particular moment. Later you find in your notes a quote that makes the same point in a better way—it's more vivid, perhaps, or more exact. On a typewriter it would take twenty minutes to replace one quote with the other and retype the whole page. On a word processor you can do it painlessly in a minute or two.

34   Equally important are such matters as variety and pace. An article that just strings together long chunks of quotes, for instance, will soon become tiresome. You must periodically alter the rhythm by converting what the speaker said into a sentence of your own, explaining his point in your words. But often the only way to get a sense of the momentum of a piece is to write several paragraphs of quotes and then read them to see if they need to be broken up. Perhaps one brief sentence of yours can create a link more tightly than the speaker did.

35   What you must do, in short, is to make an arrangement—one that hangs together from beginning to end and that moves with economy and warmth. Such a structure can only be achieved with a fair amount of trial and error. And doing this on a screen certainly beats doing it over and over on a typewriter. My last book, *Willie and Dwike,* in which I was working mainly with oral material—information that people had given me in their own words—took less than a year to write on a word processor. On a typewriter it would have taken at least two years. The difference was not only in speed and morale; it was also in control. At the end I felt that I had made exactly the arrangement that I had in mind when I started.

36   These are crucial areas of gain for a writer: time, energy, enthusiasm, output and control. I'm sure a word processor would cut a year off the writing of a Ph.D. dissertation and probably two. That's quite a bargain—in the business of writing, time is money. For the dissertation writer, the Ph.D. degree qualifies that person to enter the job market as a professor. For the free-lance writer, every completed article liberates him or her to start the next one.

37   Nor is the saving limited to the writing; it also applies to the publishing of what has been written. Normally when a writer finishes a book manuscript the publisher allows six months for it to be copyedited and typeset. In the case of *Willie and Dwike* I gave a printout of my manuscript to Harper & Row, where it was copyedited in a week. I made the changes on my screen in a few hours and gave the publisher the two disks that contained my finished book. These were converted directly into phototype and I had page proofs three weeks later.

38   I learned a lot about myself by learning to write on a word processor. I found that I could trust my powers of logic more than I ever thought I could. When you realize that you're as smart as the machine, you try to figure out how it has been programmed to "think," and you find that you don't have to be Einstein to think in the same sequential way. You say to yourself, "If I want to

do Z, the machine would probably want me to do X and Y to get there," and you do it, and the machine does it, and it's a wonderful moment. Somewhere in the depths of your humanistic soul a little spark of satisfaction goes off that you never knew was there. Logic turns out to be fun.

39   Which shouldn't be so surprising. The ability to think logically is one of the fundamental skills in nonfiction writing. Anyone who thinks logically should be able to write well; anyone whose thinking is fuzzy will never write well. I often think we should teach children simple logic before we teach them how to write.

40   I commend one thought to you as you dip your toe in the computer culture: You are more competent than you think you are. All of us liberal arts types have coddled ourselves with the notion that we can't perform mechanical tasks or understand technical processes. A lot of that is self-delusion—people will learn what they need to learn. In my case, as soon as I began to glimpse the countless ways in which a word processor could change my life I enjoyed thinking of all sorts of uses that would help me and my colleagues at work in our writing and our editing.

41   Still, resistance is strong. People listen to me and say, "I'm sure you're right—maybe next year I'll give it a try." They're afraid to give up the crutches they're sure they need to perform the act of writing. I knew, for instance, that I couldn't possibly write unless I could flick back and forth among several pieces of paper to see what I had written. I needed that continuity and I always would. Well, it turns out that I don't need it at all. On my screen I can see twenty lines at a time, and that's usually enough. If it isn't, I can bring the preceding lines into view. O.K., it's not ideal. But it's not fatal—the mind adjusts and develops new aptitudes.

42   The best way to take the plunge is to learn from another writer. Beginners assume that they have to take a computer course or immerse themselves in the instruction manual. But courses and manuals are meant mainly for office workers, who will use a word processor for office tasks. They are taught and written by people who aren't writers themselves and who don't know the cognitive steps that go into writing, revising and editing. By contrast, any writer who uses a word processor should be able to launch another writer in an hour. When I do this I demonstrate the relatively few functions that a writer needs, point out the keys that govern these functions and explain the logic that the machine uses to do what it does. Twenty minutes is generally enough. Then I sit my student down at the keyboard and tell him or her to write something. At first there is a timidity, as if to avoid striking a key that might blow the machine up. But this quickly dissolves into childlike pleasure. In fifteen minutes the beginner is writing paragraphs and adding and deleting words. All the fear is seen to have been unreasonable. At the end of an hour the worst is over.

43   Like most writers, I don't like to write; I like to have written. Now, however, I sit down to write far more willingly than I ever have before, especially if I'm facing a complex problem of organization. The opposite argument, of course, has also been made: because writing on a screen comes

so easily and looks so neat it will make many people write worse; they will assume that their beautiful-looking words, so effortlessly born, are perfect. That's also true: sloppy writers may write even more sloppily. But a certain number of sloppy writers will improve, noticing for the first time the disarray of their thoughts on the screen and knowing that they have a second chance to make their sentences—and themselves—look better. Or a third chance. The machine is forgiving: it invites you to take risks, to try things out, to fly a little. If the flight doesn't work, nobody will ever know—you can delete it and try something else. But at least you have stretched your muscles and your sense of possibility. Maybe next time you will soar.

44   When you see your words on the screen, study them closely. Remember that the two cardinal virtues of writing are clarity and simplicity. Look for clutter and prune it out. Read your sentences aloud. Do they sound like you? If they don't, fiddle with them until they do. Don't say anything in writing that you wouldn't comfortably say in conversation. If you're not a person who says "indeed" or "moreover," or who calls someone an individual ("He's a fine individual"), don't ever write it. Are you drowning in long words? Think of shorter ones. Are your sentences full of abstract nouns like "productivity"? Turn the nouns into active verbs that get real people doing real things that the reader can picture. Is a sentence stiff and pompous? Relax and write a new one right after it that expresses the warm and lovable person you really are. Then delete the earlier sentence; the stiff and pompous you will vanish into the electricity. Use the machine, in short, to capture your humanity.

45   If that's a paradox, don't knock it. ❖

Questions to Ponder

1. What techniques does William Zinsser use in this essay to break down readers' fears and apprehensions regarding using a word processor? Why are they effective?
2. Do you agree with the criticisms William Zinsser makes of his own sentences on pages 539 and 540? Do you find his revisions stronger? What further changes might you make?
3. Looking back, can you think of anything William Zinsser has overlooked about using word processors? What would you add?
4. After reading this essay, do you feel encouraged to try a word processor?

Writing Possibilities

1. Write a dialogue between a writer afraid of trying a word processor and one sold on its virtues. Who will get the last word?

2. Using William Zinsser's essay as a model, write an essay trying to convince a senior citizen of the benefits and easy use of a VCR (videotape recorder) or a microwave oven.
3. Write an essay to music lovers in which you try to convince them to switch over from records and tapes to compact discs.
4. Write a humorous essay describing your first experience using a computer, driving a car, learning to ski, or some other similar encounter.
5. Using the list you created in warm-up writing exercise 2, write an essay for college students extolling the benefits and uses of a word processor or computer.

THE NATIONAL COALITION
Winston Churchill

"I write a book the way they built the Canadian Pacific Railway," Winston Churchill explained. "First I lay the track from coast to coast, and after that I put in all the stations."

Churchill was a man of tremendous energy who wrote throughout his life. He was awarded the Nobel Prize for literature in 1953 for his impressive contribution to the English language, which took many forms: journalism, essays, histories, memoirs and biographies, autobiography, and oratory.

Through napping, Churchill found a way to compress a day-and-a-half's work into a day. He slept every afternoon. It could be at any time from 3:00 P.M. to 6:00 P.M., but he always got completely into bed and slept at least an hour. He then had a bath, and was ready to work until 3:00 A.M. If he were traveling by car, he still had his nap, either by stopping somewhere or by tying a bandage around his eyes and sleeping in transit.

Churchill awoke every morning about 8:00 A.M. and would ring a bell for his breakfast, his correspondence box, and his stenographer. His assistants report that in the early days of World War II (described in "The National Coalition," which follows), Churchill's ideas flowed out in the form of questions and "minutes" to his chiefs of staff. Often he attached his bright red label "ACTION THIS DAY" on them. These "minutes" came to be known to their recipients as "Churchill's Prayers," for they often ended, "Pray give me the facts on half a sheet of paper" (Sir John Wheeler-Bennett, Action This Day: Working with Churchill [New York: St. Martin's Press, 1969], 23).

In his books and speeches, as well as in his war minutes, Churchill displayed great interest in detail and accuracy. When writing books, he hired research assistants to feed him information and to check facts. He not only liked to get something down on paper as soon as he possibly could, but he wanted to see at once how it looked in type. As soon as a chapter was finished—and sometimes even before the facts in it had been fully checked—he would send it off to a printer. The galley proofs would then be sent back to Churchill for the next treatment. According to Maurice Ashley, in Churchill's later years it was seldom that galley proof was not revised and substantially rewritten five or six times (Maurice Ashley, Churchill as Historian [New York: Scribner's, 1968], 30). This was an expensive process, and in the end Churchill employed his own printer—and his own proofreader as well.

Churchill was equally attentive to every speech. John Colville, his assistant private secretary during World War II, reports that Churchill never spoke words that were not his own in political speeches delivered as prime minister (Wheeler-Bennett 72). Churchill rarely spoke extemporaneously, and Colville gives this eyewitness account of Churchill's speech writing process:

> A theme would unfold in his mind, and over the course of several days he would dictate sections of his speech, mainly in bed, often in a car (where he found the movement conducive to thought) and sometimes late at night pacing up and down the the Cabinet Room or his upstairs library at Chartwell. . . .
>
> When a speech had been composed, the final corrections, the insertions and deletions, were like the last touches to a picture. The draft required reading and re-reading, and it had finally to be put into speech form arranged . . . to look like the psalms. . . . [S]ince the final typing was usually being done against the clock, and he was almost invariably still in bed correcting the speech when he should have been on his way to the House, the scene before he left Downing Street with Private Secretaries urging speed, messengers holding the lift, the car's engine running and anxious Whips telephoning, was a cross between comic opera and the launching of a major offensive (Wheeler-Bennett 70–71).

Brief Warm-up Writing Exercises

1. Freewrite all you know about World War II.
2. Brainstorm a list of the first steps you would take to organize the war effort if you were named prime minister of Great Britain at the beginning of World War II.
3. Brainstorm a list of the first steps you would take if you were president or prime minister of your country at the beginning of the recent Gulf War in the Middle East.

4. Freewrite what you think your reaction would be if your country went to war.

❖

1   Now at last the slowly gathered, long-pent-up fury of the storm broke upon us. Four or five millions of men met each other in the first shock of the most merciless of all the wars of which record has been kept. Within a week the front in France, behind which we had been accustomed to dwell through the long years of the former war and the opening phase of this, was to be irretrievably broken. Within three weeks the long-famed French Army was to collapse in rout and ruin, and the British Army to be hurled into the sea with all its equipment lost. Within six weeks we were to find ourselves alone, almost disarmed, with triumphant Germany and Italy at our throats, with the whole of Europe in Hitler's power, and Japan glowering on the other side of the globe. It was amid these facts and looming prospects that I entered upon my duties as Prime Minister and Minister of Defence and addressed myself to the first task of forming a Government of all parties to conduct His Majesty's business at home and abroad by whatever means might be deemed best suited to the national interest.

2   Five years later almost to a day it was possible to take a more favourable view of our circumstances. Italy was conquered and Mussolini slain. The mighty German Army surrendered unconditionally. Hitler had committed suicide. In addition to the immense captures by General Eisenhower, nearly three million German soldiers were taken prisoners in twenty-four hours by Field Marshal Alexander in Italy and Field Marshal Montgomery in Germany. France was liberated, rallied and revived. Hand in hand with our allies, the two mightiest empires in the world, we advanced to the swift annihilation of Japanese resistance. The contrast was certainly remarkable. The road across these five years was long, hard, and perilous. Those who perished upon it did not give their lives in vain. Those who marched forward to the end will always be proud to have trodden it with honor.

3   In giving an account of my stewardship and in telling the tale of the famous National Coalition Government, it is my first duty to make plain the scale and force of the contribution which Great Britain and her Empire, whom danger only united more tensely, made to what eventually became the common cause of so many states and nations. I do this with no desire to make invidious comparisons or rouse purposeless rivalries with our greatest ally, the United States, to whom we owe immeasurable and enduring gratitude. But it is to the combined interest of the English-speaking world that the magnitude of the British war-making effort should be known and realized. I have therefore had a table made which I print on this page, which covers the whole period of the war. This shows that up till July, 1944, Britain and her Empire had a substantially larger number of divisions *in*

Land Forces in Fighting Contact with the Enemy "Equivalent Divisions"

	British Empire			USA		
	Western Theatre	Eastern Theatre	Total	Western Theatre	Eastern Theatre	Total
Jan. 1, 1940	5⅓	—	5½*	—	—	—
July 1, 1940	6	—	6	—	—	—
Jan. 1, 1941	10⅓	—	10⅓†	—	—	—
July 1, 1941	13	—	13†	—	—	—
Jan. 1, 1942	7⅔	7	14⅔	—	2⅔	2⅔‡
July 1, 1942	10	4⅔	14⅔	—	8⅓	8⅓
Jan. 1, 1943	10⅓	8⅔	19	5	10	15
July 1, 1943	16⅔	7⅔	24⅓	10	12⅓	22⅓
Jan. 1, 1944	11⅓	12⅓	23⅔	6⅔	9⅓	16
July 1, 1944	22⅔	16	38⅔	25	17	42
Jan. 1, 1945	30⅓	18⅔	49	55⅔	23⅓	79

*B.E.F. in France.
†Excludes Guerrillas in Abyssinia.
‡Excludes Filipino troops.
The dividing line between the Eastern and Western theatres is taken as a north-south line through Karachi.
The following are *not* taken as operational theatres:
  Northwest frontier of India; Gibraltar; West Africa; Iceland; Hawaii; Palestine; Iraq; Syria (except on July 1, 1941).
Malta is taken as an operational theatre; also Alaska from January, 1942, to July, 1943.
Foreign contingents—e.g., Free French, Poles, Czechs—are *not* included.

contact with the enemy than the United States. This general figure includes not only the European and African spheres, but also all the war in Asia against Japan. Up till the arrival in Normandy in the autumn of 1944 of the great mass of the American Army, we had always the right to speak at least as an equal and usually as the predominant partner in every theatre of war except the Pacific and Australasian; and this remains also true, up to the time mentioned, of the aggregation of all divisions in all theatres for any given month. From July, 1944, the fighting front of the United States, as represented by divisions in contact with the enemy, became increasingly predominant, and so continued, mounting and triumphant, till the final victory ten months later.

4   Another comparison which I have made shows that the British and Empire sacrifice in loss of life was even greater than that of our valiant ally. The British total dead, and missing, presumed dead, of the armed forces, amounted to 303,240, to which should be added over 109,000 from the Dominions, India, and the colonies, a total of over 412,240. This figure does not include 60,500 civilians killed in the air raids on the United Kingdom, nor the losses of our merchant navy and fishermen, which amounted to about 30,000. Against this figure the United States mourn the deaths in the Army and Air Force, the Navy,

U-Boat Losses

Destroyed by	German	Italian	Japanese
British forces*	525	69	9½
United States forces*	174	5	110½
Other and unknown causes	82	11	10
Totals	781	85	130

Grand total of U-boats destroyed: 996

*The terms British and United States forces include Allied forces under their operational control. Where fractional losses are shown, the "kill" was shared. There were many cases of shared "kills," but in the German totals the fractions add up to whole numbers.

Marines, and Coastguard, of 322,188.* I cite these sombre rolls of honor in the confident faith that the equal comradeship sanctified by so much precious blood will continue to command the reverence and inspire the conduct of the English-speaking world.

5   On the seas the United States naturally bore almost the entire weight of the war in the Pacific, and the decisive battles which they fought near Midway Island, at Guadalcanal, and in the Coral Sea in 1942 gained for them the whole initiative in that vast ocean domain, and opened to them the assault of all the Japanese conquests, and eventually of Japan herself. The American Navy could not at the same time carry the main burden in the Atlantic and the Mediterranean. Here again it is a duty to set down the facts. Out of 781 German and 85 Italian U-boats destroyed in the European theatre, the Atlantic and Indian Oceans, 594 were accounted for by British sea and air forces, who also disposed of all the German battleships, cruisers, and destroyers, besides destroying or capturing the whole Italian Fleet.

6   The table of U-boat losses is shown in the table on this page.

7   In the air superb efforts were made by the United States to come into action—especially with their daylight Fortress bombers—on the greatest scale from the earliest moment after Pearl Harbor, and their power was used both against Japan and from the British Isles against Germany. However, when we reached Casablanca in January, 1943, it was a fact that no single American bomber plane had cast a daylight bomb on Germany. Very soon the fruition of the great exertions they were making was to come, but up till the end of 1943 the British discharge of bombs upon Germany had in the aggregate exceeded by eight tons to one those cast from American machines by day or night, and it was only in the spring of 1944 that the preponderance of discharge was achieved by the United States. Here, as in the armies and on the sea, we ran the full course from the beginning, and it was not until 1944 that we were overtaken and surpassed by the tremendous war effort of the United States.

8   It must be remembered that our munitions effort from the beginning of

---

*Eisenhower "Crusade in Europe."

Lend-Lease in January, 1941, was increased by over one-fifth through the generosity of the United States. Through the materials and weapons which they gave us we were actually able to wage war *as if we were a nation of fifty-eight millions instead of forty-eight.* In shipping also the marvellous production of Liberty Ships enabled the flow of supplies to be maintained across the Atlantic. On the other hand, the analysis of shipping losses by enemy action suffered by all nations throughout the war should be borne in mind. Here are the figures:

Nationality	Losses in Gross Tons	Percentage
British	11,357,000	54
United States	3,334,000	16
All other nations (outside enemy control)	6,503,000	30
	21,194,000	100

Of these losses eighty per cent were suffered in the Atlantic Ocean, including British coastal waters and the North Sea. Only five percent were lost in the Pacific.

9   This is all set down, not to claim undue credit, but to establish on a footing capable of commanding fair-minded respect the intense output in every form of war activity of the people of this small island, upon whom in the crisis of the world's history the brunt fell.

10   It is probably easier to form a cabinet, especially a coalition cabinet, in the heat of battle than in quiet times. The sense of duty dominates all else, and personal claims recede. Once the main arrangements had been settled with the leaders of the other parties, with the formal authority of their organizations, the attitude of all those I sent for was like that of soldiers in action, who go to the places assigned to them at once without question. The party basis being officially established, it seemed to me that no sense of Self entered into the minds of any of the very large number of gentlemen I had to see. If some few hesitated, it was only because of public considerations. Even more did this high standard of behavior apply to the large number of Conservative and National Liberal Ministers who had to leave their offices and break their careers, and at this moment of surpassing interest and excitement to step out of official life, in many cases forever.

11   The conservatives had a majority of more than one hundred and twenty over all other parties in the House combined. Mr. Chamberlain was their chosen leader. I could not but realize that his supersession by me must be very unpleasant to many of them, after all my long years of criticism and often fierce reproach. Besides this, it must be evident to the majority of them how my life had been passed in friction or actual strife with the Conservative Party; that I had left them on Free Trade and had later returned to them as Chancellor of

the Exchequer. After that I had been for many years their leading opponent on India, on foreign policy, and on the lack of preparations for war. To accept me as Prime Minister was to them very difficult. It caused pain to many honorable men. Moreover, loyalty to the chosen leader of the party is the prime characteristic of the Conservatives. If they had on some questions fallen short of their duty to the nation in the years before the war, it was because of this sense of loyalty to their appointed chief. None of these considerations caused me the slightest anxiety. I knew they were all drowned by the cannonade.

12   In the first instance I had offered to Mr. Chamberlain, and he had accepted, the leadership of the House of Commons, as well as the Lord Presidency. Nothing had been published. Mr. Attlee informed me that the Labour Party would not work easily under this arrangement. In a coalition the leadership of the House must be generally acceptable. I put this point to Mr. Chamberlain, and, with his ready agreement, I took the leadership myself, and held it till February, 1942. During this time Mr. Attlee acted as my deputy and did the daily work. His long experience in Opposition was of great value. I came down only on the most serious occasions. These were, however, recurrent. Many Conservatives felt that their party leader had been slighted. Everyone admired his personal conduct. On his first entry into the House in his new capacity (May 13) the whole of his party—the large majority of the House—rose and received him in a vehement demonstration of sympathy and regard. In the early weeks it was from the Labour benches that I was mainly greeted. But Mr. Chamberlain's loyalty and support was steadfast, and I was sure of myself.

13   There was considerable pressure by elements of the Labour Party, and by some of those many able and ardent figures who had not been included in the new Government, for a purge of the "guilty men" and of Ministers who had been responsible for Munich or could be criticized for the many shortcomings in our war preparation. Among these Lord Halifax, Lord Simon, and Sir Samuel Hoare were the principal targets. But this was not time for proscriptions of able, patriotic men of long experience in high office. If the censorious people could have had their way, at least a third of the Conservative Ministers would have been forced to resign. Considering that Mr. Chamberlain was the leader of the Conservative Party, it was plain that this movement would be destructive of the national unity. Moreover, I had no need to ask myself whether all the blame lay on one side. Official responsibility rested upon the Government of the time. But moral responsibilities were more widely spread. A long, formidable list of quotations from speeches and votes recorded by Labour, and not less by Liberal, Ministers, all of which had been stultified by events, was in my mind and available in detail. No one had more right than I to pass a sponge across the past. I therefore resisted these disruptive tendencies. "If the present," I said a few weeks later, "tries to sit in judgment on the past, it will lose the future." This argument and the awful weight of the hour quelled the would-be heresy-hunters.

14   Although the awful battle was now going on across the Channel, and the reader is no doubt impatient to get there, it may be well at this point to describe

the system and machinery for conducting military and other affairs which I set on foot and practiced from my earliest days of power. I am a strong believer in transacting official business by *The Written Word*. No doubt, surveyed in the after-time, much that is set down from hour to hour under the impact of events may be lacking in proportion or may not come true. I am willing to take my chance of that. It is always better, except in the hierarchy of military discipline, to express opinions and wishes rather than to give orders. Still, written directive coming personally from the lawfully constituted Head of the Government and Minister specially charged with Defence counted to such an extent that, though not expressed as orders, they very often found their fruition in action.

15   To make sure that my name was not used loosely, I issued during the crisis of July the following minute:

> Prime Minister to General Ismay, C.I.G.S., and   19.VII.40.
> Sir Edward Bridges.
>   Let it be very clearly understood that all directions emanating from me are made in writing, or should be immediately afterwards confirmed in writing, and that I do not accept any responsibility for matters relating to national defence on which I am alleged to have given decisions, unless they are recorded in writing.

16   When I woke about 8 A.M., I read all the telegrams, and from my bed dictated a continuous flow of minutes and directives to the Departments and to the Chiefs of Staff Committee. These were typed in relays as they were done, and handed at once to General Ismay, Deputy Secretary (Military) to the War Cabinet, and my representative on the Chiefs of Staff Committee, who came to see me early each morning. Thus he usually had a good deal in writing to bring before the Chiefs of Staff Committee when they met at 10:30. They gave all consideration to my views at the same time as they discussed the general situation. Thus between three and five o'clock in the afternoon, unless there were some difficulties between us requiring further consultation, there was ready a whole series of orders and telegrams sent by me or by the Chiefs of Staff and agreed between us, usually giving all the decisions immediately required.

17   In total war it is quite impossible to draw any precise line between military and non-military problems. That no such friction occurred between the Military Staff and the War Cabinet Staff was due primarily to the personality of Sir Edward Bridges, Secretary to the War Cabinet. Not only was this son of a former Poet Laureate an extremely competent and tireless worker, but he was also a man of exceptional force, ability, and personal charm, without a trace of jealousy in his nature. All that mattered to him was that the War Cabinet Secretariat as a whole should serve the Prime Minister and War Cabinet to the very best of their ability. No thought of his own personal position ever entered his mind and never a cross word passed between the civil and military officers of the Secretariat.

18   In larger questions, or if there were any differences of view, I called a

meeting of the War Cabinet Defence Committee, which at the outset comprised Mr. Chamberlain, Mr. Attlee, and the three Service Ministers, with the Chiefs of the Staff in attendance. These formal meetings got fewer after 1941.* As the machine began to work more smoothly, I came to the conclusion that the daily meetings of the War Cabinet with the Chiefs of Staff present were no longer necessary. I therefore eventually instituted what came to be known among ourselves as the "Monday Cabinet Parade." Every Monday there was a considerable gathering—all the War Cabinet, the Service Ministers, and the Minister of Home Security, the Chancellor of the Exchequer, the Secretaries of State for the Dominions and for India, the Minister of Information, the Chiefs of Staff, and the official head of the Foreign Office. At these meetings each Chief of Staff in turn unfolded his account of all that had happened during the previous seven days; and the Foreign Secretary followed them with his story of any important developments in foreign affairs. On other days of the week the War Cabinet sat alone, and all important matters requiring decision were brought before them. Other Ministers primarily concerned with the subjects to be discussed attended for their own particular problems. The members of the War Cabinet had the fullest circulation of all papers affecting the war, and saw all important telegrams sent by me. As confidence grew, the War Cabinet intervened less actively in operational matters, though they watched them with close attention and full knowledge. They took almost the whole weight of Home and Party affairs off my shoulders, thus setting me free to concentrate upon the main theme. With regard to all future operations of importance, I always consulted them in good time; but while they gave careful consideration to the issues involved, they frequently asked not to be informed of dates and details, and indeed on several occasions stopped me when I was about to unfold these to them.

19   I had never intended to embody the office of Minister of Defence in a Department. This would have required legislation, and all the delicate adjustments I have described, most of which settled themselves by personal good will, would have had to be thrashed out in a process of ill-timed constitution-making. There was, however, in existence and activity under the personal direction of the Prime Minister the Military Wing of the War Cabinet Secretariat, which had in pre-war days been the Secretariat of the Committee of Imperial Defence. At the head of this stood General Ismay, with Colonel Hollis and Colonel Jacob as his two principals, and a group of specially selected younger officers drawn from all three Services. This Secretariat became the staff of the Office of the Minister of Defence. My debt to its members is immeasurable. General Ismay, Colonel Hollis, and Colonel Jacob rose steadily in rank and repute as the war proceeded, and none of them was changed. Displacements in a sphere so intimate and so concerned with secret matters are detrimental to continuous and efficient despatch of business.

*The Defence Committee met 40 times in 1940, 76 in 1941, 20 in 1942, 14 in 1943, and 10 in 1944.

20   After some early changes almost equal stability was preserved in the Chiefs of Staff Committee. On the expiry of his term as Chief of the Air Staff, in September, 1940, Air Marshal Newall became Governor-General of New Zealand, and was succeeded by Air Marshal Portal, who was the accepted star of the Air Force. Portal remained with me throughout the war. Sir John Dill, who had succeeded General Ironside in May, 1940, remained C.I.G.S. until he accompanied me to Washington in December, 1941. I then made him my personal Military Representative with the President and head of our Joint Staff Mission. His relations with General Marshall, Chief of Staff of the United States Army, became a priceless link in all our business, and when he died in harness some two years later he was accorded the unique honor of a resting-place in Arlington Cemetery, the Valhalla hitherto reserved exclusively for American warriors. He was succeeded as C.I.G.S. by Sir Alan Brooke, who stayed with me till the end.

21   From 1941, for nearly four years, the early part of which was passed in much misfortune and disappointment, the only change made in this small band either among the Chiefs or in the Defence Staff was due to the death in harness of Admiral Pound. This may well be a record in British military history. A similar degree of continuity was achieved by President Roosevelt in his own circle. The United States Chiefs of Staff—General Marshall, Admiral King, and General Arnold, subsequently joined by Admiral Leahy—started together on the American entry into the war, and were never changed. As both the British and Americans presently formed the Combined Chiefs of Staff Committee, this was an inestimable advantage for all. Nothing like it between allies has ever been known before.

22   I cannot say that we never differed among ourselves even at home, but a kind of understanding grew up between me and the British Chiefs of Staff that we should convince and persuade rather than try to overrule each other. This was, of course, helped by the fact that we spoke the same technical language, and possessed a large common body of military doctrine and war experience. In this ever-changing scene we moved as one, and the War Cabinet clothed us with ever more discretion, and sustained us with unwearied and unflinching constancy. There was no division, as in the previous war, between politicians and soldiers, between the "Frocks" and the "Brass Hats"—odious terms which darkened counsel. We came very close together indeed, and friendships were formed which I believe were deeply valued.

23   The efficiency of a war administration depends mainly upon whether decisions emanating from the highest approved authority are in fact strictly, faithfully, and punctually obeyed. This we achieved in Britain in this time of crisis, owing to the intense fidelity, comprehension, and whole-hearted resolve of the War Cabinet upon the essential purpose to which we had devoted ourselves. According to the directions given, ships, troops, and aeroplanes moved, and the wheels of factories spun. By all these processes, and by the confidence, indulgence, and loyalty by which I was upborne, I was soon able to give an integral direction to almost every aspect of the war. This was really

necessary because times were so very bad. The method was accepted because everyone realized how near were death and ruin. Not only individual death, which is the universal experience, stood near, but, incomparably more commanding, the life of Britain, her message, and her glory.

24 Any account of the methods of government which developed under the National Coalition would be incomplete without an explanation of the series of personal messages which I sent to the President of the United States and the heads of other foreign countries and the Dominion Governments. This correspondence must be described. Having obtained from the Cabinet any specific decisions required on policy, I composed and dictated these documents myself, for the most part on the basis that they were intimate and informal correspondence with friends and fellow-workers. One can usually put one's thought better in one's own words. It was only occasionally that I read the text to the Cabinet beforehand. Knowing their views, I used the ease and freedom needed for the doing of my work. I was of course hand-in-glove with the Foreign Secretary and his Department, and any differences of view were settled together. I circulated these telegrams, in some cases after they had been sent, to the principal members of the War Cabinet, and, where he was concerned, to the Dominions Secretary. Before despatching them I, of course, had my points and facts checked departmentally, and nearly all military messages passed through Ismay's hands to the Chiefs of Staff. This correspondence in no way ran counter to the official communications or the work of the Ambassadors. It became, however, in fact the channel of much vital business, and played a part in my conduct of the war not less, and sometimes even more, important than my duties as Minister of Defence.

25 The very select circle, who were entirely free to express their opinion, were almost invariably content with the drafts and gave me an increasing measure of confidence. Differences with American authorities, for instance, insuperable at the second level, were settled often in a few hours by direct contact at the top. Indeed, as time went on, the efficacy of this top-level transaction of business was so apparent that I had to be careful not to let it become a vehicle for ordinary departmental affairs. I had repeatedly to refuse the requests of my colleagues to address President Roosevelt personally on important matters of detail. Had these intruded unduly upon the personal correspondence, they would soon have destroyed its privacy and consequently its value.

26 My relations with the President gradually became so close that the chief business between our two countries was virtually conducted by these personal interchanges between him and me. In this way our perfect understanding was gained. As Head of the State as well as Head of the Government, Roosevelt spoke and acted with authority in every sphere; and, carrying the War Cabinet with me, I represented Great Britain with almost equal latitude. Thus a very high degree of concert was obtained, and the saving in time and the reduction in the number of people informed were both invaluable. I sent my cables to the American Embassy in London, which was in direct touch with the Presi-

dent at the White House through special coding machines. The speed with which answers were received and things settled was aided by clock-time. Any message which I prepared in the evening, night, or even up to two o'clock in the morning, would reach the President before he went to bed, and very often his answer would come back to me when I woke the next morning. In all, I sent him nine hundred and fifty messages and received about eight hundred in reply. I felt I was in contact with a very great man who was also a warm-hearted friend and the foremost champion of the high causes which we served.

27   The Cabinet being favorable to my trying to obtain destroyers from the American Government, I drafted during the afternoon of May 15 my first message to President Roosevelt since I became Prime Minister. To preserve the continuity of our correspondence I signed myself "Former Naval Person," and to this fancy I adhered almost without exception throughout the war.

> *Although I have changed my office, I am sure you would not wish me to discontinue our intimate private correspondence. As you are no doubt aware, the scene has darkened swiftly. The enemy have a marked preponderance in the air, and their new technique is making a deep impression upon the French. I think myself the battle on land has only just begun, and I should like to see the masses engage. Up to the present, Hitler is working with specialized units in tanks and air. The small countries are simply smashed up, one by one, like matchwood. We must expect, though it is not yet certain, that Mussolini will hurry in to share the loot of civilization. We expect to be attacked here ourselves, both from the air and by parachute and air-borne troops, in the near future, and are getting ready for them. If necessary, we shall continue the war alone, and we are not afraid of that.*
>
> *But I trust you realize, Mr. President, that the voice and force of the United States may count for nothing if they are withheld too long. You may have a completely subjugated, Nazified Europe established with astonishing swiftness, and the weight may be more than we can bear. All I ask now is that you should proclaim non-belligerency, which would mean that you would help us with everything short of actually engaging armed forces. Immediate needs are: First of all, the loan of forty or fifty of your older destroyers to bridge the gap between what we have now and the large new construction we put in hand at the beginning of the war. This time next year we shall have plenty. But if in the interval Italy comes in against us with another one hundred submarines, we may be strained to breaking-point. Secondly, we want several hundred of the latest types of aircraft, of which you are now getting delivery. These can be repaid by those now being constructed in the United States for us. Thirdly, anti-aircraft equipment and ammunition, of which again there will be plenty next year, if we are alive to see it. Fourthly, the fact that our ore supply is being compromised from Sweden, from North Africa, and perhaps from Northern*

> Spain, makes it necessary to purchase steel in the United States. This also applies to other materials. We shall go on paying dollars for as long as we can, but I should like to feel reasonably sure that when we can pay no more, you will give us the stuff all the same. Fifthly, we have many reports of possible German parachute or air-borne descents in Ireland. The visit of a United States Squadron to Irish ports, which might well be prolonged, would be invaluable. Sixthly, I am looking to you to keep the Japanese quiet in the Pacific, using Singapore in any way convenient. The details of the material which we have in hand will be communicated to you separately.
>
> With all good wishes and respect.

28 On May 18 a reply was received from the President welcoming the continuance of our private correspondence and dealing with my specific requests. The loan or gift of the forty or fifty older destroyers, it was stated, would require the authorization of Congress, and the moment was not opportune. He would facilitate to the utmost the Allied Governments obtaining the latest types of United States aircraft, anti-aircraft equipment, ammunition, and steel. In all this the representations of our agent, the highly competent and devoted Mr. Purvis (presently to give his life in an air accident) would receive most favorable consideration. The President would consider carefully my suggestion that a United States Squadron might visit Irish ports. About the Japanese, he merely pointed to the concentration of the American Fleet at Pearl Harbor.

29 On Monday, May 13, I asked the House of Commons, which had been specially summoned, for a vote of confidence in the new Administration. After reporting the progress which had been made in filling the various offices, I said, "I have nothing to offer but blood, toil, tears and sweat." In all our long history no Prime Minister had ever been able to present to Parliament and the nation a programme at once so short and so popular. I ended:

> You ask, what is our policy? I will say: It is to wage war, by sea, land, and air, with all our might and with all the strength that God can give us: to wage war against a monstrous tyranny, never surpassed in the dark, lamentable catalogue of human crime. That is our policy. You ask, What is our aim? I can answer in one word: Victory—victory at all costs, victory in spite of all terror; victory, however long and hard the road may be; for without victory, there is no survival. Let that be realized; no survival for the British Empire; no survival for all that the British Empire has stood for, no survival for the urge and impulse of the ages, that mankind will move forward towards its goal. But I take up my task with buoyancy and hope. I feel sure that our cause will not be suffered to fail among men. At this time I feel entitled to claim the aid of all, and I say, "Come, then, let us go forward together with our united strength."

Upon these simple issues the House voted unanimously, and adjourned till May 21.

30   Thus, then, we all started on our common task. Never did a British Prime Minister receive from Cabinet colleagues the loyal and true aid which I enjoyed during the next five years from these men of all Parties in the State. Parliament, while maintaining free and active criticism, gave continuous, overwhelming support to all measures proposed by the Government, and the nation was united and ardent as never before. It was well indeed that this should be so, because events were to come upon us of an order more terrible than anyone had foreseen. ❖

Questions to Ponder

1. Why does Winston Churchill go to such great lengths to establish the comparative contributions and losses of Britain and the United States in the war effort?
2. Does Winston Churchill antagonize any potential readers, or does he anticipate possible objections and counteract them in his essay? Why is acknowledging and rebutting potential opposition a good writing technique?
3. How would you evaluate Winston Churchill's address to the House of Commons? Was his communication effective?
4. How would you evaluate Winston Churchill's first letter to President Roosevelt? What was effective about it?

Writing Possibilities

1. Using Winston Churchill's essay as a model, prepare an essay outlining the best organizational plan that you can think of for your nation following a declaration of war.
2. Read other histories of Britain's first days in World War II. Then write an evaluation of Winston Churchill's essay, offering your assessment of its accuracy, its strengths, and its limitations.
3. Read the full Churchill-Roosevelt correspondence, and write an essay describing its character and any changes it undergoes as the war unfolds.
4. Winston Churchill won the Nobel Prize for literature. Using just this opening chapter of *Their Finest Hour*, isolate and describe Churchill's gifts as a writer.

LANGUAGE AND POLITICS
Mary McCarthy

I was born as a mind during 1925, my bodily birth having taken place in 1912. Throughout the thirteen years in between, obviously, I must have had thoughts and mental impressions, perhaps even some sort of specifically cerebral life that I no longer remember. Almost from the beginning, I had been aware of myself as "bright." And from a very early time reasoning was natural to me, as it is to a great many children, doubtless to animals as well. What is Pavlov's conditioned reflex but an inference drawn by a dog? . . .

[M]y own Fates may have pronounced. . . . the day I got my first library card from the Seattle Public Library—an important, indeed self-important day for me, even though I cannot call it the happiest of my life, as Napoleon is supposed to have said of the day of his First Communion. Nevertheless, I remember the feeling of power conferred on me by the small, ruled cardboard rectangle still virgin except for my name typed at the top and my signature below. I was in the main downtown branch . . . and the fiction shelves frightened me with a bewilderment of choice—a sensation bordering on panic such as one can get nowadays in a too well furnished supermarket. I felt the library card hurrying me to make up my mind. I picked a title from the shelves and advanced to the counter. It was The Nigger of the Narcissus. The librarian looked at me. She took my card and tucked another one, stamped, in a flap at the back of the volume. I had the impression that she wanted to say something, but she let me walk away. In my mind was only the vaguest notion of who Joseph Conrad was or had been.

Brief Warm-up Writing Exercises

1. A *euphemism* is a word or phrase used when we want to avoid or improve upon reality. Brainstorm a list of euphemisms for saying "She died" or "He is old."
2. Now brainstorm a list of simple and high-falutin job titles, such as *janitor* vs. *sanitary engineer* and *cop* vs. *law enforcement officer.*

3. Freewrite your answer to this question: Can language be used to conceal as well as to reveal truth?
4. Freewrite all you know about the Watergate scandal that led to the resignation of President Richard Nixon in 1974.

---

1 ❖ The other day a headline caught my attention in the financial pages of the *International Herald Tribune*. I normally don't look at the business section or the sports and avoid anything about astronauts. But that day—November 13—turning the pages I saw CHILEAN JUNTA WINS PRIVATE FINANCIAL AID. Then in smaller type: " 'Work spirit' Praised by American Banker." The news story related that private U.S. bank loans had suddenly become available for Chile—a dramatic turnabout following on the overthrow of the Allende government. The previous Friday, Manufacturers Hanover Trust had announced that it was extending a $24-million loan to a Chilean bank. According to unnamed banking sources, described as reliable, Manufacturers Hanover had lent an additional $20 million to the central bank of Santiago. In any case, the $24 million was the largest credit given to Chile by a U.S. bank since Salvador Allende took office three years ago. Altogether, eight to ten U.S. banks and two Canadian banks have offered Chile commercial loans amounting to about $150 million in the two months since Allende was overthrown.

2 You may wonder what all this has to do with language; the connection with politics is fairly clear. Well, toward the bottom of the page the writer quoted a vice-president of Manufacturers Hanover, James R. Greene, who on making the announcement spoke at length—I quote—"about the renewal of U.S. business faith in Chile." This is Greene talking: "The work spirit that I have seen in Chile leads me to fully trust that the international press will correct the negative image that is being spread about this country abroad." You will note one split infinitive, two superfluous "that's, and two cliché phrases, "work spirit" and "negative image," that also seem to be circumlocutions. Aside from the question of whether an image can be spread, like butter or like a disease or like a rumor, one asks what the speaker can be alluding to by the blanket word "negative." It is indeed a blanket covering the summary executions of thousands of oppositionists, the countless illegal arrests, the setting-up of camps, the abolition of Parliament, the suppression of left-wing political parties, the suspension of all other political parties, press censorship, purges of the universities, factories, and state enterprises. This is what the colorless "negative image" translates into, and the selection of the word "image"—in its current PR definition, not yet, I see, admitted to my dictionary, copyright 1957—assigns a kind of deniability to all those public facts, as though they were bodiless, insubstantial, mere refractions of evanescent appearance, as opposed to reality.

3 By contrast to his handling of the negative, Greene eventually defines what

he understands by the "work spirit." Something positive. Here he is again: "The fact that Chileans are working on Saturday is a very good antecedent, as far as my bank is concerned. This is very important in the financial world." So work spirit means that the forty-hour week has been abolished by the junta. He does not say, at least in the *Herald Tribune* quotes from him, that the junta has promised to return to private capital the "vast majority" of the more than three hundred foreign and domestic enterprises that were nationalized by the Allende government without compensation. Nor that it has announced that it is prepared to renew negotiations on compensation to the three U.S. companies whose copper mines were taken over—assets worth between $500 and $700 million. That, the joyful undersong of the announcement he had to make, possibly did not need to be put into words. It was tacit. But what about the word "antecedent"? Working on Saturday is a very good antecedent, he says, as far as his bank is concerned. I have been asking myself what word he was reaching for. "Precedent"? But "precedent," though slightly closer to the mark, does not make sense either. Precedent for what, unless he means working on Sunday? The thing he is trying to articulate, evidently, is that his bank takes the extension of the work week as a good sign. Then why not say so? Maybe, to his ear, sign was too commonplace a word for a $24-million occasion. Or maybe, grope as he would, he couldn't remember "sign." Not for the life of him. Was he speaking off the cuff or reading a prepared statement? The news story does not tell.

4   To get back, though, for a moment to Manufacturers Hanover—no prior knowledge of the circumstances, of Allende's murder, U.S. investments, the blood bath, would be required by a newspaper reader of Greene's quoted remarks in order to understand that something was rotten in Chile. His language inadvertently made that clear. In South Vietnam (when I was there in 1967), I noticed the same kind of thing. If I had dropped straight from Mars, I thought, into one of the daily press briefings, I would have known from the periphrastic, circumspect way our spokesmen expressed themselves that an indefensible action of some sort was going on in that country. As with Greene, just about everything they said, or, rather, "stated," was in a kind of bumbling code that quickly translated itself into plain English: e.g., for "success," read "failure." The purpose of language, somebody—probably French—said, is to conceal thought. I don't agree with the aphorism, yet the American language, as spoken today, often bears it out with comical results: the attempt to conceal an underlying thought or feeling produces almost total transparency. As when Nixon, in his letter to Senator Sam Ervin last summer about why he was not going to hand over the tapes to the Committee, said they might be subject to misinterpretation by persons "with other views"; he might as well have made an announcement that he had decided they were extremely damaging. That letter was the first confirmation of John Dean's testimony to come from what we could call a reliable independent source.

5   Of course there are people who have become so practiced in evasion, euphemism, circumlocution, and all the forms of lying that they would not

know *how* to tell the truth if an occasion favoring truth-telling should arise. Their syntax, so twisted, crippled, and deformed by these habits, is incapable of directness, and the occasional forthright statement—"I love America," "I am not a crook"—though grammatically sound as a bell, has to be construed as meaning the opposite: "I hate America," "I am a crook."

6   But this is pathology, and though many or even perhaps most public officials and corporation heads are afflicted by it, I don't think it extends yet to the population at large. In the population at large, though, you find warning symptoms of a deteriorated faculty of expression: the inarticulateness of the very young and the long-winded prosiness of the middle-aged and old. On the one hand, "I went, like, to a party"; on the other, "Thursday evening I attended a function." The common speech of the people, on which Wordsworth hoped to base a new *ars poetica*, is riddled with such curious faults. Between the two examples I have just quoted there is only a generational gap; both seek to avoid direct statement. The continual "like . . . like"—"I went, like, to a party and we smoked, like, pot"—is the sidewise, slithering, crab-gaited, youth approach, whereas the elderly widow who "attended a function" is putting her own strange distance from "Thursday I went to a party."

7   Enough has been said—and for years—about "funeral director," "passed away," "senior citizen," "home" for "house," "wealthy" for "rich." Such linguistic vulgarities, contrary to what is thought, are not restricted to emotive fields, like death and old age, where fear is being held at a distance, or, like the home and money, where reverence is duly paid. "I got my car fixed"—not really a sentimental matter—now turns into "I took my car to be repaired." In rural areas, women talk of their "hose," and "what a lovely gown"; in cities there is "panty hose." Pedantic neologisms issuing from psychiatry are fuzzing up the atmosphere: "He is highly motivated." No matter how many times I hear that, I can never understand what it means. "He has high motives"? No. "He has a lot of drive"? Closer. Maybe "He likes the work he is doing." And "relate"—which is youth jargon: "I found I couldn't relate to Physics 1B." "He is an achiever" (or "an under-achiever") at least is clear. It means he does well (or badly) in school, including sports and "activities."

8   Take the still new adverb "hopefully." People who care for language, including myself, wince every time they hear it. It floats around in the sentence, attached to nothing in particular. "Hopefully the dollar will go up." There it certainly does not modify the verb, as a good adverb should unless there is an adjective somewhere to cling to. If it modified the verb, it would be "the dollar will go hopefully up." Yet it is not a grammatical howler, so far as I can see; it is a parenthesis thrown in, on the pattern of "incidentally," which is not a desirable term either, but, being useful, has got itself accepted. (I myself prefer "by the way" or simple parenthesis marks, as in this sentence.) It must have come to us from German "hoffentlich," normally translated as "it is to be hoped"; perhaps we are indebted to German businessmen, who introduced it along with Volkswagens and Mercedes. What is melancholy about the suddenly universal "hopefully" is that it seems to point to a contrary state of mind,

that is, to an absence of hope. The speaker really fears the dollar will go down still further, and if you tell me "Hopefully we'll meet in a better world," I can pretty well understand that we won't. Its free-floating position in the sentence emphasizes that insecurity, that lack of ground for hope. It is an irony that this pathetic invading adverb should be sweeping the country at what may be the lowest point in our history.

9   Our language, once homely and colloquial, seeks to aggrandize our meanest activities with polysyllabic terms or it retreats from frankness into a stammering verbosity. Americans are slow tedious talkers, and universal semieducation has made them worse. Only the poorer blacks and a few rural whites are still able to express themselves vividly and to find the word they want without too protracted a search. Maybe this is because they never finished school. Illiteracy at the poverty level (mainly a matter of bad grammar) does not alarm me nearly as much as the illiteracy of the well-to-do. In fact, it is almost a comfort and I could wish the poor might stay untaught forever, for their own sakes and for the preservation of the language, if the price did not include other kinds of deprivation. Poor blacks, some rural white and a few gifted talkers are the only people I have heard in recent times use the language with relish. They are the only ones to enjoy talking artistically, for its own sake. Senator Sam Ervin's popularity on radio and television was based, I think, in large part, on his unabashed relish for the language; being old and rural, he sounded like a poor man. His relish for the language, sometimes positively syllabic ("eleemosynary," you could hear his tongue taste those vowels), seemed to be deeply related to his determination to get the truth of Watergate out and to his confidence that this could be done—slowly and painfully, like a tooth-extraction before the days of Novocain.

10   Senator Ervin was not always grammatical, but that enhanced the pleasure one had in him, because his grammar did not so much err as revert to older modes ("ain't," "it don't") and showed no disrespect for the forms of speech, that is, for the sinews of thought. By contrast, there was Jeb Stuart Magruder, a graduate of Williams College. Since I don't have on hand a transcript of his testimony, I will construct a characteristic but imaginary sentence: "Mr. Haldeman indicated to me that between he and I we had a problem." And here is a real exchange between him and Senator Ervin. They were talking about the "climate" prevailing in the White House. Ervin: ". . . I just could not understand why people got so fearful." Magruder: "I would characterize that at least my reaction was stronger after three years of working here than it had been before." More genuine Magruder: "We agreed, Mr. Liddy and I, that he would terminate from the committee all activities." "In November of 1971 it was indicated to me that the project was not going to get off the ground and subsequently G. Gordon Liddy came into the picture after that." Finally, "I think from my own personal standpoint, I did lose some respect for the legal process because I did not see it working as I hoped it would when I came here."

11   I put the verb "indicate" in my imaginary sentence because it came up

over and over in Magruder's testimony. The choice of the word raised interesting questions. When he said "he indicated to me" did he mean simply "he told me"? Let us look at a few examples. "John Dean indicated to me that I would not be indicted." "We indicated to Mr. Stans the problem we had with money." [Haldeman] "indicated that I should get back to Washington directly." "As I recall, we all indicated that we should remove any documents that could be damaging, whether they related at all to the Watergate or not." Of Hugh Sloan and his perjured testimony to the grand jury: "So I indicated at the meeting that I thought he had a problem and might have to do something about it. He said, you mean commit perjury? I said you might have to do something like that to solve your problem and very honestly was doing that in good faith to Mr. Sloan to assist him at that time."

12   The last extract tells the story. "Indicate" means something less and more than "told." Sloan's "you mean commit perjury?" points to the terrible difference between the two. Sloan, an honest accountant (as his conduct before the Ervin committee had already made clear), who insisted on having things named by their names, and the devious operator Magruder, still posing to the Committee as a bashful penitent freshman. Even when pressed by Sloan, he will not assent to "perjury" as the right name for what he has in mind. ". . . something like that," he says. So must we conclude that "indicate" in that crowd meant "tip off"? Possibly, but it is hard to see how, in some of the circumstances, this was done. When John Dean let Magruder know that he was not going to be indicted, what form of words did he use? Or did he wigwag the message? And when Haldeman indicated to him, by long-distance telephone, that he should get back to Washington right away, how did he put it, so that Magruder would understand the order without being told it was one? Did he say "The weather is beautiful in Washington at this time of year, Jeb. The forecast for tomorrow is sunny and mild"? From Magruder's parlance alone, you would get the feeling of secretive men conscious of bugging devices everywhere. It was not surprising to learn that Liddy in California, the morning after the break-in, warned Magruder to find a safe phone. Nor, finally, that Nixon was tapping *himself.* And if all essential communications were coded, in this involute fashion, "indicated," never stated ("indicateur," in French, is the common slang word for "informer," "police spy"), no wonder there has been so much contradiction in the Watergate testimony as to who said what; they were all bent on not saying anything to each other that could be pinned down to a concrete meaning. Imprecision was the rule, and the coverup did not begin June 18 but had been practiced on a daily basis in the ordinary transmission of messages. Indeed, what we call talk for them consisted almost exclusively of messages. This was true no doubt even of banter.

13   John Mitchell had his own code, personalized, initialed JNM, like a monogram on a City Hall mobster's shirt sleeve. It was less bureaucratic than Magruder's, not so stamped by office routines. The expression "White House horror stories," for instance, was to be understood as an allusion to Charles Colson. Another favorite phrase, "in hindsight," mystified me. It cannot be

code, but it is not English. What he means is "looking back," or, more starchy, "in the light of my present knowledge." You cannot say "in hindsight," any more than you can say "in foresight." For fun, I looked the noun up in the big *Oxford English Dictionary*. The original sense was the backsight of a rifle, and the word was first used by Mayne Reid in 1851 in a work called *Scalp Hunting*: "When you squint through her hindsights." The second reference for the word, still in the primary sense, is Farmer's *Americanisms*, 1889. The mystery is cleared up. You can see John Mitchell squinting through the backsight of his rifle at the Watergate affair, putting a bead on that wild Indian, Colson, on Jeb Magruder. That peculiar expression (not used by any other witness) is his enigmatic signature, hence, after all, a kind of code. Will it find its way into the *OED*?

14   Of course if he liked that word so much, if the picture gave him such dour satisfaction, he could have said "through hindsight." His lazy mind did not think it out. In lighting on the wrong preposition, he was a typical American of today. The breakdown of our language, evident in the misuse, i.e., the misunderstanding of nouns and adjectives, is most grave, though perhaps not so conspicuous, in the handling of prepositions, those modest little connectives that hold the parts of a phrase or a sentence together. They are the joints of any language, what make it, literally, articulate. As you know from experience in learning a foreign language, they are the hardest part to get right. You may have a pretty good vocabulary and have mastered the verb forms, the subjunctive, even genders, but you are still horribly uncertain about "de" and "à," "en" and "dans," "zu" and "nach," "aus" and "auf." Whether to say "Je pense de vous," or "Je pense à vous" (sometimes an almost imperceptible difference), "zu Hause," "nach Hause," "zu Bett," "im Brett"? They cannot be learned by mastering general rules; memorizing sentences containing them may be helpful but is no sure guide to a new sentence; the application of logic is useless, for their peculiarity is to defy logic, to be capricious. If you are like me, you will never really get hold of them in all their aberrant motion; even if you have spoken the language for fifteen years, doubt remains.

15   This means that they are the quintessential feature of a language; unlike nouns, verbs, and adjectives, they cannot be exchanged against their opposite numbers in a second or third language. In short, they are stubbornly idiomatic, from *idios* ("one's own, private, peculiar"). Though I said, just now, that logic is useless to a foreigner who is seeking to master them, they do express the inner logic of a particular language—a logic that is, precisely, different from the alien logic one is uselessly trying to apply. They are a birthright.

16   It is obvious that America, with its doors so long open to new citizens, would have a hard time maintaining the purity of those little particles of speech. Yet in fact our prepositions held out quite valiantly throughout the nineteenth century and through the first decades of the twentieth. I would date the deterioration from the forties; at least I first became aware of it in 1945–46 when I went to teach in a college and discovered from my students' papers that many of those young people did not have any idea what preposition was called

for in a given circumstance. "Tolstoy in his progenitors and his disciples," one student wrote. To change "progenitors" to "predecessors" and "disciples" to "followers" only took a little practice in mind-reading—yes, the student agreed happily, that was what he had been trying to say, he guessed. But that "in"! Impossible to penetrate the thought process that had been working there. Some relation between Tolstoy and those who preceded him as well as those who followed him was adumbrated but remained inexpressible.

17 That prepositions point out relationships between members of a sentence is plain. In classical languages much of this work was done by declension of the noun. I have always liked the notion I came upon long ago in a Greek grammar that the declension was a visual thing for the Greeks. The noun was pictured as standing straight up (nominative), lying on its side (ablative), leaning (dative); I forget what the genitive position was. This innocent clarity of vision, an exercise of both the imaginative and the analytical faculties, has much to do with the beauty of Greek literature and also, I would guess, with the perspicuousness of Greek philosophy and Greek political thought. One thinks of Socrates: the fanciful stories and myths he invented, to lay bare, finally, a relation or sequence admitted by the hearer to be ineluctable. Also his idea that knowledge is an act of recovery from the storehouse of the mind; teaching was merely prompting the pupil to recognize something he had known all along, though he had not known he knew it, till Socrates showed him. The slave boy in the *Meno*. A thought, when fully grasped, should induce a feeling of recognition. This implies, of course, that our common universe, on close examination, makes sense, that there are connections, if only in the brain.

18 One reason for the loss of clarity in our current speaking and writing must be the fact that the classical languages are no longer taught in schools. In fact, the loss of control over prepositions—the articulate parts of speech—seems to have coincided with the disappearance of Latin as a "subject" in public high schools. Up through the war, at least in New England, in the mill towns (not just in Boston), Latin was still taught—Greek sometimes too—by vigorous unmarried old ladies. When they died or retired, it went. In New England, in former days, the teaching of Latin was considered indispensable to a truly civic education; it was thought to form democratic habits of mind. Whether it did or not, the dropping of it from the program of free universal education certainly deepened the chasm between classes. And whatever it did or did not do toward conserving democratic habits, Latin surely promoted clear, analytic thinking and helped us in our language to distinguish the relations between members of a sentence.

19 Some of this training in logic and economy has been delegated to mathematics. In the college I speak of, where I taught literature back in the mid-forties, many of my best students were math and physics majors. They had no particular gift for literature, but they knew how to follow a sequence of thought, and if I had asked it of them, they could probably have taken a sentence apart and put it back together. It was usually a relief to read their

papers. Unfortunately, today's readers and writers cannot all be math and physics majors.

20 The disappearance of classics is obviously not the only factor in the atrophying of the power to communicate. On the grade-school level, there used to be parsing and diagramming of sentences. I wonder whether that still exists, and very much doubt it. In my schools, we had to do it every day. Some who were bored by parsing did not mind diagramming. We also had to memorize poetry, but that too has gone, I suppose.

21 Yet if Latin is no longer given and English is not taught as rigorously as it once was, that is not enough to account for the dimensions of what has happened. The public was startled and shocked by the language-murder committed before television cameras during the Watergate hearings by White House and Cabinet functionaries with college degrees. It is true that the mixture of euphemism, circumlocution, and a kind of insolent barbarity of phrasing gave an insight into a new mentality that could take an ordinary citizen aback. But the grammar, the clichés? Where had the public been during the last few decades—in a cloister?—that it could have been troubled by "at that point in time"? It cannot have been paying attention to its own speech or its neighbor's. Most people sound like Jeb Magruder. Ninety percent of the letters I get from Americans—strangers, I mean—are at best half-literate. And these are from citizens who read books (that is why they are writing to me), from sub-editors working on magazines and in publisher's offices, from college professors who have drafted questionnaires, from agents who want to sign me up for lecture tours, who have an idea for a movie. If this sample of the population is a culture-conscious minority, what must the majority write like?

22 I have plenty of evidence that it was not always so. I have read logs kept by ship's captains describing the sea, the weather, the ports and islands visited. These old skippers were not Melvilles, but they could write clear and plain. Nor can I conclude that most of them had had advantages, a superior education. Maybe they had not even had parsing in their village schools. I have gone through a mass of papers found in a barrel in a Massachusetts house. The family were storekeepers, and many of the papers are commercial: inventories, records of the dollar they "gave" for a pig, what five bolts of calico cost this winter, what they paid the servant. But they also kept letters. A member of the family would go to New York on the steamboat and report back on the harbor, the streets, the dwellings, the inhabitants, the strangers he met in the boarding-house, the sermons he heard preached. In good sober English, neat legible handwriting, and with a certain power of description, especially where the sermons were concerned. I have read my great-great-uncle's journal, which he started when he was a student at Dartmouth College before the Civil War and continued into his old age, out in the Middle West, where he went into the real-estate business. He was certainly not an interesting man; in his youth he went through a religious period that brought on paroxysms of conventional feelings; he too was a great church-attender and carefully wrote down a description of each preacher—height, estimated weight, complexion, voice—a

detailed account of the sermon and his own responses to it. When old, he was interested mainly in figures—the temperature outside, snow measurement, wind velocity, his wife's weight, which he recorded in the journal once a week. Yet, except for an occasional spelling lapse (he was a college drop-out), the journal is written in very acceptable, if colorless English. No clichés; he was a cliché himself, you could say, but his mild pen gave no offense. Today, one of his descendants cannot write a letter to the telephone company asking for service to be suspended without tying himself into knots so convolute that it would take a Houdini to arrange his escape from the opening clause.

23   Now it is possible that this breakdown in communication will soon be felt throughout the world. The Americans may only have pioneered it, as they have done with computers, the electrified kitchen, and pollution. If it is an effect of modern civilization which is being noticed first in America, then the causes must be larger than any merely local and parochial phenomena, such as the American character with its tendency to pomposity, the dropping of Latin, the permissive approach to the teaching of English. Indeed, those last may be more effects than causes of a world-wide revolution that will end in the dethronement or abdication of the word.

24   That of course is the gospel Marshall McLuhan has been preaching, although he speaks of the obsolescence of print rather than of the word itself. But if print is condemned, the word, it seems to me, will not survive long. It would be easier to reinstitute Latin in the schools and have everybody parsing and diagraming than to revert to an archaic age where words were carried by chant and gesture. Whatever can be said in favor of television as a "warm" or "hot" medium, it cannot reproduce the conditions of the Homeric world in your living-room. It cannot act as a preserver and transmitter of meaning. Far more than print, it lacks memory, and memory, of course, was a highly developed faculty in pre-literate civilizations, almost like an extra organ of the body. It still is among primitive peoples. Contemporary man's memory is not improving now that he looks at TV in the evening instead of reading a book or the newspaper. It is getting worse, and television itself is partly responsible for that. Not just the distraction caused by the intrusion of the commercials but also the flickering of the image, the mechanical failure obliging you to turn the dial, the necessity of concentrating on a small square area—all this makes nearly anything seen on television far more unmemorable than something seen on a movie screen, in a darkened house, surrounded by the silent presences of other movie-goers. And if certain pictures first seen on TV retain their peculiar ghostly black-and-white vividness, that is because usually you have seen them afterwards in the newspaper: Kent State, the shooting of Oswald. Nor will tape-recorders insure permanence; in the public domain we are seeing that demonstrated. Future generations may develop an aural memory, but the very popularity of taping today shows that modern people do *not* remember what they hear, and feel the need to have it played back. The same, in the visual field, can be said of the camera; few tourists today remember what they see.

25   The decay of language must be part of a whole syndrome in which formerly healthy human faculties—speech, sight, hearing, taste, locomotion, even touch—have been to some degree vitiated by technological advance. This is more evident with the eye, the ear, the feet, the tongue as an organ of taste, the fingers—who but a professional can feel a stone, a piece of material, or tell leather from plastic? Smell seems to be an exception; this sense may have *developed* with modern civilization, despite air pollution. In the Middle Ages people were less sensitive to bad smells, I think; nowadays Americans profess to have very delicate nostrils, which are offended, when abroad, by the stench of bad drains, Venetian canals, B.O. And the recent work of Saul Bellow shows the primacy he accords to his nose—what Mr. Sammler has against women, more than the way they talk, is the way they smell.

26   With speech, though, it is not clear how or why machines should have affected it; we have not yet invented a machine that will do our talking for us. And as for writing, have the typewriter, the ball-point, the felt pen really done more than lame our handwriting? True, thanks to the telephone, ordinary people write less than they did and those who write—or dictate—are mainly located in offices. Hence the householder, obliged to write a letter, copies the language of the business communications he receives or that of the social column of his local paper: "I attended a function," "I was present at the interment." Lack of practice in writing probably has as a side-effect an impairment or loss of control of speech.

27   Yet there must be something beyond that. I would guess that our incompetence with words had to do with consciousness-lowering. A reduced consciousness of what is happening, of sights and sounds and textures, is first of all imposed on us by present-day conditions: driving in a car you see less than when you walk; living in a city, in an air-conditioned apartment, you hear less than your ancestors did—no cock's crow, bird song, rustling of leaves, roar of waterfall. The chief noises you hear are sirens and the refrigerator. But aside from these deprivations (felt as such if felt at all) there are sights and noises you *will* not to see or hear, sensations you *will* not to notice—TV commercials, crowding, ugly bodies, ugly clothes, traffic jams, your neighbor's rock or his classical music. You simply turn them off, and this soon becomes an automatic matter. Your switch is always in the down position. If you want to change that, you find you have to sign up for consciousness-raising sessions or turn on with drugs.

28   But language is a consciousness-raiser. The problem there is that the power of using and understanding language, like all power, carries responsibilities with it. You consent to having it or you don't. And most people today would rather not have it. You can't exactly blame them. If they agreed to use and understand language clearly, this would only exacerbate all those aches and pains of contemporary civilization by putting them into *words*. It is true that this can give relief but not on a daily basis. Better the primal scream than intelligible words that lead nowhere. Better delegate language to experts and specialists, i.e., intellectuals.

29   Language on occasion may be a substitute for action (in mourning, for instance) but in the long run if it is not linked to action it becomes insupportable. "Don't just keep talking. *Do* something!" This explains, I think, the current dislike felt for intellectuals by the silent majority which Agnew knew how to play on. They are grudged the power of articulate speech which has been delegated to them in a world that has become unspeakable, where action is required, but none is forthcoming. Of course our intellectuals are some of the worst sinners against language; the fall-out in academic circles is asphyxiating, and some of this must be the result of specialization, the loss of touch with common everyday utterance implied by the delegation of powers. One of the amusing sidelights of Watergate was the discovery that Haldeman, Ehrlichman, Krogh, and a few others considered themselves an intellectual elite. Haldeman was proud of his language skills, and Ehrlichman showed an open intellectual contempt for the workhorse politicians of the Senate. If the public came to understand, from their jargon, that these were brains-trusters, this would help explain the absence of grief at their departure.

30   In any case, it is impossible to believe that the misuse and abuse of English on the part of ninety percent of the population are not to some extent voluntary. The numerous handbooks on correct usage, though they sell, I believe, have about as much "relevant impact" as Emily Post's or Amy Vanderbilt's etiquette manuals, which sell too. I think people must read all these books for entertainment.

31   George Orwell foresaw the dangers for a free society of cant, jargon, and euphemism. He was thinking mainly of official and party hypocrisy, which a courageous writer could unmask while pointing to the right way by his own steadfast plain-spoken example. What he missed, I think—perhaps he came too early—was the element of consent in the public. A general will to confusion. He analyzed the phenomenon of double-think but saw it as something inculcated in the enslaved masses by training and repetition. That is not happening to us—unless you count the indoctrination practiced by advertising—and exposure (Orwell's remedy) of verbal manipulation and malpractice has no effect. How many times has Nixon been exposed as a liar? And nobody cared, except the exposers. Nixon, for most, is just a fact, and words, his own or anybody else's, do not affect him. What has brought him down, if he is brought down, is a delightful turn of technology—the tapes.

32   Unlike Orwell, I do not have a remedy. A few men and women in public life who spoke and wrote clearly might help, since people are imitative or, as the current phrase goes, need "role models." But I think any real improvement would have to be effected by the popular will.

33   A final comment. It is curious that the sciences of linguistics and semiology—both highly abstruse—should have come into vogue just at this time, when the structures they so learnedly analyze—sentences—are a gruesome mass of rubble. On the professorial level, this corresponds to the in roads of "hopefully" as denoting the utter absence of hope.

Questions to Ponder

1. Why do you think people—particularly college freshmen—think big (four and five syllable) words are better than short, simple ones?
2. For what reasons might politicians wish to conceal the truth (reality) from their constituents, each other, and even themselves?
3. Do you agree with Mary McCarthy that public schools should return to teaching Latin? Defend your response.
4. What recommendations would you make to reverse the decline in language skill?

Writing Possibilities

1. Find an article in a newspaper, and using Mary McCarthy's handling of the article on Chile as a model, analyze the language used for what it says and does not say in an essay designed for your state's journalism organization.
2. Watch videotapes or read transcriptions of recent presidential debates. Take note of the language used by each candidate; then write a report to the League of Women Voters, presenting your findings and recommendations.
3. Compare recent presidential debates with transcriptions of the Lincoln-Douglas debates in 1858. Write an essay summarizing any differences you note in subject matter and language use.
4. Write a three-part argument about language featuring (a) a teenager speaking slang, (b) an older person speaking in pompous and wordy phrases, and (c) a middle-aged person speaking for plain speaking.

Notes on Punctuation
Lewis Thomas

In 1970 I had a telephone call from Franz Ingelfinger, the editor of the New England Journal of Medicine. Ingelfinger said he had read [a copy of speech I had made] and liked it, parts of it anyway, although he didn't agree with all of it, and he wanted me to try writing some essays for the Journal in the same general style. The terms were attractive enough: I would have to write one essay each month, due on Thursday of the third week, no longer than the space of one Journal page (around a thousand words), on any topic I liked. There would be no pay, but in return he would promise that nobody would be allowed to edit any essay. They would print them or not, but not change them.

I could not say no.... I had not written anything for fun since medical school and a couple of years thereafter, except for occasional light verse and once in a while a serious but not very clear or very good poem. Good bad verse was what I was pretty good at. The only other writing I'd done was scientific papers, around two hundred of them, composed in the relentlessly flat style required for absolute unambiguity in every word, hideous language as I read it today. The chance to break free of that kind of prose, and to try the essay form, raised my spirits, but at the same time worried me. I tried outlining some ideas for essays, making lists of items I'd like to cover in each piece, organizing my thoughts in orderly sequences, and wrote several dreadful essays which I could not bring myself to reread, and decided to give up being orderly. I changed the method to no method at all, picked out some suitable times late at night, usually on the weekend two days after I'd already passed the deadline, and wrote without outline or planning in advance, as fast as I could. This worked better, or at least was more fun, and I was able to get started....

I think writing essays, especially writing short essays, is kind of like [an experiment in the mind]. Although I usually think I know what I'm going to say, most of the time it doesn't happen that way at all. At some point I get misled down a garden path. I get surprised by an idea that I hadn't anticipated getting, which is a little like being in a laboratory.

Brief Warm-up Writing Exercises

1. Freewrite what you find hardest or easiest about punctuation.
2. Brainstorm two lists: (a) the punctuation marks you feel comfortable using and (b) the punctuation marks you are uncertain about using.
3. Freewrite a paragraph in which you correctly use all ten punctuation marks: period, colon, semicolon, comma, dash, question mark, exclamation point, quotation marks, ellipses, and parentheses.

---

1 ❖ There are no precise rules about punctuation (Fowler lays out some general advice (as best he can under the complex circumstances of English prose (he points out, for example, that we possess only four stops (the comma, the semicolon, the colon and the period (the question mark and exclamation point are not, strictly speaking, stops; they are indicators of tone (oddly enough, the Greeks employed the semicolon for their question mark (it produces a strange sensation to read a Greek sentence which is a straightforward question: Why weepest thou; (instead of Why weepest thou? (and, of course, there are parentheses (which are surely a kind of punctuation making this whole matter much more complicated by having to count up the left-handed parentheses in order to be sure of closing with the right number (but if the parentheses were left out, with nothing to work with but the stops, we would have considerably more flexibility in the deploying of layers of meaning than if we tried to separate all the clauses by physical barriers (and in the latter case, while we might have more precision and exactitude for our meaning, we would lose the essential flavor of language, which is its wonderful ambiguity)))))))))))).

2 The commas are the most useful and usable of all the stops. It is highly important to put them in place as you go along. If you try to come back after doing a paragraph and stick them in the various spots that tempt you you will discover that they tend to swarm like minnows into all sorts of crevices whose existence you hadn't realized and before you know it the whole long sentence becomes immobilized and lashed up squirming in commas. Better to use them sparingly, and with affection, precisely when the need for each one arises, nicely, by itself.

3 I have grown fond of semicolons in recent years. The semicolon tells you that there is still some question about the preceding full sentence; something needs to be added; it reminds you sometimes of the Greek usage. It is almost always a greater pleasure to come across a semicolon than a period. The period tells you that that is that; if you didn't get all the meaning you wanted or expected, anyway you got all the writer intended to parcel out and now you have to move along. But with a semicolon there

you get a pleasant little feeling of expectancy; there is more to come; read on; it will get clearer.

4   Colons are a lot less attractive, for several reasons: firstly, they give you the feeling of being rather ordered around, or at least having your nose pointed in a direction you might not be inclined to take if left to yourself, and, secondly, you suspect you're in for one of those sentences that will be labeling the points to be made: firstly, secondly and so forth, with the implication that you haven't sense enough to keep track of a sequence of notions without having them numbered. Also, many writers use this system loosely and incompletely, starting out with number one and number two as though counting off on their fingers but then going on and on without the succession of labels you've been led to expect, leaving you floundering about searching for the ninethly or seventeenthly that ought to be there but isn't.

5   Exclamation points are the most irritating of all. Look! they say, look at what I just said! How amazing is my thought! It is like being forced to watch someone else's small child jumping up and down crazily in the center of the living room shouting to attract attention. If a sentence really has something of importance to say, something quite remarkable, it doesn't need a mark to point it out. And if it is really, after all, a banal sentence needing more zing, the exclamation point simply emphasizes its banality!

6   Quotation marks should be used honestly and sparingly, when there is a genuine quotation at hand, and it is necessary to be very rigorous about the words enclosed by the marks. If something is to be quoted, the *exact* words must be used. If part of it must be left out because of space limitations, it is good manners to insert three dots to indicate the omission, but it is unethical to do this if it means connecting two thoughts which the original author did not intend to have tied together. Above all, quotation marks should not be used for ideas that you'd like to disown, things in the air so to speak. Nor should they be put in place around clichés; if you want to use a cliché you must take full responsibility for it yourself and not try to job it off on anon., or on society. The most objectionable misuse of quotation marks, but one which illustrates the dangers of misuse in ordinary prose, is seen in advertising, especially in advertisements for small restaurants, for example "just around the corner," or "a good place to eat." No single, identifiable, citable person ever really said, for the record, "just around the corner," much less "a good place to eat," least likely of all for restaurants of the type that use this type of prose.

7   The dash is a handy device, informal and essentially playful, telling you that you're about to take off on a different tack but still in some way connected with the present course—only you have to remember that the dash is there, and either put a second dash at the end of the notion to let the reader know that he's back on course, or else end the sentence, as here, with a period.

8   The greatest danger in punctuation is for poetry. Here it is necessary to be as economical and parsimonious with commas and periods as with the words themselves, and any marks that seem to carry their own subtle meanings, like

dashes and little rows of periods, even semicolons and question marks, should be left out altogether rather than inserted to clog up the thing with ambiguity. A single exclamation point in a poem, no matter what else the poem has to say, is enough to destroy the whole work.

9   The things I like best in T. S. Eliot's poetry, especially in the *Four Quartets,* are the semicolons. You cannot hear them, but they are there, laying out the connections between the images and the ideas. Sometimes you get a glimpse of a semicolon coming, a few lines farther on, and it is like climbing a steep path through woods and seeing a wooden bench just at a bend in the road ahead, a place where you can expect to sit for a moment, catching your breath.

10 Commas can't do this sort of thing; they can only tell you how the different parts of a complicated thought are to be fitted together, but you can't sit, not even take a breath, just because of a comma. ❖

Questions to Ponder

1. How does Lewis Thomas structure this essay?
2. What is his approach to each paragraph? What does Thomas gain by this approach?
3. Do you agree or disagree with Lewis Thomas's comments on each punctuation mark? If you disagree, which marks do you use differently—and why?
4. Do you think punctuation usage changes over time, just as language does? What marks might be likely to change, and what might these changes be?

Writing Possibilities

1. Write about the punctuation marks as if they were traffic signs for writing: a stop sign for the period, red flashing light for the comma, and so on.
2. Using Lewis Thomas's essay as a model, try to write a sentence or paragraph on each punctuation mark, making your sentences themselves exemplify proper use of the mark. You might call it "Further Notes on Punctuation" or "Personal Notes on Punctuation."
3. Do research on how punctuation in the English language has changed over the years, and write a light essay or a serious report presenting your findings.
4. Interview your teachers about what they find to be the most common punctuation errors students make. Then ask your fellow students the same question. Write a letter to your state's English journal sharing your findings and suggesting possible ways to help writers overcome these errors.

Concerning Footnotes

Carol Kammen

"Concerning Footnotes" was written as one of a series of essays about the ethics and mechanics of researching, writing, and presenting local history. My concern is that the information passed along within a community needs to be reliable and that other people who might be interested in a subject be able to find their way to the original source. Local history defines what a community's past has been and how the present has been created. If the information in a town's history is not accurate, a false picture can easily circulate, and once something has become part of the public memory, it is difficult to make corrections.

In addition, much of the source material that local historians use is in private hands. I hope that by encouraging local historians to state the locations of their sources, even if it means noting that the letters or diaries belong to a neighbor and are kept in the dresser drawer, it will make tracing that material at a later date somewhat easier. My other hope is that people who own documentary materials, either through family inheritance or by happenstance, will realize the value of those items to historians and to the community and will consider donating original documents to a nearby archive or historical society.

There is a general bias against footnotes, as indicated by the initial anecdote. Many local historians believe footnotes (or parenthetical documentation) are only necessary for professional historians—or for students. I know that some local historians believe footnotes destroy the flow of local history and that their presence signals to the reading public that the work is pedantic or dull. Also, I did have the conversation I recount in which I was told that footnotes were too expensive to add to a work of local history. This latter comment is generally no longer true because of computer technology that allows writers to create endnotes with no trouble at all, and footnotes with ease.

The problem I had in writing this essay is that the "nitty-gritty" of footnoting is not very interesting; that is, it is not something many people really want to read or think about.

Brief Warm-up Writing Exercises

1. Brainstorm a list of types of information that generally require parenthetical documentation or footnotes.
2. Freewrite on the uses that footnotes or parenthetical documentation serve.
3. Make a list of kinds of writing that generally do *not* use footnotes or parenthetical documentation.

---

1   A lovely but stubborn man I once knew insisted that the pamphlet we were working on should have no footnotes. "Those little numbers," he sputtered, "only confuse people and put off the average reader. They get in the way." I protested but I was rather young at the time and he was eighty. He prevailed and there were no footnotes. I have felt apologetic about that publication ever since. Footnotes should not instill guilt and they certainly should not induce anxiety, yet they often create both feelings.

2   Footnotes are like the rungs of a ladder; each one allows the reader to move along with a writer's progress through the source material and the secondary literature. Footnotes are a road map showing where a historian has been: they are a trust left to those who come after us that they may understand how we know what we write and why we conclude that which we conclude. Footnotes are our badge of honesty, one generation to the next. Without footnotes, history is more an art form: that is, history appears to be the creation of one individual mind. With footnotes, the historian is accountable to the past and to the future and history becomes a responsible discipline that can be replicated, that is honest, that can be a shared human experience.

3   A good footnote tells the reader who first said a thing, on what piece of evidence or on which of several pieces of information an opinion has been based, and what gives a writer the authority to move an argument forward from one point to another. A good footnote contains specific information showing how a statement can be made, and where evidence can be found. It should tell in what letter, located in which collection, in what archive we can find a quote. It should tell in whose book, with what title, published when and where and on what page we can discover a similar or dissimilar argument. A footnote should allow us to unpeel a work of local history to see how the layers were built up, thereby creating the whole.

4   Footnotes for works of local history can be written in many styles; simplicity should be the rule for us. When quoting a letter written by Calista Hall, a historian simply states the following:

Calista Hall to Pliny Hall, 16 August 1849, in the Smelzer Collection, Department of Manuscripts and University Archives, Cornell University, Ithaca, New York.

When crediting something from a diary, the notation should read:

Belle Cowdry Diary, 6 February 1857, page 28, DeWitt Historical Society of Tompkins County, Ithaca, New York.

These citations show that the material quoted from, or the material that gives you a reason to assert something, can be found in these places. Readers interested in seeing the quotation in its original context or collateral information can write or visit these repositories and judge for themselves how the original information bolsters that which was footnoted.

5 The use of a footnote requires some judgment. Where there are a group of references to be footnoted in one paragraph, they may be clustered together into one note, the number appearing at the end of the block of material in the text. All other footnotes follow these basic forms:

Calista Hall, letter of 16 August 1849, quoted in Carl N. Degler, *At Odds: Women and the Family in America from the Revolution to the Present* (Oxford and New York: Oxford University Press, 1980), 211.

and

Carol Kammen, ed., "The Letters of Calista Hall," *New York History* 43 (April 1982): 209–234.

In each case, the footnote tells us where the quotation or the information can be found.

6 Other footnotes expand upon these basic formulas by adding the number of the volume when quoting something that has appeared in a series, or adding other useful information that will help the reader locate the source. If Calista Hall's letters were still in private hands, as is much of the material that local historians use, the footnote would state:

Calista Hall to Pliny Hall, 16 August 1849, letter in private collection of Mrs. Nellie Smelzer of Lansing, New York.

The reader is told to the best of our ability where we found the information used. If we consulted church records, we might note where in the church the records were kept:

Minutes of the Ladies Aid Society, Federate Church, Brooktondale, New York; records kept in the bottom drawer of the file in the pastor's study.

Records in private hands require us to be as specific as possible about their location at the time the materials were consulted.

7 There is one particular footnoting problem that most local historians face, and this concerns statements found in our town and county histories. Those

books are rarely footnoted themselves, and yet they contain a great deal of material upon which local historians depend. To footnote directly to a county history, however, is to lead the reader nowhere in particular, for the writers (or compilers, as many were called) of county histories do not tell us how they knew what they wrote down. To question their source of information is not to question their veracity, but footnoting directly to one of those tomes is not good enough.

8 My personal rule is to use material in a county history only when I have other source material that corroborates that information. For example, in the "Four County History," formally entitled the *History of Tioga, Chemung, Tompkins, and Schuyler Counties, New York,* published in Philadelphia in 1879, there is mention of slaves having been held in Tompkins County prior to the end of slavery in New York state in 1827. In an article, I would never simply cite the "Four County History" as my source of knowledge about slavery but would note that evidence of slavery can be found in census compilations, where Tompkins County is credited with having ten slaves in 1820 and none thereafter. So my footnote would include a citation to the published census figures. Such a footnote could read something like this:

"Census of the County of Tompkins," *Ithaca Republican Chronicle,* 21 February 1821, p. 3; "Village of Ithaca," *American Journal* (Ithaca, New York), 24 September 1823, p. 3; "Census of Ithaca," *The Ithaca Journal,* 5 January 1825, p. 3; and *Census for the State of New York* (Albany, 1855), ix.

It may be noted that with primary material leading the reader directly to the sources, the inclusion of the county history, where the mention of slavery is vague at best, is unnecessary.

9 What of a statement in an unfootnoted town or county history that cannot be verified? If it is something that I want or need to use, I would then state in the footnote where the information came from and that I have been unable to verify it elsewhere, but that even while I cannot confirm it, I have no reason to doubt it, either. Then I use the material as I would any other and don't worry about it.

10 What should be footnoted? There is no firm rule that covers every case. Instead there are any number of situations that require us to give credit. When someone is quoted directly, a footnote is needed. When an author is quoted indirectly or his or her material is drawn upon, credit is needed. When a fact is mentioned that is otherwise unknown or beyond common knowledge, a footnote to the source is needed. For example, it is generally known that once there were slaves within my county, and this fact need not demand a citation. When I categorically state that there were ten slaves, however, it is incumbent upon me to tell the reader why I used the number ten rather than twelve or eight. My sources directed me to state ten, and I did so with conviction. I therefore credit my sources.

11 A footnote is needed any time an argument is developed that coincides

with an argument or disagrees with a contention of another author who has written on a particular subject.

12   We need a footnote when something written is a revision of previously held ideas. Any time an author advances knowledge beyond that which was previously known, a footnote is needed. When we deviate from that which has been previously stated, we should explain to our readers what evidence induces us to think otherwise.

13   If material used is gathered from an individual in an oral interview, that person should be noted or credited in a footnote. An interview with an old-time resident of the area about a flood or education or family history might yield useful information. An appropriate footnote will tell who told you the information used, when you were told, and something about the authority of that individual. My footnote for a 1935 flood could take one of these forms:

Conversation, 16 April 1984, with Sally Smith, who was forced from her home by the 1935 flood.

or

Interview with Paul Smith, 1935 flood survivor, 16 April 1984.

or

Casual conversation with Paul Smith regarding the 1935 flood, 16 April 1984.

This last form indicates that the information gained from Smith was not the result of a planned interview but was more informal in nature—in this case, I talked with Smith while I was standing in line at the grocery store.

14   Footnotes are important, and they are relatively simple to write. They document things other people have said, borrowed ideas, and items that have caused you to think differently. Footnotes should lead to sources, and they also show the transmission of an idea. They lead, sometimes, to more information on a subject. They do not need to scare a reader or a writer.

15   "But what," a woman asked me not long ago, "do we do when we cannot footnote our material?" She added that in some instances footnotes would be expensive to add to a text, and in other instances they would be inappropriate to add. Footnotes cost extra if they are placed at the bottom of the page, but as end notes following a chapter or at the end of a book they add little to the overall cost. "When are they inappropriate?" I asked. The woman replied: "In a church bulletin that might carry a historical announcement, in a program, perhaps, or souvenir pieces from a community. What then should be done?"

16   It seems to me that there are two solutions to this problem. The first is to take one copy of the text, whatever it might be, annotate it with references, and place this special copy in the nearest archive. This annotation can be done on

17 The second solution is what I call the "sneaky" footnote. This is a way of footnoting material that usually does not receive such careful treatment. A writer of local history in the public press is a person who is faced with the problem of giving credit in a medium where editors and others would frown upon the insertion of a real footnote. In such a case, the sneaky footnote is better than nothing. This is a footnote, or as much of a footnote as possible, that is written directly into the text. It usually does little for the graceful flow of the article, but it does manage to give credit where credit is due, and it directs readers to the appropriate source.

18 "As Calista Hall wrote to her husband, on August 16, 1849, in a letter donated by Nellie Smelzer to the Cornell Archives" is one way to begin a statement and give credit at the same time. Another way is to introduce a fact by noting that it "appears in the section on the Town of Caroline in the 'Four County History' " and still another is to note that historian Carl Degler quotes Calista Hall in his 1980 book *At Odds*. In each case, there is enough information to get an interested reader to the right archive, where the index of holdings will lead to the letter in question, or to the author's name and book title. In each case, there is enough information to be helpful but not too much apparatus to put off an editor, who might regard footnotes as pedantic and antithetical to his or her idea of what should appear in a newspaper.

19 It is particularly important that local historians be conscientious about footnotes, because often the materials with which we deal are outside common repositories and therefore unknown to others. Our footnotes do more than reveal our sources; through them we share knowledge of local materials with others engaged in similar or related studies.

20 By writing accurate footnotes, by annotating special copies of publications that are not to be footnoted, by inserting a sneaky footnote into material not generally dealt with in this way, we local historians keep faith with those on whom we leaned—and from whom we learned—and we keep faith with those who come after, offering our footnotes as a token of openness and honesty, one generation to another. Our responsibility, I believe, is to "leave footnotes unto others as we would have footnotes left unto us." If this sounds like a hard and fast rule, so be it. Consider how much easier our task would be today if the historians who preceded us had followed that rule. I can think of no more important dictum for local historians to follow. It keeps us honest, and it is our link of trust with the future. "Leave footnotes unto others as we would have footnotes left unto us." ❖

Questions to Ponder

1. What myths or misconceptions might arise about a town's history? How could such myths be discredited—or corrected? What role would sources play in such correction?

2. To which disciplines besides history do Carol Kammen's words "Concerning Footnotes" also apply?
3. When you use parenthetical documentation to acknowledge your sources, for what other uses might you use footnotes?
4. Why does Carol Kammen's opening anecdote make an effective way to introduce her subject? What other openings might she have employed?

Writing Possibilities

1. Using Carol Kammen's essay as a model, write an essay for students in your major, focusing on the special documentation problems they may encounter.
2. Write an "advisory warning" to first-year college students, reminding them of information they should be sure to take down when doing their research, and pitfalls to avoid when using parenthetical documentation or footnotes.
3. Choose a dramatic moment in your town's history, and read about it in your local archives. (*Hint:* Read histories, newspaper accounts, official accounts, reports, letters—anything you can find, including information from interviews.) Share your findings in a piece for your local historical society, faithfully documenting your sources.

Student Essay
LIPSTICK KISSES

Jennifer C. Miller

I think the best way to come up with ideas is to try freewriting. Freewriting, if you haven't already tried it, is simply writing down whatever comes to your mind as you think of it. Your subconscious seems to work in mysterious ways, so all the wonderful ideas that are percolating while you were busy doing other things can finally come out.

Another good time to come up with new ideas is just when you are drifting off to sleep or just when you are waking up. Again, your mind is finally freed from all the restraints a busy day puts on it.

I freewrote the first draft of "Lipstick Kisses." The piece became stronger as a result of ideas from my writing group. It was here that someone suggested the idea of using italics to separate visually the two voices I was using in this essay: my four-year-old voice and my current (more mature) viewpoint as a college student. My writing group also challenged my first ending. Group members said it seemed too "easy" and asked if I could really stomach Doritos, or horses. I knew they were right. I pushed myself to give a deeper and more truthful conclusion.

Brief Warm-up Writing Exercises

1. Freewrite about your first memories of your mother, your father, or an important family member.
2. Brainstorm a list of words, smells, sights, sounds, or occurrences in the present that can evoke strong memories from your past.
3. Describe a childhood fear, habit, or anxiety that you have overcome—or are trying to overcome.

DRAFT

1   My earliest memory is of my father and me lying in the living room on a blanket where we had fallen asleep the night before. There's a bag of Doritos a few feet from our heads, and we eat those for breakfast. Mom is gone, at work, I suppose. We laugh conspiratorially. Mom would never allow Doritos for breakfast.

2   The rest of my first five years is a murky swamp of muddied images and tumultuous emotions. I remember pressing lipstick kisses on Daddy's roughly bearded cheek, and I remember being called "kiddo." And the presents he gave me . . . there was the turquoise Indian necklace one Christmas, and the plastic, amazingly lifelike replicas of all different kinds of horses for one birthday. That was the one thing I knew my daddy could never forget about me—we both had a fierce passion for horses.

3   Grandma and Grampa owned about a half-dozen half-wild all-white horses and one old, gentle brown mare for the grandkids to ride. Daddy always rode the wildest of the white stallions. He could handle them,

make them obey. Then, I thought my daddy could do anything. I loved him with all my heart, I adored him, and I believed in him. I hated anyone who didn't love my daddy as much as I did. That included my mom.

4   I hated my mom when she left my daddy. Couldn't she see that he was everything? And I couldn't even stay with Daddy; I had to go with her. Just when I thought things couldn't possibly get any worse, my little sister was born. Great. Now I had to share.

5   The most important event in my life happened when I was four and my parents were divorced. The strange thing is, I never realized that until a few short months ago. When my mother left my father, I didn't really understand what was going on; all I knew was that she wouldn't let me see my daddy very much any more. But then Mom remarried, my step-father adopted us, and I never saw Daddy again.

6   I thought, until a few months ago, that the divorce never really had much of an impact on my life. I figured that the media exaggerated case studies concerning children of divorced parents, because I certainly had never felt "affected." As far as I was concerned, I had lucked out that I had a great new dad in my step-father, and I was a normal, well-adjusted adult. Now I realize that a divorce can never be forgotten.

7   The event that churned up a million old memories was one simple question. My boyfriend asked me to marry him. As soon as those words fell from his lips, a chilling fear gripped my heart. What happened to all the skyrockets and fireworks that were supposed to go off when a girl gets proposed to by her one and only? Instead of feeling like singing, I felt like running away to the darkest, loneliest place in the world, curling up and crying.

8   After days of soul-searching, I came tot he realization that I was scared to death of real flesh-and-blood commitment. I was afraid my boyfriend would desert me, I was afraid I would leave my boyfriend, and I was afraid that one or the both of us would turn into a monster. Each night, after putting all these thoughts in the back of my mind for the day, terrifying images of daddy would race through my mind. The

tall, good-looking Air Force officer transformed into a gaunt, shifty-eyed drug addict of my nightmares.

9   I saw Daddy, cattleprod in hand, whipping the brown mare until she reared again and again, panic-stricken and pained. Her eyes were huge and rolling; his eyes were laughing and glittering, hard. I remember now the arguments that I had blocked out, stuffing my head under the pillow or working in my dot-to-dot book, all the while humming. "Why can't you take her just a couple of days she wants to see you child support go to court this can't continue" and on and on and on. Now I remembered the rejection I felt, knowing that my daddy didn't want to see me. Now he had his new wife, Ruby, and he had a new little girl, Tena. I wondered if she got to wear her mommy's lipstick, too. I still bet she couldn't leave as good of kisses as I could

10 While my mother remarried and I had a relatively happy childhood, I realize now that the divorce has affected my life so strongly that I will probably never completely escape its effects. Even now, my greatest fear is rejection and abandonment. To prevent people from leaving me, I become what I think they want me to be. If a person expects me to be a mature, intelligent student, then that's who I am. If the guy sitting next to me in class wants me to be a dizzy chick, then that's who I am. I can't show anger, because if I get angry at someone, they may not want to be my friend any longer. My parents want me to achieve, so I strive to do well in my studies and take part in many extracurricular activities. I have to get a good job someday, you know.

11 While being a very congenial person thirty-six hours a day makes you a lot of fun acquaintances and even a few pretty good friends, it doesn't make up for the resentment that builds inside. The pressure I feel to excel and conform on the outside doesn't compare to the pressure to be loved from the inside. It's a very slow process, learning to trust in people all over gain. Even though I know my boyfriend would do absolutely anything in the world for me, a trickle of fear sometimes runs through the back of my mind. Just an innocent word from him, yet a word which reminds me of my father, will click with an

unfortunate (unhappy?) memory. And the horses . . . well, I guess they've lost their magic.

12   But I have to remember not to get caught up in the tragedies of the past. As I am discovering, it's important to deal with how they affect my life today, but my fears can't rule my every thought and action. I have to move forward. And speaking of moving forward, it's time to end this. I hear a bag of Doritos calling my name.

◆ ───────────────────────────────

1   *My earliest memory is of my father and me lying in the living room on a blanket where we had fallen asleep the night before. There's a bag of Doritos a few feet from our heads, and we eat those for breakfast. Mom is gone, at work, I suppose. We laugh conspiratorially. Mom would never allow Doritos for breakfast.*

2   *The rest of my first five years is a murky swamp of muddled images and tumultuous emotions. I remember pressing lipstick kisses on Daddy's roughly bearded cheek, and I remember being called "kiddo." And the presents he gave me . . . there was the turquoise Indian necklace one Christmas, and the plastic, amazingly lifelike replicas of all different kinds of horses for one birthday. That was the one thing I knew my daddy could never forget about me—we both had a fierce passion for horses.*

3   *Grandma and Grampa owned four half-wild all-white horses and one old, gentle brown mare for the grandkids to ride. Daddy always rode the wildest of the white horses. He could handle them, make them obey. Then, I thought my daddy could do anything. I loved him with all my heart. I adored him, and I believed in him. I hated anyone who didn't love my daddy as much as I did. That included my mom.*

4   *I hated my mom when she left my daddy. Couldn't she see that he was everything? And I couldn't even stay with Daddy; I had to go with her. Just when I thought things couldn't possibly get any worse, my little sister was born. Great. Now I had to share.*

5   The most important event in my life happened when I was four and my parents were divorced. The strange thing is, I never realized that until a few short months ago. When my mother left my father, I didn't really understand what was going on; all I knew was that she wouldn't let me see my daddy very much any more. But then Mom remarried, my stepfather adopted us, and I never saw Daddy again.

6   I thought, until a few months ago, that the divorce never really had much of an impact on my life. I assumed that the media exaggerated case studies concerning children of divorced parents, because I certainly had never felt "affected." As far as I was concerned, I had lucked out that I had a great new dad in my stepfather, and I was a normal, well-adjusted adult. Now I realize that a divorce can never be forgotten.

7 The event that churned up a million old memories was one simple question. My boyfriend asked me to marry him. As soon as those words fell from his lips, fear gripped my heart. What happened to all the skyrockets and fireworks that were supposed to go off when a girl gets proposed to by her one and only? Instead of feeling like singing, I felt like running away to the darkest, loneliest place in the world, curling up and crying.

8 After days of soul-searching, I came to the realization that I was scared to death of real flesh-and-blood commitment. I was afraid my boyfriend would abandon me or I would leave my boyfriend, and I was afraid that one or the both of us would turn into a monster. Each night, after putting all these thoughts in the back of my mind for the day, terrifying images of Daddy would race through my mind. The tall, good-looking Air Force officer transformed into the gaunt, shifty-eyed drug addict of my nightmares.

9 I saw Daddy, cattleprod in hand, whipping the brown mare until she reared again and again, panic-stricken and pained. Her eyes were huge and rolling; his eyes were laughing and glittering, hard. I remember now the arguments that I had blocked out, stuffing my head under the pillow or working in my dot-to-dot book, all the while humming. "Why can't you take her just a couple of days she wants to see you child support go to court this can't continue" and on and on and on. Now I remembered the rejection I felt, knowing that my daddy didn't want to see me. Now he had his new wife, Ruby, and he had a new little girl, Tena. I wondered if she got to wear her mommy's lipstick, too. I still bet she couldn't leave as good kisses as I could.

10 Even though my mother remarried and I had a relatively happy childhood, I realize now that the divorce has affected my life so strongly that I will probably never completely escape its effects. Even now, my greatest fear is rejection and abandonment. To prevent people from leaving me as my daddy did, I become what I think they want me to be. If my professor expects me to be a mature, intelligent student, then that's who I am. If the guy sitting next to me in class wants me to be a dizzy chick, then that's who I am. I can't show anger, because if I get angry at someone, they may not want to be my friend any longer. My parents want me to achieve, so I strive to do well in my studies and take part in many extracurricular activities. I have to get a good job someday, you know.

11 While being a very congenial person thirty-six hours a day makes you a lot of fun acquaintances and even a few pretty good friends, it doesn't make up for the resentment that builds inside. The pressure I feel to excel and conform on the outside doesn't compare to the urgent need to be loved I feel inside. It's a very slow process, learning to trust in people all over again. Even though I know my boyfriend would do absolutely anything in the world for me, a trickle of fear sometimes runs through the back of my mind. Just an innocent word from him, yet a word which reminds me of my father, will click with an unfortunate memory. And the horses . . . well, I guess they've lost their magic.

12 But I have to remember not to get caught up in the tragedies of the past.

As I am discovering, it's important to deal with how they affect my life today, and my fears can't rule my every thought and action. I have to move forward. That doesn't mean that I will ever be able to accept what my father became or what he did to our family, but I know that I can overcome the effects the divorce had on me. I've finally allowed another man to get as close to me as my father did. It is still difficult to open my heart completely to just anyone, but with my fiancé, I have. I'm still working on that, too. Little by little, I'm mastering those feelings that have limited me for so long. ❖

Questions to Ponder

1. Where do you hear distinctive voices in this essay?
2. Do you find the use of italics effective? What do these italicized sections represent?
3. How has Jennifer Miller created a vivid portrait of her father? Of herself at two different ages? How do you see each of these people?
4. Which ending of "Lipstick Kisses" do you prefer? Why?
5. Why is "Lipstick Kisses" an appropriate and eye-catching title for this essay?

Writing Possibilities

1. Using Jennifer Miller's essay as a model, write of your first childhood memories of a loved one in one voice, followed by mature reflection on the experience in another one.
2. Do research into the effect of divorce on children, and write an objective report sharing your finding with parents.
3. Following extensive reading on the effect of divorce on children or teenagers, write a "How to Cope with Your Parents' Divorce" manual, offering the best concrete advice you can muster.
4. Describe an experience in the present; then step back, and write how this experience triggers memories of the past. (*Hint:* Try italics to indicate the separate sections.)

Short Story
MATERIAL
Alice Munro

[I write my first drafts in longhand and struggle to develop my stories from] the horrible first draft. . . . And then I just revise and revise and revise. . . .

What is important to me about the story is not what happens. . . . It's like a view of reality—a kind of reality that I can go into for a while, and I know right away if I can go into it [further] or not. Then, once I'm into it, I'll find out what happens. It's getting into it that's important, not caring what happens. A story is a spell, rather than a narrative. . . .

I no longer feel attracted to the well-made novel. I want to write the story that will zero in and give you intense, but not connected, moments of experience. I guess that's the way I see life. People remake themselves bit by bit and do things they don't understand. The novel has to have a coherence which I don't see any more in the lives around me.

Brief Warm-up Writing Exercises

1. Brainstorm a list of characteristics commonly associated with writers.
2. Now freewrite what you think writers are *really* like.
3. Freewrite your answer to this question: What is a writer's material?

1 ❖ I don't keep up with Hugo's writing. Sometimes I see his name, in the library, on the cover of some literary journal that I don't open—I haven't opened a literary journal in a dozen years, praise God. Or I read in the paper or see on a poster—this would be in the library, too, or in a bookstore—an announcement of a panel discussion at the University, with Hugo flown in to discuss the state of the novel today, or the contemporary short story, or the new nationalism in our literature. Then I think, will people really go, will people who could be swimming or drinking or going for a walk really take

themselves out to the campus to find the room and sit in rows listening to those vain quarrelsome men? Bloated, opinionated, untidy men, that is how I see them, cosseted by the academic life, the literary life, by women. People will go to hear them say that such and such a writer is not worth reading any more, and that some writer must be read; to hear them dismiss and glorify and argue and chuckle and shock. People, I say, but I mean women, middle-aged women like me, alert and trembling, hoping to ask intelligent questions and not be ridiculous; soft-haired young girls awash in adoration, hoping to lock eyes with one of the men on the platform. Girls, and women too, fall in love with such men, they imagine there is power in them.

2   The wives of the men on the platform are not in that audience. They are buying groceries or cleaning up messes or having a drink. Their lives are concerned with food and mess and houses and cars and money. They have to remember to get the snow tires on and go to the bank and take back the beer bottles, because their husbands are such brilliant, such talented incapable men, who must be looked after for the sake of the words that will come from them. The women in the audience are married to engineers or doctors or businessmen. I know them, they are my friends. Some of them have turned to literature frivolously, it is true, but most come shyly, and with enormous transitory hope. They absorb the contempt of the men on the platform as if they deserved it; they half-believe they do deserve it, because of their houses and expensive shoes, and their husbands who read Arthur Hailey.

3   I am married to an engineer myself. His name is Gabriel, but he prefers the name Gabe. In this country he prefers the name Gabe. He was born in Romania, he lived there until the end of the war, when he was sixteen. He has forgotten how to speak Romanian. How can you forget, how can you forget the language of your childhood? I used to think he was pretending to forget, because the things he had seen and lived through when he spoke that language were too terrible to remember. He told me this was not so. He told me his experience of the war was not so bad. He described the holiday uproar at school when the air raid sirens sounded. I did not quite believe him. I required him to be an ambassador from bad times as well as distant countries. Then I thought he might not be Romanian at all, but an impostor.

4   This was before we were married, when he used to come and see me in the apartment on Clark Road where I lived with my little daughter, Clea. Hugo's daughter too, of course, but he had to let go of her. Hugo had grants, he traveled, he married again and his wife had three children; he divorced and married again, and his next wife, who had been his student, had three more children, the first born to her while he was still living with his second wife. In such circumstances a man can't hang onto everything. Gabriel used to stay all night sometimes on the pull-out couch I had for a bed in this tiny, shabby apartment; and I would look at him sleeping and think that for all I knew he might be a German or a Russian or even of all things a Canadian faking a past and an accent to make himself interesting. He was mysterious to me. Long after he became my lover and after he became my husband he remained, remains,

mysterious to me. In spite of all the things I know about him, daily and physical things. His face curves out smoothly and his eyes, set shallowly in his head, curve out too under the smooth pink lids. The wrinkles he has are traced on top of this smoothness, this impenetrable surface; they are of no consequence. His body is substantial, calm. He used to be a fine, rather lazy-looking, skater. I cannot describe him without a familiar sense of capitulation. I cannot describe him. I could describe Hugo, if anybody asked me, in great detail—Hugo as he was eighteen, twenty years ago, crew-cut and skinny, with the bones of his body and even of his skull casually, precariously, joined and knitted together, so that there was something uncoordinated, unexpected about the shifting planes of his face as well as the movements, often dangerous, of his limbs. He's held together by nerves, a friend of mine at college said when I first brought him around, and it was true; after that I could almost see the fiery strings.

5   Gabriel told me when I first knew him that he enjoyed life. He did not say that he believed in enjoying it; he said that he did. I was embarrassed for him. I never believed people who said such things and anyway, I associated this statement with gross, self-advertising, secretly unpleasantly restless men. But it seems to be the truth. He is not curious. He is able to take pleasure and give off smiles and caresses and say softly, "Why do you worry about that? It is not a problem of yours." He has forgotten the language of his childhood. His lovemaking was strange to me at first, because it was lacking in desperation. He made love without emphasis, so to speak, with no memory of sin or hope of depravity. He does not watch himself. He will never write a poem about it, never, and indeed may have forgotten it in half an hour. Such men are commonplace, perhaps. It was only that I had not known any. I used to wonder if I would have fallen in love with him if his accent and his forgotten, nearly forgotten, past had been taken away; if he had been, say, an engineering student in my own year at college. I don't know, I can't tell. What holds anybody in a man or a woman may be something as flimsy as a Romanian accent or the calm curve of an eyelid, some half-fraudulent mystery.

6   No mystery of this sort about Hugo. I did not miss it, did not know about it, maybe would not have believed in it. I believed in something else, then. Not that I knew him, all the way through, but the part I knew was in my blood and from time to time would give me a poison rash. None of that with Gabriel, he does not disturb me, any more than he is disturbed himself.

7   It was Gabriel who found me Hugo's story. We were in a bookstore, and he came to me with a large, expensive paperback, a collection of short stories. There was Hugo's name on the cover. I wondered how Gabriel had found it, what he had been doing in the fiction section of the store anyway, he never reads fiction. I wondered if he sometimes went and looked for things by Hugo. He is interested in Hugo's career as he would be interested in the career of a magician or popular singer or politician with whom he had, through me, a plausible connection, a proof of reality. I think it is because he does such anonymous work himself, work intelligible only to his own kind. He is fas-

cinated by people who work daringly out in the public eye, without the protection of any special discipline—it must seem so, to an engineer—just trying to trust themselves, and elaborating their bag of tricks, and hoping to catch on.

8   "Buy it for Clea," he said.
9   "Isn't it a lot of money for a paperback?"
10 He smiled.
11 "There's your father's picture, your real father, and he has written this story you might like to read," I said to Clea, who was in the kitchen making toast. She is seventeen. Some days she eats toast and honey and peanut butter and Oreos and creamed cheese and chicken sandwiches and fried potatoes. If anybody comments on what she is eating or not eating, she may run upstairs and slam the door of her room.
12 "He looks overweight," said Clea and put the book down. "You always said he was skinny." Her interest in her father is all from the point of view of heredity, and what genes he might have passed on to herself. Did he have a bad complexion, did he have a high I.Q., did the women in his family have big breasts?
13 "He was when I knew him," I said. "How was I to know what had happened to him since?"
14 He looked, however, very much as I would have thought he would look by now. When I saw his name in the newspaper or on a poster I had pictured somebody much like this; I had foreseen the ways in which time and his life would have changed him. It did not surprise me that he had got fat but not bald, that he had let his hair grow wild and had grown a full, curly beard. Pouches under his eyes, a dragged-down look to the cheeks even when he is laughing. He is laughing, into the camera. His teeth have gone from bad to worse. He hated dentists, said his father died of a heart attack in the dentist's chair. A lie, like so much else, or at least an exaggeration. He used to smile crookedly for photographs to hide the right top incisor, dead since somebody at high school pushed him into a drinking fountain. Now he doesn't care, he laughs, he bares those rotting stumps. He looks, at the same time, woebegone and cheerful. A Rabelaisian writer. Checked wool shirt open at the top to show his undershirt, he didn't use to wear one. Do you wash, Hugo? Do you have bad breath, with those teeth? Do you call your girl students fond exasperated dirty names, are there phone calls from insulted parents, does the Dean or somebody have to explain that no harm is meant, that writers are not as other men are? Probably not, probably no one minds. Outrageous writers may bounce from one blessing to another nowadays, bewildered, as permissively reared children are said to be, by excess of approval.
15 I have no proof. I construct somebody from this one smudgy picture, I am content with such clichés. I have not the imagination or good will to proceed differently; and I have noticed anyway, everybody must have noticed as we go further into middle age, how shopworn and simple, really, are the disguises, the identities if you like, that people take up. In fiction, in Hugo's business,

such disguises would not do, but in life they are all we seem to want, all anybody can manage. Look at Hugo's picture, look at the undershirt, listen to what it says about him.

> Hugo Johnson was born and semi-educated in the bush, and in the mining and lumbering towns of Northern Ontario. He has worked as a lumberjack, beer-slinger, counterman, telephone lineman and sawmill foreman, and has been sporadically affiliated with various academic communities. He lives now most of the time on the side of a mountain above Vancouver, with his wife and six children.

16   The student wife, it seems, got stuck with all the children. What happened to Mary Frances, did she die, is she liberated, did he drive her crazy? But listen to the lies, the half-lies, the absurdities. *He lives on the side of a mountain above Vancouver.* It sounds as if he lives in a wilderness cabin, and all it means, I'm willing to bet, is that he lives in an ordinary comfortable house in North or West Vancouver, which now stretch far up the mountain. *He has been sporadically affiliated with various academic communities.* What does that mean? If it means he has taught for years, most of his adult life, at universities, that teaching at universities has been the only steady well-paid job he has ever had, why doesn't it say so? You would think he came out of the bush now and then to fling them scraps of wisdom, to give them a demonstration of what a real male *writer,* a creative *artist,* is like; you would never think he was a practicing *academic.* I don't know if he was a lumberjack or a beer-slinger or a counterman, but I do know that he was not a telephone lineman. He had a job painting telephone poles. He quit that job in the middle of the second week because the heat and the climbing made him sick. It was a broiling June, just after we had both graduated. Fair enough. The sun really did make him sick, twice he came home and vomited. I have quit jobs myself that I could not stand. The same summer I quit my job folding bandages at Victoria Hospital, because I was going mad with boredom. But if I was a writer, and was listing all my varied and colorful occupations, I don't think I would put down *bandage folder,* I don't think I would find that entirely honest.

17   After he quit, Hugo found a job marking Grade Twelve examination papers. Why didn't he put that down? Examination marker. He liked marking examination papers better than he liked climbing telephone poles, and probably better than he liked lumberjacking or beer-slinging or any of those other things if he ever did them; why couldn't he put it down? *Examination marker.*

18   Nor has he, to my knowledge, ever been the foreman in a sawmill. He worked in his uncle's mill the summer before I met him. What he did all day was load lumber and get sworn at by the real foreman, who didn't like him because of his uncle being the boss. In the evenings, if he was not too tired, he used to walk half a mile to a little creek and play his recorder. Black flies bothered him, but he did it anyway. He could play "Morning," from *Peer Gynt,* and some Elizabethan airs whose names I have forgotten. Except for one:

"Wolsey's Wilde." I learned to play it on the piano so we could play a duet. Was that meant for Cardinal Wolsey, and what was a *wilde*, a dance? Put that down, Hugo. *Recorder player.* That would be quite all right, quite in fashion now; as I understand things, recorder playing and such fey activities are not out of favor now, quite the contrary. Indeed, they may be more acceptable than all that lumberjacking and beer-slinging. Look at you, Hugo, your image is not only fake but out-of-date. You should have said you'd meditated for a year in the mountains of Uttar Pradesh; you should have said you'd taught Creative Drama to autistic children; you should have shaved your head, shaved your beard, put on a monk's cowl; you should have shut up, Hugo.

19   When I was pregnant with Clea we lived in a house on Argyle Street in Vancouver. It was such a sad gray stucco house on the outside, in the rainy winter, that we painted the inside, all the rooms, vivid ill-chosen colors. Three walls of the bedrooms were Wedgwood blue, one was magenta. We said it was an experiment to see if color could drive anybody mad. The bathroom was a deep orange-yellow. "It's like being inside a cheese," Hugo said when we finished it. "That's right, it is," I said. "That's very good, phrase-maker." He was pleased but not as pleased as if he'd written it. After that he said, every time he showed anybody the bathroom, "See the color? It's like being inside a cheese." Or, "It's like peeing inside a cheese." Not that I didn't do the same thing, save things up and say them over and over. Maybe I said that about peeing inside a cheese. We had many phrases in common. We both called the landlady the Green Hornet, because she had worn, the only time we had seen her, a poison-green outfit with bits of rat fur and a clutch of violets, and had given off a venomous sort of buzz. She was over seventy and she ran a downtown boardinghouse for men. Her daughter Dotty we called the harlot-in-residence. I wonder why we chose to say *harlot;* that was not, is not, a word in general use. I suppose it had a classy sound, a classy depraved sound, contrasting ironically—we were strong on irony—with Dotty herself.

20   She lived in a two-room apartment in the basement of the house. She was supposed to pay her mother forty-five dollars monthly rent and she told me she meant to try to make the money baby-sitting.

21   "I can't go out to work," she said, "on account of my nerves. My last husband, I had him six months dying down at Mother's, dying with his kidney disease, and I owe her three hundred dollars board still on that. She made me make him his eggnog with skim milk. I'm broke every day of my life. They say it's all right not having wealth if you got health, but what if you never had either one? Bronchial pneumonia from the time I was three years old. Rheumatic fever at twelve. Sixteen I married my first husband, he was killed in a logging accident. Three miscarriages. My womb is in shreds. I use up three packs of Kotex every month. I married a dairy farmer out in the Valley and his herd got the fever. Wiped us out. That was the one who died with his kidneys. No wonder. No wonder my nerves are shot."

22   I am condensing. This came out at greater length and by no means dolefully, indeed with some amazement and pride, at Dotty's table. She asked

me down for cups of tea, then for beer. This is life, I thought, fresh from books, classes, essays, discussions. Unlike her mother, Dotty was flat-faced, soft, doughy, fashioned for defeat, the kind of colorless puzzled woman you see carrying a shopping bag, waiting for the bus. In fact, I had seen her once on a bus downtown, and not recognized her at first in her dull blue winter coat. Her rooms were full of heavy furniture salvaged from her marriage—an upright piano, overstuffed chesterfield and chairs, walnut veneer china cabinet and dining room table, where we sat. In the middle of the table was a tremendous lamp, with a painted china base and a pleated, dark red silk shade, held out at an extravagant angle, like a hoop skirt.

23   I described it to Hugo. "That is a whorehouse lamp," I said. Afterwards I wanted to be congratulated on the accuracy of this description. I told Hugo he ought to pay more attention to Dotty if he wanted to be a writer. I told him about her husbands and her womb and her collection of souvenir spoons, and he said I was welcome to look at them all by myself. He was writing a verse play.

24   Once when I went down to put coal on the furnace, I found Dotty in her pink chenille dressing gown saying good-bye to a man in a uniform, some sort of delivery man or gas station attendant. It was the middle of the afternoon. She and this man were not parting in any way that suggested either lechery or affection and I would not have understood anything about it, I would probably have thought he was some relative, if she had not begun at once a long complicated slightly drunk story about how she had got wet in the rain and had to leave her clothes at her mother's house and worn home her mother's dress which was too tight and that was why she was now in her dressing gown. She said that first Larry had caught her in it delivering some sewing he wanted her to do for his wife, and now me, and she didn't know what we would think of her. This was strange, as I had seen her in her dressing gown many times before. In the middle of her laughing and explaining, the man, who had not looked at me, not smiled or said a word or in any way backed up her story, simply ducked out the door.

25   "Dotty has a lover," I said to Hugo.

26   "You don't get out enough. You're trying to make life interesting."

27   The next week I watched to see if this man came back. He did not. But three other men came, and one of them came twice. They walked with their heads down, quickly, and did not have to wait at the basement door. Hugo couldn't deny it. He said it was life imitating art again, it was bound to happen, after all the fat varicose-veined whores he'd met in books. It was then we named her the harlot-in-residence and began to brag about her to our friends. They stood behind the curtains to catch a glimpse of her going in or out.

28   "That's not her!" they said. "Is that her? Isn't she disappointing? Doesn't she have any professional clothes?"

29   "Don't be so naive," we said. "Did you think they all wore spangles and boas?"

30   Everybody hushed to hear her play the piano. She sang or hummed along

with her playing, not steadily, but loudly, in the rather defiant, self-parodying voice people use when they are alone, or think they are alone. She sang "Yellow Rose of Texas," and "You Can't Be True, Dear."

31   "Whores should sing hymns."
32   "We'll get her to learn some."
33   "You're all such voyeurs. You're all so mean," said a girl named Mary Frances Shrecker, a big-boned, calm-faced girl with black braids down her back. She was married to a former mathematical prodigy, Elsworth Shrecker, who had had a breakdown. She worked as a dietician. Hugo said he could not look at her without thinking of the word *lumpen,* but he supposed she might be nourishing, like oatmeal porridge. She became his second wife. I thought she was the right wife for him, I thought she would stay forever, nourishing him, but the student evicted her.
34   The piano-playing was an entertainment for our friends, but disastrous on the days when Hugo was home trying to work. He was supposed to be working on his thesis but he really was writing his play. He worked in our bedroom, at a card table in front of the window, facing a board fence. When Dotty had been playing for a bit, he might come out to the kitchen and stick his face into mine and say in low, even tones of self-consciously controlled rage, "You go down and tell her to cut that out."
35   "You go."
36   "Bloody hell. She's your friend. You cultivate her. You encourage her."
37   "I never told her to play the piano."
38   "I arranged so that I could have this afternoon free. That did not just happen. I arranged it. I am at a crucial point, I am at the point where this play *lives or dies.* If I go down there I'm afraid I might strangle her."
39   "Well don't look at *me.* Don't strangle *me.* Excuse my breathing and everything."
40   I always did go down to the basement, of course, and knock on Dotty's door and ask her if she would mind not playing the piano now, because my husband was at home and was trying to work. I never said the word *write,* Hugo had trained me not to, that word was like a bare wire to us. Dotty apologized every time, she was scared of Hugo and respectful of his work and his intelligence. She left off playing but the trouble was she might forget, she might start again in an hour, half an hour. The possibility made me nervous and miserable. Because I was pregnant I always wanted to eat, and I would sit at the kitchen table greedily, unhappily, eating something like a warmed-up plateful of Spanish rice. Hugo felt the world was hostile to his writing, he felt not only all its human inhabitants but its noises and diversions and ordinary clutter were linked against him, maliciously, purposefully, diabolically thwarting and maiming him and keeping him from his work. And I, whose business it was to throw myself between him and the world, was failing to do so, by choice perhaps as much as ineptitude for the job. I did not believe in him. I had not understood how it would be necessary to believe in him. I believed that he was clever and talented, whatever that might mean, but I was not sure

he would turn out to be a writer. He did not have the authority I thought a writer should have. He was too nervous, too touchy with everybody, too much of a showoff. I believed that writers were calm, sad people, knowing too much. I believed that there was a difference about them, some hard and shining, rare intimidating quality they had from the beginning, and Hugo didn't have it. I thought that someday he would recognize this. Meanwhile, he lived in a world whose rewards and punishments were as strange, as hidden from me, as if he had been a lunatic. He would sit at supper, pale and disgusted; he would clench himself over the typewriter in furious paralysis when I had to get something from the bedroom, or he would leap around the living room asking me what he was (a rhinoceros who thinks he is a gazelle, Chairman Mao dancing a war dance in a dream dreamt by John Foster Dulles) and then kiss me all over the neck and throat with hungry gobbling noises. I was cut off from the source of these glad or bad moods, I did not affect them. I teased him sourly:

41   "Suppose after we have the baby the house is on fire and the baby and the play are both in there, which would you save?"

42   "Both."

43   "But supposing you can just save one? Never mind the baby, suppose *I* am in there, no, suppose I am drowning *here* and you are *here* and cannot possibly reach us both—"

44   "You're making it tough for me."

45   "I know I am. I know I am. Don't you hate me?"

46   "Of course I hate you." After this we might go to bed, playful, squealing, mock-fighting, excited. All our life together, the successful part of our life together, was games. We made up conversations to startle people on the bus. Once we sat in a beer parlor and he berated me for going out with other men and leaving the children alone while he was off in the bush working to support us. He pleaded with me to remember my duty as a wife and as a mother. I blew smoke in his face. People around us were looking stern and gratified. When we got outside we laughed till we had to hold each other up, against the wall. We played in bed that I was Lady Chatterley and he was Mellors.

47   "Where be that little rascal John Thomas?" he said thickly. "I canna find John Thomas!"

48   "Frightfully sorry, I think I must have swallowed him," I said, ladylike.

49   There was a water pump in the basement. It made a steady, thumping noise. The house was on fairly low-lying ground not far from the Fraser River, and during the rainy weather the pump had to work most of the time to keep the basement from being flooded. We had a dark rainy January, as is usual in Vancouver, and this was followed by a dark rainy February. Hugo and I felt gloomy. I slept a lot of the time. Hugo couldn't sleep. He claimed it was the pump that kept him awake. He couldn't work because of it in the daytime and he couldn't sleep because of it at night. The pump had replaced Dotty's piano-playing as the thing that most enraged and depressed him in our house. Not only because of its noise, but because of the money it was costing us. Its

entire cost went onto our electricity bill, though it was Dotty who lived in the basement and reaped the benefits of not being flooded. He said I should speak to Dotty and I said Dotty could not pay the expenses she already had. He said she could turn more tricks. I told him to shut up. As I became more pregnant, slower and heavier and more confined to the house, I got fonder of Dotty, used to her, less likely to store up and repeat what she said. I felt more at home with her than I did sometimes with Hugo and our friends.

50   All right, Hugo said, I ought to phone the landlady. I said he ought. He said he had far too much to do. The truth was we both shrank from a confrontation with the landlady, knowing in advance how she would confuse and defeat us with shrill evasive prattle.

51   In the middle of the night in the middle of a rainy week I woke up and wondered what had wakened me. It was the silence.

52   "Hugo, wake up. The pump's broken. I can't hear the pump."

53   "I am awake," Hugo said.

54   "It's still raining and the pump isn't going. It must be broken."

55   "No, it isn't. It's shut off. I shut if off."

56   I sat up and turned on the light. He was lying on his back, squinting and trying to give me a hard look at the same time.

57   "You didn't turn it off."

58   "All right, I didn't."

59   "You did."

60   "I could not stand the goddamn expense any more. I could not stand thinking about it. I could not stand the noise either. I haven't had any sleep in a week."

61   "The basement will flood."

62   "I'll turn it on in the morning. A few hours' peace is all I want."

63   "That'll be too late, it's raining torrents."

64   "It is not."

65   "You go to the window."

66   "It's raining. It's not raining torrents."

67   I turned out the light and lay down and said in a calm stern voice, "Listen to me, Hugo, you have to go and turn it on, Dotty will be flooded out."

68   "In the morning."

69   "You have to go and turn it on *now.*"

70   "Well I'm not."

71   "If you're not, I am."

72   "No, you're not."

73   "I am."

74   But I didn't move.

75   "Don't be such an alarmist."

76   "*Hugo.*"

77   "Don't *cry.*"

78   "Her stuff will be ruined."

79   "Best thing could happen to it. Anyway, it won't." He lay beside me stiff

and wary, waiting, I suppose, for me to get out of bed, go down to the basement and figure out how to turn the pump on. Then what would he have done? He could not have hit me, I was too pregnant. He never did hit me, unless I hit him first. He could have gone and turned it off again, and I could have turned it on, and so on, how long could that last? He could have held me down, but if I struggled he would have been afraid of hurting me. He could have sworn at me and left the house, but we had no car, and it was raining too hard for him to stay out very long. He would probably just have raged and sulked, alternately, and I could have taken a blanket and gone to sleep on the living room couch for the rest of the night. I think that is what a woman of firm character would have done. I think that is what a woman who wanted that marriage to last would have done. But I did not do it. Instead, I said to myself that I did not know how the pump worked, I did not know where to turn it on. I said to myself that I was afraid of Hugo. I entertained the possibility that Hugo might be right, nothing would happen. But I wanted something to happen, I wanted Hugo to crash.

80   When I woke up, Hugo was gone and the pump was thumping as usual. Dotty was pounding on the door at the top of the basement stairs.

81   "You won't believe your eyes what's down here. I'm up to my knees in water. I just put my feet out of bed and up to my knees in water. What happened? You hear the pump go off?"

82   "No," I said.

83   "I don't know what could've gone wrong, I guess it could've got overworked. I had a couple of beers before I went to bed elst I would've known there was something wrong. I usually sleep light. But I was sleeping like the dead and I put my feet out of bed and Jesus, it's a good thing I didn't pull on the light switch at the same time, I would have been electrocuted. Everything's floating."

84   Nothing was floating and the water would not have come to any grown person's knees. It was about five inches deep in some places, only one or two in others, the floor being so uneven. It had soaked and stained the bottom of her chesterfield and chairs and got into the bottom drawers and cupboards and warped the bottom of her piano. The floor tiles were loosened, the rugs soggy, the edges of her bedspread dripping, her floor heater ruined.

85   I got dressed and put on a pair of Hugo's boots and took a broom downstairs. I started sweeping the water towards the drain outside the door. Dotty made herself a cup of coffee in my kitchen and sat for a while on the top step watching me, going over the same monologue about having a couple of beers and sleeping more soundly than usual, not hearing the pump go off, not understanding why it should go off, if it had gone off, not knowing how she was going to explain to her mother who would certainly make it out to be her fault and charge her. We were in luck, I saw. (*We* were?) Dotty's expectation and thrifty relish of misfortune made her less likely than almost anyone else would have been to investigate just what had gone wrong. After the water level went down a bit, she went into her bedroom,

put on some clothes and some boots which she had to drain first, got her broom and helped me.

86 "The things that don't happen to me, eh? I never get my fortune told. I've got these girl friends that are always getting their fortune told and I say, never mind me, there's one thing I know and I know it ain't good."

87 I went upstairs and phoned the University, trying to get Hugo. I told them it was an emergency and they found him in the library.

88 "It did flood."

89 "What?"

90 "It did flood. Dotty's place is under water."

91 "I turned the pump on."

92 "Like hell you did. This morning you turned it on."

93 "This morning there was a downpour and the pump couldn't handle it. That was after I turned it on."

94 "The pump couldn't handle it last night because the pump wasn't on last night and don't talk to me about any downpour."

95 "Well there was one. You were asleep."

96 "You have no idea what you've done, do you? You don't even stick around to look at it. I have to look. I have to cope. I have to listen to that poor woman."

97 "Plug your ears."

98 "Shut up, you filthy moral idiot."

99 "I'm sorry. I was kidding. I'm sorry."

100 "Sorry. You're bloody sorry. This is the mess you made and I told you you'd make and you're bloody sorry."

101 "I have to go to a seminar. I am sorry. I can't talk now, it's no good talking to you now, I don't know what you're trying to get me to say."

102 "I'm just trying to get you to *realize*."

103 "All right, I realize. Though I still think it happened this morning."

104 "You don't realize. You never realize."

105 "You dramatize."

106 "*I* dramatize!"

107 Our luck held. Dotty's mother was not so likely as Dotty to do without explanations and it was, after all, her floor tiles and wallboard that were ruined. But Dotty's mother was sick, the cold wet weather had undermined her too, and she was taken to hospital with pneumonia that very morning. Dotty went to live in her mother's house, to look after the boarders. The basement had a disgusting, moldy smell. We moved out too, a short time later. Just before Clea was born we took over a house in North Vancouver, belonging to some friends who had gone to England. The quarrel between us subsided in the excitement of moving; it was never really resolved. We did not move much from the positions we had taken on the phone. I said you don't realize, you never realize, and he said, what do you want me to say? Why do you make such a fuss over this, he asked reasonably. Anybody might wonder. Long after I was away from him, I wondered too. I could have turned on the pump, as I have said, taking responsibility for both of us, as a

patient realistic woman, a really married woman, would have done, as I am sure Mary Frances would have done, did, many times, during the ten years she lasted. Or I could have told Dotty the truth, though she was not a very good choice to receive such information. I could have told somebody, if I thought it was that important, pushed Hugo out into the unpleasant world and let him taste trouble. But I didn't, I was not able fully to protect or expose him, only to flog him with blame, desperate sometimes, feeling I would claw his head open to pour my vision into it, my notion of what had to be understood. What presumptuousness, what cowardice, what bad faith. Unavoidable. "You have a problem of incompatibility," the marriage counselor said to us a while later. We laughed till we cried in the dreary municipal hall of the building in North Vancouver where the marriage counseling was dispensed. That is our problem, we said to each other, what a relief to know it, incompatibility.

108   I did not read Hugo's story that night. I left it with Clea and she as it turned out did not read it either. I read it the next afternoon. I got home about two o'clock from the girls' private school where I have a part-time job teaching history. I made tea as I usually do and sat down in the kitchen to enjoy the hour before the boys, Gabriel's sons, get home from school. I saw the book still lying on top of the refrigerator and I took it down and read Hugo's story.

109   The story is about Dotty. Of course, she has been changed in some unimportant ways and the main incident concerning her has been invented, or grafted on from some other reality. But the lamp is there, and the pink chenille dressing gown. And something about Dotty that I had forgotten: When you were talking she would listen with her mouth slightly open, nodding, then she would chime in on the last word of your sentence with you. A touching and irritating habit. She was in such a hurry to agree, she hoped to understand. Hugo has remembered this, and when did Hugo ever talk to Dotty?

110   That doesn't matter. What matters is that this story of Hugo's is a very good story, as far as I can tell, and I think I can tell. How honest this is and how lovely, I had to say as I read. I had to admit. I was moved by Hugo's story; I was, I am, glad of it, and I am not moved by tricks. Or if I am, they have to be good tricks. Lovely tricks, honest tricks. There is Dotty lifted out of life and held in light, suspended in the marvelous clear jelly that Hugo has spent all his life learning how to make. It is an act of magic, there is no getting around it; it is an act, you might say, of a special, unsparing, unsentimental love. A fine and lucky benevolence. Dotty was a lucky person, people who understand and value this act might say (not everybody, of course, does understand and value this act); she was lucky to live in that basement for a few months and eventually to have this done to her, though she doesn't know what has been done and wouldn't care for it, probably, if she did know. She has passed into Art. It doesn't happen to everybody.

111   Don't be offended. Ironical objections are a habit with me. I am half-

ashamed of them. I respect what has been done. I respect the intention and the effort and the result. Accept my thanks.

112   I did think that I would write a letter to Hugo. All the time I was preparing dinner, and eating it, and talking to Gabriel and the children, I was thinking of a letter. I was thinking I would tell him how strange it was for me to realize that we shared, still shared, the same bank of memory, and that what was all scraps and oddments, useless baggage, for me, was ripe and usable, a paying investment, for him. Also I wanted to apologize, in some not-outright way, for not having believed he would be a writer. Acknowledgment, not apology; that was what I owed him. A few graceful, a few grateful, phrases.

113   At the same time, at dinner, looking at my husband Gabriel, I decided that he and Hugo are not really so unalike. Both of them have managed something. Both of them have decided what to do about everything they run across in this world, what attitude to take, how to ignore or use things. In their limited and precarious ways they both have authority. They are not *at the mercy*. Or think they are not. I can't blame them, for making whatever arrangements they can make.

114   After the boys had gone to bed and Gabriel and Clea had settled to watch television, I found a pen and got the paper in front of me, to write my letter, and my hand jumped. I began to write short jabbing sentences that I had never planned:

115   *This is not enough, Hugo. You think it is, but it isn't. You are mistaken, Hugo.*
116   That is not an argument to send through the mail.
117   I do blame them. I envy and despise.
118   Gabriel came into the kitchen before he went to bed, and saw me sitting with a pile of test papers and my marking pencils. He might have meant to talk to me, to ask me to have coffee, or a drink, with him, but he respected my unhappiness as he always does; he respected the pretense that I was not unhappy but preoccupied, burdened with these test papers; he left me alone to get over it. ❖

Questions to Ponder

1. What differences does the narrator see between the two men in her life, Hugo (the writer) and Gabe (the engineer)? What similarities does she discover?
2. How does the narrator's view of Hugo change in the course of this story? What causes this change?
3. What criticisms does the narrator make of herself? Do you agree? How do you see her?
4. Why is it true that what is "all scraps and oddments, useless baggage" to a nonwriter can be "ripe and usable, a paying investment" to a writer?

Writing Possibilities

1. Using Alice Munro's story as a model, write a story in which a first-person narrator talks about two relationships in his or her life.
2. Write a story in which an ordinary moment—like Alice Munro's incident with the water pump—becomes a turning point in a relationship.
3. Write a story in which you contrast an artist of some kind with characters who are not artists.

CHAPTER 10

Touchstones

Art proceeds out of an exquisite awareness of life.

Norman Cousins

Human curiosity counts among the highest social virtues (as indifference counts among the basest defects), because it leads to the disclosure of the causes of character and temperament and thereby to a better understanding of the springs of human conduct. . . . Observation . . . is a moral act and must inevitably promote kindliness—whether we like it or not. It also sharpens the sense of beauty. An ugly deed—such as a deed of cruelty—takes on artistic beauty when its origin and hence its fitness in the general scheme begins to be comprehended. . . . Observation endows our day and our street with the romantic charm of history, and stimulates charity—not the charity which signs cheques, but the more precious charity which puts itself to the trouble of understanding.

Arnold Bennett

I try to leave myself very blank—a kind of sounding board, all the time very open to catch a vibration, a tone from something or somebody. . . . Every so often I'll catch, out of the corner of my eye, off balance, a flash impression of

605

something—a spark of excitement. . . . I get strange, my hair rises on the back of my head when I begin to sense something.

Andrew Wyeth

I think you spend your whole life learning how to listen. And what you're listening for is something nobody else can hear. So nobody else can tell you how to do it. That's what makes it difficult, what makes it exciting, and what makes it never finished. That means you're always beginning the whole thing.

W. S. Merwin

It is astounding how after days of being with people—sometimes out of necessity, social or economic—a good and exciting idea becomes pale and wan, vague, and not worth writing. It is just as outstanding and thrilling when, after a day or so of solitude, silence, daydreaming and loafing, the same idea comes alive again, beautiful and bright like a wilted plant that has been given a good soaking in the rain.

Patricia Highsmith

Some writers achieve the incremental process, by which a story attracts to itself what belongs in it, by continual rewriting; the basic idea becomes enlarged with each revision. Other writers, I one of them, find the story grows outside of consciousness. Work is done on the story with the conscious mind and then it is pushed down for a day or several days or more, after perhaps a few notes have been taken to capture the story's development. When it next rises into consciousness it always seems to have changed and to have added new elements. The big risk is in deciding when to begin writing; although here, too, the most important thing is to keep the idea as whole as possible in one's mind: flexible, not pinned down irrevocably, until the idea can be gradually manipulated into its final form in words.

Nancy Hale

To believe your own thought, to believe that what is true for you in your private heart is true for all men [and women], that is genius.

Ralph Waldo Emerson

The one great rule of composition—is to speak the truth.

Henry David Thoreau

How does an artist help us to live? By telling the absolute truth, no matter how dispiriting, and at the same time somehow insinuating that the shape and energy of truth breeds the appetite not only to live but to change life.

Jack Kroll

The writers who we say are for all time . . . have one very important characteristic: they are going toward something, are summoning you toward it, too, and you feel not with your mind, but with your whole being, that they have some object.

Anton Chekhov

Writers need not offer solutions, but insights.

Anonymous

And I wanted to show you that you can spur yourself beyond your limits if you are in the proper mood. A warrior makes his [or her] own mood . . . anything can serve to get you into it.

Don Juan

The beginning of style is character. . . . Therefore, if you wish your writing to seem good, your character must seem at least partly so. And since in the long run deception is likely to be found out, your character had better not only seem good, but be it. Those who publish make themselves public in more ways than they sometimes realize. Authors may sell their books: but they give themselves away.

F. L. Lucas

Technique is the consequence of a vision, not its cause.

Cynthia Ozick

The material never saves a work of art, the gold it is made of does not hallow a statue. A work of art lives on its form, not on its material; the essential grace it emanates springs from its structure, from it organism.

José Ortega y Gasset

Imagination applied to the whole world is vapid in comparison to imagination applied to detail.

Wallace Stevens

A whole essay might be written on the danger of thinking without images.

Samuel Taylor Coleridge

Atmosphere is the result of presenting the physical details in such a way as to create emotional reactions. . . .

Peggy Simson Curry

Make the strange real, or the real strange. Establish situations; then cut loose.

Nancy Price

Of course you know that when I mime walking upstairs I never saw anyone climbing stairs like that. Many say it is a haunting image of the reality of climbing stairs, yet one does not climb stairs like that. It is the feeling of climbing stairs. I do not say I mime things I have not seen in some way, but miming takes place inside. You become the other. By sympathy. It isn't copying.

Marcel Marceau

[I]t may come clearer by comparing this stillness I'm talking about to the short stories of Isaac Babel or Hemingway, or to Jerzy Kosinski's *Steps*, works that evoke emotion because the artist has not tried to capture emotion itself but conveys successfully the facts from which emotion is made and leaves our imagination free. It is the difference between the photo of a man caught at the precise instant he is being made aware of a tragedy in his life, and the same man weeping after hearing the news. The first photo would help us understand a particular man. The second is everybody's soap opera. . . .

William Kennedy

We are allowed to come to our awareness and feelings with that special sense of surprise that comes when an author has taken none of the easy routes to our minds and hearts.

Anonymous

Astonish me, take trouble over it.

Colette

Writing is rewriting.

Anonymous

The impromptu is what begins to happen at about the twentieth draft.

John Ciardi

Nothing but fine execution survives long.

Gerard Manley Hopkins

[F]ear your admirers! Learn in time, from your first steps, to hear, understand and love the cruel truth about yourselves. Find out who can tell you that truth and talk of your art only with those who can tell you the truth.

Konstantin Stanislavsky

The work of art stands up by itself, and nothing else does. . . . Ancient Athens made a mess—but the Antigone *stands up. . . . [King] James I made a mess—but there was* Macbeth. *. . . Art for art's sake? I should just think so, and more so than ever at the present time. It is the one orderly product which our muddling race has produced.*

E. M. Forster

Clean white paper waiting
            under a pen
is the gift beyond history
    and hurt and heaven

John Ciardi

Credits

PHOTOS

Page 4 AP/Wide World. Page 10 The Bettmann Archive. Page 19 AP/Wide World. Page 35 Culver Pictures. Page 41 AP/Wide World. Page 70 Star Tribune/Minneapolis/St. Paul. Page 86 The Granger Collection, New York. Page 94 Courtesy Alfred A. Knopf, Inc. Photo: Peter Simon. Page 111 Culver Pictures. Page 124 UPI/Bettmann. Page 174 Photo: Miriam Berkley/Published by Alfred A. Knopf, Inc. Page 184 Alinari/The Louvre/Art Resource, New York. Page 202 Alinari-Art Reference Bureau/Art Resource, New York. Page 213, top Courtesy Mark Johnson; bottom Jane Scherr, University of California, Public Information Office. Page 217 UPI/Bettmann. Page 224 AP/Wide World. Page 250 L. A. Hyder. Page 270 The Granger Collection, New York. Page 279 AP/Wide World. Page 335 UPI/Bettmann. Page 338 AP/Wide World. Page 343 Photo: Koby-Antupit/Pantheon Books. Page 401 Brown Brothers. Page 409 Harvard University News Office. Page 434 Courtesy Mihaly Csikszentmihalyi. Page 442 AP/Wide World. Page 449 Courtesy Gretel Ehrlich. Photo: Press Stephens. Page 453 AP/Wide World. Page 459 Reuters/UPI/Bettmann. Page 491 UPI/Bettmann. Page 503 Photo: Donald E. Johnson/Reprinted by permission HarperCollins Publishers Inc. Page 522 Linda Fry Poverman. Page 534 Photo: Thomas Victor/Reprinted by permission HarperCollins Publishers Inc. Page 546 Acme/UPI/Bettmann. Page 560 The Granger Collection, New York. Page 573 Courtesy Lewis Thomas. Page 590 Photo: Jerry Bauer/Published by Alfred A. Knopf, Inc.

SELECTIONS

Headnotes not specifically credited below are published by permission of their authors to Barbara Lounsberry for *The Writer in You*.

Page 4 Excerpt from *An American Childhood* by Annie Dillard. Copyright © 1987 by Annie Dillard. Reprinted by permission of Harper & Row Publishers, Inc.

Page 10 Headnote from "Interview with the Paris Review," No. 93, Fall 1984. Reprinted by permission.

Page 10 From *Reading Myself and Others* by Philip Roth. Copyright 1975 by Farrar, Straus & Giroux, Inc. Reprinted by permission.

Page 14 Headnote from *Second Words: Selected Critical Prose* (Boston: Beacon Press, 1982). Reprinted with permission from the author.

Page 15 From "High School Beginnings" by Margaret Atwood. Reprinted with permission from the author.

Page 19 From *The Friday Book: Essays and Other Nonfiction* by John Barth. Copyright © by John Barth. Reprinted by permission of The Putnam Publishing Group.

Page 31 "Musical Beginnings" by Warren Wortham. Reprinted by permission.

Page 36 "Professions for Women" from *The Death of the Moth and Other Essays* by Virginia Woolf. Copyright © 1942 by Harcourt Brace Jovanovich, Inc., and renewed 1970 by Marjorie T. Parsons, Executrix. Reprinted by permission of the Publisher.

Page 41 From *Selected Stories* by Nadine Gordimer. Copyright © 1965 by Nadine Gordimer. Reprinted by permission of Viking Penguin, a division of Penguin Books USA, Inc.

Page 60 Headnote from "To Be Reborn: An Interview with May Sarton" by Karla Hammond. *The Bennington Review*, No. 3, December 1978. Reprinted by permission.

Page 61 From *Journal of a Solitude* by May Sarton. Copyright © by May Sarton. Reprinted by permission of W.W. Norton & Company, Inc.

Page 64 "On Keeping a Notebook" from *Slouching Towards Bethlehem* by Joan Didion. Copyright © 1966, 1968 by Joan Didion. Reprinted by permission of Farrar, Straus & Giroux, Inc.

Page 71 "The Imagination Works Slowly and Quietly" from *If You Want to Write*. Copyright © 1987 by Brenda Ueland. Reprinted by permission of Gray Wolf Press.

Page 76 From *Writing with Power: Techniques for Mastering the Writing Process* by Peter Elbow. Copyright © 1981 by Oxford University Press, Inc. Reprinted by permission.

Page 81 "Lifeguarding: Fun in the Sun?" by Kelly Linnenkamp. Reprinted by permission.

Page 96 From *Trust Me* by John Updike. Copyright © 1987 by John Updike. Reprinted by permission of Alfred A. Knopf, Inc.

Page 115 "The Search for Marvin Gardens" from *Pieces of the Frame* by John McPhee. Copyright © 1972 by John McPhee. Reprinted by permission of Farrar, Straus & Giroux, Inc.

Page 125 From *Practicing History* by Barbara Tuchman. Copyright © 1981 by Alma Tuchman, Lucy T. Eisenberg, and Jessica Tuchman Matthews. Reprinted by permission of Alfred A. Knopf, Inc.

Page 136 "The Tailors of Maida" by Gay Talese. Reprinted by permission.

Page 147 From *Works and Lives: The Anthropologist as Author* by Clifford Geertz. Copyright © 1988 by the Board of Trustees of the Leland Stanford Junior University. Reprinted by permission of the publishers, Stanford University Press.

Page 158 "Employee Stock Ownership Plans: New Players in the Leveraged Buyout Game" from *Draftings in Economics: Major Themes*, The University of Northern Iowa journal of student research and writing, editor Barbara Lounsberry, 5 (2), 1990. Reprinted by permission of the University of Northern Iowa Board of Student Publications.

Page 178 Copyright © 1989 by Julian Barnes. Reprinted by permission of The Helen Brann Agency, Inc.

Page 208 From *The World of John McNulty* (New York: Doubleday, 1957). Reprinted by permission of Faith McNulty.

Page 214 From *Metaphors We Live By* by George Lakoff and Mark Johnson. Copyright © 1980 by The University of Chicago Press. Reprinted by permission.

Page 218 Headnote and "Double-Sunrise" from *Gift From the Sea* by Anne Morrow Lindbergh. Copyright © 1955 by Anne Morrow Lindbergh. Reprinted by permission of Pantheon Books, a division of Random House, Inc.

Page 226 "Why We Can't Wait" from *Letter From Birmingham Jail* by Martin Luther King, Jr. Copyright © 1963, 1964 by Martin Luther King, Jr. Reprinted by permission of Harper & Row, Publishers, Inc.

Page 240 "An Analysis of 'Letter from Birmingham Jail,'" early and late drafts, by Lisa Battani. Reprinted by permission.

Page 251 "'Really, Doesn't Crime Pay?'" from *In Love and Trouble*. Copyright © 1973 by Alice Walker. Reprinted by permission of Harcourt Brace Jovanovich, Inc.

Page 265 Excerpt from *The Kandy-Kolored Tangerine-Flake Streamline Baby* by Tom Wolfe. Copyright © 1963, 1964, 1965 by Thomas K. Wolfe, Jr. and New York Herald Tribune, Inc. Reprinted by permission of Farrar, Straus & Giroux, Inc.

Page 271 From *One Writer's Beginnings* by Eudora Welty. Copyright © 1983, 1984 by Eudora Welty. Reprinted by permission of Harvard University Press.

Page 274 "Seeing Red," early and late drafts by Cordell Waldron. Reprinted by permission.

Page 289 From *The Woman Warrior: Memoirs of a Girlhood Among Ghosts* by Maxine Hong Kingston. Copyright © 1975, 1976 by Maxine Hong Kingston. Reprinted by permission of Alfred A. Knopf, Inc.

Page 308 Headnote excerpted from *Contemporary Authors,* vol. 110, edited by Hal May. Copyright © 1984 by Gale Research Inc. All rights reserved. Reprinted by permission of the publisher.

Page 309 From *Hunger of Memory* by Richard Rodriguez. Copyright © 1982 by Richard Rodriguez. Reprinted by permission of David R. Godine, Publisher, Boston.

Page 323 "Milk Run" by Donna Roazen. Reprinted by permission.

Page 325 "One Story—Thirteen Points of View" by Nancy Price. Reprinted by permission.

Page 336 From *A Moveable Feast* by Ernest Hemingway. Copyright © 1964 by Mary Hemingway. Reprinted with permission of Charles Scribner's Sons, an imprint of Macmillan Publishing Company.

Page 338 Headnote from V.S. Naipaul, "On Being a Writer," *The New York Review of* Books," April 1987, page 7. Reprinted by permission.

Page 339 From *Finding the Center: Two Narratives* by V.S. Naipaul. Copyright © 1984 by V.S. Naipaul. Reprinted by permission of Alfred A. Knopf, Inc.

Page 343 From *Lying: Moral Choice in Public and Private Life*. Copyright © 1978 by Sissela Bok. Reprinted by permission of Pantheon Books, a Division of Random House, Inc.

Page 357 Headnote, first drafts, and selection—"Small Towns: A Close Second Look at a Very Good Place," 1987, Iowa Humanities Board. Reprinted by permission.

Page 376 "Labor Unions: A Part of Our Past or Future?" from *Draftings in Economics: Major Themes*, The University of Northern Iowa journal of student research and writing, editor Barbara Lounsberry, 5 (2), 1990. Reprinted by permission of the University of Northern Iowa Board of Student Publications.

Pages 392, 393 Headnote to "Cover Girl," and "Cover Girl" by Nancy Price. Reprinted by permission.

Page 403 "Why I Write" from *Such Such Were the Joys* by George Orwell. Copyright © 1953 by Sonia Brownell Orwell, renewed 1981 by Mrs. George K. Perutz, Mrs. Miriam Gross, Dr. Michael Dickson, Executors of the Estate of Sonia Brownell Orwell. Reprinted by permission of Harcourt Brace Jovanovich, Inc.

Page 410 Reprinted from *The Panda's Thumb, More Reflections in Natural History* by Stephen Jay Gould. Copyright © 1980 by Stephen Jay Gould. Reprinted by permission of W.W. Norton & Company, Inc.

Page 416 "The Brady Plan: An Attempt to Solve the Mexican Debt Crisis" from *Draftings in Economics: Major Themes*, The University of Northern Iowa journal of student research and writing, editor Barbara Lounsberry, 5 (2), 1990. Reprinted by permission of the University of Northern Iowa Board of Student Publications.

Page 436 Excerpted from *Flow: The Psychology of Optimal Experience* by Mihaly Csikszentmihalyi. Copyright © 1990 by Mihaly Csikszentmihalyi. Reprinted by permission of HarperCollins Publishers.

Page 442 Headnote excerpted from *Contemporary Authors New Revision Series*, vol. 23, edited by Deborah A. Straub. Copyright © 1988 by Gale Research Company. Reprinted by permission of the publisher.

Page 442 From *Crossing Open Ground*. Copyright © 1984, 1988 by Barry Holstun Lopez. Reprinted by permission of Charles Scribner's Sons, an imprint of Macmillan Publishing Company. (First appeared under a different title in *Harper's*, Dec. 1984.)

Page 449 Headnote, and "About Men" from *The Solace of Open Spaces* by Gretel Ehrlich. Copyright © 1985 by Gretel Ehrlich. Reprinted by permission of the publishers, Viking Penguin, a division of Penguin Books USA Inc.

Page 454 Excerpted from *The Managerial Woman* by Margaret Hennig and Anne Jardim. Copyright © 1976, 1977 by Margaret Hennig and Anne Jardim. Used by permission of Doubleday, a division of Bantam, Doubleday, Dell Publishing Group, Inc.

Page 459 Headnote, 1982 Nobel Address. Copyright © The Nobel Foundation.

Page 460 "The Sea of Lost Time" from *Innocent Erendira and Other Stories* by Gabriel García Márquez. English translation copyright © 1978 by Harper & Row, Publishers, Inc. Reprinted with the permission of the publisher.

Page 475 From "Telling It Like It Maybe Is" by William Kloefkorn. Reprinted by permission.

Page 486 Headnote from *A Continuous Harmony: Essays Cultural and Agricultural*. Copyright © 1970 by Harcourt Brace Jovanovich. Reprinted by permission.

Page 487 From *The Gift of Good Land: Further Essays Cultural and Agricultural*. Copyright © 1981 by North Point Press. Reprinted by permission.

Page 491 Headnote from *Solzhenitsyn: A Pictorial Autobiography* (New York: Farrar, Straus, & Giroux, Inc., 1974). Reprinted by permission.

Page 492 "First Cell, First Love" from *The Gulag Archipelago 1918–1956: An Experiment in Literary Investigation—I–II* by Aleksandr I. Solzhenitsyn. Translated by Thomas P. Whitney. English translation Copyright © 1974 by Harper & Row, Publishers, Inc. Reprinted by permission of the publisher.

Page 501 Copyright © 1989 by The New York Times Company. Reprinted by permission.

Page 503 Headnote excerpted from *Letters of E.B. White* collected and edited by Dorothy Labrano Guth. Copyright © 1976 by E.B. White. Reprinted by permission of HarperCollins Publishers.

Page 505 "Death of a Pig" from *The Second Tree From the Corner* by E.B. White. Copyright © 1947, 1954 by E.B. White. Reprinted by permission of Harper & Row, Publishers, Inc.

Page 512 "Of Cows and Men," early and late drafts, by Brad Williams. Reprinted by permission.

Page 522 Headnote from *Leslie Marmon Silko* by Per Seyersted. (Boise: Boise State University Western Writers Series, 1980). Reprinted by permission.

Page 523 From *The Man to Send Rain Clouds* edited by Kenneth Rosen. Copyright © 1974 by Kenneth Rosen. Reprinted by permission of Viking Penguin, a division of Penguin Books USA Inc.

Pages 534, 535 Headnote, and "Writing—and Rewriting—with a Word Processor" Copyright © 1976, 1980, 1985 by William K. Zinsser. Reprinted by permission of the author.

Page 548 Excerpted from *The Finest Hour*, Volume II by Winston Churchill. Copyright © 1949 by Houghton Mifflin Company. Copyright renewed © 1976 by Lady Spencer-Churchill, the Honourable Lady Sarah Audley, the Honourable Lady Soames. Reprinted by permission of Houghton Mifflin Company.

Page 560 From Mary McCarthy, *Occasional Prose* (New York: Harcourt Brace Jovanovich, 1985). Reprinted by permission.

Page 573 Headnote from *The Youngest Science: Notes of a Medicine Watcher* by Lewis Thomas. Copyright © 1983 by Lewis Thomas. Reprinted by permission of the publisher, Viking Penguin, a division of Penguin Books USA, Inc.

Page 574 From *The Medusa and the Snail* by Lewis Thomas. Copyright © 1979 by Lewis Thomas.

Page 578 From *New York History*, No. 83, January 1985, pages 73–77. Reprinted by permission.

Page 583 "Lipstick Kisses," early and late drafts, by Jennifer C. Miller. Reprinted by permission.

Page 590 From *Something I've Been Meaning to Tell You* by Alice Munro. Copyright © 1974 by Alice Munro. Originally published by McGraw-Hill Ryerson Limited. Reprinted by arrangement with Virginia Barber Literary Agency, Inc. All rights reserved.

Instructor's Manual to accompany

THE WRITER IN YOU:

A WRITING PROCESS READER

Barbara Lounsberry

University of Northern Iowa

HarperCollins*Publishers*

CONTENTS

INTRODUCTION												v

Section 1

    SAMPLE SYLLABI

    FOR A 16-WEEK SEMESTER (MWF) 1

    FOR A 16-WEEK SEMESTER (TTH) 13

    FOR A 10-WEEK QUARTER (MWF) 23

    FOR A 10-WEEK QUARTER (TTH) 31

Section 2

    GUIDELINES FOR USING EACH CHAPTER			38

Section 3

    ANSWERS TO "QUESTIONS TO PONDER"			45

INTRODUCTION

This manual is designed to be as helpful as possible to teachers using <u>The Writer in You: A Writing Process Reader</u> in their writing courses.

Organizing a reader that deals with a recursive process, such as writing, is difficult. How can one set forth the stages of the writing process in a sequential fashion when those processes are not lock-step sequential? How does one lay out the stages of a process which varies from writer to writer but inevitably involves repeated doubling-back, regular backing and filling?

The solution I have hit upon is simple. I have set forth the stages of the writing process in a logical order, but then ask teachers and students not to read each chapter completely before moving on to the next, but to <u>cycle through the reader as many times as possible.</u>

The second general principle I hope teachers will adopt is to feel free to treat Chapters 4 through 7--"Finding the Form," Finding a Voice," "One True Sentence," and "Generating"--in any order that best suits them. I am most aware that some students will not find the best form, voice, or opening for a piece of writing until they have "generated" a great deal of material. Other students will find that they begin best, like Hemingway, with one true sentence. Still other students will want consciously to select a form or a voice before they begin.

In short, teachers should feel comfortable moving backward and forward in the reader, assigning selections that best enhance their course designs, as well as making numerous circuits through the stages. By doing this, they will be modeling the recursive process that they are teaching!

In order to help teachers as much as possible, I have designed 4 syllabi for using The Writer in You in college writing courses. Designed to fit both 16-week semester and 10-week quarter courses, as well as Monday-Wednesday-Friday and Tuesday-Thursday schedules, these syllabi are given in Section 1.

Section 2 follows with a few short tips for using each of the reader's chapters. Here I particularly point out selections which work well when assigned and discussed as pairs.

The long Section 3 which concludes this manual supplies answers to the Questions to Ponder which follow each selection.

The Writer in You contains the best wit and wisdom I can summon on that highly personal and rewarding act: writing. My hope is that the professional and student essays and short stories will be so rewarding in themselves that students will want to read on and on . . . to see what they can discover next. My hope is that they will find in this reader many techniques to try in their own writing, as well as much encouragement to be daring truth seekers, both in their college papers and in writing on their own.

Section 1

SAMPLE SYLLABI FOR A SEMESTER

AND A QUARTER

The following are sample syllabi for using *The Writer in You* in 16-week semester writing courses and in 10-week quarter courses. Syllabi are given for courses taught three days a week or two days a week:

Sample Syllabus for 16-Week Semester
(Monday, Wednesday, Friday)

Week 1
   Monday: Introduce Course
           Assign: Opening of Chapter 1.
                Introduction: A Writer's
                Beginnings & Annie Dillard,
                "An American Childhood"
           Do: Brief Warm-up Writing Exercise
              1, 2, or 3 for Dillard's essay
              at end of hour

   Wed.: Introduce "Personal Experience" Paper
          Present & Practice Invention
                  Strategies
           Assign: Opening of Chapter 2. Finding
              the Subject: The Figure in
              the Carpet & May Sarton,
              "Journal of a Solitude"

   Fri.: More practice of Prewriting
                    Strategies
          Assign: Joan Didion, "On Keeping a
              Notebook" & Philip Roth, "My
              Baseball Years"

Week 2
Mon.: Introduce "thesis" or "controlling idea"
  Assign: Warren Wortham, "Musical Beginnings" & Kelly Linnenkamp, "Lifeguarding: Fun in the Sun?"

Wed.: Discuss thesis and the importance of vivid, sensory details (with reference to Wortham & Linnenkamp essays)
  First Draft of Personal Experience Paper Due
  Begin Responding to Drafts in small peer writing groups
  Assign: John Barth, "Some Reasons Why I Tell The Stories I Tell The Way I Tell Them Rather Than Some Other Sort of Stories Some Other Way"

Fri.: Opening minutes: ask students to list the vivid details they remember from John Barth's essay
  Continue responding to First Drafts in Small Groups
  Assign: Opening of Chapter 5. Finding a Voice; Donna Roazen, "Milk Run" & Nancy Price, "One Story--Thirteen Points of View"

Week 3
Mon.: Ask students their responses to "Milk Run" and "One Story--Thirteen Points of View" as an introduction to a general discussion of "Voice" in writing in general, and in their Personal Experience papers in particular. Allow time at the end of class for students to experiment with changing the voice or tone of their Personal Experience paper-in-progress.
  Assign: Cordell Waldron, "Seeing Red"

Wed.: Opening minutes: ask students to freewrite their responses to "Seeing Red." Ask several students to read their freewritten responses.
Presentation on revising and proofreading
Assign: Opening of Chapter 9. Revising and Proofreading: Backing and Filling & William Zinsser, "Writing--and Rewriting--with a Word Processor"

Fri.: Presentation on sharpening diction and avoiding wordiness
Assign: Gay Talese, "The Tailors of Maida"

Week 4
Mon.: Second Drafts of Personal Experience Paper Due
Begin responding to Second Drafts in small groups (making distinction between responses involving revision and those related to proofreading)
Assign: Brenda Ueland's "The Imagination Works Slowly and Quietly"

Wed.: Continue small group responses to Second Drafts
Assign: John Updike's "One More Interview"

Fri.: Polished Personal Experience Paper Due
Introduce the Report
Assign: Opening of Chapter 3. Researching: The Deeper the Richer & Henry James, "The Art of Fiction"

Week 5
Mon.: Practice Invention Strategies for Finding a Report Topic
Assign: John McPhee, "The Search for Marvin Gardens"

Wed.: Opening minutes: have students list the kinds of research McPhee used for his article "The Search for Marvin Gardens"
Session (perhaps in the library) on using compact discs for searches and other research techniques
Assign: Barbara Tuchman, "In Search of History"

Fri.: Opening minutes: underscore the differences between primary and secondary sources and have students make a list under these headings of the sources they plan to tap for their reports.
Discuss the sections of a Report: Abstract, Table of Contents, Labeled Sections, Bibliography of Works Cited or References, Optional Appendices

Explain internal documentation

Assign: Carol Kammen, "Concerning Footnotes"

Week 6

Mon.: Focus on developing the Report sections--types of evidence; specificity of detail--all presented in an objective voice
Assign: Jon Shepherd, "Employee Stock Ownership Plans: New Players in the Leveraged Buyout Game"

Wed.: Opening minutes: discuss Shepherd's use of voice, sources, and section headings in "Employee Stock Ownership Plans"
Presentation on Introductions & Titles
Assign: Opening of Chapter 6. One True Sentence & Ernest Hemingway, "A Moveable Feast"

Fri.: First Drafts of Reports Due
Respond to first drafts in small groups
Assign: Cori McNeilus, "Labor Unions: Part of Our Past or Future?"

Week 7

Mon.: Opening minutes: discuss McNeilus's use of voice, sources, and section headings in "Labor Unions"
Continue responding to first drafts of reports in small groups
Assign: Steven Armbrecht's "The Brady Plan: An Attempt to Solve the Mexican Debt Crisis"

Wed.: Opening minutes: discuss Armbrecht's use of voice, sources, and section headings in "The Brady Plan"
Introduce the Abstract & allow in-class time for writing the report Abstract
Assign: Julian Barnes, "Shipwreck"

Fri.: Opening minutes: ask students to list the sources Barnes tapped in order to write "Shipwreck"
Putting it all together: Abstract, Table of Contents, Report Sections, Bibliography of Works Cited or References, Appendices
Explain parallel construction (in reports & sentences); if time, do brief in-class exercise on paralleling
Assign: Plato, "The Allegory of the Cave"

Week 8

Mon.: Opening minutes: discuss Plato's Allegory as it applies to revision and their reports
Second Draft of Report Due
Respond to second drafts in small groups
Assign: Mary McCarthy, "Language and Politics"

Wed.: Opening minutes: discuss ways of polishing diction
Continue responding to Second Drafts of Reports in small groups
Assign: Lewis Thomas, "Notes on Punctuation"

Fri.: Opening minutes: discuss "Notes on Punctuation" with students, underscoring the points Thomas makes regarding each punctuation mark and entertaining student questions on punctuation.

Week 9
Mon.: Polished Report due
Introduce Informed Opinion Paper
Practice prewriting invention strategies for finding paper topics
Assign: Opening of Chapter 4. Finding the Form & George Orwell's "Why I Write" (in Chapter 7)

Wed.: Continue practicing prewriting invention strategies for finding a subject for an Informed Opinion Paper and then developing its points
Assign: Peter Elbow's "The Open-ended Writing Process"

Fri.: Opening 20-25 minutes: practice Elbow's Open-ended Writing Process with one possible subject for an Informed Opinion Paper
Presentation of possible ways to structure an Informed Opinion Paper & types of supportive evidence
Assign: Opening of Chapter 7. Generating & Sissela Bok, "Lying" (in Chapter 6)

Week 10
Mon.: Opening minutes: have students write down the opinion Bok advances in "Lying," her method of structuring her essay, and the sources she taps.

Presentation on finding a voice for presenting one's opinion

Assign: Carol Bly, "Small Towns: A Close Second Look at a Very Good Place"

Wed.: Opening minutes: have students write down the opinion(s) Bly advances in "Small Towns," her method of structuring her essay, the sources she taps, and the voice she adopts.

Assign: Tom Wolfe, "The Kandy-Kolored Tangerine-Flake Streamline Baby"

Fri.: First Drafts of Informed Opinion Paper Due
Respond to First Drafts in small groups

Assign: Gretel Ehrlich, "About Men" and Anne Jardim & Margaret Hennig, "Managerial Woman"

Week 11

Mon.: Opening minutes: have students write down the opinion Gretel Ehrlich advances in "About Men," her method of structuring her essay, the sources she taps, and the voice she adopts. Then do the same for the assigned excerpt from <u>Managerial Woman</u>.

Continue responding to First Drafts in small groups

Assign: Winston Churchill, "The National Coalition"

Wed.: Opening minutes: have students write down the opinion(s) Churchill advances in "The National Coalition," his method of structuring his essay, sources tapped, and voice adopted.

Presentation on acknowledging and rebutting opposing opinions & on Logos, Pathos, & Ethos in writing—with reference to Churchill's work.

    Assign: Stephen Jay Gould, "The Panda's Thumb"

Fri.: Opening minutes: have students write down the opinion(s) Gould advances in "The Panda's Thumb," his method of structuring his essay, sources tapped, and voice adopted.
Discuss Gould's Logos, Pathos, and Ethos in "The Panda's Thumb"
    Assign: George Lakoff and Mark Johnson, "Concepts We Live By" and Anne Morrow Lindbergh, "Double-Sunrise"

Week 12

Mon.: Opening minutes: discuss the structure of Lindbergh's "Double-Sunrise" and her Logos, Pathos, and Ethos
Presentation on agreement of subjects, pronouns, verbs, and nouns

    Assign: Opening of Chapter 8. Sustaining the Call & Wendell Berry, "Home of the Free"

Wed.: Opening minutes: have students write the opinion Wendell Berry advances in "Home of the Free," the structure and voice he selects, and the sources he taps. Discuss his Logos, Pathos, and Ethos.
Second Drafts of Informed Opinion Paper Due
Respond to Second Drafts in small groups
    Assign: William Kloefkorn, "Telling It Like It Maybe Is"

Fri.: Opening minutes: discuss the voice and structure of Wlliam Kloefkorn's "Telling It Like It Maybe Is"
Continue responding to Second Drafts in small groups

Week 13
Mon.: Polished Informed Opinion Papers due
Introduce the Critical Review of an article or book and offer students a choice of articles to review
Assign: Martin Luther King, Jr., "Letter from Birmingham Jail" and Lisa Battani's "An Analysis of 'Letter from Birmingham Jail'"

Wed.: Opening minutes: have students write the opinion(s) King advances in his "Letter from Birmingham Jail."
Discuss each section of Lisa Battani's analysis of "Letter from Birmingham Jail," noting on the board additions students would make to each section--and any divergent opinions.

Assign: Ruth Wisse, "Romance of the Secret Annex"

Fri.: Opening minutes: have each student make a list of the major ideas and opinions Ruth Wisse advances in her review of The Diary of Anne Frank: The Critical Edition.

Allow students to work on writing the opening ("Summary") section of their reviews in class, giving individual assistance as required.

Assign: Mihaly Csikszentmihalyi, "Flow" and Barry Lopez, "Landscape and Narrative"

Week 14

Mon.: Opening minutes: ask students to freewrite how they think Csikszentmihalyi's "Flow" relates 1) to the writing process, and 2) to evaluating articles and books. Structure remainder of class around an analysis of Barry Lopez's "Landscape and Narrative," making lists on the board of Strengths of this essay, Limitations, and Recommendations regarding the essay.

Assign: E. B. White, "Death of a Pig"

Wed.: Opening minutes: have each student brainstorm three lists: 1) Strengths of White's essay "Death of a Pig," 2) Limitations or Weaknesses in the essay, and 3) Recommendations each would make to strengthen the essay or for its use or audience. Collect these lists.

First Draft of Critical Review due While students are responding to these First Drafts in small groups, make a list on the board of the class's Critical Review of White's essay from the lists collected. Share this with the class in the closing 5 minutes of class.
Assign: Brad Williams, "Of Cows and Men"

Fri.: Opening minutes: have each student brainstorm three lists: 1) Strengths of Brad Williams's essay; 2) any Limitations or Weaknesses noted; and 3) Recommendations for improving the Weaknesses or regarding its use or audience. Collect these lists.

While students are continuing to respond to First Drafts of their Critical Reviews in small groups, make a list on the board of the class's Critical Review of "Of Cows and Men," using the collected lists. Share this with the class in the closing 5 minutes of class.
Assign: Maxine Hong Kingston, "At the Western Palace"

Week 15
 Mon.: Opening minutes: have each students brainstorm three lists: 1) the Strengths of Kingston's "At the Western Palace"; 2) any Limitations or Weaknesses noted; and 3) Recommendations for improving the Weaknesses or regarding its use or audience.
Begin a group Critical Review of Kingston's "At the Western Palace" by soliciting one item from each student's list.
Focus: ways to discuss the nuances of writing.
Assign: Longinus, "On the Sublime"

 Wed.: Opening minutes: brief discussion of Longinus's essay
Second Draft of Critical Review Due
Respond to Second Drafts in small groups
Assign: John McNulty's "Come Quick. Indians!"

 Fri.: Opening minutes: brief discussion of how McNulty's language and sentence style capture (and change with) his subject.
Continue responding to Second Drafts of Critical Reviews in small groups.

IM-11

Week 16

Mon.: Polished Critical Reviews due
Begin review & celebration of student work by sharing copies of superior Personal Experience papers and Reports
Assign: Alice Walker, "Really, <u>Doesn't</u> Crime Pay?"

Wed.: Opening minutes: discuss the pleasures of Alice Walker's short story and its experimental (or innovative) qualities
Continue review & celebration of student work by sharing copies of superior Informed Opinion Papers and Critical Reviews
Assign: Alice Munro, "Material"

Fri.: Discuss Munro's story and relate it to a Course Summary: material and what we do with it. Have students read aloud and interpret the "Touchstones" (quotations) in Chapter 10 in terms of what they have learned about the writing process.

<u>Final Exam:</u> A final in-class essay in which students are asked to describe the writing process in general, what they have learned during the semester about their <u>own</u> writing processes, and the conditions under which they write best.

Sample 16-Week Semester Syllabus
(Tuesday, Thursday)

Week 1
- Tues.: Introduce Course
  - Assign: Opening of Chapter 1. Introduction: A Writer's Beginnings & Annie Dillard, "An American Childhood"
  - Do as many of the Brief Warm-up Writing Exercises for Dillard as possible.

- Thurs.: Introduce Personal Experience Paper
  - Present & Practice Invention Strategies
  - Assign: Opening of Chapter 2. Finding the Subject: The Figure in the Carpet; May Sarton, "Journal of a Solitude"; and Joan Didion, "On Keeping a Notebook"

Week 2
- Tues.: Introduce "thesis" or "controlling idea"
  - Discuss the importance of vivid, sensory details
  - Assign (or use in class): Warren Wortham, "Musical Beginnings," Kelly Linnenkamp, "Lifeguarding: Fun in the Sun?" and Philip Roth, "My Baseball Years"

- Thurs.: Opening minutes: Discuss thesis and vivid, sensory details in Roth's "My Baseball Years"
  - First Draft of Personal Experience Paper Due
  - Begin Responding to Drafts in small peer writing groups
  - Assign: Opening of Chapter 5. Finding a Voice, Donna Roazen's "Milk Run," Nancy Price's "One Story--Thirteen Points of View," &

John Barth's "Some Reasons Why I Tell The Stories I Tell The Way I Tell Them Rather Than Some Other Sort Of Stories Some Other Way"

Week 3

Tues.: Opening minutes: ask students to list the vivid details they remember from John Barth's essay.
Discuss the role of "voice" in writing in general, and in their Personal Experience Papers in particular.
Continue responding to First Drafts in small groups.
Assign: Opening of Chapter 9. Revising and Proofreading: Backing and Filling & William Zinsser, "Writing--and Rewriting--with a Word Processor"

Thurs.: Presentation on revising and proofreading
Use the two versions of Cory Waldron's essay in Chapter 5 as illustration, or the two drafts of Jennifer Miller's "Lipstick Kisses" in Chapter 9.

Assign: Brenda Ueland, "The Imagination Works Slowly and Quietly" and Virginia Woolf "Professions for Women"

Week 4

Tues.: Second Drafts of Personal Experience Paper Due
Presentation on sharpening diction and avoiding wordiness
Begin responding to Second Drafts in small groups (making distinction between responses involving revision and those related to proofreading).

　　　　　Assign:　John Updike, "One More
　　　　　　　　　　Interview"

　Thurs.:　Continue small group responses to
　　　　　　　　　　　　　Second Drafts

　　　　　Assign:　Opening of Chapter 3.
　　　　　　　　　　Researching: The Deeper
　　　　　　　　　　the Richer & Henry James,
　　　　　　　　　　"The Art of Fiction"

Week 5
　Tues.:　Polished Personal Experience Papers
　　　　　　　　　　　　　　　　Due
　　　　　　　Introduce Report, including its
　　　　　　　structure: Abstract, Table of
　　　　　　　Contents, Labeled Sections,
　　　　　　　Bibliography of Works Cited or
　　　　　　　References, Optional Appendix or
　　　　　　　　　　　　　Appendices
　　　　　　　Use Invention Strategies for finding
　　　　　　　　　　　　　Report topics
　　　　　Assign:　Barbara Tuchman, "In Search
　　　　　　　　　　　　of History"

　Thurs.:　Session (if possible in the library)
　　　　　　on using compact discs for searches
　　　　　　as well as other research techniques.

　　　　　Assign:　John McPhee, "The Search for
　　　　　　　　　　Marvin Gardens" and Carol
　　　　　　　　　　Kammen, "Concerning
　　　　　　　　　　　　Footnotes"

Week 6
　Tues.:　Opening minutes: have students list
　　　　　　the kinds of research McPhee used for
　　　　　　his article "The Search for Marvin
　　　　　　Gardens." Then, after reviewing the
　　　　　　difference between primary and
　　　　　　secondary sources, have students list
　　　　　　under these headings the sources they
　　　　　　plan to tap for their reports.

　　　　　　　　　　IM-15

Explain and illustrate internal documentation.

Assign: Jon Shepherd, "Employee Stock Ownership Plans: New Players in the Leveraged Buyout Game"

Thurs.: Focus on ways to develop Report sections: types of evidence, specificity of detail--all presented in an objective voice.
Discuss Jon Shepherd's use of voice, sources, section headings, and section development in "Employee Stock Ownership Plans"
First Drafts of Reports Due
Begin responding to First Drafts in small groups

Assign: Cori McNeilus, "Labor Unions: Part of Our Past or Future?"

Week 7

Tues.: Opening minutes: discuss McNeilus's use of voice, sources, and section headings in "Labor Unions"
Continue responding to First Drafts of Reports in small groups

Assign: Steven Armbrecht, "The Brady Plan: An Attempt to Solve the Mexican Debt Crisis"

Thurs.: Opening minutes: discuss Armbrecht's voice, sources, section headings, and section development in "The Brady Plan"

Presentation on Introductions, Titles, and Abstracts
Presentation on parallel construction (in Reports & sentences); if time, do brief in-class exercise on paralleling.

Assign: Opening of Chapter 6. One
         True Sentence & Ernest
         Hemingway, "A Moveable
         Feast"

Week 8
 Tues.: Second Drafts of Report Due
         Respond to Second Drafts in small
                                  groups

         Assign: Julian Barnes, "Shipwreck"

 Thurs.: Opening minutes: ask students to
         list the sources Barnes tapped in
                 order to write "Shipwreck"
         Continue responding to Second Drafts
                 of reports in small groups
         Assign: Lewis Thomas, "Notes on
                                Punctuation"

Week 9
 Tues.: Opening minutes: discuss "Notes on
         Punctuation" with students, with
         special reference to their Reports.

         Polished Report Due
         Introduce Informed Opinion Paper
         Practice invention strategies for
                  finding paper topics.
         Assign: Opening of Chapter 4.
                  Finding the Form and George
                  Orwell's "Why I Write"
                        (in Chapter 7)

 Thurs.: Read in class Peter Elbow's "The
         Open-ended Writing Process" in
         Chapter 2. Then practice Elbow's
         process for one possible subject for
                  an Informed Opinion Paper.
         Presentation on possible ways to
         structure an Informed Opinion Paper
              & types of supportive evidence.
         Assign: Opening of Chapter 7.
                  Generating and Sissela
                  Bok, "Lying" (in Chapter 6)

Week 10

Tues.: Opening minutes: have students write down the opinion(s) Bok advances in "Lying," her method of structuring her essay, and the sources she taps.

First Draft of Informed Opinion Paper Due

Respond to First Drafts in Small Groups

Assign: Carol Bly, "Small Towns: A Close Second Look at a Very Good Place"

Thurs.: Opening minutes: have students write down the opinion(s) Bly advances in "Small Towns," her method of structuring her essay, the sources she taps, and the voice she adopts. Continue responding to First Drafts in small groups.

Assign: Tom Wolfe, "The Kandy-Kolored Tangerine-Flake Streamline Baby"; Gretel Ehrlich, "About Men"; & Margaret Hennig and Anne Jardim, "Mangerial Woman"

Week 11

Tues.: Opening minutes: have students write down the opinion Gretel Ehrlich advances in "About Men," her method of structuring her essay, the sources she taps, and the voice she adopts. Then do the same for the assigned excerpt from <u>Managerial Woman</u>. Presentation and exercise on acknowledging and rebutting opposing opinion; presentation on Logos, Pathos, & Ethos in writing.

Assign: Winston Churchill, "The National Coalition"

Thurs.: Opening minutes: have students write down the opinion(s) Churchill advances in "The National Coalition," his method of structuring his essay, sources tapped, and voice adopted.

    Assign: Stephen Jay Gould, "The Panda's Thumb"; George Lakoff and Mark Johnson, "Concepts We Live By"; and Anne Morrow Lindbergh, "Double-Sunrise"

Week 12

Tues.: Opening minutes: have students write down the opinion(s) Gould advances in "The Panda's Thumb," method of structuring his essay, sources tapped, and voice adopted.
Discuss Gould's Logos, Pathos, and Ethos in "The Panda's Thumb."
Second Drafts of Informed Opinion Paper Due
Respond to Second Drafts in groups

    Assign: Opening of Chapter 8. Sustaining the Call & Wendell Berry, "Home of the Free"

Thurs.: Opening minutes: have students write the opinion(s) Wendell Berry advances in "Home of the Free," the structure and voice he selects, and the sources he taps. Discuss his Logos, Pathos, and Ethos.
Continue discussion of Second Drafts of Informed Opinion Papers in small groups.
    Assign: William Kloefkorn, "Telling It Like It Maybe Is"

Week 13

Tues.: Polished Informed Opinion Paper Due
Introduce the Critical Review of an article or book and offer students a choice of articles to review.

Assign: Martin Luther King, Jr., "Letter from Birmingham Jail" and Lisa Battani's "An Analysis of Letter from Birmingham Jail'"

Thurs.: Opening minutes: have students write the opinion(s) King advances in his "Letter from Birmingham Jail." Discuss each section of Lisa Battani's analysis of "Letter from Birmingham Jail," noting on the board additions student would make to each section--and any divergent opinions.

If time, allow students to work on the Summary section of their Critical Reviews in class.
Assign: Ruth Wisse, "Romance of the Secret Annex"

Week 14
Tues.: Opening minutes: have each student brainstorm four lists: 1) the major ideas and opinions Ruth Wisse advances in her review of The Diary of Anne Frank: The Critical Edition; 2) Strengths of Wisse's review; 3) Limitations or Weaknesses of the Review; and 4) Recommendations each would make to strengthen the review or for its use or audience. Collect these unsigned lists.

First Draft of Critical Reviews Due
While students are responding to these First Drafts in small groups, make a list on the board of the class's Critical Review of Wisse's essay from the lists collected. Share this with the class in the closing 5 minutes of class.

Assign: Mihaly Csikszentmihalyi, "Flow" and Barry Lopez, "Landscape and Narrative"

Thurs.: Opening minutes: have each student brainstorm four lists: 1) the ideas and opinions Barry Lopez advances in "Landscape and Narrative"; 2) the Strengths of Lopez's essay; 3) any Limitations or Weaknesses in the essay; 4) Recommendations for strengthening the essay or for its further use or audience. Continue responding to First Drafts of Critical Reviews in small groups. While students are working in groups, make a list on the board of the class's Critical Review of Lopez's essay from the lists collected.

Assign: E. B. White, "Death of a Pig" and Brad Williams, "Of Cows and Men"

Week 15

Tues.: Opening minutes: Divide the class in half and have one-half brainstorm 3 lists regarding E. B. White's essay "Death of a Pig" and the other 3 lists regarding Brad Williams's "Of Cows and Men": 1) the Strengths of the essay; 2) any Limitations or Weaknesses noted; and 3) Recommendations to strengthen the essay or for its further use or audience.

Outline a Critical Review of each essay on the board, drawing at least one item from each student's listings. Focus: ways to discuss the nuances of writing.

Assign: Longinus, "On the Sublime" and John McNulty, "Come Quick. Indians!"

Thurs.: Opening minutes: brief discussion of how McNulty's language and sentence style capture (and change with) his subject.
Second Drafts of Critical Review due.

IM-21

Begin responding to Second Drafts in small groups.

    Assign: William Kloefkorn, "Telling It Like it Maybe Is" and Mary McCarthy, "Language and Politics"

Week 16
  Tues.: Opening minutes: have students freewrite their responses to William Kloefkorn's essay "Telling It Like It Maybe Is."
  Discuss Kloefkorn's advice in respect to their Critical Reviews in progress.
  Continue responses to Second Drafts in small groups.

    Assign: Alice Munro, "Material"

  Thurs.: Polished Critical Reviews due. Discuss Alice Munro's "Material" in terms of what it suggests about writers and the writing process as a lead into the Course Summary. If time, bring in copies of exemplary Personal Experience Papers, Reports, and Informed Opinion Papers to distribute to the class as a celebration and commemoration of their work.

    Assign for Final: Chapter 10. Touchstones

Final Exam: A final in-class essay in which students are asked to describe the writing process in general, and what they have learned during the semester about their _own_ writing processes and the conditions under which they write best.

Syllabus for 10-Week Quarter
(Mondays, Wednesdays, Fridays)

Week 1
- Monday: Introduce Course
  - Assign: Opening of Chapter 1. Introduction: A Writer's Beginnings & Annie Dillard, "An American Childhood"
  - Do: As many of the Brief Warm-up Writing Exercises for Dillard's essay as possible.

- Wed.: Introduce Paper #1
  - Present & Practice Invention Strategies
  - Assign: Opening of Chapter 2. Finding the Subject: The Figure in the Carpet & May Sarton, "Journal of a Solitude"

- Fri.: Introduce "thesis" or "controlling idea" & the importance of vivid, sensory details
  - Read Warren Wortham's "Musical Beginnings" in class, with special reference to "thesis." If time, read Kelly Linnenkamp's essay "Lifeguarding: Fun in the Sun?" in class, noting changes in "thesis" and use of vivid details.
  - Assign: Joan Didion, "On Keeping a Notebook" & Philip Roth, "My Baseball Years"

Week 2
- Mon.: First Draft of Paper #1 Due
  - Describe small group work; then break into small groups to respond to First Drafts.
  - Assign: Assign Opening of Chapter 5. Finding a Voice; Donna Roazen, "Milk Run" & Nancy Price, "One Story--Thirteen Points of View"

Wed.: Opening minutes: Ask students their responses to "Milk Run" and "One Story--Thirteen Points of View" as an introduction to a general discussion of "voice" in general, and in their papers-in-progress in particular.

Presentation on revising and proofreading.
Assign: Chapter 9. Revising and Proofreading: Backing and Filling & William Zinsser, "Writing--and Rewriting--with a Word Processor"

Fri.: Presentation on sharpening diction and avoiding wordiness followed by in-class exercise
Assign: Gay Talese, "The Tailors of Maida"

Week 3

Mon.: Polished First Paper Due
Introduce Paper #2 (involving research)
Practice Invention Strategies for finding a paper topic
Assign: Opening of Chapter 3. Researching: The Deeper the Richer & Henry James, "The Art of Fiction"

Wed.: Session (perhaps in the library) on using compact discs for searches and other research techniques
Assign: Barbara Tuchman, "In Search of History"

Fri.: Opening minutes: underscore the difference between primary and secondary sources and have students make a list under these headings of the sources they are tapping (or plan to tap) for their papers.

Explain & illustrate internal
documentation and use of a
bibliography (with special reference
   to their papers-in-progress).
   Assign: Carol Kammen, "Concerning
             Footnotes" & Jon Shepherd,
             "Employee Stock Ownership
             Plans: A New Player in the
             Leveraged Buyout Game"

Week 4
  Mon.:   Opening minutes: discuss Shepherd's
          use of voice, sources, and section
          headings in "Employee Stock Ownership
                                        Plans"
          Presentation on Introductions & Titles

          Assign: Opening of Chapter 6. One
                    True Sentence & Ernest
                    Hemingway, "A Moveable Feast"

  Wed.:   First Draft of Paper #2 Due
          Short presentation on developing
          paragraphs: types of evidence & need
                         for specific details
          Begin responding to First Drafts in
          small groups, asking students to focus
          particularly on introductions and
                    paragraph development.
          Assign: Cori McNeilus, "Labor Unions:
                    Part of Our Past or Future?"

  Fri.:   Opening minutes: discuss McNeilus's
          introduction, paragraph development,
          voice, & use of sources in "Labor
                                       Unions"
          Explain parallel construction and its
          use in essays, reports, and sentences.
          Do brief in-class exercise on
                    paralleling.

          Assign: Mary McCarthy, "Language and
                                       Politics"

Week 5
  Mon.:   Polished Paper #2 Due

Introduce Paper #3
Practice Invention Strategies for finding paper topics
Assign: Opening of Chapter 4. Finding the Form & Peter Elbow, "The Open-ended Writing Process"

Wed.: Opening 20-25 minutes: practice Elbow's Open-ended Writing Process with one possible subject for Paper #3--allowing the writing to take whatever form it takes.
Presentation on forms of writing (in general) and ways to structure essays (in particular).
Assign: Opening of Chapter 7. Generating & George Orwell, "Why I Write"

Fri.: First Draft of Paper #3 Due
Respond to First Drafts in small groups
Assign: Mihaly Csikszentmihalyi, "Flow" & Barry Lopez, "Landscape and Narrative"

Week 6

Mon.: Opening minutes: have students list the main idea(s) Lopez advances in "Landscape and Narrative." Use this list as a springboard for a discussion of the relationship of Csikszentmihalyi's "Flow" to Lopez's ideas, noting that both involve trying to regulate (or focus upon) the relationship of outer and/or inner "reality." Relate this to the writing process and to students' papers-in-progress.
Presentation on Logos, Pathos, & Ethos in writing

Assign: E. B. White, "Death of a Pig" & Brad Williams, "Of Cows and Men"

Wed.: Opening minutes: ask students to freewrite on E. B. White's Logos, Pathos, & Ethos in "Death of a Pig" or on the Logos, Pathos, & Ethos of Brad Williams in "Of Cows and Men." Develop the comparison on the board.

Read Lewis Thomas's essay "Notes on Punctuation" in class, asking specific students to read each paragraph aloud. Discuss Thomas's remarks on each mark as you go, underscoring key points and encouraging student questions.

Fri.: Polished Paper #3 Due
Introduce Paper #4 (involving research)
Practice Invention Strategies for finding paper topics
Assign: Winston Churchill, "The National Coalition"

Week 7

Mon.: Opening minutes: have students write down the opinion(s) Churchill advances in "The National Coalition," his method of structuring his essay, sources tapped, and voice adopted.

Presentation on acknowledging & rebutting opposing opinions--with reference to Churchill's essay; brief in-class exercise practicing this technique.
Assign: Sissela Bok, "Lying"

Wed.: Opening minutes: have students write down the opinion(s) Bok advances in "Lying," her method of structuring her essay, and the sources she taps. Discuss her anticipation and rebuttal of opposing views on her subject.

Divide the class in thirds. Ask the students in group 1 to write on Bok's

use of logical appeals (Logos) in her essay; the students in group 2 to write on Bok's use of emotional appeals (Pathos) in her essay; and the students in group 3 to write on Bok's Ethos in "Lying." After allowing them to work for 15 minutes, collect evidence under each heading on the board with an eye for analyzing which appeal Bok employs most fully and successfully.
Assign: Steven Armbrecht, "The Brady Plan: An Attempt to Solve the Mexican Debt Crisis"

Fri.: First Draft of Paper #4 Due
Respond to First Drafts in small groups
Assign: Stephen Jay Gould, "The Panda's Thumb"

Week 8
Mon.: Opening minutes: have students write down the opinion(s) Gould advances in "The Panda's Thumb," his method of structuring his essay, sources tapped, and voice adopted. Divide the class into 3 groups. Ask the students in group 1 to write on Gould's use of logical appeals (Logos) in "The Panda's Thumb"; the students in group 2 to write on Gould's use of emotional appeals (Pathos) in his essay; and the students in group 3 to write on his Ethos in his essay. (Be sure students are writing on a different appeal than they focused on for the Bok essay.)
Assign: Opening of Chapter 8. Sustaining the Call & Wendell Berry, "Home of the Free"

Wed.: Opening minutes: have students write the opinion(s) Wendell Berry advances in "Home of the Free," the structure

and voice he selects, and the sources he taps. Discuss his Logos, Pathos, & Ethos.
Presentation on agreement of subjects, verbs, pronouns, and nouns in writing, followed by brief in-class exercise allowing students to practice the principles described.
Assign: Margaret Hennig & Anne Jardim, "Managerial Woman"

Fri.: Opening minutes: have students list the opinion(s) Anne Jardim & Margaret Hennig advance in "Managerial Woman" and then freewrite whether they agree or disagree with their position. Ask for representative freewrites to be read as a way of moving into a discussion of the Logos, Pathos, and Ethos in this brief excerpt.
Polished Paper #4 Due
Introduce Paper #5 (perhaps a critical review)
Offer students a choice of articles to review
Assign: Martin Luther King, Jr., "Letter from Birmingham Jail" & Lisa Battani, "An Analysis of 'Letter from Birmingham Jail'"

Week 9
Mon.: Opening minutes: discuss each section of Lisa Battani's analysis of "Letter from Birmingham Jail," noting on the board additions students would make to each section--and any divergent opinions.
Discuss the characteristics of a good "Summary" of an article or book. Then allow students in-class time to work on the Summary section of their critical reviews, giving individual assistance as required.
Assign: Ruth Wisse, "Romance of the Secret Annex"

Wed.: Opening minutes: have each student make a list of the major ideas and opinions Ruth Wisse advances in her review of <u>The Diary of Anne Frank: The Critical Edition</u>. Then, as a group, discuss (and place on the board) a list of: 1) the Strengths of Ruth Wisse's review; 2) Limitations or Weaknesses in the review; and 3) Recommendations for strengthening the review, or for its use by its audience or suitability for other audiences.
Presentation on diction: "Gas vs. Petroleum and Work vs. Employment: Anglo-Saxon & Latin influences on the English language
Assign: Longinus, "On the Sublime"

Fri.: Opening minutes: brief discussion of Longinus's essay as it relates to ways of discussing the nuances of writing.

First Drafts of Paper #5 due
Respond to First Drafts in small groups
Assign: Julian Barnes, "Shipwreck"

<u>Week 10</u>
Mon.: Opening minutes: ask students to brainstorm 3 lists: 1) the Strengths of Julian Barnes's "Shipwreck"; 2) Limitations or Weaknesses of Barnes's essay; and 3) Recommendations for strengthening the weaknesses noted or for its use by its audience, or other audiences. Solicit items from each student's list in making a group review of Barnes's "Shipwreck."

Read John McNulty's essay "Come Quick. Indians!" aloud in class. Facilitate a class review of the Strengths and Limitations of McNulty's essay, with special focus on his use of language and sentence fragments. Make a list

IM-30

              of any Recommendations the class would make regarding audiences for this work, or for strengthening the weaknesses noted.

Fri.: Polished Paper #5 due.
Course Summary: Review & Celebration of writing done. Share with students copies of superior work done on each of the first 4 paper assignments.

      Assign for Final: Chapter 10.
                            Touchstones

<u>Final Exam:</u> A final in-class essay in which students describe the writing process in general, and then what they have learned during the quarter about their <u>own</u> writing processes and the conditions under which they write best.

<u>Sample Syllabus for 10-Week Quarter</u>
      (Tuesdays & Thursdays)

Week 1
Tuesday: Introduce Course
Introduce Paper #1
Assign: Opening of Chapter 1. Introduction: A Writer's Beginnings & Annie Dillard, "An American Childhood"
Do: As many of the Brief Warm-up Writing Exercises for Dillard's essay as possible.

Thursday: Practice Invention Strategies
Introduce "thesis" or "controlling idea" & the importance of vivid sensory details

          Assign: Opening of Chapter 2. Finding the Subject: The Figure in the Carpet, May Sarton, "Journal of a Solitude" & Joan Didion, "On Keeping a Notebook"

Week 2

Tues.: First Draft of Paper #1 Due
Describe small group work; then break into small groups to respond to First Drafts

       Assign: Chapter 9. Revising and Proofreading: Backing and Filling & William Zinsser, "Writing--and Rewriting--with a Word Processor"

Thurs.: Read both drafts of Kelly Linnenkamp's Chapter 2 essay "Lifeguarding: Fun in the Sun?" in class, noting changes in thesis and use of vivid sensory details.

Presentation on sharpening diction and avoiding wordiness followed by an in-class exercise

       Assign: Philip Roth, "My Baseball Years"

Week 3

Tues.: Polished First Paper Due
Introduce Paper #2 (involving research)
Practice Invention Strategies for finding a paper topic
       Assign: Opening of Chapter 3. Researching: The Deeper the Richer & Henry James, "The Art of Fiction"

Thurs.: Session (perhaps in the library) on using compact discs for searches and other research techniques you go, underscoring key points and encouraging student questions.

  Thurs.: Polished Paper #3 Due
         Introduce Paper #4 (involving research)
         Practice Invention Strategies for finding paper topics

         Assign: Winston Churchill, "The National Coalition"

Week 8

  Tues.: Opening minutes: have students write down the opinion(s) Churchill advances in "The National Coalition." After listing these on the board, discuss his method of structuring his essay, sources tapped, and voice adopted.
Presentation on acknowledging & rebutting opposing opinions--with reference to Churchill's essay; brief in-class exercise practicing this technique.
         Assign: Steven Armbrecht, "The Brady Plan: An Attempt to Solve the Mexican Debt Crisis"

  Thurs.: Opening minutes: have students write down the opinion(s) Armbrecht advances in "The Brady Plan," his method of structuring his essay, sources tapped, and voice adopted. Collect these.

        First Draft of Paper #4 Due
While students are responding to these First Drafts in small groups, make a list on the board of class's analysis of Armbrecht's essay, from the sheets collected. Share this with the class in the closing 5 minutes of class.

         Assign: Sissela Bok, "Lying"

Week 9
  Tues.: Opening minutes: have students list the opinion(s) Bok advances in her essay and then freewrite whether they find themselves agreeing or disagreeing with Bok--and why. Ask for at least one on each side to be read as a way of introducing a:

  Presentation on Logos, Pathos, and Ethos in Writing. In last 5 minutes of class ask students to analyze the appeals present in their current paper-in-progress and to state which (if any) appeals they hope to develop more extensively as they move to their polished submission. Have students hand these in.
  Assign: Carol Bly, "Small Towns: A Close Second Look at a Very Good Place"

  Thurs.: Opening minutes: ask students to freewrite their assessment of Bly's essay "Small Towns" in terms of her use of logical appeals (logos), emotional appeals (pathos), and ethical appeals (ethos).

  Polished Paper #4 Due
  Introduce Paper #5 (perhaps a critical review)
  Offer students a choice of articles to review
  Assign: Opening of Chapter 8. Sustaining the Call & Martin Luther King, Jr., "Letter from Birmingham Jail" & Lisa Battani's "An Analysis of 'Letter from Birmingham Jail'"

Week 10
  Tues.: Opening minutes: discuss each section of Lisa Battani's analysis of "Letter from Birmingham Jail," noting on the

IM-36

board additions students would make to each section--and any divergent opinions.
First Drafts of Paper #5 Due
Respond to First Drafts in small groups

Assign: Ruth Wisse, "Romance of the Secret Annex"

Thurs.: Polished Paper #5 Due (also accepted Friday)
Course Summary: Review & Celebration of writing done. Share with students copies of superior work done on each of the first 4 assignments.

Assign for Final: Chapter 10. Touchstones

<u>Final Exam:</u> A final in-class essay in which students are asked to describe the writing process in general, and then what they have learned during the quarter about their <u>own</u> writing processes and the conditions under which they write best.

Section 2

GUIDELINES FOR USING EACH CHAPTER

The following are general suggestions for using each chapter of <u>The Writer in You</u>. Many of the selections have been placed next to each other in the chapters because they work well together as pairs. These selections might be assigned and discussed together. Those selections which provide early and late drafts are indicated with an asterisk (*).

Chapter 1. A Writer's Beginnings

This chapter focuses on childhood memories and first writing efforts. It is designed to suggest to students the variety of ways writers come to writing and to encourage them to begin writing themselves. It will be especially useful for teachers who like to begin writing courses with personal writing. The essays are also useful as illustrations of the use of vivid details.

<u>Possible Pairs</u> (to assign & discuss):

Annie Dillard, "An American Childhood"
Philip Roth, "My Baseball Years"
   (male & female treatment of baseball)

Margaret Atwood, "High School Beginnings"
*John Barth, "Some Reasons Why I Tell The Stories The Way I Tell Them Rather Than Some Other Sort of Stories Some Other Way"
   (humorous backward glances at schooldays)

*John Barth, "Some Reasons . . ."
*Warren Wortham, "Musical Beginnings"
   (both deal with music as career choices)

Virginia Woolf, "Professions for Women"
Nadine Gordimer, "Not for Publication"
   (describe obstacles to self-actualization)

Chapter 2. Finding the Subject:
The Figure in the Carpet

This chapter is devoted to prewritng invention strategies and to early efforts at writing. Teachers who ask students to keep journals might assign the May Sarton and Joan Didion selections to enhance students' appreciation of writers' journals and notebooks. The remaining selections work to suggest the quiet deliberation and exploration writers engage in as they begin to find their particular subject matter and start to trace the figures they will pursue.

<u>Possible Pairs</u> (to assign & discuss):

May Sarton, "Journal of a Solitude"
Joan Didion, "On Keeping a Notebook"
  (journal vs. notebook keeping)

Brenda Ueland, "The Imagination Works Slowly and Quietly"
Plato, "The Allegory of the Cave"
  (the slow apprehension of truth)

Peter Elbow, "The Open-ended Writing Process"
*John Updike, "One More Interview"
  (a writer's gradual warming to his or her subject)

Chapter 3. Researching: The Deeper the Richer

This chapter is designed to survey a variety of forms of research: observation and on-site research; interviews; primary source research; secondary source research; and research in the fields of history, economics, and anthropology.

<u>Possible Pairs</u> (to assign & discuss):

Henry James, "The Art of Fiction"
John McPhee, "The Search for Marvin Gardens"
  (John McPhee seems to be a writer who follows Henry James's counsel to be "one of whom . . . nothing is lost"; his essay on Monopoly and Atlantic City is not only ingenious, but it illustrates primary, secondary, & on-site research)

Barbara Tuchman, "In Search of History"
Gay Talese, "The Tailors of Maida"
  (Talese's family history illustrates Tuchman's precepts regarding primary, secondary, and on-site research--as well as the importance of distilling information.)

Barbara Tuchman, "In Search of History"
Clifford Geertz, "Being There: Anthropology and the Scene of Writing"
  (research and writing in the fields of history & anthropology)

Clifford Geertz, "Being There: Anthropology and the Scene of Writing"
*Jon Shepherd, "Employee Stock Ownership Plans: New Players in the Leveraged Buyout Game"
  (studying American business as if it were a tribal culture)

John McPhee, "In Search of Marvin Gardens"
*Jon Shepherd, "Employee Stock Ownership Plans: New Players in the Leveraged Buyout Game"
  (American business as game)

Barbara Tuchman, "In Search of History"
*Julian Barnes, "Shipwreck"
  (history and art history; Barnes practices what Tuchman preaches)

Chapter 4. Finding the Form

This chapter moves from Longinus's discussion of suiting form to content to metaphor as form, the letter as form, the critical review as form, and an illustration of innovative form in the short story. The selections by Longinus, McNulty, Lakoff & Johnson, Lindbergh, and Battani illustrate a variety of essay forms, from the informal and personal (McNulty) to the highly formal (Longinus).

<u>Possible Pairs</u> (to assign & discuss):

Longinus, "On the Sublime"
John McNulty, "Come Quick. Indians!"
  (McNulty's personal essay illustrates
  Longinus's precepts regarding form matching
  content)

George Lakoff and Mark Johnson, "Concepts We Live By"
Anne Morrow Lindbergh, "Double-Sunrise"
  (Lakoff & Johnson illustrate the viability of
  collaborative writing while Lindbergh's
  essay is constructed from a metaphorical
  concept such as Lakoff & Johnson describe)

Martin Luther King, Jr., "Letter from Birmingham Jail"
*Lisa Battani, "An Analysis of 'Letter from Birmingham Jail'"
  (Battani's essay can be used as a model of a
  form for writing a critical review of an
  article or book)

Chapter 5. Finding a Voice

Seven different approaches to locating voice in a piece of writing are offered here. They include heuristic devices, such as Tom Wolfe's recommendation to begin works as letters, and student Cory Waldron's deliberate shift in point-of-view in the "Little Red

Riding Hood" story, as well as Nancy Price's exercise of rewriting Donna Roazen's short story "Milk Run" from thirteen different points of view. Internal ways of finding one's voice are explored by Eudora Welty, and Maxine Hong Kingston and Richard Rodriguez show how they have found ways to sound the voices of their Chinese and Hispanic traditions.

<u>Possible Pairs & Trios</u> (to assign & discuss):

*Maxine Hong Kingston, "At the Western Palace"
Richard Rodriguez, "Mr. Secrets"
  (the voices of diverse cultures)

Donna Roazen, "Milk Run"
Nancy Price, "One Story--Thirteen Points of
                                        View"

*Cory Waldron, "Seeing Red"
  (vivid--and changing--points of view)

<u>Chapter 6. One True Sentence</u>

    This chapter centers on the truth as both motivator and talisman for writing. If we can get our students to focus on telling the truth about their subjects, matters such as form and voice may fall naturally into place.

<u>Possible Pairs</u> (to assign & discuss)

Ernest Hemingway, "A Moveable Feast"
V. S. Naipaul, "Finding the Center"
  (Naipaul's essay illstrates Hemingway's
  counsel regarding the importance of
  beginning with "one true sentence")

*Sissela Bok, "Lying"
*Carol Bly, "Small Towns: A Close Second Look
                            at a Very Good Place"
  (Bly's essay offers a practical and
  refreshing illustration of Bok's message)

*Cori McNeilus, "Labor Unions: A Part of Our Past or Future?
Nancy Price, "Cover Girl"
   (efforts to tell the truth about their subjects)

Chapter 7. Generating

This chapter explores the process of generation, from what motivates writers to write, to ways of achieving creative "flow," to making do with one's natural materials.

Possible Pairs (to assign & discuss)

Stephen Jay Gould, "The Panda's Thumb"
*Steven W. Armbrecht, "The Brady Plan: An Attempt to Solve the Mexican Debt Crisis"
   (Natural and man-made attempts to find structural solutions to critical problems)

Mihaly Csikszentmihalyi, "Flow"
Barry Lopez, "Landscape and Narrative"
   (Lopez demonstrates the abstract concepts of "Flow")

Barry Lopez, "Landscape and Narrative"
Gretel Ehrlich, "About Men"
   (Here Ehrlich illustrates Lopez's counsel regarding exterior and interior landscapes)

Gretel Ehrlich, "About Men"
Margaret Hennig & Anne Jardim, "The Managerial Woman"
   (to engage the battle of the sexes)

Chapter 8. Sustaining the Call

This chapter is for advanced students, or for those wishing to consider the challenges of sustaining a work over an extended period of time, or sustaining oneself as a writer during adversity. Tips for writing about literature are given in William Kloefkorn's opening essay, "Telling It Like It Maybe Is: The Poet as Critic."

Possible Pairs (to assign & discuss):

Wendell Berry, "Home of the Free"
Aleksandr Solzhenitsyn, "First Cell, First
     Love" (To prime discussions on freedom,
       responsibility, and literacy)

Aleksandr Solzhenitsyn, "First Cell, First
                                       Love"
Ruth Wisse, "Romance of the Secret Annex"
   (Two prisoners of war)

Ruth Wisse, "Romance of the Secret Annex"
*Lisa Battani, "An Analysis of 'Letter from
          Birmingham Jail'" (in Chapter 4.)
   (examples of two reviews)

E. B. White, "Death of a Pig"
*Brad Williams, "Of Cows and Men"
   (giving voice to the ordinary; making
    the ordinary extraordinary)

Chapter 9. Revising and Proofreading: Backing and Filling

Aspects of revising and editing are presented here, from the joys of writing (and re-writing) with a word processor to the essential attention which must be given to language, punctuation, and footnotes. The reader closes with a student essay which experiments with different typefaces (as well as voices), and with Alice Munro's provocative short story on the writer, aptly titled "Material."

Possible Pairs (to assign & discuss):

Winston Churchill, "The National Coalition"
Mary McCarthy, "Language and Politics"
   (Language & Politics in the 1940s and 1970s)

Lewis Thomas, "Notes on Punctuation"
Carol Kammen, "Concerning Footnotes"
   (The fine points of writing)

Section Three

ANSWERS TO QUESTIONS TO PONDER

Chapter 1. Introduction: A Writer's Beginnings

For Annie Dillard's "An American Childhood":

1. <u>What did Annie Dillard discover about drawing as a young girl</u>?

    Dillard discovered that drawing bound her attention "to both the vigor and the detail of the actual world" (paragraph 2).

    <u>How long did it take to do a drawing</u>?

    Drawing took as long as Dillard (the drawer) cared to give it. She could do a gesture drawing in 45 seconds or spend all morning on a sustained study.

2. <u>In what ways might writing be like drawing</u>?

    Writing, too, draws our attention "to both the vigor and the detail of the actual world" (paragraph 2).

    <u>How long does it take to write about something</u>?

    It takes as long to write about something as the writer chooses to give. As Dillard says about drawing, writing about something takes "not an infinite amount of time, but more time than [the writer] first imagine[s]" (paragraph 7).

How many different ways are there to write about something?

There are as many different ways to write about something as there are writers writing. There are also as many ways to write about something as one writer can imagine--not an infinite number, but more than the writer might first think.

3. What keeps people from giving close attention to their lives as they unfold?

Three obstacles keep people from paying close attention to their lives. The first is over-scheduling. Students are often so busy rushing from class to work to study and back to class again that they have no time to see the world they are racing through or to reflect upon their experiences. A second barrier to close attention is fear of change. If we really see ourselves and our world, we may find that we need to change something--ourselves or the world, or both--and this takes effort. Some people seem deliberately to wear blinders to avoid upsetting their lives. Socrates offered the definitive comment on this form of chosen oblivion when he said, "The unexamined life is not worth living." A third reason many students fail to pay close attention to their lives is that no one has ever suggested that they should. They may have never enjoyed the benefits of close attention. Stopping to smell the lilacs, of course, becomes its own reward; the heavenly scent can transport one to an altered state. Writing assignments which encourage close attention enhance the quality of life itself.

What conditions are necessary in order for you really to concentrate on an assignment? A person? An event?

In answering this question, students should consider whether they need to be alone to concentrate on an assignment, a person, or an event--or if they focus better:

- in a crowd of strangers;
- surrounded by many, a few, or one other friend(s);
- with "background" music or noise or in complete silence.

They should reflect on whether they can better concentrate on an assignment, person, or event outdoors, in a public place, or in the privacy behind a closed door. They should consider whether they can concentrate best in the morning, afternoons, or evenings. Students should be encouraged to list the benefits and liabilities of each choice, to experiment with varying conditions for writing, and to report back their findings. They may discover that different writing projects call for different writing conditions at the same time they are finding their own optimal writing times and modes. When they have trouble concentrating or writing, they will learn to vary their writing situation in hopes of surprising themselves into something new (see the Introduction to Chapter 8. Sustaining the Call).

4. <u>How is learning to see related to learning to write</u>?

Seeing, one might say, precedes, coincides, and even follows writing. We see something that we want to write about. We see it again (and sometimes anew) when we attempt to evoke it upon the page. After summoning it forth onto paper, we often see new facets (details or relationships or meanings) which cause us to layer in more features in subsequent <u>re-visions</u>--just as Annie Dillard shaded in her baseball mitt's contours and its "billion grades of light and dark" (paragraph 5). The more astutely we perceive at each stage of seeing/understanding, the more individual our evocations of experience will be. To that degree, tuning up one's senses is the most fundamental prewriting activity we can do.

For Philip Roth's "My Baseball Years"

1. To Philip Roth, how is baseball like great literature, especially great fiction? What do they have in common?

    According to Roth, baseball (like literature) has thrills and spaciousness, suspensefulness, heroics, nuances, characters, narrators with interesting points of view, a peculiar hypnotic tedium, and often involves a mythic transformation of the immediate (paragraph 7). Like fiction, baseball could excite Roth's imagination, hold his attention as much with "minutiae as high drama" (paragraph 8) and move him to ecstacy and tears.

2. According to Roth, what is the source of baseball's appeal to people from all classes, races, and walks of life?

    Baseball, like great writing, "reache[s] into every class and region of the nation and [binds] millions upon millions of [people] together in common concerns, loyalties, rituals, enthusiasms, and antagonisms" (paragraph 3). Rich and poor, men and women, children and grownups can join together to exalt over a new star or to trash the opposing team. In this leveling arena, the greatest fan is he or she who loves and narrates the story best.

3. What does Philip Roth do in "My Baseball Years" to make baseball and his childhood come alive for you the reader?

Roth gives many specific details which paint word pictures of his childhood love for baseball. He lists the hours he spent playing baseball from ages 9 to 13 (40 hours a week) and tells us the kind of player he was (flashy but erratic). He illustrates this point by describing his success at the whiz-bang catch but inevitable failure at the high pop fly hit right at him. He tells us the specific kinds of baseball he played --softball, hardball, and stickball pickup games--and of his keen disppointment in failing to make the high school team. He describes in detail Ruppert Stadium where he watched the Newark Bears take on their "hated enemy from across the marshes," the Jersey City Giants (paragraph 5). Roth then moves from the specific facts of his childhood obsession to the more abstract considerations of the mythic, patriotic, and aesthetic dimensions baseball added to his life. Yet even here he returns to describe at length a <u>specific</u> emblematic moment involving Red Barber, Rex Barney, and a prematurely eaten hot dog.

4. <u>Could another writer (or you) make a case for the appeal of another sport</u>?

Without a doubt.

<u>What is the appeal of basketball?</u> <u>Hockey?</u> <u>Volleyball?</u> <u>Swimming?</u>

The appeal of basketball lies in the ease with which novice fans can follow the ball, yet the complexity of defenses and offenses it offers for more savvy viewers. Its appeal lies in the literal handful of players to watch on each team--as opposed to the larger mobs of masked and helmeted men required for baseball, hockey, and football. Perhaps basketball's whole appeal is in the fact that one need not wear a hat. Then there are the stunning leaps and glides and 180-degree and 360-degree turns, slams, dunks, and slamdunks; the passes round the back and through the unsuspecting opponent's legs; the sense of Baryshnikov freed from the choreography of The Firebird to be a firebird of his own making. There is the appeal of a winter sport, firing our winter stay-at-home evenings, and the politeness of the season's finale in June--just when we want to go outside.

[Similar celebrations could be made of hockey, volleyball, swimming, or other sports and hobbies.]

5. Why might the patriotism fostered by baseball be "a more humane and tender" brand of patriotism than that associated with war?

Roth compares the humane and tender form of patriotism fostered by baseball to the patriotism generated during World War II which he describes as "grounded in moral virtue and bloody-minded hate" (paragraph 4). Roth particularly seems to mind the self-righteous zeal of America's military patriotism, the fixing of "a bayonet to a Bible"--surely an inhumane and (indeed) unchristian act (paragraph 4). Baseball might be a more tender and humane form of patriotism because one does not literally kill the umpire--or the teams and players one despises. Indeed such is the individualizing (rather then generalizing) nature of the game that one comes to know intimately the tics and scratches, the feints and furies of despised as well as beloved players, and this can bring a tenderness even to one's hates. The atmosphere of baseball, Roth also reminds us, is lyrical rather than martial. It invites imaginative revery rather than lockstep conformity. Self-righteousness also has little place in baseball where today's hero is tomorrow's goat.

For Margaret Atwood's "High School Beginnings"

1. <u>Why does a writer suddenly start writing? List some possible reasons</u>.

   A writer might start writing for any number of reasons, including:

   . being invited to write by a family member, friend, teacher, or writing group;

   . having something to say that <u>must</u> be expressed;

   . feeling the wish just to "fool around" with language and form--without any end writing "product" in mind;

   . having a desire consciously to imitate other writers and work the writer has read;

   . being presented with material so inviting that it begs to be written;

   . having the wish to exercise and, in the process, exorcise one's emotions;

   . receiving repeated encouragement to write.

2. <u>Does a person have to have visible role models in order to become a writer</u>?

   No. Margaret Atwood became a poet, essayist, and novelist with only scattered Canadian foremothers to guide her.

   <u>Would visible role models help</u>?

   Most writers say that having visible role models helps. Alice Walker writes: "In my own work I write not only what I want to read . . . I write all the things I <u>should have been able to read</u>" ("Saving the Life That Is Your Own," <u>In Search of Our Mother's Gardens</u>. New York: Harcourt Brace

IM-51

Jovanovich, 1983: 13). At the least, models demonstrate that the goal one aspires to is attainable. At best, they illuminate the path by showing what methods and approaches can (or cannot) work. Models may also forthrightly describe subjects and techniques yet to be explored. (See Virginia Woolf's "Professions for Women" in Chapter 1.)

What other kinds of role models might there be besides visible ones?

Writers seeking material and inspiration usually find them wherever (and however) they can. Models that are not visible might include: anonymous letters or diaries found in a historical society or archive, works by long dead and forgotten writers discovered in a library, or works or artists in other art forms.

3. What might be the effects of encouragement (or lack of encouragement) on the beginning writer?

Most human beings are like orchids. They bloom with encouragement and attention. Deny the proper soil and water and they droop and die. Hearing even, "I can't understand this, dear, but I think it's good" was enough to keep teenage Margaret Atwood writing. Peter Elbow speaks of believing and doubting as two distinct processes. My experience tells me that the ratio of belief, support, and encouragement to doubt, denial, and discouragement for beginning writers should be something like 95 percent encouragement to 5 percent doubt, with the ratio becoming less and less one-sided as the writer gains more confidence and experience. Teachers can always find some encouraging words to give beginning writers, even if they are only in praise of the choice of subject or the ambitiousness of the approach. Discouragement can cause writers never to dare to write again, or if they dare, never to risk themselves in ways which may lead to something interesting--or unexpected.

4. How does Margaret Atwood make her "High School Beginnings" come alive for you?

Atwood uses specific details to make her senior year of high school come alive. She tells us the color of her high school guidance book (gray) and lists the five careers it offered to female students. She describes girls who took typing as having very thin eyebrows, smoking cigarettes in the washroom, chewing gum, and tending to vanish from school--a vivid portrait that undoubtedly rings true to many of her readers' own high school memories. Atwood depicts her first poems, not only as "dark and brooding," but she further helps us to imagine them by saying they were like those of Poe and Byron. When she comes to describing the Home Economics opera she wrote, she gives the names of her family of characters (Orlon, Nylon, Dacron, and their father, Old King Coal) and the opera's crisis and resolution. Atwood even shows that (paradoxically) one can use imprecise details to achieve a humorous (and vivid) effect. When she says that she learned in high school home economics to have "a green thing, a white thing, a brown thing and a yellow thing" on every dinner plate, she creates a vision in our minds of a plate of vague and inedible colored clumps. Clearly Atwood also uses satirical humor to breathe life into her high school beginnings.

For John Barth's "Some Reasons Why I Tell The Stories I Tell The Way I Tell Them Rather Than Some Other Sort Of Stories Some Other Way"

1. In what ways do the circumstances of our birth (our birth order, for example, or the

ease or difficulty of our birth) affect the kind of person we become?

Studies show that birth order often has a significant (though varying) effect on a child's development. Only children may be taciturn since they are raised with no siblings to talk to. Middle children are often described as mediators, balancing the demands of older and younger siblings, while the youngest child in a large family may be babied, lost in the crowd, or aggressive--to be noticed. In "Some Reasons Why I Tell The Stories The Way I Tell Them" John Barth says that being a twin caused him to share a language with his twin sister "before speech and beyond speech" (paragraph 3). He says he grew up being unnaturally conscious of language because for him speech was for others. When students reflect on the effect their birth order has upon their personalities they will usually discover that other factors also become important including the treatment they were given by their parents and siblings; the quality of their homes and community environments, and key events in their lives.

2. How can a poor early education (in grade school or high school) be overcome?

A poor early education in grade school, high school, or undergraduate school can be overcome by hard work later in life. John Barth worked hard at Johns Hopkins University to learn about the Renaissance and the Enlightenment, two of many terms (and eras) which were completely new to him in college. Martin Luther King, Jr., doubled his efforts at Morehouse College in Atlanta when he learned that the inferior education he had received from Atlanta's segregated school system had caused him to be deficient in reading. King went on to earn a doctoral degree in theology. (See the headnote to "Letter from Birmingham Jail" in Chapter 4.)

3. <u>What are some ways to tell whether you possess "genuine apprentice talent" for a field of work--or simply "makeshift amateur flair"?</u>

   John Barth tells us that one way he discovered that he possessed a makeshift amateur flair for music (rather than "genuine apprentice talent") was that he soon found limitations to his abilities (paragraph 24). He observed that other musicians could do easily what he could do only with great difficulty--or not at all. Mozart could compose in his head while most of us nonmusicians could not compose even with the most sophisticated technical assistance available. Barth also was not particulary troubled by the discovery of his musical limitations. This is probably another sign of flair as opposed to genuine calling. He tells us that when he turned to writing fiction in college, he "was toiling uphill with much slippage and misstep, but not quite falling" (paragraph 36). That "not quite falling" was enough to allow him to sense the possibilities of improvement with added practice. It was enough to increase his curiosity and make exploring the boundaries of possibility an absorbing experience. (See "Flow" in Chapter 7.) Barth had found that he had simply begun with the wrong medium: he was an arranger, not of music, but of words.

4. <u>In what ways are writers like musicians? Are writers "arrangers" of words?</u>

   Musicians' materials are notes, pauses, and accent marks, while writers' materials are words, pauses, and punctuation. Musicians create within certain traditional forms-- such as the song, concerto, symphony, and opera--but they often extend these classical forms with new (or hybrid) forms all their own. Writers do the same. They may begin to write a poem, but end up writing an essay or novel. Often their creations are ingenious blends of forms new and old (see <u>Moby-Dick</u> or James Agee's <u>Let Us Now Praise Famous Men</u>). Musicians, finally, compose for diverse instruments, each instrument (whether it be a human voice or an oboe) possessing its own range of possibilities. Musicians also compose for specific audiences and purposes. ("Silent Night" was written for a specific Christmas eve church service.) Writers, too, choose to write in different voices, and their audiences and purposes for writing influence the shape of their works. In short, writers (as John Barth discovered) are indeed arrangers of words.

For Warren Wortham's "Musical Beginnings"

1. <u>Musicians create with notes, while writers create with words. In what ways might their composing processes be similar</u>?

   - A composer might begin with a "theme" in his or her head whose possibilities cry out to be explored. The theme could be a series of notes (a musical motif) or (for the writer) an image, phrase, or complete thesis statement.

   - In developing a theme the composer explores the directions the theme wishes to go: repetitions, variations, inversions, modulations to other keys or octaves, resolution, nonresolution, etc. The writer does the same.

   - Limits exist on both available notes and available words. Both music and writing offer enough choices to be interesting to the composer/writer (and to create surprises for the reader), but few enough to make selection possible. (See "Flow" in Chapter 7.)

- A composer of either music or words might abandon a piece of work (temporarily or permanently) if its possibilities seem quickly exhausted, prove too predictable, or become uninteresting.

- Composers with notes and composers with words both rely on reader/interpreters who can interpret their works badly or well.

<u>In what ways might their composing processes be different?</u>

- At first glance one might think that notes are fewer than words (which seem infinite). One might conclude from this that composing with notes (music) is easier than composing with words (writing). This is not quite true. The possible variations on the 13 notes on the piano (8 white keys and 5 black keys) are many. Add to this the extensions of different octaves and keys and possibilities roughly analogous to the variations possible with the 600,000 words of the English language come into sight.

- One true difference between composing with notes and composing with words is that notes are essentially more abstract than words. An "A" note does not evoke an automatic association in its hearer as does, for example, the word <u>apple</u>. Given fewer concrete associations, composers of music may have to work slighly harder than wordsmiths at establishing a musical context in which "A" will evoke a specific response or image.

2. <u>What lessons do you think Warren Wortham has learned so far in his musical career?</u>

From the testimony of his essay, Warren Wortham seems to have learned:

IM-57

- to try to relax when he is composing either music or a college paper so that his ideas and feelings will flow.

- that freewriting (see Introduction to Chapter 2) is one way he can achieve this flow.

- that if he pushes too hard to write either a song or an essay, he will not find what he is after.

- that composing just for himself actually enhances his more public compositions--by capturing ideas/themes/feelings.

- that it is a good habit to record any idea that may surface (paragraph 3).

- that it is beneficial to attempt to compose in a variety of styles, with a variety of purposes, and for a variety of audiences.

- that "sampling"--bringing in diverse voices and sounds--can be done in writing as well as music.

- that composing is sometimes easy and sometimes difficult.

- that though he loves composing, there is a business (professional) side to it.

- that it is reinforcing to share one's compositions with others. Indeed the response can often be reinforcing beyond one's greatest expectations.

- creating with music or words can lead one to other people, places, and opportunities.

- that musical composers can experience the equivalent of writer's block.

- that music (like writing) takes "plenty of hard work and practice" (paragraph 6).

- that doing what you love can pay off.

- that meeting and working with famous people can be a learning experience.

- that composers must trust their own instincts and be wary of outside pressures to change their style and subjects.

3. <u>What is the central idea (or thesis) of Warren Wortham's essay?</u>

    Warren Wortham's central idea is: Writing music is both a love and and a business (paragraphs 1 & 9).

4. <u>Can you imaginatively reconstruct the process Warren Wortham might have gone through to get from his first to his final draft</u>?

    Warren Wortham's first freewrte is a meditation on his composing process: how he writes his songs. After these first good sentences, it appears that he had expressed his ideas and feelings, and so didn't know where to go from there. Should he (and could he) continue offering more such meditations? Finding a central idea (thesis)--writing music is both a love and a business--seemed to give a focus to what he wanted to write about, which was his life in music. The central idea may also have suggested a pattern (structure) for unfolding his experience. Warren solved his development problem by turning to a chronological structure. This enabled both him and his reader to track his development as a musician. Along the way he also found he could add in his insights into his own creative process. When he had brought his career up to the present (at the end of his essay's eighth paragraph), he must have felt that he wanted to do more than just stop with his forthcoming album. Thus he added two more paragraphs that look to the future, reflect on what he has learned, and reiterate in a heightened context his central idea that he composes for love--and money.

5. <u>From the evidence of "Musical Beginnings," does Warren Wortham seem to be an artist?</u>

   Yes.

   <u>What artistic qualities does he reveal?</u>

   The artistic qualities Warren Wortham displays include:

   - an early love of his medium--music.

   - the desire and ability to teach himself to play different instruments and to compose in a variety of styles.

   - the ability to create interest in his work, both the interest of audiences and of other musicians.

   - experience in writing in a variety of forms for different audiences and purposes.

   - the experience of one piece of work leading to another.

   - an intuitive need to protect his musical vision from outside pressures.

   - the tendency to keep working whatever happens.

   - the sense of fluid boundaries or borders which he crosses easily.

For Virginia Woolf's "Professions for Women"

1. <u>What were the "phantoms" Virginia Woolf battled as a writer?</u>

Virginia Woolf called her first phantom "the Angel in the House." This Angel was the image of woman as a sympathetic, charming, tender, conciliating, and (above all) pure creature who never had a mind of her own. This image of what a woman <u>should be</u> would have kept Woolf from telling the truth in her writing. This phantom was always encouraging her toward falsehood.

Woolf's second phantom was the extreme conventionality of the male sex which condemned women who spoke the truths about their own bodies and passions. As of 1941, Woolf had not succeeded in killing this phantom.

<u>When you sit down at your writing table, what "phantoms" keep you from having a mind of your own and expressing what you think to be the truth? A representative of one or more social institutions (such as a teacher, minister, or boss)? Some part of yourself?</u>

"Phantoms" which keep students from developing minds of their own or telling the truth as they have come to know it might include:

- stern parents who forbid the expression of certain feelings or thoughts in the house. (The "phantom" might be the image of such a parent or relative.)

- a religion which forbids certain behaviors or subjects for discussion. (The "phantom" might be a minister, priest, nun, or rabbi.)

- teachers who condemned early efforts at expression.

- an employer who might object to employees declaring themselves in print.

- the "phantom" of conventional or "received wisdom" which dictates what should be thought and said on almost every occasion.

- a personal fear that if they tell the truth they will be rejected by others--or by society in general.

- the fear that if they express a truth that they may be forced to act upon it--and they do not feel ready to do so at this time.

- the fear that comes because no one has yet dared to write on this subejct.

- the fear that what they write will never be as wonderful as they want it to be.

2. <u>Do men have different "phantoms" to overcome than women?</u>

   Men will have many of the same "phantoms" to overcome as women, but many undoubtedly will have additional phantoms arising from their own role conditioning.

   <u>If so, what are they?</u>

   For many men such "phantoms" might be:

   - the tough guy or macho phantom (call it the Marlboro man) who will encourage men to lie about, repress, or mask their emotional vulnerabilities. The current guise of this spectre is the voice that whispers: "They <u>say</u> they want kinder, gentler men--but they really don't mean it."

   - the phantom of the enraged feminist which will encourage caution, timidity, and (most of all) sensitivity in speaking of any girl, woman, or woman's issue.

   - the phantom that says they cannot write about women's subjects because they are men.

Why might they differ?

It is likely that men's and women's "phantoms" will differ because of their different sex role conditioning. Western societies tend to encourage women to lay bare their emotions and their vulnerabilities at the same time these societies are counseling denial of these very (appealing) traits in men. Conversely, like the male locker room, sex and profanity have only recently been opened to women writers. The early venturers are traversing gingerly. Women similarly have been discouraged from declaring personal ambition, something routinely expected of American and Canadian boys and men.

3. Can you recall any insights you have had, or striking images or phrases that have come to you in moments when you have let your imagination "sweep unchecked . . . in the depths of [your] unconscious"?

   Insights students might have could include:

   - some newly recognized truth about a person or event in their lives: Dad wasn't as great a guy as Mom always said he was (or vice versa); someone's (or their own) action cannot be justified; they really did what they did out of fear (or ignorance); someone really didn't have their best interests at heart.

   - a feeling or idea that lay behind an event, action, or conflict.

   - the role of other people or things in an event, action, or conflict.

   - an image or phrase that sums up the moment.

   What feelings came along with these "discoveries"?

Feelings will generally come along with new insights. Occasionally fear, uneasiness, or even dread may accompany a newly discovered truth. However, usually new insights are accompanied by a shock of recognition (Eureka!) followed by a release of energy. Insight usually is exhilarating and spurs one to want to dwell, share, and even act on the insight.

4. <u>Has the world changed since the 1940s, or do you think women writers are still discouraged from speaking the truth about their passions and the experiences of their bodies?</u>

More than 50 years have passed since Virginia Woolf made her speech. In general, women writers in the United States and Canada today are not discouraged from writing the truths about their bodies and their passions. In the United States, Supreme Court decisions in the 1960s liberalized what could be published, and this liberal climate spilled over to films, theater, television, music, art, and other media. The second wave of feminism which occurred in the late 1960s also had the effect of encouraging women to speak the truths of their lives. Nevertheless, much depends on the individual woman writer's environment, upbringing, and personal inclinations. Erica Jong has attempted to write truthfully about women's sexual impulses, as have Toni Morrison, Alice Walker, Doris Lessing, Margaret Atwood, Adrienne Rich, May Sarton, Nancy Price, and many other contemporary writers.

<u>Do you think men are discouraged as well? What has (or has not) changed?</u>

Men may be discouraged from writing about the emotions that accompany their passions and body experiences. What has changed have been laws and a young writer's access to multiple media. What has not changed is the time required to come to self-knowledge.

5. <u>What are the phantoms to be slain and rocks to be dashed against in other professions (besides writing)?</u>

   Fields requiring physical prowess or beauty bring with them the phantoms (fears) of injury and the phantoms of aging to slay. Other fields, such as medicine or law enforcement, involve the phantom of death-- of patients, of lawbreakers (or yourself). These spectres of death must be slain if doctors or officers are to operate successfully. Researchers and journalists are often haunted by the phantoms of error, knowing as they do how easily human error occurs. If they let the fear of error dominate them, they will never dare to experiment or report. Other fields may offer the phantom of lost identity or of loss of individual power. Clearly each field harbors its phantoms.

For Nadine Gordimer's "Not for Publication"

1. <u>What is the "initiation" Praise is about to begin when Miss Graham-Grigg takes him off to Father Audry to study</u>?

   Praise appears to be preparing to undergo some sort of puberty rite or tribal initiation into manhood.

   <u>Why do you think this initiation is important to him?</u>

   Such an initiation would be important to Praise for at least three reasons: 1) it represents a bonding experience with others his own age; 2) it is part of his tribal (cultural) identity; and 3) coming of age is an important matter to every young person.

2. <u>What are the signs that Praise is not being completely transformed by Miss Graham-Grigg and Father Audry?</u>

Praise's physical appearance is the first (and most obvious) sign that he is not being completely transformed. Good nutrition cannot totally make up for years of malnutrition (we learn in paragraph 39). Gordimer also emphasizes the lasting imprint of Praise's early environment by noting that Praise "had never grown out of the slight stoop of the left shoulder where the weight of the old man's hand had impressed the young bone" (paragraph 35). As the story unfolds, Gordimer's narrator tells us that Praise is thinking back to his tribal initiation, and we see in his moments of breakdown that his identity has not been completely assimilated.

3. <u>Why do you think Praise is embarrassed to have Father Audry come in with a glass of hot milk?</u>

Praise is embarrassed when Father Audry brings him a glass of hot milk because it singles him out; it is one more sign that he is different from the other boys at the school. The passage before the reference to the hot milk (in paragraph 41) reveals that Praise is feeling more and more isolated as he advances further in his studies. Indeed his fellow students seem to recognize this themselves and never ask him to play cards. They pass a cigarette to him in silence.

<u>Why does he cry, and why does he shrink in fear when Father Audry reaches out his hand</u>?

I suspect that Praise cries because he wishes to understand what Father Audry and Miss Graham-Grigg intend for him, and cannot, and because he wishes Father Audry and Miss Graham-Grigg would understand the importance of his tribal initiation to him.

This they do not understand. Praise seems to shrink with fear when Father Audry reaches out his hand as an instinctive, subconscious response to white intercession. He is afraid. Gordimer's narrator describes Praise as acting out of "collective memory" (paragraph 50). Indeed in paragraph 47 Father Audry's own grimace as he tries to recall geometry repeats Praise's earlier grimace of humiliation at being discovered unable to write (paragraph 5). This "grimace" in Father Audry's face causes "a jump, like a single painful hiccup, in Praise's body" (paragraph 47). This profound body remembrance of humiliation is associated with victimization (paragraph 5).

4. <u>What do you think happened to Praise after he left Father Audry? Where do you think he may have gone? What in the text leads you to your conclusion</u>?

Gordimer gives us few clues as to what happened to Praise Basetse. Readers can only use their imaginations and speculate. As we reread the story's last paragraph we begin to wonder if we should believe Praise's family when they tell Father Audry they have not seen him, or Miss Graham-Grigg's report that he is not back at the Protectorate. Could Praise's family be hiding him? Could Miss Graham-Grigg? Or could the Chief be hiding Praise from Miss Graham-Grigg--away among his tribesmen? Perhaps Praise has returned to his tribe after all. Perhaps he is no longer a displaced tribesman. On the other hand, perhaps Praise has come full circle and has returned to the streets of Johannesburg--as he earlier predicted (paragraph 4). The more the reader ponders over these possibilities the more the reader realizes that his precise whereabouts during the interim are not important. What seems to be important is that Praise has become Prime Minister, but his road to this office had to be his own--not the roads of even well-intentioned others like Father Audry and Miss Graham-Grigg.

5. <u>Why is Miss Graham-Grigg critical of the Christian missionaries who came to Africa--so critical that she has established a secular school in the tribal village in opposition to the mission school?</u>

   Gordimer's narrator tells us that Miss Graham-Grigg was critical of the Christian missionaries in South Africa because "they stressed Christ's submission to humiliation, and so had conditioned the people of Africa to humiliation by the white man" (paragraph 5).

6. <u>Is Father Audry right when he suggests that what Miss Graham-Grigg wants in Praise is "someone who will turn out to be an able politician without challenging the tribal system"?</u>

   Father Audry seems to be accurately summarizing Miss Graham-Grigg's wish to preserve the tribal system (see paragraph 24).

   <u>How does this differ from his view?</u>

   Gordimer's narrator tells us that Father Audry's view is that the tribal chiefs will have to go, while Miss Graham-Grigg "saw no reason why Africans shouldn't develop their own tribal democracy instead of taking over the Western pattern" (paragraph 25). In the event recounted in the story, Father Audry's rather than Miss Graham-Grigg's view seems to have triumphed--at least for the moment. Praise Basetse is "Prime Minister," not "Chief."

   <u>What position do you take?</u>

   Students may have a variety of views on this question. Gordimer's story provides an excellent <u>context</u> for such a discussion.

7. <u>Is there just one way to make a prime minister</u>?

   There would appear to be as many paths to the prime ministry as there are to heaven.

   <u>Is there just one way to make a writer</u>? <u>How many ways do you suppose there are</u>?

   Similarly there is not just one way to become a writer. There would appear to be countless (and unaccountable) paths to either calling. Perhaps Praise offers the best model for both prime ministers and writers-in-the-making: have good fortune; study hard; but ultimately be true to your own personal intuitions as they find echo in your cultural heritage and traditions.

Chapter 2. Finding the Subject: The Figure in the Carpet

For May Sarton's "Journal of a Solitude"

1. <u>Why is it that we often do not really "see" things until we are alone</u>?

   To "see" means more than just visually to perceive; more abstractly, it means "to understand." Lamentably, we often have to be alone before we truly "see" in either sense of the word. This is because when we are rushing about from place to place we usually do not have time to look intently at our surroundings. Other people, with their inevitable demands for our time, attention, and conversation, similarly distract us from deep understanding of our world--as well as observations of it. As May Sarton insists, it is in moments of solitude that we most often find time truly to be awake to nature and our household environments. Similarly, in solitude we find open, undisturbed spaces for reflection--which leads to finer and deeper insights and understandings.

2. <u>What</u> <u>are</u> <u>the</u> <u>benefits</u> <u>of</u> <u>making</u> <u>an</u> "<u>open</u> <u>place</u>, <u>a</u> <u>place</u> <u>for</u> <u>meditation</u>" <u>in</u> <u>our</u> <u>lives</u>?

   The benefits of making an open space in our lives (daily) for observation and reflection include:

   - fuller sensory experience.

   - time to savor the gifts of the subconscious--dreams, waking reveries, and intuitions--collected immediately upon rising.

   - the opportunity for creative play of our full capacities.

   - discovery of new solutions to problems--indeed, discovery of the availability of muliple options--or that what we perceived as a "problem" or "conflict" is not of such consequence.

   - a calmness or serenity--not to mention a lower blood pressure--than when under pressure of a fully scheduled day.

   <u>How</u> <u>might</u> <u>writing</u> <u>be</u> <u>part</u> <u>of</u> <u>that</u> "<u>meditation</u>"?

   Writing channels our meditations in more (or less) controlled fashion depending on whether we are freewriting, mapping, idly fooling with words or phrases, or immersed in earnest composition.

3. <u>What</u> <u>aspects</u> <u>of</u> <u>your</u> <u>life</u> <u>exhaust</u> <u>you</u>?

   Exhausting aspects of students' lives might include:

   - keeping up with all their course assignments.

   - traveling to and from school or work.

   - dealing with certain teachers, employers, friends, or loved ones.

- dealing with a disability or illness.

- simply keeping up their rooms, apartments, houses, cars, or lives.

What parts exhilarate you?

Exhilarating aspects of life might include:

- the experience of nature.

- discovery of new ideas.

- successful completion of college papers and projects.

- encounters with interesting or inspiring people.

- success in school, job, or the social arena.

- the afterglow from jogging, swimming, or some other form of physical exercise.

- the sense of loving and being loved.

What plan can you develop to increase the time you spend in the latter and decrease the time spent in the former?

Once the exhausting aspects of life are identified, students should be encouraged to brainstorm strategies to reduce the time spent on these draining activities. Often such strategies involve changing jobs, courses, majors, and even friends. When change is impossible, plans can focus on ways to limit necessary encounters, ways to make encounters as mutually nourishing as possible, and ways to reward oneself following the experience--to ameliorate the inevitable exhaustion as much as possible. Once the exhilarating aspects of life are identified, students can focus on such plans for increasing these experiences as:

- repeating these experiences.

- taking more courses from exhilarating teachers or in an exhilarating area of study.

- reading more by an exhilarating author.

- doing continued research or writing in an area.

- deliberately seeking more contact with exhilarating or inspiring people.

- working out more.

4. <u>Why is preparing to write--thinking, brainstorming, mapping, going over your notes, making your coffee or tea--actually an essential part of the writing process</u>?

    Prewriting activities are an essential part of the writing process because they initiate the first (and subsequent) play of the subject, and its possibilities, in our consciousness. It is in this vital time of preliminary "fooling around" that connections are made and relationships are discovered, where we begin to sense <u>what</u> we have to say on our subject and <u>how</u> we might say it. In subsequent days of writing, prewriting activities stoke the writing generator for maximal <u>re-vision</u> and output. (See Chapter 7. Generating.) The value of prewriting activities cannot be overestimated.

    <u>Do you use these prewriting activities to their fullest potential?</u>

    Most students do not.

For Joan Didion's "On Keeping a Notebook"

1. <u>What can we learn about ourselves from the facts we jot down in our notebooks? From IM-72</u>

<u>the scenes and dialogue we record?</u> <u>From the sayings we find worth noting?</u>

We can learn what kinds of facts interest us--their types and geographical range. Are we interested in local facts, state facts, regional facts, national facts, international facts, or extraterrestrial facts? Do we find ourselves noting facts about nature? About people? About institutions? Some combination of all three? Are we taken by mundane facts (the average rainfall of our state or community) or bizarre facts (that Arnold Schwarzenegger wants to buy an Army landrover)? By facts of high seriousness--or humor? By observing the kinds of facts we are drawn to we begin to discover our subject matter as writers.

The same is true of the scenes and dialogue we record and the sayings we find worth noting. Sometimes writers even make direct use of diary or notebook jottings. Virginia Woolf described in her 1919 diary a "woman of doubtful character" making a scene by walking out of a restaurant. She later used this scene in her novel <u>Jacob's Room</u>.

2. <u>In what ways might one writer's notebook be of value to another writer?</u>

One writer's notebook or diary is valuable to another writer to the extent that it reveals what interested that writer. Often it represents the raw material which appears later in actual or (more often) transmuted form in the writer's published works. Frequently a writer's notebook will also supply another writer with insights into the creative process.

<u>In what respects might it be of no value at all?</u>

Joan Didion suggests that "your notebook will never help me, nor mine you" (paragraph

17). Didion means, perhaps, two things by this. Another writer's <u>material</u> will be of little help to us as writers, for we must find our own material. Furthermore, another writer's notebook can never serve for us the critical function it serves for writers like Joan Didion: to provide clues of "how [past experience] felt to [that writer]" (paragraph 8). Perhaps, however, Didion overstates her case. Because every writer's imagination can be likened to a compost heap, distilling the raw materials of experience, who is to say what one writer may find of use in another writer's notebook--or of what value it will be?

3. <u>Why is it helpful for a writer to keep in touch with his or her earlier "selves"?</u>

First of all, those earlier experiences and "selves" are <u>material</u> which can be drawn upon, directly or indirectly, for later writings. A writer describing the effects of divorce on young children in either fictional or nonfictional works would be assisted by memories of his or her own recalled experience of parental divorce. Secondly, writers write with their sensibilities. All previous experiences (and "selves") contribute to that evolving sensibility. The more writers understand their sensibilities, the more nuances they can bring to their writing.

4. <u>How does Joan Didion make her notebook come alive for the reader?</u>

Didion makes her notebook come alive through the use of arresting <u>specific examples</u> (of all kinds) of materials in her notebook. Her opening scene in the hotel bar overhearing a conversation about "That woman Estelle" piques our interest in both the speaker and the girl in the plaid Peck & Peck dress at the other end of the bar who is clearly Joan Didion. Later scenes involving the rich are also mysteriously romantic and morally engaging. Arresting, too, are the examples Didion offers of factual entries in her notebook, such as that 720 tons of soot fell on every square mile of New York City in 1964 or that Ambrose Bierce spelled Leland Stanford's name Leland $tanford (paragraph 12). Didion's vivid examples do more, however, than reveal how interesting notebook entries can be. They also repeatedly underscore her central idea (thesis) "On Keeping a Notebook": that notebooks provide the writer with access to earlier selves.

For Brenda Ueland's "The Imagination Works Slowly and Quietly"

1. Why does rushing cause writers to lose ideas --or treat them superficially?

    Brenda Ueland tells us that when we are "so quick, snappy and efficient about doing one thing after another . . . [we] have not time for [our] own ideas to come in and develop and gently shine" (paragraph 4). She quotes Tolstoy's assertion that ideas that have not fully matured in our consciousness can only "dimly" present themselve to us (paragraph 7). If we hurry, we often fail to sense these dim (but important) flickerings, and so we miss the very truth that is ours to tell. Even if a dimly flickering truth is glimpsed, rushing its telling can cause its deeper shades of meaning to be ignored in favor of its superficial surface attractions.

2. When a writer is given a deadline a month away for a writing assignment, when ideally should the writer begin work?

    Ideally, the writer should begin immediately such prewriting activities as brainstorming, mapping, freewriting, and employing the reporter's formula to explore possible subjects and their possibilities for development.

<u>Can you map out the best schedule for you for completing this project</u>?

An ideal schedule for completing a writing project within a month might be:

Days 1 & 2: Brainstorm, map, freewrite and/or use other prewriting strategies to find your paper subject and possible central idea (thesis) and developmental possibilities.

Days 3 - 10: Conduct any necessary research: library & archive; interviews; on-site visitations. Immediately order via inter-library loan materials not available.

Days 11 - 18: Distill research material and write the first draft

Days 19 & 20: Put the draft away and don't look at it.

Day 21: Look at your first draft with new eyes and begin making any major <u>revisions</u> in its thesis or development.

Days 22 - 26: Continue revising the paper, showing it to others if possible to see if it is meeting readers' needs.

Days 27 & 28: Put second draft away and don't look at it.

Day 29: Look at second draft with new eyes for final <u>revisions</u>. When these are made, begin careful proofreading of this third draft of the paper following the recommendations given in the opening of Chapter 10. Revising and Proofreading: Backing and Filling.

Day 30: Ask your roommate or another close friend or relative to proofread your final draft, looking for any errors in standard edited English.

Day 31: Turn the paper in with confidence knowing that it has lived (and grown) in your consciousness for a full month.

3. <u>What is the best way to ensure yourself time every day to allow the imagination to work slowly and quietly</u>?

The best way to ensure this quiet time for reflection and creativity is to make it a part of your daily schedule. Students may need to experiment to discover the time of day in which they most need and can best lend themselves to this quiet revery. Some students will find they will want to rise a half-hour or hour earlier than they have in the past to allow for a post-breakfast period of writing or revery. Others may want to add a late afternoon or evening walk to their daily lives as an occasion for solitary reflection. Still others will find that the hour just before bed is when they are at their reflective and creative best. Whatever or whenever time is allotted, making it habitual is the way of making reflection and creation habitual.

For Peter Elbow's "The Open-ended Writing Process"

1. <u>Why is "getting lost" one of the best ways to find new material</u>?

"Getting lost" means getting past "what is on the top of your mind," past the cliches and received wisdom of a lifetime into the deeper truths which underlie (or contradict) such surface truths (or falsehoods). Inviting "maximum chaos" opens the way for ideas, feelings, and images to combine in new (and often surprising) ways (paragraph 1). Inviting disorientation is a way deliberately to abandon traditional moorings in hopes of seeing new sights in new ways.

2. _Should writers, then, deliberately seek to lose themselves at times (so they don't know quite where they are going with a piece of writing) so that they can discover new insights or writing styles?_

Yes.

What are some ways to do this?

Peter Elbow's open-ended writing process provides maximum safety and control during this process of "getting lost," for the writer knows the sea voyage of getting lost will be followed by a period of focusing, of finding the focus of the new material discovered. Freewriting is part of this process and one of the best methods of uninhibited exploration. Mapping and brainstorming can also lead into exotic associational branches. Sometimes just quiet revery--Virginia Woolf's letting her thoughts drop deep into the subconscious to play among the rocks and eddies--can be a fine way of "getting lost." Elbow's suggestions of abruptly changing writing voices, or forms, or intellectual positions represent other ways of inviting the subject and its elements to bounce off each other in new and interesting ways.

3. _If you always write on the surface of what you know, are you in danger of being superficial--falling into cliche_ (Brenda

Ueland's "automatic verbiage")--instead of being profound and original?

Yes. Our surface knowledge often has not been carefully examined. By subjecting received wisdom, clichés, or other surface knowledge to rigorous examination, we often will uncover unexpected grounds to support, reject, or modify what we thought we knew or understood.

4. How long do you find you have to work before you get past what is on top of your mind into something more unusual, unexpected, or true?

The length of time will vary with each writer, but many writers say they have to work at least two or three hours before they begin to be so immersed in their material that new insights and discoveries can be made. (See Tom Wolfe's headnote and introduction to "The Kandy-Kolored Tangerine-Flake Streamline Baby" in Chapter 5 and Mihaly Csikszentmihalyi's "Flow" in Chapter 7.)

What processes are involved in reaching this richer insight?

One process is that of being contrary. To get past the surface, received wisdom, the too-easy phrase or judgment, try questioning all such insights. Are there not occasions when a stitch in time does not save nine? Can't I burst my jeans even after I've repaired them--saving me nothing? Do parents really know best? When might they not know best? Raising questions, then, is a good way of pushing your thoughts into deeper and more original territory. Exploring your thoughts through freewriting, brainstorming, mapping, or quiet revery are other helpful processes.

5. As you look back over the experiences you described in warm-up exercises 1 and 2, what process did your emotions or ideas go through as they passed from one state to another? What forces caused the changes or the deepening perspective?

   Students might discover that the very process of writing about their mood permitted them to vent it, subject it to analysis, and end up seeing it in new and richer perspective. The forces involved might be those of release, analysis, and reconstruction or reinterpretation.

6. Why is the ability to summarize and to synthesize--to find the center of gravity or point of a piece of writing--a valuable ability to have?

   The ability to summarize or synthesize allows a person to cut through supporting reasons and details to the essence or heart of any matter. It is thus a great time saver and reveals a precision of mind. Leaders in every field often have this ability, for they are able to see not only the individual parts, but how the parts join to create the whole system (or organizational vision). Once the summary or synthesis has been made, the individual or group can study it and determine future directions.

For Kelly Linnenkamp's "Lifeguarding: Fun in the Sun?"

1. What would you say is the "central idea," or thesis, of Kelly Linnenkamp's first draft?

   The thesis of Kelly Linnenkamp's first draft is: "an event that occurred during my first month in this position made me realize how much responsibility was actually upon my shoulders and that a knowledgeable team of people can act like a well-oiled machine in times of emergency" (paragraph 1).

How does she refocus it by the time she's written her final draft?

Kelly's refocus is to abandon her concern for the other lifeguards and their action as a "well-oiled machine" to focus even more upon the effect of the experience on herself. In this sense, simplifying her focus/thesis allowed her to probe what remained more deeply.

What is her new central idea?

Kelly's new central idea is: "While I enjoy the fringe benefits of being a lifeguard, an event that occurred during my first month in this position made me realize how much responsibility was actually upon my shoulders. But it also assured me that I was capable of dealing with an emergency without panicking and making the situation even worse" (paragraph 1).

2. What details in this essay reveal that Kelly was conscientious about her job?

Kelly tells us that she "had to keep track of an unusually large number of swimmers" (paragraph 3) and that she and another guard took "the expected precautions" when rotating positions (paragraph 4). When the diving accident occurs, we learn that her first thought, as a result of her training, was that a spinal injury was possible (paragraph 5) and that she immediately took the appropriate steps. She "gave three sharp whistles, indicating that [she] had an emergency, swiftly climbed down from [her] chair, and slid into the water" (paragraph 5). She tells us that she slid into the water rather than dove in because "a dive entry would have made waves that could worsen a potential spinal injury" (paragraph

5). After assisting the swimmer out of the pool, Kelly and her fellow lifeguards "applied a cold pack" to her broken nose while they awaited the ambulance (paragraph 5). After the incident, Kelly tells us that her conscientiousness was motivated, in part, by the realization that improper care might have led to a lawsuit against the city (paragraph 6). In the final line of her essay, she underscores the concept of <u>conscientiousness</u> when she declares: "Even though it shook me up, I feel that my first rescue as a lifeguard made me more conscious of my actions and improved my self-confidence and performance in a job that many people feel is all fun in the sun."

3. <u>Kelly says she likes to use descriptions that involve the human senses. What passages in her essay evoke the reader's sense of smell, touch, taste, sight, or hearing?</u>

   Smell: "the ever-present cocoa butter scent of tanning lotion being spread on like jelly on a slice of toast wafted up to me" (paragraph 2).

   Touch: "wafted up to me on the slight breeze that was blowing" (paragraph 2)

   "the summer heat" (paragraph 3)

   "Pushing my sunglasses back onto my nose after they slid down on a trail of perspiration, I adjusted my towel" (paragraph 4)

   "I . . . swiftly climbed down from my chair, and slid into the water. It had occurred to me that a dive entry would have made waves that could worsen a potential spinal injury." (paragraph 5)

"She was . . . holding her nose" (paragraph 5)

"I had to grip the arms of the lifeguard's chair to keep from shaking" (paragraph 6)

"it shook me up" (paragraph 7)

Taste: "the ever-present cocoa butter scent of tanning lotion being spread on like jelly on a slice of toast" (paragraph 2)

Sight: "A 'healthy' golden tan, sun-glitzed hair" (paragraph 1)

"tanning lotion being spread on like jelly on a slice of toast" (paragraph 2)

"Swiftly, I made my way through the jungle of swimmers and sunbathers to the next chair" (paragraph 4)

"Instantaneously, I saw the body floundering in the water to regain buoyancy" (paragraph 5)

"a red-headed girl about eleven years old" (paragraph 5)

"her nose had already started to swell and turn purple" (paragraph 5)

Hearing: "It's eleven minutes after three, ninety-eight degrees, and sunny." The D.J.'s voice faded into the familiar drone of Top 40 music that boomed out of the loudspeakers each afternoon (paragraph 2)

> "Shouts and laughter of swimmers filled the air along with the constant sounds of splashing water" (paragraph 2)

> "the springing of a diving board after a safely executed dive or jump has a familiarity to it like that of the voice of a parent" (paragraph 5)

> "I heard the spring of the lowest, closest diving board, except with an unfamiliar thud. Instantaneously, . . . I heard a spectator saying, 'She hit her head on the board'" (paragraph 5)

> "I gave three sharp whistles" (paragraph 5)

> "She was crying" (paragraph 5)

> "My heart seemed to pound out of my chest" (paragraph 6)

4. <u>Is writing in any way like lifeguarding</u>?

Yes. At first glance writing may seem like a romantic and glamourous occupation. Furthermore, writing has literally saved some people's lives.

<u>Does our enjoyment of a good piece of writing often make us forget the considerable training and attention that goes into the attractive product?</u>

Yes.

For Plato's "The Allegory of the Cave"

1. <u>What is an allegory</u>?

An allegory is a form of extended metaphor

IM-84

in which persons, actions, and objects in a narrative, either in prose or verse, are equated with meanings that lie outside the narrative itself. Allegory attempts to create a dual interest, one in the events, characters, and setting presented, and the other in the ideas they are intended to convey or the significance they bear (C. Hugh Holmon & William Harmon, <u>A Handbook to Literature</u>, 5th ed. New York: Macmillan, 1986).

<u>Why is allegory sometimes useful for a writer?</u>

Abstract ideas are sometimes difficult for readers to grasp. By presenting ideas in the form of a story, writers often can make their ideas easier to understand--for themselves as well as for their readers.

2. <u>If people knew only a dark and chained existence, why would they want to change their condition?</u>

Some would not. Some, however, with powerful imaginations would imagine what it would be like not to be chained and to move about the cave unfettered. Some might imagine an existence outside of the cave. Still others might imagine a world that was not dark. Curious about the source of light creating the shadows on the cave wall, they would long to trace the source of that light to its origins. Throughout history human beings have always sought to improve their living conditions.

3. <u>Is it possible to be "in the dark" on some topics and "enlightened" about others?</u>

Yes. Teachers might ask students to make two lists, one of subjects about which they feel relatively "enlightened," and the other subjects about which they feel very much 'in the dark."

Making these two lists is a useful excercise and lists will be very individual. Typically, students will feel relatively enlightened about: specific sports, television, movies, popular music, and perhaps even their majors. They will admit to ignorance of distant countries and cultures, brain surgery, rocket science, and other scientific or technical subjects. By pushing students to describe what they do and do not know about even the subjects they feel "relatively enlightened" about, teachers can help students see that shades (or degrees) of knowledge exist as we pass from the darkness of ignorance along the path to Platonic essences.

4. What steps are necessary for "enlightenment"?

Socrates would say that recognizing that what we have taken as substance is only shadow is the first step toward freeing ourselves from the chains of ignorance. He also demonstrates the importance of asking questions of our experience as a method of determining substance from shadow; indeed, of making ever more precise discriminations. Clearly, Socrates sees "enlightenment" as the result of a progressive outward (and upward) journey; however, his allegory implies that the potential for knowledge (or "enlightenment") exists from the beginning in human beings. All that is necessary is that education draw it out.

5. What is the responsibility of those who have become enlightened?

Socrates says it is the responsibility of those who have become enlightened to return to the cave and share their wisdom with their fellow citizens (paragraph 57).

6. Why does Plato believe political leadership should be required of enlightened ones?

Socrates insists that those who have been enlightened, once they return to the cave and accustom themselves once again to seeing in the dark, "will see ten thousand times better than the inhabitants of the den, and . . . will know what the several images are, and what they represent, because [they] have seen the beautiful and just and good in their truth. And thus our State . . . will be a reality, and not a dream only, and will be administered in a spirit unlike that of other States, in which men fight with one another about shadows only and are distracted in the struggle for power, which in their eyes is a great good" (paragraph 61).

For John Updike's "One More Interview"

1. <u>What are the qualities of a good journalist?</u>

Good journalists seek to establish good rapport with the persons they interview. They try to present themselves as sympathetic, trustworthy, and even admiring audiences for their interviewee's words. When interviewing an ill-at-ease or hostile source, they seek to overcome the source's reservations by conveying their intentions to be fair in their treatment of the source and the subject. In any situation, a good journalist seeks to convey great interest in what the source will say, and to take thorough notes while the source is speaking. Good journalists have questions prepared to ask--in order to gather all the information they will need. They also do thorough research on their sources and subjects before the interview. In writing up the story, a good journalist will be fair and accurate. Good journalists do not make up quotes or scenes, nor do they quote out of context if this would give an inaccurate picture of the source. Good journalists write in a lively, vivid-yet-precise style.

<u>How does the newspaper reporter in this story measure up to these qualities?</u>

While the reporter seems to have done some research (paragraph 9), his research is not up-to-date (paragraphs 10 & 11). As an interviewer, he also leaves a great deal to be desired. He repeatedly is silent and acts bored during the interview, and he often fails to take notes of the actor's words (paragraph 19). He asks very few questions and often seems to minimize or trivialize the actor's confessions, rather than encouraging them (paragraphs 20, 22, 39, 47). At times he even refuses to look at the actor while he is speaking (paragraph 15). The reporter was fortunate that this actor "was at that awkward age almost too old for romantic leads but not old enough for character parts" and thus needed the publicity. Another actor might have terminated the interview at the reporter's first rude response.

2. <u>In the first four paragraphs of the story, what signs are there that the actor and the reporter have different language styles?</u>

The reporter alternates between silence and slang: "It would provide, you know, an angle." His imprecise "you know" makes him seem almost illiterate. His language is that of an adolescent, but he is not an adolescent. The actor, in contrast, seems highly literate, intelligent, and urbane. His remark that interviews are "so intrinsically imprecise. So sadly prurient" reveals his intelligence and also his brooding wit. Indeed his four opening sentences reveal that he is capable of suiting his language to his mood. He can be disarmingly confessional: "I can't stand interviews"; charmingly suggestive: "So sadly prurient"; or--when both fail--he can meet his audience on its own level: "O.K." The actor's language suggests he is capable of wide ranges of thought and expression, a fact the remainder of the story bears out.

<u>Is this significant?</u>

The differences between the reporter and actor in mental and linguistic range are highly significant for they are early signs of the lack of sympathy which will grow between the two as the story unfolds. The reporter seems to appreciate neither the actor's wit nor the emotional experience he undergoes as he drives through his hometown. The reporter's lack of enthusiasm for the interview is amusing in itself, for it is the opposite of the fawning, gushing, or naive interview style readers would tend to expect. The reporter's taciturn skepticism also functions to place the actor's loquaciousness in high relief--as if the reporter's stoicism perversely causes the actor to break every rule for the interview he establishes (in paragraph 5).

<u>What does the language of each reveal about him?</u>

The reporter's language seems to suggest he is still more of a jock than a wordsmith. His slang, imprecision, and overriding taciturnity suggest that he is uncomfortable in the presence of a man who uses language with considerable sophistication and range. The actor's language, on the other hand, reveals that he is quite drawn to the impetuous (and unwise) confessional statement.

3. <u>How does the actor's attitude toward his subject change as the story unfolds?</u>

The actor warms to his subject the longer he is engaged with it. Indeed, at the end of the story he is so immersed in recapturing his early youth that he does not wish to stop.

What happens to him?

The further he goes, the more of his past presents itself and "he wanted to cruise forever through this half of town, the car dipping in a kind of obeisance at every intersection" (paragraph 68).

Why do writers often warm to their subjects as they get into them?

As with John Updike's actor, once immersed in their subject they find that a range of (often unexpected) possibilities suggest themselves and call out to be explored. One might say that the rich possibilities of the material itself take over.

4. *What evidence is there in the story that the actor has kept in touch with (or lost touch with) the "selves" he was as a teen?*

With the spur of his childhood setting, the actor is able to recall himself after a date at two in the morning, "all lightheaded and [his] face full of lipstick," going to Smoky Moser's diner for a hamburger (paragraph 21). He recalls himself cruising the streets in his parents's old Dodge on Sundays, "looking for action" (paragraph 25). He recalls himself submitting to haircuts (paragraph 27), hiding in the shrubbery (paragraph 34), playing in the sandbox (paragraph 34), suffering from acne (paragraph 38), and watching himself smoking in the mirror of the corner variety store (paragraph 52). He recalls the self who wore corduroy shirts and reindeer sweaters inside-out (paragraphs 55, 59), and finally, in an epiphany, he recalls Ermajean, his teenage love (paragraphs 60-66). As Updike writes: "The actor felt swamped by love; he was physically sickened, to think that such a scene had once been real, and that a self of his had been there to play a part" (paragraph 66).

Chapter 3. Researching: The Deeper the Richer

For Henry James's "The Art of Fiction"

1. <u>Why is experience never limited--or complete?</u>

    Henry James asserts that experience is never limited because the mind's imagination can take one's experience very far. Such an imagination "converts the very pulses of the air into revelations." Thus, though a writer's experiences may <u>seem</u> limited, what that writer's imagination can do with these experiences is without limit. Similarly, the imaginative possibilities are never complete so long as the writer's imagination and sensibility function.

2. <u>What are the characteristics of an imaginative person?</u>

    James says that an imaginative person is "one . . . on whom nothing is lost." Such a person "takes to itself the faintest hints of life [and] converts the very pulses of air into revelations." An imaginative person should also be daring, should be "blessed with the faculty which when you give it an inch takes an ell." Such a bold imaginer cultivates "the power to guess the unseen from the seen, to trace the implication of things, to judge the whole piece by the pattern, . . . [to feel] life in general so completely that [they] are well on [their] way to knowing any particular corner of it."

3. <u>Why do you think James believes that the faculty of boldness ("when you give it an inch it takes an ell") is a greater source of strength in a writer than money or social position?</u>

    Money and social position can give one access to many experiences; however, having

IM-91

experiences is not enough. A writer must do something with them. It is here that the power to boldly imagine shines.

4. **How can we guess the unseen from the seen? When you have correctly predicted the outcome (of an athletic event, science experiment, or meeting), what factors were significant to you in making your projection?**

   In guessing the unseen from the seen--whether it be the outcome of an athletic event, science experiment, or meeting--one carefully assesses the visible evidence, imaginatively projects as many possible scenarios or outcomes as one can, and then selects the one most likely to fit the current context. Guessing the unseen from the seen involves perceiving patterns, analyzing psychologies, and being conscious of dynamic interactions. Finally, however, such guessing involves a bold leap of intuition or faith. Nevertheless, the greater sensitivity one has to the nuances of the visible reality, the more likely one is to intuit the future with precision.

5. **What value might there be in striving to reach James's ideal of being "one . . . on whom nothing is lost"?**

   The value of being one on whom nothing is lost is considerable--even if one does not become a writer. The most obvious value is the richness of life which would come from increasing one's perception of life. Nature would be sensed acutely, as well as the social and institutional arenas. On a practical level, one who does not miss subtexts and nuances of communications would make fewer mistakes and treat people better than one missing the feelings or messages lurking beneath the surface of daily conversation. In any kind of work, one might draw on the rich perceptions of life to enhance any project. For a writer (or another kind of artist), being one on whom nothing is lost would signify an unlimited supply of material for one's art.

For John McPhee's "The Search for Marvin Gardens"

1. <u>What kinds of research are showcased in this article</u>?

   "The Search for Marvin Gardens" showcases at least three kinds of research: 1) on-site observation; 2) on-site interviews; and 3) library research into the histories of Atlantic City and the monopoly game.

2. <u>In what ways does John McPhee seem to be one on whom nothing is lost?</u>

   McPhee seems to have assimilated all there is to know about Atlantic City, its past grandeur and present decline, as well as the essential history of the monopoly game. Having assimilated it all, he can then elaborate it in this (most) imaginative form.

3. <u>Where would you look to find information about Charles Darrow and the invention of the Monopoly Game? About other inventions or famous people?</u>

   One might begin with an encyclopedia. Other sources would include biographies and autobiographies (if they exist) and books and articles about games. One might even check the game box itself for information on its inventor and invention. Information on famous people can also often be found in <u>Who's Who</u>, <u>Who Was Who</u>, or the <u>Dictionary of National Biography</u>.

4. <u>What details suggest that McPhee is fantasizing his "best-of-seven series for</u>

IM-93

the international Monopoly singles championship of the world"?

Perhaps the first clue that McPhee is having fun with his contrapuntal Monopoly game with his "tall, shadowy" opponent (paragraph 3) is when he asserts that he uses "the Hornblower & Weeks opening and the Zuricher defense" (paragraph 5). Since these are unknown in the game of Monopoly--indeed they sound like satiric chess moves--we begin to suspect that this is a hyperbolized "best-of-seven series for the international singles championship of the world" (paragraph 5). The statistics in paragraph 16 also should raise doubts in careful readers' minds: 2,428 games in a single season? Tying at 1,199 games each? What is the likelihood of either?

For Barbara Tuchman's "In Search of History"

1. What are the purposes and value of the four kinds of sources Barbara Tuchman describes: (1) secondary sources; (2) primary sources; (3) unpublished material; and (4) on-the-spot research?

    Barbara Tuchman considers secondary sources to be "helpful but pernicious" (paragraph 19). She uses them as guides at the start of a project "to find out the general scheme of what happened," but she does not take notes from them because she "does not want to end up simply rewriting someone else's book" on World War I or II (paragraph 19). Secondary sources can also give the researcher a general sense of the positions taken on the subject, positions which might be acknowledged--or refuted.

    Tuchman prefers primary sources to secondary sources. These are the diaries, memoirs, letters, reports, and other firsthand documents regarding an event or subject.

Tuchman asserts that she uses only material from primary sources because by reading the original documents she is able to draw her own conclusions and make her own selections. (With secondary sources, the material has been selected for one.) Tuchman reminds us that "even an untrustworthy source is valuable for what it reveals about the personality of the author," especially if that person is an actor in the event (paragraph 20).

Tuchman calls <u>unpublished material</u> "the most primary source of all" (paragraph 21). These materials, often in private hands or buried in archives, may not have been examined by any other researcher and thus provide the writer with the opportunity for discovering and reporting something new. Tuchman suggests that there is "an immediacy and intimacy" about unpublished materials that "reveals character and makes circumstances come alive" (paragraph 21).

The value of <u>on-site</u> research is that it often answers questions which reading cannot answer, questions about the terrain, and about cultural attitudes and behaviors. Mistaken assumptions quickly reveal themselves in the light of the physical context. On-site research is an attempt to comply with the admonition: "You had to be there." It is an attempt to walk in your subject's shoes.

2. <u>What can a researcher do to "distill" information?</u>

Tuchman says that a researcher "must do the preliminary work for the reader" (paragraph 15). By this she means "assemble the information, make sense of it, select the essential, discard the irrelevant--above all, discard the irrelevant--and put the rest together so that it forms a developing dramatic narrative" (paragraph 15). Writers might choose a form other than the narrative, but they should still distill their research following Tuchman's advice. Distilling also means being able to identify people, locate places, define difficult terms, and do anything else to make the material accessible for one's reader. (See the section on "Distilling: The Process of Taking Good Notes" at the opening of Chapter 3.)

3. When is research completed on a writing project?

Theoretically, research is never completed. One might always hope to find another article to read on the subject, or person to interview. Because of this unending nature of research, writers early on must learn to set arbitrary cut-off points for their research projects. Such points should be realistic and reasonable. Due dates of papers often force researchers to limit their research only to materials available in local libraries and through immediate inter-library loan. Time constraints may make on-site research impossible for a project and limit efforts to locate unpublished materials. Similarly time constraints might cause a researcher to research everything that has been written on a subject up to a certain date or during a certain decade or year. Good researchers seek to be thorough, but Barbara Tuchman is right when she writes that: "The most important thing about research is to know when to stop. . . . One must stop before one has finished; otherwise, one will never stop and never finish" (paragraph 25).

4. What is the danger of using too many four- and five-syllable Latin words in your sentences?

Latin words are often sonorous, but abstract (and thus difficult). As Barbara

Tuchman says about the sentence "His _presentation_ is not _vitiated historically_ by efforts at _expository simplicity_" (Latin words italicized): "one has to read it three times over and take time out to think, before one can even make out what it means" (paragraph 11).

For Gay Talese's "The Tailors of Maida"

1. What sources do you think Gay Talese tapped to get and verify this story? (Cite specific details that suggest certain kinds of research.)

    Talese's father, Joseph Talese, was the primary source for this story. As the 8-year-old apprentice whose error precipitated the crisis, Joseph was able to recall (with renewed mortification and admiration) the precise words and actions of Cristiani and the mafioso. On his research trip to Paris, Talese was able to verify Joseph's story with his uncle Antonio, Cristiani's son, who was also an eyewitness to the scene. He undoubtedly gained more details from this second eyewitness. Talese further double-checked the story with surviving relations and tailors in Maida during his 3 research trips to that city. During this on-site research, he could see the town square and the old tailor's shop with his own eyes and check on what had changed since 1911 and what had remained the same. Such vivid details as those involving the ringing church bells, the balconies, and the passeggiatas may have come from his own personal observations. Other details such as Talese's discussion of the region's fare bella figura syndrome (paragraph 11) and his digressions to the 1815 assasination of Napoleon's brother-in-law Joachim Murat (paragraph 12) and to Vincenzo Castaglia's American cousin, Frank Costello, came from his reading of secondary sources, historical books and articles on Maida and southern Italy.

2. <u>Why do you think Talese chooses to tell about the ill-fitting band jacket and the jacket with too-narrow sleeves before he gets to his major story involving the Italian mafioso? What does he gain by doing this?</u>

These two brief introductory incidents reveal Cristiani's pride in his creations, his ingenuity in concealing tailor errors, indeed his unwillingness to <u>acknowledge</u> tailor errors. Readers thus are primed for Cristiani's brilliant response to the later, greater crisis involving the <u>mafioso</u>.

3. <u>Do the phrases and sentences in Italian strengthen or weaken this piece?</u>

Many students will agree that the occasional phrases or sentences in Italian contribute to the story's Italian atmosphere and, as a result, to the story's authenticity. Many will find the Italian proverb regarding the donkey-- <u>Lavar la testa al'asino e acqua persa</u> (Washing a donkey's head is a waste of water)--particularly effective in its Italian form. Here Talese gains credibilty and humor.

4. <u>Was the tailor wrong to do what he did?</u>

Strictly speaking, Cristiani commits fraud when he seeks to pass off his wing-tipped knee design as new fashion. Despite this fact, most readers will delight in Cristiani's ingenuity, for his opponent is a fearsome, gun-toting <u>mafioso</u>, and he is protecting an 8-year-old boy.

<u>Why do we find this story funny?</u>

This story is funny because--as with Jack the giantkiller or David and Goliath--we see a tiny hero defeat a dreaded foe, with only the tools of his wit and his trade. The victory is unexpected and we delight when it happens. The humor of this story also rests in Talese's creation of character and in his dry narrative tone. The vainglorious Cristiani is a funny character and the revelation of the mafioso's vulnerability is also surprising--and funny.

For Clifford Geertz's "Being There: Anthropology and the Scene of Writing"

1. What are the challenges of doing on-site, "being there" research?

   According to Clifford Geertz, the challenges of doing on-site research include "a willingness to endure a certain amount of loneliness, invasion of privacy, and physical discomfort; a relaxed way with odd growths and unexplained fevers; a capacity to stand still for artistic insults, and the sort of patience that can support an endless search for invisibile needles in infinite haystacks" (paragraph 28). Geertz also mentions the balance on-site researchers try to maintain between an excessive subjectivity and unattainable objectivity and of the need to avoid ethnocentrism (paragraph 18).

   What are the challenges of writing up research gathered in the field, that is, "being there" in the writing?

   The challenges of "being there" in the writing include the capacity "to convince us that what [you] say is a result of [your] having actually penetrated (or, if you prefer, been penetrated by) another form of life" (paragraph 8). This involves rhetorical strategies. It involves construction of a "writerly identity" (paragraph 15). It involves "developing a way of putting things--a vocabulary, a rhetoric, a pattern of argument--that is connected to that identity in such a way that it seems to come from it as a remark from a mind" (paragraph 15). It involves the difficult challenge of "constructing texts ostensibly scientific out of experiences broadly biographical. . . . Finding somewhere to stand in a text that is supposed to be at one and the same time an intimate view and a cool assessment is almost as much of a challenge as gaining the view and making the assessment in the first place" (paragraph 18). Ultimately, the challenge of being there in the writing means considering the <u>writing</u> of the research as important as the gathering of the research.

<u>Which kind of "being there" is easier for you?</u>

Some students will find the on-site gathering of information easier than writing up what they have gathered. Others will find the writing easier than the gathering, and still others will find both tasks equally challenging.

2. <u>What leads Clifford Geertz to suggest that researchers and writers in fields outside English tend to pay little attention to the writing side of their work?</u>

Geertz offers 3 reasons why researchers and writers in fields outside of English have tended to pay little attention to the writing side of their work. He states that concern with literary questions has been thought to contribute to an "unhealthy self-absorption" (paragraph 2). Secondly, he suggests that these researchers and writers tend to believe that rhetorical strategies are important only for writers of fiction, poetry, and drama (paragraph 3). Finally, he observes that some believe that focusing on "the ways in which knowledge claims are advanced undermines our capacity to take any of these claims seriously" (paragraph 4). All of these views Geertz calls unreasonable yet prevalent.

How would this inattention affect the quality of their work?

Inattention to the writing side of the equation can (and has) result(ed) in poor texts. Such texts often lack voice (a writerly identity) and consistency of tone or argument. They may lack any sense of audience and thus be written in ponderous impenetrable prose. In general, such texts reveal that the writer had no sense of the options available to the skillful writer.

3. In what way is the writer present in an essay even when it is written in third person?

The writer makes the choice of this narrator's identity, the voice or tone in which the narrator speaks, the consciousness the narrator shows of the work's audience, and the diction and rhetorical strategies which unfold.

For Jon Shepherd's "Employee Stock Ownership Plans: New Players in the Leveraged Buyout Game"

1. What are some of the best sources for finding current financial information?

Sources for finding current financial information include: a) Annual reports of businesses and corporations; b) current income tax forms; c) Moody's Manual and the Value Line (for stocks and bond information); d) The Wall Street Journal; and e) financial magazines such as Barrons, Business Week, and Forbes.

2. <u>Which form of internal (parenthetical) documentation is Jon Shepherd using?</u>

   Jon Shepherd is actually following the style of the <u>Journal of Economics</u>, the most distinguished journal in the field of economics. The style used by this journal resembles APA style, the style used by the American Psychological Association, in many respects, but does not follow it exactly. When a student's discipline has no prescribed stylebook, teachers might suggest the student adopt APA style (if the discipline is in the social sciences or education), MLA style (if the discipline is in the humanities), the <u>Chicago Manual of Style</u>, or follow the style of the most admired journal in the field--as Jon Shepherd did here.

   <u>What kinds of information does he document?</u>

   Shepherd documents all statistics, quotations, and information he wishes to acknowledge came from other sources.

3. <u>Is Jon Shepherd for ESOPs? Against them? Neutral? How can you tell? List supporting details for each position before making your final decision.</u>

   Jon Shepherd seems to be seeking a neutral position. His essay describes a phenomenon which has not yet reached its full potential. Shepherd describes its uses without advocating its use. In his second section on "Leveraged versus Unleveraged ESOPs," Shepherd's neutrality is especially apparent. While he notes that "Employees almost always benefit when a leveraged ESOP is established to prevent a takeover attempt," he asserts that these same leveraged ESOPs "almost always hurt existing stockholders" (paragraph 8). In his third section on "The Friendly ESOP Buyout" he poses an example of a successful ESOP buyout

(Healthtrust) with "a more sobering" situation for workers and company (Weirton Steel). It is only in his fourth section on "Unions and ESOPs" that Shepherd seems to leave his neutral position to criticize union leaders' responses to ESOPs.

4. <u>What are the advantages of raising a series of questions in an introduction--as Jon Shepherd does at the end of his first paragraph?</u>

The advantage of posing questions--particularly tantalizing or intriguing ones--is that even reluctant readers become curious to learn the answers. Good questions thus are good hooks for the reader's attention. They draw the reader into the work and make the reader want to read more.

<u>Are there any disadvantages?</u>

There are 3 pitfalls to avoid when considering the question (or multiple question) technique. Avoid:
a) writing dull or patronizing questions;
b) overdoing this device (readers will not sit still for more than 3 or 4 consecutive questions; their minds cannot retain them); and
c) tantalizing the reader too long before answering the questions.

<u>Does he ever answer his questions? Where?</u>

Jon Shepherd answers his 4 questions <u>in order</u> in four sections of his essay. The origins of ESOPs are given in section one on "Advantages of Stock Ownership Plans." The answer to his second question is given in this same section through the Polaroid illustration and through others mentioned in paragraph 5. Shepherd's third and fourth questions are answered respectively by his sections on "The Friendly ESOP Buyout" and "Hostile ESOP Buyouts."

For Julian Barnes's "Shipwreck"

1. <u>What evidence suggests that Géricault was a thorough researcher of his subject?</u>

   Julian Barnes tells us that Géricault read Savigny and Corréard's <u>eyewitness account</u> of the shipwreck and then arranged to meet and question them. "He compiled a dossier of the case. He sought out the carpenter from the <u>Medusa</u>, who had survived, and got him to build a scale model of his original machine. On it he positioned wax models to represent the survivors. . . . Recognizable portraits of Savigny, Corréard, and the carpenter are included in the final picture" (paragraph 34).

2. <u>You learned from Julian Barnes's author's note that the paragraphs on Géricault's painting techniques were late additions. How do these paragraphs strengthen (or weaken) "Shipwreck"?</u>

   These two paragraphs strengthen "Shipwreck" in several ways. First of all, they give us further images of Géricault. We learn that he was "tallish, strong and slender, with admirable legs" and that he wore a short beard and a tasselled Greek cap (paragraph 58). When we learn that he used surprisingly small brushes and heavy, fast-drying oils, his skill and daring in painting his large figures directly onto the canvas "with only an outline drawing for assistance" become even more noteworthy (paragraph 58). Barnes uses his second paragraph to disabuse readers of the sense that the final portrait was inevitable; rather, he places his readers in Géricault's place during the process of creation to help them realize that "the painter isn't carried fluently downstream towards the sunlit pool of that finished image, but is trying to hold a course in an open sea of contrary tides" (paragraph 59). Painters (and

IM-104

writers), in short, are always facing shipwreck.

3. <u>Why is it a good idea to share your drafts with others--particularly with experts on the subject--as Julian Barnes did?</u>

   Experts can catch errors in fact or interpretation which could cause you embarrassment--or a lawsuit--if they appeared in print. Experts might also recommend further sources or approaches which would enhance the work. Even the most ordinary, inexpert lay reader can offer insights or observations which are invaluable to the writer.

4. <u>Locate some examples of the nineteenth-century language Barnes adopts in Part I, and contrast this language with the twentieth-century language of Part II. Why is each form suited to its part?</u>

   The nineteenth-century language Barnes adopts is more formal than the casual twentieth-century diction of Part II. In the first line of "Shipwreck" Barnes uses the archaic word <u>portent</u> rather than the more modern word <u>omen</u>. Nineteenth-century speakers and writers justified their formality with their sense of the stately passage of time. They had (and took) the time to write sentences like this: "But these manoeuvres were cumbrously done, and by the time the six-oared barge was let down, it was in vain" (paragraph 2). Or "Since the boats it carried were not capacious enough to contain the whole personnel, it was decided to build a raft and embark upon it those who could not be put into the boats" (5).

   The gracious length of nineteenth-century sentences and their formal diction is abandoned in the opening two paragraphs of Part II for short, fast, twentieth-century speech: "How do you turn catastrophe into art? Nowadays the process is automatic. A nuclear plant explodes? We'll have a play on the London stage within a year. A President is assassinated? You can have the book or the film or the filmed book or the booked film." Students will note that Barnes uses contractions in Part II (We'll have a play . . .), while such casual, speeding constructions are eschewed for the sentences of Part I. Furthermore, sentences such as "You can have the book or the film or the filmed book or the booked film" hint at the bombarding options assaulting (and sometimes confusing) the twentieth-century sensibility. Julian Barnes thus matches his sentence form to his century in "Shipwreck."

5. <u>What are the similarities between Géricault's research-and-composition process as a painter and your research-and-composition process as a writer?</u>

Both painters and writers may read <u>primary</u> and <u>secondary</u> accounts of subjects they wish to explore. They may conduct <u>interviews</u> with <u>eyewitnesses</u> and have <u>scale models</u> or drawings made to assist their visualization of the subject. Both may carry out <u>on-site research</u> to attempt to get the "feel" of the setting and action.

Composition methods are also similar. Painter and writer both engage in preliminary sketches which lead to finished works. Along this less-than-clear path, however, they will both make false starts and wrong turns. To reach the final masterpiece, great concentration and dedication are required. Sometimes writers will even be tempted to shave their heads and lock themselves in their rooms in order to resist social distractions from their work.

Chapter 4. Finding the Form

For Longinus's "On the Sublime"

1. In Sappho's ode, does her trembling, frenzied emotion gain force because it is contrasted with her lover's "blissful" calm?

    Yes.

    How does contrast help to accentuate emotions and descriptions?

    Contrast sets an object or emotion in high relief. On a desert plain, the smallest tree becomes an oasis. In a silent room, the slightest sound is magnified. When one person is in a fury, the smallest tear running down the cheek of another can convey the greater anguish.

2. How would Sappho's ode be different if she depicted both herself and her lover distraught by love's frenzy?

    Sappho's ode would be completely different. She would have to add lines to show her lover's frenzy. Then she might feel inclined to add more stanzas at the end revealing whether the two frenzied lovers moved beyond interior frenzy to outward action.

3. Can writers gain surprising and often stunning effects by joining words together that do not seem easily or naturally joined, like Homer's line about the sailors, "they are carried close from under death"?

    Yes.

    Does the fact that we pause and wonder what "from under death" means add to or detract from the power of the image?

IM-107

For many readers it will add to the power of the image, for when they pause and think about death as something overriding, indeed as something overcoming or overwhelming like a wave, they will sense the precariousness of the human condition and be moved by the truth of this image. Readers may also find that wondering about the meaning of "from under death" is not unlike wondering about death itself. Both cause us to pause, wonder, and (perhaps) experience dread.

Why can writing be effective when it is a little strange?

Writing can be effective when it is a little strange because that strangeness makes the reader pause . . . and reflect . . . and see the world in new ways.

4. What is meant by matching form to content?

Matching form to content means that the structure or rhythm of a line, or of a whole work, reinforces the ideas or sense being conveyed. The last line of Euripides's description of Dirce being dragged by a bull is presented in two-word phrases separated by commas:

               And if he chanced
To twist or turn, he dragged along as one
The oak, the rock, the woman, intertwined.

Readers feel Dirce bounce from oak to rock, twisting and turning in protracted agony. Form here seems not only to match but also to enhance content. (See also the next selection, John McNulty's "Come Quick. Indians!")

For John McNulty's "Come Quick. Indians!"

1. Why do you think John McNulty takes so much time and space describing the layout of the

town of Andover, the Phillips Academy, his friend Nicky, and his boss Sam Resnick before he begins telling what it was like to be a silent-movie piano player? What does he gain by this?

The success of John McNulty's story depends on his ability to evoke a bygone place and time. In his introductory 12 paragraphs he is able to remind us that films once came by train and were run for two days only. They were shown by an "operator" who would climb up an iron ladder to the "operating room." McNulty recalls forgotten stars of the silent era, such as Mary Miles Minter, and reminds us that while silent movie theaters had no popcorn machines or concession stands of any kind, they did have pianos-- and piano players.

McNulty's success also depends upon his ability to engage our affection for this youthful piano player (himself), and he does this by presenting himself as an ordinary boy having a chocolate milk shake with his good friend Nicky, ambling over to the railroad station to pick up the film, and loitering in the theater lobby in order to be pointed to appreciatively by the patrons. The reader would not be prepared to appreciate his wizardry as a piano player without this gentle priming.

2. What sort of person does 19-year-old John McNulty seem to be? What words and phrases in this memoir create your picture of him? Do you like him?

McNulty presents himself as a most likable youth, a kind of piano-playing Huck Finn who confesses his faults and underplays his virtues. McNulty starts off by admitting that he was (and still is) "a singularly bad piano player" (paragraph 2). However, his later description of himself in action makes us doubt this by story's end. McNulty also tells us that he behaved in a "swanky" way out of pride for his profession (paragraph 3). This and later admissions of ego only make McNulty more attractive because they reveal his affection for a (now gone) way of life. The fact that he likes the other characters in the story, Nicky and Mr. Resnik, and that they, in turn, like him adds to our admiration of him--and to the sense of this bygone era as an idyllic time.

3. *Why does McNulty resort to so many short and abbreviated sentences in this piece, sentences like, "Nice quiet music, then. Until the dog shows up"?*

McNulty seems to be imitating the short, jerky movements of silent films.

In what contexts might sentence fragments be effective?

Sentence fragments might be effective to underscore fragmented thoughts. Here form would equal content. They might also be effectively used to convey haste, or speed--as John McNulty uses them here in "Come Quick. Indians!." Humorous effects can also be created by fragments, because of their incomplete and haphazard quality.

4. *John McNulty obviously has a wide-ranging vocabulary. He can speak of a "tidy escriture" and toss in an "agitato" and a "heimgemacht" when he wishes, but for most of this piece he chooses to be simple and informal, almost studiedly unstudied. Does the youthful slangy style of this piece work for you?*

Yes.

How is it suited to its subject?

McNulty's casual style is suitable for an affectionate boyhood reminiscence. Indeed such pieces, when written for The New Yorker, were called "casuals." Through this informal, almost offhand style, McNulty is able to celebrate his friend and his early career without making too much of them.

Why do you think McNulty occasionally drops high-falutin' words into this context?

McNulty occasionally dazzles us with his verbal virtuosity out of sheer relish for the language--and also to bring humor to his story. When he uses the word agitato, for example, it is to contrast with the youthful slang "thing," and to tweak gently the noses of those with musical pretensions: "That was a thing played alternately with the left and right hand, agitato, as they'd call it at Carnegie Hall." When we learn that the commandant at the fort reads, not a hastily scribbled note, but a "tidy escriture," we enjoy the elegant language just for itself.

5. **McNulty wraps up this piece in one swift sentence. Does this work for you?**

Yes.

Does it make an effective end?

This sentence is effective in two ways. The first phrase--"I play 'When You Come to the End of a Perfect Day'"--provides the conclusion to the account of a perfect day from McNulty's lost youth. The quick second phrase--"and Nicky and I go out and have a milk shake before the night show"--continues McNulty's tack of understating an experience he is obviously celebrating. This ending is amusing in its abruptness and is a brilliant illustration of the power of understatement. By constantly deprecating his abilities as a piano player, as well as the whole era of silent movies, McNulty avoids sentimentalizing his subject--and the past.

For George Lakoff's and Mark Johnson's
"Concepts We Live By"

1. <u>Do you agree with Lakoff and Johnson that arguing is like war?</u>

   Often arguing does seem to be a battle.

   <u>Where might the analogy collapse?</u>

   Sometimes, however, arguing can assume the quality of witty repartee relished by all participants. At such times arguing is not war as much as it is verbal <u>play</u>. In other instances, arguing can be a person's primary form of communication. In such cases arguing would be more like an <u>outlet</u> or an <u>evacuation</u> than like <u>war</u>. The more kinds of arguments students can imagine, the more they will see that the war metaphor only suits a portion of them.

2. <u>Do some people think of love as war?</u>

   Yes.

   <u>If your thinking is shaped by the metaphor "Love is war," what might some of your thoughts, actions, and statements be?</u>

   People who think of love as war might <u>lay siege</u> to their beloveds, <u>cut off their lines of communication</u> with others, <u>wear down their defenses</u>, <u>starve them into submission</u>, and finally claim them as <u>spoils of war</u>. They might speak of the "battle of the sexes" or of defeat or victory in love. They might think or speak of declaring a truce with a loved one.

   <u>How would they be different from those of one who thought of love as a "collaborative work of art"?</u>

   Those who think of love as a collaborative work of art would think and act in terms of cooperation rather than competition. They might speak of adding new dimensions to their relationship or of highlighting or accenting certain facets of their love. As with writing collaborations, the more they work together the greater depth and nuance they often will find in their collaborative effort. Indeed they may find that one enhances the other and makes a whole greater than the sum of the parts.

3. What do we mean in Western cultures when we use the metaphor "Time is money"?

   The metaphor "Time is money" reveals the materialistic value American culture tends to place on time. It implies that every second of existence is quantifiable, is equivalent to hard cash.

   In what ways is time like money?

   Those who think that time is money speak of "wasting" time, "saving" time, and "spending" time. They budget their time and they set a value on their time (often called a consultant's fee or even a minimum wage).

   What other ways are there to think of time?

   Time is often likened to a river, flowing inexorably to the sea of mortality or ultimate consciousness. The river (time) seems sometimes to be rushing and other times to be lazy--or even stagnant. This river (time) is fed by countless creeks and streams but ends ultimately in some vast unity or abyss.

4. What common metaphors shape your life?

   One way teachers can help students discover metaphors which shape their lives is to ask each student to write a "metaphor poem" beginning: My life is a _____

   or

My life is like a _____
(See brief warm-up writing exercise 3.)

5. <u>In what ways is writing a "solo" activity?</u>

Writing is a solo process to the degree that individual words, phrases, and sentences—not to mention whole ideas, theses, and rhetorical strategies—can come from individual minds.

<u>In what ways is it a "collaborative" process?</u>

Writing is a collaborative process to the degee that all good writers collaborate, at least mentally, with their intended readers as they write. Even when writers are writing diaries or notebooks or poems or songs just for themselves, they are writing for (and thus picturing and collaborating with) a future reader who is themselves. The more mental collaboration that goes on between writers and their intended audiences (anticipating needs, hesitations, or outright opposition), the more successful the piece of writing is likely to be. Writing becomes directly collaborative when "solo" writers share their early drafts with others and invite their responses. This is inviting readers to informal collaboration. Often this informal feedback is formalized by formal collaboration on specific writing tasks.

<u>How might it be limiting to think of writing as one or the other?</u>

It is limiting to think of writing as only a solo, or as only a collaborative, activity for writing usually consists of a complex and dynamic interaction between the two. When collaborating is really working, it is hard to trace the source of any of a work's elements.

For Anne Morrow Lindbergh's "Double-Sunrise"

1. What stage of love does the double-sunrise seashell represent for Anne Morrow Lindbergh?

   For Anne Morrow Lindbergh the double-sunrise seashell represents the stage of first love.

2. Why do you think it is important that such love be "freely given"?

   Lindbergh thinks of this pure first love as a "gift" (paragraph 1). One doesn't expect it, yet there it is. Pure love cannot be compelled from another. When pure love is given, Lindbergh writes, "Nothing is demanded of you in payment, no social rite expected, no tie established . . . . The smile, the act, the relationship is hung in space in the immediacy and purity of the present" (paragaraph 2).

3. Do you agree with Anne Morrow Lindbergh that most people wish to be "loved alone," that is, without any interference from the world and other people?

   I suspect most students would agree with Lindbergh that most people wish at some time to be "loved alone."

   Explain the reasons for your agreement or disagreement.

   As Lindbergh implies, the desire to be loved alone, without any interference from other people or events, has its roots, perhaps, in our first moments of life when we seem to need only our mother's (or another's) body for nurture and support. Perhaps all subsequent love relationships become efforts to re-create this primal experience. Another reason most people wish to be loved alone is that such love can serve as protection from the buffets and bruises of the world, indeed, as a haven or escape from life's storms.

4. **Why is it that such moments of pure love alone cannot last?**

   Lindbergh reminds us that such pure moments are fragile and easily damaged (paragraph 3). She reminds us that two individuals--whether they be husband and wife, mother and child, or friend and friend--do not exist in a vacuum. The demands of others, of one's multiple social roles, and simply of daily living can soon weigh down or damage that original simple-and-pure love. Pure love **forever** is thus a myth. As Lindbergh's friend told her: "there is no one-and-only; there are just one-and-only moments" (paragraph 13).

5. **Like Anne Morrow Lindbergh, do you think best with a pencil (or pen) in your hand or at a word processor?**

   Many students will agree that the process of writing helps them define (and refine) their thoughts. Students who say "no" to this question should be encouraged to describe the conditions under which they think best. With a paint brush or tool in their hands? When walking, or jogging, or driving alone? While cooking? Sewing? Cleaning? Lying in the grass--or in bed--thinking?

   How does writing help us to know what we think and to clarify our thoughts?

   From our shifting (and often frantic) thoughts and feelings, writing forces us to choose specific images or lines of inquiry and then follow them. By thus subjecting our thoughts to the discipline of choice, we are able to direct and control them. When we declare a thought (or feeling) on paper, we begin to own it. In owning it we begin to explore it, and in this process often find ourselves clarifying, qualifying, and subtilizing our initial perception.

For Martin Luther King, Jr.'s "Letter from Birmingham Jail"

1. What are the advantages of the letter as a form of communication? What does King gain by writing a letter, rather than an essay or magazine article or book?

    A letter is both a more personal and a more direct form of communication than an essay or magazine article. King's letter is directed to the eight Alabama clergymen who publicly criticized his nonviolent protest activities; thus his letter seems to be aimed only at eight people. As with the letters of St. Paul on which his letter is modeled, however, this letter actually has a wider audience; it is aimed at the legions who shared the eight clergymen's beliefs. Thus King's "letter" is really an essay seeking to gain the direct, personal engagement of a letter.

2. What are King's four steps in a nonviolent campaign?

    King advocates four steps for an admirable campaign:
    a) collection of facts to determine whether injustice exists;
    b) negotiation to end the injustice;
    c) self-purification (should negotiations fail); and
    d) nonviolent direct action. (paragraph 6)

    Why is each step necessary?

    King believed each step must be fully explored before moving on to the next. Facts must be complete and accurate before an assessment of injustice can be made. If the facts document individual instances, or

a pattern, of injustice, honest and
extensive efforts should be made to work
within the system to bring about the end of
such injustice. Self-purification is the
step often omitted by many demonstrators.
King (and Ghandi before him) insisted that
his followers undergo a series of workshops
on nonviolence in which they would prepare
to submit their bodies to blows and their
spirits to insult and the ordeals of jail
and legal punishment. It is only after all
three steps have been essayed that a nonviolent sit-in, march, or other demonstration
should begin.

Do most protestors follow all four steps?
Why or why not?

Many protestors do not follow King's four
steps. Some omit the third step of self-
purification while others find themselves
willing to plea-bargain or otherwise escape
the full legal consequences of their civil
disobedience. Still others shortchange the
fact-gathering and negotiation steps,
preferring their own versions of the "facts"
or failing truly to negotiate in good faith
for the changes they desire. The standards
King sets with his four steps are high; to
execute fully each step is difficult. It
requires both hard work and an open heart.

Why are King's four steps a helpful
guideline for evaluating admirable and less-
than-admirable political protest?

Because King's four steps set the standard
for admirable nonviolent passive resistance
campaigns, each new abortion, nuclear plant,
or civil rights protest can be measured
against them.

3. What are the three distinctions King draws
between "just" and "unjust" laws?

According to King, "Any law that degrades

human personality is unjust" (paragraph 16). By extension, any law which elevates human personality is just. Secondly, "an unjust law is a code that a numerical or power majority compels a minority group to obey but does not make binding on itself" (paragraph 17). A just law, in comparison, would be "a code that a majority compels a minority to follow and that it is willing to follow itself" (paragraph 17). Finally, an unjust law is one inflicted on a minority that had no say in its enactment (paragraph 18). A just law would be one created with full participation of all people.

<u>Do you agree with him on this?</u>

Yes.

<u>Can you think of any laws today that would be "unjust" according to King's definitions?</u>

Some may argue that recent laws denying 18-, 19- and 20-year-olds the right to drink are unjust according to the first two of King's definitions: they degrade 18-, 19-, and 20-year-olds and they are made by a majority which is unaffected by the law. Even more recent state laws requiring high school drop-outs to forfeit their drivers' licenses are arguably unjust according to all three of King's distinctions.

4. <u>King refers often to such great religious and political leaders of the past as Jesus, St. Paul, St. Augustine, Thomas Jefferson, and Abraham Lincoln. What does he gain by such references?</u>

By referring to Catholic, Protestant, and Jewish philosophers, King reveals an astute appreciation of his audience which included Catholic, Protestant, and Jewish clergy. By referring to Jesus, St. Paul, Thomas Jefferson, and Abraham Lincoln, King succeeds in equating his cause (including his civil disobedience) with theirs. Since most readers admire Jesus, Paul, Jefferson, and Lincoln, King hopes they will transfer their support of these historical figures to him and his cause. To this degree he is resting his own protest on documents dear to most Americans' hearts: the Bible, the Declaration of Independence, the Emancipation Proclamation, and the Gettysburg Address.

<u>Does he lose anything?</u>

The only risk King takes in alluding frequently to philosophers and religious and political leaders of the past is that some of his readers may be unfamiliar with some of these figures. He clearly considers the risk (and stretching the reader) worth it, and he protects himself from completely baffling his audience by ranging his allusions from the highly familiar (Jesus, Thomas Jefferson, and Abraham Lincoln) to those less well known (Reinhold Niebuhr and Paul Tillich). Teachers might ask students if everything in a piece of writing should be easy, or on the same level.

5. <u>King repeatedly acknowledges the criticisms made of him and the Birmingham protest, and then rebuts them. Is this rhetorical technique--acknowledgment and rebuttal--an effective one?</u>

Yes.

<u>What would you lose if you gave your side first and then presented the other side?</u>

If writers give their sides first and <u>then</u> the opposing opinions, the reader ends with the opposition's view in mind rather than with the writer's view. In addition, if the opposing views are presented last, the writer has no chance to refute or rebut them.

For Lisa Battani's "An Analysis of 'Letter from Birmingham Jail'"

1. **What are some ways to preview an essay, article, or book?**

   To preview a work, readers should look at the title and the chapter or section titles (or headings) to see how the work is structured. Then they should read quickly over the first paragraph and the last paragraph--and perhaps the first sentences of each section or chapter in between--to gain an overall sense of the work before they begin reading the full piece in earnest.

2. **Why is it usually a good idea to read with a pencil or pen in hand--to mark key phrases or sentences, or to make notes to yourself in the margins?**

   To mark key words, sentences, or paragraphs as one reads is to become an active reader. Rather than passively assimilating the words, the reader-with-pencil is constantly interacting with the words on the page-- questioning them, looking up new words in the dictionary, underscoring central or meaningful concepts. Readers-with-pencil will have richer experiences with texts than those without. As a result, they stand a good chance of remembering what they read. They will stand a good chance of making texts their own.

3. **How do you decide what to include and exclude when summarizing someone's work?**

   When summarizing a work students should try to state the work's central idea (or premise) in one sentence if possible, and then any supporting points or arguments, also in one or two sentences each.

   What can be excluded? What must not be excluded?

IM-121

In such summaries, small details and supportive examples and illustrations can be excluded. What must _not_ be excluded is the main theme or premise of the work.

4. What are the benefits of the four-part form Lisa Battani has chosen for her analysis?

    By placing a Summary of an article or book first, readers make sure they have thoroughly understood the work, in all its nuances, before they begin to analyze it. The succeeding sections force the reader to analyze and evaluate, to focus consecutively on the work's Strengths, its Limitations, and upon recommending any action to correct weaknesses or limitations noted or to adapt the work to a wider (or different) audience. Thus the benefit of this four-part form is that it serves as a heuristic for the evaluator.

5. When summarizing a work written in the past, what is the advantage of using the historical present (King states, he expresses disappointment, he notes) instead of the past tense (King stated, he expressed disappointment, he noted)? What does a writer gain by this?

    The past is removed from us. It is not as immediate as the present. By using the historical present writers gain the sense of immediacy of the work's words--even when the words were written years (or centuries) before. The justification for using the present tense is that Dr. King's text spoke in 1963 and it speaks to us, even today.

6. Do you agree with Lisa Battani's opinions regarding the strengths and limitations of King's letter? What further examples could you cite to support her points? What other strengths and limitations might be added?

    Many readers will agree with Lisa Battani's

analysis of the <u>Strengths</u> of Dr. King's letter. In addition, she might have discussed Dr. King's overall ethos in the letter. She might have described how he presents himself as a sincere and loving minister honestly and earnestly seeking to answer his fellow clergymen's concerns. Indeed he seems to embody the principles he advocates as he challenges Americans with their best principles--and with love.

Some readers might disagree with Lisa Battani's suggestion that Dr. King would have enhanced his letter by referring to other minorities besides blacks. These readers might argue that Dr. King would have diffused his focus had he made his call more general.

For Alice Walker's "Really, <u>Doesn't</u> Crime Pay?"

1. <u>What is innovative about the structure of this story?</u>

   It is unusual for a short story to be constructed as excerpts from a notebook.

   <u>What two time periods does this story cover?</u>

   The two time periods covered in this story are May 1958 to August 1961 and the month of September 1961. May 1958 to August 1961 represents the period during which Myrna met Mordecai Rich, gave herself and her work to him, was abandoned by him, and subsequently had a mental breakdown and was institutionalized. The September 1961 time period which opens the story presents Myrna newly released from the hospital and moved into her new and more elegant home. When the story resumes after the flashback to 1958, it is later in September 1961 and Myrna has begun to write again. Indeed she seems to have started a writer's notebook.

How does the form of this story (dates plus page numbers) enable you to follow the time changes in this story?

The dates place the story in time. The page numbers reveal the progression of events within the months and years.

2. What do you think Myrna (the narrator of this story) wants out of life? What lines or details in the story lead you to your conclusion?

Myrna wants to be a writer. (She says so in paragraph 11.) Although she says she is "not a serious writer" (paragraph 1), we learn that she has written for more than 20 years and that her writing would easily fill a small shed (paragraph 44). Myrna writes in her grape arbor (paragraph 11), and she at least writes outlines of stories she someday wants to complete (paragraph 17).

3. Compare and contrast the two men in Myrna's life. How are they different from each other?

Ruel, Myrna's husband, is a Southern farmer and businessman on the rise. Having come from poverty, he seems dedicated to achieving all the material symbols of middle-class success. If Ruel is a Southern businessman, Mordecai Rich is a Northern vagabond conman. (His name, thus, is ironic.) Rich says he is an artist, but he creates nothing himself; he only steals Myrna's work. He does, however, seem to be a better lover than Ruel.

Do they have anything in common?

Despite their considerable differences, Ruel and Mordecai Rich share two traits. Both are insensitive to Myrna's real needs and both exploit her--although in different ways. Ruel treats Myrna as a possession.

He seems to want her to be a conventional, wealthy, perfumed wife and mother of his children. Mordecai Rich exploits Myrna both sexually and artistically.

4. <u>How does the story of the one-legged woman and her husband relate to Myrna and Ruel?</u>

    Myrna's story of the one-legged woman is a reflection of her own life condition. Both Ruel and the husband in Myrna's story are more concerned with social acceptance than with their wives' needs. Both women sacrifice themselves for their husbands in vain, for neither husband is capapble of appreciating the sacrifice. The woman in the story sacrifices her leg; Myrna amputates the artist within her. One might say that she amputates her art. A major difference between Myrna's story and her life is the respective endings. While the one-legged woman hangs herself in despair, Myrna attempts first to retaliate against her husband, and then to move toward resuming her art and leaving him forever.

5. <u>Alice Walker refers to smells often in this story. Why do you think Myrna keeps herself smothered in expensive fragrances and lotions?</u>

    Myrna seems to keep herself smothered in expensive fragrances because her husband (Ruel/Rule) prefers her this way. She tells us that he came home from Korea a war hero and a "glutton for sweet smells" (paragraph 8). Just as Ruel wants to forget the past (paragraph 11), he seems to want to cover up his past poverty with sweet odors. Similarly he does not wish to see Myrna for what she is but prefers her to be a walking magazine ad for rich creams and fragrances.

    <u>What smells does she really prefer?</u>

    It is hard to determine what smells Myrna

prefers. This is a sign that she has not yet established her own identity. We know she detests the rich fragrances and lotions that Ruel prefers. However, even when she mentions natural odors such as sweat, she is seeing herself through Mordecai Rich's fantasy--not her own reality. She states: "Already I see myself as he sees me. . . . I smell of sweat. I glow with happiness" (paragraph 46).

6. Why do you think Myrna in 1958 was able to get only as far as outlines for her stories?

    Ruel's criticisms seem to have undermined Myrna's confidence in herself as a writer. "No wife of mine is going to embarrass me with a lot of foolish, vulgar stuff," he has told her (paragraph 34).

7. Do you think Myrna will ever leave Ruel?

    Yes. In the last paragraph of her notebook she seems to suggest that she will (paragraph 70).

    What does the fact that we are reading her book mean about her writing?

    The fact that we are reading her autobiography from her notebook suggests that she, at least, is writing again and has completed a work of 223 pages. She has moved beyond outlines,

8. To what does the story's title, "Really, Doesn't Crime Pay?", refer? How many crimes are there in this story? Why is each necessary?

    There are at least four crimes in this story --all of which seem to pay. Students may think first of Mordecai Rich's crime of theft. Far from being punished, his crime seems to pay off in publication in a national magazine. His crime really does pay! Like Mordecai, the husband in Myrna's short story of the one-legged woman is guilty of <u>neglect</u> and <u>deceit</u>. He also does not seem to suffer in society's eyes for these crimes.

Myrna also is guilty of a crime, that of attempted murder of her husband, Ruel. Although she is banished temporarily to a mental ward, far from punishing her for her crime, Ruel showers her with clothes and perfumes and luxuries of all kinds. Thus crime pays for Myrna materially, if not spiritually.

Perhaps Walker's title also points to a more subtle crime: society's insensitivity to women's needs. This crime manifests itself in various guises, Walker's story implies, and continues undetected.

Chapter 5. Finding a Voice

For Tom Wolfe's Introduction to "The Kandy-Kolored Tangerine-Flake Streamline Baby"

1. <u>Why do you think Tom Wolfe had trouble at first trying to write his custom car story?</u>

   Wolfe says that he "had a lot of trouble analyzing what [he] had" (paragraph 4). He was struggling to understand both what his story <u>was</u> and what <u>voice</u> would be appropriate for telling it. In short, he was looking to reconcile content, form, and voice.

2. <u>What was it about writing the "Dear Byron" memo that freed him to find his voice?</u>

   The "Dear Byron" memo freed Wolfe from the paralysis of writing for a faceless national audience. When his audience was one person --whom he knew--he could focus more directly and thus his fears decreased.

3. **Why do you think it took a couple of hours of work before Tom Wolfe could tell that something "was beginning to happen"?**

   Often it takes several hours of work for writers to get so deep into their material that pleasing and surprising connections can be made and relationships discovered.

   What was beginning to happen?

   As writers warm to their subjects they get beneath the surface of conventional wisdom and begin to see and treat the subject for what it really is rather than how it is expected to be treated. Only after these hours of immersion can the writer sense the possibilities in the material.

4. **What are some of the distinctive characteristics of Tom Wolfe's voice and writing style?**

   Tom Wolfe's voice is casual and spontaneous. He achieves this spontaneity by using contractions, which speed the flow of his sentences, and by the use of a deliberate offhand diction. "I don't mean for this to sound like `I had a vision' _or anything_," he writes (paragraph 1; emphasis mine); "I had been through _the whole Ph.D. route_ at Yale, in American Studies, _and everything_" (paragraph 2; emphasis mine). Wolfe also achieves liveliness by inserting exclamations into his account as a kind of running commentary: "Strange afternoon!"; "Mommy!" (paragraph 1); "Nutty!" (paragraph 3). Sometimes he will even use italics to add extra emphasis to an exclamation: _Holy beasts!_ (paragraph 3). A final hallmark of Wolfe's style is his penchant for turning nouns into extended hyphenated adjectivals, such as "the frightened chair-arm-doilie Vicks Vapo Rub _Weltanschaung_" (paragraph 1). Wolfe has serious (and often learned) cultural commentary to offer; his success lies in his ability to serve up these cultural insights in a zippy, pop, spontaneous-sounding prose.

For Eudora Welty's "Finding a Voice"

1. <u>What words would you choose to describe the voice or tone of this piece?</u>

    The voice of this essay is that of a gentle, loving sensibility feeling its way toward truth. The voice is tentative and accumulative, seeming almost to come from the subconscious or from a dream. "Now the whole assembly--some of it still in the future--fell, by stages, into place in one location already evoked, which I saw now was a focusing point for all the stories," she writes (paragraph 2). "The stories connected most provocatively of all to me, perhaps, through the entry into my story-telling mind of another sort of tie--a shadowing of Greek mythological figures, gods and heroes that wander in various guises, at various times, in and out, emblems of the characters' heady dreams" (paragraph 3).

    <u>Does the voice seem suitable and effective?</u>

    This gentle voice is highly suitable for Welty's delicate probing of her writing process. In fact, a fine tension is created between the strength and firmness of Welty's final assertions and the delicacy by which she attains them.

2. <u>As you look back over your own life and work, what patterns or themes do you discover?</u>

    Students will discover many patterns or themes in their lives and work: themes of love and of loss; themes of fear or anxiety or failure; themes of illness or death;

themes of victory or rising levels of growth and achievement; themes of persistence.

3. <u>What are your affinities (the things you are drawn to)</u>?

    Each student will have a different answer to this question. Ask students to brainstorm their own lists, or freewrite their answers.

4. <u>In what way is the imagination like a Geiger counter</u>?

    The imagination is like a Geiger counter in that it tends to quicken (or intensify) when it nears material of special interest or importance.

5. <u>Why are creators more interested in the "freedom ahead" than their work in the past</u>?

    Once writers have revised, polished, and proofread a work until they can think of nothing more that will enhance it, they must submit it to its audience and begin a new work. The old work is then left behind as the writer seizes the freedom to explore the possibilities of a new work.

    <u>What does Eudora Welty mean when she says, "[D]uring the writing of any single story, there is no other existing"</u>?

    When writing a story, writers immerse themselves in the story's atmosphere and vision. They are so concerned with exploring the possibilities of this story that they cannot think of any other work. (See the introduction to Chapter 7. Sustaining the Call.)

For Cory Waldron's "Seeing Red"

1. <u>How would you describe the grandmother in Cory Waldron's story</u>?

The grandmother in Cory Waldron's version of "Little Red Riding Hood" is not a sweet old lady. She is a post-modern complainer.

What is her personality like?

Cory Waldron's grandmother is self-absorbed. She feels sorry for herself, frequently speaking of her "poor, arthritic fingers" (paragraph 2) and of "fret[ting] her poor heart away" (paragraph 6). She is also outraged by such aspects of contemporary society as microwave cooking, designer fashions, rock lyrics, and sexual freedom.

How has Cory succeeded in making her voice and personality distinctive in this short piece?

Cory succeeds in making the grandmother's voice effective by giving her distinctive exclamations, such as "my foot" (paragraph 2) and "Bah" (paragraphs 2, 4, 11). He also makes her voice distinctive by having her continuously debunk (in a surprising and outrageous fashion) the Red Riding Hood storyline as most people know it. After saying "Anyway, she was coming to visit me with a basket of goodies," the grandmother adds: "You could hardly call them goodies" (paragraph 3). After noting that Frances Lucretia "was skipping along the trail, whistling merrily all the way," she adds: "Probably whistling one of those nasty pop songs full of sex, drugs, and other smutty lyrics" (paragraph 4). As the above passages suggest, the most characteristic trait of this grandmother's voice is its poor-me whine.

2. What surprises does this story offer?

As suggested above, Cory Waldron repeatedly surprises the reader, not only by his grandmother's less-than-sweet personality, but by her worldliness. He seems to have snatched this innocnet Grimm's fairy tale into the 1990s world of microwaves and Gucci capes. He surprises us, then, with a new take on every moment of the story. Waldron also creates surprises (and seems post-modern) by tossing in references to other fairy tales as well, such as "The Three Pigs," "Snow White and the Seven Dwarves," "Cinderella," and "The Princess and the Frog."

3. <u>Do you find Cory Waldron's second closing more effective than his first?</u>

   Yes.

   <u>Which phrases and sentences strike you as improvements?</u>

   In his second ending, Cory seems to have more fully imagined the final scene. Giving the hunter and Frances Lucretia dialogue brings the scene to life. In addition, the new sentences--"They leave me sitting here in my little old house, staring at the wolf guts all over my carpet. I don't think I'll ever get my floor clean again"--are nicely in keeping with the grandmother's self-centered complaining nature, as is the other new line, "But does she ever think about me?"

4. <u>Why is humor difficult to write?</u>

   Humor is difficult to write for two reasons. In the first place, every line must be funny --or at least surprising or delightful--or the humor falls flat and dies. Humor is also difficult because it is so subjective. What is funny to one person may seem juvenile or strained to another.

For Maxine Hong Kingston's "At the Western Palace"

1. **From reading just the first paragraph of "At the Western Palace," how can the reader tell that this memoir is being told from a non-Western point of view, in a very distinctive voice?**

   The names Brave Orchid and Moon Orchid are clues that this is not going to be a Western story. In the second half of the paragraph, when Kingston's narrator tells us that "Brave Orchid would add her will power to the forces that keep an airplane up," we begin to see that we are hearing a distinctive non-Western voice with a distinctively non-Western point of view.

   What effect does this voice have on you?

   Many readers will find this voice arresting, interesting, and often humorous in its unusual perspective.

2. **What is the difference between Brave Orchid and her American children?**

   Brave Orchid maintains many Chinese traditions and views which her Americanized children do not follow.

   Between Brave Orchid and her sister, Moon Orchid?

   Brave Orchid seems stronger, more self-confident, and self-assertive than her sister, Moon Orchid. (This difference is even suggested in their names.) Perhaps Brave Orchid's experience in making a life for herself as an immigrant in America has strengthened her and made her enterprising and resilient. Moon Orchid, in contrast, has led a rather sheltered life, waited on by many servants. Her psyche seems more delicate than Brave Orchid's. Coming to

America in one's youth and coming to America in one's old age also would make quite a difference.

How does Maxine Hong Kingston convey these differences?

Kingston's narrator conveys the differences between Brave Orchid and her children and between Brave Orchid and Moon Orchid by reporting what each says and does. Brave Orchid's children can drive cars and they disdain many of their mother's Chinese traditions. They often try to distance themselves from her schemes. The narrator reveals the differences between the two sisters, Brave Orchid and Moon Orchid, by contrasting Brave Orchid's impressive industry with Moon Orchid's ability only to fold towels, and by revealing Brave Orchid's thoughts regarding her less able sister.

3. What are the small signs in Moon Orchid's first moments in the United States that her hold on reality is tenuous?

In the first description of Moon Orchid we learn that she has "fluttering hands" (paragraph 6). She hovers over the customs inspector's unwrapping of her gifts "surprised at each reappearance as if she were opening presents after a birthday party" (paragraph 6). She then speaks inaudibly to her daughter through the glass (paragraph 8) and keeps exclaiming to Brave Orchid "You're so old." Separately these details seem insignificant, easily attributable to Moon Orchid's old age or lack of familiarity with America. Taken together they seem clear signs that Moon Orchid's displacement is beginning from her first moment in America.

4. How might this episode be told by Moon Orchid? By Brave Orchid's daughter? By Moon Orchid's doctor-husband? In each case

<u>how would the selection of details and the voice, tone, and pace change?</u>

Moon Orchid's narration would probably become more fragmented and paranoid as the story unfolded. She would understandably see her sister as tyrranical and overbearing. Her narration might ultimately fade away. Brave Orchid's daughter might narrate this story in a tone of exasperation --perhaps bemused, perhaps not. Moon Orchid's husband might be defensive in telling the story. He might portray himself as the innocent party.

For Richard Rodriguez's "Mr. Secrets"

1. <u>Why is "Mr. Secrets" an accurate title for Richard Rodriguez's essay?</u>

   The title "Mr. Secrets" accurately reflects Richard Rodriguez's essay in that we learn that he is called that by his mother (paragraph 37). We also learn that his cultural and family traditions encourage reticence about personal and family matters.

   <u>Does the title have more than one meaning?</u>

   The title "Mr. Secrets" is ambiguous because one of the points Richard Rodriguez makes in this memoir is that it was only in writing for the <u>public</u> that he was able to reveal the personal secrets of his life. Thus in many ways he no longer is Mr. Secrets. He is public about his private life. Furthermore, he found, paradoxically, that such "<u>written</u> words heighten the feeling of privacy" (paragraph 42). Thus Rodriguez manages to be public and private at the same time.

2. <u>Why is it appropriate for someone who thinks of himself as "Mr. Secrets" to place his (often unspoken) thoughts in parentheses?</u>

IM-135

The parentheses visually suggest the separation and enclosure of private thoughts which almost seem whispered to the reader.

How does form match content here?

Form (the parentheses) does match content (private thoughts).

Is this often a sign of good writing?

Yes.

3. Why is it that by making private feelings public through the act of writing, the young writer "no longer need feel all alone or eccentric"?

   Richard Rodgriguez says that "the act of revelation helps the writer better understand his [or her] own feelings. . . . By finding public words that describe one's feeling, one can describe oneself to oneself. One names what was previously only darkly felt" (paragraph 41). By making these feelings publicly intelligible, the writer feels intelligible to others and thus not alone. What may have seemed eccentric when undefined seems less eccentric when made intelligible to oneself and others.

4. Why is it that the personal (the individual) can become, paradoxically, the universal? How does this happen?

   Ralph Waldo Emerson wrote: "To believe your own thought, to believe what is true for you is true for all people, that is genius." By writing of his family Christmas, Richard Rodriguez invites his readers to bring forth their own Christmas memories and particularly to recall moments that were like (or very different from) his. Similarly, Rodriguez's description of his parents' secrets, questions, and rebukes will recall our own. Thus his individual story will have a universal resonance. His story has enough space to allow the truths of our lives to come in.

5. <u>Why is it that the public voice a writer may sound in a piece of writing may not be the same voice his or her family members know and recognize?</u>

   One reason that a writer's public voice may not be the voice that his or her family members recognize is that the writer's audience has changed and the voice has changed to suit it. Rodriguez writes that "In the company of strangers now, I do not reveal the person I am among intimates" (paragraph 48). The public voice sounded may also differ from the writer's "family voice" because, as with Rodriguez, it is speaking of subjects never confronted by the family. "Intimacy grooved our voices in familiar notes;" Rodriguez writes, "familiarity defined the limits of what could be said" (paragraph 46). A final reason family members may not recognize a writer's public voice is that the medium of writing inevitably changes the human voice. Rodriguez writes: "Even when I quote them accurately, I profoundly distort my parents' words. (They were never intended to be read by the public.)" (paragraph 36).

   <u>Is there something wrong or false in this?</u>

   This is an inevitable process: there is nothing wrong or false about it.

6. <u>How does Richard Rodriguez make the voices and personalities of himself and his family seem distinctive to us? What details and expressions help to etch them sharply in our minds?</u>

   Rodriguez makes his mother's public and private voices distinctive by stressing their difference in pitch: "My mother must

IM-137

use a high-pitched tone of voice when she addresses people who are not relatives," he writes (paragraph 9). Taciturnity, in contrast, is what distinguishes his father's personality, although the occasional questions both parents raise also help reveal them. Rodriguez creates a sense of his brother's and sisters' personalities by describing the subjects of their dinner table conversation--Woody Allen movies, real estate tax laws, yoga classes (paragraph 48). (They are upper middle class successful.) He occasionally generalizes his siblings by saying, "Someone remembers at some point to include her in the conversation. Someone asks how many pounds the turkey was this year" (paragraph 48). However, he reveals the greater intimacy he feels with his younger sister than with his older sister by <u>describing</u> himself and his younger sister gossiping and laughing and talking of mutual friends, while he <u>quotes</u> his older sister's discomfiting questions about his writing (paragraphs 50-55) and her revealing admission that she and her 13-year-old son "read all the same books" (paragraph 60). Rodriguez establishes his older brother's personality for us in the brief scene in which the brother assumes the role of Santa's helper, "making us laugh with his hammy asides" as, cigar in hand, he passes out gifts (paragraph 64). Rodriguez's own voice and personality come through across the memoir. He is sensitive, reflective, indeed anguished about his family's acceptance of his writing and about the difficulties of speaking of the unspoken.

For Donna Roazen's "Milk Run"

1. <u>From reading just the first paragraph, what is your impression of Salty Dog? Which details in the paragraph contribute to this impression?</u>

IM-138

Salty Dog seems to be an experienced trucker who has survived many mishaps. The sense of his experience comes from both the range of delicate and dangerous items he has hauled (cut-glass and nitroglycerine) and the statement that "it ain't like he got his Class-One yesterday" (sentence 2). A sense of unflappability is conveyed in the phrase "he don't get too nervous about things" (sentence 1). However, the later assertion that Salty Dog came away from three jacknives and one head-on collision with "a ruined dispostion" is our first clue that the unflappable Salty Dog is affected by his experiences (sentence 4).

2. <u>What specific details in the last paragraph suggest that Salty Dog has been changed by his milk run down Boneyard Mountain?</u>

That Salty Dog's survival may have made a religious convert out of him is suggested by the details that he has shaved his head and taken up meditation--not to mention a vegetarian diet.

3. <u>How would you describe Willy, the narrator of this story? Do you think he is perceptive? Imperceptive? Naive? Ignorant? Wise? Which details in the text lead you to your conclusion?</u>

Willy seems to be an imperceptive narrator. When he first sees Salty Dog hanging on the wheel, cutting to the left and right and getting red in the face, he does not conclude that something is wrong (paragraph 2). Indeed Willy tends to want to avoid facing trouble. "I decided to get my mind on other things," he tells us in paragraph 2, and in paragraph 3 he confesses: "To tell the truth, I didn't want to ask [why Salty Dog didn't slow or brake] because I had an idea the answer would spoil my day." In the story's final paragraph, Willy's imperception is underscored by the fact that he does not seem to understand that Salty Dog's changed appearance and behavior are related to his brush with death on Boneyard Mountain and that Willy <u>enjoys</u> watching trucks go by.

4. <u>What is the effect of understatement in this story, such as Willy's "I was thinking how it might be nice to be a farmer instead of a trucker . . ." or "I didn't want to ask because I had an idea the answer would spoil my day . . ."</u>?

These dry understatements add humor to the story. By understating, they invite the reader to imagine what Willy is really thinking, which is, in the first case, that he wishes he wasn't seated in this runaway truck, and in the second, that Willy really suspects that the truck's brakes and steering have failed.

5. <u>Do you consider the nonstandard English ("Salty Dog, he don't get too nervous . . .") and the off-color diction ("he is running shit green in circles . . .") offensive--or necessary to this story? How would you defend your answer?</u>

Many students will conclude that the nonstandard English is necessary to lend authenticity to the story and to reveal that Willy isn't too bright. There may be more debate regarding the effect, necessity, and offensiveness of such off-color phrases as "he is running shit green in circles." Some students might suggest that the farmer's running "shit green" links him in fear and anxiety with Willy and Salty Dog who are sitting in puddles they have evacuated.

<u>Chapter 6. One True Sentence</u>

For Ernest Hemingway's "A Moveable Feast"

1. <u>Why do you think Ernest Hemingway spends the first two paragraphs describing the Paris setting before he begins to talk about his writing?</u>

   These first two paragraphs contain one true sentence after another about Paris in the 1920s and Hemingway's experience of it. After we learn in paragraph 3 of Hemingway's way of beginning by writing "one true sentence, . . . the truest sentence you know," we discover, with pleasure, that he has been demonstrating this method. A second justification for Hemingway's opening paragraphs is that they set the scene and provide details he will make use of later, such as the fact that he would squeeze the orange peels into the fire when he was having trouble starting a new work. At the end of the excerpt, when Hemingway explains that after writing he was free to walk anywhere in Paris, the reader knows what to imagine for Hemingway has already provided the description.

2. <u>How did Hemingway handle the moments when he had trouble getting started with a piece of writing?</u>

   Hemingway says that when he had trouble starting a new piece of writing he would sometimes squeeze orange peels into the fire and sometimes stand and stare out the window over the roofs of Paris, and always tell himself not to worry. "You have always written before, and you will write now," he would remind himself. "All you have to do is write one true sentence. Write the truest sentence that you know" (paragraph 3).

3. <u>Why might it be "good and severe discipline" to write one piece about each true thing you know?</u>

   It is "good and severe discipline" to write

IM-141

one piece about each true thing we know because this forces us both to limit our focus and to explore this one truth in depth. Indeed it is a way of regulating skill with anxiety and interest in such a way as to create a "flow" experience. (See "Flow" in Chapter 7.)

4. Why is it often a good practice to stop work when you know what you are going to say next, or when you know where the piece of writing is going to go next?

Hemingway offers two good reasons for stopping writing when one knows what is going to come next. The first is that this technique assures writers that they will be able to go on the next day (paragraph 3). They will not be starting from scratch each dawn. This takes a great deal of the anxiety out of writing. Secondly, Hemingway recognized that if he stopped when he had a general idea of what was going to come next, his subconscious "would be working on it and at the same time [he] would be listening to other people and noticing everything" (paragraph 4). Notice here that Hemingway is consciously trying to take Henry James's advice (in Chapter 3) and be "one . . . on whom nothing is lost."

For V. S. Naipaul's "Finding the Center"

1. What does V. S. Naipaul's opening sentence--"Every morning when he got up Hat would sit on the banister of his back verandah and shout across, 'What happening there, Bogart?'"--tell us about Hat?

Naipaul's opening sentence suggests that Hat has time on his hands when he gets up each morning and that, perhaps, he is lonely and is seeking company.

2. What do you think it was in Naipaul's first

IM-142

sentence that "provoked" his second: "Bogart would turn in his bed and mumble softly, so that no one heard, 'What happening, Hat?'"

Hat's question demands an answer--from both Naipaul and Bogart. The sentence caused Naipaul to picture, not only Hat sitting on the banister and shouting his questions, but Bogart being awakened by the shout and responding in a much different fashion.

3. What does Naipaul's second sentence tell us about Bogart?

This second sentence tells us that Bogart is concerned enough to give some response to Hat's greeting, but that he is either too sleepy or too diffident to respond in a way that anyone (including Hat) could hear. This is the first sign of Bogart's mysterious isolation.

4. Does every detail of a place or subject have to be included to make a sentence true?

No. V. S. Naipaul found that just a few details--a banister, a verandah, a greeting --were enough to evoke the whole of his life in Port of Spain in the 1930s.

For Sissela Bok's "Lying"

1. Can you think of examples from your own life of each of these forms of lying--clearly intended lies; "white lies"; exaggerations; euphemisms; evasions; misleading gestures; and silence?

Typical examples students might cite could include:

- Clearly intended lies -- Telling parents that a friend's parents will be home to gain permission to attend a party or an overnight. Telling a lie to relatives or acquaintances to keep them from coming to an event.

- "White lies" -- Telling lies to avoid hurting others' feelings, such as telling a friend you like her dress or hair (when asked) when, in truth, you don't.

- Exaggerations -- Telling "fish stories" such as that an experience was more dangerous, frightening, or competitive than it actually was.

- Euphemisms -- Describing a garbage collector as a sanitary engineer or a secretary as an administrative assistant.

- Evasions -- Pretending not to hear a question or remark, or answering it indirectly.

- Misleading gestures -- Nodding or smiling in support when one really is unsympathetic or unsupportive of what is being said. Shrugging one's shoulders to suggest one doesn't know, when one does.

- Silence -- Not taking the time or making the effort to assert another truth or perspective. Letting a racist or sexist joke or slur stand.

2. Are there any kinds of "fibbing" or lying that are defensible? If your answer is "yes," which kinds?

Some students might say that "white lies" to spare a person's feelings are defensible. Others might say that job euphemisms which enhance an employee's self-esteem are not only defensible but invaluable. Some might suggest that exaggerations to make an anecdote better are unobjectionable and that some silence can express disapproval as well as support. Some might even say that outright lies might be necessary, such as in the case of persons with fatal illnesses. Sissela Bok would ask students to look at each instance carefully to see whether the lies can withstand the test of publicity or whether alternatives are not available.

3. <u>How can we influence the amount and kinds of duplicity in our lives?</u>

    Bok says we can influence the amount and kinds of duplicity in our lives by "decid[ing] to rule out deception whenever honest alternatives exist, and becom[ing] much more adept at thinking up honest ways to deal with problems" (paragraph 4. She says that we "can learn to look with much greater care at the remaining choices" when deception seems like the only way out and we can make use of the test of publicity when faced with different choices (paragraph 4). Finally, Bok urges us to beware of those who would deceive us, and "make clear [our] preference for honesty even in small things" (paragraph 4).

4. <u>What is the "test of publicity," and how can it be used to help us govern our participation in duplicity?</u>

    The test of publicity is whether bringing our lie (or deceptive practice) into the light of public scrutiny would make us uncomfortable or generate legal or moral censure. Would we want anyone to know that we cheated on an exam, lied on our résumé or income tax form, or kept silent while colleagues or superiors misled others. If what one is contemplating doing cannot stand the test of publicity, one should reconsider doing it.

5. <u>What social and institutional pressures encourage lying and duplicity?</u>

    As Sissela Bok indicates, government and media officials who tolerate giving (and taking) information "off the record" encourage disinformation. Indeed this practice has encouraged "trial ballooning," floating an idea in the press without taking responsibility for it. In business, the pressures of unrealistic profit margins can cause employees to collude, engage in creative accounting, and other deceptive practices to make sales quotas. In education, pressures placed on students to get high SAT or ACT scores or superior grade points can cause students to cheat on tests or take only those courses in which they can do well. Pressures can cause students and professors to fake research to win grants, appointment, promotion, tenure, or recognition. A society that idolizes youth places pressure on its members to lie about their ages, just as military and religious institutions and employers who are intolerant of homosexuality have forced generation after generation of human beings to lie about their sexual orientation.

For Carol Bly's "Small Towns: A Close Second Look at a Very Good Place"

1. <u>Does the first sentence of Carol Bly's essay seem to be true and strong?</u>

   Carol Bly's sentence is true, blunt, and strong. She clearly has this preference, so it is true, and she pulls no punches in her against-the-grain reverse cosmopolitanism. Her sentence's opening words, "Let me say," however, are more suited to her speech context than they are eye-catching words for an essay.

2. <u>What hard truths does Carol Bly offer in her author's note?</u>

   In her author's note Carol Bly asserts that American society as a whole, and liberal arts folk in particular, look down their noses at social workers because their work carries the stigma of "lower class." This is a pity, she suggests, for social workers learn a set of "interactional skills" which can help people move through the ethical stages, make small towns more expressive, and even bring peace to the world.

<u>In her essay?</u>

In her essay, Bly offers the following blunt assertions:

- that "human beings don't benefit from access to culture nearly so much as we pretend" (paragraph 1).

- that it is better for children to imagine storms and ships than to be shown museum paintings of them (paragagraph 1).

- that art does not keep us from "promoting insane public policies" (paragraph 1).

- that nature does not teach compassion either (paragraph 2).

- that old stereotypes of farmers and of rural life have long been exploded by writers, artists, and sociologists (paragraph 3).

- that many films, however, still cling to the old stereotypes (paragraph 3).

- that sophisticated family-therapy processes can help make rural towns freer and more expressive (paragra 4).

- that "half the people who say they love the country really don't" (paragraph 5).

- that "people's hearts are in their groups and families" (paragraph 6).

- that people in the Midwest do not hold the

major powerlines or have much of a data base; their habit is "not to start changes, but to keep [their] chins up" (paragraph 7).

- that in each of us there is both a leader and a follower (paragraph 11).

- that people who see all change as frightening and hopeless can become people "whose curiosity is greater than their fear of change and whose willingness to take a risk is greter than their sense of hopelessness" (paragraph 11).

- that twentieth century psychological savvy can turn a blocked person into a free person (paragraph 11).

- that we need to associate <u>leadership</u> with <u>psychological</u> <u>good</u> <u>health</u> (paragraph 11).

- that "imagination, as well as experience, is a teacher" (paragraph 15).

- that "imagination is what is missing from rural habit" (paragraph 14).

- that we depress the imagination and emotion when we summarize one another's conversations (paragraph 18), engage in small talk (paragraph 19), and talk about sensational events that have nothing to do with our lives (paragraph 22).

- that asking people for more data on the subject invites them to refine, enlarge or correct their original remarks (paragraph 24).

- that asking questions to gain more data and to ascertain others' feelings and trying energetically to imagine what others are saying are rarely done (paragraph 25).

. that when anger is spoken about accurately "much of its desperate quality disappears" (paragraph 49).

   <u>Do you agree with these assertions?</u>

   Many students will agree with most of Bly's assertions. Some may dispute, however, her notion that Midwesterners lack data bases, power, and the inclination to initiate change (paragraph 7). Specific examples might be cited to support each of these counter assertions.

3. <u>Why does Carol Bly's use of specific details of small-town life (a John Deere 300 tractor, for example) enhance her credibility?</u>

   Bly's highly specific details--from the recipe for the church's funeral-sandwich spread to the quarter-inch woodgrain paneling in the VFW (Veterans of Foreign Wars) lounge--convince us that she was there, that she knows intimately whereof she speaks.

   <u>What additional functions do such vivid specific details serve?</u>

   Bly's use of vivid details also re-creates five small scenes of rural life for us. The details themselves are often amusing or touching; whatever their emotional effect, however, they encourage us to participate imaginatively in small-town life. Thus Bly's form reinforces her call for greater imagination in small-town and rural America.

4. <u>Why do you think people resort to summarizing other people's conversations, talking about sensational faraway events, or retreating into small talk rather than speaking the truths of their hearts?</u>

   Carol Bly suggests several reasons for the diminishing quality of much small-town

IM-149

conversation. She notes that many people are afraid to express themselves fully for fear of being put down by others. She states that schools and other social institutions tend to reinforce these fears, encouraging young people to believe that "wrap-up philosophies" are correct and high emotional response is not (paragraph 18). Thus people develop poor communication skills because those are the only communication strategies they are explosed to and thus know. Such strategies of small talk, summarizing, and sensationalism can also be used as shields (to avoid connection) and as weapons (to put people down).

5. How does asking questions allow people to attach their feelings to their appropriate causes?

By asking questions--of others, or ourselves--we invite others (and ourselves) to expand on and refine initial ideas. During this process of expansion and refinement we often discover the true sources of our feelings. Actually, this questioning process is at the heart of individual or small group revision of writing as well as of speaking.

6. Does Carol Bly's blunt speaking strike you as refreshing?

Yes.

Is her speech an example of the practice she is advocating?

Yes.

For Cori McNeilus's "Labor Unions: A Part of Our Past or Future?"

1. Compare the first draft of the opening of Cori McNeilus's essay with her final

version. Which opening do you consider stronger, and why?

Most students will agree that Cori McNeilus's second opening is stronger than her first. Her first opening contains five multi-syllabic Latinate words-- <u>experienced</u>, <u>tremendous</u>, <u>technology</u>, <u>industrial</u>, and <u>revolution</u>--which give it an air of ponderousness. In addition, the first words of this sentence--Many countries experienced-- are dull hooks for the reader's attention. Perhaps most importantly, the sentence offers a tame and tepid truth which would neither surprise nor challenge readers. McNeilus's second opening, in contrast, offers a short, blunt truth about unions in present-day America: they have fallen on hard times. In this direct declaration, McNeilus conveys the thesis of her essay in language any reader can understand. In the eleven words of this stark sentence, eight are of one syllable and the remaining three words have only two. Some students might even suggest that McNeilus could achieve an even more eye-catching opening by eliminating her five opening words, which set the timeframe of her essay, to start with her central word, <u>unions</u>: Unions have fallen on hard times.

2. <u>In this essay, does Cori McNeilus seem pro-union, anti-union, or neutral? On what passages do you base your opinion?</u>

Cori McNeilus seems to be striving for neutrality in this essay. Her tone is sympathetic to and supportive of unions at the same time she is taking them sharply to task for a number of failings. Students might be asked if this rhetorical strategy is effective. Is it a good idea to offer sympathetic support when you are asking a person (or organization) to change? Is this approach more likely to get results than scathing criticism? Than sarcasm? Than an

"I told you so" voice? McNeilus achieves her stance of concerned neutrality by repeatedly presenting the hard truths of the current situation and then offering constructive suggestions about what can be done. She ends her first section on "Industry Changes," for example, by stating: "In order to increase membership, union leaders must unionize white-collar and high-tech sectors" (paragraph 4). Her "Conclusion" is filled with <u>coulds</u>, <u>shoulds</u>, <u>mights</u>, and <u>musts</u>. She enhances the reader's sense of her balance and fairness by stressing the positive, as well as the negative, side of the growth of immigrant and minority participation in the workforce, and, in her conclusion, by acknowledging at least one union which is bucking the general trends.

3. <u>What techniques does Cori McNeilus use to convince us that she knows what she is talking about? Could she do anything more to enhance her credibility?</u>

McNeilus relies predominantly on statistics to buttress her case. Indeed students might be asked if her first paragraph is so loaded with statistics that it is overwhelming. McNeilus enhances her credibility by using her statistics precisely and by using recent (rather than decades' old) sources. Her division of her essay into four factors contributing to union decline also helps convince the reader that she appreciates the complexity of the union dilemma. Students might feel that McNeilus could do even more in her conclusion to find and present other unions, besides the International Union of Electronic Workers, that are responding imaginatively to present and future labor realities. Interviews and direct quotations from union workers, union officials, union regulators, employers, and labor historians might also enhance her credibility.

For Nancy Price's "Cover Girl"

1. <u>What details in the story reveal Kim Cordelia's attitude toward her job?</u>

   Many details reveal that Kim Cordelia sees beyond the glamor of her career. She "sighs" when the modeling agency calls (paragraph 1), and she is not interested in buying the <u>Vogue</u> magazine with her face on the cover (paragraph 3). Her confident professionalism is revealed in the fact that she doesn't listen to the ad man and photographer; rather, she runs herself through her own pre-shot checklist--like a computer (paragraph 6). She knows how to "tuck her toes under and how to make a pattern of herself in space" (paragraph 6). She does it again at the end of the story with the high school boy, Don Fisk (paragraph 20).

2. <u>Which details disclose how Kim Cordelia is treated by her employers?</u>

   That Kim is treated as an object, a commodity, rather than as a person with a personal history and feelings is revealed in the "metalic" model agency voice which summons her to a "shoot" (paragraph 1) and by the fact that no one helps her as she "drag[s] her cases upstairs to the studio" (paragraph 4). During the photograph session the photographer calls her fat (paragraph 5), and both he and the ad agency man order her around: "They looked at her as if she were the shape of a woman that would set off their arrangements of ideas, like an empty vase" (paragraph 8). Once she has served her function for them, she is forgotten: "no man at the studio asked her where she was going or if she wanted company" (paragraph 8).

   <u>By the men at Epcot?</u>

IM-153

The men at Epcot all treat her as a "gorgeous," desirable commodity that can enhance their status in the eyes of other men (paragraphs 15, 16, 25). Price writes that "Heads turned as she passed; men paused in mid-word" (paragraph 11). She also reveals that, like the men at the ad agency, these men also have no real interest in Kim as a person. No one even cared to know what her "very fascinating unique job" might have been (paragraph 27), nor that she was really Kathy Knudsen of Lander, Missouri (paragraph 9).

3. What change takes place during this short story?

   A homely high school boy, a surrogate for Kim's own shy and homely former self, is given attention and grows in self-confidence and self-esteem as a result. Don Fisk also gains a lesson in the art of kissing (paragraph 31) and watches Kim disappear into the darkness with a "tremendous, triumphant smile on his face" (paragraph 31).

4. Do you consider Nancy Price's first sentence a true and effective opening for this story?

   Yes. The one-word first sentence, our heroine's name with a question mark after it, encourages readers to wonder about Kim—something no one else in the story seems to do. It is a question seeking an answer, and the longer second sentence which follows establishes the cold, mechanical nature of the modeling business and Kim's blasé but resigned attitude toward it.

Chapter 7. Generating

For George Orwell's "Why I Write"

1. What do you think George Orwell means when

__he says in paragraph 2 that he had the "power of facing unpleasant facts"?__

In the context of his first two paragraphs Orwell's assertion that he had the power of facing unpleasant facts seems to refer to facing the sad truths of his youth: paternal neglect, loneliness, and unpopularity throughout his school days. His ability to face the unpleasant is especially underscored by his admission that he "developed disagreeable mannerisms" that contributed to his social rejection and that from the beginning his literary ambitions were related to the feeling of being "isolated and undervalued" (paragraph 2). Such willingness to reveal less-than-flattering facts about himself is continued in his confession that his writing provided a way in which he "could get my own back for my failure in everyday life" (paragraph 2).

__How might that be of value to a writer?__

Writers must always tell the truth, even when the truth is unpleasant. Orwell's ability to tell the brutal truth about himself is part of the powerful ethos he develops in his essays. Readers feel that if he can be so honest about __himself__, he will be equally honest about his other subjects, be they the truth about poverty in England and France, the Spanish Civil War, or totalitarianism in all of its forms.

2. __Do you agree with George Orwell that a writer's subject matter will be determined by the age in which he or she lives?__

   Yes and no. Writers vary greatly in their interest in and the attention they pay to their times. The subject matter of some may be narrowly focused--on their own town or region, for example, or on one biographical, historical, or scientific topic--and thus the larger issues of "the age" may seem somewhat peripheral. Nevertheless, Orwell is accurate in asserting that even the most private or hermetic subject is influenced by the times.

<u>If you agree, what are some examples of subject matter of our age?</u>

Students might list the following as some subjects of our age:

- world cooperation and conflict, be it economic, political, social, environmental, scientific, cultural, etc.

- cultural heritage and cultural diversity.

- moral and ethical dilemmas raised by scientific and technological breakthroughs (genetic engineering, death with dignity, pharmaceutical abortion, surrogate mothering, preserving some wilderness).

- male and female relations.

- the viability of marriage and the family.

- racism, sexism, ageism.

- the human rights and peace movements.

- the future of eastern Europe, the Soviet Union, China, the Middle East, South Africa, Africa in general, Central and South America, and our own ongoing democracy.

3. <u>Do you agree with George Orwell that writers before they even begin to write acquire an "emotional attitude" from which they will never completely escape?</u>

Yes. Our genetic makeup and environment interact in complex ways to shape our emotional and intellectual responses to experience. We may respond with fear or courage, enthusiasm or paralysis, sympathy or hatred, or with hundreds of other emotions to everything from cats to catastrophe.

<u>From this essay, what do you suspect was Orwell's emotional attitude?</u>

Orwell's sense of early failure seems to have exerted a powerful influence on both his choice of subject matter and his emotional attitude toward it. He chose to write about the unpopular, despised, and ignored--those down and out and homeless in England and France, coal miners in northern England, and those oppressed by "bullies" of all kinds. Orwell states that he had a "natural hatred of authority" (paragraph 10) and that his "starting point [was] always a feeling of partisanship and a sense of injustice" (paragraph 11). He thus seems to champion the underdog, the despised, and the ignored. However, he brings the same brutal honesty to writing about the despised as he does to writing about himself and his own experience. The result is treatment which, far from sentimental or celebratory, is compassionate yet brutal at the same time.

<u>What is yours?</u>

Asking students to freewrite the answer to this question would be most worthwhile.

4. <u>Do you agree with George Orwell that the majority of people abandon individual ambition by age 30 and that it is only a minority of "gifted, wilful people who are determined to live their own lives to the end . . ."?</u>

While I suspect Orwell is more right than I want to acknowledge, I would maintain that "the majority of people" maintain the potential for self-actualization throughout their lives and thus are capable of culti- vating themselves and their personal goals at any moment when conditions are ripe for personal growth. This could come at age 40, 80, or never.

<u>Do you consider yourself in the majority or in the minority--and why?</u>

Teachers might poll students by secret ballot on this question and use the results to stimulate discussion of the truth of Orwell's assertion. (Orwell, of course, was acutely conscious of the abandonment of personal ambition under the pressures of social conformity.)

5. <u>Do you endorse George Orwell's contention that the four motives for writing are (1) sheer egoism, (2) aesthetic enthusiasm, (3) historical impulse, and (4) political purpose?</u>

Yes and no. If we accept Orwell's use of the word "political" in the widest possible sense to include religious and moral (altruistic) purpose, we might ask Orwell to broaden his understanding of "sheer egoism" to include, not only the desire "to seem clever, to be talked about, to be remembered after death, [and] to get [one's] own back," but such positive aspects of egoism as self-definition and self-challenge (the "because it's there" motive).

<u>Which of Orwell's four motives do you think is strongest in you?</u>

As with questions 3 and 4, having students freewrite their answers to these questions could be a valuable step toward self-knowledge.

For Stephen Jay Gould's "The Panda's Thumb"

1. <u>How might writers resemble nature in being</u>

able to do amazingly much with limited raw material?

Human beings, of course, are part of nature; thus it is not surprising that writers, like pandas, can fashion extraordinarily successful forms from limited materials. Indeed as Mihaly Csikzentmihalyi will argue in "Flow" in this chapter, paradoxically it is by setting limits, restricting options, and otherwise manipulating possibilities that creative breakthroughs can occur. Necessity (i.e., limitation) is indeed the "mother" of invention. Writers can borrow a lesson from the panda and the orchid and (a) identify their natural materials/resources, and (b) experiment with limiting them further, manipulating them to play off each other in unusual ways. Fusions may occur!

2. Should we worry about the need to "jury-rig" our writing from our (necessarily) limited set of available components?

No. Richness exists in even the most limited experience. Indeed, the writer's subject may be limitation.

What can we do to enlarge the set of components?

Students can read, travel, and observe to enlarge their "set of components." As Henry James suggests in Chapter 3, an individual can strive to be "one . . . on whom nothing is lost." Beyond that, writers can consciously introduce components of other subjects, forms, and media into their writing in hopes of discovering and creating something new.

3. Is "self-fertilization" as poor a strategy for long-term survival for writers as it is for orchids?

Probably--although most writers can go a
long way exploring their own natural
materials. (Indeed, most student writers
are only on the threshold of such
exploration.)

<u>How can writers achieve "cross-
fertilzation"?</u>

Writers can achieve "cross-fertilization" by
reading other writers (and in a variety of
fields); going to art galleries and museums;
listening to music and to people; and
watching films and television.

For Steven W. Armbrecht's "The Brady Plan: An
   Attempt to Solve the Mexican Debt Crisis"

1. <u>What fuunction does Steven Armbrecht's early
   section on the "History of the Mexican Debt
   Crisis" serve?</u>

   Steven Armbrecht's early section giving the
   "History of the Mexican Debt Crisis"
   provides the historical context for better
   appreciating the recent Brady initiative.

2. <u>What is the value of creating subsections
   with titles in an extended essay like this
   one?</u>

   Titled subsections provide clues to an
   essay's structure and development--for the
   writer as well as the reader. They assist
   readers previewing an article and allow
   readers to focus on specific sections of
   special interest to them. The longer an
   essay is, the more titled subsections assist
   readers in gaining a sense of the whole.

3. <u>What is the value of isolating and setting
   in specific goals and features, such as
   those of the Brady plan?</u>

   Setting off (and in) specific features of a

law, bill, or plan gives special emphasis to these features. It enables readers to take in the key features at a glance and return to them easily for further (or future) reference. Students can number features, as Steven Armbrecht does in his first draft, or simply use periods (bullets, as they are often called) as he prefers in his final version.

4. For an audience of interested laypeople, what do you think would be the best ratio of information (facts) to analysis/interpretation?

   An audience of interested laypeople may need more facts than analysis, since they may know next to nothing about the subject. Facts without interpretation, however, may be both overwhelming and meaningless since no context is supplied for understanding the facts. By writing with one's specific audience always in mind, writers can supply interpretation whenever necessary.

   Does Steven Armbrecht generate enough of each?

   Steven Armbrecht handles the fact/interpretation ratio quite well. His first three sections--"History of the Mexican Debt Crisis," "Early Attempts to Solve the Debt Crisis," and "The Brady Plan"--provide the factual background which prepares readers to evaluate for themselves his analysis of "Problems of the Brady Plan," "Other Aspects of the Brady Plan," and possible "Conclusions" which might be drawn.

For Mihaly Csikszentmihalyi's "Flow"

1. Why does focusing (or concentrating) require imposing mental limits or rules?

   When we focus or channel our attention, it

IM-161

is as if we draw mental lines out of which we will not let our attention stray. We consciously "tune out" outside distractions such as the sounds of the television, radio, or stereo, and even of people talking to us. When we are really concentrating we actually do not hear them. We also rule out, or tune out, distractions of the body. Thus in a period of creative flow we do not feel tired or hungry; indeed we seem to lose all self (and other) consciousness.

2. <u>What goal might you set for yourself that would be challenging--but not too challenging?</u>

    Some goals students might set for themselves in respect to writing might include:

    - writing in a diary, journal, or writer's notebook for 15 minutes a day (or 20 or 30).
    - freewriting 10 to 15 minutes a day and then seeing if they want to take that day's writing further.
    - practicing writing possible central idea (thesis) statements on 4 subjects that interest them (or that are in the news). They could take the debate form of "Resolved, that _____."
    - writing a letter or brief note to someone each day--even if it is only to congratulate them on something well done.
    - writing a haiku each day (or a four-line poem).
    - reading 30 minutes a day.

3. <u>What kinds of feedback are there?</u>

    There are at least three kinds of feedback. We can receive <u>feedback from other people</u> in the form of formal evaluations or grades, or through less formal responses such as compliments, invitations to repeat or develop the work further, or (perhaps best of all) receipt of others' undivided attention. By sharing our work-in-progress with others, we can tap into this form of external feedback which often helps us refine or refocus our efforts. Such external feedback is augmented by two kinds of internal feedback. The sense of surprise or discovery which Peter Elbow describes in Chapter 2 is one of the best forms of feedback writing gives us. The discoveries of our minds (of what we think and feel) are so interesting in themselves that we want to continue making them (or to press them even further). The sense of exhilaration or pleasure which comes when one has written a satisfying phrase or sentence, or has hit upon just the right word or image to capture one's thought, is another satisfying form of feedback. Feeling in "flow" is another highly rewarding form of <u>internal feedback.</u> A related form of internal feedback is that which seems to come from <u>the work itself</u> rather than from the feelings we have before, during, and after working. When writers speak of a a work "taking on a life of its own," they are speaking of this kind of feedback which comes from the terms, structure, or relationships set in motion in the work. Having imagined vivid characters, for example, some writers speak of having to race along trying to get down all that these characters do and say. Similarly, in an essay a line of thought or a mood might take one very far, or into unexpected quarters. All three forms of feedback can be valuable. It is because of this feedback that we often discover that one piece of work leads to another.

<u>What sorts of feedback would help you know if you are meeting your goal?</u>

Feedback might include: (a) positive or encouraging responses from readers; (b) a go-ahead or an acceptance of a piece by an editor; (c) the sense that the work is moving in interesting directions; (d) the sense that the work will open other possibilities of work; (e) internal excitement or anxiety. (Norman Mailer says he writes best when he is mildly depressed.)

Teachers can help students make decisions about _when_ to seek outside feedback and _how_ to seek it. Responses given too soon can keep a writer from creating; feedback delayed too long is often too late to be fully used. If students can learn to ask for just the kind of feedback they need at a given point--perhaps just on the idea itself or on the introduction--they can learn to control the tension between creation and response in ways best suited to their needs.

4. _What might you do to increase the challenge for yourself in a certain area of your life?_

Students might increase the challenges of _writing_ by:

- experimenting with _length_ of works. Compress a 10-page paper into a 5-page paper. Expand a 5-page paper into a lengthier study.
- experimenting with using less familiar _forms_. (If you are comfortable writing the "How to" essay, challenge yourself to a "Comparison & Contrast" essay. If you are comfortable writing essays, challenge yourself to write reports.)
- experimenting with changing the _tone_ or _voice_ of a piece of writing.
- writing the opposing point of view on an issue about which you have strong opinions.
- asking for an honest response to your work from the best writer you know.
- tailoring a piece for submission to a specific magazine, journal, or editor, and then submitting it.
- reading more challenging writers, such as Shakespeare, Henry James, and William Faulkner.

5. <u>Why do you think the experience of setting and achieving goals makes people deeper, richer, and happier human beings?</u>

   Mihalyi Csikzentmihalyi argues that when we set realistic goals and achieve them, we automatically increase our skills. This greater skill involves the knowledge, insight, and experience gained, as well as physical prowess, and as a result we become deeper, richer human beings than we were before. Achieving goals is also reinforcing. It makes habitual the process of self-reinforcement and personal growth, the by-products of which are usually self-confidence and happiness.

For Barry Lopez's "Landscape and Narrative"

1. <u>Why do you think Barry Lopez chose to begin and end his essay with stories about wolverines</u>?

   Barry Lopez may have chosen to begin and end his essay with stories of wolverines because these stories illustrate the points he makes about the necessary relationship between landscape and narrative, between outer and inner truths, between life and story. The opening wolverine story not only allows us "to learn more about fierceness" (paragraph 1), but illustrates the profound exhilaration and renewal of purpose which seem to come when a story explores truthfully relationships of the outer and inner landscapes in forms and language suited to them. Lopez's concluding story reinforces his first for it shows how another people respond with dignity and austerity to the first wolverine story.

2. <u>Why do beginning writers often focus too generally rather than on the specific relationship of one element to another</u>?

IM-165

Beginning writers often feel they have to tell the "big story" or the "whole story" to tell any story at all. They often think those are the only stories there are. When they begin to realize that a small moment often can reveal more truth about a person or a landscape than a whole biography or topography, then they are ready to do some interesting work.

<u>Why is focusing on relationships (both exterior and interior) one way to generate material?</u>

Barry Lopez suggests that it is by focusing on relationships--of the light on snow, of one animal and one man, of one person to another, or of the outer to the inner landscape--that one can make discoveries of truths that resonate on many levels. Such focusing leads to stories of the authentic complexity of life, of its paradoxes, ironies, and contradictions (paragraph 19).

3. <u>In Barry Lopez's view, what are the qualities of the best storytellers?</u>

According to Barry Lopez, the best storytellers aim "to evoke honestly, some single aspect of all the land contains. . . . As long as the storyteller carefully describes the order before him, and uses his storytelling skills to heighten and emphasize certain relationships, it is even possible for the story to be more successful than the storyteller himself [or herself] is able to imagine" (paragraph 16). The best storytellers, he tells us, have "respect for both the source and the reader" (paragraph 20), and a humility before the mysteries to be told which deepens the story's intimacy (paragraph 6).

4. <u>Do you agree with Barry Lopez that a person's interior landscape (one's ideas,</u>

intuitions, and speculations) responds to
the character of the exterior landscape?
If you agree, why might this be so?

Yes. John Barth makes a similar point in
his essay in Chapter 1, "Some Reasons Why I
Tell the Stories the Way I Tell Them Rather
Than Some Other Sort of Stories Some Other
Way." Speaking of being raised on the flat,
marshy tidewaters of Maryland, he explains
that "in a landscape where nothing and
almost nobody was distinguished; where for
better or worse there was no pressure from
nature or culture to stand out; where
horizontality is so ubiquitous that anything
vertical--a day beacon, a dead loblolly
pine--is ipso facto interesting, the
abstract wish to distinguish oneself
somehow, anyhow, seems pardonable"
(paragraph 16). Barth continues: "Your
webfoot amphibious marsh-nurtured writer
will likely by mere reflex regard many
conventional boundaries and distinctions as
arbitrary, fluid, negotiable: form versus
content, realism versus irrealism, fact
versus fiction, life versus art" (paragraph
17). As with Barth and Lopez, each person's
inner thoughts, intuitions, and speculations
take shape, color, and texture from (or in
reaction to) the outer environment. This is
a natural interactive process which occurs
often without our realizing it.

If you disagree, why do you believe this
interior response may not occur?

Students who disagree should be encouraged
to write their opposition in an
argumentative essay or in a letter to Lopez.

5. Do you agree with Barry Lopez that stories
have the power to "nurture and heal, to
repair a spirit in disarray"?

Yes.

How do they do this?

IM-167

Many students will have had the experience of being tired before hearing a story, or before the start of a film or a play, but being filled with energy when the story (play, film) was over. It is as if we draw energy from the story itself, or from the actors or storytellers, or that imaginative energy itself is contagious. Similarly, as Barry Lopez observes, "Inherent in the story is the power to reorder a state of psychological confusion through contact with the pervasive truth of those relationships we call 'the land'" (paragraph 13). The story does this, according to Navajo tradition, by reproducing the harmony of "the land" in the individual's confused interior. In this way stories can renew our sense of the purpose of life and can cause us to think of mundane tasks with pleasure (paragraph 5).

<u>What stories (from books, films, or life) have healed you?</u>

Teachers might ask students to list films (or plays or songs) which have energized them. A short list of films might include:
- <u>Flash Dance</u>
- <u>All That Jazz</u>
- <u>Dirty Dancing</u>
- <u>Thelma and Louise</u> (for women)
- <u>Top Gun</u> (for men)

Students' lists of stories that have nurtured or healed them will be quite person-specific. Teachers might describe works that have served this purpose for authors in the past, such as <u>The Consolation of Boethius</u>, John Stuart Mills's writings, and T. S. Eliot's poem "The Waste Land."

For Gretel Ehrlich's "About Men"

1. <u>What traditional views of the cowboy does Gretel Ehrlich call into question in this essay?</u>

Gretel Ehrlich's essay asks us to reconsider the myth of the cowboy as a stern, humorless, silent and solitary, trigger-happy macho man.

2. <u>By debunking the romantic myth of the cowboy does Gretel Ehrlich make the real cowboy more or less attractive to you? Why?</u>

   Ehrlich makes the real cowboy more complex and (thereby) more interesting, believable, and (therefore) attractive than the Marlboro man--who wasn't true anyway.

3. <u>Why does being a cowboy involve generation and nurturing even more than killing and violence?</u>

   As Ehrlich explains, the cowboy's "part of the beef-raising industry is to birth and nurture calves and take care of their mothers" (paragraph 2). They also birth lambs (paragraph 4). Film and television "westerns" which portray endless cattle rides have left out the beginning when the cattle get born. In point of fact, the cowboy's goal is to protect, not to kill, the animals.

4. <u>How can writers be nurturers of their own gifts and still be masculine--even "tough"?</u>

   Writers can be nurturers of their own gifts and still be tough and masculine by recognizing and owning their own complexity including the fact that they, like ranchers, can be "midwives, hunters, nurturers, providers, and conservationists all at once" (paragraph 4)--or at least in different contexts. If writers can learn from Barry Lopez's essay "Landscape and Narrative" to observe themselves <u>in their relationship</u> to others (and to the landscape), they will begin to observe when they are tough and when they are soft and when all becomes intertwined and "their strength is also a softness, their toughness, a rare delicacy" (paragraph 8).

For Margaret Hennig's and Anne Jardim's
                "Managerial Woman"

1. <u>According to Margaret Hennig and Anne Jardim, how do early experiences with team sports contribute to the success of a manager?</u>

    Margaret Hennig and Anne Jardim maintain that boys begin to develop the personal skills needed in management early "in an outdoor classroom to which girls traditionally have had no access" (paragraph 10). These "outdoor classrooms" are such team sports as football, baseball, and hockey. Through these traditionally all-male sports, Hennig and Jardim believe that boys learn not only the importance of winning, but how to plan, take criticism, cooperate with people they don't like, and influence fellow players, authorities, and even the rules. Jardim and Hennig believe women are at a disadvantage in management careers because of their limited access to such team experiences.

2. <u>Do you find any weaknesses in Margaret Hennig's and Anne Jardim's argument? If so, what might these be?</u>

    Margaret Hennig and Anne Jardim offer an interesting theory for women's different orientation to careers in management. They seem to me particularly persuasive in their claims that women are less experienced in competitive situations than men are, and that girls' childhood activities rarely require continued association with people they do not like.

    Time may be blurring the sharp sexual lines of the authors' argument. As more and more girls participate in team sports such as baseball, basketball, soccer, swimming, and track, Jardim's and Hennig's argument loses some force. Nevertheless, teachers can inquire of those women with youthful experience in team sports if they feel Jardim's and Hennig's assertions regarding managerial skills learned are valid. Another weakness some students might cite is Jardim's and Hennig's assumption that girls learn no personal skills from their style of play. Surely a case might be made for girls learning to influence peers, authorities, and even the rules through their activities.

3. <u>In what ways is business management not like team sports?</u>

It seems to me that business management can be more cutthroat than the most dangerous team sport. The stakes are higher and more serious in business than in sports. Losing in team sports can mean the loss of jobs; losing in business can bring harm to hundreds, even millions, of people. One might argue as well that some company heads might have and insist upon corporate styles which do not place primary value on "winning."

4. <u>What are the parallels between generating in the business world and generating in writing?</u>

Generating in the world of business and in the world of writing both require imagination. Both require planning and research, including skill in dealing with primary and secondary sources. Producing in business often means revising one's first plan (or draft) and getting input from others in the process--just as writers do. Success often involves an infinite capacity to revise. Finally, when the business product is complete it is shared with the world which either buys or ignores it. In truth, writing is used by business managers in most stages of generating products and services, from initial brainstorming of ideas, to specifications, memos, reports, to final advertising and instructional copy. A successful business manager undoubtedly is a successful generator of writing.

For Gabriel García Márquez's "The Sea of Lost Time"

1. <u>Why does it seem as if Gabriel García Márquez's story could go on and on and on</u>?

    Gabriel García Márquez's story is both episodic and fantastical. As a result, it seems as if he could keep adding indefinitely new changes from the sea and new visitors to the town. The story seems as inexaustible as the sea.

2. <u>How does Márquez seem to generate this story?</u>

    This story seems to be generated by smells. The smell of roses from the sea begins the story and leads to other smells, and other visitors, both of whom occasion activity in the town. Thus action seems to arrive naturally on currents of the sea, of air, and land.

3. <u>If an allegory is a form in which persons, objects, and actions in a story are equated with ideas outside the story itself, of what historical or political situation might "The Sea of Lost Time" be an allegory?</u>

    "The Sea of Lost Time" might be read as an allegory of the United States's economic invasion of Latin America.

4. <u>If you think of "The Sea of Lost Time" as a story of South America's (or Colombia's) plight, what might Mr. Herbert represent</u>?

<u>His money? His sleep? The smell of roses?
The sea of lost time itself? What details
in the story lead you to your conclusion?</u>

Mr. Herbert might represent the United
States, and his money, the wealth of the
U.S. corporations seeking footholds in Latin
America. Like Mr. Herbert, the United
States at first seemed to represent an
economic boon for Latin America; U.S.
dollars would solve all the countries'
problems, just as Mr. Herbert offers to
solve each person's problems. In the wake
of the U.S. corporations came a circus of
other entrepreneurs and hustlers and
sightseers just as occurs in Márquez's
allegory. Finally, however, Mr. Herbert
goes to sleep. This may represent U.S.
neglect or turning away from Latin
America after obtaining a foothold. When
Mr. Herbert wakes up, the town is just the
same as it was before, garbage is fermenting
in the streets, and the people are starving
(paragraphs 166, 170). Márquez may be
suggesting that the intrusion of the United
States into Latin America was a bitter
error. It was an illusion, a smell of
roses from the sea which ultimately
represented lost time.

5. <u>How does Gabriel García Márquez make his
fantastical world seem real?</u>

Márquez begins his stories with realistic
details: "Toward the end of January the sea
was growing harsh." As the details
continue, they become increasingly exotic;
however, because Márquez's narrator treats
them as totally unexceptional, we enlarge
our sense of the world of the story to
include them as well.

<u>Chapter 8. Sustaining the Call</u>

For William Kloefkorn's "Telling It Like It
            Maybe Is: The Poet as Critic"

1. <u>How do William Kloefkorn's six lessons for
   hog calling apply to writing</u>?

   William Kloefkorn's first lesson for hog
   calling, "Swallow the microphone," suggests
   that writers should not be timid about
   expressing their ideas and feelings.
   Writing is an act of assertion, and writers
   should not shy away from it. As F. Scott
   Fitzgerald told an aspiring writer: "You
   must tear your love story from your heart
   and put it on the page for people to see."
   Kloefkorn's second lesson, "Sustain the
   call, though it might seem to you that eons
   are passing," also applies to writers. As
   this chapter suggests, writers must find
   ways to sustain the life of their works for
   as long as it takes to complete them. This
   takes energy, stamina, and dedication.
   Kloefkorn's third lesson, "Assume a pose,"
   conveys the message of Chapters 4 and 5 of
   this reader: that writers must assume a
   voice and a form for their works and make
   these stylistic choices with their audience
   as well as the subject in mind. Once the
   pose is assumed, Kloefkorn's fourth lesson
   comes into play: "Vary the pitch suddenly
   and drastically, providing a surprise not
   unlike discovery." Readers delight in
   variety and surprise; they despair the
   single pitch. Kloefkorn's final rules, "Be
   anecdotal" and "Be political," relate to the
   writer's sense of audience. "Be anecdotal"
   betrays Kloefkorn's own predilection as
   a writer, speaker, hog caller and gentle
   human being to increase his intimacy with
   his audience by telling amusing, folksy
   stories. "Be political" reveals the wisdom
   behind the folksy raconteur. Writers could
   do worse than to heed these six maxims.

2. <u>What is the advantage of embedding
   instruction in a story</u>?

The advantage, of course, of embedding instruction in a story is that the audience will be entertained as well as instructed. Indeed, the story may make the lessons more accessible and palatable.

3. <u>According to William Kloefkorn, what do writers and critics have in common?</u>

   According to Kloefkorn, writers <u>must</u> be critics, if only critics of their own work. Kloefkorn notes that both writers and critics make use of "touchstones," lines from other works which serve as standards against which to measure their own and others' offerings. For Kloefkorn, such touchstones are lines which "cause the heart to quicken, the mind to reach, [or] the scalp to detach itself most pleasurably and most painfully from the bone" (paragraph 54).

4. <u>This essay is the published version of a keynote speech William Kloefkorn gave at a conference of high school and college writers. What form and voice does Kloefkorn adopt for this occasion?</u>

   Having been in the audience, I can testify that the form William Kloefkorn adopted was that of the tall tale, and the voice he evoked sounded very much like Garrison Keillor's telling about Lake Wobegon on the old "Prairie Home Companion" radio show. Kloefkorn's voice was low and folksy, and, like Mark Twain, he milked every line for its dramatic or humorous worth.

   <u>Do you find them effective for his audience?</u>

   Yes. He was loved.

For Wendell Berry's "Home of the Free"

1. <u>What spurred Wendell Berry to write this essay?</u>

The apparent inspiration for this essay was Wendell Berry's receipt of two advertisements which he found to be most disconcerting.

Can advertisements and newspaper articles, television shows and films sometimes inspire fine commentary?

Yes. Berry's essay is proof.

2. Does "free" for Wendell Berry mean free from responsibility?

No. Wendell Berry does not wish to be free of "the natural conditions of the world and the necessary work of human life" (paragraph 5). To be truly free of these, he points out, would be to be dead (paragraph 7).

3. What (and whose) definition of "freedom" does Wendell Berry contrast with the advertisements for space capsule tractors and condominiums?

Berry contrasts the two advertisements' definitions of "freedom" with that of seventeenth century poet John Milton who said that "To be free is precisely the same thing as to be pious, wise, just and temperate, careful of one's own, abstinent from what is another's, and thence, in fine, magnanimous and brave" (paragraph 11).

What are the differences between these definitions?

As Wendell Berry makes clear, the two contemporary ads define "freedom" as being free of nature and work. He reminds us that implicit in the ads is the assumption that there are people who are "too good to do work that other people are not too good to do" (paragraph 6). In short, the advertisements encourage us to believe that we can be free of the responsibilities of living in this world, of taking care of ourselves and others. Berry calls this definition a deadly illusion. In contrast, Berry finds Milton's definition of freedom one which corresponds to reality. True freedom, for Berry and Milton, is "living in this world, as you find it, and . . . taking responsibility for the consequences of your life in it" (paragraph 12). Thus freedom and responsibility are intimately related to Milton and Berry, while freedom without responsibility is the call of the contemporary ad.

4. <u>What does Wendell Berry consider necessary behavior (and thinking) for "sustaining the call"?</u>

   To sustain the call of <u>this</u> world, rather than the call of the grave, Wendell Berry calls for living responsibly in it. He calls for returning to the tradition of freedom articulated by John Milton which means being "temperate, careful of one's own [and] abstinent from what is another's." It means cleaning up after ourselves and not objecting to the "chores" of daily living. It means not passing on to others, or to other generations, our own responsibilities.

5. <u>Do you agree with Wendell Berry, or do you think he is too harsh with those who are seeking comfort and ease</u>?

   I agree with Wendell Berry.

For Aleksandr Solzhenitsyn's "First Cell, First Love"

1. <u>Why is Aleksandr Solzhenitsyn's double-question opening effective? How does it draw you into his essay</u>?

   Aleksandr Solzhenitsyn's opening is effective because his two queries have the effect of increasing our curiosity about his subject. If we have passed quickly over his title, his question makes us stop and ponder it; indeed to ask Solzhenitsyn's question of ourselves: "How is one to take the title of this chapter?" The two questions together also increase the intimacy between Solzhenitsyn and each of his readers, for he seems to have jumped into our minds: "A cell and a love in the same breath?" By his third sentence he is on intimate (you) terms with each of us.

2. <u>What does Aleksandr Solzhenitsyn achieve by repeatedly addressing the reader as "you" and assuming that the reader was imprisoned too?</u>

By addressing the reader directly as "you," Solzhenitsyn not only increases the intimacy between himself and his reader, but insists that what happened to him could have happened to the reader (i.e., to us). Solzhenitsyn achieves universality through this route. Indeed, his "you" refuses to allow readers to distance the horror he recounts.

3. <u>How did Aleksandr Solzhenitsyn sustain himself in prison?</u>

Solzhenitsyn sustained himself in many ways while in prison and exile. As he tells us in this chapter, one source of sustenance was dreaming during interrogation of his first cell (paragraph 13). This first cell meant the company of his fellow prisoners which proved sustaining as well. As he eloquently expresses it: "Now for the first time you were about to see people who were not your enemies . . . who were traveling your road, and whom you could join to yourself with the joyous word 'we'" (paragraph 20). Finally Solzhenitsyn sustained himself in prison by maintaining his curiosity regarding "every detail of the cell" (paragraph 38), and by the thought of telling his story, first to them, then to the world.

4. **How does Aleksandr Solzhenitsyn create a vivid picture of Soviet prison cells?**

   Solzhenitsyn creates a memorable picture of Soviet prison cells by marshalling not only the vivid details of his own personal experiences, but also by including precise details from accounts of other prisoners which he gathered in his exhaustive research. In one paragraph alone (paragraph 8), he gives us the colors, the sounds, the dimensions, the temperatures, even the wattage of the light bulbs of four different cells in different parts of Russia. We learn that "lice-laden, bedbug-infested lock-up[s]" could be found at police stations, railroad stations, and even (or, perhaps, especially) ports.

For Ruth Wisse's "Romance of the Secret Annex"

1. **This review of The Diary of Anne Frank: The Critical Edition appeared in The New York Times Book Review. How does Ruth Wisse introduce her readers to her subject in her first two paragraphs?**

   In her first paragraph, Ruth Wisse presents those new to the story of Anne Frank with the facts about Anne's two years of hiding from the Nazis in an Amsterdam attic and about the diary that was found after her capture and extermination in Bergen-Belsen. She reminds both old and newcomers to Anne's story that although Anne's diary is found in the children's section of most bookstores, it has given millions of readers "their first, and probably sharpest images of Jewish experience under Nazi occupation." After presenting these basic facts regarding *Anne Frank: The Diary of a Young Girl*, as well as an assessment of its influence, Wisse moves in her second paragraph to introduce the book she is to review, a new Critical Edition of the text. In this paragraph she explains the reasons for this book's publication, gives a brief overview of part of its contents, and offers an assessment of this work's interest and value.

Do you find the introduction adequate?

Yes. In fact it is a model of concise history, description, and judgment. Wisse gives all the information a new reader would need without insulting those who know and revere Anne's Diary.

2. What role do you think writing played in Anne Frank's life during her years in hiding?

Wisse tells us that "writing was [Anne's] vocation" (paragraph 4). Thus it played a central role in Anne's life. In her diary Anne was able to daydream about figure skating, write unsent letters to real and imaginary friends, try out jokes, and vent her anger at her older sister and her mother. More importantly, she was able to keep track of the changes that were happening to her body and mind as she entered her teenage years. She believed the Dutch Minister of Education who said that "the history of the war would be based not on official documents alone but on ordinary records of private individuals" (paragraph 3). Her diary has borne out his statement. The Critical Edition reveals that Anne's diary was much more than a vehicle for killing the long hours of hiding. Rather, the diary represents the writing and rewriting of a serious writer.

3. How does Ruth Wisse structure this review?

The structure of this review is complex, yet logical. The first paragraph is given over to the history of the well-known <u>Diary</u>; the second, to the appearance and significance of the new <u>Critical Edition</u> under review. In her third paragraph, Wisse continues describing the three texts which are included in the <u>Critical Edition</u> and assures readers that the new material leaves "the familiar author substantially unchanged, except for deeping our appreciation of her craft." In the central paragraphs of her review (paragraphs 4-6), Wisse elaborates on Anne's artistry. Paragraph 7 is devoted to Otto Frank's editing of his daughter's <u>Diary</u>, and paragraph 8 exonerates him for cutting "Anne's most explicit passages about sex" in order to get the <u>Diary</u> published. In the final paragraph, Wisse anticipates and answers reader questions regarding the betrayal of the Franks by indicating that the new <u>Critical Edition</u> leaves their betrayer's identity still unknown.

<u>Do</u> <u>you</u> <u>find</u> <u>this</u> <u>structure</u> <u>effective</u>?

Yes. Wisse gives us just the information we need, when we need it. Readers first will wonder what is in the new <u>Critical Edition</u>, and then whether the new work changes our understanding of Anne and her family. It is both chronologically and dramatically appropriate to end with the betrayal which ended Anne's writing career.

4. <u>Do</u> <u>you</u> <u>agree</u> <u>that</u> <u>history</u> <u>will</u> <u>(and</u> <u>should)</u> <u>be</u> <u>based</u> <u>on</u> "<u>ordinary</u> <u>records</u> <u>of</u> <u>private</u> <u>individuals</u>"?

Yes--as well as on public records, ordinary or extraordinary.

<u>Explain</u> <u>the</u> <u>reasons</u> <u>for</u> <u>your</u> <u>answer</u>.

History, today, is no longer only the record of kings and generals. The lives of the ordinary deserve recounting alongside the lives of the extraordinary. Today's New History recognizes this fact and would especially applaud Anne's splendid *Diary*.

For E. B. White's "Death of a Pig"

1. **What does E. B. White gain by speaking of his own "sense of personal deterioration" as well as that of the pig?**

   White achieves two effects by speaking of his own deterioration. In the first place, he enhances the significance of the pig's death through the implication that more than merely the pig was affected by the event. This underscores the deepest theme of the essay: that the death of White's pig represented a failure in the natural order.

2. **Why do you think E. B. White compares his pig's death to ancient tragedy in paragraph 2 and throughout the essay? What does he gain by doing this?**

   By describing the natural cycle of raising and then butchering a pig as a "familiar scheme," an "antique pattern," "a tragedy enacted on most farms with perfect fidelity to the original script" (paragraph 2), he is able to suggest an old and universal ritual that he and his pig failed to uphold. He then is able to draw on this metaphor of tragedy in suggesting that his failure (and his pig's) transformed tragedy into heartbreaking farce. By this admission he is able to bring in the many wry and comical facets of the event in a respectful way.

3. **Is Fred, the dog, a necessary character in this essay?**

   Yes.

   What function does he serve?

Fred is necessary because he was one of the three major players in the scene--the others being White and the pig. Through Fred, White is able to acknowledge the more ghoulish aspects surrounding death (since Fred is a "notorious ghoul"). In addition, against Fred's relish for all aspects of the illness and death, White's sensitive response to the occasion stands out in higher relief.

4. <u>Does this essay seem to have "voice"? Do you feel you know the person who wrote it?</u>

Yes!

<u>How would you describe this person and "voice"?</u>

The voice which emerges from this essay is that of a wise and sensitive, animal-loving man who has deep appreciation of the natural world he lives in and its natural cycles. White's immediate admission of his "sense of personal deterioration" and his chiding of himself for his failure to save his pig make us like him, sympathize with him, and believe fully all he tells us. That White possesses exquisite senses of irony and humor is also most apparent.

<u>How does White's voice suit his subject?</u>

White's voice is so perfect for his subject that it is impossible to imagine this piece without the sensitive, reflective, wise yet humble, slightly chagrined voice which is able to place an ordinary barnyard loss in its proper perspective. No pig (except, perhaps, Wilbur) has received a nobler remembrance.

5. <u>How can one sustain a call by speaking of the failure to do so?</u>

Denying one's ability to reach a goal is a powerful rhetorical device. Such denials (or admissions of failure) have the paradoxical effect of spurring readers to complete the action or imaginative leap which the writer claims to be unable to achieve. Thus E. B. White is paying homage to the natural cycle of birth and death at the same time he is lamenting his failure to uphold it. Similarly he is acknowledging by his failure the existence of suffering in a suffering world (paragraph 3).

For Brad Williams's "Of Cows and Men"

1. <u>Does Brad Williams's opening paragraph draw you into his essay?</u>

    Yes.

    <u>What makes it effective?</u>

    Brad Williams's opening sentence is an invitation: "Would you like to go visit the cows?" The question form makes readers stop and wonder if they, indeed, would like to make such a visit. His next sentences place him right into his readers' minds: "Hmmn . . . . did she say cows?" Their informality ("Hmmm . . . Naaah") increases the intimacy of writer and reader just as Williams's use of dialogue ("Uhhhm--I don't think so, Mom") adds liveliness and humor to the essay's opening. All in all, this is a most sophisticated, and effective, opening.

2. <u>Why do you think Brad Williams spends so many paragraphs setting up his visit to the cows before actually getting there? Does this strengthen or weaken his essay?</u>

    The title of Brad Williams's essay is "Of Cows and Men." What he realized in the process of revising his essay was that the piece was at least as much about "men" as it was about cows. He discovered that this essay was, indeed, <u>more</u> about his family than it was about that bovine family, the Cows. The cows provide the occasion for celebrating his own family. Therefore the opening paragraphs in which he establishes the personalities of his mother, his father, his little brother, and himself are vital to the essay. They strengthen the essay by establishing the charm of this family.

3. <u>Does this essay have "voice"? Do you feel like you know the person who wrote it?</u>

Yes.

<u>How does Brad Williams's voice differ from E. B. White's voice in "Death of a Pig"?</u>

While E. B. White's voice is somber and meditative, earnest and self-deprecating, Brad Williams's voice is nimble, casual, and often witty. While White's piece carries an overriding tone of lament, Williams's conveys an air of convivial enjoyment. The voice we hear in Brad Williams's essay is that of one who habitually processes all experience through a lively sensibility, one he is willing to share with us as it encounters parents and cows. Williams's voice is upbeat. He is capable of appreciating his parents, the cows, and even his little brother, Brent. Both Williams and White gain reader sympathy by admitting their own fears and failures. Both also have a delicate and richly humane comic sense. We might think of Brad Williams's voice in "Of Cows and Men" as a voice untouched yet by suffering and loss.

<u>How does Brad Williams's voice suit his subject?</u>

Brad Williams's perceptive, lively, amused and amusing voice is most appropriate for this portrayal of his lively, perceptive, and amusing family, and the lively and amusing, if not particularly perceptive, cows. His voice matches his subject.

4. <u>What makes the title of this essay appropriate? Is this essay as much about men (and women) as about cows?</u>

    As suggested in the answer to question 2, "Of Cows and Men" is at least as much about Brad Williams's family as it is about the cows. Therefore his title, with its witty play on John Steinbeck's famous title <u>Of Mice and Men</u>, is most appropriate. "Men," of course, must be understood in a generic sense, since Williams's mother is one of the most delightful characters in the essay.

5. <u>What does Brad Williams do to sustain this simple story?</u>

    During his revising process, Brad Williams hit upon two techniques which worked effectively to sustain a reader's interest in his narrative. The first was to establish his family members' personalities through <u>dialogue</u>. He did this spontaneously with his mother in his essay's opening; it took him longer to see he could re-create his father (and the nature of their relationship) through his father's kidding reprimands (and his equally playful retorts). Only a slip of dialogue was needed to create the portrait of unflappable Brent at essay's end. The second technique which Williams uses repeatedly to sustain reader interest in his essay is his vivid and fresh descriptions of each moment. The reader easily visualizes the "dozen jam-packed tubs of grass clippings, each weighing about 75 pounds" (paragraph 6) and the "moving wall of brown, black, and white" which is the cows descending upon the clippings (paragraph 15). Such language manages to be vivid, fresh, and surprising at the same time.

For Leslie Marmon Silko's "Yellow Woman"

1. <u>What makes Leslie Marmon Silko's opening sentence effective? Does it make you want to read on?</u>

   Leslie Marmon Silko's opening sentence is sensuous and erotic: "My thigh clung to his with dampness, and I watched the sun rising up through the tamaracks and willows." Readers are eager to read on. They want to know who this man is, who this woman is, and whether they were making love under the tamaracks and willows. Readers will be hoping for a romantic, not to mention erotic, story.

2. <u>What is truth and what is legend, and where do the two intersect in this story?</u>

   This is the intriguing question that this story raises. While our narrator insists that she is not Yellow Woman (paragraphs 16, 27), and that the story she recounts is a "true" and recent event, the story partakes of many elements of the Yellow Woman legends. Our narrator, a young woman, goes away with a mysterious man (spirit) from the north and lives with him for a time and then returns. He, in point of fact, calls her "Yellow woman" (paragraphs 12, 17, 31, 49, 55, 83) and tells her "some day they will talk about us, and they will say 'Those two lived long ago when things like that happened'" (paragraph 39). Thus this story provides a vehicle for teachers and students to discuss where "truth" and "legend" intersect.

3. <u>Why do the young woman and man do what they do? Can you explain what might motivate each?</u>

   If the story is read as a legend, psychological motivation has little bearing. Yellow Woman and the ka'tsina spirit go away together because that is what they always do. To this degree they seem to enact a story beyond their understanding in which they exert little personal volition. If, on the other hand, "Yellow Woman" is treated as an encounter between realism and myth, the young woman might be seen as a romantic young mother tired of her multiple roles of wife, mother, and daughter, who seizes the opportunity to escape her responsibilities temporarily by fleeing with a convenient romantic and dangerous figure. We learn in the story that the young woman is taken with the legends of Yellow Woman. This interest, and her romantic, escapist temperament, may have motivated her to try to reenact the legend. We do not have access to the mind of Silva, the mysterious thief of women and cattle. We might assume that he steals cattle to support his physical needs, and that he steals women for the same reason. This story provides teachers and students much to discuss regarding whether Silva rapes Yellow Woman and whether she acquiesces in her own victimization.

4. <u>What feelings does Leslie Marmon Silko evoke in you through this story?</u>

The power of this story lies in the fact that Silko succeeds in evoking in the reader the same romantic and sensuous longings for the past as her narrator possesses. As we read, we, too, are fascinated by the mystery of Silva and the power of Yellow Woman. The attractions of escaping daily responsibilities are understandable, particularly if we can become legendary and escape responsibility for our actions at the same time. "Yellow Woman" represents a most attractive and, perhaps, most dangerous fantasy.

<u>Chapter 9. Revising and Proofreading: Backing and Filling</u>

For William Zinsser's "Writing--and Rewriting--With A Word Processor"

1. <u>What techniques does William Zinsser use in this essay to break down readers' fears and apprehensions regarding using a word processor? Why are they effective?</u>

   The first technique Zinsser uses is to acknowledge immediately his readers' apprehensions. "There's nobody more filled with anxiety than a writer who has been told that he should start writing with a word processor," he begins. Even more effective than this sympathetic acknowledgment is Zinsser's depiction of himself as "a mechanical boob" (paragraph 4). Readers can't help but feel that if a man who can't refill a stapler can learn to use a word processor, then they can too. Finally, Zinsser systematically acknowledges and refutes every argument against word processing that nay-sayers might marshall, from fears that the machine will make their writing mechanical (paragraph 11), to worries about spilling Danish pastry on the equipment (paragraph 9). By the end of his essay, Zinsser has effectively stripped away all our arguments and soothed all our fears.

2. <u>Do you agree with the criticisms William Zinsser makes of his own sentences?</u>

   Yes.

   <u>Do you find his revisions stronger?</u>

   Yes.

   <u>What further changes might you make?</u>

   I would correct the sentence fragment in Zinsser's revised version by placing a colon after the word "fact": "But what really troubled him was an even more shocking fact: the time when his friends deserted him was the time when he needed them most." I would also reconsider using the word "But" to begin three sentences.

The "Buts" give his excerpt a casual, spontaneous quality, but technically they give him more sentence fragments. Wouldn't "However" be more effective in the first case: "However, that no longer seemed to happen in America"? Would it be as equally satisfying in the remaining instances? I would also press him for more details regarding Spanish and Italian treatment of the ill. Dropping in with a loaf of bread doesn't seem like quite a rich enough picture.

3. Looking back, can you think of anything William Zinsser has overlooked about using word processors? What would you add?

The only facet of becoming a word processing writer that is missing from William Zinsser's essay is a discussion of price, or of how to rent or gain access to word processors if one cannot afford to buy one. Zinsser must have consciously decided not to open up the vast and changing area of price and access. Nevertheless, once he has convinced a reader of the merits of word processing, the immediate question on the reader's mind is: how do I gain access to one of these marvelous machines? Unless readers can afford to follow Zinsser's lead, and hie themselves to an IBM store, he offers them no guidance at all.

4. After reading this essay, do you feel encouraged to try a word processor?

Yes.

For Winston Churchill's "The National Coalition"

1. Why does Winston Churchill go to such great lengths to establish the comparative contributions and losses of Britain and the United States in the war effort?

Clearly Churchill wants to set the record straight and gain recognition for his countrymen and women for the significant effort they made in the war. Since the entry of the United States into the war helped significantly to turn the tide of battle against Germany, a popular assumption would have been that the United States bore the brunt of the war effort. It is this view that Churchill seeks to address by showing his comparative tables of contributions and losses.

2. <u>Does Winston Churchill antagonize any potential readers, or does he anticipate possible objections and counteract them in his essay?</u>

Far from antagonizing readers, Churchill seems to bend over backwards to anticipate and diffuse potential opposition. Regarding the matter of comparative war effort, for example, he writes: "I do this with no desire to make invidious comparisons or rouse purposeless rivalries with our greatest ally, the United States, to whom we owe immeasurable and enduring gratitude. But it is to the combined interest of the English-speaking world that the magnitude of the British war-making effort should be known and realized" (paragraph 3). Churchill is equally diplomatic, even generous, in his treatment of members of the British parties which opposed him. He writes that: "The party basis being officially established, it seemed to me that no sense of Self entered into the minds of any of the very large number of gentlemen I had to see. . . . Even more did this high standard of behavior apply to the large number of Conservative and National Liberal Ministers who had to leave their offices and break their careers, and at this moment of surpassing interest and excitement to step out of official life, in many cases forever" (paragraph 10).

Why is acknowledging and rebutting potential opposition a good writing technique?

Acknowledging contrary views and seeking to refute them is wise for two reasons. First, it shows an awareness of audience and their needs. Secondly, it shows that the writer is not narrow-minded, seeing only his or her position. By acknowledging and rebutting opposing points of view, writers show that they have considered all perspectives on the subject and have come to their present position through careful weighing of all points of view.

3. **How would you evaluate Winston Churchill's address to the House of Commons? Was his communication effective?**

Winston Churchill's address to the House of Commons is eloquent and stirring. His use of the question motif--"You ask, what is our policy? . . . You ask, what is our aim?"--is particularly effective when coupled with his short and dramatic replies. Churchill points out the grave stakes of the crisis, and places the concept of survival in the larger context of survival of the tradition that the British Empire represented. He draws on the support of God and calls for the support of men for a cause for which he can only offer "blood, toil, tears and sweat,"--a phrase which remains among the the most celebrated and memorable in history.

4. **How would you evaluate Winston Churchill's first letter to President Roosevelt? What was effective about it?**

Churchill's first letter is a masterpiece of diplomacy. His first sentence acknowledges his new position as Prime Minister in a modest and wry manner. In the next 7 sentences he swiftly and vividly describes the current crisis: "The small countries are simply smashed up, one by one, like matchwood." In the next two sentences, Churchill warns the President about waiting too long to enter the battle. When he comes to his requests, however, he is a practical politician asking only that Roosevelt "proclaim non-belligerency" rather than requesting full entry at that time. He then makes six direct requests for aid, giving the reasons for each request and the plans for repayment in a concise and persuasive fashion. He ends with his good wishes and respect. Having read this communication, Roosevelt would be clear about the present state of the war from Britain's perspective, and about Britain's needs. Undoubtedly he would also have been impressed with Churchill's command of the crisis and his determination to "continue the war alone" unafraid. Such a letter would encourage the President to reply in kind.

For Mary McCarthy's "Language and Politics"

1. Why do you think people--particularly college freshmen--think big (four and five syllable) words are better than short, simple ones?

   Because our beginning "Dick & Jane" readers are composed mainly of one-syllable words, students understandably grow up equating the use of multi-syllabled words with elevated education and (therefore) intelligence. Smart people use big words, is the popular fallacy. Thus first semester freshmen sometimes think they can demonstrate their new intellectual status by using expensive, Latinate verbiage. The faster they are disabused of this notion the better.

2. For what reasons might politicians wish to conceal the truth (reality) from their constituents, each other, and even themselves?

The many motives for concealment all reduce to one: unease at the test of publicity. (See Sissela Bok's essay, "Lying," in Chapter 6.) If colleagues or constituents knew of their action, or lack of action, the politicians would have no substantive defense and could be censured. They would lose respect, votes, and ultimately their jobs. Thus, when politicians are engaged in unspeakable acts, they usually do not speak of them even to themselves, or, as Mary McCarthy's analysis of the langauge of Watergate reveals, their language becomes distant and obscure.

3. <u>Do you agree with Mary McCarthy that public schools should return to teaching Latin?</u>

    Yes. I agree with McCarthy and Lewis Thomas and others who remind us that studying Latin not only gives us access to an important culture, but enables us to appreciate the roots of many of the words we use daily. Of even greater importance is McCarthy's belief that we might regain some clarity in our use of language, as well as control over prepositions, if we return to the study of classical languages (paragraph 18).

4. <u>What recommendations would you make to reverse the decline in language skill?</u>

    This question would be a good one for class discussion and for a series of essays or letters. Sound recommendations might include (1) reading an hour a day; (2) writing for an hour every day; (3) delivering a brief speech every day; (4) limiting the hours of television viewing; (5) studying classical and modern languages; (6) most of all, <u>using</u> language in a variety of forms, for a variety of purposes, for a a variety of audiences.

For Lewis Thomas's "Notes on Punctuation"

1. <u>How does Lewis Thomas structure this essay?</u>

   Each of Lewis Thomas's opening 7 paragraphs is devoted to discussion and demonstration of a specific punctuation mark: the parenthesis, comma, semicolon, colon, exclamation point, quotation mark, and dash. Thomas devotes his eighth paragraph to the dangers of overusing punctuation in poetry and his ninth to T. S. Eliot's sublime use of semicolons, especially in the <u>Four Quartets</u>. He concludes his "Notes on Punctuation" by returning to the comma and its possibilities--and impossibilities.

2. <u>What is his approach to each paragraph?</u>

   In each paragraph devoted to a punctuation mark, Thomas discusses each mark's use at the same time he is wittily demonstrating it.

   <u>What does Thomas gain by this approach?</u>

   Through this approach Thomas manages to entertain as well as enlighten. Readers benefit doubly, for they hear Thomas's notes and see the punctuation in action. Thomas undoubtedly hopes that his readers will better remember his observations if they are given in this visible and risible manner.

3. <u>Do you agree or disagree with Lewis Thomas's comments on each punctuation mark? If you disagree, which marks do you use differently --and why?</u>

   For the most part, I agree hardily with Thomas's observations regarding use of the punctuation marks. However, he surely is being sportif in his handling of the parenthesis. Students should be assured that no handbook (not even <u>Fowler's</u>) recommends piling up right-hand parentheses at the end of a sentence.

4. **Do you think punctuation usage changes over time, just as language does?**

   Yes.

   What marks might be likely to change, and what might these changes be?

   Certain usages of the comma might be abandoned, such as the current use of commas around appositives or after (or around) phrases such as **moreover**, **however**, and **nonetheless**. In addition, one sees so many run-on sentences in print that one fears the period may be losing hold.

For Carol Kammen's "Concerning Footnotes"

1. **What myths or misconceptions might arise about a town's history?**

   Early town histories were often written to lure new settlers. Thus they often tended to accentuate (and even exaggerate) the positive, ignore the negative, and omit whole facets and factions.

   How could such myths be discredited--or corrected? What role would sources play in such correction?

   If myths or errors are contained in previous town histories, they can be corrected by reexamining previous sources and by uncovering new sources of information. Such sources might include newly discovered letters or diaries, old newspapers, church bulletins or published sermons, and society or organization minutes. Information in these sources can be checked against other materials, such as census reports, tax records, and birth, marriage, and death certificates. Once information is verified for accuracy, it should be written up and deposited in the local historical society, and shared in speeches and newspaper articles with the community. The greater the error or myth, the more urgent it is to correct the public misconception.

2. <u>To which disciplines besides history do Carol Kammen's words "Concerning Footnotes" apply?</u>

   Carol Kammen's counsel "Concerning Footnotes" applies to every discipline, including the sciences. Future researchers in every field need to know the sources we use and how we have come to know what we know.

3. <u>When you use parenthetical documentation to acknowledge your sources, for what other uses might you use footnotes?</u>

   When parenthetical documentation is employed, footnotes can be used to provide the reader with supplementary information, including interesting digressions not suitable for the text proper.

4. <u>Why does Carol Kammen's opening anecdote make an effective way to introduce her subject?</u>

   Carol Kammen's opening anecdote is a true story that dramatizes the attitude she hopes her essay will counter. Since many of the readers of Kammen's essay will be elderly local historians who dislike footnotes, this anecdote is aimed specifically at them. Kammen is gentle with the ancient historian who shunned footnotes--calling him "lovely but stubborn"--yet she firmly asserts her counter position. Thus her opening is neither harsh nor threatening. Rather it humanizes and makes interesting the rather dry subject of footnotes.

   <u>What other openings might she have employed?</u>

Numerous openings might be effective. (See Chapter 6. One True Sentence.)

For Jennifer Miller's "Lipstick Kisses"

1. <u>Where do you hear distinctive voices in this essay?</u>

    The opening section in italics gives the voice of Jennifer Miller moving deeper and and deeper into her childhood memory and persona. What begins as "My earliest memory of my father" becomes, by the end of the first section, "Great. Now I had to share." The section in regular type which follows is in the voice of Jennifer Miller as she is today, a college student soon to be married. The word "nightmares" at the end of this section (paragraph 8) returns Jennifer to a new voice of dreams that regresses, like the first voice, to long-repressed memories of arguments and feelings of rejection. The final four paragraphs of the essay return us to the mature voice of the author.

2. <u>Do you find the use of italics effective?</u>

    Yes.

    <u>What do these italicized sections represent?</u>

    The italics help signal flashbacks in time and voice to the early Jennifer Miller still inside the present adult "Presidential Scholar." They are helpful guides to the reader who must follow Miller's changes in time, place, and mindscape.

3. <u>How has Jennifer Miller created a vivid portrait of her father?</u>

    Just a few specific details, skillfully developed, bring Jennifer's father vividly to life in this essay. We know him by the passions he shared with his daughter--a love of Doritos and of horses--by the name he called her--"kiddo"--and by one conspiratorial early morning moment they shared. Even this scene of falling asleep together on the living room floor carries a certain ominous air, suggests a certain rebellious irresponsibility in the father which is underscored in his love for wild horses and in Jennifer's dream of his whipping them.

How has Jennifer Miller created a vivid portrait of herself at two different ages?

Jennifer creates a vivid portrait of herself at two ages again through a few revealing details and actions, as well as through her changing voices. She allows us to see her as a child of five laughing "conspiratorially" with her father, receiving a turquoise Indian necklace from him, and "pressing lipstick kisses on [his] roughly bearded cheek" (paragraph 2). Later, she shows us herself doing her dot-to-dot book while humming to block out her parents' arguments. When she speaks in the voice of the five-year-old child, when she says "I hated my mom when she left my daddy" (paragraph 4), we believe her. Jennifer uses the same techniques to show herself today. "If my professor expects me to be a mature, intelligent student, then that's who I am," she writes. "If the guy sitting next to me in class wants me to be a dizzy chick, then that's who I am" (paragraph 10). The honesty of these scenes in which she is willing to show herself and her parents in less-than-favorable light convinces us of their truth and helps us to understand and sympathize with the writer.

4. Why is "Lipstick Kisses" an appropriate and eye-catching title for this essay?

"Lipstick Kisses" is an appropriate title for this essay because it unites the two voices in the story, the 5-year-old Jennifer Miller pressing lipstick kisses on a father who would soon leave her, and the 21-year-old Jennifer Miller who is trying to learn to trust in the love of her fiance. "Lipstick Kisses" is an eye-catching title because it seems to promise a story of romance. The phrase itself is provocative, inviting readers to ponder the difference between ordinary kisses and lipstick kisses.

For Alice Munro's "Material"

1. What differences does the narrator see between the two men in her life, Hugo (the writer) and Gabe (the engineer)?

In the beginning of her story, the narrator sees many differences between Hugo and Gabe, her first and second husbands. The writer, Hugo, seems to her to be vain and quarrelsome, bloated, opinionated, and untidy (paragraph 1), a "brilliant . . . incapable man who must be looked after for the sake of the words that will come from [him]" (paragraph 2). Hugo is also unfaithful and a liar. While the writer, Hugo, is "held together by nerves," Gabe, the engineer, seems to be "substantial and calm" (paragraph 4). He says he enjoys life (paragraph 5) and he seems utterly natural and unthreatened by Hugo's fame. Indeed, unlike Hugo, he is neither curious nor self-conscious (paragraph 5).

What similarities does she discover?

At the end of her story, the narrator comes to feel that her very different husbands share important similarities. "Both of them have managed something," she discovers. "Both of them have decided what to do about everything they run across in this world, what attitude to take, how to ignore or use things. In their limited and precarious ways they both have authority. They are not <u>at the mercy</u>. Or think they are not" (paragraph 113).

2. <u>How does the narrator's view of Hugo change in the course of this story? What causes this change?</u>

After haranguing her former husband for most of the story, the narrator sits down and reads his story and discovers to her surprise that it is both good and honest. She sees in the story their neighbor Dotty "lifted out of life and held in light, suspended in the marvelous clear jelly that Hugo has spent all his life learning how to make" (paragraph 110). She recognizes Hugo's gift as "a special, unsparing, unsentimental love" (paragraph 110) and wishes to write him to acknowledge she was wrong in not believing that he would be a writer. Yet this new appreciation does not hold. When she comes to write the letter, she changes her view again, believing that the ability to immortalize Dotty in art is "not enough" to justify the harm he did her (and others) in life. Alice Munro leaves the narrator (and us) pondering this question.

3. <u>What criticisms does the narrator make of herself? Do you agree?</u>

The narrator confesses to us that she lacks the imagination or good will to reach beyond clichés regarding people, including artists (paragraph 15). This lack of imagination or good will is made clear in her failure to recognize during her marriage to Hugo that he was a true writer. "He did not have the authority I thought a writer should have," she tells us. "He was too nervous, too touchy with everybody, too much of a showoff. I believed writers were calm, sad peple, knowing too much" (paragraph 40). The narrator is also critical of her handling of the pivotal argument with Hugo over the water pump. "I could have taken a blanket and gone to sleep on the living room couch for the rest of the night. I think that is what a woman of firm character would have done," she tells us. Are we, then, to believe our narrator lacks firm character?

How do you see her?

Yes, our narrator does seem to lack an original imagination, good will, and firm character. This does not, however, make her an unattractive character. What is attractive about the narrator is her honesty. What is attractive, and believable, about the narrator is the way she is groping her way toward a richer understanding of life. The fact that she has trouble thinking beyond clichés regarding people is shown in her early failure to appreciate Gabe's authority, as well as Hugo's. Her lack of good will is seen in her inability to overcome her past anger at Hugo's destructiveness to acknowledge to him that she was wrong not to recognize that he would be a writer. Her lack of firmness of character is seen in her changing views of Hugo; but she is approaching authority here.

4. Why is it that what is "all scraps and oddments, useless baggage" to a nonwriter can be "ripe and usable, a paying investment" to a writer?

This is the nature of the artistic process. The writer is first of all paying attention in a certain way. The writer is trying to be "one . . .on whom nothing is lost" (as Henry James counseled in Chapter 3). The writer also plans to use this material in ways which are of little interest to nonwriters.